Yeats

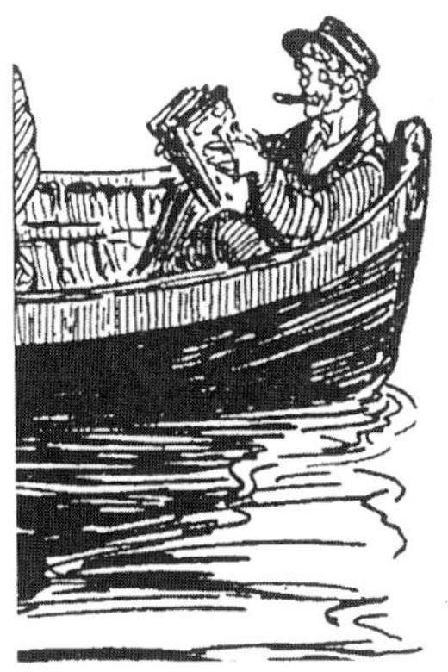

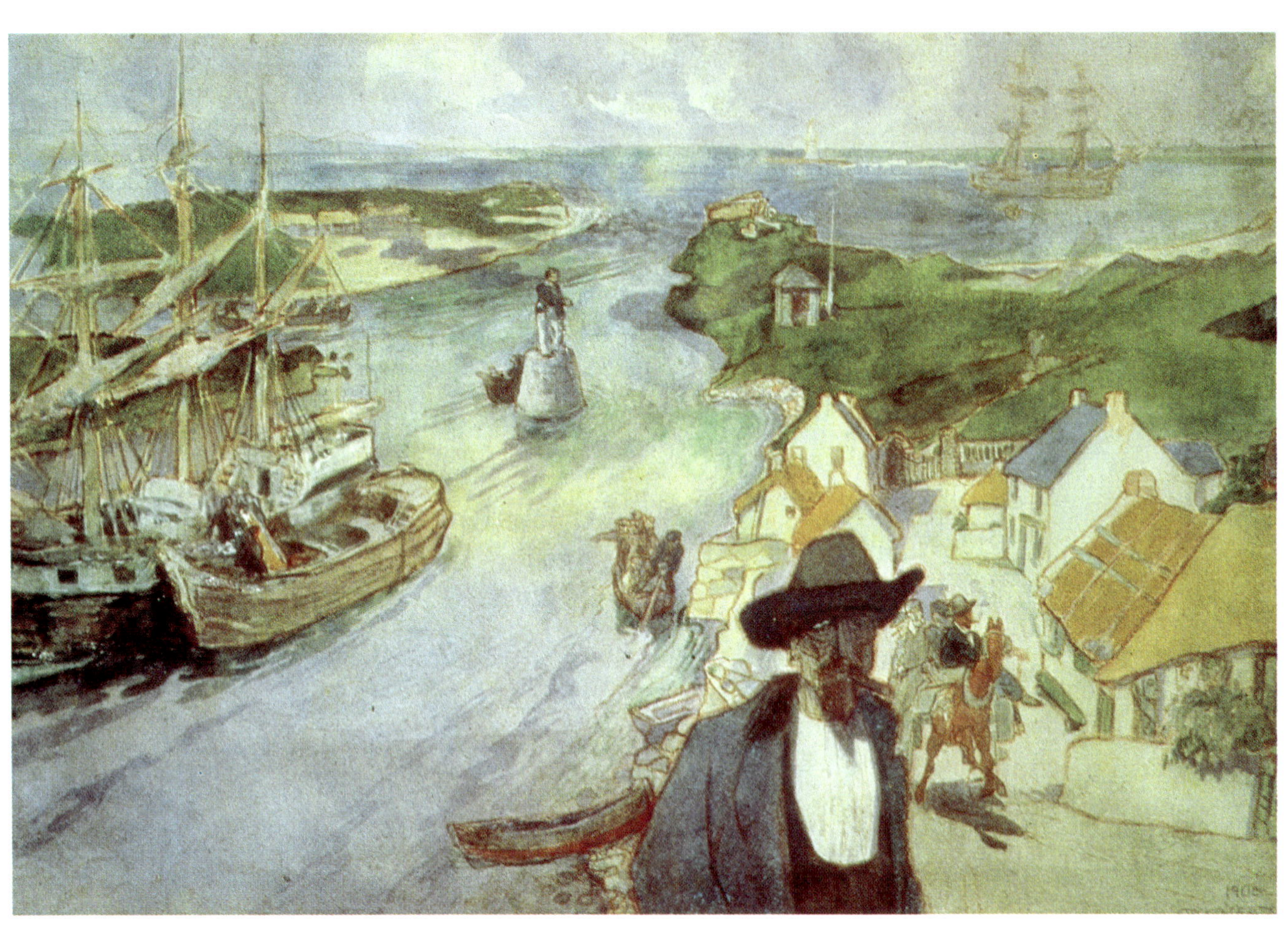

Yeats

PORTRAIT
OF AN
ARTISTIC FAMILY

HILARY PYLE

NATIONAL GALLERY OF IRELAND
in association with
MERRELL HOLBERTON
PUBLISHERS LONDON

First published in 1997, in association with the National Gallery of Ireland, by
Merrell Holberton Publishers Ltd
Willcox House, 42 Southwark Street, London SE1 1UN

Hardback ISBN 1 85894 040 0
Paperback ISBN 0903 162 938

Produced by Merrell Holberton Publishers
Designed by Roger Davies

Printed and bound in Italy

Jacket/cover illustration: Jack B. Yeats, *The singing horseman*, 1949 (NGI 4524)
Back jacket/cover illustration: John Butler Yeats, *William Butler Yeats*, 1900 (NGI 872)
Frontispiece: Jack B. Yeats, *Memory Harbour*, 1900 (Michael B. Yeats Collection)

Contents

Author's Ackowledgements

Originally this book was envisaged as two separate small books, an update of *Jack B. Yeats in the National Gallery of Ireland*, published in 1986, and a companion volume, *John Butler Yeats in the National Gallery of Ireland*, which would include the watercolour by W.B. Yeats in the Gallery's collection. The recent acquisition of several important items, however, made it clear that, put together, the two books could become one book about the art of the Yeats family as it is represented – and it is represented well despite many gaps – in the National Gallery of Ireland.

W.B. Yeats has been extolled and will go on being extolled over many a year. Those who nurtured him and shared his growing have more slowly been earning their due in biographies, John Butler Yeats in the splendid work by William Murphy, and Lily and Elizabeth in essential publications by Joan Hardwick and Gifford Lewis. Anne Yeats was the subject of a major exhibition at the Royal Hibernian Academy two years ago. This book now aims to break new ground by bringing all these personalities together with an emphasis on the unique nature of their art.

Anne Yeats has spent a great deal of her life encouraging and assisting research into those who have gone before her. I am in perpetual debt to her. Her ready interest in the many questions that arose, and her cooperation in the attempt to solve them, made the research immensely pleasurable. It is through her generosity that we now have the Jack. B. Yeats archive in the National Gallery of Ireland, a source of much enlightenment, and with it Jack Yeats's library and material relating to the Cuala Press and Cuala Industries, as well as a rare watercolour by Elizabeth Yeats.

Since I began writing, some lovers of the Yeatses have quickly and generously come forward with very special additions to the Yeats collection. These new additions are all included in the book.

Among others, I wish to thank my colleagues Brian Kennedy, Adrian Le Harivel and Fionnuala Croke for assistance in various ways; Máighréad McParland and Niamh McGuinne for advice on matters of conservation; and Niamh Gogan in the Library for spontaneous cheerful help. I am particularly grateful to Roy Hewson and Marie McFeely for their tireless and scrupulous work in photographing the collection and pursuing companion images.

My thanks also to Michael Kenny, Gifford Lewis, William Murphy, Cian hÉigeartaigh, Homan Potterton, Rex Roberts, Theo Waddington, Dr James White, the librarians in the various libraries I have consulted, and owners who in the past have opened their collections to me, so increasing my knowledge and understanding of all the Yeatses. Paul Holberton has been a very sympathetic editor. Raymond Keaveney's enthusiasm for the initial concept I put to him of a Yeats Museum has never waned, and I thank him for inviting me to write this book.

Its publication represents the first stepping stone *en route* to a long awaited Yeats Museum within the National Gallery of Ireland. Dedicated to the most notorious of the artistic Yeatses, Jack B. Yeats, it it hoped (to quote from his book *Sligo*) that 'it will have a Museum interest, without the permanent mill stone effect of a sure enough Museum'.

HILARY PYLE

Foreword

Since the middle of the nineteenth century the Yeats family have contributed on a virtually continuous basis to the cultural life of Ireland, in writing, theatre, painting and printing. Thanks to the generosity of the Yeats family and other individuals and corporations, the National Gallery of Ireland today possesses the most comprehensive collection of artworks by the family, embracing paintings, watercolours, drawings, sketchbooks, embroidery and other media.

It is intended to assemble this splendid collection in one location within the National Gallery of Ireland's complex of buildings on Merrion Square, to constitute a 'Yeats Museum'. This museum within a museum, in the first instance, will be temporarily located on the ground floor of Francis Fowke's 1864 building, where it will be housed for three years. In the year 2000 the museum will move to a new location in the planned extension on Clare Street which is being designed by the firm of Benson & Forsyth. The space provided here will be purpose-built to show the material off to best advantage.

The current publication has been compiled to provide the visitor with a commentary on the collection, providing a detailed analysis of the oil paintings, watercolours and drawings, together with more concise accounts of other material. Hilary Pyle's erudite text outlines the careers of the various members of the family as they moved from Dublin to London to Sligo to New York and back again. Her exhaustive exegesis of the works themselves supplies the reader with a keen insight into their meaning and context, enriching the experience of the visitor and whetting the appetite of the uninitiated. The text is complemented by a visual survey of the collection provided by the photographs of Roy Hewson.

RAYMOND KEAVENEY
Director of the National Gallery of Ireland

Introduction

Unlike other remarkable families of the nineteenth century, such as the Wordsworths, Brontës and Rossettis, who did their flourishing in one lifespan, the Hones and the Yeatses have tended to produce creative people from generation to generation. The first notable Yeats may have been the Yeates who illustrated that splendid propagandist volume *The History of the Coronation of the most high, most mighty and most excellent Monarch, James II ... of 1685.*[1] If the artist who conceived *The Manner of the Champions performing the Ceremony of the Challenge* (fig. 1) was some kind of relative, John and Jack Yeats, who came after him, were capable of representing equally spirited personages and steeds (fig. 2).

The Yeats family is known to have been in Ireland since the seventeenth century. They cherished their connection with an even older Irish family, the Butlers.

However, the nineteenth-century philosopher of the family, John Butler Yeats (JBY), may have ruminated on the fact that the family name could derive from the word 'gate'. For him it would have to have been an open gate. His father, William, a red-headed rector who hunted and carried out his ministry at Tullylish, County Down, where JBY grew up, did everything to encourage him mentally and artistically. William Butler Yeats was "always on the lookout for the beautiful and the pleasing", JBY wrote in his manuscript memoirs. He remembered his mother (née Corbet) writing poetry. From this secure childhood, augmented with stories about his father's background in Sligo and carefree student days at Trinity College, Dublin, JBY was sent at the age of ten to a puritanical school at Seaforth near Liverpool, "managed by a fear of God and Miss Emma". Two years later he went to the Atholl Academy

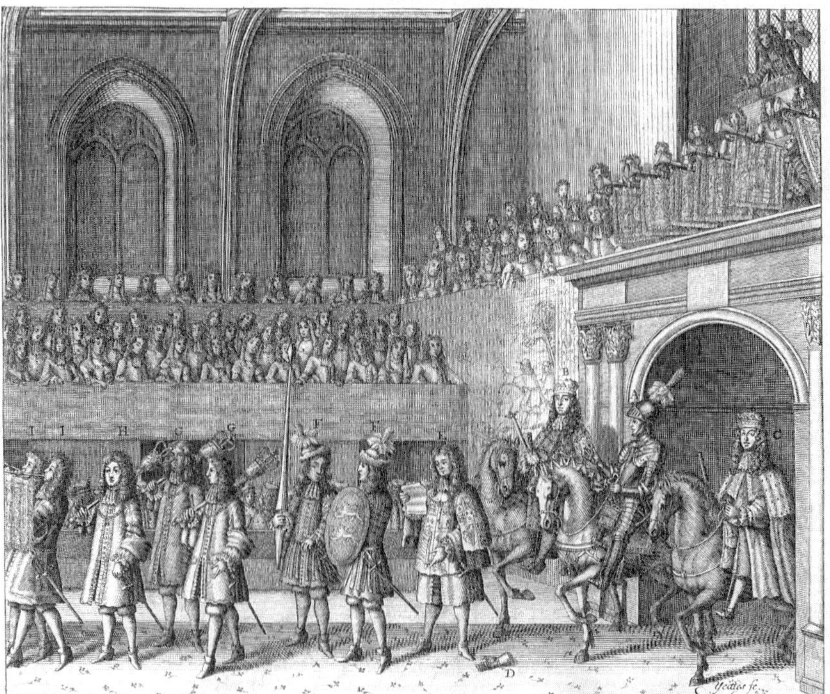

Fig. 1 Yeates, *The Manner of the Champions performing the Ceremony of the Challenge,* engraving, *ca.* 1685

Right
John Butler Yeats, *Susan L. Mitchell* (detail), 1899 (see p. 94)

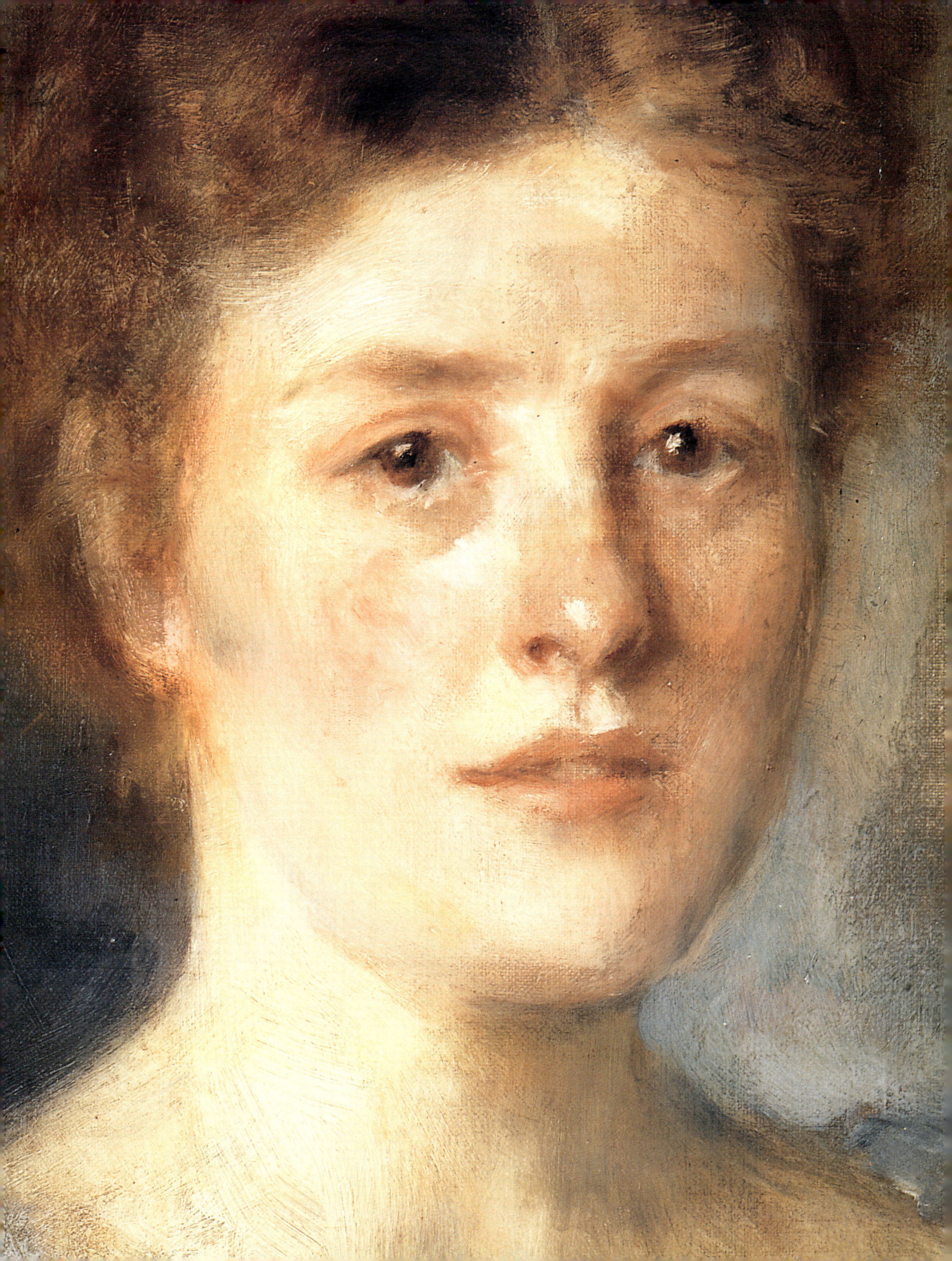

it is unlikely that such resounding idealism affected all who listened to him, JBY himself continued to reiterate his fervent belief in truth specifically in connection with his art. Quite late in life he told his son William Butler Yeats (WBY), "Truth seen in passion is the substance of poetry. And to him who has not the vision of truth the poetry tells nothing."[3]

He undertook "the task of Self-Culture" and humbly strove to improve his painting technique throughout his days. He had been drawing from infancy. The gift was recognized at school, where he experienced "a continual intellectual intoxication" from form and colour around him in the classroom.[4] While working for the Trinity Entrance, he covered a compendium of algebra (figs. 2 and 3) with pen-and-ink horses, fancy heads and portraits. He loved to do caricature (a true man of an age which enjoyed absurdities). A large sketchbook with pen-and-ink studies of characters in 1860s' costume[5] – a Mrs Brown (fig. 4) and others blown mischievously by the wind, and sketches based on Hogarth – was probably filled when he was thinking tentatively of making a career in art. He had had a favourable start at the Four Courts as protégé of his father's friend Isaac Butt (see p. 102), conscious that other young and not so young men stood idly waiting

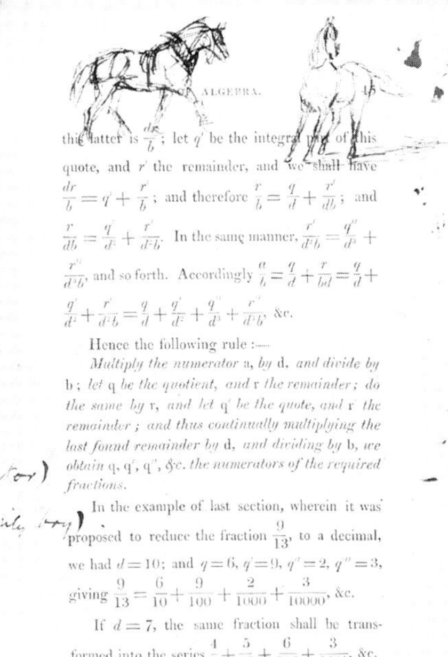

Fig. 2
J.B. Yeats,
Early drawing
of horses in an
algebra
compendium
(NGI Yeats
Archive)

on the Isle of Man, an even sterner establishment, but where he thrived intellectually and where despite waning belief he found that his father's insistence on honesty in thinking was echoed. This education at a distance from home may have been the cause of a rootlessness that later made it difficult for him to settle in one place for any great length of time.

JBY's open mind and dislike of superstition led him to read Darwin and John Stuart Mill at university. He was excited, too, by Comte's logical positivism, and after doing brilliantly in his degree at Trinity College he rejected the Church, for which he had been intended. He took to the law, became a student at the King's Inns, and, skilled in argument, was elected auditor of the Law Students' Debating Society of Dublin. In his inaugural address in November 1865 he pronounced the attainment of truth and the "task of Self-Culture" to be imperative for those on the threshold of their lives, quoting Mill, Schiller and Shakespeare ("let your reason serve to make the truth appear where it seems hid, and hide the false, seems true") to support his views.[2] The pursuit of truth and beauty was not uncommon in an age when science was disturbing more orthodox and long established tenets. But while

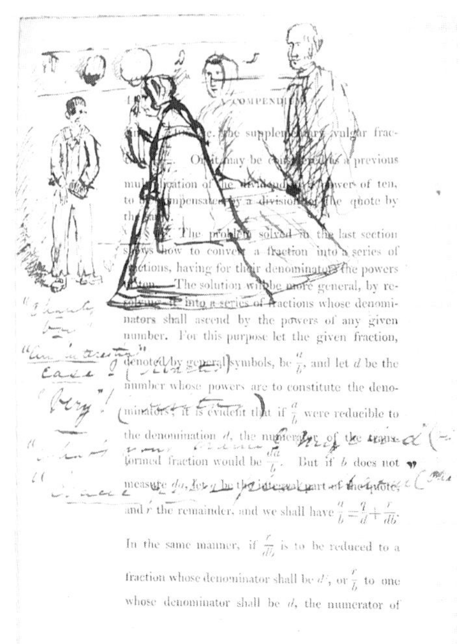

Fig. 3
J.B. Yeats,
Early drawing
in an algebra
compendium
(NGI Yeats
Archive)

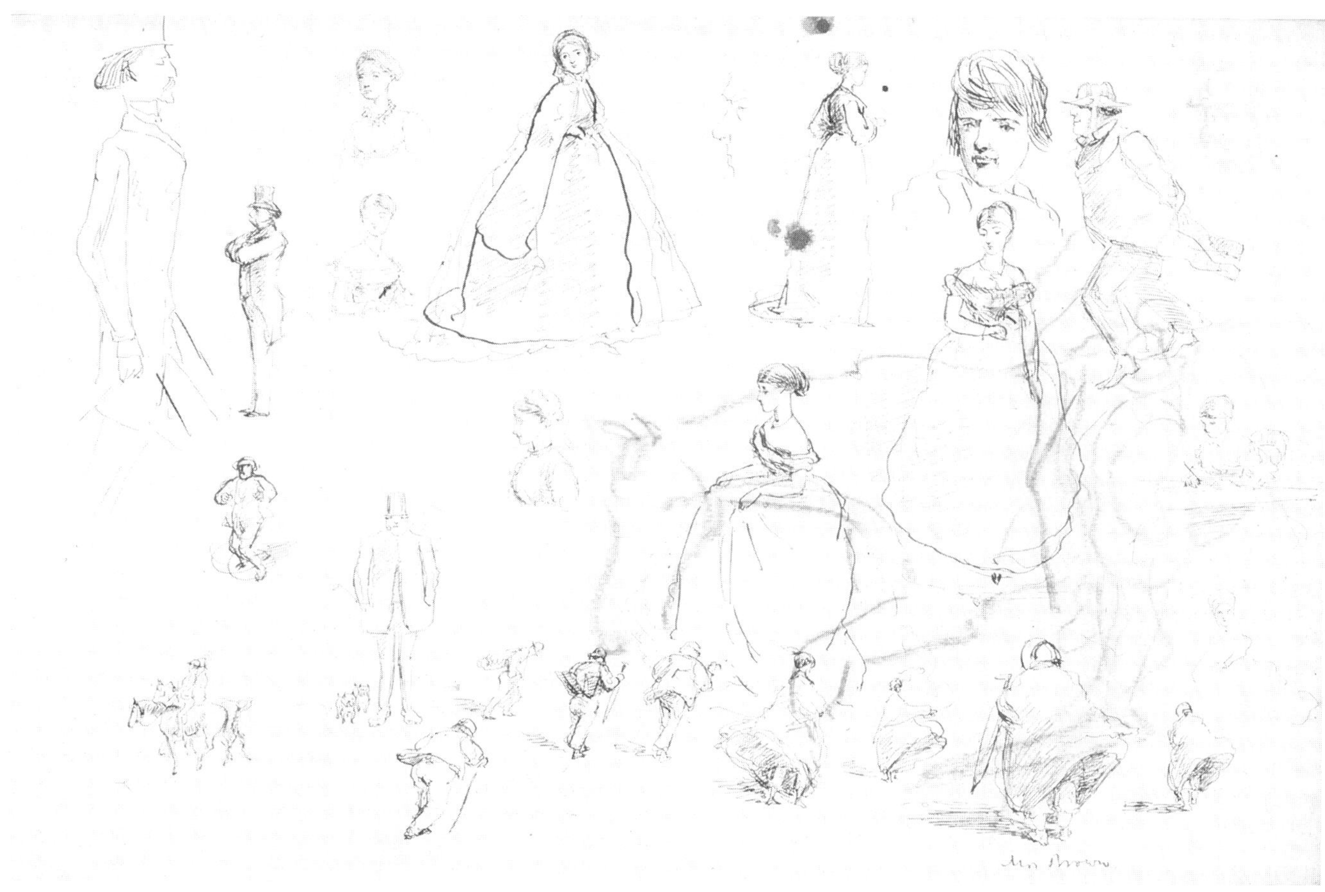

Fig. 4 J.B. Yeats, *Mrs Brown* and other drawings from a
Sketchbook, 1860s (Anne Yeats Collection)

for cases to come to hand; but at trials it was his pencil rather than his legal sense that was busy, his sketches of the participants in the court dramas entertaining his colleagues around him.

Then one day the joke rebounded. His satirical portrait found its way into the hands of its subject – the humourless defending counsel – who was not amused, and JBY realised that a change of career was desirable. He had been encouraged by friends to send drawings to the editor of *Fun*, who was interested in them. Early in 1867 he set out for London, where he received further encouragement from Richard Doyle, the illustrator, and the sculptor John Henry Foley. He had inherited a small income from family lands at Thomastown in County Kildare which enabled him to enrol at Heatherley's Art School.

JBY was already a father when he became a student once again. Upon winning a prize in political economy at Trinity College after graduation, he had spent the

money looking up George Pollexfen, his closest friend
at the Atholl Academy, in Sligo. At school he had been
captivated by Pollexfen's ability to tell riveting stories
(JBY tried all his life to write short stories, but never
succeeded). Pollexfen's loneness as an individual, and
his intrinsic melancholy, JBY found compelling; though
the Sligo boy shared none of JBY's intellectual interests
and took to a career as a horse-trainer (fig. 5). (In later
years he would become obsessed with the occult and
astrology.) JBY found that George's sister shared
facets of his schoolfellow's character that he had found
intriguing. Visiting the Sligo of his ancestors must also
have touched roots that moved him (the emotion trans-
mitted to three of his children). He married Susan Mary
Pollexfen (see p. 54) a year later, and with her begot the
remarkable family that engaged his attention, both
admiring and critical, until the day of his death.

JBY never failed to be fascinated by creative women,
or women out of the ordinary, and though posterity has
preserved little of actual fact about Susan Pollexfen,
apart from accounts of her inherited melancholy, she
must have attracted JBY not only with her beauty but
with an originality of mind as well. Their first son,
William Butler Yeats, was born nearly two years later
in Dublin. Susan Mary (Lily) was born at Enniscrone,
County Sligo, in August 1866; and Elizabeth Corbet
(Lolly) and John Butler Yeats Junior (Jack B. Yeats) were
born after the family had moved to London. Two other
children did not survive – Robert (Bobbie) was
regarded by JBY as the brightest of the bunch and one
wonders what he might have become.

At Heatherley's JBY became friends with Nettleship,
Ellis (see further p. 48) and Sydney Hall (all to be successful minor artists), and they formed a 'brotherhood',
George Wilson taking the place of Hall (later the artist
of the Parnell Commission) when he left to become an
illustrator. They shared an interest in Browning, Blake
and the Pre-Raphaelites, and acknowledged the solitary
nature of the artist. JBY's original themes, scrupulously
finished, attracted attention. He visited the studio of
Frederick Sandys, who liked his work. He was himself
visited by George Watts, 'the English Michelangelo',
prominent and popular (fig. 6), whose best portraits had
a poetic immediacy JBY would aim for in his own

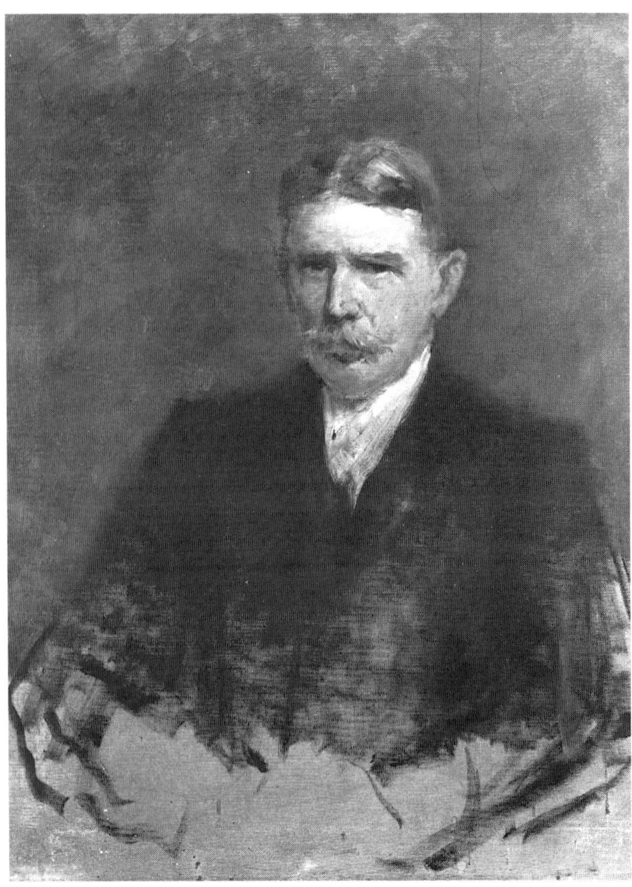

Fig. 5 J.B. Yeats, *George Pollexfen, ca.* 1902 (Michael B. Yeats
Collection)

Right
John Butler Yeats, *John O'Leary* (detail), 1904 (see p. 118)

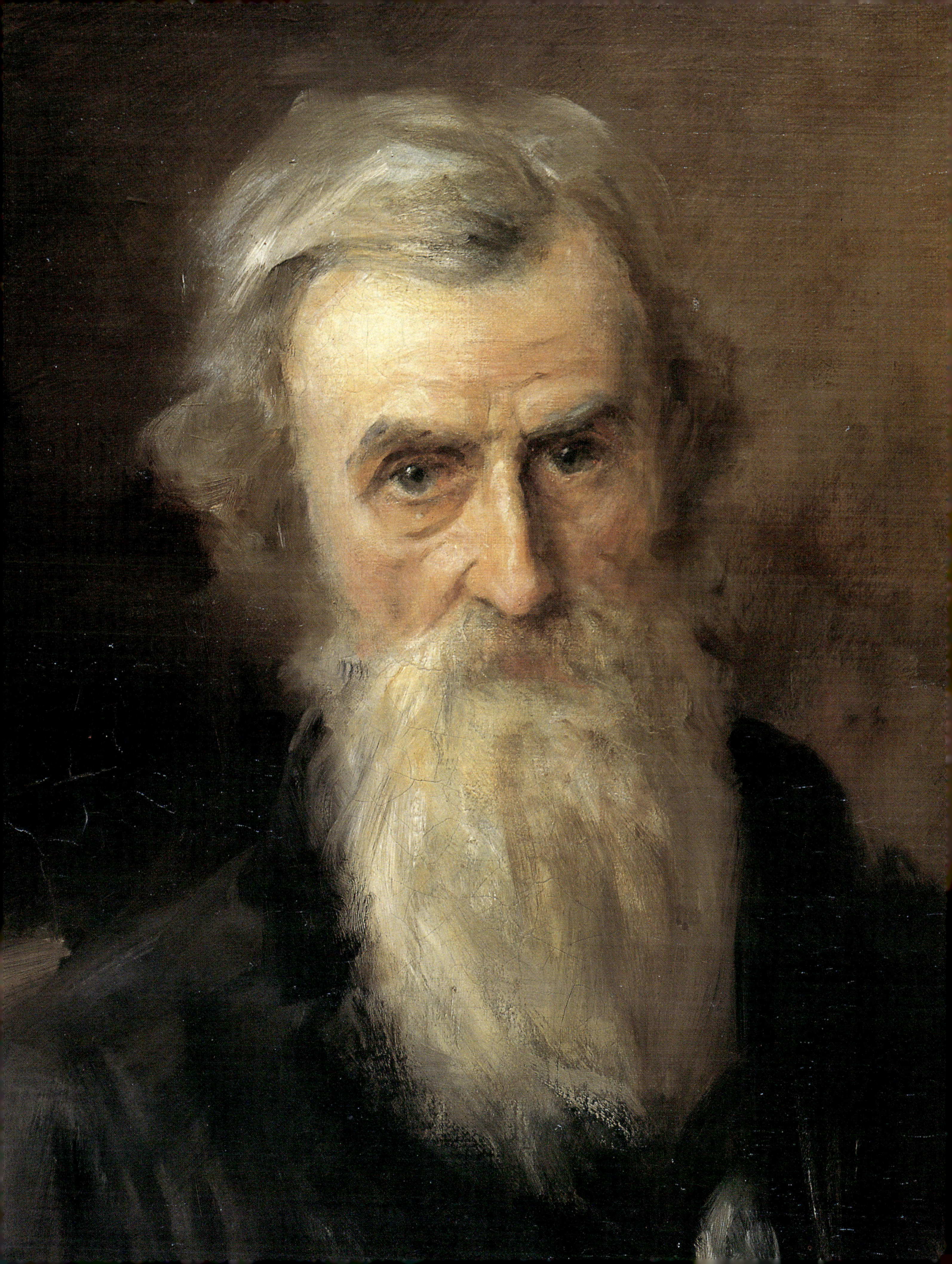

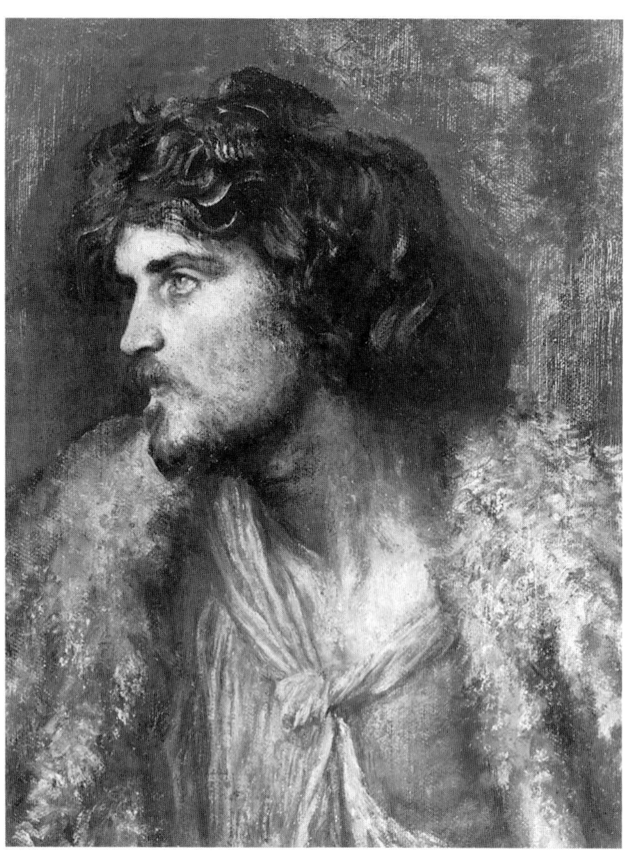

Fig. 6 G.F. Watts, *The Prodigal Son*, 1872 (Trustees of the Watts Gallery, Compton)

portraits. But he was shy of Rossetti and Browning, both valuable connections, who were receptive to his *Pippa* (p. 50). Some inborn misgiving in JBY, which seemed to seize him on occasions of success, prevented him from following up their invitations. He told WBY not long before he died, "I did so want to put myself right with your mother and her family. That was why I turned from the things of the imagination and did not go to see Rossetti." The Pollexfens would never accept his rejection of a respectable career for what they regarded as a bohemian life. Since he was naturally gifted and potentially an excellent barrister, the family could have enjoyed a very comfortable life.

This constant struggle between his duty as a husband and father and his aspirations as an artist undermined his career, so that he succeeded in both only in an idealistic way. He continued as a student, sharing a studio for a time with Ellis, where he worked with models and learned to make them talk. He moved from Heatherley's to the Slade to become the pupil of Edward Poynter, recently returned from Paris, whose Ingres perfection appealed to him. His own flawless technique in chalk (something he would never achieve in oil) impressed Poynter, who encouraged a reluctant JBY (now in his early thirties) to move on to oil. JBY was nurturing his intellect, reading recent poetry by Newman, and remaining friendly with his academic friends Todhunter and Dowden.

In about 1873 JBY became a professional journeyman for a time, painting portraits in Kerry, Laois and the South of England. He described this form of commercial work to Lady Gregory (see further pp. 17 and 112) as "a ghoulish and horrible industry", confessing to have done many posthumous portraits from photographs, for which he said people in Dublin had "an appetite". "The dining hall at the King's Inns has many of these horrors flaunting in ghastly mockery, beside portraits done straight from the living sitters." The practice of copying portraits, though, stood him in good stead further into his career, and was one of his few practical assets. Living sitters saw another side of the artist. His friend Dowden who sat as model described JBY at work: "He gets so thoroughly into the 'fluid and attaching' state, every glance at one's face seems to give him a shock, and through a series of such shocks he progresses … and all the while he is indulging in endless gossip of the peculiar *Yeatsian* kind".[6] The trivial traits of character he brooded on, according to Dowden, were analysed in a series of Aristotelian classifications.

JBY made attempts to advance himself. In May 1876 he approached Isaac Butt, by this time leader of the Irish Party in the House of Commons, for a portrait (see p. 102), in order to launch himself properly as a portrait painter; but it was not long before he decided to paint landscape seriously, and then he was distracted once more by tantalizing subjects that stimulated his mind, such as *Eurydice* or *The Nihilist*. The Royal Academy, which was his goal, receded perpetually. He only ever had two pieces accepted, *Nieta* in 1879 and a subject picture in 1887.

Towards the end of the 1870s Dowden, always encouraging, found him some work in Dublin; and, when his portrait of Dowden's daughter (see p. 56) was a great success in the Royal Hibernian Academy, he returned there, leaving his son Jack with the Pollexfen grandparents in Sligo and bringing the rest of the family to Howth first, and then Terenure. His studios at York Street and, from late 1883, no. 7, St Stephen's Green, became meeting places for artists, poets and philosophers. "Canvases were stacked everywhere round the walls," Katharine Tynan recalled.[7] "They were used to conceal many things – the little kitchen and tea-table arrangement at one end, Mr. Yeats's slippers and the dressing-room of the family." Sarah Purser (fig. 7) lunched with him, Osborne looked in, and Dowden continued to sit for a portrait.

It was a promising time, in a city where Yeats's name was familiar and a modest living from portraiture was possible. JBY knew the right people and was an attractive personality. He was already a member of the Dublin Sketching Club. He taught sporadically at the Metropolitan School of Art, sending his daughters there for a short time and instructing WBY there when he had left High School. Quirks of character still intrigued him, and he attended the trial of the Invincibles to make drawings. He worked at commissions from friends and acquaintances, exhibiting portraits and fancy paintings

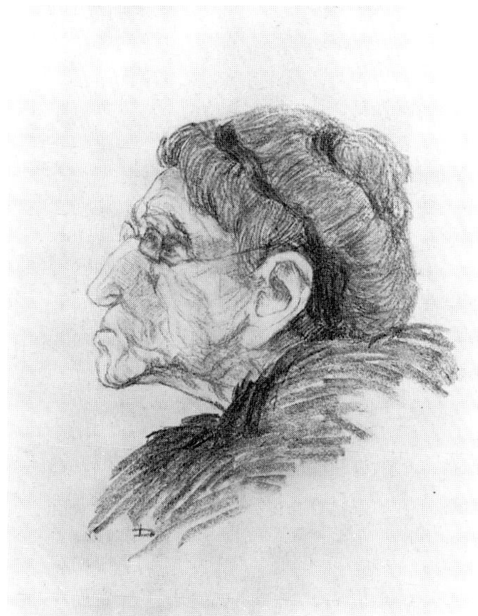

Fig. 7
L. Davidson,
Sarah Purser
(NGI 3281)

at the RHA; and his local subjects, where he observed the socially deprived of Dublin, were topical and strongly painted.

His style had progressed from its post-Pre-Raphaelite emphasis with an overloading of paint, in the previous decade, to something freer and more tonal as he felt the influence of Whistler. At all stages of his career JBY had an eye to what was modern, looking at leading painters critically and taking from them what he admired. But his penchant for intellectual discussion and theoretical monologue led him into bad habits, where he neglected to finish paintings or harassed them beyond retrieval, which upset clients and himself. ("Every artist knows how difficult it is to make up one's mind that a picture is finished," he would say, "for a picture is never finished, since it is never perfect, and perfection is the artist's goal.")[8] About this time he developed the portrait sketch, for which he became famous, in a more finished technique, separating it from notions of caricature or illustration. His original and expressive work with pencil derived from his natural skill with chalk, together with an accuracy and delicacy as a pen-and-ink artist. But it also rose out of an affinity with Whistler's ability to transmit in his paintings a sketchlike quality that he approved. "Every work of art should survive after all the labour bestowed on it, and *survive as a sketch*," he believed. "To the last it must be something struck off at a first heat." His sketches of intellectuals at the Contemporary Club (see pp. 64–70) have that element of living immediacy.

JBY received a serious blow in 1885 when his uncle Matthew, who managed the small estate in Kildare on which he depended, died, leaving his financial matters in a perilous state. The artist took advantage of the Land Commission offer to dispose of the land and departed for London, determined to make good this time as the illustrator he had intended to be twenty years before. But from the start the move was doomed. His wife had a stroke, and then a second one; and it quickly became obvious that JBY was no better suited to seeking out publishers in London than he had been to attracting patrons for his portraits in Dublin.

However, there was a difference now in that his children were fully grown and helped to shoulder the responsibility of which JBY was incapable. WBY, already making a name for himself as a poet, made contact with publishers, interesting them in illustrations by his father and brother. Lily trained as an embroideress and worked for years at Kelmscott House, the Oxford-shire workshop of William Morris's daughter. Eliza-beth was housekeeper and later a Froebel teacher. She kept an account of what Jack (at art school) contributed from the drawings he sold, and the two brought samples of their father's work around the publishing houses. JBY executed commissions for Fisher Unwin and Dent, he illustrated for his son and his drawings appeared in *Leisure Hour*.

In London's artistic neighbourhood of Bedford Park, to which they had returned, the family made a noticeable impact despite their dire poverty. "The intensity and individualism of genius itself could never wash out of the world's memories the general impres-sion of Willie and Lily and Lolly and Jack," wrote G.K. Chesterton, "names cast backwards and forwards in a unique sort of comedy of Irish wit, gossip, satire, fam-ily quarrels and family pride. I knew the family more or less as a whole in those days."[9] In the room next to JBY's studio was his wife, not totally oblivious of the scene and always the concern of all as well as provid-ing a conceptual link with Sligo. JBY, constantly aware

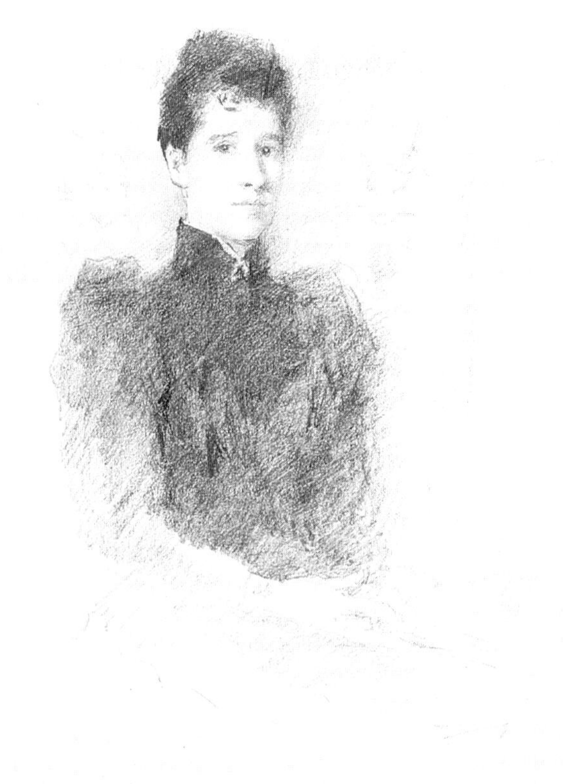

Fig. 8 J.B. Yeats, *Elizabeth (Lolly) Yeats, ca.* 1895 (Anne Yeats Collection)

of her delicacy, was hesitant to make sorties from home, but found an outlet for his intellect in conversation evenings at the Calumet Club, a group of artists and philosophers of the district who met regularly.

Though he was painting hardly at all, JBY was elected Associate of the Royal Hibernian Academy (ARHA) in 1893. His distinctive work of the period was in wash, illustrations for reproduction where he showed himself more suited to poetry than to narrative, his images of musicians being romantic yet individual. Within the house at Blenheim Road in Bedford Park he had a ready-made subject-matter in his children, whose portraits he painted and sketched during this decade when they were proving themselves: WBY, the poet (see pp. 88, 96), creating a new national literature;[10] Lily, embroiderer and designer, JBY's constant model (see p. 98 and fig. 9), who was growing psychic in visions and dreams; Elizabeth (fig. 8) and Jack (see pp. 60 and 78) artists of different calibre, both innovators in their own fields, Elizabeth publishing a valuable art instruction manual, Jack already "solitary in his habits", "the most serious person in the house by far ... the only one who lives by jokes", JBY claimed.[11]

JBY, at the instigation of Lady Gregory (see p. 112), whom he had met at Jack's first exhibition in the Haymarket, London, was tempted to spend the summer of 1898 in Dublin, making sketches of Irish luminaries for her. He worked in his studio, as well as teaching for May Manning; and he was a natural teacher. He found a rapport with Clare Marsh, who learned much from him in the matter of stylistic expression, and would surpass him in technique, if not in imagination. "In painting the chief thing is to make oneself think," he advised her. "You must not imitate a thing *directly* but rather translate it into the language of painting." His tip about portrait painting sheds light on his own method. "You should be a little kind and courtly to ... failings ... this is artistic truth and it is also good behaviour."[12]

This sojourn had encouraged him to start painting oil portraits again, and he even tackled a nude after an interval of twenty years, telling Rosa Butt (see p. 100), "the nude is the highest achievement of our art". His failure to get even one picture accepted by the Royal Academy was the occasion for Sarah Purser's insistence

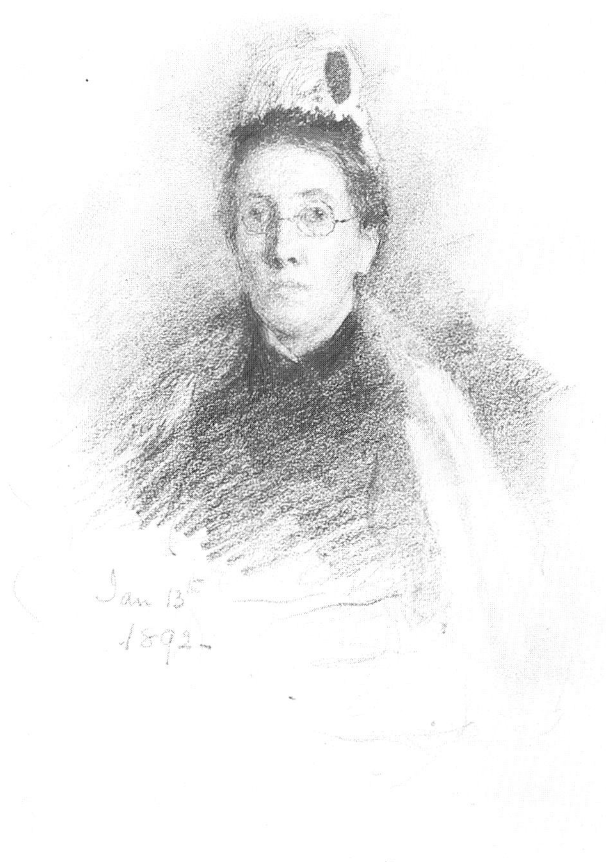

Fig. 9 J.B. Yeats, *Susan Mary (Lily) Yeats,* January 13th 1892 (Anne Yeats Collection)

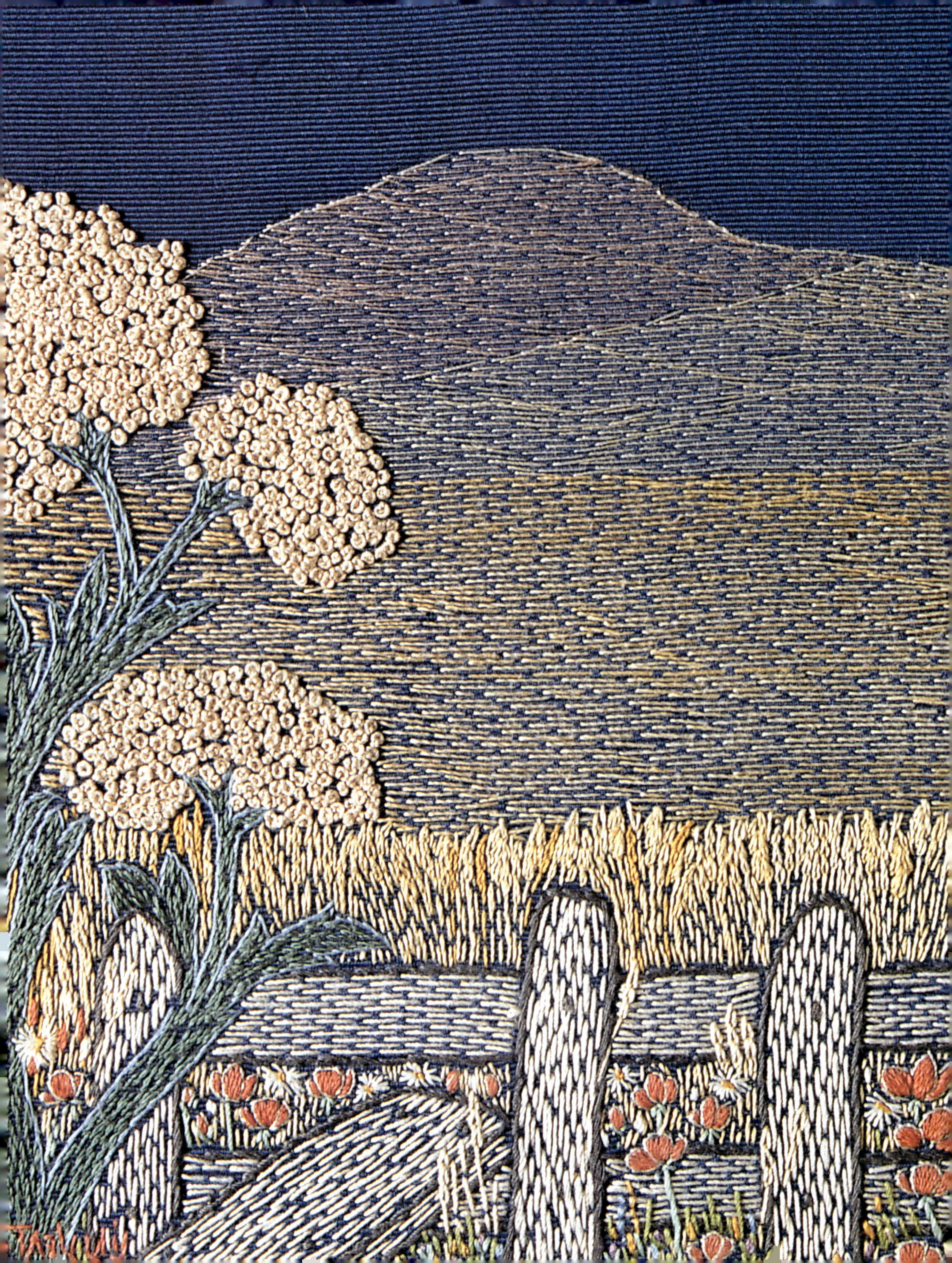

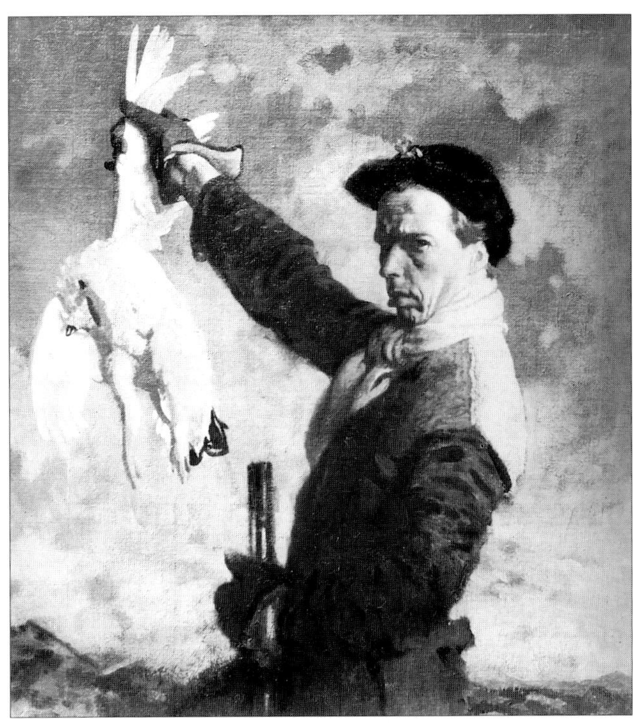

Fig. 10 W. Orpen, *The dead ptarmigan (self-portrait)*, *ca.* 1909 (NGI 945)

Left
Susan Mary (Lily) Yeats, *Cornfield with poppies* (detail), 1941 (see p. 154)

on arranging the historic selection of his work and that of Nathaniel Hone back in Dublin, late in 1901.[13] JBY again returned to Dublin where two formidable portrait painters, Walter Osborne (who soon and tragically died) and William Orpen (fig. 10) – younger than JBY's younger son – were potential rivals. But he received commissions almost at once from John Quinn, who was bewitched by the Irish cultural revival, and Hugh Lane (see p. 130), building the corpus of an Irish modern art collection, both of whom saw him as the visual exponent of the creators of the new ethos. It was an ideal situation for a man at sixty as energetic as he was.

Home Rule, it was ardently believed, lay round the corner, and JBY had always been an advocate of Home Rule. One son was laying the foundations of a national theatre. The other was exhibiting innovative art with a nationalist theme. His daughters were enticed over from England into the craft industry, to design embroidery suitable to the nationalistic fervour, and to found the Cuala Press, where Irish poetry and prose were printed. With several Yeatses around, it is not surprising that there was some confusion. JBY had already found himself mixed up with Jack when they both illustrated in London; and the *Freeman's Journal*, reporting the private view of the newly opened Abbey Theatre in December 1904, referred to the portraits "painted by Mr. W.B. Yeats"![14] Nevertheless the old artist was fêted in his own right, and had, it seemed, won honourable and independent declining years in the land of his ancestors. However, "by constantly searching for the moment of magic in terms of revealing his sitter's inner soul or radiance," James White has written, "he lived on the brink of success which never quite seemed to become fact".[15] Added to this, and because of it, as an impractical dreamer he allowed himself to be preyed on by Lane and Quinn, who paid him pitiful fees for his portraits, less than a third of what they offered to Orpen or Shannon. His own lack of confidence led him generally to charge only what he regarded as the minimum, £10 for a head and £20 for a portrait with hands, when he knew he could ask £20 and £30 for each.

He did paint the incomparable portraits he had always known he could paint (the faulty technique has not barred them from posterity). Yet materially he knew himself to be a failure. Privately he was acutely sensitive to the "destructive" criticism, which he perceived to be "a special accomplishment" of "the vivacious city" in which he now lived.[16] He may have felt uneasy, too, living on the stage that the rôle of father of his family necessitated. He even turned against Jack's reserve, calling him "cold, and a little self complacent".[17] When Lane and the artist Sarah Cecilia Harrison had collected a sum to send him to Italy (rather tactlessly, since Lane's new protégé, Mancini, over whom he was enthusing, was an Italian), JBY suddenly decided to use the money to go to New York with Lily (fig. 11), on her way there to exhibit the Cuala products.

John Quinn took JBY under his wing. Before long he made a permanent home with the Petitpas sisters, "a stranger among strangers", as he described himself to Susan Mitchell (see p. 94),[18] analysing the essentially solitary nature he had always assigned to the artist and its paradoxical need to be at the same time with people. He never saw his family again, with the exception of WBY, who visited the United States with his wife the year after JBY's granddaughter Anne Yeats, also a painter (see pp. 270–73), was born. Almost immediately he was sketching in the law courts. John Quinn commissioned his own portrait and a few other commissions followed.

JBY had tended to associate with fringe artistic groups wherever he lived, and in New York he joined the anti-academic Ashcans, who favoured modernistic colour and expression, but who were themselves bypassed following the introduction of avantgarde European painting to America at the Armory Show in 1913. JBY exhibited some work with them, as the New York Independents, but he was not selected for the Armory Show, in which his son Jack was represented. The 'impressionistic' manner he had cultivated, and taken pride in during his final phase in Dublin, was not sufficiently modern: he would always, with his enthusiasm for Rubens, Romney and Hogarth, manifest an instinctive link with the Old Masters.

However, in America his 'impressionism' now gave way to a more 'expressionist' manner, where his colour

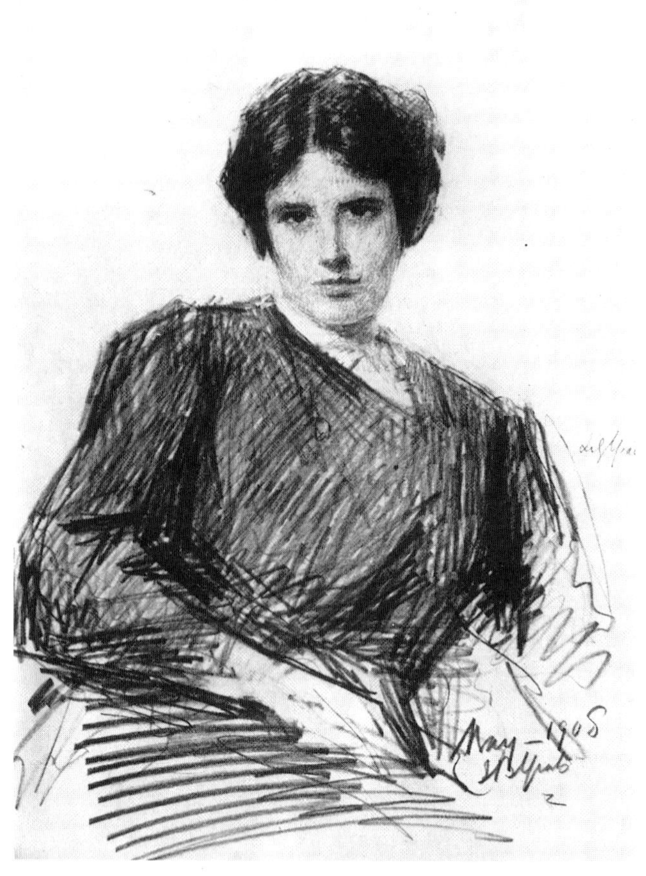

Fig. 11 J.B. Yeats, *Sketch portrait of Lily Yeats in New York,* May 1908 (Sligo County Library and Museum)

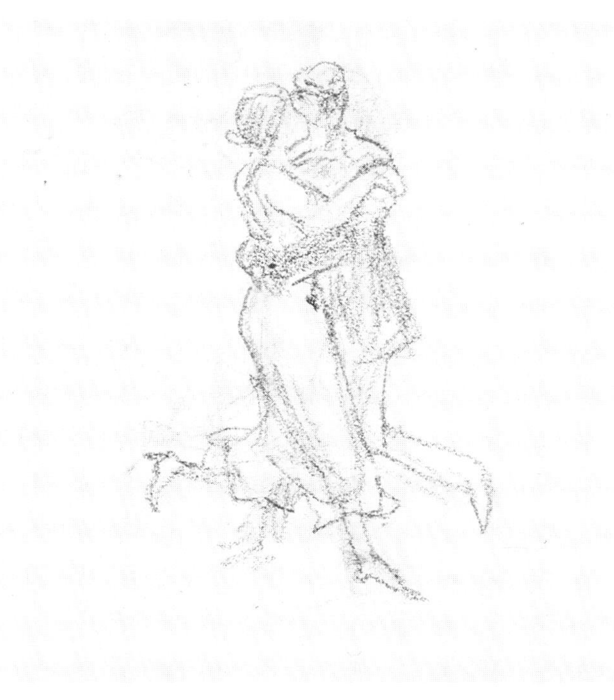

Fig. 12 J.B. Yeats, *Sketch of dancers,* New York *ca.* 1916 (Anne Yeats Collection)

took on a kind of brash energy. His drawing, too, exchanged the tentative exploration of the inner person for a confident affirmation of the outer self (fig. 12).

Much of JBY's work in America was lecturing – to men's clubs and women's societies, and to Irish organizations such as the Sinn Fein Society of New York. His writings at last became important. His lectures, letters and memoirs, and his essays in the tradition of Lamb and Hazlitt, were found worthy of publication by an audience for whom his conversation, admired at home, was phenomenal. He discovered Dostoyevsky and French novels. Every thinking or creative Irishman or -woman who visited New York sought him out; and he had continual intellectual stimulation in the composition of his final definitive self-portrait, commissioned by John Quinn (see p. 150).

George W. Russell (A.E.; see pp. 86 and 114) praised JBY towards the end of his life for "a humanity which delights in the humanity of others", and said, "I have liked people after seeing his portraits of them." JBY from his New York seclusion could have offered him an explanation: "When the artist imitates," [for him all art was imitation] "love seems to take the pencil out of his hand and finish the picture."[19] Despite the vicissitudes in his life, JBY had never abandoned his pursuit for artistic truth. In his final consideration he realised that what he had been running away from in life was the finite. His ceaseless search had brought him ultimately to realise the existence of an Art that was infinite.

JBY shared with all his children a natural affinity for the pen that comes to hand, or chalk. Lily was to perfect the needle as artistic implement, Elizabeth the printing press. WBY, for all his dedication to the literary pen, showed his sensitivity to watercolour and pastel. But it was Jack who, like his father, mastered the formalities of oil, and after great dedication and effort. It did not come easily for either artist, and yet both ultimately advanced the history of Irish art through that medium because of their originality and refusal to be trapped by convention.

When he was not sketching, JBY was writing, though without the stylistic replenishment of which his painting was capable. In words, he remained the eminent

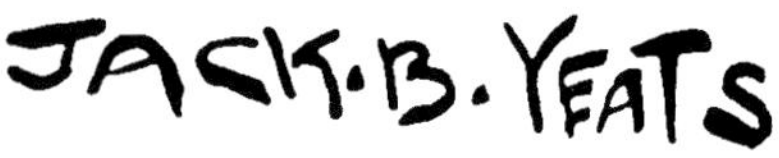

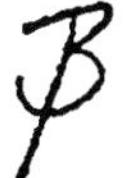

Fig. 13 Jack B. Yeats signature from an oil painting

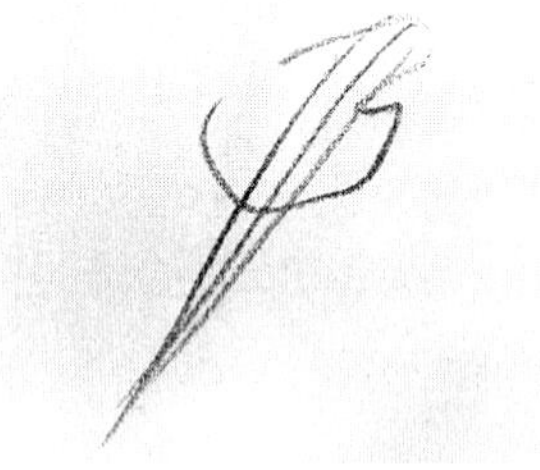

Fig. 14 Jack B. Yeats monogram from a watercolour

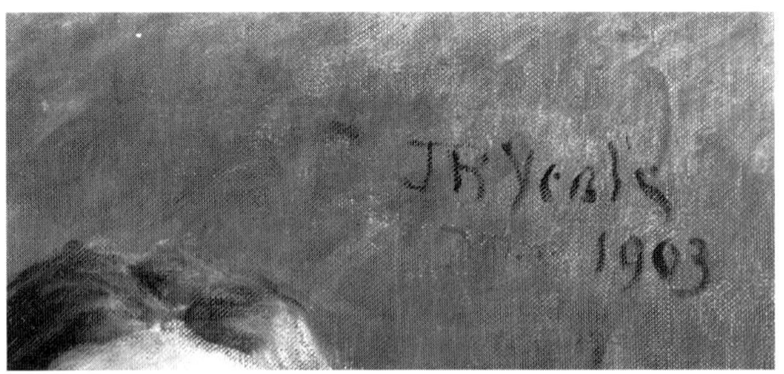

Fig. 15 Jack B. Yeats monogram from one of his books, 1930s

Fig. 16 John Butler Yeats signature from an oil painting

Jack B. was christened John Butler – like the others inheriting a family name – and, though he was always called Jack, he continues to be mistaken for his father and *vice versa*. To avoid confusion, from the beginning of his career (with one or two very early exceptions) he took care to sign himself 'Jack B. Yeats'. He signed all his oil paintings JACK B. YEATS – in capital letters (fig. 13). When he wished to be brief, on drawings or watercolours, he used a monogram devised from his initials JBY, in pencil or pen (figs. 14, 15). Some years after his death, this monogram was converted into a stamp in London by his dealer, Victor Waddington, to use on unsigned drawings, so some drawings bear this stamp.

'J.B. Yeats' is how his father signed himself, when he did not simply apply initials (fig. 16). Yet confusion will still arise between the works of father and son as a result of their both being referred to loosely as 'J.B. Yeats'.

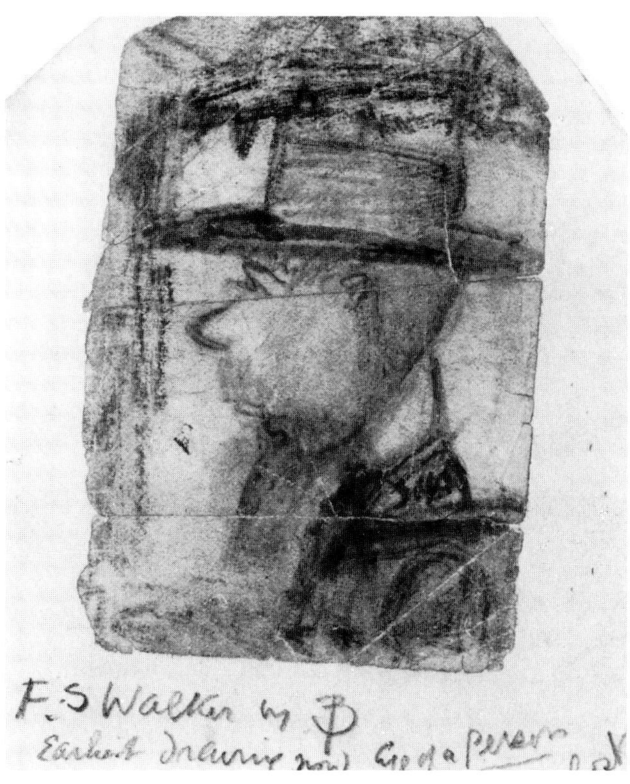

Fig. 17 Jack B. Yeats, *F.S. Walker*, an early drawing (NGI Yeats Archive)

Victorian. Both of his sons inherited the dual gift: W.B. Yeats, who had less inclination to practise art, has a marked visual element in his verse; Jack's preoccupation with words grew alongside his visual genius from his youth, when he earned his living as a cartoon artist, working for almost every illustrated paper in London. He contributed to *Punch* once, in 1896, under his own name, and then, from 1910 for the next thirty years, under the pseudonym 'W. Bird'. He wrote juvenile plays and books, collected ballads and published them with his own illustrations, and, at the age of sixty, he started a career as a serious writer of novels and books. These were admired by Beckett. At the same time he was painting regularly, and had yet to arrive at his most important canvases.

As a boy Jack Yeats had the advantage of living apart from the intellectual 'high' of his father, brother and sisters, and he developed a leisurely independence. He was born in London while JBY was still a student: his father's finances were precarious (he relied on a small private income) and Mrs Yeats's health was delicate and her disposition melancholy, so it was fortunate for Jack that his practical Pollexfen grandparents – with their odd relatives (whom WBY studied with interest) – decided to offer him a home in Sligo, a small country town in the west of Ireland, on the shores of the Atlantic. In this way Jack escaped any manifest influence from his father, though in later life when questioned why he took to his profession he would say: "I painted because I am the son of a painter".

Jack was practical, too, and, being objective and detached, could enjoy the company of all he met. He went to the local school. He rode into Sligo town seated beside his respected merchant grandfather in the pony trap; and he learned all there was to know about the docks where his grandfather's boats came in, and about Sligo town with its local characters and events.

He was drawing from an early age (fig. 17). His first known sketch, on an envelope, is of horses.[20] When he rejoined the family on their move to London in 1887, his sense of comedy inspired a drawing of a stained-glass window with St Valentine steaming open a love letter. His earlier illustrations to *Beauty and the Beast* have a similar mischievousness.[21]

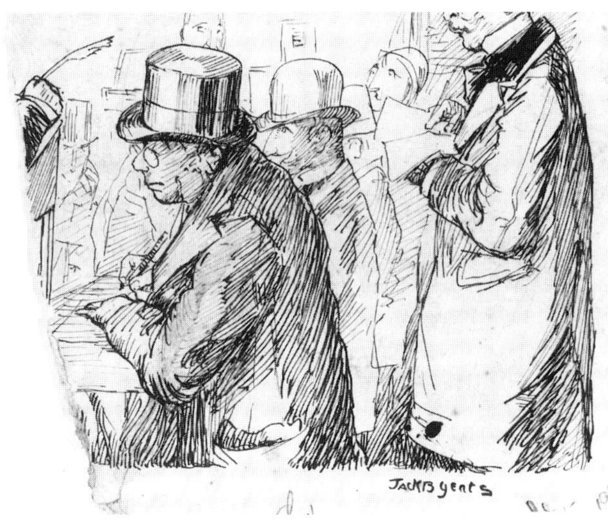

Fig. 18 Jack B. Yeats, *Old Quaritch, publisher, at a book sale*, 1890 (NGI Yeats Archive)

Details of Jack Yeats's subsequent movements may be found in the Chronology and, when they are relevant, with the descriptions of the pictures. He attended various art schools in London for short periods, where, through Fred Brown, and perhaps the painter and etcher Alphonse Legros, he came indirectly under the influence of the New English Art Club and its liberal policy. Legros underlined his own method of memory drawing in his teaching, and memory was to become a feature of Yeats's later work. At South Kensington the young artist learned the value of a clear line in drawing (fig. 18).

Yet the most worthwhile art training for Jack Yeats was gained though apprenticeship. He was contributing to the illustrated magazine *The Vegetarian* from the age of sixteen, producing decorative borders, cartoons with comic captions and straight drawings. Later he spread to other journals such as *Paddock Life*, *Chums* and *Judy*, illustrating sports events and developing his flair for visual comedy. He continued to work unremittingly at this specialized form of journalism for the next ten years, with a spell as a commercial poster artist in Manchester.

Beardsley and Phil May, one of the more distinctive black-and-white illustrators, had a passing influence on him, as did Harry Furniss, with whom he worked for some years. The more famous Continental poster artists of the 1890s affected his work indirectly. After phases of experimentation, Yeats developed a personal manner, which was highly regarded, but was not yet outstanding. Subsequently his literary bent led him to collect printed ballads, with their crude woodcut illustrations, and this with other influences led him to the unmistakeably individual idiom of *A Broad Sheet* and the *Broadsides*, which was to have such an influence on contemporary Irish art as a whole.

He may not have been as oblivious to the dramatic developments in Paris as he claimed to be. There is a curious similarity between his work of the late 1890s, in watercolour, and that of Edgar Degas twenty years previously, in the emphasis they both placed on empty space and in a fascination with subjects viewed from an oblique angle. Both were conservative artists with firm roots in the nineteenth century and with an interest in horse-racing and theatre – Yeats in the more popular working-man's stage of the time. Yeats's watercolour *Waiting* (fig. 19),[22] with its figures active about the perimeter of the shaped and shadowed foreground, like other works of 1897 suggests some contact with the French artist (fig. 20) which he never acknowledged.

The similarity, perhaps fortuitous, does not end there. Degas's remarks about memory, late in life, form a parallel with Yeats's less formal concepts. "It's all very well to copy what you see, but it's much better to draw what you see only in your mind," Degas reasoned. "During such transformation, the imagination collaborates with the memory. You reproduce only what strikes you, which is what is necessary."[23] According to Degas, both memory and imagination may be freed, in this way, from the 'tyranny' of nature. Yeats was more dogmatic in a letter to Joseph Hone. "No one creates …. The artist assembles memories."[24] In 1922 he told the Irish Race Congress in Paris that "the finest picture in the world will give the finest moment finest felt by the finest soul with the finest memory".[25]

This is the typical kind of non-statement that Yeats took pleasure in. Yet these apparently carelessly

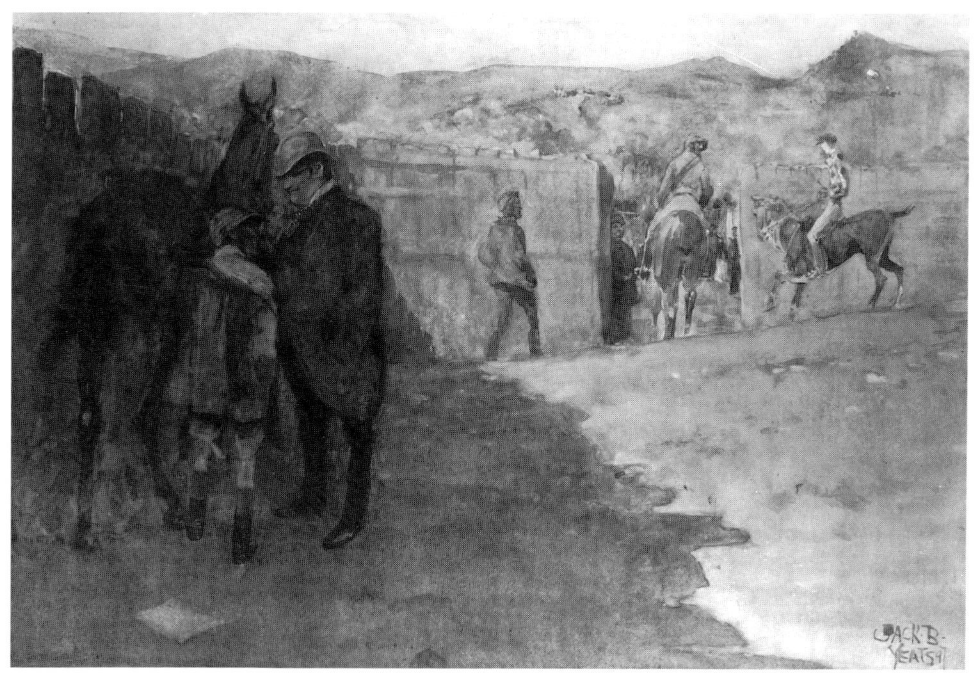

Fig. 19 Jack B. Yeats,
Waiting, 1897
(private collection)

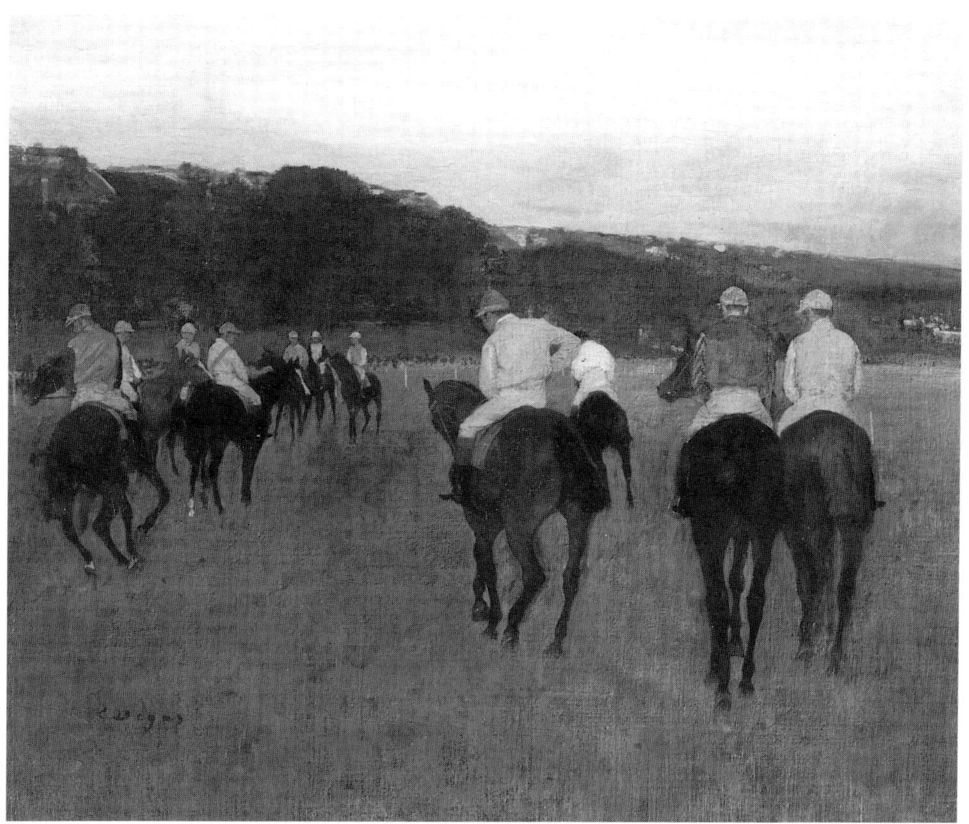

Fig. 20 Edgar Degas,
Racehorses, 1874 (Museum
of Fine Arts, Boston)

scattered words, we can be sure, were selected particularly because they conveyed what was most important to him in his own work. Emotion and imagination (emanating from the 'soul', the source of intellective and inspirational power), joining with memory to depict a real moment, are what make a picture, he suggests. Memory itself was interpreted freely by Yeats. In his book *Sligo* he added, "About this memory business. Buy or steal your memories instead of stuffing yourself with your own."[26]

Memory began to impress him as an artistic implement, we know, from about 1900, when he painted the large watercolour *Memory harbour* (frontispiece).[27] But memory needs to be trained and cultivated, and already he had begun building up a collection of small notebooks (Rowney Ringbacks, measuring 9×13 cm),[28] filled with sketches of people and incidents mainly, sometimes of a particular corner of scenery, and all made on the spot.

He set these sketches with a wash of colour when he reached home. The sketchbooks cover a period of about twenty years in detail, after which they become sporadic. But Yeats continued to refer to them until the end of his life for ideas for oil paintings. Occasionally a sketch sets out the theme of a larger picture. More often it is only the initial inspiration. Thus his principle of 'Memory-plus' evolved, allowing room for the influence of dream, emotion and retrospective perception, while at the same time retaining the integrity of the original memory.

After his move to Devon, Jack Yeats abandoned the black-and-white profession – which was finally imperilled by the camera – to concentrate on watercolour, working as intensely in the new medium as he had done with the demands of a journal's deadline. He held exhibitions in London and Dublin regularly, the same exhibitions in both cities, with a few changes. In 1904 he showed also in New York. There was nothing private about his art, except for his actual working of it, which he kept strictly to himself.

He was punctilious in the regularity with which he showed, but he had little inclination to be associated with other artists, other than in contributing, which he did readily, to group shows. He had no leanings towards the academic and yet was content to represent himself in the Royal Hibernian Academy, as in other society exhibitions on both sides of the Irish Sea, and to be elected a member of the Academy when the time came.

JBY described the life his son lived while in Devon: "I have had a radiant fortnight with Jack and his wife," he wrote to Rosa Butt in 1900. "They are so quietly happy and busy. Each in their own way that one asks oneself is it possible that any kind of trouble should ever find them out. – Jack at work either on pictures or a great undertaking which occupies all his evenings [fig. 21] – A Circus with puppets and horses and men – a most laughable thing, Jack explains. A Country Circus tries to imitate life ancient and modern – he imitates the circus."[29]

Jack's life was full, according to his father – "very busy with his art work and gardening and chicken rearing. He knows everybody and attends all the country sports and meetings – finding all his material for art in this kind of life ... he toils incessantly and cannot express all he thinks. – Behold a happy man."[30]

His isolation, through choice, from other artists was due partly to his literary bent, partly to temperament. Some contemporary painters expressed their admiration for him – A.E., Evie Hone, Sickert – in their various ways. Though Yeats never commented on Sickert's painting, certain facets in his own early figurative oils indicate that the interest was mutual. The Austrian Expressionist Kokoschka took notice of him at a later date – again an artist with obvious affinities. But Orpen, Osborne and Lavery, his famous co-nationals of differing ages, he seems to have ignored.

His path led away from them and, in his leisurely way, to a level of innovation none of them could have contemplated. He absorbed more than he cared to admit from what he saw when in London, and from viewing Lane's Continental pictures displayed in Dublin – "things," J.M. Synge wrote, "I connect so directly with life of Paris".[31] Did Yeats hold the Manets in his mind? His own small works (fig. 22) were hanging in another room in the newly created Municipal Gallery in Dublin.

His close friends were generally writers: John Masefield, J.M. Synge (fig. 23), Thomas Bodkin in his early

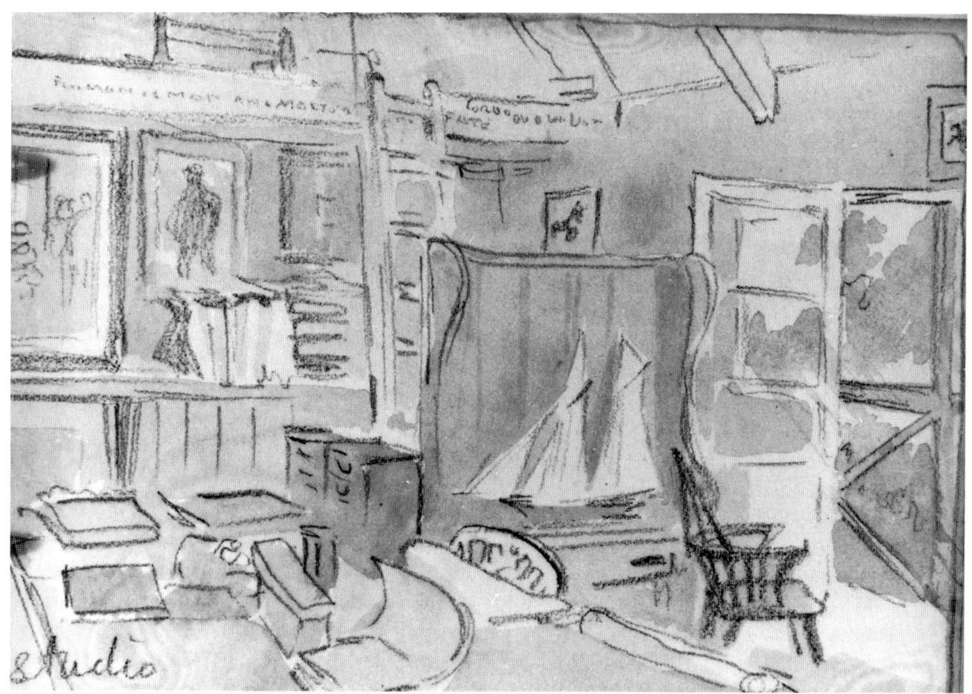

Fig. 21 Jack B. Yeats,
My studio, sketchbook, 1899
(NGI Yeats Archive)

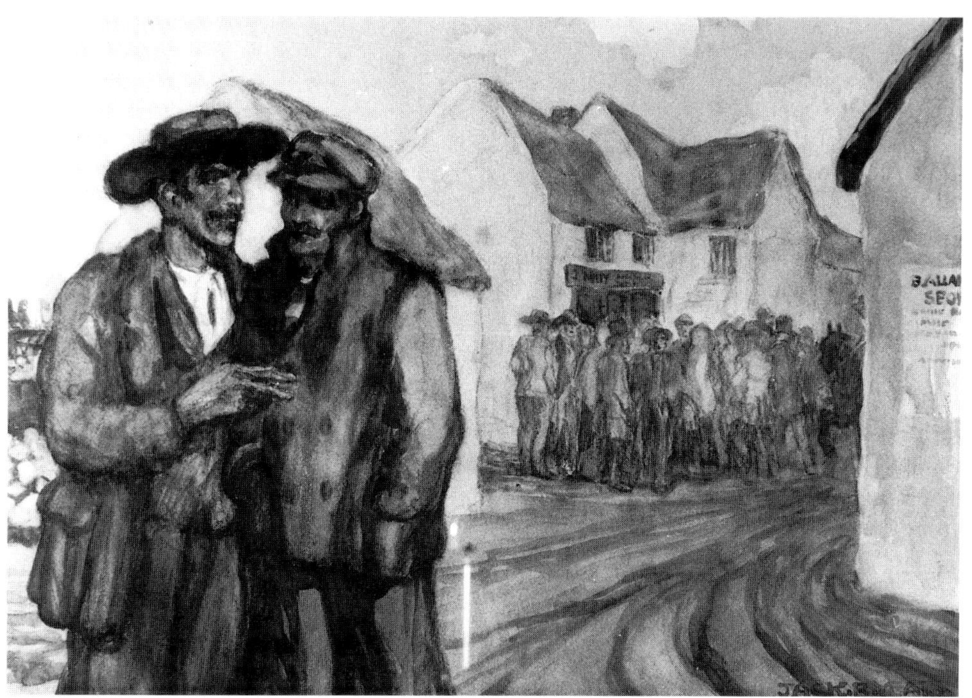

Fig. 22 Jack B. Yeats,
The day of the sports, 1904
(Hugh Lane Municipal
Gallery, Dublin)

poetic days, Samuel Beckett and Thomas MacGreevy; or kindred spirits like Arnold Harvey, a Church of Ireland priest who was Robert Gregory's tutor and afterwards a bishop; and in his final years, the young architect Niall Montgomery. Montgomery was conscious of Jack Yeats's affability when he was a newcomer to one of Sarah Purser's formidable evenings. He attended Yeats's 'At Homes' on Thursday afternoons, often meeting distinguished visitors (Sir John Rothenstein and others) to Dublin. He discovered that the artist's gentle manner masked a merciless wit and a predilection for cruel stories, particularly about politicians. A Republican, he initially manifested a dislike of Cosgrave and the Free Staters, but in the end he disliked even more "that fellow from 42nd Street" – De Valera.[32]

Yeats's most significant associations, however, belong to his days in Devon. Masefield supported his interest in the miniature theatre of the middle and late Victorian period, melodrama for children, which Yeats elevated to a minor art form during the revival of the private presses. He fed Yeats's endless hunger for sea fantasy and shared his pleasure in pirates. Synge stimulated his love of his country.

Jack Yeats was an obvious illustrator for Synge, and he added an attractive dimension to the books on Aran, Wicklow, West Kerry and Connemara that makes them visually alive today when traditional life of those times has been virtually forgotten. His stark linear style, totally objective, because he had been observing from a distance in Devon for years, was in sympathy with Synge's cultivated, pleasantly intellectual manner, with its touch of the heroic. They were in the vicinity of Clifden about the time that Marconi, who was half Irish, was making his historic communications by wireless telegraphy there, yet their sole concern was with the old pattern of life they had come to study, and with its living exponents.

Synge's academic tendencies might have presented a barrier to the more carefree Yeats; yet the playwright seemed to engender in the artist a realisation that it was time he pursued his Irish subjects on a deeper level than he had done in the anecdotal watercolours, for all their captivating artistry.

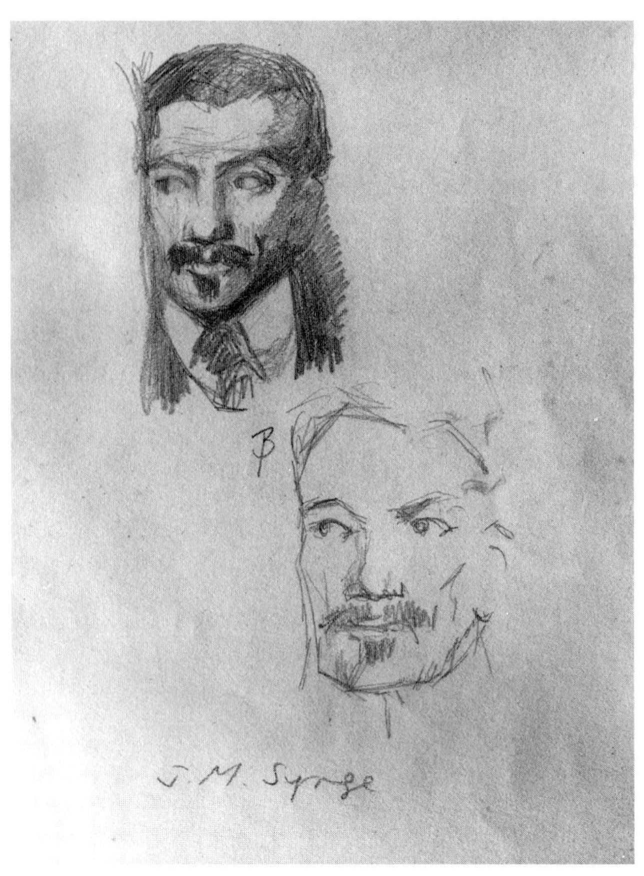

Fig. 23 Jack B. Yeats, *Sketch portrait of J.M. Synge*, 1905 (NGI Yeats Archive)

Right
Jack B. Yeats, *The priest* (detail), 1913 (see p. 198)

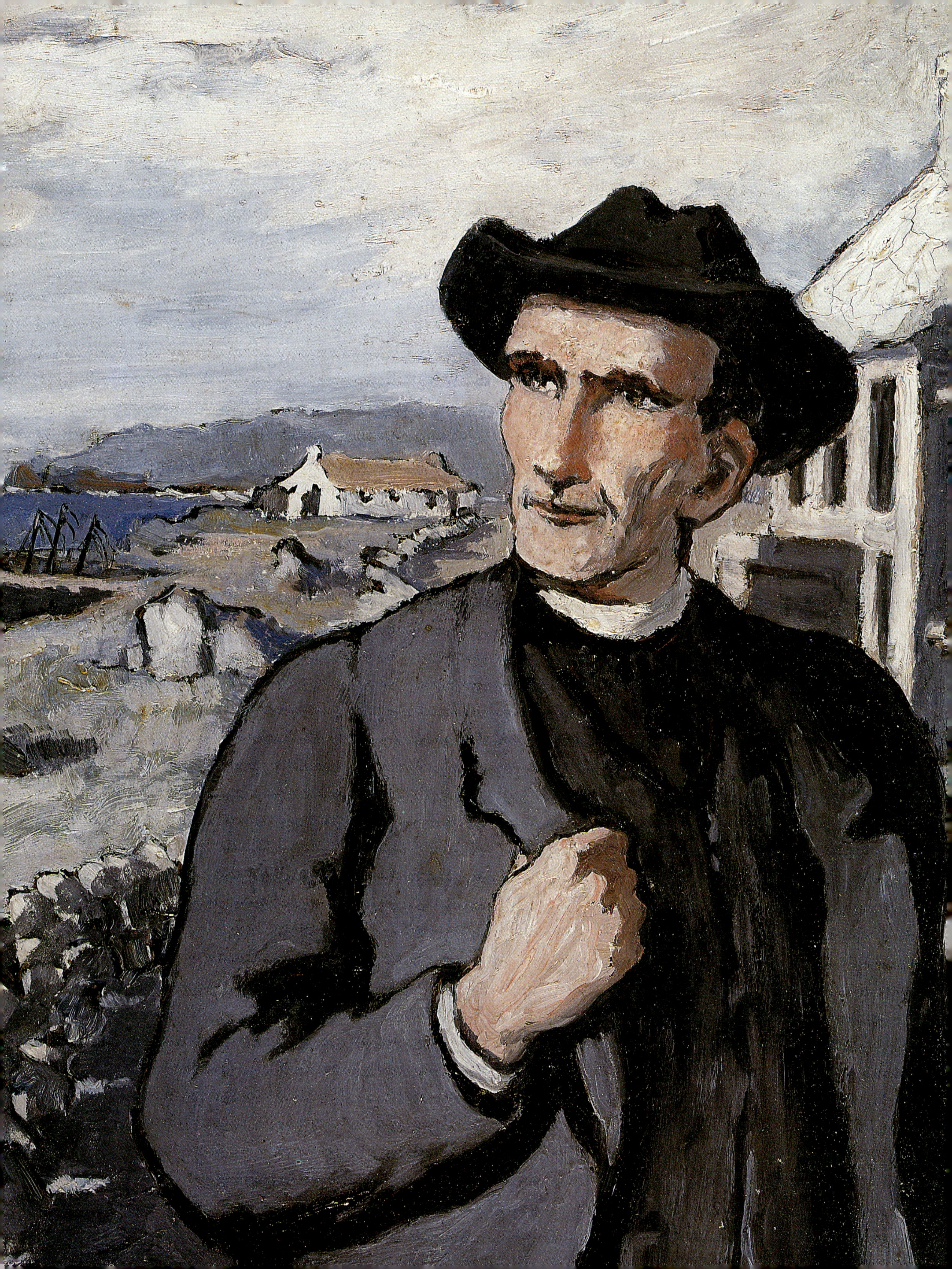

So he turned to oil, oils that developed in a forceful way out of the few heavily stylized examples at the beginning of the new century, to the strong illustrative small-scale landscapes and subjects after 1910 (when he returned to Ireland), in which his main intention was to record truthfully the reality of the Irish ethos. He first settled by the sea at Red Ford, near Greystones in County Wicklow. He moved to Dublin when the events of 1916 convinced him that the reality he sought was more than the eyes could see, and that the Irish character needed more complex expression in paint than had been hitherto attempted. The urban paintings of the 1920s may have a narrative element still, but in gesture, mood and honesty (and humour) of subject-matter, they carry a profound awareness of the challenge of modern Ireland and of the individuality of those who are challenged. The painterly development of these years is huge, as though something brewing in the artist had finally but not too suddenly erupted, and released him from the leisurely objectivity that had been his wont. (It parallels a similar mature transmutation in the work of his father and his brother.) Jack Yeats's illness around the time of the Easter Rising led to increased introspection and an interest in dream, stimulated by the current vogue for spiritualism and the surreal. Perhaps his visit to Paris for the Irish Race Congress in 1922 opened his eyes more fully to the potential of colour.

Alongside the loosened brush, the flowing pigment, Yeats was permitting his own emotions to enter the paintings. The spreading oil of 1922, transformed through a new understanding of light and colour by 1925, appeared in 1928 almost to be from another hand. On 9 August 1927 Jack Yeats could write, "I am having a kind of new birth. I have been running with my head loose for two or three years now and my work is as I wish it to be."[33] Yet the same Yeats was there, painting at his studio in Pembroke Street, and then moving to his final workplace and home in Dublin's most beautiful Georgian square, Fitzwilliam Square.

By 1930, he was ready with his revised personal idiom to channel themes of fantasy, through images culled from years of observation, on to panel or canvas. The heroics of his youth were fused together with the reality for which he had abandoned them. Memory, itself enhanced, became a major theme. Companion to this, the written word was especially important to him at this period, when he was publishing his original prose and plays.

His scale progressively enlarged, like his expression. The 1940s were his most prolific period, when he attained a metaphysical plane, sometimes of great personal intensity, nourished still by memory and by continual observation from nature. The deep blue of the indigo paint which he used constantly at this period was an inspiration, with its suggestive colour as well as its oily smell and tackiness. He described the colour in *Ah Well* as "a great arc ... everlasting, unfading". His final paintings, of 1955 – two years before his death on 28 March 1957 – are light and fluid, verging on the abstract.

Yeats always invited viewers to interpret the pictures for themselves, and it is hoped that visitors to the National Gallery will continue to take up this invitation. While he frequently told stories about his work, he intended his commentaries as glosses rather than as binding truths. One admirer met him towards the end of his life at an exhibition. Attempting to understand a canvas, he turned to discuss it with the man standing beside him, only to find that he was speaking with the artist himself. "I can't explain that picture," Yeats said. "It simply happened."[34] Art for him could still be equated with Life,[35] "like a polished dagger of beauty leaping, by its own volition, from the scabbard of crepe-bound dull-witted obscurity".[36]

He continually reaffirmed Life as his source. "Some people are afraid of a stylish sky. Nature drawing up its embattled and highly coloured wonders to proclaim that when it comes to glory, profundity, high spots, tiger stripes, and whirlygigging refulgences the palette of the painter ... is but a half a half-brother to the towering jars of luminosity spilling themselves through the cracks in the firmaments."[37]

During his last two years, when he lived in the Portobello Nursing Home in Dublin, he painted nothing.[38] He told Victor Waddington a few months before he died, "Everything I vowed to paint is painted ... there is no unfinished work for me."[39] He had

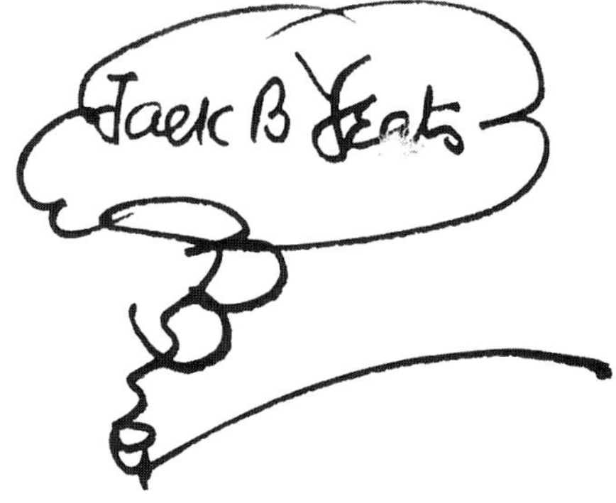

"no desire to linger on and on," he said, "... as a painter who can no longer paint." He said too, "there is nothing funny in the long hours spent here", and a life without humour for Jack B. Yeats was not Life.

The collection of his work in the National Gallery of Ireland represents Jack B. Yeats in all his creative phases, and owes much to the generosity of individual donors over the years. Yeats is an artist of surprises. Elusive. Idiosyncratic. Deeply joyous. Confronting tragedy, small and universal. Flagrant with imagination. Erotic in his use of paint. Yet his feet were always planted, as he willed, in the green of earth. It was the soft air of the Irish landscape that passed through his nostrils (fig. 24).

When viewed in the context of Irish art of their period, the Yeatses can be seen as leaders in shaping the course of the culture to come. JBY and Jack were considerable and influential as painters. Alongside them, WBY, Lily and Lolly must appear as minor artists, yet within the family whole, their importance cannot be measured. WBY, author of but a handful of surviving visual images, was his father's favourite image and the accustomed butt of his wisdom. He devilled for his young brother when Jack was starting out as an illustrator. Lily, like WBY, though her skilled embroidered pictures are not widely known, was an inspirational subject for JBY. Elizabeth, influence on a generation of writers and women artists, drew material for her Press largely from the work of her brothers.

Quite apart from this was their practical interdependence, at a crucial point in their creativity the entire family depending on Elizabeth who earned a comfortable income from teaching. The interaction of their individual persona which has been much discussed seems to have been integral to the creative energy of the family.

Anne Yeats, heir and custodian to this awesome lineage, has worked alone in her generation, though still with family support from the start. Soon after WBY's marriage to Georgie Hyde-Lees, Lily had a dream in which she saw a high stone tower with, on the top of it, a herald blowing a trumpet. Out of the trumpet came words rather than music, the trumpet blasting the refrain, 'The Yeatses are not dead'.[40] When their daughter, Anne was born, Lily interpreted the dream as a portent foretelling the event.

Working alone, introducing European concepts into Irish art in her own way, Anne Yeats's development at the same time has shown remarkable similarities with the Yeats artists of the previous generation. Slow to work in oil, she started first with lighter and graphic media, probing for her own individuality. She has recounted how she had as much difficulty as any one in understanding her uncle Jack's late paintings, so she sat down in front of one of his canvases in the Dublin Municipal Gallery and looked at it, observing for twenty minutes, until at last the excitement of pigment fell into place and the content was clear. Like the rest of the family, in art or in poetry, she has progressed during her career from strongly defined graphic imagery to a more mysterious colourful manner, spacious, lingering in metaphor, the most recent canvases excelling those that have gone before.

Besides her unique contribution to modern Irish art, Anne Yeats and her brother Michael B. Yeats have been generous with their heritage, Michael making his collection of family portraits and memorabilia available for exhibitions which could not have been mounted without them, and recently Anne presenting the Jack B. Yeats Archive to the National Gallery of Ireland for the formation of a Yeats Museum. So the projected derivation of the family name, 'gate', which so happily describes the attitude of JBY when conceived as an open gate, can be seen to describe equally well the frame of mind of the present-day Yeatses.

NOTES

1 By Francis Sandford (printed Thomas Newcomb, 1687).

2 *An Address delivered before the Law Students Debating Society of Dublin in the Lecture Hall, King's Inns, November 21st 1865* by the auditor John Butler Yeats, A.B., Dublin (Dollard) 1865.

3 *Passages from the Letters of John Butler Yeats*, selected by Ezra Pound, Dublin (Cuala Press) 1917, p. 22.

4 J.B. Yeats, *Essays Irish and American*, Dublin/London (Talbot Press/Fisher Unwin) 1918: 'Watts and the Method of Art', p. 76.

5 Anne Yeats Collection.

6 E. Dowden, *Fragments from Old Letters* II, London/New York 1914, p. 24.

7 *Memories*, London (Eveleigh, Nash & Grayson) 1924, pp. 277–28.

8 *Frank Potter* (unpublished manuscript), quoted in Murphy 1978, p. 116.

9 *Autobiography*, London (Hutchinson) 1936, pp. 141–42.

10 The Irish Literary Society was founded at no. 3, Blenheim Road in December 1891.

11 1 December 1891. J.B. Yeats, *Letters from Bedford Park: A Selection from the Correspondence (1890–1922) of John Butler Yeats*, ed. W. Murphy, Dublin (Cuala Press) 1972.

12 See 'Clare Marsh Remembered', *Irish Arts Review Yearbook* 1988, pp. 89–92.

13 John O'Grady, *The Life and Work of Sarah Purser*, Dublin (Four Courts Press) 1996, pp. 90–91, 97–98.

14 M. O hAodha, *Pictures at the Abbey*, Dublin (Dolmen Press) 1983, p. 12. The portrait of John O'Leary (NGI 595) is entered in the *Catalogue of Pictures in the National Gallery of Ireland* (1914) under 'Yeats (William Butler)', though it is entered correctly in the same catalogue in the *National Historical and Portrait Gallery* section as by J.B. Yeats RHA.

15 *John Butler Yeats and the Irish Renaissance*, Dublin (National Gallery of Ireland) 1972, p. 7.

16 J.B. Yeats, *Essays Irish and American*, Dublin/London (Talbot Press/Fisher Unwin) 1918: 'Watts and the Method of Art', pp. 88, 94.

17 To Rosa Butt, 4 December 1907, Bodleian Library, Oxford.

18 Hilary Pyle, '"A Stranger among Strangers": John Butler Yeats in New York', *American-Irish Historical Society, The Recorder*, XLIV, 1983, p. 95.

19 'Why there are Artists' by J.B. Yeats, typescript (New York, n.d.) p. 18 (National Gallery of Ireland Archive).

20 *Ca.* 1879–81: H. Pyle, *Jack B. Yeats: His Watercolours, Drawings and Pastels*, Dublin (Irish Academic Press) 1993, no. 1. See W. Murphy, *Prodigal Father*, Ithaca and London (Cornell UP) 1978, p. 148 for a childhood sketch of his grandfather.

21 National Library of Ireland, MSS 12160, p. 49, and 4595.

22 H. Pyle, *Jack B. Yeats: His Watercolours, Drawings and Pastels*, Dublin (Irish Academic Press) 1993, no. 58.

23 G. Jeanniot, 'Souvenirs sur Degas', *Revue Universelle*, LV, 1933, p. 158.

24 7 March 1922, University of Kansas Libraries.

25 'Ireland and Painting', *Ár nÉire*, IX, 1922, pp. 189–90.

26 *Sligo*, London (Wishart) 1930, p. 28.

27 H. Pyle, *Jack B. Yeats: His Watercolours, Drawings and Pastels* Dublin (Irish Academic Press) 1993, no. 206.

28 National Gallery of Ireland, Yeats Archive, presented by Anne Yeats, 1996.

29 JBY to Rosa Butt, November 1900, Bodleian Library, Oxford, MS Eng. Lett. e.87.

30 *Idem eidem*, 14 June 1900.

31 J.M. Synge, 'Good Pictures in Dublin: The New Municipal Gallery', *Manchester Guardian*, 24 January 1908. Reprinted in J.M. Synge, *Collected Works II. Prose*, ed. A. Price, London (Oxford University Press) 1966, pp. 390–92.

32 Niall Montgomery to author, summer 1967.

33 Jack B. Yeats to W. Blaikie Murdoch (Trinity College MSS Collection).

34 Aidan Murray, Carlow, to author, April 1986.

35 See *The Green Wave*. 'I have known some men who might be called works of Art.' *Collected Plays*, ed. R. Skelton, London (Secker & Warburg) 1971, p. 331.

36 Sheila in *The Deathly Terrace*, Act 2, *Collected Plays*, p. 100.

37 Nardock, *ibid.*, Act 3, *Collected Plays*, p. 113.

38 Victor Waddington to Fred and Eleanor Reid, 23 April 1957 (National Gallery of Ireland Y2-7).

39 *Idem eisdem*.

40 W.M. Murphy, *Family Secrets: William Butler Yeats and his Relatives* Dublin (Gill & Macmillan) 1995, p. 385.

Chronology

1839
16 MARCH
JOHN BUTLER YEATS (JBY) born at Tullylish, County Down, son of Revd William Butler Yeats of Sligo and Jane Grace Corbet of Dublin.

1849–57
JBY educated near Liverpool and at the Atholl Academy, Isle of Man. First drawings and caricatures in pen and ink.

1857–62
JBY to Trinity College, Dublin, to study for the ministry, but his reading of Darwin, Comte and Mill decided him against ordination. Made lifelong friendships with John (later Bishop) Dowden, and Edward (later Professor) Dowden and (Dr) John Todhunter, both poets.

1862
SPRING JBY graduated. In September he visited George Pollexfen in Sligo and became engaged to his sister Susan Mary Pollexfen.
Enrolled at King's Inns, Dublin.
Revd William Butler Yeats died at Sandymount Castle, leaving JBY properties in Thomastown, County Kildare, and Dorset Street, Dublin.

1863
JUNE JBY enrolled at the Inner Temple, London.
10 SEPTEMBER JBY married Susan Pollexfen at St John's Church, Sligo.

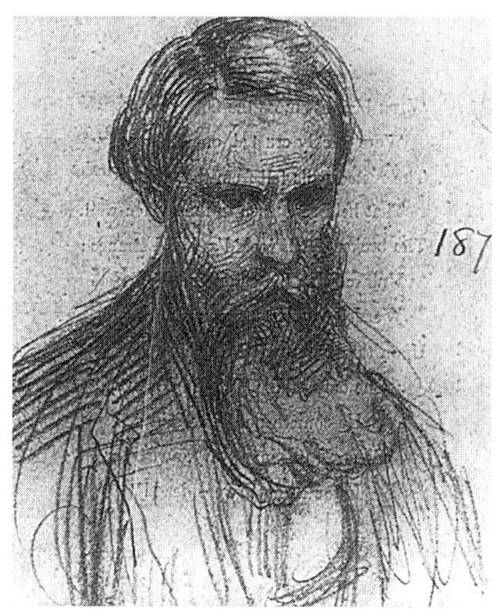

Fig. 25 J.B. Yeats, pencil self-sketch, *ca.* 1875 (Michael B. Yeats Collection)

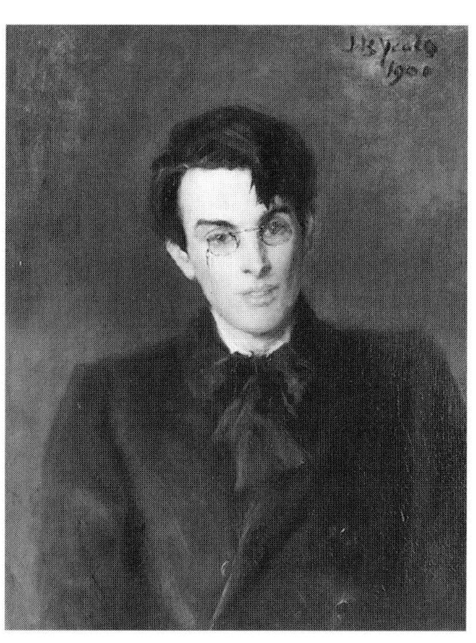

Fig. 27 J.B. Yeats, *W.B. Yeats*, 1900 (NGI 872)

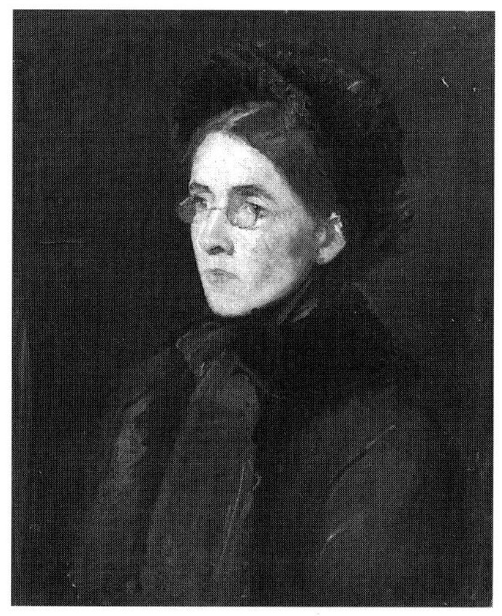

Fig. 26 J.B. Yeats, *The artist's wife (Susan Mary, née Pollexfen)*, *ca.* 1875 (NGI 1179)

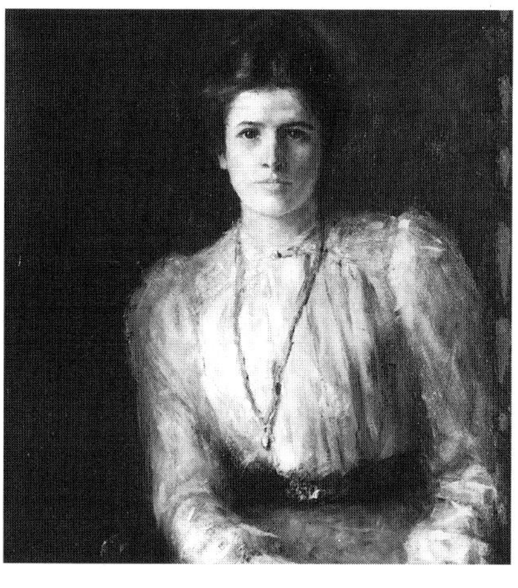

Fig. 28 J.B. Yeats, *Susan Mary (Lily) Yeats*, 1900–01 (NGI 1180)

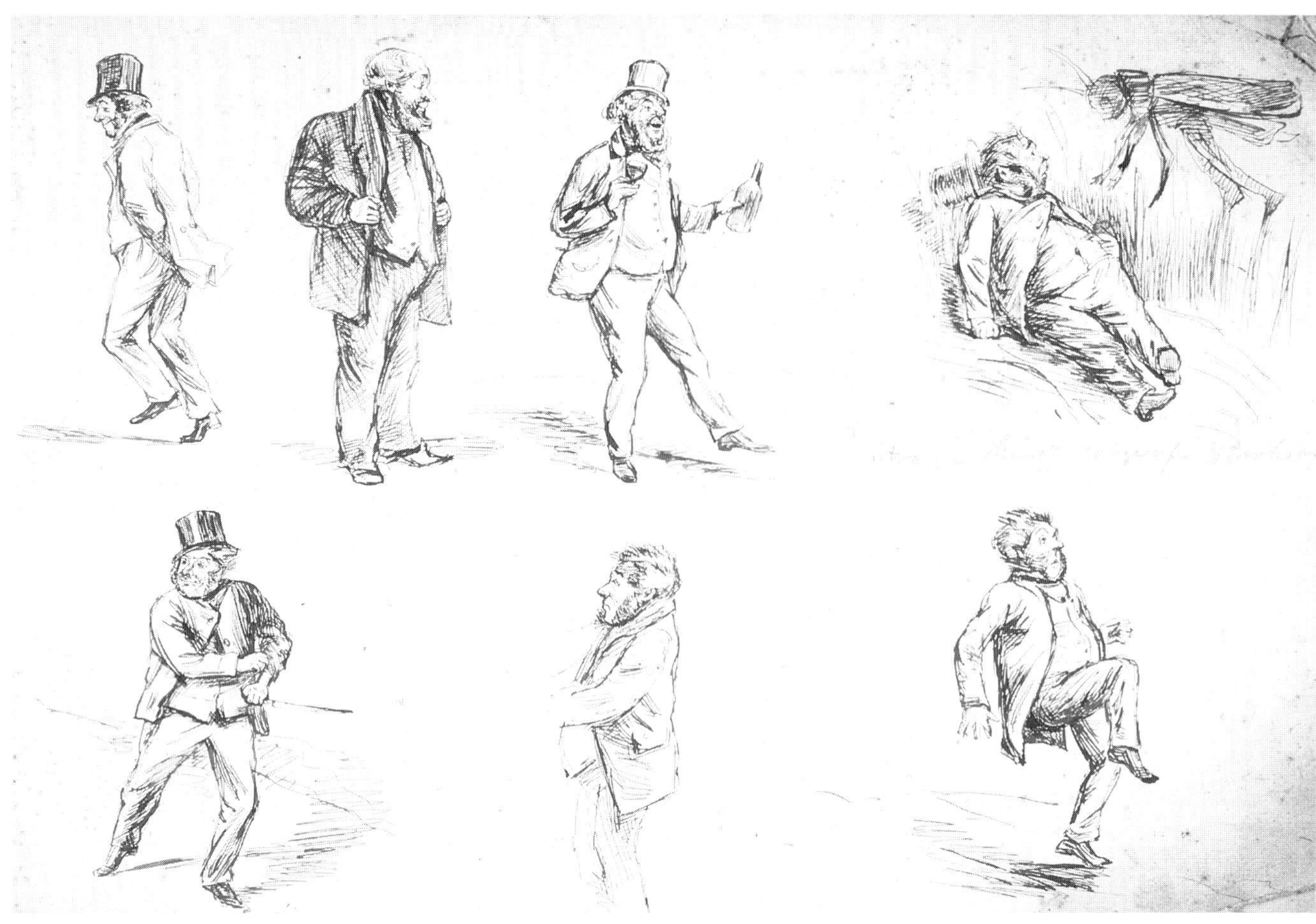

Fig. 29 J.B. Yeats, *Comic sketches*, *ca.* 1866 (Anne Yeats Collection)

1865

13 JUNE
WILLIAM BUTLER YEATS (WBY)
born at Sandymount, Dublin.
JBY's address as Auditor to the King's
Inns Debating Society revealed a
passion for truth and an innate belief
in self-culture.

1866

JANUARY JBY admitted to the Bar.
Sketched at the Four Courts.
25 AUGUST
SUSAN MARY YEATS (LILY)
born in Sligo.
Edward Dowden and John Todhunter
persuaded JBY to send satirical
sketches (fig. 29) to Tom Hood, editor
of *Fun*, who invited him to London.

1867

JBY's sketches accepted for *Fun* and
the family moved to live at no. 23,
Fitzroy Road, near Regent's Park,
London.
JBY enrolled at Heatherley's Art
School, Newman Street. His growing
nationalism excited by Fenian
executions.

1868

JBY visited the studio of Frederick
Sandys, who admired his pictures.
11 MARCH
ELIZABETH CORBET YEATS
(LOLLY) born in London.

1869

JBY formed an artistic brotherhood
with Nettleship, Ellis and Hall (and
later Wilson), declaring a common
interest in Blake, Browning and the
Pre-Raphaelite ideals, as well as a
belief in the solitary nature of the
artist. At the end of May he went to
Antwerp with Dowden.

1870

JBY shared studio with Ellis till June.
George Watts visited him about now.
Commission from Todhunter to
illustrate Browning's *Pippa Passes*.

1871

29 AUGUST
JOHN BUTLER YEATS (JACK B.)
born in London.

1872

JBY left Heatherley's for the Slade to
study under Edward Poynter, who
advised him to work in oil instead of
chalk.
23 JULY JBY moved his family to
Sligo, where they lived for two years
while he returned to London.
Edward Dowden arranged some
portrait commissions in Dublin.

1873

JBY painted Mrs Hoare in Richmond,
the Herberts in Killarney, the Cosbys
at Stradbally Hall and portraits in
Sligo.

1874

JBY's family returned to London, to
live at no. 14, Edith Villas, North End.

1875

JBY's *Portrait of Gracie Yeats* refused by
the Royal Academy.
Commission for *The Lute girls* from
Dowden.

1876

JBY's *Portrait of Todhunter*.
He joined Dublin Sketching Club.
MAY JBY approached Isaac Butt,
leader of the Irish Party in the House
of Commons, for a portrait, which he
made in chalk.
He burnt *The red girl* and started
again. Painting landscape near Slough.

1878

Todhunter joined group painting from
the nude in JBY's studio.
NOVEMBER Browning called after
seeing *Pippa* and *In a gondola*.

1879

JBY moved to no. 8, Woodstock Road,
Bedford Park, London.
SUMMER JBY teaching his children
to paint in Branscombe, Devon.
Portrait of Hester Dowden refused by
the Royal Academy.
OCTOBER In Dublin JBY did chalk
Portrait of Charles Fitzgerald; and
started on portrait of Edward
Dowden.
Jack lived mainly with his
grandparents in Sligo until 1886.

1881

JBY's *Portrait of Hester Dowden* praised
at the Royal Hibernian Academy.
JBY and his family moved to Howth,
County Dublin, while he rented a
studio in the city at York Street. WBY
attended High School.

1883

SPRING JBY sketched at the trial of
the Invincibles.
MAY Lily and Elizabeth enrolled at
Dublin Metropolitan School of Art.
The family moved house to Terenure,
and JBY took a studio at no. 7, St
Stephen's Green, painting portraits
and watercolours.

1884

MAY WBY attended Metropolitan
School of Art for two years.
DECEMBER Whistler exhibited at
Dublin Sketching Club exhibition.

1885

JBY and WBY invited to join the
Contemporary Club where they met
John O'Leary, the Fenian leader,
released from his sentence of exile.

1886

WBY's 'Mosada' published in the
Dublin University Review and reprinted
as a pamphlet with frontispiece
portrait by JBY.
The Pollexfens sold Merville and
moved to Charlemont, Sligo.
JBY returned to London, to no. 58,
Eardley Crescent, South Kensington,
later joined by his family (Jack in the
summer of 1887).

1887

JBY's watercolour *The girl with the
basket* shown in the Royal Academy.
JBY elected ARHA. His drawings
published anonymously in *Good Words*
and *Leisure Hour*.
Susan Yeats suffered two strokes.
Jack attended art classes at South
Kensington School of Art, under
Thomas Armstrong. Later studied at
the Chiswick School of Art; and,
under Fred Brown, at the Westminster
School of Art.

1888

MARCH–APRIL The family moved
to no. 3, Blenheim Road, Bedford
Park, London.
APRIL Jack began illustrating for *The
Vegetarian*.
DECEMBER Lily employed as an
embroideress with May Morris at
Kelmscott House, Oxfordshire.

1889

JANUARY Maud Gonne introduced
to Blenheim Road by John O'Leary;
start of her friendship with WBY.
JBY painted WBY in competition with
H.M. Paget.
Lolly teaching at kindergarten
(Froebel system) in Bedford Park.

1891

Jack began illustrating for *Ariel* and
Paddock Life. His first book of
illustrations. JBY's last oil paintings
for seven years.

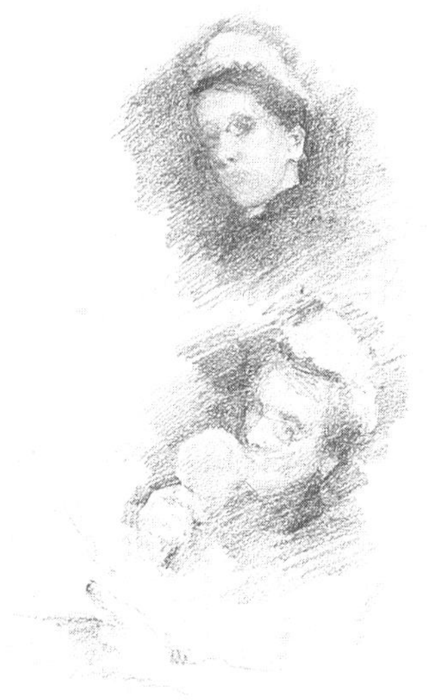

Fig. 30 J.B. Yeats, *Sketch of Susan Mary Yeats, ca.* 1890 (Anne Yeats Collection)

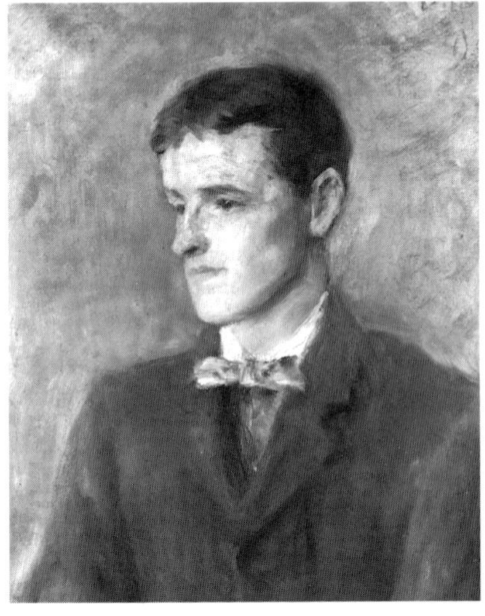

Fig. 31 J.B. Yeats, *Jack B. Yeats*, 1890 (NGI 4040)

1892

JBY elected RHA.
Lily becoming aware of her psychic dreams and visions.
NOVEMBER Death of William Pollexfen in Sligo.
Jack designing for David Allen & Sons in Manchester.

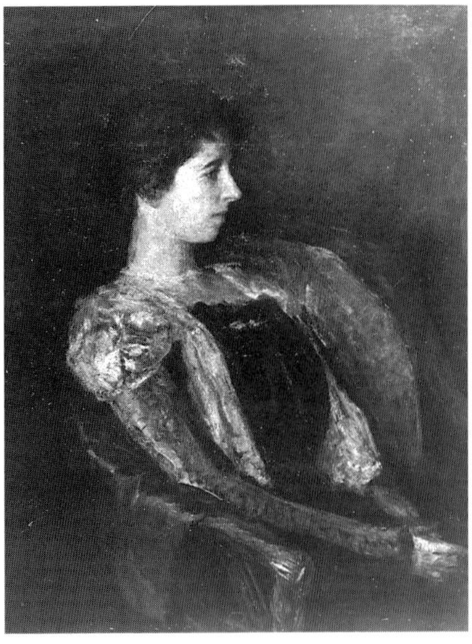

Fig. 32 J.B. Yeats, *Elizabeth Corbet (Lollie) Yeats, ca.* 1899 (Michael Yeats Collection)

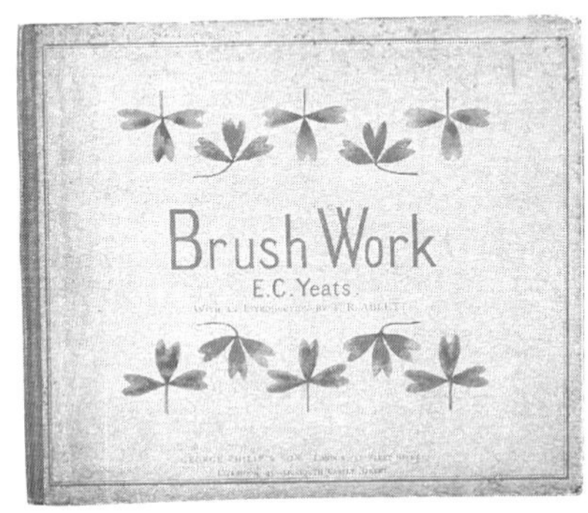

Fig. 33 Elizabeth C. Yeats, *Brush Work*, 1895 (Anne Yeats Collection)

1893

FEBRUARY WBY published *The Works of William Blake* with Edwin Ellis (formerly a member of JBY's Pre-Raphaelite brotherhood).

1894

Lily left May Morris's workshop. Sat as model for the illustrations to Daniel Defoe that JBY was preparing for Dent.
Jack a staff artist with *Lika Joko*. He married Mary Cottenham White (Cottie) in August and left Bedford Park to live at Chertsey, in Surrey.

1895

Lolly teaching brushwork painting. She published *Brush Work* (fig. 33), the first of four manuals demonstrating her technique.
Jack exhibited *The Strand races, West of Ireland* (a watercolour) at the Royal Hibernian Academy in Dublin.
OCTOBER Lily to France for fourteen months.

1897

WBY's breakdown in health took him to Coole Park to convalesce. He made his pastel views of Coole (fig. 34) about this time.
JBY met Lady Gregory who commissioned a sketch portrait from him of WBY.
Susan Mitchell came to live with Yeats family for two years as Lily's companion.
Jack turned from black-and-white journalism to concentrate on watercolour.
NOVEMBER Jack's first solo watercolour exhibition at the Clifford Gallery, Haymarket, London.

1898

SUMMER JBY taught in May Manning's studio in Dublin and completed Lady Gregory's commission for further pencil portraits.
Jack travelled to Italy, visiting Como and Venice. Witnessed the 1798 centenary celebrations at Carricknagat in Sligo.
Lily exhibited a flower painting at the Royal Hibernian Academy.

1899

Jack's first *Sketches of Life in the West of Ireland* exhibitions in London and Dublin. Visited Coole, the Aran Islands and Paris. His first memory sketches.
JBY began painting oil portraits once more.
Lily began exhibiting with the Arts and Crafts Society of Ireland. Jack also exhibited, showing bookplates.

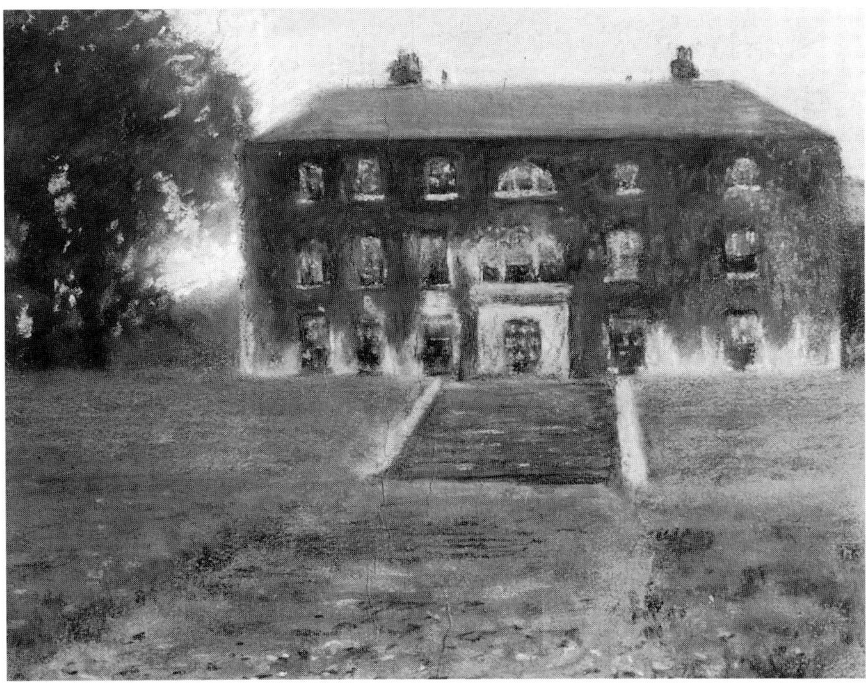

Fig. 34 W.B. Yeats, *Coole House, ca.* 1897 (Michael Yeats Collection)

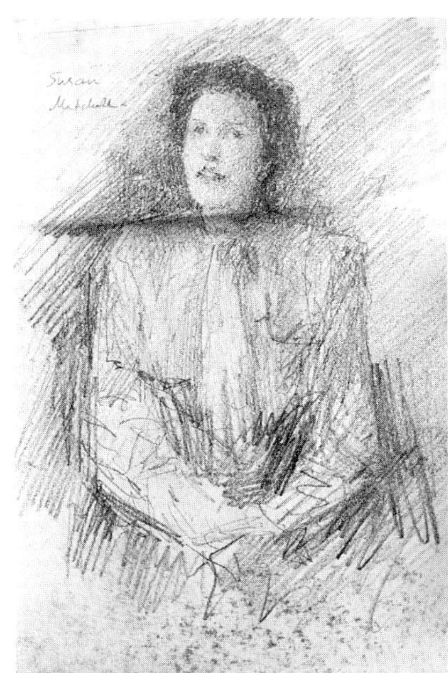

Fig. 35 J.B. Yeats, *Susan L. Mitchell,*
ca. 1897 (Sligo County Library and
Museum)

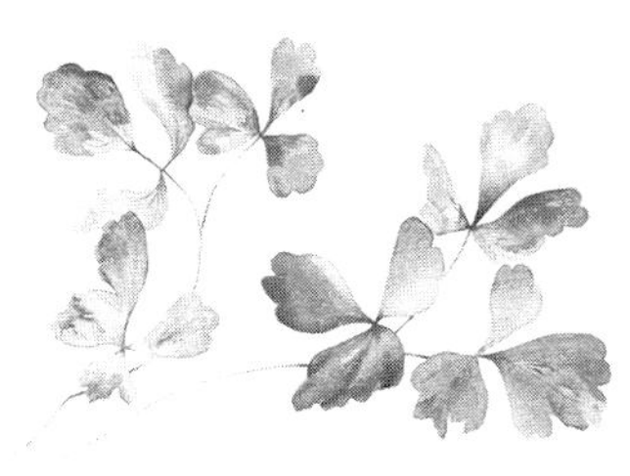

Fig. 36 Elizabeth C. Yeats,
Example of brushwork drawing
(Anne Yeats Collection)

1900

3 JANUARY Death of Susan Yeats.
Jack painted *Memory harbour*
(frontispiece). He continued to exhibit
his watercolours both in London and
Dublin.
APRIL JBY to Paris for two weeks to
visit Edwin Ellis and his wife. He
attended the Romney exhibition in the
company of Sarah Purser.
JULY JBY and Lily visited Jack in
Devon.
Elizabeth published *Elementary Brush
Work Studies*, the last of her manuals
(fig. 36).

1901

JBY's *Portraits of Lily and Lolly* rejected
by the Royal Academy, as a result of
which Sarah Purser arranged a joint
exhibition of his and Nathaniel Hone's
paintings in Dublin, at no. 6, St
Stephen's Green.
John Quinn bought portrait of WBY
and commissioned three more.
Jack published *James Flaunty*, a play
for miniature theatre.

1902

Jack edited *A Broad Sheet* monthly
with Elkin Mathews, Pamela Colman
Smith co-editing the first twelve
issues. Met John Masefield.
Elizabeth trained with the Women's
Printing Society in Westminster and,
with Lily, joined Evelyn Gleeson in
founding the Dun Emer Industries.
JBY moved from Bedford Park to
Churchtown, County Dublin.
DECEMBER JBY's first short story
appeared in *A Celtic Christmas.*

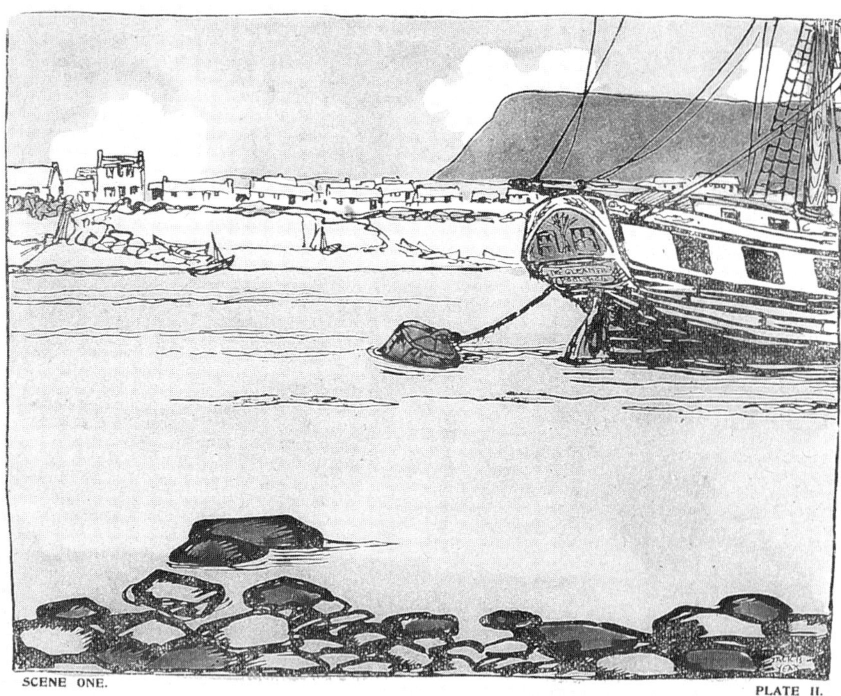

Fig. 37 Jack B. Yeats, *The Treasure of the Garden*, Scene I, 1903 (NGI Yeats Archive)

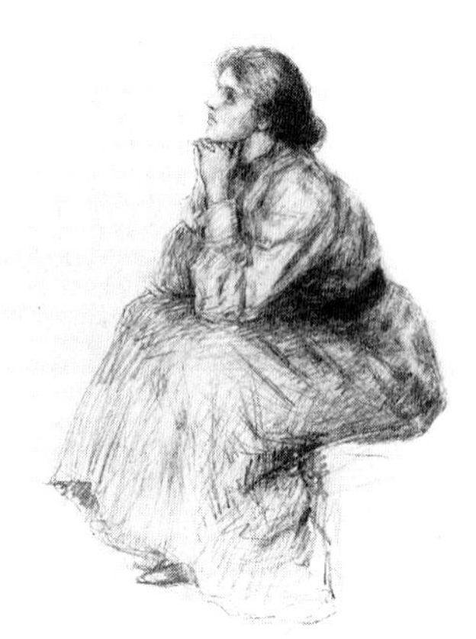

Fig. 38 J.B. Yeats, *Máire Nic Shiubhlaigh sketched at rehearsal, ca.* 1904 (NGI Photo Archive)

1903

SPRING Hugh Lane commissioned twenty portraits from JBY for his proposed modern gallery. Helped JBY to lease his studio at no. 7, St Stephen's Green.
Jack published *The Treasure of the Garden* for miniature theatre (fig. 37). With Cottie commissioned to design most of the sodality banners for the new cathedral at Loughrea, embroidered by Lily and her assistants at Dun Emer.
Elizabeth published *In the Seven Woods* by WBY, the first book from the Dun Emer Press.

1904

Jack travelled to New York to exhibit at the Clausen Galleries.
JBY lost the Lane portrait commission to Orpen. He lectured at Hugh Lane's *Exhibition of Paintings for a Gallery of Modern and Contemporary Art* at the RHA (to which Jack presented three works). Painted portraits for the foyer of the new Abbey Theatre (fig. 38).

1905

Jack visited the Whistler exhibition in London. In June, toured South Connemara and Mayo with the dramatist J.M. Synge.
Lily and Elizabeth exhibited at the Irish Industrial Exhibition in New York.

1906

JANUARY JBY lectured at the Watts exhibition organized by Lane.
Jack painted his first landscape in oil. Published *The Fancy* with Masefield.

1907

JBY spoke at the Abbey Theatre (fig. 39) debate about Synge's controversial *Playboy of the Western World*.
16 MARCH Death of John O'Leary.
Jack saw London performance of *Playboy of the Western World*.
Jack and Cottie holidayed on the Rhine.
Hugh Lane and Sarah Cecilia Harrison raised a fund to send JBY to Italy.
29 DECEMBER Lily, accompanied by JBY, travelled to New York to exhibit and sell craftwork.

1908

JANUARY JBY sketched at Harry Thaw murder trial, New York.
6 JUNE Lily, unable to persuade JBY to come with her, sailed for home.
Last Dun Emer publications (including first number of *A Broadside*) before split with Evelyn Gleeson.
Cuala Industries established in July.
First Cuala Press book published, and second issue of *A Broadside*, published monthly until May 1915.

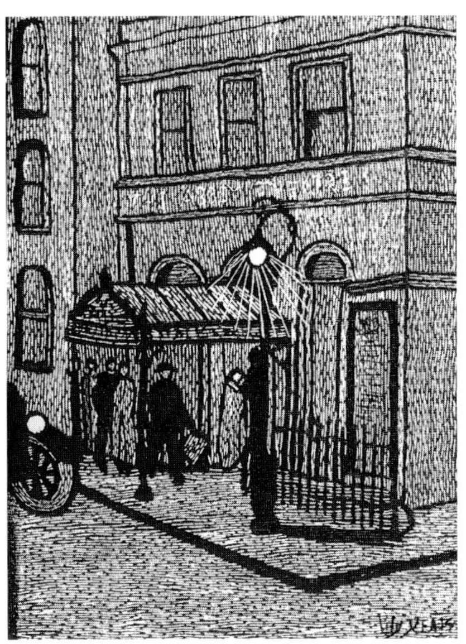

Fig. 39 Lily Yeats, *The Abbey Theatre*, embroidery (Anne Yeats Collection)

1909

Death of J.M. Synge.
Jack exhibited in London with the Allied Artists Association.
OCTOBER JBY moved to Petitpas boarding house in New York, where he lodged for the rest of his life. Lasting friendship with John Sloan and Robert Henri, of the Ashcan School (fig. 41).
Elizabeth designed stamps for Women's National Health Association of Ireland.

1910

JBY exhibited at the New York Independents' second show.
Elizabeth selling Cuala arts and crafts in Oxford, Beaconsfield and London.
Jack moved back to Ireland in June, to Greystones in County Wicklow. Painting consistently in oil. Began contributing to *Punch* under the pseudonym 'W. Bird'.
Lily present at George Pollexfen's death. Jack attended his funeral, his last visit to Sligo for many years.

1911

3 FEBRUARY John Quinn commissioned JBY's self-portrait in oil. JBY published articles in *Harper's Weekly* and started writing philosophical letters to WBY which would eventually be published. Elizabeth in Italy and Switzerland for three months.

1913

17 FEBRUARY *International Exhibition of Modern Art*, in which Jack Yeats was represented, opened at New York Armory.
Abbey Theatre linen handkerchief designed, with JBY sketches of players.
Jack learning Irish. Contributed to *Irish Art* at Whitechapel Art Gallery in London. Painting landscape in Kerry.

1914

Jack elected ARHA. Attended Pearse's nationalist meetings making sketches.

1915

JANUARY JBY knocked down and unable to work for some months.
Jack painted *Bachelor's Walk, in memory* and *Before the start*.
Jack elected RHA. Start of lengthy period of illness and depression.
Lily exhibited embroidery (fig. 42) at the Irish Literary Society, and commissioned by WBY to embroider one of Sturge Moore's designs.

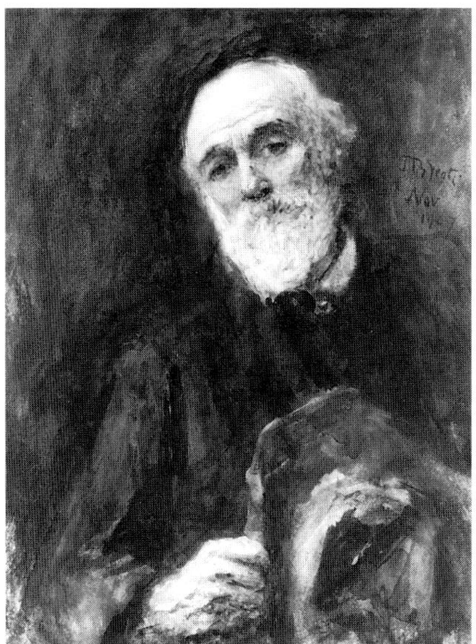

Fig. 40 J.B. Yeats, *Self portrait*, November 1907 (NGI Yeats Archive Photo)

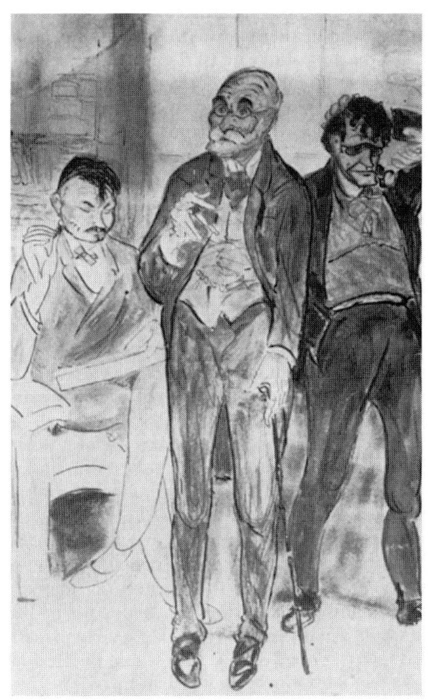

Fig. 41 Marjorie Organ, *Studio evening – Robert Henri, JBY, John Sloan* (private collection)

1916

The Easter Rising. Four of Jack's pictures destroyed in the Royal Hibernian Academy conflagration. Gradual recovery of health. Painted landscape at Roundstone in Connemara. First 'half-memory' sketches (fig. 43).
Death of JBY's friend John Todhunter.
OCTOBER JBY started afresh on *Self-portrait* commissioned by Quinn.

1917

MARCH Thoor Ballylee bought by WBY.
30 APRIL JBY's *Selected Letters* edited by Ezra Pound published by Elizabeth at the Cuala Press. JBY writing his memoirs.
OCTOBER WBY married Georgie Hyde-Lees (George) in London.
AUTUMN Jack left Wicklow to live at no. 61, Marlborough Road in Dublin.

1918

JBY's *Essays* published by Talbot Press and Fisher Unwin.

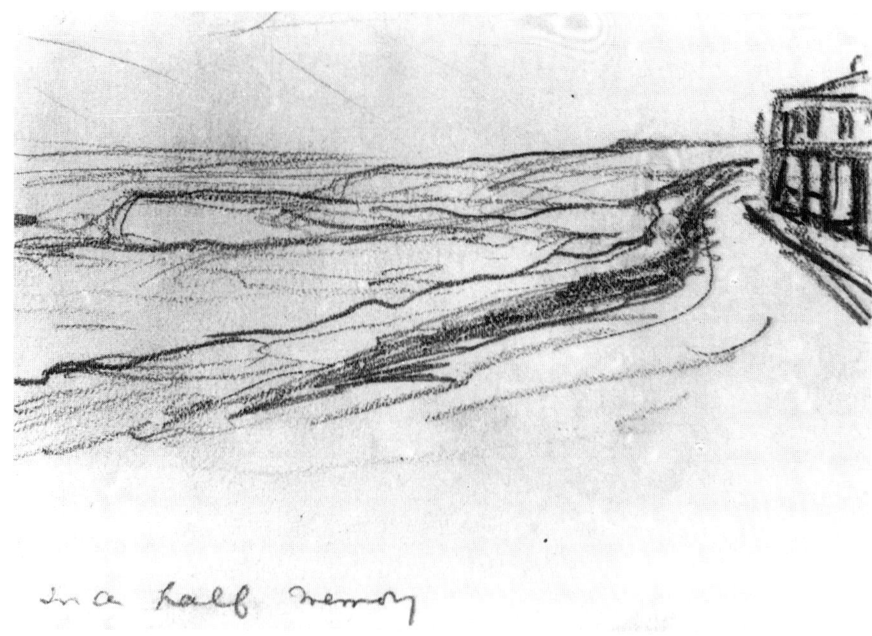

Fig. 43 Jack B. Yeats, *In a half memory*, sketchbook, 1916 (NGI Yeats Archive)

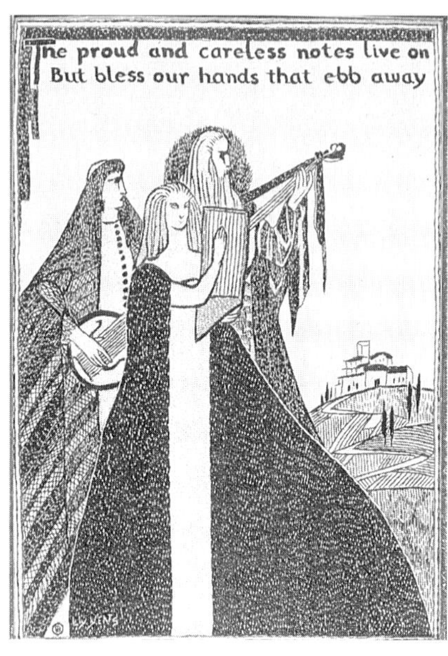

Fig. 42 Lily Yeats, *The proud and careless notes live on*, embroidery
(Anne Yeats Collection)

1919

26 FEBRUARY
ANNE BUTLER YEATS born.
JBY making 'self-sketches' (fig. 44) as preliminary to his *Self-portrait* (fig. 45). Cuala preparing *Further Letters*, edited by Lennox Robinson.
Susan L. Mitchell lecture on JBY in Dublin.
Jack painting landscape in West Cork.

1920

JANUARY JBY met his daughter-in-law George Yeats, visiting New York with WBY, his last meeting with members of his family.
Jack closed his Dublin exhibition in sympathy with the nationalist protest against the official refusal to recognize the status of political prisoners.
Painted landscape in Galway and Clare.

1921

Jack elected a member of the Glasgow Society of Painters and Sculptors. Exhibited with the Independent Artists, New York.

1922

WBY spoke on Irish literature, Jack on Irish painting at the Irish Race Congress in Paris.
3 FEBRUARY JBY died in New York.

1923

AUGUST Cuala Industries moved to the basement of WBY's house in Merrion Square, Dublin because of the Troubles.

1924

Death of John Quinn, American patron of JBY and Jack.

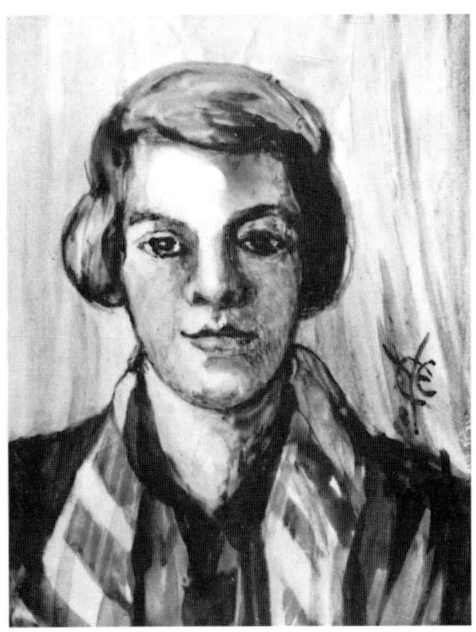

Fig. 44 Elizabeth Corbet Yeats, *Anne Yeats* (Anne Yeats Collection)

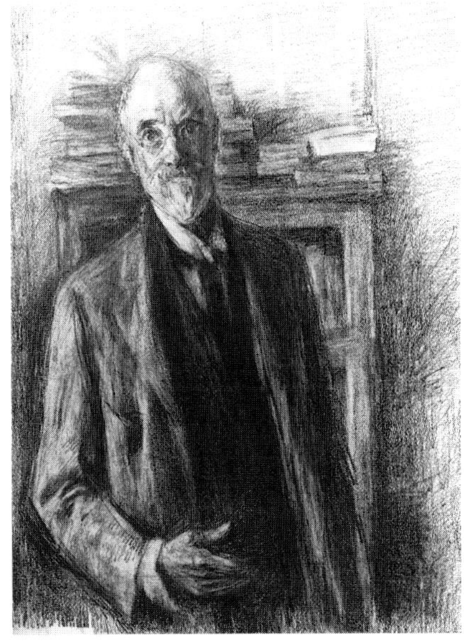

Fig. 45 J.B. Yeats, Study for final *Self-portrait* (NGI Photo Archive)

1925

25 FEBRUARY Cuala Industries reopened at no. 133, Lower Baggot Street.
Jack hand-coloured Cuala Prints (fig. 46) for the last time. Expressed confidence in his new oil style to WBY.

1926

Elizabeth Yeats teaching her niece Anne Yeats brush painting and an appreciation of the power of pure colour.

1928

Lily and Elizabeth to Birmingham to the Arts and Crafts exhibition.

1929

Jack moved to live at no. 18, Fitzwilliam Square, Dublin.

1930

Jack published his first major prose work, *Sligo*. Exhibited in Toronto. He was visited by Samuel Beckett, who was interested in his paintings.
The Liffey Swim bought by the Haverty Trust and presented to the National Gallery of Ireland.

1932

Barbizon Museum of Irish Art, New York, opened by WBY.
Anne Yeats entered Royal Hibernian Academy Schools, studying under MacGonigal, Lily Williams and Tisdall.

1933

Jack published *Apparitions* (plays) and *Sailing, Sailing Swiftly* (a novel).

1935

Anne Yeats assistant designer (later chief stage designer) to the Abbey Theatre.

1936

Jack published *The Amaranthers*.
Painted *Donnelly's Hollow*, the first of his major canvases of personal reminiscence.

1937

Cuala, originally a women's co-operative, reorganized with a board of directors, including George and WBY (hitherto advisory editor).
Jack painted *In memory of Boucicault and Bianconi*, *Helen* and *A race in Hy Brazil*, among other notable works.
Anne training at the Paul Collin School of Theatre Design in Paris.

1939

JANUARY Death of WBY at Cap Martin in France.
Jack's play *Harlequin's Positions* produced by the Abbey Experimental Theatre. Jack awarded a medal at San Francisco World Fair (fig. 47).
Appointed a governor of the National Gallery of Ireland.
Cuala awarded a Certificate of Merit at the New York World Fair.

1940

JANUARY Death of Elizabeth (Lolly) Yeats. Cuala Press taken over by George.
Jack elected a member of the London Group. Contributed to *British Painting since Whistler* at the National Gallery, London, and to Victor Waddington's exhibition of Irish artists in Waterford and Cork. Painted *Tinkers' encampment – the blood of Abel*.
Anne Yeats freelance stage designing in Dublin and Cork while studying painting with Keating at the National College of Art.
Jack advised Anne to paint life around her instead.

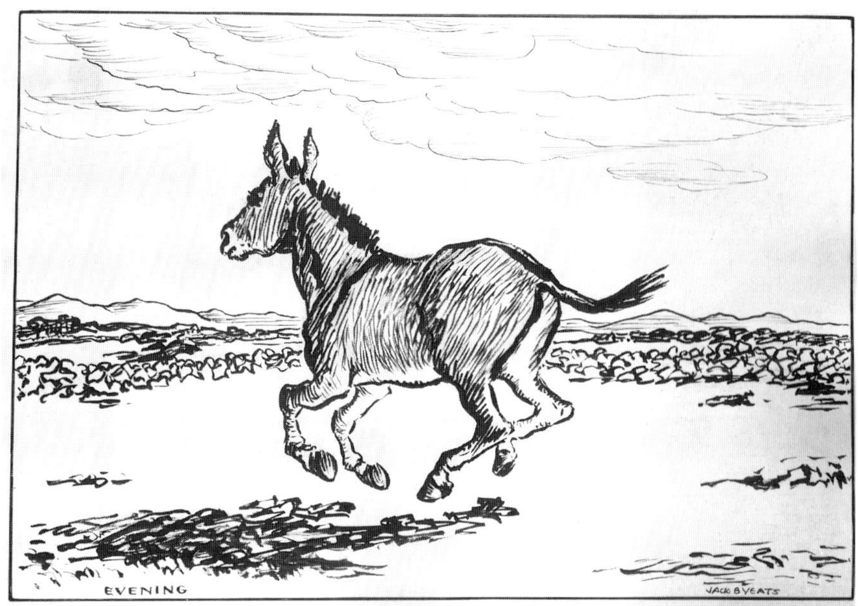

Fig. 46 Jack B. Yeats, *Evening,* Cuala Print (NGI Yeats Archive Photo)

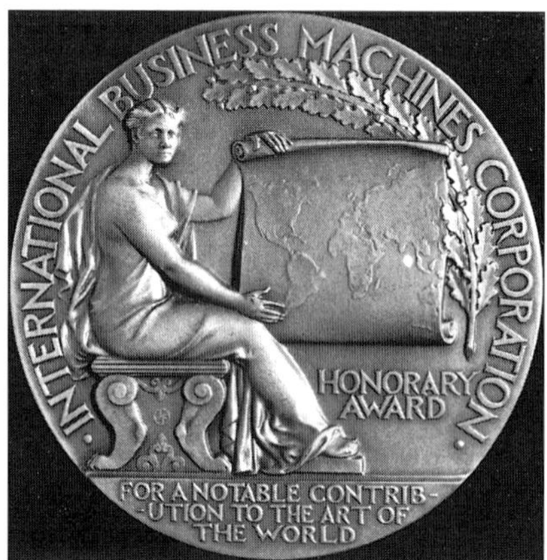

Fig. 47 Medal awarded to Jack B. Yeats at San Francisco World Fair, 1939

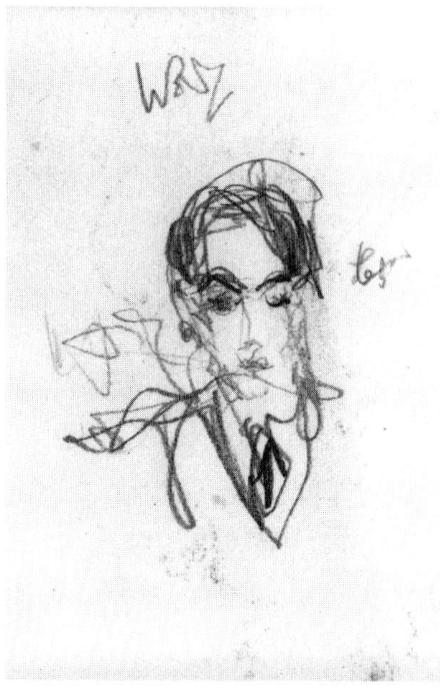

Fig. 48 Jack B. Yeats, *Sketch of W.B. Yeats from memory, ca.* 1948 (NGI Yeats Archive)

1941

Anne Yeats turning from stage design to concentrate on painting.

1942

Jack shared exhibition with William Nicholson at the National Gallery, London. His play *La La Noo* produced at the Abbey Theatre. Published *Ah Well.*

1943

Jack's first one-man exhibition with Victor Waddington, Dublin. Jack and Anne contributed to the first Irish Exhibition of Living Art.

1944

Jack published *And to You Also.*

1945

Jack B. Yeats National Loan Exhibition at the National College of Art, Dublin. Jack painted *Rise up Willie Reilly.* Anne exhibiting regularly, perfecting watercolour wax technique. Cuala Press closed after printing a new edition of *The Aran Islands* by J.M. Synge.

1946

Jack awarded D.Litt. by Trinity College, Dublin.
Men of destiny bought by the Committee of the *Jack B. Yeats National Loan Exhibition* for the National Gallery of Ireland.
Anne Yeats's first one-person exhibition.

1947

Death of Cottie. Jack painted *The great tent has collapsed.*
His last novel, *The Careless Flower,* published. Awarded D.Litt. by the National University of Ireland.
Anne joined committee of Irish Exhibition of Living Art, to which she was contributing regularly. Second visit to Paris, studying School of Paris painters who became a strong influence.

1948

Jack B. Yeats Loan Exhibition (Arts
Council of Great Britain) at the Tate
Gallery, London, Aberdeen and
Edinburgh.
Anne Yeats painting studies of
women and solitary people.

1949

Death of Lily Yeats. Jack painted *There
is no night*.
Jack's play *In Sand* produced at the
Abbey Theatre. Awarded Diploma of
the Accademia Culturale Adriatica,
Milan.

1950

Jack invested *Chevalier de la Légion
d'Honneur*. Painted his last major work
of reminiscence, *The showground
revisited* (fig. 49). Anne painting
regularly in oil.

1951

Jack's *American Retrospective Exhibition*
toured the United States.
Began to spend winters in Portobello
Nursing Home.

1954

Jack exhibited at the Galerie Beaux-
Arts in Paris.

1955

Jack attended his last Dublin
exhibition, held at Waddington
Galleries. Moved permanently to live
at Portobello House.

1956

Jack's last exhibition, in Belfast.
Visited by John Berger. Letter from
Kokoschka in November.
Anne Yeats illustrated *Margadh na
Saoire* by Máire Mac an tSaoi, later
illustrating poetry by Denis Devlin
and Kinsella, and other books.
First visit to Sicily.

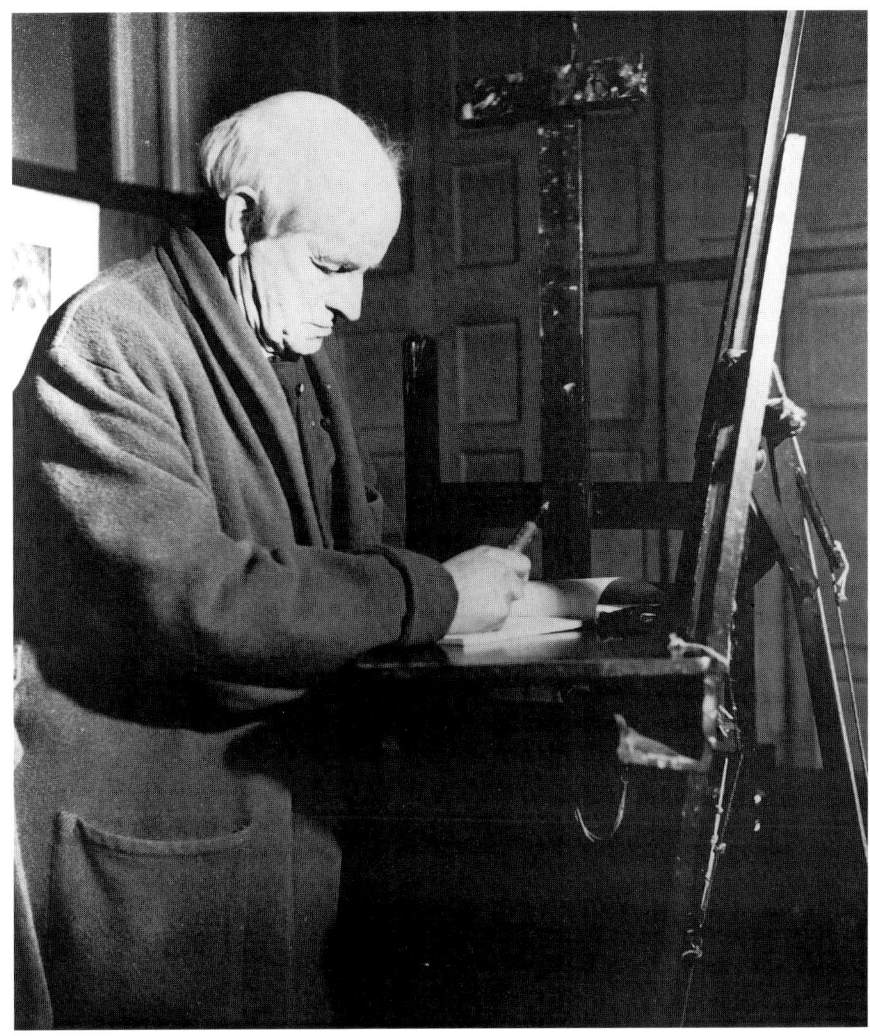

Fig. 49 W. MacQuitty, *Portrait photograph of Jack B. Yeats in his studio*, 1950
(NGI Yeats Museum Y6)

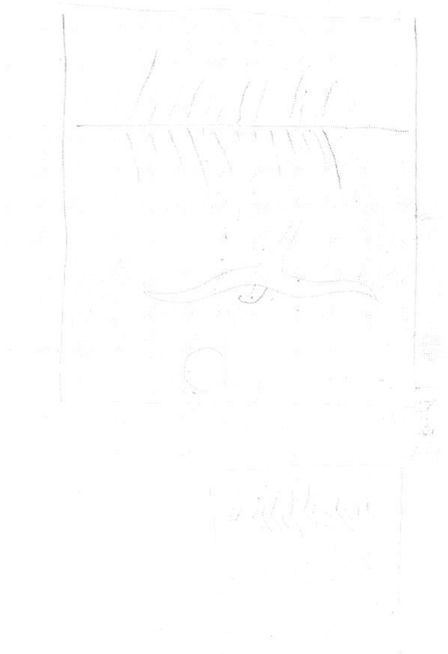

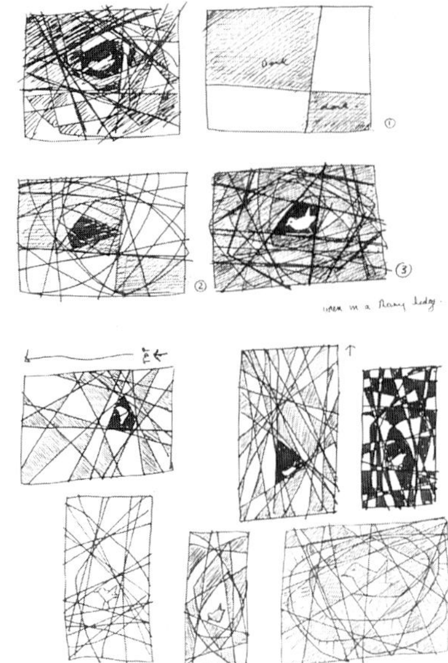

Fig. 50 Anne Yeats,
Wren in a thorny hedge, sketchbook
(Anne Yeats Collection)

Fig. 51 Anne Yeats, Preliminary sketch
for *Call down the hawk*, sketchbook, 1992
(Anne Yeats Collection)

1957
28 MARCH Death of Jack B. Yeats.

1963
Anne's third one-person show in
Dublin. Contributed to *Twelve Irish
Painters* exhibition, New York. From
1963 to 1968 making lithographs of
still life and other subjects.

1965
Anne painted *The bird* (later *The hunted
bird*), a subject she would develop
further (fig. 50). A visit to Sicily
resulted in paintings 'ordering chaos'.

1968
Anne developing new technique with
butter muslin and oil.

1970
Anne revived Cuala Press with Liam
Miller of Dolmen Press, Dublin.
Reprints series of *Broadside characters*
and other books.

1971
Jack B. Yeats Centenary Exhibition at the
National Gallery of Ireland in Dublin
and in New York. Anne and Cottie
represented in *Jack B. Yeats and his
Family* exhibition in Sligo County
Museum.

1970s
Anne painting still life, birds and cats
using cloth technique.

1972
*John Butler Yeats and the Irish
Renaissance* exhibition at the National
Gallery of Ireland, commemorating
the fiftieth anniversary of JBY's death.

1979
Anne painted series of *String paintings*.
Exhibition in Caen.

1984, 1989
Anne has one-person exhibitions in
Sligo.

1986
AUTUMN Cuala Press closed.

1992
Anne commissioned to paint *The hawk*,
commemorating her father, WBY, for
Samuel Beckett Theatre, Trinity
College, Dublin (fig. 51).

1995
JANUARY Anne Yeats's *Retrospective
Exhibition*, RHA Gallagher Gallery.

*Works
by the Yeats Family*

John Butler Yeats 1839–1922

JBY was admitted to the Bar in January 1866 and devilled for Isaac Butt (see p. 102), his father's friend from college days. One of his first assignments, in February 1866, was the Fitzgerald Will Case. The issue was whether the late Lord Fitzgerald, a man of notorious reputation, was of sound mind when he made his will. Isaac Butt appeared on behalf of the plaintiff, while James Whiteside, QC, was one of the barristers who acted for the defendant.

JBY took his sketchbook to court, which was to become his regular practice. He sketched the profile of the sixty-year-old Whiteside as he leaned forward to emphasize a point, gesticulating. Whiteside had a lean face beneath his wig, small bright eyes, a long nose, fleshy mobile lips and a pronounced chin. The drawing has an element of caricature and dwells on the idiosyncrasy of the man, though it was evidently true to life.

This sketch provides an interesting example of the artist's early, untrained working methods. The figure was outlined first very roughly in light pencil, still clearly visible in the lower half of the drawing. The barrister's face was later strengthened with sepia, moulding and shading added very lightly and the wig filled in in rapid detail. The body is roughly sketched.

James Whiteside (1804–1876) entered Trinity College in 1822 and was called to the Bar at the Inner Temple ten years later. He quickly acquired a reputation as an advocate of exceptional ability, and became a Queen's Counsellor in 1842 and later a judge. He represented Trinity College in Parliament in 1851, and the following year was appointed Attorney General. A change of government put him out of office a few years later, but he returned in 1866 and was appointed Chief Justice of the Queen's Bench. A marble bust portrait of James Whiteside by Patrick MacDowell was exhibited at the Royal Academy in 1861 and is now in Trinity College.

Another, slightly smaller, pencil caricature made by JBY during the same court case – of Chief Baron Palles – is in the collection of the Honourable Society of the Benchers, King's Inns, Dublin.

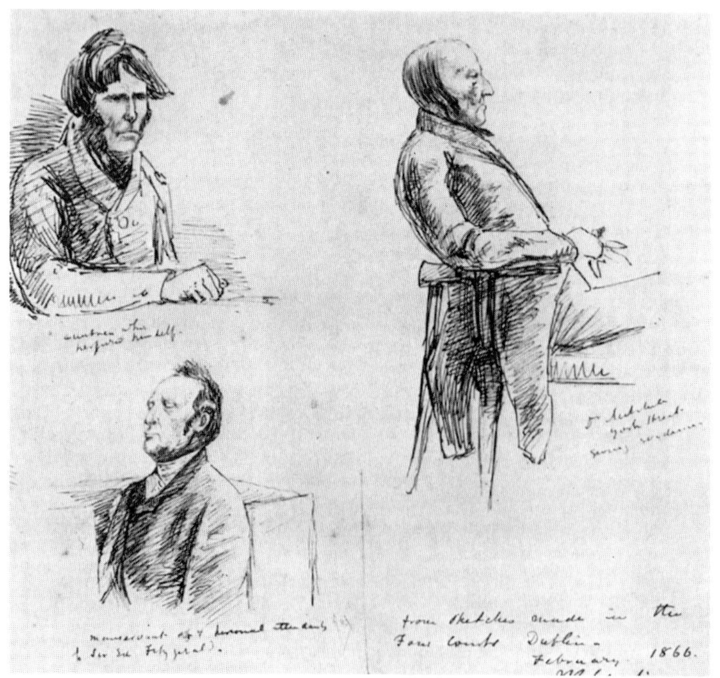

Fig. 52 J.B.Yeats, *Sketches made during the Fitzgerald Will case,* pencil, 21.5 × 19.5 cm (Michael B. Yeats Collection)

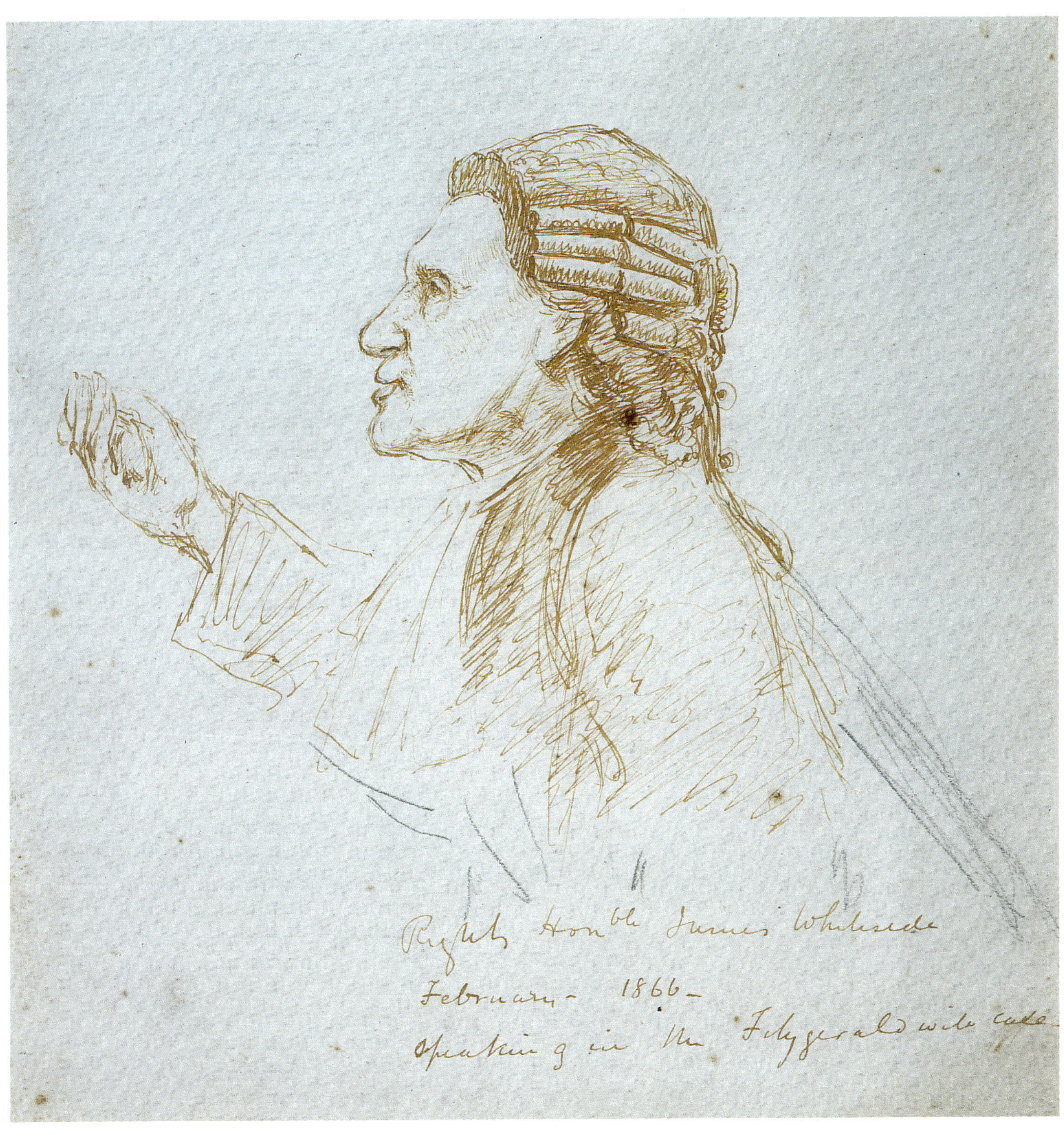

In the spring of 1870 Dr John Todhunter commissioned from JBY a drawing of 'Pippa' from Robert Browning's series of narrative poems *Bells and Pomegranates.* First published between 1841 and 1846, these poems were still immensely popular. *Pippa Passes*, the first in the series, tells how a girl from the silk mills in Asolo spends her New Year's holiday, passing through the lives of others, imagining herself into their situations and so influencing them, though she in no way envies their preferable lot.

At the time, JBY was sharing a studio with Edwin Ellis at no. 74, Newman Street, London, near J.T. Nettleship – a member of the informal Brotherhood they had set up – who had recently published a collection of essays on Browning's poetry. Todhunter sent a deposit of £5 to JBY in late February. On 2 March, JBY told him that he had a fresh design for the work which he would begin to paint at once. A month later he promised to start work immediately. On 24 April he informed Todhunter that he planned to add pines to the picture and to dress Pippa in nothing but white, and spoke of another new design. He was also ready to accept the remaining £5 of the fee. Then in June he told Todhunter the picture was a failure, "You will have little for your money except the feeling that you by this commission have helped me *enormously*." By early August the picture was "still merely in its commencement".

JBY went to Sligo for his customary summer holiday and came back to find that *Pippa* had deteriorated. "I found the face of Pippa *black*, greenish black, nearly all over. I have painted it in and out since ever so many times, but it has not come right." He hoped to finish it in a few days. On 30 December the picture was hung in the Dudley Gallery where it attracted a great deal of attention, notably from the artist Dante Gabriel Rossetti. After the show JBY worked on *Pippa Passes* for another year. Todhunter finally received it in April 1872, two years after the commission. Browning admired the picture when he saw it in Todhunter's possession and called on JBY, who was out and never returned Browning's call.

The gouache shows Pippa, a Rossetti-type beauty, wandering through a wood in early light. She throws her head back, cradling it in her arms. Her thick auburn hair falls heavily, away from her head. Her mouth is slightly open with a dreamy expression, her eyes gaze abstractly at the viewer. Her full white sleeves, pink sash, peasant apron and blue skirt sway as she seems to float rather than walk past a knotted tree with raised roots. Behind her the russet trunks of pine trees are visible along a woodland path. Autumn leaves whirl at her feet. The wood is dim, but light falls on the figure, highlighting her face, the drapery of her garments and her bare legs.

In 1972, when the picture was removed from the original panel, the name Isabella Pollexfen was revealed, written in pencil on the wood. Isabella Pollexfen, one of Susan Yeats's younger sisters, stayed with the Yeats family in London as companion and helper while the family was growing. She was close to Oliver Madox Brown, the precocious novelist and artist who died tragically young in 1874, and she eventually married the artist John Varley.

Fintan Cullen further compares the attitude of Pippa with that of Danaë in Frederick Sandys's *Danaë in the brazen chamber*, painted in 1867. Yeats was a student at Heatherley's Art School when he first visited Sandys in his studio in June 1868, where Sandys praised his work. Yeats continued to visit Sandys to discuss art, telling his friend Edward Dowden that over Sandys's work "there was a kind of splendid melancholy".

Dr Todhunter lent *Pippa* to the Dublin Industrial Exhibition in 1873. The following lines from Browning's poem, the verse chanted by Pippa as she sets out, were printed in the catalogue as an accompaniment to the painting.

> But let the sun shine! Wherefore repine?
> – With thee to lead me O Day of mine,
> Down the grass-path, grey with dew,
> Under the pine-wood, blind with boughs,
> Where the swallow never flew
> As yet, nor cicole dared carouse –
> Dared carouse!

Pippa Passes

1870–72, gouache on paper, originally laid down on wooden panel from which
it was removed in 1972, 48 × 34 cm, NGI 3531

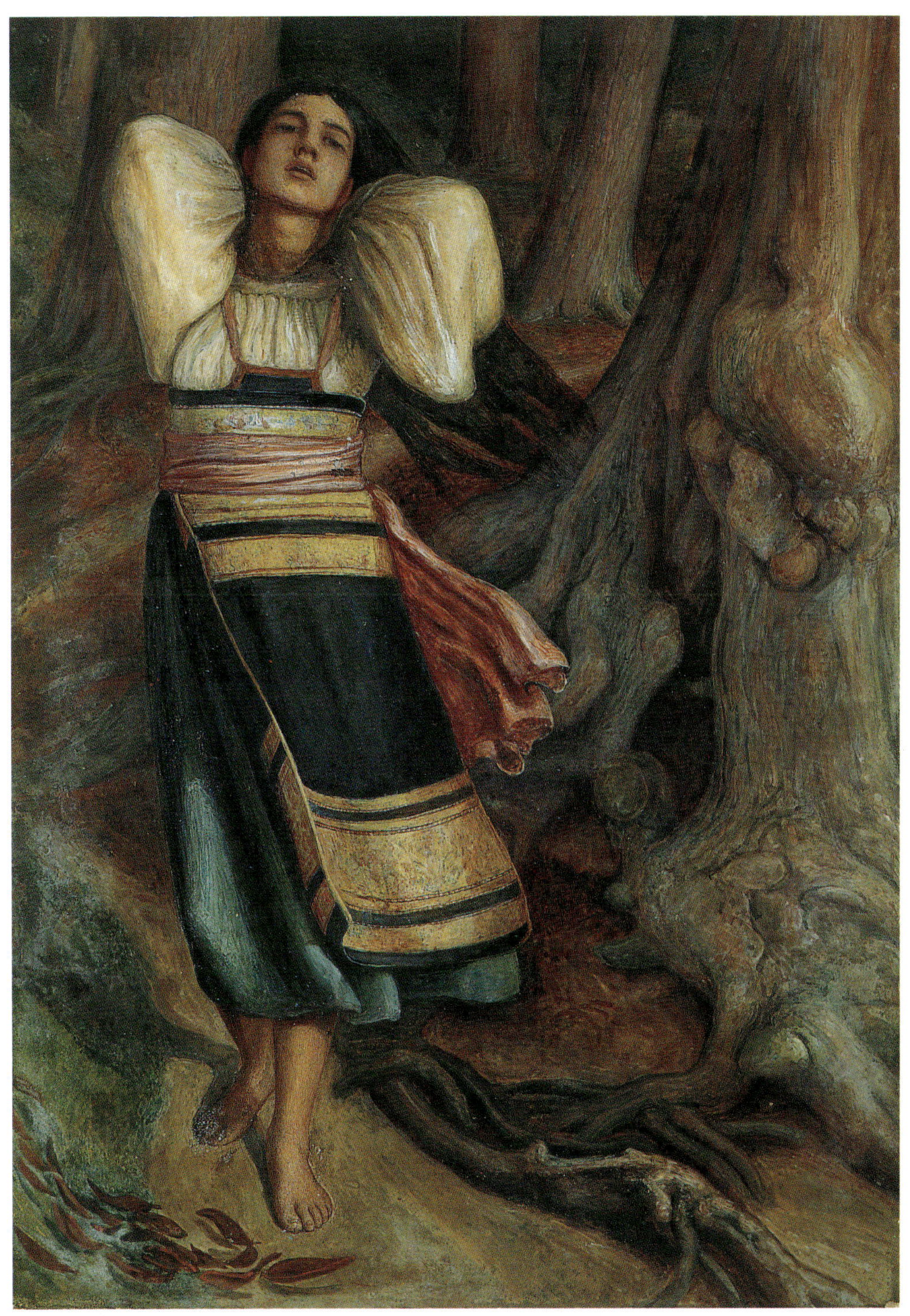

Thiis must be the chalk head of *Pippa* ordered by Edward Dowden in July 1870, taking the subject from Robert Browning's dramatic poem 'Pippa Passes', published nearly thirty years earlier (see also previous page). Black chalk was JBY's preferred medium at the time – he was complete master of it. The drawing is a splendid study of Pippa, or Felippa, the "black-eyed, pretty singing ... gay silk-winding girl", in the ecstasy of dreaming herself into the lives of others while she passes through Asolo on New Year's Day. The artist has placed her head and shoulders in the centre of the drawing, occupying nearly the whole vertical space. Her head is tilted back and, though her eyes engage the viewer, her lips are parted as in a trance. Behind her is a landscape of gentle, grassy slopes, and swallows dip to the right and left of her head:

> There goes a swallow to Venice – the stout sea-
> farer!
> Seeing those birds fly, makes one wish for wings.

Just two birds are shown, leaving the background free from distraction, while to the left, at neck level, are two sunflower heads, the 'flowerets' of which Pippa has announced herself queen. Light falls from the right on to her head. The bone structure is beautifully described.

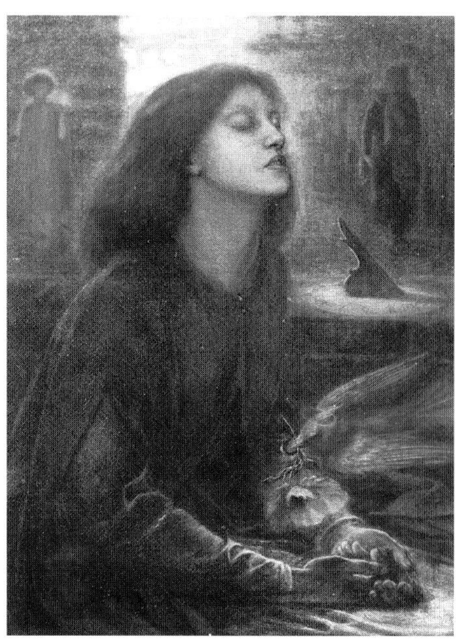

Fig. 53
D.G. Rossetti, *Beata Beatrix*, 1864–66, oil on canvas, 86.4 × 66 cm (Tate Gallery, London)

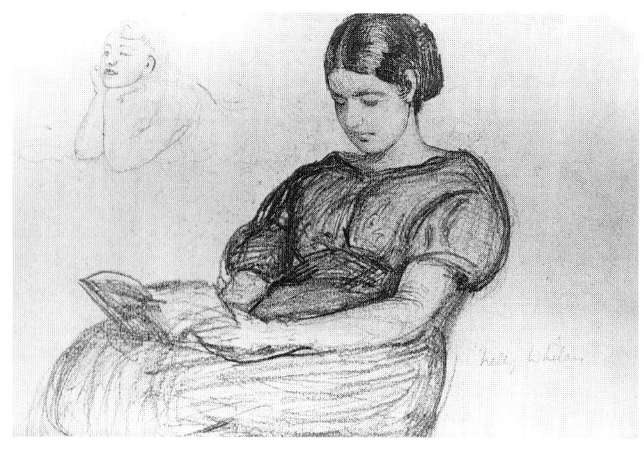

Fig. 54 J.B. Yeats, *Nelly Whelan, ca.* 1870 (Michael B. Yeats Collection)

As for the larger watercolour (previous page), JBY used Nelly Whelan as model (JBY to Dowden, 22 September 1870: TCD MSS), whom he also sketched in pencil about this time (see fig. 54). The artist has enhanced her features in pursuit of the Rossetti ideal that tantalized him during his student days. His line, strengthened during his training at Heatherley's, provides an organic rhythm on which the composition pivots. The drawing, on unevenly cut paper, was lined by the artist with lightweight paper before it was mounted on board, thus enabling him to extend the lower edge and straighten the lower line of the image with minor shading in black chalk.

The mood of *Pippa* is so close to that of Dante's Beatrice in Rossetti's *Beata Beatrix* (fig. 53) – based on drawings of Rossetti's dead wife, Elizabeth Siddal – that it is tempting to assume that JBY had seen the picture. Rossetti was interested in JBY's work, sending his brother William Michael to Fitzroy Road to invite JBY to visit him. JBY, who was very much in awe of the older painter, never took up the invitation; but it is not inconceivable that he visited Rossetti's studio or some other venue with Nettleship when the painting was on view but Rossetti was not present. JBY, however, never aimed for such heights of colour and sensuousness as Rossetti. His style at the time was more in the region of Watts's best work, but with a puritan quality that gave it an air of individuality.

Pippa

1870, black chalk on cream paper, originally mounted on board,
35 × 38 cm, NGI 3253

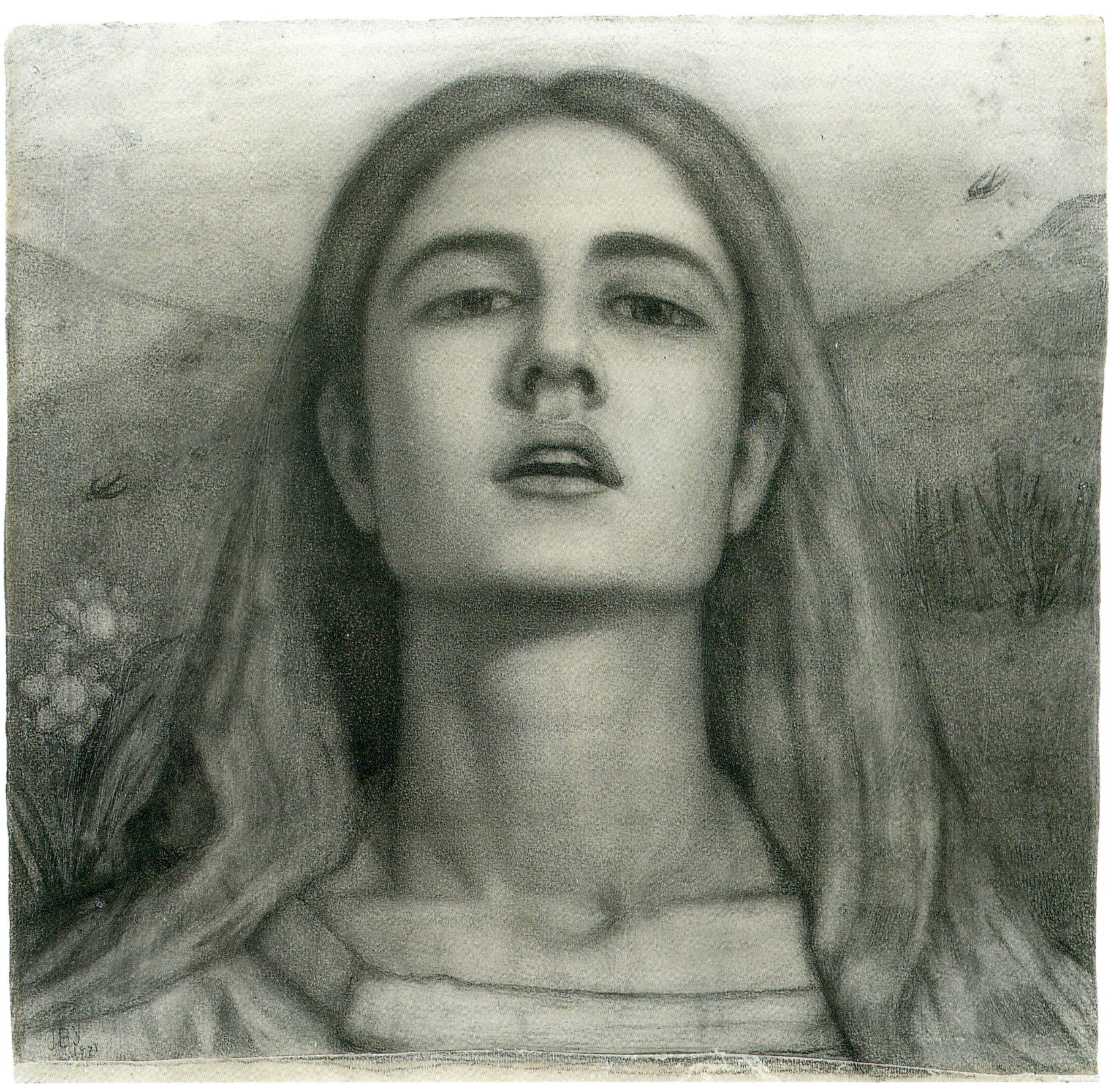

During what he called his "apprenticeship", JBY received enormous support, both moral and practical, from his friends Dowden (poet and critic) and Todhunter (doctor *cum* connoisseur), who were anxious to see him launched on his career as an artist. In June 1870 a Mr W.T. Grahame, unknown to the artist, sent £25 to Todhunter, asking him to commission pictures from Yeats and his friend Nettleship. Todhunter decided that Yeats was to receive £20 for a picture that, according to Grahame's stipulation, must be of "moonlight". A full six months later, in typical fashion, JBY had hardly begun it, and a year later it was not yet ready.

Part of the problem may have been that JBY was working for a man he had never seen, a situation that always made him ill at ease. As well as this, Yeats's idealistic aims made it impossible for him to envisage that he had done all that he could to make a perfect picture. The "landscape" Dowden commissioned, which this painting is believed to be, fared little better than the "moonlight" picture. It must have taken about a year and, when Dowden received it in November 1871, JBY was apologetic about the execution, "so very unsatisfactory", "I began the picture in the snow, when the whole place was hung and festooned and draped with a luxuriance of dead leaves. This indeed was the great attraction. Interruptions occurred, and I finished the picture when the spring winds were on every side of me with great dispatch, dislodging and carrying off the dead leaves, except a few that still stood out and *flecked* the brown gloom as I have painted them."

The gouache shows a woodland, with a narrow path at the right bottom edge disappearing between two large trees. Behind the more mature trees in the foreground is a grove of saplings, and there is much low growth in the foreground. The artist has articulated the space cleverly by dividing it into rough thirds with the trunks of the larger trees, creating a compositional interest which is necessary where there is no human activity to enliven it.

His other resource is light, which he has treated originally. Rather than taking a position facing the wood, he seems to stand under the trees, allowing light to filter from the sky through the top of the picture, so lighting the back- and foregrounds from wherever it enters. It suggests a familiarity with the Barbizon painters, though JBY gives a pictorial quality to his study, treating the trees individually as if in an illustration, imbuing the picture with some unseen presence, a quality which relates it stylistically to the *Pippa* paintings in the tradition of the Pre-Raphaelites.

JBY was justly admired for his portraits, but he told his daughter years later, "I have always wished to be a landscape painter".

Landscape

1871, gouache on paper, originally lined and attached to a stretcher
backed by canvas, 25.2 × 35.1 cm, NGI 3254

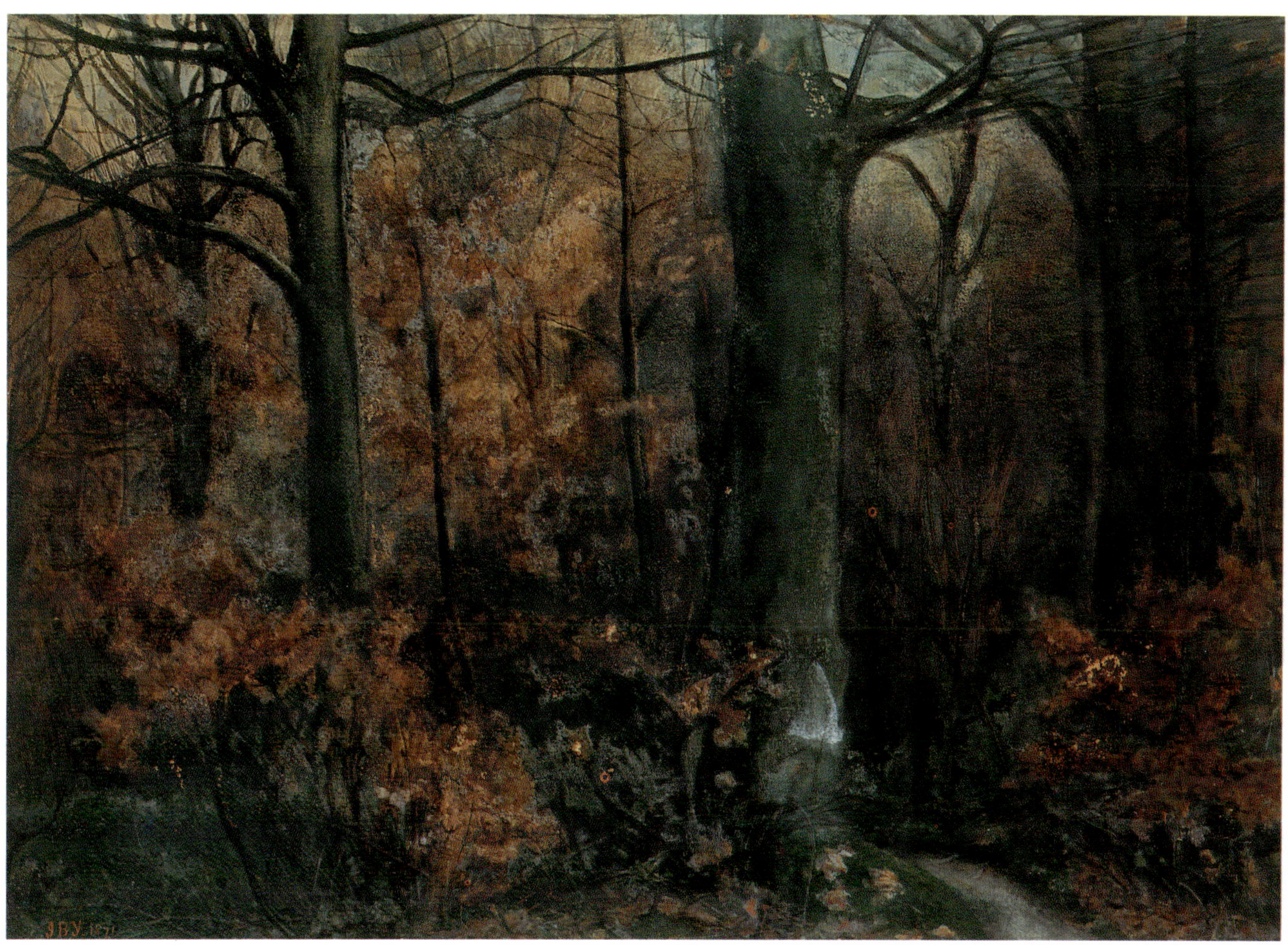

John Butler Yeats met his future wife, Susan Mary Pollexfen (1841–1900), when visiting his old school friend George Pollexfen in Sligo in September 1862. The couple became engaged almost immediately, married on 10 September 1863 and went to live in Sandymount, Dublin, while JBY completed his studies as a law student. Much has been written about their incompatibility and the extremes to which JBY put his wife after abandoning the legal profession for a perilous career as an artist; but there was some irresistible attraction between them. Katharine Tynan relates in her *Memories* (1924) how, when she visited the family in Dublin, JBY looked at his quiet wife and said, "I always knew she would be the mother of a poet". She tells a subsequent story of a man meeting JBY in the street, who asked how Mrs Yeats was, not knowing that she was dead. "He just stared at me, burst into tears and ran away."

This bust portrait was probably painted about 1875, when Susan was in her early thirties. The family had recently been reunited in London (Susan and the children had been in Sligo for over two years while JBY found work in various places) and JBY was also painting a portrait of his sister Gracie, who had come to London to help with the family. He had made some romantic pen portraits of his wife in 1867 (fig. 55), in which she wears a bonnet as in this portrait. He made various drawings of her during the 1870s (see fig. 56), but this is the only known oil portrait.

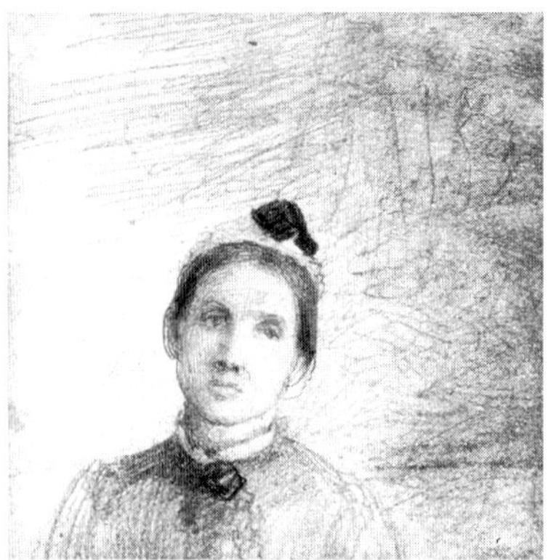

Fig. 56   J.B. Yeats, *Susan Yeats, ca.* 1878, pencil, 24 × 16.5 cm (Anne Yeats Collection)

Susan wears what is probably her Sunday bonnet, with a small brim and broad ribbons tucked behind her ears and tied under the chin. It matches her black, fur-collared coat. The effect, with her plain rimmed spectacles and withdrawn expression, is sober – a married woman dressed properly – neglecting fashion, yet charming. She is seen three-quarters face. She has an oval face with firm jawline, a high forehead bordered by straight brown hair parted in the middle (as was the mode), clearly marked dark eyebrows, and unmatched eyes – one grey, one hazel. Her lips are pursed beneath her straight nose. Her skin is fair and rendered radiant in the painting. As with other portraits of sitters wearing black, JBY has painted the background red-brown, touched with vandyke-brown to tone with her hair, giving the formal portrait a warmth it might otherwise lack.

The paint is not as thick as in some of the other early portraits, though there is some craquelure. JBY has handled his brush freely within the contained image. There is a tenderness in this image – a good-looking woman of great potential, isolating herself at the same time as submitting to current conventions, and resigned to the instability of life with an improvident artist. About ten years later she suffered a stroke, followed by a second one, and remained an invalid until her death.

On the reverse Lily Yeats has appended a note giving the date of Susan Yeats's birth, marriage in St John's Church, Sligo, and death, adding, "I think that the likeness is very good, but it always seemed to me to be over life size. The only remark my mother ever made about it was it had a woodland rustic air."

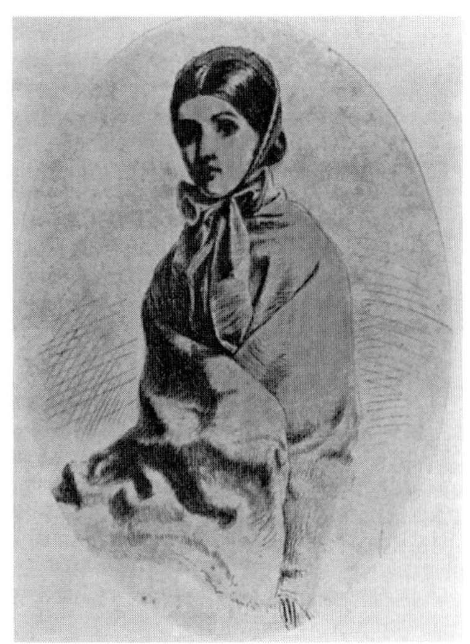

Fig. 55 J.B. Yeats, *Susan Yeats,* 1867, ink, 27 × 18 cm (Michael B. Yeats Collection)

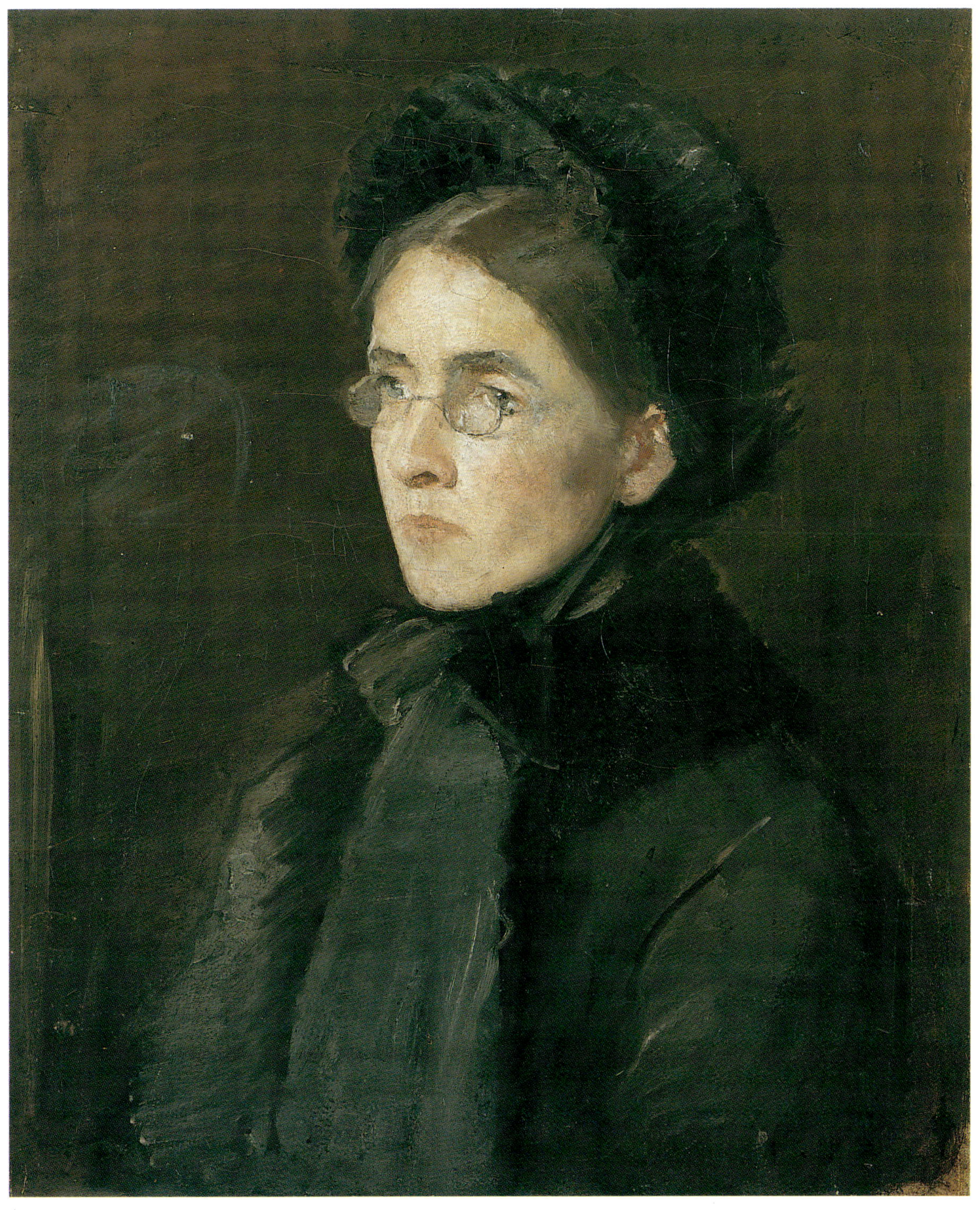

John Butler Yeats made several splendid children's portraits towards the end of the 1870s, including an oil of his daughter Lily (fig. 57) and one of Charles Fitzgerald, done in chalk (exh. RHA 1880). That of Hester Dowden (1868–1949; eldest child of JBY's old friend Edward Dowden, Professor of English Literature at Trinity College, Dublin, and his wife Mary Clerke) was ready for the Royal Academy in 1879. JBY travelled over to Dublin to collect it so as to offer it for exhibition. However, the painting was rejected. Whether JBY felt bruised by yet another failure, or he decided to do some repainting, it was two years before the picture was exhibited – accepted by the Royal Hibernian Academy in Dublin where it was much admired.

JBY's child portraits are all challenging. They seem to assert a belief in the power of the human personality from birth and, while full of the charm of innocence, they are just as intriguing as his studies of adults. Hester Dowden, shown in a three-quarter-length view, sits up straight, her mittened hands clasped tightly. Her black medieval-style hat – perhaps one of the products of the current aesthetic movement – is pushed back from her head to form a kind of halo, revealing neatly combed and parted hair. She is turned slightly to the right, but her deep-blue bright eyes look straight at the viewer from a heart-shaped face of radiant complexion.

Yeats has painted the young girl in a strong light, which throws up the detail of her black stuff dress with its broad velvet bands – the artist has made much of it – and which dwells on her lace ruff collar and cuffs. While he has moved away from the symbolism of his daughter's portrait (of some two years earlier) towards a greater naturalism, the light still plays a noticeable rôle in this image of youth's freshness and promise, and the more so because the background is a very dark brown, a curtain or drape, out of which obscure warmth the form of the erect young figure emerges.

Hester – or 'Essie' – Dowden was very close to her poet father during these formative years, accompanying him on long walks around Howth and the outskirts

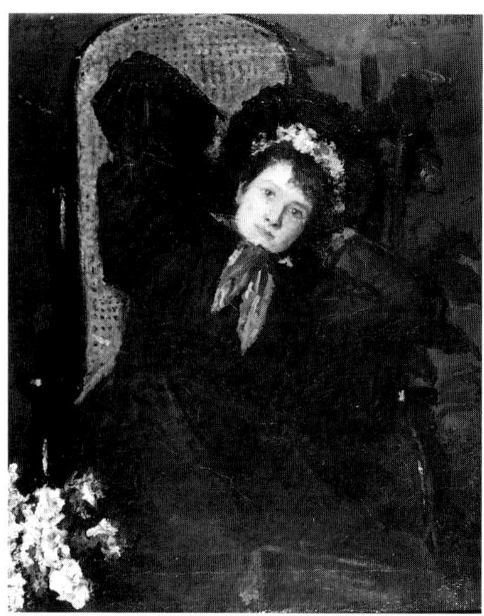

Fig. 57   J.B. Yeats, *My daughter, ca.* 1877, oil on canvas, 85 × 49.5 cm (Hugh Lane Municipal Gallery, Dublin)

of Dublin. Though Dowden felt she lacked originality, she followed an interesting career. After her marriage to the Reverend Travers Smith of St Bartholomew's Church, she acquired a reputation as a spiritualist. Her most noted publication was *One Step Higher, Automatic Writings*, 1937. A.E. (George Russell) did not quite approve of her, telling a correspondent in 1920, "The centre of spiritualism in Dublin is a Mrs Travers Smith, FitzWilliam Street. I believe she has published something about it which attracted attention because she got a message from Sir Hugh Lane who was drowned in the *Lusitania* and there was considerable controversy over it. She is quite honest and a clever woman, a daughter of the late Professor Dowden."

When Yeats's picture was shown at the exhibition shared with Hone in 1901, the critic of *The Irish Times* thought the portrait of Essie Dowden "the most successful work of art among Mr. Yeats's contributions".

Hester Dowden as a child

1879, oil on canvas, 76 × 63 cm, NGI 1395

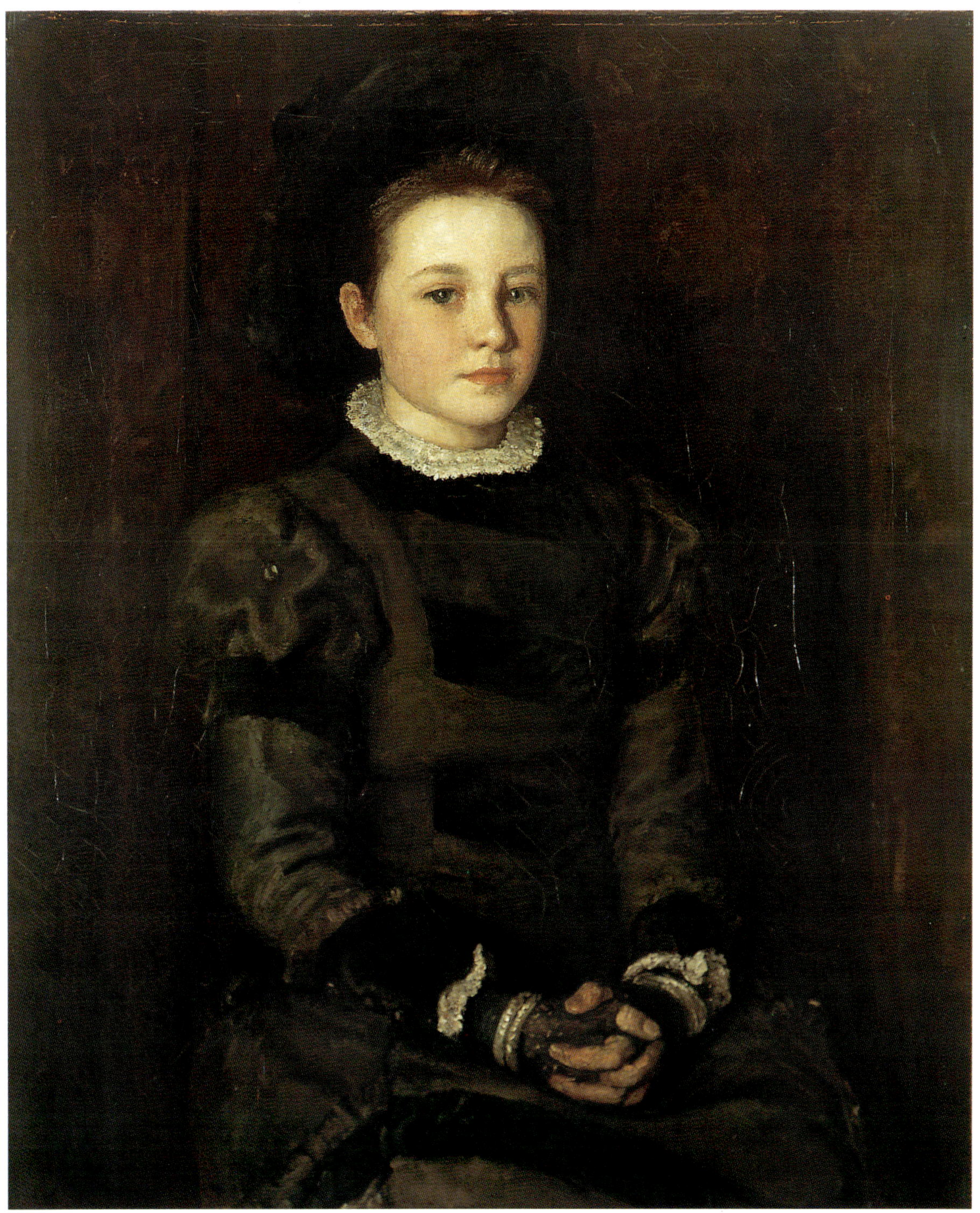

In June 1879 JBY wrote to his uncle Matt, "I want to come to Dublin to paint portraits, to put my sickle into the harvest. I think I shall succeed. *I have practised very hard at painting faces and draperies all winter ...* I hear an immense income is to be made in Dublin by portrait painting. Friends are constantly urging me to come over." It was two years before he moved to Dublin, though he worked there periodically and exhibited at the Royal Hibernian Academy from 1880. His *Portrait of the eldest daughter of Edward Dowden Esq.* (see previous page), shown in 1881, was widely praised and could only further his career.

It was perhaps because of the success of this portrait that he was commissioned to paint an oil of Frances Elizabeth Euphemia ('Effie') Geoghegan (1872–1956). Sarah Purser was probably involved. Effie Geoghegan's grandmother was a Purser, her aunt and uncle were married to a brother and a sister of Sarah Purser. Sarah Purser herself was a member of the Dublin Sketching Club, as was JBY; she sometimes lunched with him in his York Street studio, which had by then become a meeting point for artistic Dublin. A portrait of an only child must have seemed to Sarah Purser of prime benefit to both painter and client. Elizabeth Geoghegan, Effie's mother, had not long been widowed. Effie's father, John Geoghegan, had spent his career in the Indian Civil Service, but died in 1877 at the age of forty, too young to have enjoyed retirement.

The picture is one of JBY's typical child portraits, a mixture of innocence and independence of spirit. Effie wears a becoming dress of a deep blue, with a white-fringed bow at the neck and white-fringed cuffs, the sleeve touched with green where it catches the light.

She sits in a wooden library chair which is turned towards the left. She herself faces the viewer, placing her lovely childish hands on the arm of the chair (the painting of these belies the view that JBY was incapable of painting hands). Her lap is filled with flowers she must have been picking in the garden – marigolds, nasturtiums, carnations. No doubt, harking back to JBY's more symbolic phase, some passing reference to the ephemerality of life can be read here – though this 'flower' was to live to a ripe old age. JBY is also following a common convention in comparing the freshness of youth with the vivacity of newly plucked blossoms. Effie's complexion, shining palely from a low-lit interior, betrays her early upbringing in the Indian climate. Her brown eyes stare mutinously from a heart-shaped face, framed by long, dark-brown hair held back firmly by an Alice band. This may be the painting JBY exhibited in the Royal Hibernian Academy of 1882 with the title *Bored*.

The portrait is charming and well constructed. The brown chair, gleaming with polish and reflection, frames the young girl's figure; the upright of the chair's arm leads the spectator's eye straight to the sitter's face while also creating interesting shapes in the centre and lower parts of the picture. Nevertheless this is a classic example of JBY never knowing when a painting was complete. The pigment has been piled on in an attempt to strengthen the image, and has led to craquelure about the surface. The sitter, who lived unmarried in Dublin for the rest of her life, had a high regard for the portrait. She never parted with it, and she left it to the National Gallery in her will.

Frances Elizabeth Geoghegan as a child

ca. 1882, oil on canvas, 46 × 36 cm, NGI 1343

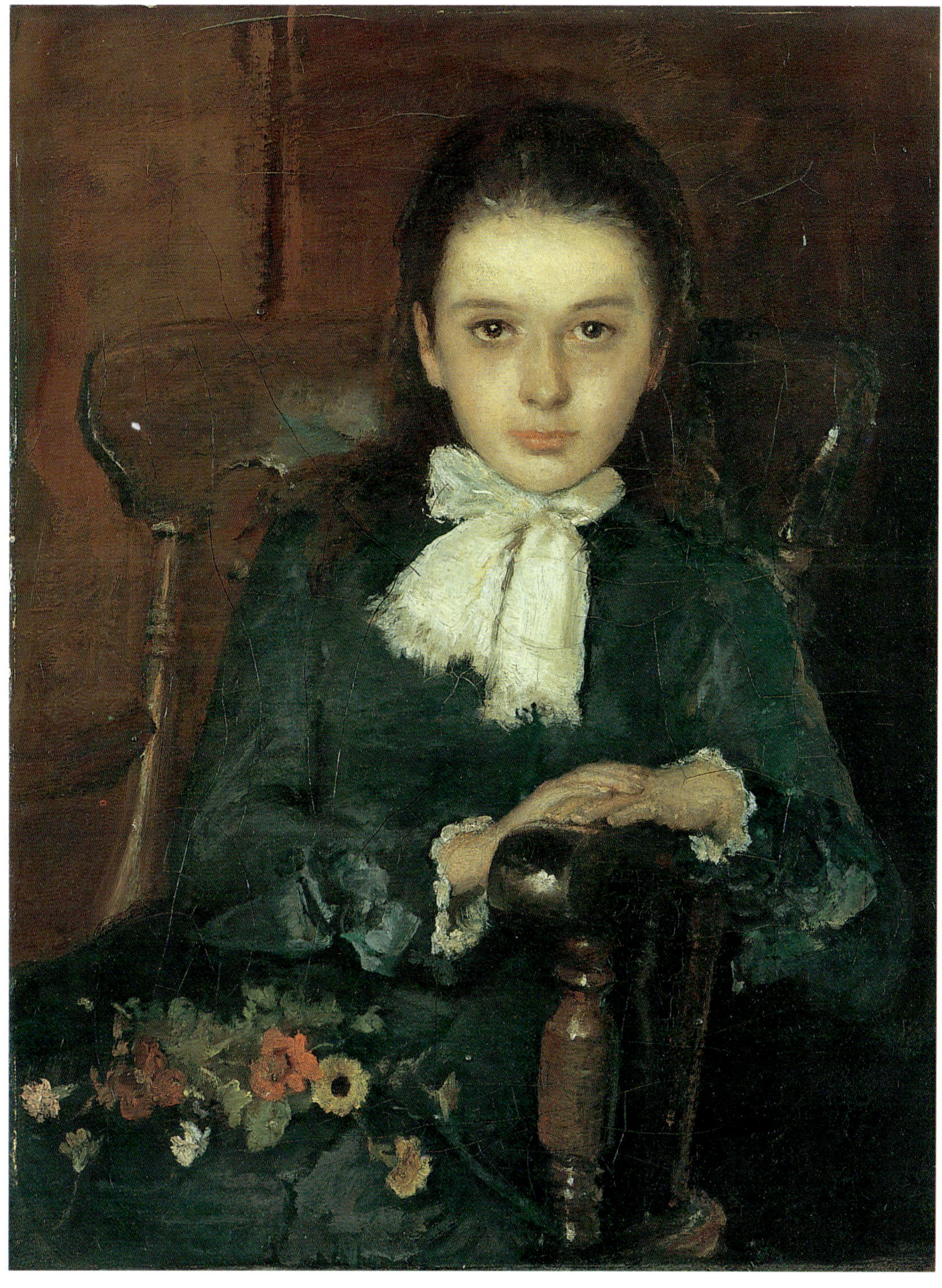

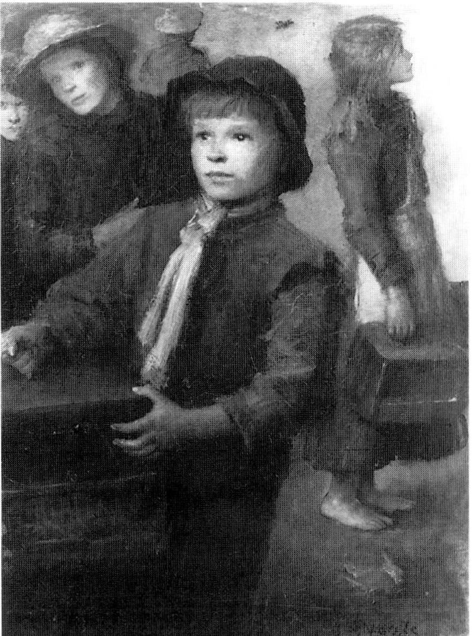

Fig. 58 J.B. Yeats, *The bird market, ca.* 1886, oil on canvas, 63.5 × 48 cm (Hugh Lane Municipal Gallery, Dublin)

This half-length portrait of the artist's younger son, Jack, as a boy of twelve or thirteen, is unusual among the child portraits of this period; the technique seems closer to JBY's oil paintings of more than a decade later. The picture is loosely painted in light tones, a reminder that when JBY holidayed with his children in Devon he refused to give them any black for their paintings because "there was no black in Nature". JBY, established in Dublin, could put his modernist notions into practice when he was not dealing with a commission. The occasion for the portrait may have been a visit to Sligo for the annual holiday – Jack now lived with his Pollexfen grandparents and was being educated in Sligo, so his mother may have wanted a likeness to keep in Dublin. Or the portrait may have been painted in the York Street studio when Jack was visiting the family.

One explanation for the fluidity of the paint in this picture might be that JBY went back to the painting years later. However, the brushwork is smooth and does not dance as it does in the mature portraits (he uses a short expressive stroke about the face, and a longer diagonal slant on the garments). The artist is not so provocative with colour as he would be later, but he has learned the value of a modern tonality. Another explanation for the stylistic change (see also fig. 58) is that Yeats used the occasion to test an abiding attraction to Whistler, parallelling his *Nocturnes* and *Arrangements in grey and black* (the most famous being the portrait of his mother) with an *Etude* in fawn. JBY later described Whistler to WBY as "a poet painter" (in contrast with Sargent, "a prose painter"); he was invited by Knoedler's Gallery to contribute an introduction to a Whistler exhibition. But already, in 1884, he had contrived to bring an exhibition of Whistler watercolours and paintings (including the famous *Mother*) to Dublin.

Judging by later sketches and oil-paintings, the *Etude*, if one may call it that, is, for all its wistful poetry, a good likeness of Jack. Jack was a store of wit and tomfoolery in the right company, but he was remarkable also for his moments of withdrawal. JBY experimented with differing aspects of personality in portraits of WBY, but always seemed to strike a balance between kindly good-humour and a slight distancing in Jack. Jack's high-domed head is covered with short golden-brown hair, falling over his forehead in an uneven fringe not long enough to disguise the vaguely anxious expression. His deep-blue eyes, meeting the viewer, have a far-away look that was typical throughout his life. His complexion is fair and rosy. While probing into his essential character, JBY does not detract from his son's boyishness.

Posed to the left, with his head turning back at a characteristic angle, Jack is wearing a respectable light-grey suit, the top button fastened as was the fashion, and a handkerchief in his top pocket. His left arm, stretched across the lower part of the picture, is not finished – perhaps he moved and there was no time to pose anew. JBY has painted him in daylight, to avoid any strong shadows which might interfere with the tonal harmony. The creamy-beige ground, shot with light or darker tones, complements the youthful image by unifying the golden brown of the boy's hair and the grey of his coat, so extending the interior mood of pensive tranquillity.

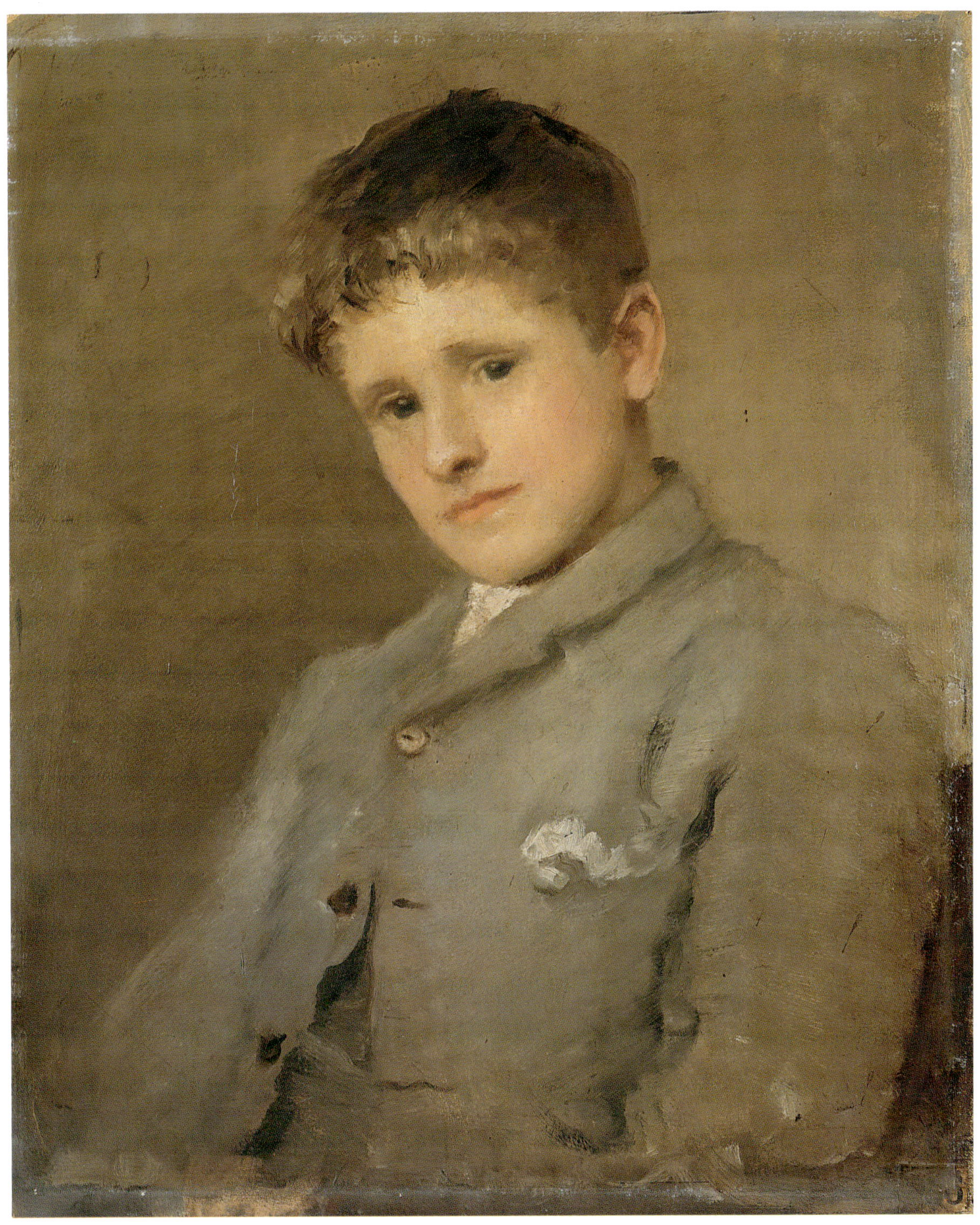

bust of a soldier, head bare, standing to attention with an exaggerated expression of zeal. He wears a short moustache, which curls down on each side of his taut mouth. The artist views the man from one side, a three-quarter view, capturing the fanatic gleam in the visible eye as the soldier looks away to the right.

The drawing has much in common with JBY's half-tone illustrations of the 1890s, when he contributed to the magazine *Leisure Hour* (fig. 59), illustrating for WBY, Frederick Langbridge, and others, as well as offering original subjects of his own invention for reproduction. This ample-sized work, however, is a character study rather than an attempt at pictorial narrative. Rather than being a straight illustration for a story or poem, it is more likely to have been inspired by some literary quotation, and designed as a subject picture, such as was popular at the time.

The slight touch of cynicism in his reading of the character suggests that JBY approached the subject in a mood of irony – he was very opposed to war. Despite his initial intention to live by portraiture, JBY continued to do genre pictures in the contemporary mode, showing them in the Royal Hibernian Academy, some in chalk and on paper. The paper used here was acquired through the Dublin Sketching Club, of which he had been a member for nearly ten years. *A young man of his country's service* is carried out in monochrome grey, reinforced here and there with black chalk, and with the hatching about the nose and the outline of the eyes detailed in ink.

JBY had by now moved to a new studio at no. 7, St Stephen's Green, which became a centre for the family and for the many visitors who went to enjoy his conversation. He believed that his oil technique was improving, though he was totally impractical and unable to make a living from the few commissions for portraits which he arranged in an unbusinesslike way. His uncle Matthew, who managed his Thomastown estate genially, helping JBY with loans, had died in the summer, leaving the artist in the hands of a more exacting agent. Impatient with his lack of success at portraits, and uncertain of his future in Dublin, JBY in this monochrome study may have been anticipating the change, which would take place the following year, to a new career as a black-and-white illustrator in London.

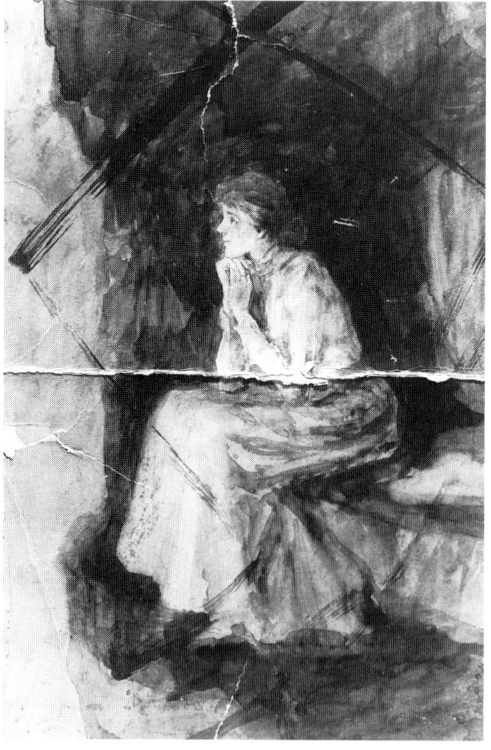

Fig. 59 J.B. Yeats, Study for *Dania* in 'The Dreams of Dania', *Leisure Hour*, 1896, wash drawing, 36 × 25 cm (Hugh Lane Municipal Gallery, Dublin)

A young man of his country's service

1885, black chalk, pencil and monochrome wash on watercolour paper,
stamped on verso *Dublin Sketching Club*, 35.7 × 25.6 cm, NGI 19,238

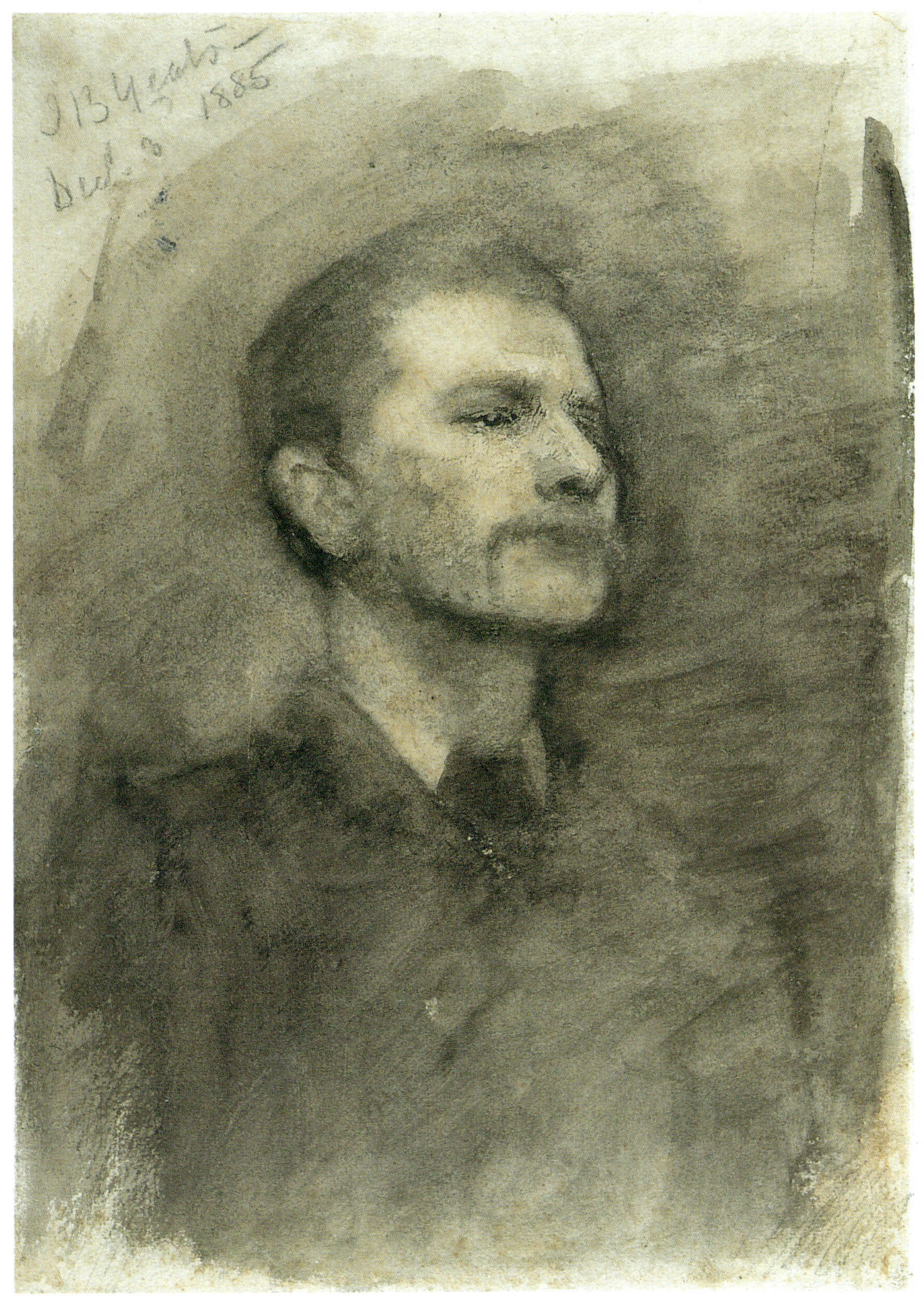

The Contemporary Club was founded in Dublin on 21 November 1885 by Charles Hubert Oldham (1860–1926), a colleague of JBY's friend Dowden at Trinity. Oldham, a mathematician and scientist, had been in the habit of inviting students and lecturers to his college rooms for informal discussions over a pipe and a cup of tea on Saturday nights. The subjects were topical, mainly literature and politics; but the authorities disapproved of Oldham's openly expressed opinions (he was to found the Protestant Home Rule Association in 1886), and he was compelled to move out of College to rooms at no. 116, Grafton Street. The group re-formed as the Contemporary Club (the name indicative of a mutual interest in live and, particularly, Irish issues) at Oldham's new rooms, which were above Ponsonby's bookshop, right opposite the entrance to the College. WBY – then an art student, but manifesting gifts as a writer – and JBY were invited to join. Douglas Hyde and Michael Davitt were early members.

Initially membership was limited to fifty, though all were welcome to what was a 'wrangling' club, in the accepted sense, devised to bring men of every shade of opinion together to exchange views. "In Ireland harsh argument which had gone out of fashion in England was still the manner of our conversation," WBY recalled in *Autobiographies*; "and at this club Unionist and Nationalist could interrupt one another and insult one another without the formal and traditional restraint of public speech." He was one of the more heated speakers, while his father sat in a corner listening and sketching. JBY's sketches of members and guests in session obviously intrigued the arguers. The Club acquired a selection, and framed them in two groupings, hanging them in the club rooms (which moved later to Lincoln Chambers at the back of the College), and lending them to the artist's Dublin exhibition in 1901.

The first group of pencil portraits includes William Morris (1834–1896) (NGI 6078), the socialist poet and artist, undoubtedly the most illustrious visitor in the early days, who was invited to lecture to the Contemporary Club on 9 April 1886. He had recently gained notoriety when he was arrested during the formation of the militant Socialist League, but he soon returned to his passive socialism and to literature. For some years he had been lecturing widely on various aspects of his lifelong theme, that true art belongs to the domain of moral, social and political doctrine. JBY, as a student living at Woodstock Road in London's Bedford Park, had decorated the bathroom walls with Morris wallpaper. He was obviously familiar with Morris's major work, *Earthly Paradise*, completed in 1870, and named on this drawing, but on the occasion of his visit to Dublin he felt that Morris had no genuine philosophy. Morris attracted a great crowd but little understanding at the Contemporary Club. While JBY sketched him, WBY monopolized him, talking of literature.

Lily Yeats, in her memoir of the years she spent working with Morris's daughter, describes William Morris's "fine head and shoulders" set on a body that was "much too short". He was below average height and powerfully made, though Burne-Jones and Rossetti both used him as a model in sacred pictures because of his beautiful head; and JBY in his sketch has concentrated on the noble features.

The artist has outlined details of beard, shoulder, bust and the chair in which he sits, with a strong rippling black line. As in all the Contemporary Club drawings, the study is extraordinarily delicate, picking out essential areas with a fine pencil, working some parts more strongly but keeping the shading light. Fintan Cullen describes this technique as "Whistlerian" – favouring "quick execution and concentration on the head, the outer areas being treated with what almost approaches disdain".

JBY captures William Morris from a different viewpoint in NGI 6079, with a study of Professor Sullivan, President of University College, Cork, inserted above. He painted an oil of Morris in about 1891, which went to New York (JBY to Lily, 11 May 1916), but its whereabouts are now unknown.

Just over a week after the Contemporary Club lecture, on 17 April 1886, Yeats sketched the English radical Arnold White (NGI 6080), who was visiting the Club. He lies back full length in an armchair, his eyes closed. The top right-hand corner of the drawing has been cut out, and a left-profile head-and-shoulders portrait of Mohini Chatterji (1858–1936), done on a different occasion, pasted in. Mohini, a native of Calcutta of

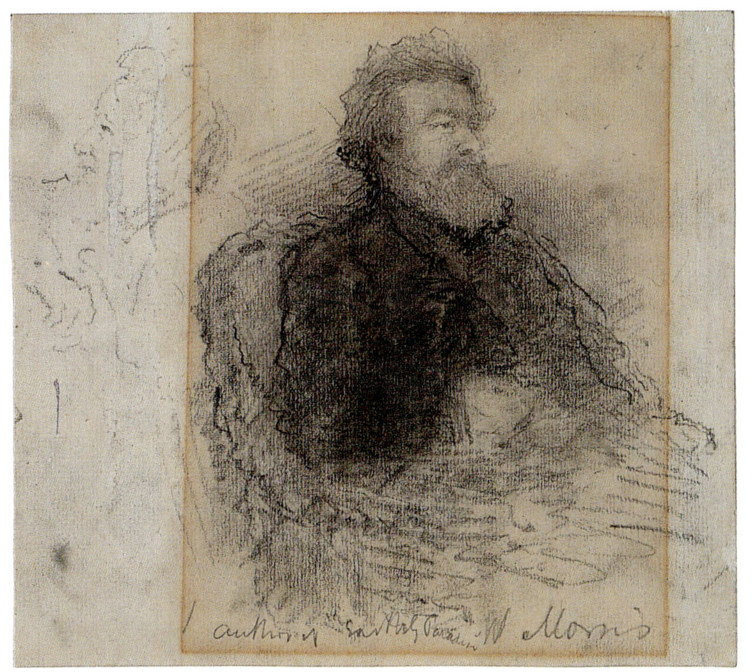

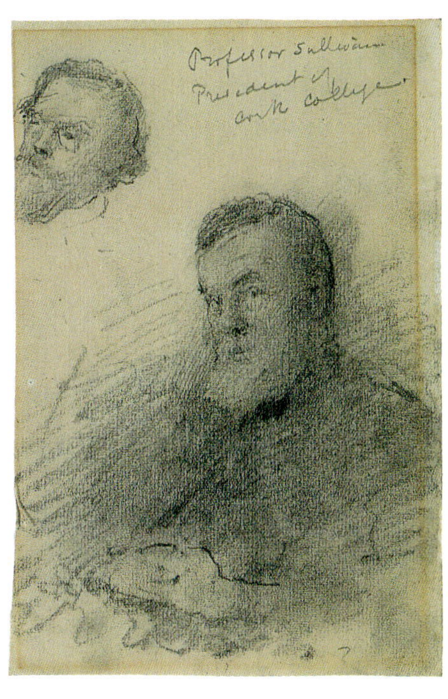

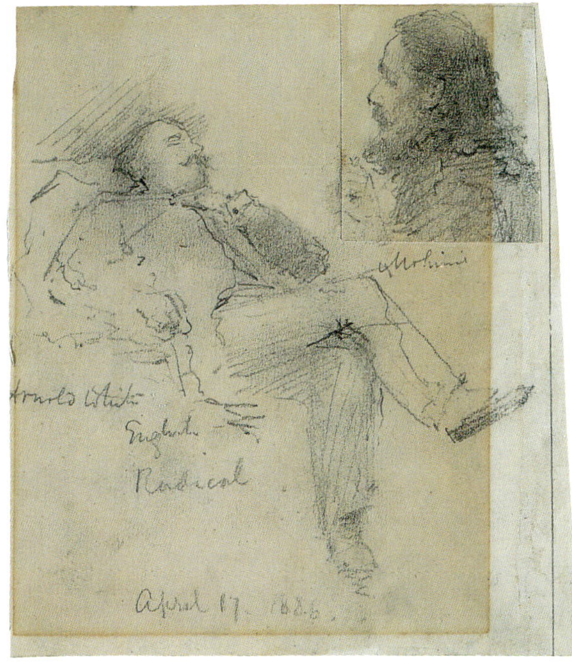

ABOVE LEFT

William Morris at the Contemporary Club

April 1886, pencil on buff paper, 16.8 × 19 cm, NGI 6078

ABOVE RIGHT

Professor Sullivan, President of University College, Cork, and William Morris

Pencil on paper, 16.9 × 11.5 cm, NGI 6079

BELOW LEFT

Arnold White and Mohini Chatterji

April 1886, pencil on paper, 16.9 × 14.6 cm, NGI 6080

the Brahmin caste, had recently joined the Theosophical Society of Madras, and was sent to Europe in advance of Madame Blavatsky and Colonel Olcott, to prepare the way for their theosophical teaching. He was invited to lecture in Dublin towards the end of 1885 by Charles Johnston of the Hermetic Society, and was an enormous influence on WBY.

The Fenian leader, John O'Leary (1830–1907; see also pp. 76, 82 and 118), a favourite subject for JBY, is seen in right profile in NGI 6081, leaning forward, untidy hair topping his wrinkled forehead, his hairy eyebrow obscuring a deep-set eye. "God in Heaven, I'd sooner march on Kerry," he is exclaiming; and the artist has captured the emotion of the moment by interpolating rapid jerks of movement with his pencil, at the same time suggesting a certain amusement on the part of the speaker. John O'Leary was arrested in Dublin in 1865 because of views expressed in the nationalist newspaper he edited. After serving five years, he was released on condition that he would not return to Ireland until the original term of twenty years had expired. With time his views modified, and when he came back to Dublin he rapidly established himself in the centre of liberal, nationalist and creative thought there,

attending the Contemporary Club regularly.

The National Library of Ireland has a drawing of O'Leary in a similar pose, at a club meeting on 12 June 1886; and there is another profile sketch of O'Leary by JBY in Lady Gregory's copy of *Samhain* (October 1901; New York Public Library, Berg Collection).

Dr MacDonnell (NGI 6082) of the Royal College of Surgeons leans forward a little remonstrating with his finger as he "reasons" with Mr Russell (who is not represented but is probably the MP seen in NGI 7357). Mr Taylor (NGI 6083), reclining with his hands tightly clasped, was one of the more colourful characters in the Club. Queen's Counsel, defender of hopeless cases, and famed for his eloquence and brilliant cross-examination, John F. Taylor was nevertheless unsure of himself and apt to erupt, especially when WBY, who would argue contentiously, provoked him. In *Reveries*, WBY has described his "coarse red hair, his gaunt ungainly body, his still movements as of a Dutch doll, his badly rolled shabby umbrella. And yet with women, as with O'Leary, he was gentle, deferential, almost diffident." JBY in the drawing captures his bold bright eye, his high-domed brow, and intent look, containing the vital image within a typical wandering line.

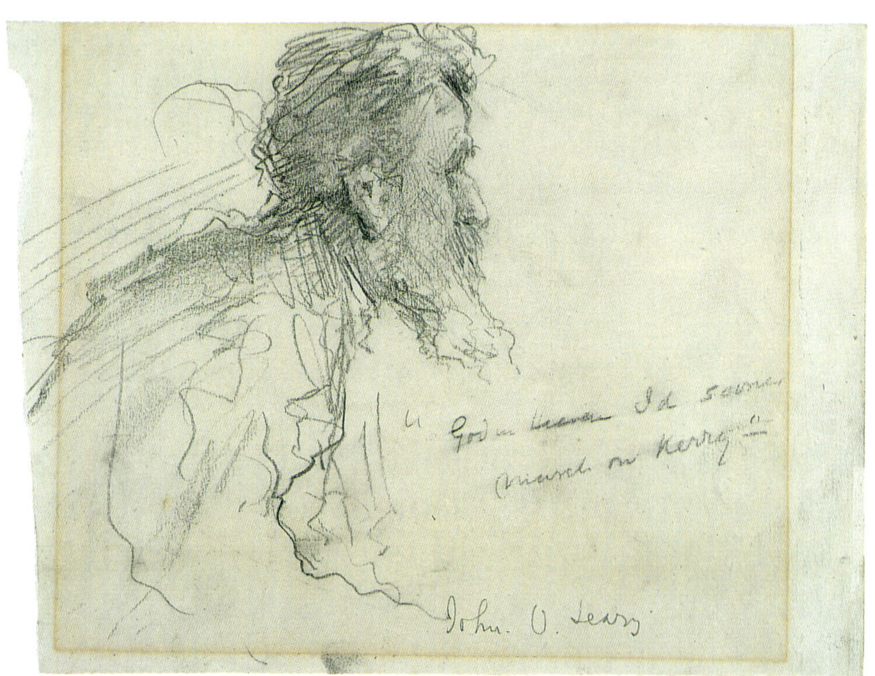

John O'Leary

Pencil on unevenly cut paper,
16.8 × 22 cm, NGI 6081

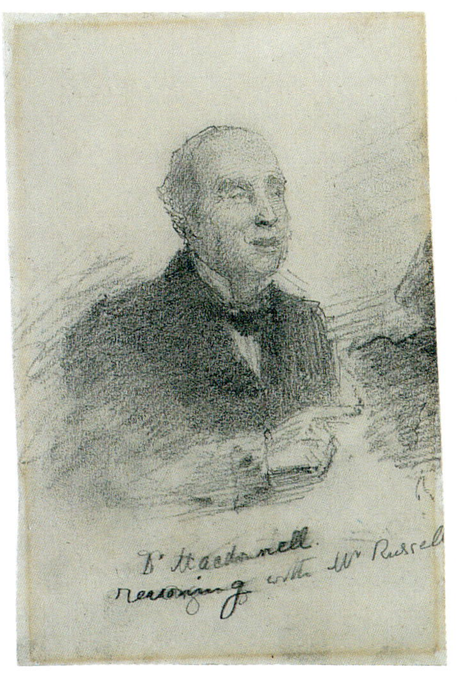

Dr MacDonnell reasoning with Mr Russell

Pencil on paper, 16.8 × 11 cm, NGI 6082

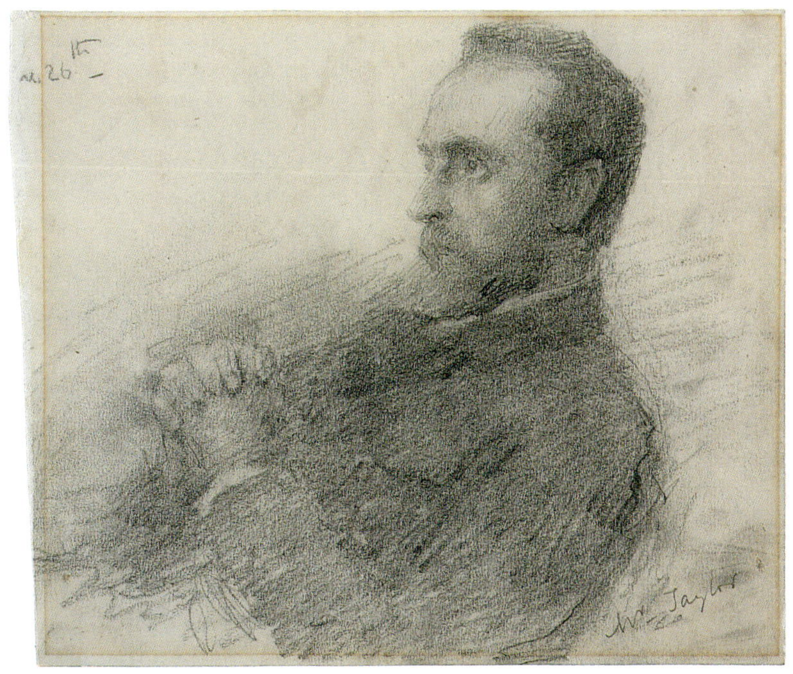

Mr Taylor

Pencil on paper, 16.8 × 20.3 cm, NGI 6083

One of the successes of JBY's sketches at the Contemporary Club was the way he captured the club atmosphere, each member comfortably ensconced in a favourite chair, debating with spirit, or listening, ready to express a view. Arthur Patton (NGI 7357) has been caught in right profile, arms akimbo as he engages with fellow parliamentarian T.W. Russell, a little way away from him. (Between the two men, the head and shoulders are thought to be of John Taylor, the red-headed barrister, involved in another conversation.) Patton, who was canvassing in Dublin at the time for his seat at Westminster, smiles slightly under his neat moustache, wrinkling his heavy-lidded eye, and looking pleased. Russell, whose short straight hair stands back from a bulging forehead above his penetrating eyes, leans to one side as he seems to question something Patton has been saying. A Unionist, he later became a minister in the Liberal Government. While the heads are delicately described, with strong cross-hatching in the shadows behind, the artist hardly bothers with the bodies; but the back of a chair by Patton's elbow suggests that he has been leaning on it.

William Thomas Stead (1849–1912) (NGI 7358), of the Pall Mall Club, London, is represented more formally, the drawing unevenly cut at the edge, probably when it was taken from JBY's sketchbook. He listens, looking straight ahead, quietly, not yet drawn into the debate.

The drawing (NGI 7359) is of Charles Hubert Oldham (1860–1926), the originator of the Club, who sits in an armchair with his left elbow balanced on a small table beside him, his arm and hand stuck up in the air. His right arm is lightly indicated, raised to his head. Perhaps he lifts it as he prepares to argue out some point; but for the moment he listens with total concentration, his eyes like sheep's pellets, his lips firm. He is cleanshaven, except for a wide moustache, his face with its straight jaw, and with the smooth hair brushed high, making a pale square above the dark loop of his body. Oldham has been described by Mary Macken as "the kindest of men", who was "invulnerable to wordy attack and constantly gave offence where he least intended to". From a formidable Dublin family, one sister a vigorous pioneer for women's university education, and another a musician and scholar married to R.I. Best (see p. 136), he himself moved from mathematics and physics to become the first Professor of Commerce in University College, Dublin. He was one of the group who founded the *Dublin University Review* in 1885, where WBY had his first poems published, and it was he who introduced WBY to the poet Katharine Tynan. At the time of the sketch he was a dedicated follower of John O'Leary, actively adopting his ideals and pacifist stance.

Mr Bailey (NGI 7360), who in later life hosted parties for the Dublin literary élite, leans to one side, putting his left hand up to adjust his monocle as he stares into space; while the poet Alfred Percival Graves (1846–1931) (NGI 7361) is seen in right profile, his left hand supporting the side of his head as he gazes intently into the distance, pensive, melancholic, his large eye drooping sadly beneath an arched brow.

Graves, Dublin-born and earning his living as an inspector of schools in northern England, had recently published his collection *Songs of Old Ireland*, with the popular ballad 'Father O'Flynn'. Later he collaborated with the musician C.V. Stanford in producing *Songs of Erin* (1892). During the 1890s he lived in London, and contributed to *Punch*; and he became an active member of WBY's newly formed Irish Literary Society.

Mr Crooks and Mr Doherty (NGI 7362) are seen from a little distance (there are faint outlines of two other men sitting behind them). Mr Crooks is almost full length, leaning forward with a frown on his face, his eyes concentrated on some unseen speaker to the viewer's left. He seems to clench his hands grimly; while Mr Doherty, the engineer who widened O'Connell Bridge (originally Carlisle Bridge) in 1880, gazes towards the artist, with a touch of amusement. His bulky coat has been darkened about his chest, placing him firmly in the foreground.

Mr Bailey, Mr Walker and Mr Hogg (NGI 7363) sit in a row, perhaps listening to an invited speaker, with a young unidentified man sitting behind. Mr Bailey is in almost the same position as in NGI 7360 but here he appears more animated, leaning forward with interest. James Walker, printer of the *Dublin University Review*, a Presbyterian and Parnellite who toured Ulster with

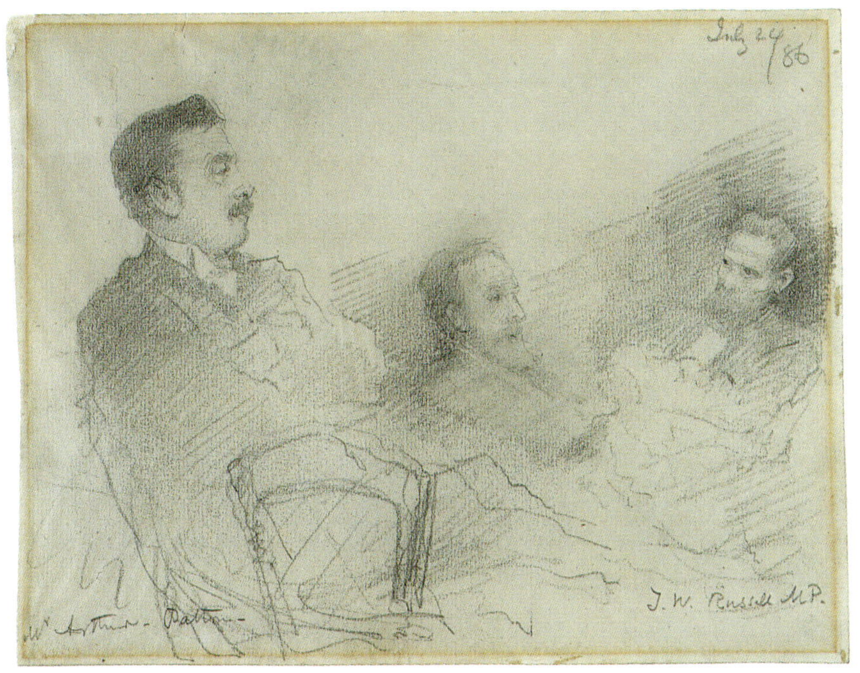

Arthur Patton, Mr Taylor (?) and T.W. Russell MP

Pencil on paper, 16.7 × 21.7 cm, NGI 7357

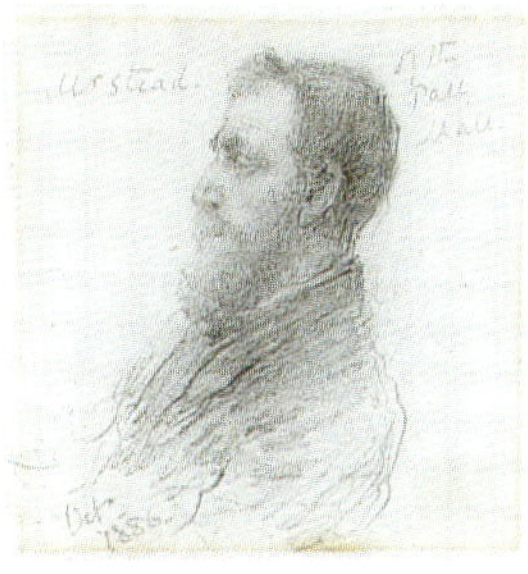

William Thomas Stead, of the Pall Mall Club, London

Pencil on unevenly cut buff paper, 7.8 × 7.8 cm, NGI 7358

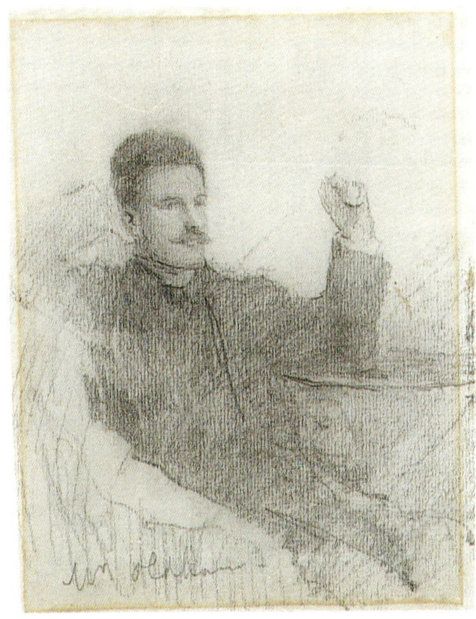

Mr Oldham

Pencil on buff paper, 16.6 × 13 cm, NGI 7359

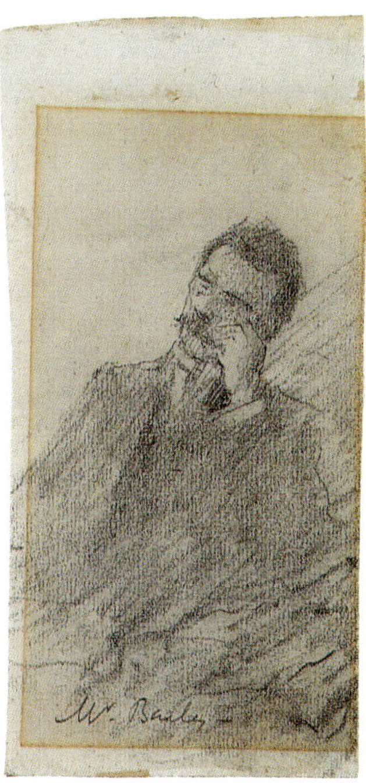

Mr Bailey

Pencil on unevenly cut buff paper, 16.5 × 7.9 cm, NGI 7360

Oldham in 1885 and 1886 to recruit for the Protestant Home Rule Association, looks down as he listens, his arms folded. Mr Hogg could be the 'J. Hogg Esquire' who lent *Rufus* to JBY's *Loan Collection of Pictures* shown in Dublin in 1901. He is smoking a cigar he has lowered from his mouth in order to take in and weigh up what he is hearing. His heavy-lidded eyes under hairy eyebrows seem to brood ominously above a sceptical mouth. Not for nothing did WBY write in *Reveries* that the Contemporary Club had taught him to "play with hostile minds".

George Coffey and Mr McNiffe (NGI 7364) sit near one another, the bearded McNiffe in the right foreground perhaps speaking, since Coffey is looking at him. Mr McNiffe is nearly bald, and his broad high-domed forehead has been described with a single stroke by the artist, using shading to indicate a fringe of hair to each side, above a neat ear. George Coffey (1857–1916), who is lean and dark, with a shapely beard, gazes at him from behind. His dark serious eyes glow, perhaps in disbelief at what he hears. A close friend of

Douglas Hyde at Trinity College, he became an archaeologist, and was appointed Keeper of Antiquities in the National Museum of Ireland. JBY's portrait of him was exhibited in the Royal Hibernian Academy in 1887.

In the drawing below, Mohini Chatterji (NGI 7365) is shown almost completely in profile. (There is a sketch note in the top left corner portraying his head as it turns towards the artist.) Mohini holds his hand against his head to enable him to concentrate, two fingers extended perhaps to position his ear, the others folded. "He sat there beautiful, as only an Eastern is beautiful," WBY wrote in *Autobiographies*, "making little gestures with his delicate hands, and to him alone among all the talkers I have heard, oratory, and even the delight of ordered words, seemed nothing, and all thought a flight into the heart of truth." Mohini opened up a philosophy that "seemed at once logical and boundless". The young poet's Indian images in *The Wanderings of Oisín* were owed to him, and he remembered Mohini Chatterji in old age in a poem entitled with his name.

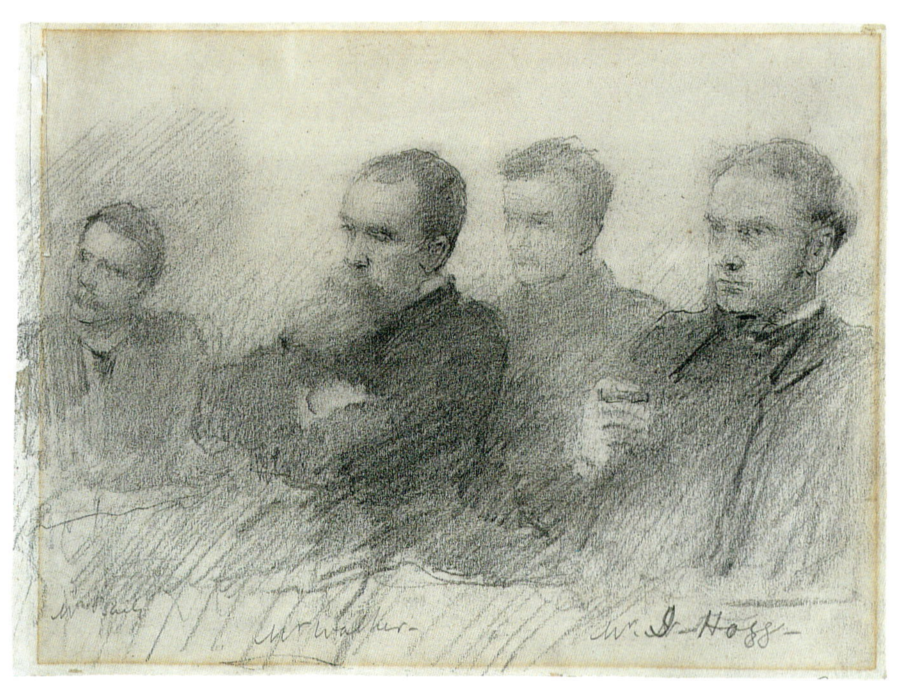

Mr Bailey, Mr Walker and Mr J. Hogg

Pencil on buff paper, 16.7 × 23 cm, NGI 7363

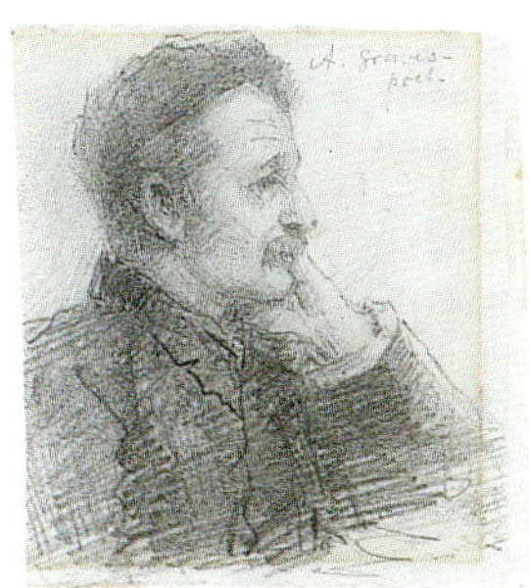

Alfred Percival Graves

Pencil on paper,
7.8 × 7.2 cm, NGI 7361

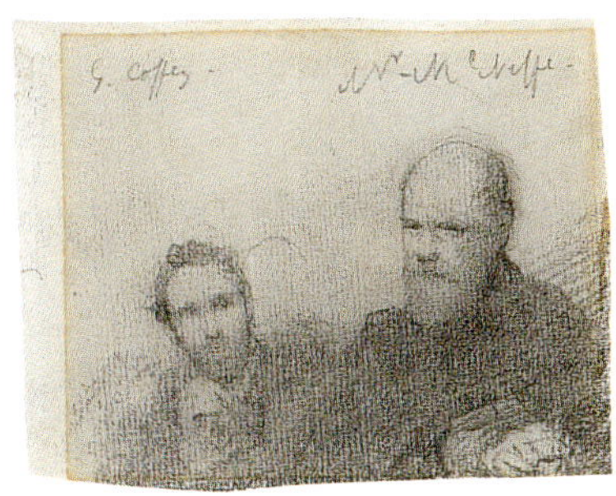

George Coffey and Mr McNiffe

Pencil on unevenly cut buff paper,
7.9 × 10.3 cm, NGI 7364

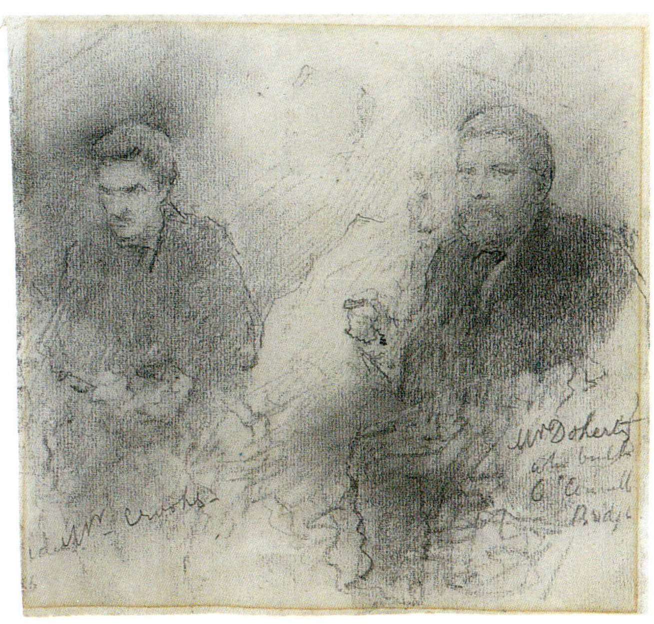

Mr Crooks and Mr Doherty

Pencil on paper, 16.7 × 18 cm, NGI 7362

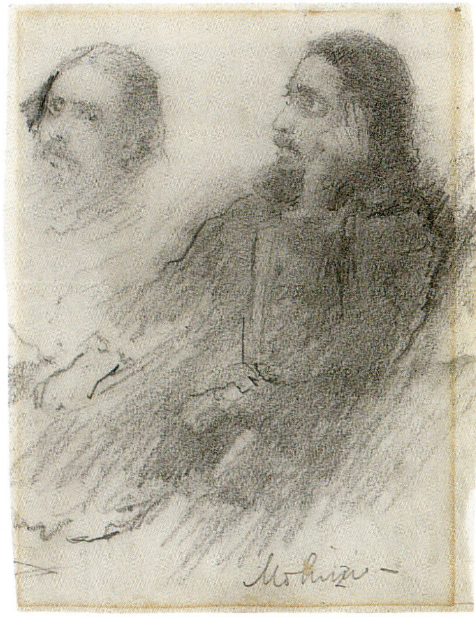

Mohini [Chatterji]

Pencil on unevenly cut paper, 16.7 × 13.4 cm,
NGI 7365

JBY drew and painted many portraits of his elder son William Butler Yeats (1865–1939). Despite their disagreements, and WBY's intimidating manner, he produced the warmest and most romantic likenesses of him that exist. He appreciated – even manipulated – his appearance: "It was ... his insistence," WBY wrote,

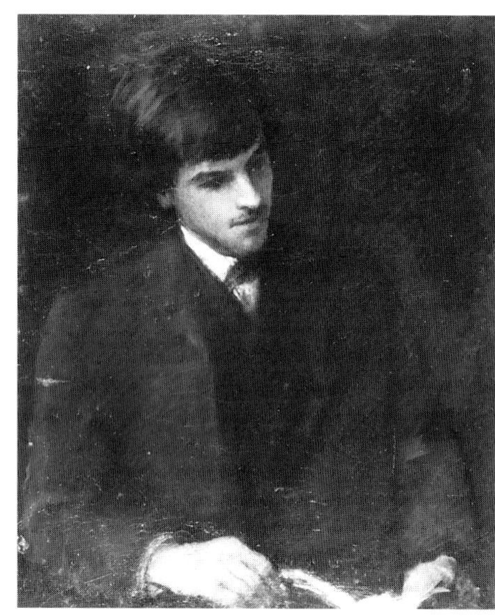

Fig. 60 J.B. Yeats, *Portrait of W.B. Yeats*, *ca.* 1886, oil on canvas, 76.5 × 65 cm (Hugh Lane Municipal Gallery, Dublin)

"that kept me bearded". This pencil portrait probably dates from 1886, when the beard was not fully grown.

The year 1886 was the year when WBY won recognition as a poet with the publication of his dramatic poem 'Mosada' in the June issue of the *Dublin University Review.* JBY drew him in pen and ink in January (Michael B. Yeats Collection), and the youthful oil portrait of the young poet, reading a book, caught in a reverie (fig. 60), must have been painted this year too. This pencil study may have been a preliminary to the oil, though it is very different in mood, redolent, even at this early stage, of a Colossus. The poet is seen from the side, in left profile, his head slightly bowed, deep in thought, his hands clasped in his lap. It is a Shelleyan image, the face sensitively described, the new whiskers which sprout tenderly on upper lip and chin causing no intrusion. An even light bathes the young skin, while the inspired eye gleams. Around this centre of focus, the untidy dark hair and the coat built up with firm strokes from a thick soft lead confirm the poetic image. Katharine Tynan saw him at this date as "a gentle dreamer", "beautiful to look at with his dark face, its touch of vivid colouring, the night-black hair, the eager dark eyes".

The sitter's private mood is not engineered. From an early age WBY composed verses, murmuring to himself after he had done his school exercises at night, soon forgetting where he was, his voice growing louder and louder until his sisters protested. His daughter Anne Yeats has told how, when travelling on the top of a tram in Dublin, he would sit by himself and appear to be lost in a trance as he composed.

'Mosada' was reprinted as a pamphlet in October 1886, JBY insisting on contributing another version of his pen-and-ink portrait for a frontispiece (engraved on zinc by Lewis). "I was alarmed at the impudence of putting a portrait in my first book," WBY told John Quinn later, "but my father was full of ancient and modern instances." Though Gerard Manley Hopkins found the poem to be "a strained and unworkable allegory", he admired the drawing and thought that JBY was a fine draughtsman. At Katharine Tynan's suggestion he called on JBY in his studio to listen to his theories on art.

JBY made other studies of WBY with his beard (Michael B. Yeats Collection); and in 1889 painted a portrait in competition with H.M. Paget, an illustrator and one of the members of the Calumets, the conversation club that JBY joined on his return to Bedford Park. Shortly afterwards WBY took a razor, and became a clean-shaven poet.

Pencil portrait of William Butler Yeats

1886, pencil on paper, 15 × 23.5 cm, NGI 3256

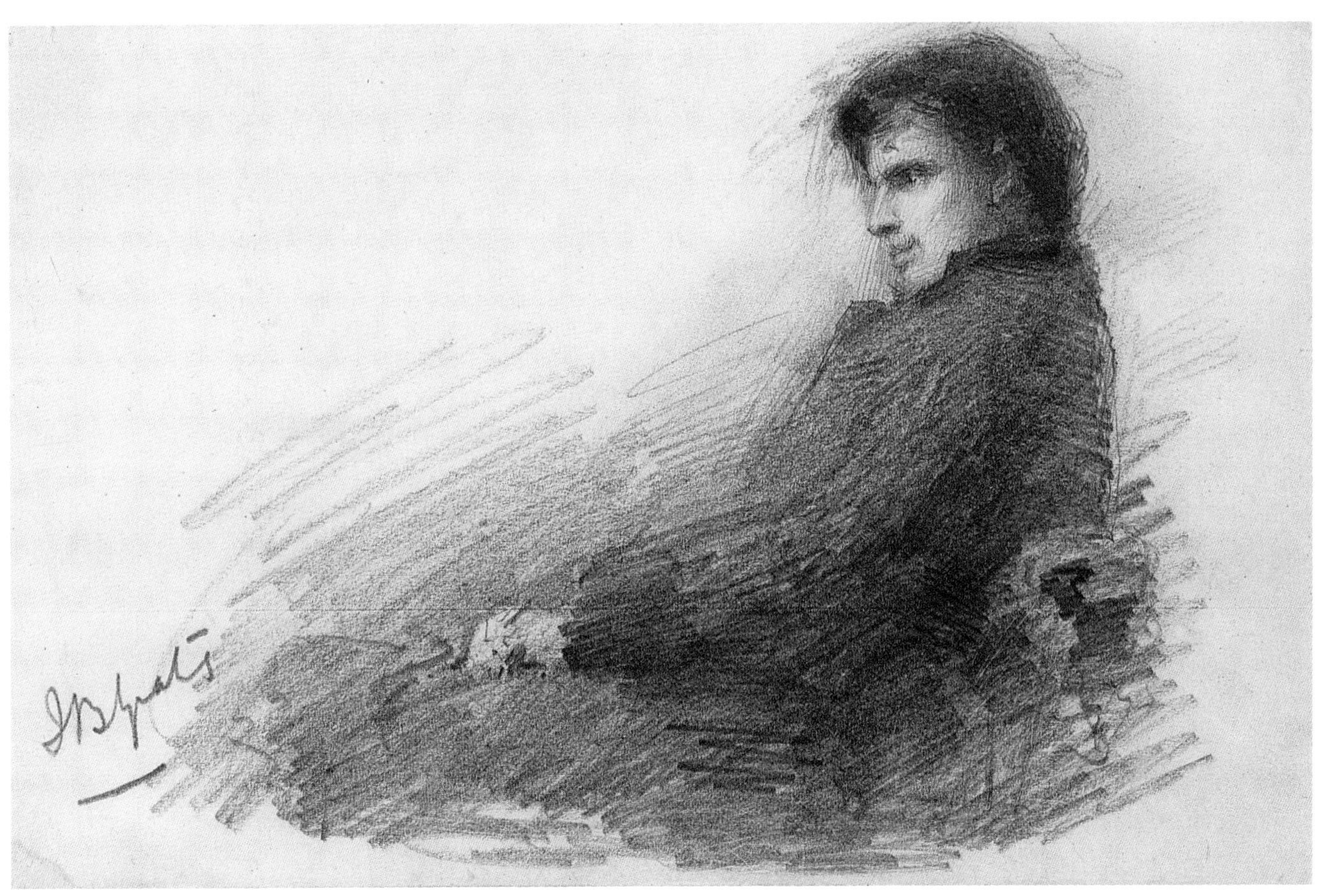

The sitters for these sketches (three obviously posed while one was taken unawares) have been unidentified since they were presented to the Gallery by Miss Digby in 1944. It is assumed that they have some connection with JBY's friend and patron Todhunter, whose second wife was a Digby. Judging from photographs of Todhunter and his wife (figs. 61 and 62), NGI 7683 and 2986 may be portraits of the couple. The *Standing lady* wears a fringe and a dress with a lace collar identical with that worn by Dora Louisa Digby Todhunter in the photograph. The lady in *Lady and gentleman in conversation* may also be Dora Todhunter, while *Gentleman smoking a cheroot* looks like a slightly younger Todhunter, without his shaggy beard.

The date 1886–87 is suggested tentatively. John Todhunter, like JBY, had recently moved to London. A gifted dilettante, who started life in a grocery firm and then decided to be a doctor, his interest at Trinity in music, poetry and philosophy brought him into the company of JBY and the Dowdens. He commissioned pictures (see pp. 48 and 52) in the early 1870s from JBY – who was still a student. Abandoning medicine to write poetry and plays, he became a member of the Dublin Sketching Club, and in Bedford Park, with JBY, joined a group of aesthetes who met regularly. Todhunter was one of the founders of the Irish Literary Society in London.

JBY did not like Dora Todhunter, pretty and hospitable though she was. He dubbed her "that she-dragon of contention" because she loved to argue. Todhunter, he felt, had not realised his potential: he and Dowden, he told WBY (14 August 1915), were "wild birds who lost in captivity their gift of song".

If these are the Todhunters, JBY has represented them spiritedly, having the 'she-dragon' pose like a saint in NGI 7683, as in a play, one arm on her hip, the other perhaps holding a vase, while she raises her eyes. Light pours on to the left side of her face. NGI 3257 and the other two drawings create imaginative depths in the background with the erratic build-up of shading in every direction. The lady who takes the centre in NGI 3257 wears a dark jacket with a mandarin-type collar, and turns her eyes to a moustached gentleman on the right, who is speaking, probably at some conversation

evening. The characters emerge slowly out of the pencilwork.

The gentleman in evening dress (NGI 2986) has pulled up a chair to straddle it backwards as he poses after a dinner, still in such a jovial mood that he does not remove his top hat, and he beams as ash grows on his slim cheroot. When it was restored in December 1972, another sketch was revealed on the verso side of this drawing, the head and shoulders of a man with a large moustache wearing a tam-o'-shanter.

Finally, the *Seated lady*, in a Windsor chair (NGI 2727), seems apart, a pensive woman, her soft hair twisted into a bun behind her peaky face. This may be a Digby relative: houses at the time were full of female relatives, particularly unmarried ones. JBY has worked diligently at her black dress and the shading behind, isolating her head, and highlighting her nose and cheekbones, so as to increase the mood of *tristesse*.

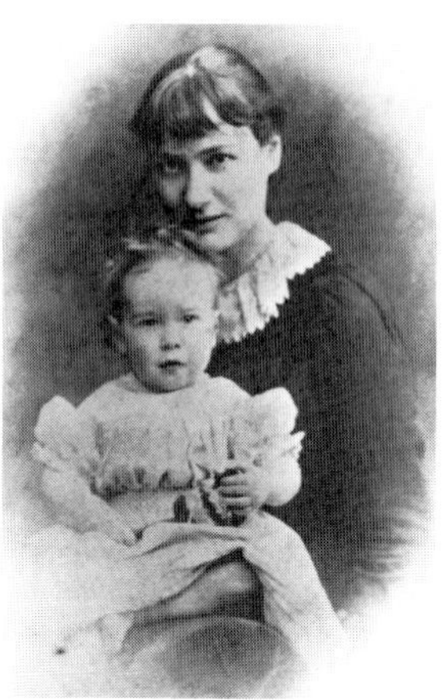

Fig. 61 Dora Digby Todhunter (Photo NGI Archive)

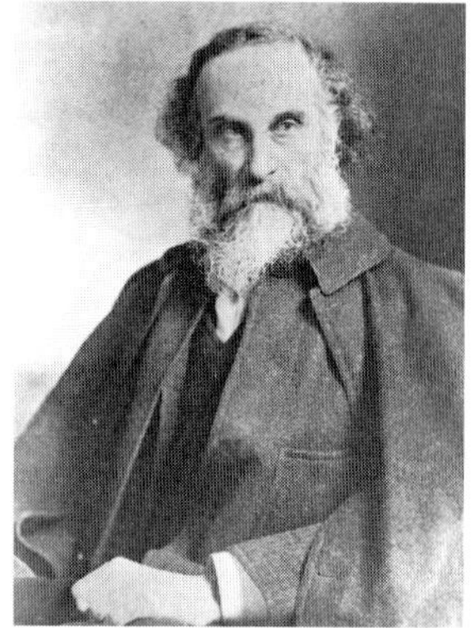

Fig. 62 John Todhunter (Photo NGI Archive)

*Lady and
gentleman in
conversation*

Pencil on paper,
23.5 × 15 cm, NGI 3257

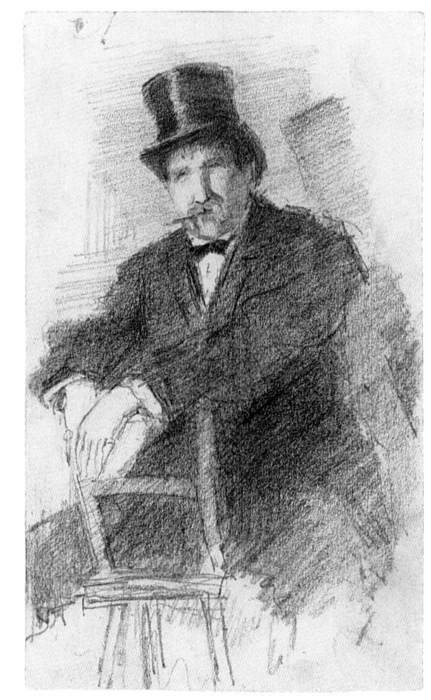

*Gentleman
smoking a
cheroot*

Pencil on paper,
19.3 × 11.7 cm,
drawing on verso
of a man wearing
a tam-o'shanter,
NGI 2986

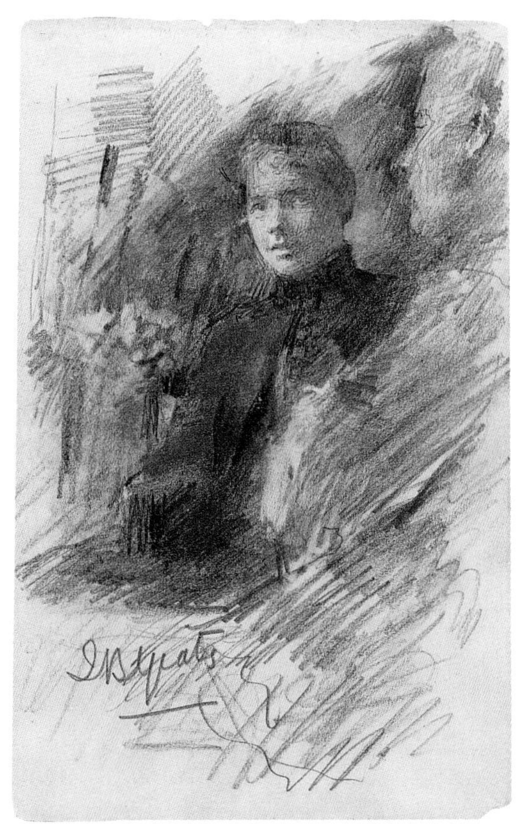

*Seated
lady*

Pencil on
paper,
23.5 × 15 cm,
NGI 2727

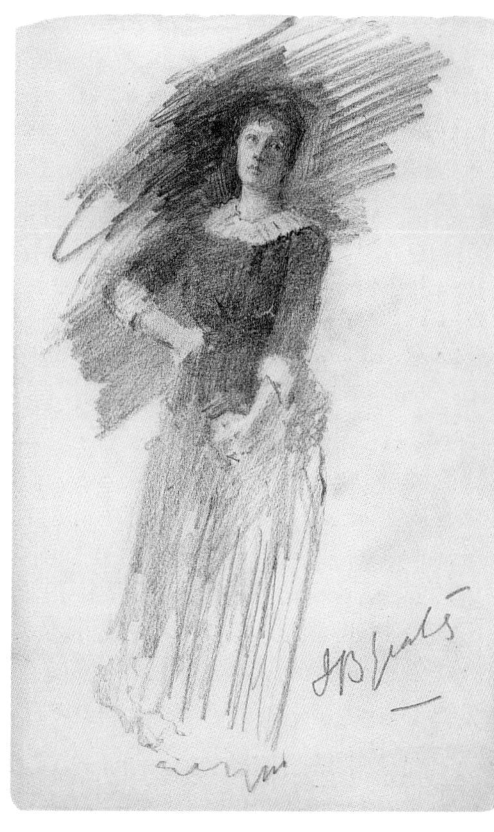

*Standing
lady*

Pencil on
paper,
23.5 × 15 cm,
NGI 7683

J ohn O'Leary (see also pp. 66, 82 and 118) might be regarded as the most spectacular presence in Dublin's Contemporary Club. An intellectual, passionately nationalist, but more moderate in his political opinions since his prolonged exile, he had a charismatic effect on the Home Rulers among its members, and was a particular influence on WBY, whose first poems he helped to publish in the United States. WBY described O'Leary in *Reveries* (1915) as "the handsomest old man I had ever seen" (fig. 63). He visited O'Leary and his sister Ellen at their house in Leinster Road; Douglas Hyde, Katharine Tynan and John F. Taylor were other regular visitors, and inspired by him. WBY noted O'Leary's room full of books, always shabby second-hand copies, and many in Irish. "He seemed to consider politics almost wholly as a moral discipline," Yeats wrote. He never complained about his prison sentence, with all its hardships. "He had the moral genius that moves all young people ... here was something as spontaneous as the life of an artist." Though his temper was hot he never bore grudges, and WBY recalled, "It became my delight to rouse him to these outbursts for I was the poet in the presence of his theme."

The Contemporary Club must have commissioned the portrait before JBY left Dublin late in 1886, relieved of the estate which had hung like an albatross round his neck, but now pressurised into making his profession lucrative. Perhaps he started painting in Dublin, and completed the portrait in London in 1887, which was when he inscribed the date. It was exhibited in the Royal Hibernian Academy that year. It was the first of three portraits of O'Leary by JBY (see pp. 82 and 118). The artist has presented a formal – almost confrontational – half-length image, O'Leary seated in a chair of which only part of the arm is seen. An elderly man with a weatherbeaten face, his hair is still light brown and luxuriant, parted and brushed over to the right of his forehead, while his wiry spade-like beard buries the lower part of his face. His lips seem to speak from a

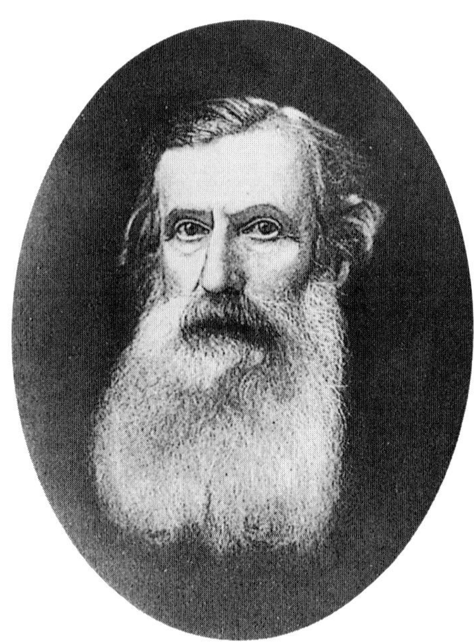

Fig. 63 *John O'Leary*, photograph *ca.* 1887, (National Museum of Ireland)

forest of hair. His penetrating eyes, set beneath shapely lids and mobile brows, above a long nose, stare out of the painting in astonished enquiry, but look as ready to jest as to argue.

It is a dark painting, strangely like an Old Master given JBY's advance during the 1880s to a lighter palette and Whistlerian harmony. However, it is conceivable that in painting the portrait JBY was thinking of the setting in which the portrait would hang, and that he regarded such a formal pose appropriate to the rooms of the Contemporary Club. The black of O'Leary's coat is relieved by the warm skin colour of his sensitively painted hands, by the sparkle of the monocle or *pince-nez* he cradles in one, and by the gleam of the white page of the book he holds open with the other. O'Leary, it appears, has been disturbed as he reads. In this way JBY refers to the patriot's impressive library, and to the way in which he kept his essential spirit and his ideals alive throughout the tribulations he suffered, at the same time as he captures a particular moment with the immediacy he always sought in his portraits.

John O'Leary

1887, oil on canvas, 92 × 71 cm, NGI 1963

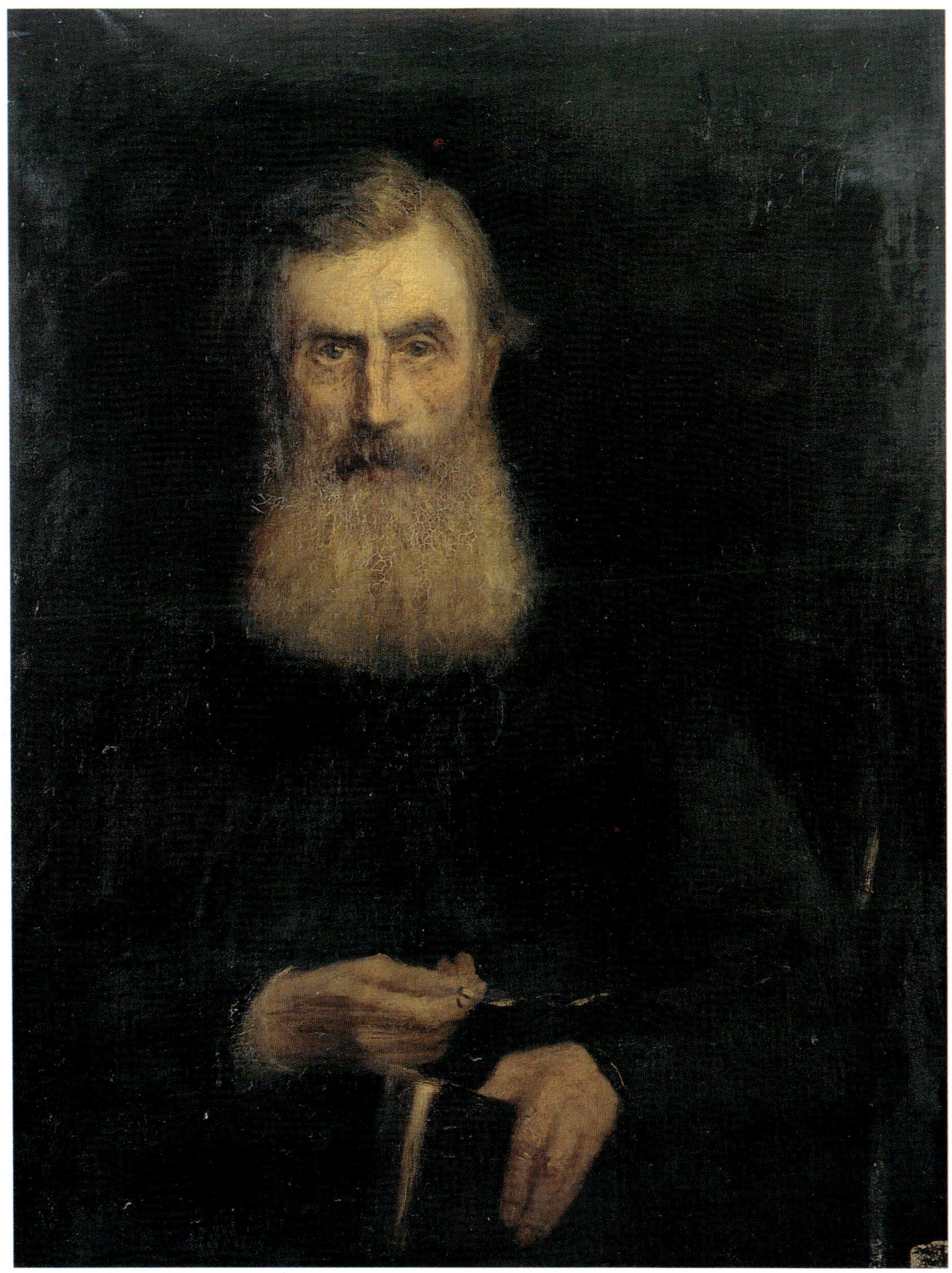

This bust portrait of Jack B. Yeats, JBY's younger son, as a youth of eighteen or nineteen, was painted at Bedford Park in London, where the family had moved in 1888. Jack was a student at art college, but already selling designs and working as a pen-and-ink illustrator for journals (see fig. 64). Christened John Butler, he had distinguished himself from his father quite early on by signing his work 'Jack B. Yeats', a form to which he always adhered except when he

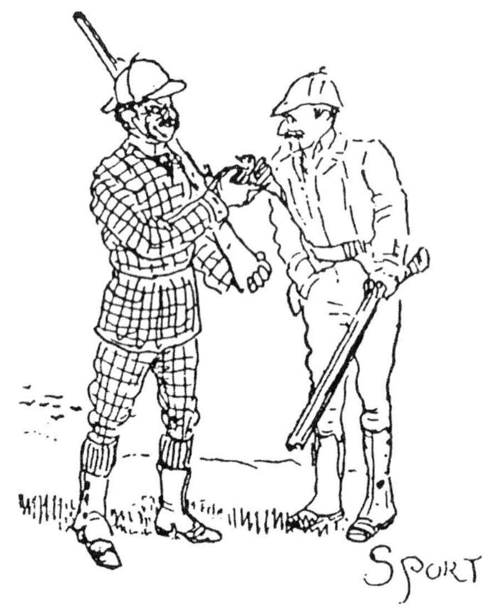

Fig. 64 *The first of September* or *What a partridge felt*, in *The Vegetarian*, 13 September 1890

used a monogram of his initials. In September 1890 he received his first commission to illustrate a book. His father, who had hoped to earn a steady income in London with his black-and-white work, was having little success in selling his drawings, and had few commissions for portraits. He had not exhibited at the RHA since 1887.

The portrait is at once gauche and subtle, and offers a masterly interpretation of an adolescent character in formation. Jack, unlike WBY, had little of the poseur in him, but was an unusual mixture of a doer and a dreamer. JBY represents him in a dreamy moment, his head turned half to one side, his lit-up eyes becoming a focus for the composition. As in the earlier portrait (see p. 60) he wears subdued plain clothing, a grey coat, white shirt and grey-blue bow tie. His hair is short with a neat middle parting, fringing the top of his wide brow carelessly. His fair colouring and vivid, deep-set, blue eyes complement the grey-blue of his garments. Both of the dominant tones, the grey blue and the brown ochre, are echoed in the background – something that would become normal practice with JBY a decade later. Indeed the entire portrait has an air of experiment, the looseness of image and pigment anticipating the freedom of style that marks the Lane and Quinn commissions.

The face has been painted rapidly, with tossing strokes, yet preserving the transparency of the young man's fresh young skin and pink cheeks. The coat painted with a broader brush, going in different directions, adds stability in a picture where the paint seems to be constantly moving. The whole movement is peaceful, the portrait benign and visionary. The slight aura about the head was another feature JBY would develop in his impressionist portraits, as an intimation of the sitter's imaginative persona. Like NGI 1142 (p. 61), the painting is perhaps unfinished, though the artist has added his initials and the date.

The portrait was given by the artist to his friend and agent Victor Waddington in 1952; and, fittingly, presented by Victor Waddington to the National Gallery in 1971, to grace the occasion of the Jack B. Yeats Centenary Exhibition.

1890, oil on canvas, 61 × 51cm, NGI 4040

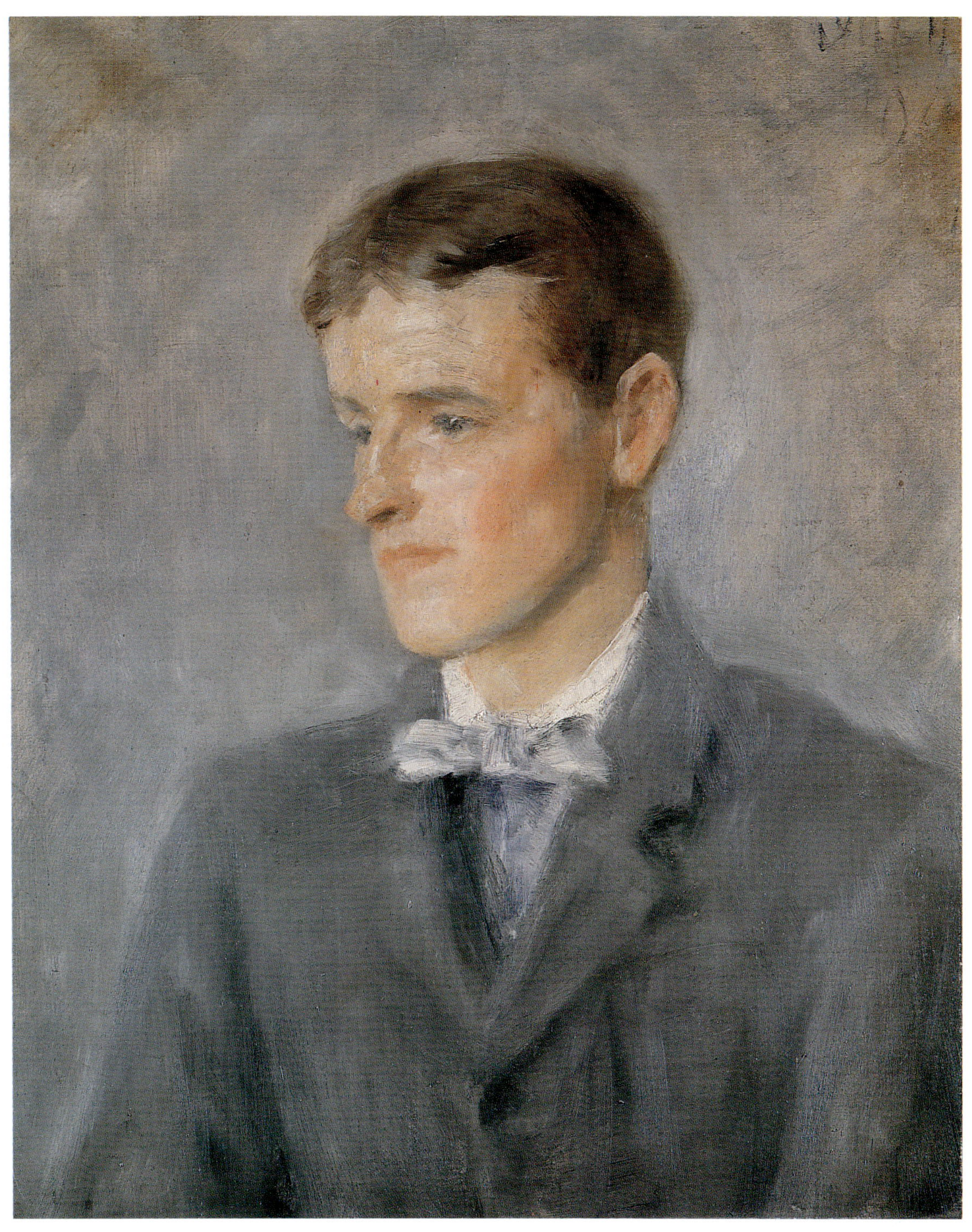

JBY used to say that between 1890 and 1897 he never lifted a brush; and it is true that this portrait, that of John O'Leary (p. 83) and one of the lawyer Acheson T. Henderson (fig. 65), were among his last oils for some years, owing to circumstance no doubt rather than choice. He was elected to full membership of the Royal Hibernian Academy in 1892, but did not exhibit again until 1895, when he showed some portrait sketches and an illustration. He still continued to hope for a breakthrough in black-and-white illustration.

The portrait of Violet Osborne (1866–1893) was evidently commissioned on the occasion of her engagement to W.F.P. Stockley in 1891. Violet Osborne was the younger sister of Walter Osborne, himself a portrait painter, who had painted her at the age of seventeen or eighteen. Osborne was a good friend of JBY in Dublin – they probably met at the Contemporary Club.

JBY has painted a half-length likeness in a favourite pose, seated at a slant to the left, the head looking back full face to the viewer. The young woman fills the whole of the right side of the canvas, her half-opened fan, of a cream colour, reaching to the left corner, and above it, in the empty space by her shoulder, the artist's signature – flamboyantly – with the date. The picture has the air of a society portrait, because of the prominent fan, the black-lace evening jacket, and the bangle (perhaps an engagement gift) and the ring with a single red stone, which are displayed on the bare arm stretching across the lower part of the canvas, the lady's elbow resting on a table edge.

At the same time, the artist seems captivated with this capable-looking and attractive young woman, whose serious brown eyes gaze out at the spectator with a hypnotic gleam, from a rather tense face, beneath a crown of auburn hair. She has regular features and a pretty mouth, and JBY has painted the background a browny green to set off her fair skin and the unusual colour of her hair. Despite the portrait's formality, one gets the impression of a compelling personality. Tragically, Violet Osborne was to die two years later in childbirth, in Canada, where the couple had gone to live. This picture may be the *Portrait of a lady* lent by Walter Osborne to JBY's Dublin exhibition in 1901.

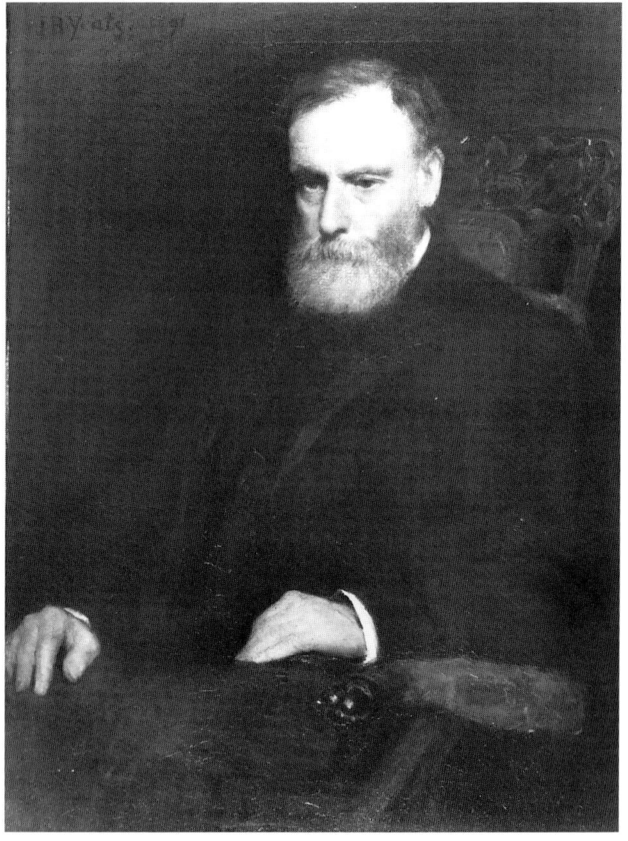

Fig. 65 J.B. Yeats, *Portrait of Acheson T. Henderson Q.C.I,* 1891, oil on canvas, 91.5 × 71 cm (Ulster Museum, Belfast)

Violet Osborne

1891, oil on canvas, 61 × 51 cm, NGI 4032

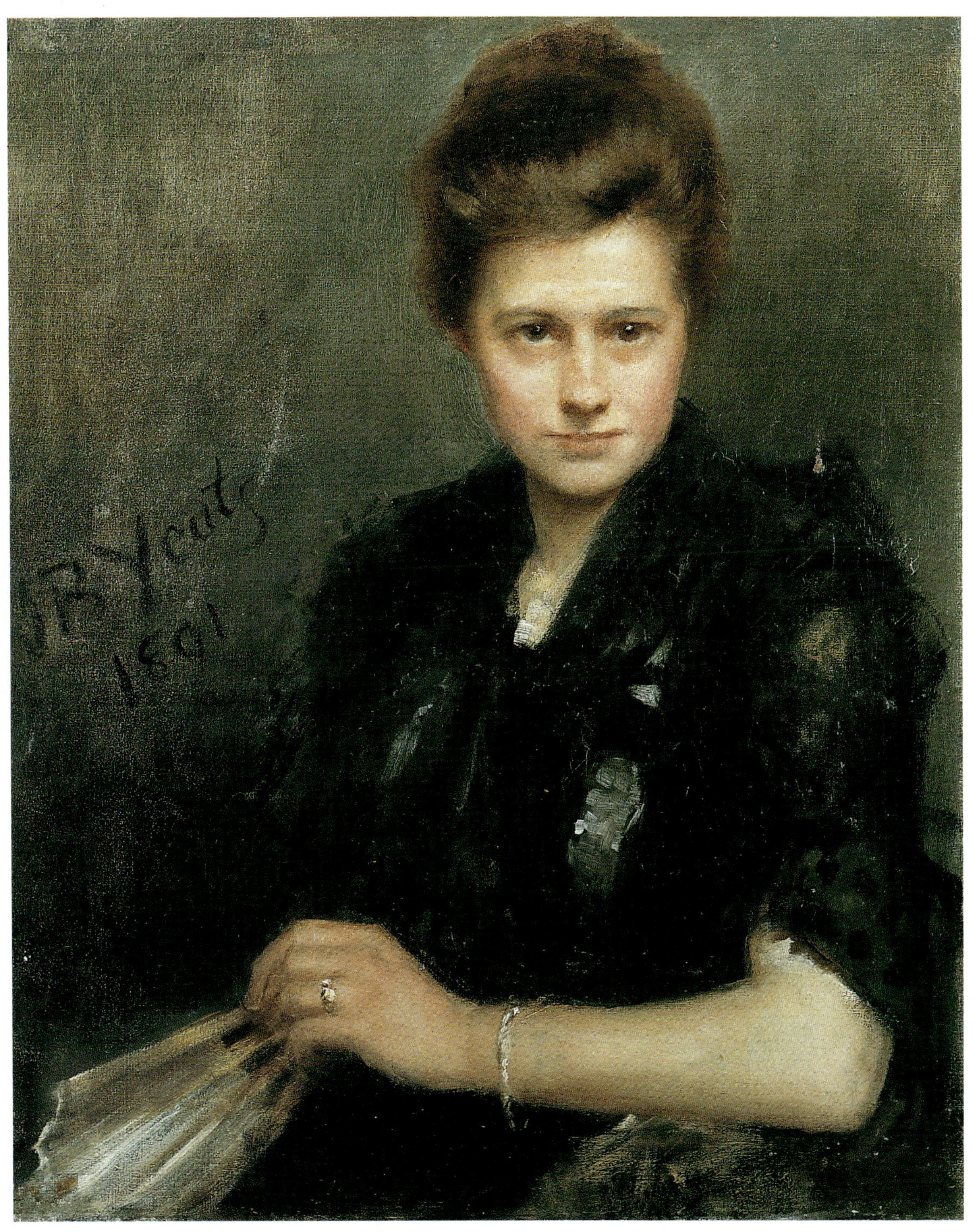

This second oil portrait of John O'Leary (see p. 76) by JBY was commissioned by a group of O'Leary's friends in 1891, and must have been finished by November, when JBY had to write to O'Leary to remind him that he had not yet received a fee. O'Leary lent the portrait to JBY's Dublin exhibition in 1901, and bequeathed it to the National Literary Society, who presented it almost immediately to the National Gallery as O'Leary wished.

The National Literary Society was only one of O'Leary's interests. Born in Tipperary in 1830, it was while he was a student in Dublin that he became involved in revolutionary politics, partly under the influence of James Stephens. He had served a term in prison before he went to Paris a few years later to study medicine at the Ecole de Médicine, a course he never finished – in fact, from the number of colleges he attended, it seems he was a perpetual seeker of know-ledge. At the Ecole he became friendly with Whistler, who was fascinated with his "booming Tipperary accent", and he was friendly also with the poet Swin-burne, with Poynter (later JBY's master in London), and with George Du Maurier. Whistler encouraged his interest in art; and no doubt owning this portrait by JBY mattered greatly to the Fenian hero. He and JBY had many conversations on every topic while he was sitting, having known each other since 1885 in Dublin and Lon-don, where they shared the same intellectual circles.

In this portrait JBY sees O'Leary as the thinker, and gives him an ascetic, almost priestly appearance. He sits in an armchair, turned slightly to the left, with head bowed, one hand emerging from a white cuff to rest over the other on his crossed knee (his hands slim and sensitive, with long fingers). His hair is receding from his brow, which commands the light. His eyes, set deep and dark under his thoughtful eyebrows, look troubled, and his nose, like a hawk's beak, adds to his ascetic appearance. JBY has created a simple profound image, working with a lighter brush than before, though he has not yet abandoned a traditional palette.

George Coffey, reviewing JBY's 1901 exhibition in *The Daily Express* (21 October 1901), called the painting "a great portrait", "probably the finest portrait painted by an Irish artist in recent years". In *The Irish Times* E.J. Gwynn disagreed. "The artist has spent all his care and time – too much time even – on the head," he wrote. "He has made up his mind to show you the enthusiast brooding over his single dominant idea; everything – the heavily knitted brow, the commanding nose, the great beard sunk on the chest – contributes to the expression of an absorbing thought and a frustrated purpose. There Mr. Yeats's interest stops; the rest of the figure and the chair are alike mere background to relieve the head ...." He was seeing the emergence of JBY's penultimate, most celebrated style.

John Quinn was anxious to buy the portrait, and JBY did offer to make a copy. "I could easily get permission to make one & would do it for £30", he replied. But the offer was not taken up and it was 1904 when he painted the famous large oil of O'Leary for Quinn (see p. 118). H.M. Paget, JBY's close friend of the time in Bedford Park, painted O'Leary's portrait in 1890 (Crawford Gallery, Cork).

John O'Leary

1891, oil on canvas, 91 × 71 cm, NGI 595

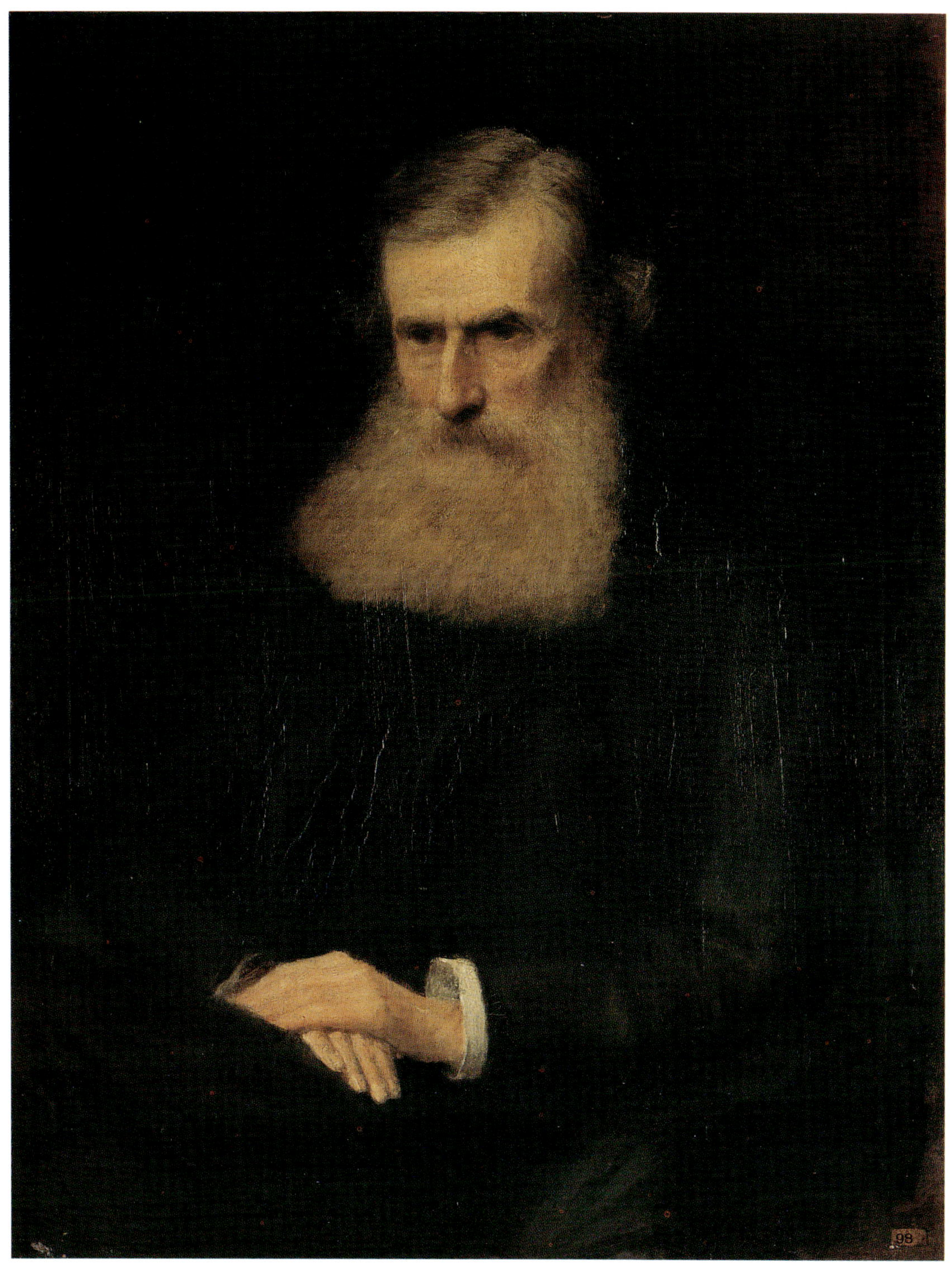

The date of this pencil portrait of Douglas Hyde (1860–1949) has been read as both 1895 and 1898, but must be taken to be 1898, when JBY was fulfilling a commission for pencil portraits from Hyde's aunt Augusta Gregory. JBY did not meet Lady Gregory until 1897, when she commissioned a sketch of Hyde with others, including a study of his own son, from the artist, and this sketch comes from her collection. JBY had known the Irish scholar in the Contemporary Club in Dublin, and both would have been glad to renew their acquaintance, though according to JBY's report to Lady Gregory (18 June 1898) the meeting was not lengthy. While his sketches of WBY and Russell (see following pages) were good, he thought, he was not so sure about that of Douglas Hyde. "At the time his wife (who understands art, being artist or art student) seemed quite satisfied; he was an impatient sitter – having come off a long railway journey and about to undertake another."

Impatient or not, Hyde turns and slants slightly as he leans on the arm of his chair and makes pleasant conversation. His eyes and head look keenly and warmly at the artist.

As was his practice in his sketches, JBY has concentrated on the neat head, worked in firm soft pencil. The hair is parted a little off centre, the moustache is luxuriant, perhaps waxed to stand out beyond the span of his face. Again, and as usual, the forehead shines, as does the tip of the nose, leading the viewer's eye upwards to receive an impression of a powerful intellect. There is no gleam of light in the eyes, however; rather they are like deep, humorous, friendly pools.

Hyde's body is rendered fluidly in rapid shading, like a ghost image beneath his completed head. His left elbow is leaning on the side of the chair, the hand dangling towards the top of a leg flung over the other at an angle. His right arm stretches down to the corner of the drawing in an awkward gesture, perhaps holding a cigarette, or he may have shifted and adopted a different pose, and the artist had no opportunity to adjust the arm. All of this adds to the vitality and movement of the drawing. He is seen against a white ground, with some hatching from shoulder level downwards.

Douglas Hyde was born in Roscommon, the son of a Church of Ireland clergyman. He was educated at home, when he spoke Irish with the local people, and at Trinity College, Dublin, where he studied Latin, Greek, Hebrew, French, German and English as well as Irish. He was intended for the Church, but when he realised that he had no vocation turned to the law. As a student, and later, he collected Irish stories and poetry, which he would publish as *Love Songs of Connacht* and *Religious Songs of Connacht,* using the pseudonym An Craoibhín Aoibhinn.

He had distinguished himself by founding the Gaelic League in 1893. As its first president, he was launched into a pursuit of Irish culture, both traditional and modern, which would have inestimable effects on his contemporaries and their ethos (see further p. 134).

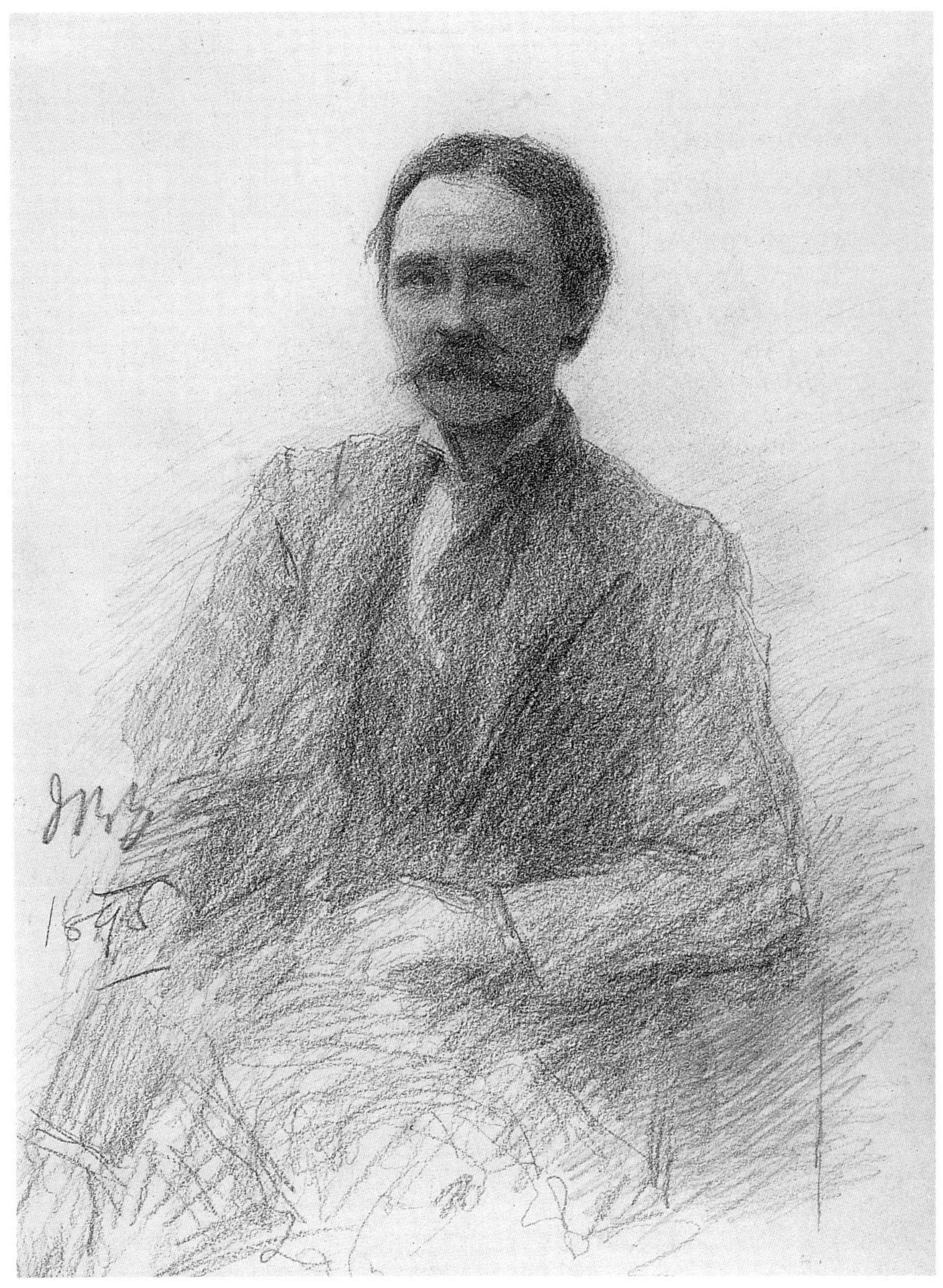

This study of the poet and painter A.E. or George Russell (1867–1935), who was as highly respected for his practical activities in journalism and political economy as for his original mystic art, comes from Lady Gregory's collection, probably commissioned at the same time as the portrait of WBY (see next). It was drawn in January 1898, and no doubt in Dublin. Russell, whom JBY had known since he was a youth at art school with WBY, had recently left his employment with Pim's, the Dublin drapers, to become a banks' organizer in the west of Ireland, engaged by Horace Plunkett of the Irish Agricultural Organisation Society. He returned to Dublin in mid-January (when the portrait would have been done) from what he described to W.K. Magee as "a desolate bogland with priests as my advisers and an ardent young Parnellite to balance". But he had doubled the number of banks. He wears his great-coat or 'ulster', with button-on cape, which he must have lived in during his misty trip. His hands emerging from the drapes, and clasped loosely, are roughly indicated, but JBY brings the attention to his long fingers. He described him to Lady Gregory as "a long-fingered visionary" (18 June 1898).

The image of an eager bearded young man is similar to that in his oil portrait painted in 1903 (see p. 114). (Russell later became more portly and was recorded as such in portraits by Estella Solomons and Hilda Roberts.) Here Russell is seen at a slightly different angle, and in different garments, seated on a high-backed chair, his legs crossed. He is turned just slightly to the right, rather than being seen full face. His hair is untidy and ruffled, as if he had just come in and sat down – which was probably the case – and his eyes, looking straight out of the drawing at the artist, seem about to laugh behind his *pince-nez*. His eyes also shine as if lit with some inner fire, and are the riveting point of the drawing.

His thick beard, his nose with its large nostrils, his large ear, and his parted lips – no doubt describing the terrible drive on a frosty road from Ballina to Belmullet – are drawn delicately, as is the whole image, shaded in smoothly with an even tone, except for a muted light down the left side. There is lively expres-

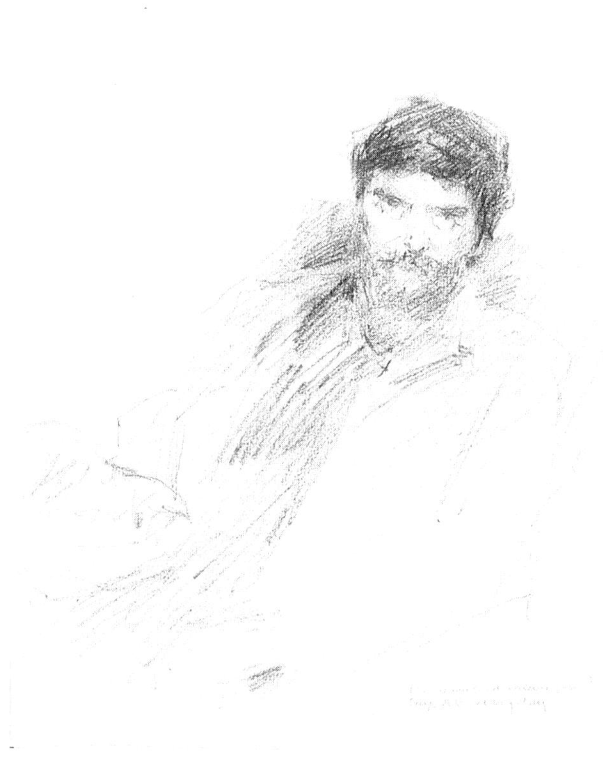

Fig. 66 J.B. Yeats, *Portrait of G.W. Russell*, from an undated sketchbook (Collection Anne Yeats)

sion in the outline, which momentarily thickens in curves and wiggles, giving the drawing a harmonious rhythm. It is a very sympathetic portrait, a subject rendered with affection.

Russell was a well loved man. Born in Lurgan, County Armagh in 1867, he had been brought up in Dublin from the age of eleven, and from 1880 attended the School of Art, where he first met WBY. He joined the Dublin lodge of the Theosophical Society in the late 1880s and lived for some years in a theosophist ('ideal') household in Ely Place, and later in Eustace Street. At the time of the drawing he had published his second collection of poems, *The Earth Breath*, and among other activities he was Irish editor of *The Internationalist*, a short-lived journal which ran from October 1897 until March 1898.

Pencil portrait of George William Russell (A.E.)

1898, pencil on paper with a faint watermark, 31.8 × 25.2 cm, NGI 2943

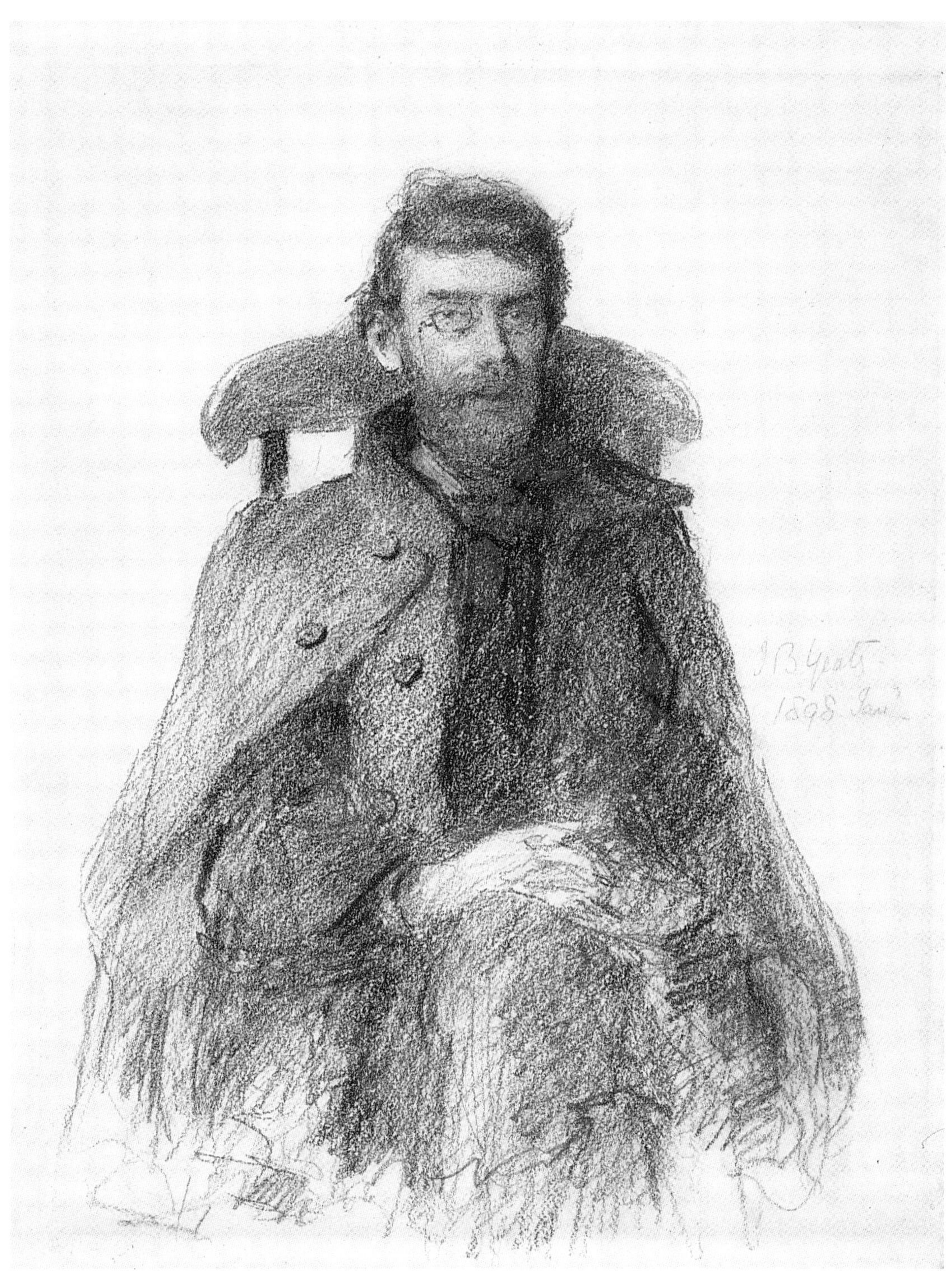

This sketch portrait of WBY, commissioned by Lady Gregory in 1897, is unusual in that JBY has used the wash technique generally associated with his illustrations. It is a three-quarter-length portrait, the figure seated in a chair. The poet's mouth is half open, as if about to speak, but his dark eyes look away dreamily. He concentrates his brow in thought: his hands dangle over the ends of the chair arms in a relaxed way, the fingers about to tighten on the wood. JBY welcomed any new image WBY might present, and here depicts him wearing a dark suit, with a large velvet bow tied over his floppy shirt. The artist seems to look down on the long scholarly shape, who has been posed at an angle, turned to the right. WBY, who was shortly to launch his Irish Literary Theatre on Dublin, was ill at the time of this portrait, and convalesced with Lady Gregory, whom he had recently met, at Coole Park.

There is a poetic flow in the image, reinforced by the monochrome watercolour that obscures the initial pencil, and which has been made substantial with gouache highlights. It is like a mini oil painting, and close to the monochrome wash study the artist had made in November 1896, which was frontispiece to WBY's *The Tables of the Law*, published in June 1897. JBY thought this new drawing might also be reproduced; and initially it bothered him. He wrote to Lady Gregory on 9 December 1897, "My drawing of Willie does not satisfy me. I did it by lamplight – *dim* lamplight. I should like a chance of doing him by daylight", and, the following day, "I do not regard this sketch as final. Its being done so quickly is due to Willie's urgency, who wants it for his forthcoming volume, at least if you and he prefer it to the one by Russell."

The "forthcoming volume" may have been the new edition of *The Celtic Twilight*, which did not appear until 1902, but which has as frontispiece the 1896 watercolour portrait from *The Tables of the Law*. In this likeness of 1898 the writer is not in such a trance. The lean cheek bones, the darkness of the eyes and the dark hair flopping over the side of his brow, though, are still a part of the image. The artist has played more with the effects of light, so alleviating the dim poetic aura.

JBY made the sketch that eventually satisfied him at

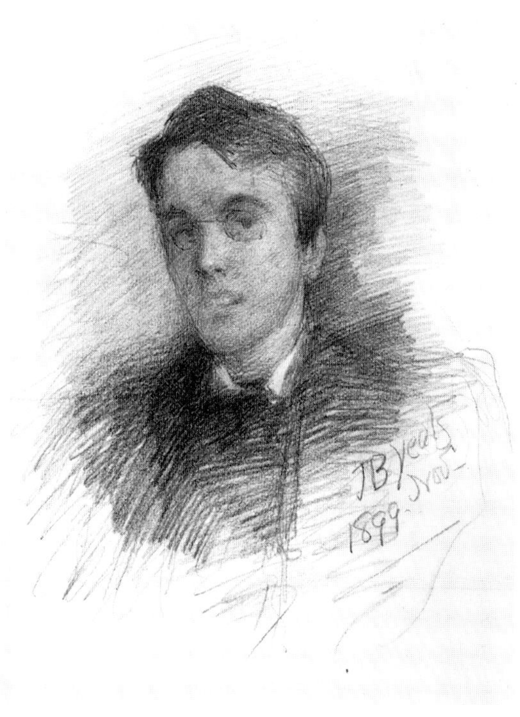

Fig. 67 J.B. Yeats, *Portrait of W.B. Yeats*, November 1899, wash drawing, 35 × 25 cm (Birmingham Museum and Art Gallery)

George Russell's home in Rathmines, on WBY's thirty-third birthday, 13 June 1898. On the strength of Lady Gregory's commission he was spending the summer of 1898 in Dublin, staying in lodgings in Hume Street, and teaching at May Manning's school. The end result he regarded as the best sketch of Willie he had done. However, writing about the drawings he did for her, he told Lady Gregory (20 June 1898), "I feel very apprehensive as to how you will regard Willie's. With him I have never succeeded. Some *uncertainty of intention* always hangs over my pencil …. I shall no doubt some day get a good portrait of Willie. The medium (Chinese white and charcoal gray) as used is always a treacherous one, since when dry it looks different from what it did when put on fresh." He need not have been so concerned; Lady Gregory was full of praises for the portrait, and he told her gratefully, "We artists live by praise, it is the sign to us that we have expressed ourselves adequately" (11 July 1898).

Wash study portrait of William Butler Yeats

1898, monochrome watercolour with gouache, mounted on board, 35.6 × 25.3 cm, NGI 2942

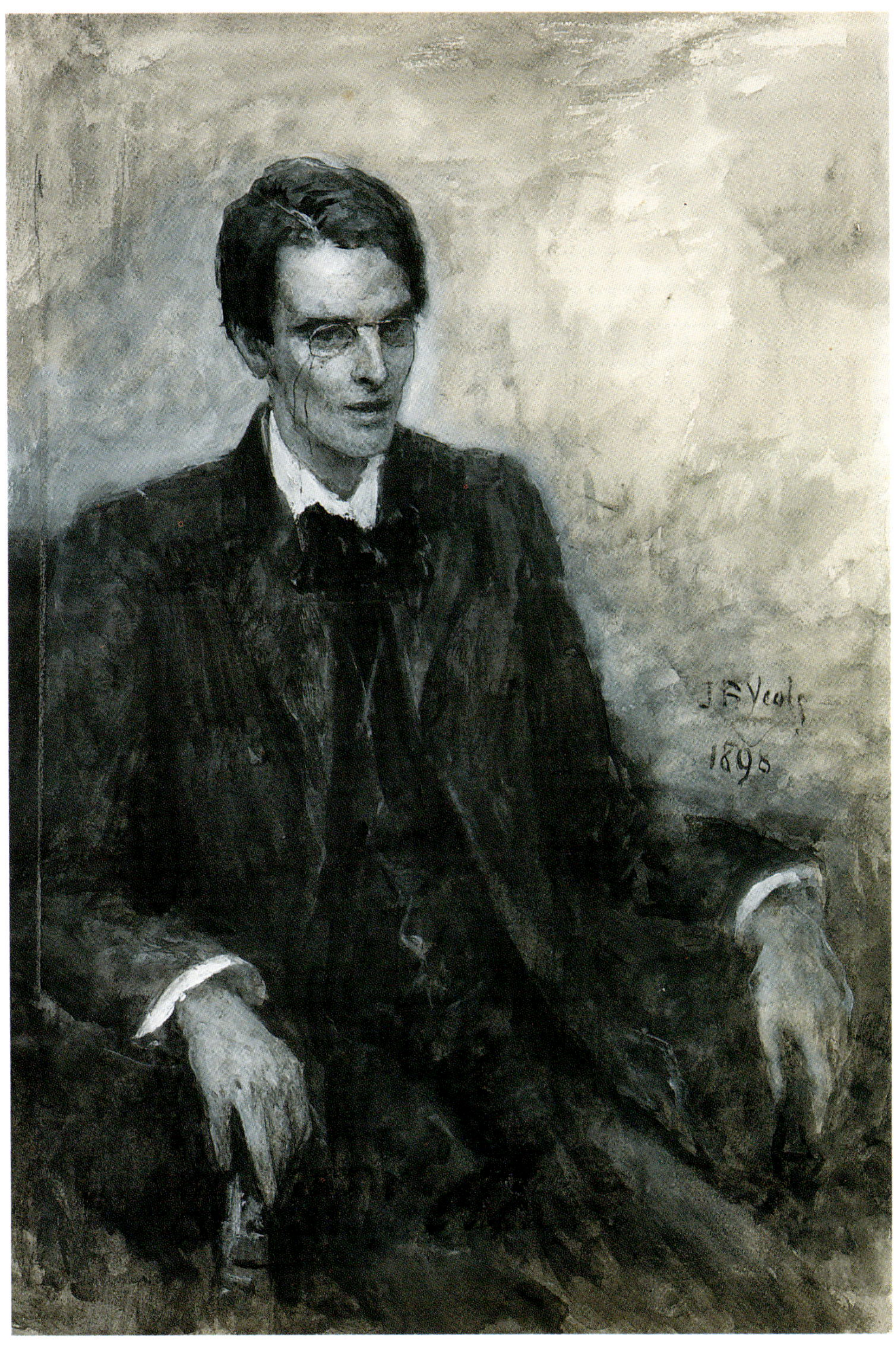

Lady Gregory never fully penetrated the reserve of JBY's younger son, Jack B. Yeats (1871–1957), but she issued a warm invitation to him and his wife Cottie to visit Coole, where they stayed with her for the first time in April 1899. She had been pleased with JBY's sketch portrait of WBY, and would have received that of Jack, posted to Gort from London, with equal pleasure, since it would appear to be a sympathetic likeness.

JBY made fewer studies of Jack than of WBY, and never seemed to feel the need to make anything other than a realistic image – or perhaps he was not encouraged to. He wrote to Lady Gregory on 27 May 1899, "I have done a sketch of Jack, which in point of skill is the best I have done yet. The mouth, however, is not quite right. There is an ill-favoured want of proportion about the upper lip, to which I have not yet done full justice. When he returns from Paris, whither he departed yesterday, I will put this all right." And he added: "I think you have done a great deal with Jack ... he has ideas, ambitions, hopes, that he never had before ... I gather this from his wife as well as himself. Jack having this very short upper lip is not quick at *explaining himself.*"

He has sketched a head with bust, looking into the left distance contemplatively, his forehead slightly wrinkled, though the mouth is confident, almost wilful, the chin firm. Another pencil portrait made at the same time (Michael B. Yeats Collection) is more serene, equally withdrawn, but with similar decided composure. JBY offered it also to Lady Gregory, who chose the sketch now in the National Gallery. His response was (16 June 1899), "You have selected the portrait of Jack which I thought the best. The other one (received here yesterday) is no good, but for some reason Lilly and his wife liked it …."

He later wrote of Jack (*Christian Science Monitor*, 2 November 1920), "He has the habits of a man who knows his own mind": and it is this image that he has projected in the sketch, the hair neatly cut and parted, tie a little loose, but all adding up to a neat and conventional appearance. The face has been shaded delicately, nurturing the lights, the main illumination being on the forehead, with bright points in the eyes, which

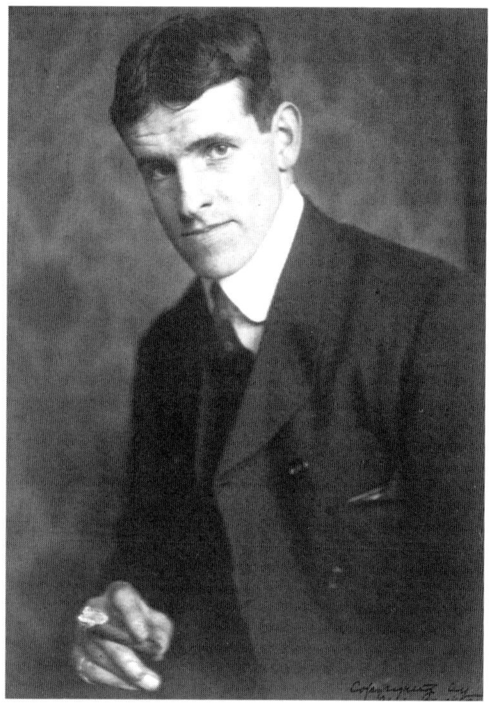

Fig. 68 Jack B. Yeats, March 1907, studio photograph by Alice Boughton (Irish Academic Press)

are expressive and dreamy. The nose, when examined, is the weakest point, and less finished than in the companion sketch.

The latter has been rendered against a plain ground, while here JBY has worked the background with heavy criss-cross shading, which overflows into the roughly described coat. The head, blurred along the right side and merged in with the shadow, rises out of the gloom, alert and living, but nevertheless retaining the meditative mood.

Jack Yeats had by now left his career as a cartoonist and illustrator, where he had reached the top of his profession and could command what fee he wished. He had settled in Devon, painting in watercolour at the time, and had adopted the Irish theme, 'Life in the West of Ireland', that would soon identify him as one of the key figures in the Irish cultural renaissance. He had recently held his second exhibition in London and Dublin.

Pencil portrait of Jack B. Yeats

1899, pencil on paper, 29 × 22.8 cm, NGI 2945

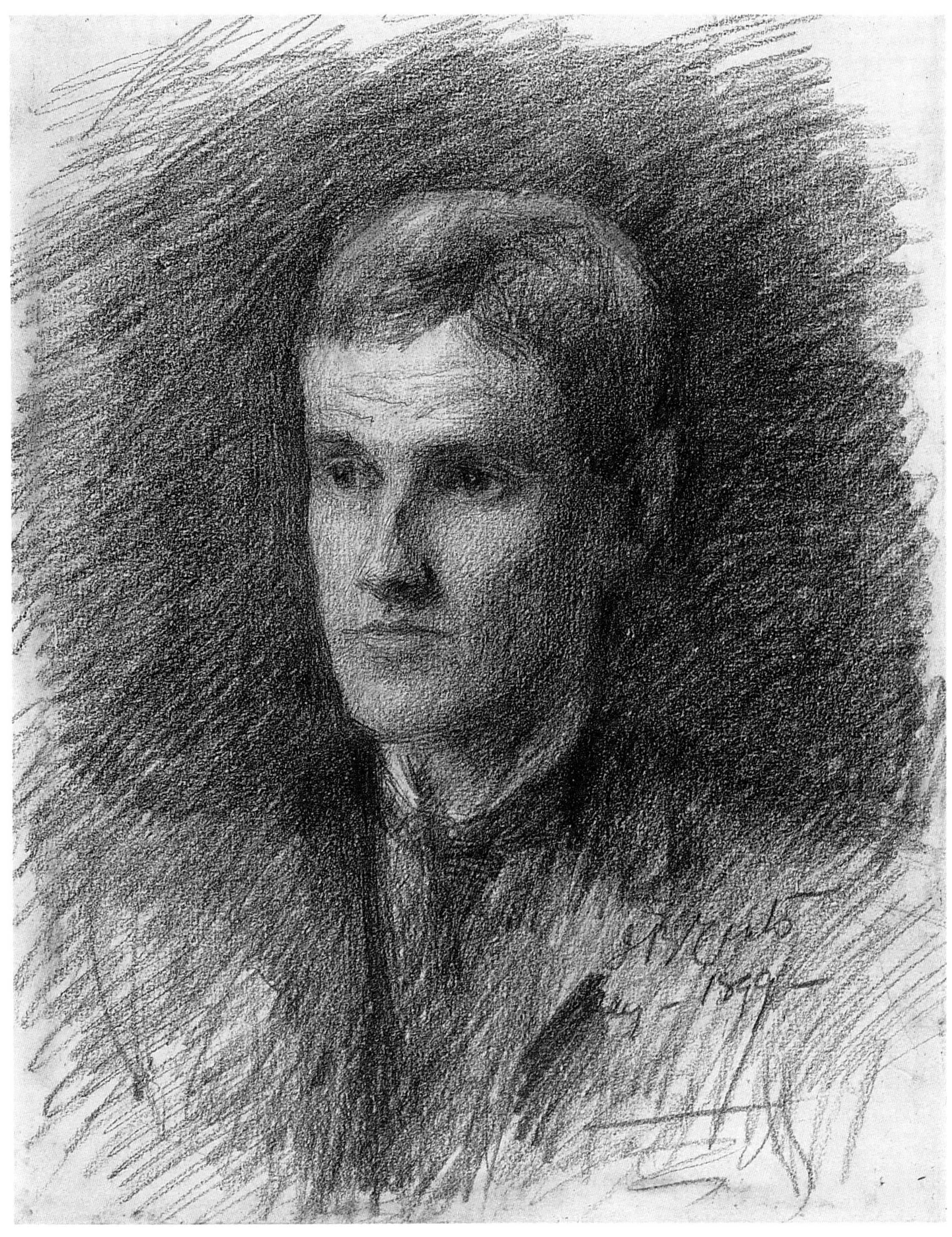

mong the sketch portraits commissioned by Lady Gregory from JBY while he lived in London was a likeness of Edward Martyn (1859–1923), of Tulira Castle, County Galway. A connoisseur and collector, Martyn was to bequeath his Corot *Willows* and a Monet landscape, as well as two Degas pastels, to the National Gallery of Ireland.

The vigour of the pencilwork which all but rains on the body of the sitter, leaving the head calm and isolated, places the drawing close to the pencil portrait of Jack B. Yeats of July 1899; and it is not inconceivable that this drawing was done about the same time. JBY would have enjoyed the sitting – Martyn was a playwright as well as an aesthete, and he had just bought a magnificent pugilist watercolour by Jack.

But he was also a quiet man, a Catholic landowner who was a bachelor and something of a recluse. JBY may have done all the talking. The full lips of the plump man in this bust portrait are firmly closed; though his eyes seek those of the artist, and he appears to listen with attention to whatever is being said. Turned very slightly to the left, his head is inclined in enquiry. His pensive eyes gaze from behind his *pince-nez*. Apart from his broad forehead, revealed by sparse, receding hair, his face is in light shadow. JBY may have found this the best way to suggest his retiring personality, and he has used fine detailed pencilwork to build up his sensitive face. Behind it, active dark graphite strokes push his gentle genial head forward out of the shadow. Like the other early pencil studies of the emerging leaders of the Irish renaissance done for Lady Gregory, this sympathetic portrayal can be seen to be laying the foundations of style for JBY's great oil portraits.

Martyn wears a neat wing collar, a dark tie and – roughly indicated – a plain coat, giving him a not unpriestly appearance. An Oxford graduate with political interests (he was a member of Sinn Fein from its foundation, and later president), he was a devoted Catholic, and was one of the initiators of An Túr Gloine, the Dublin stained-glass studio where so many original artists worked (see fig. 69). He was a patron of Loughrea Cathedral, and supervised its artwork, and he founded the Palestrina Choir in the Pro-Cathedral in Dublin.

His play *The Heather Field* had been produced in Dublin in May 1899, along with WBY's controversial drama *The Countess Cathleen*; and at the same time, with Lady Gregory, the two men launched the Irish Literary Theatre, which was committed to presenting Irish and Gaelic plays yearly. Martyn was high in the estimation of the writer George Moore; and JBY, when doing a nude picture of *Echo pursued by a satyr* the following year (a theme that obsessed him), talked of discussing the idea with Edward Martyn.

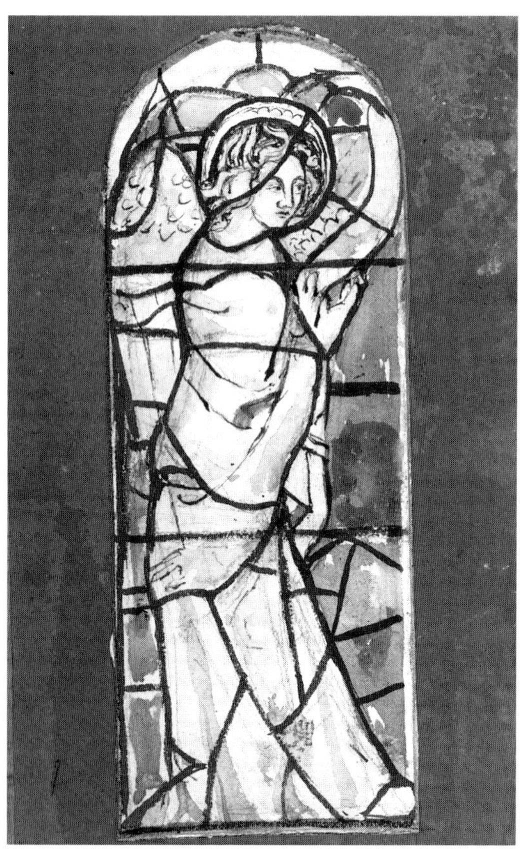

Fig. 69 *Archangel Gabriel*, watercolour design for An Tur Gloine, NGI 18, 467

1899, pencil on Whatman paper, 28.3 × 22.8 cm, NGI 2941

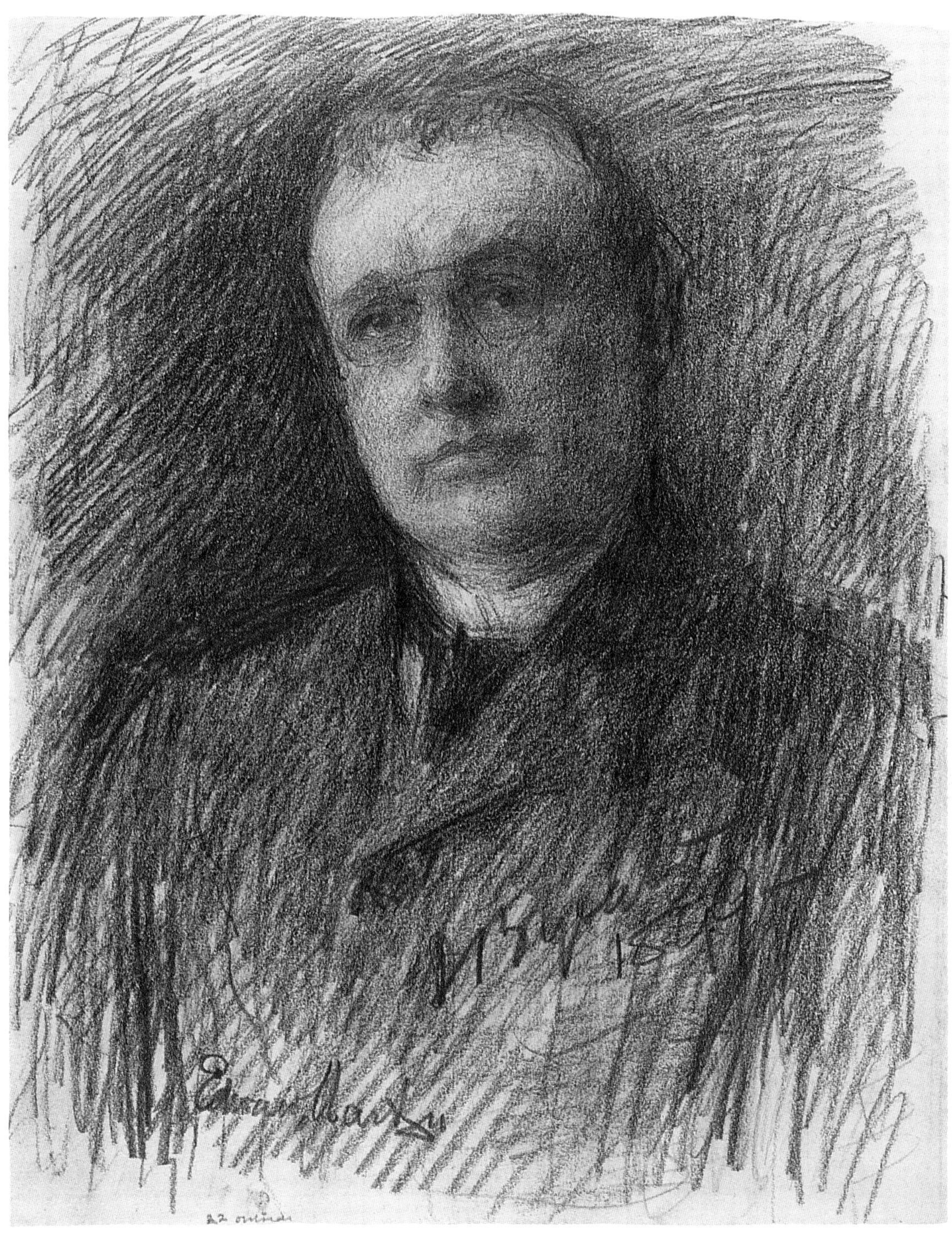

W hile Lily Yeats was recovering from typhoid in 1897, Susan Langstaff Mitchell (1866–1926) came to lodge at Blenheim Road as her companion. With Sligo/Leitrim origins, she had been brought up in Dublin and Birr, and was vaguely related to the Yeats family. Her infectious personality and her gifts as a singer made her a welcome addition to the household. The picture was painted before she returned to Ireland in the summer of 1899.

For Susan Mitchell life in Bedford Park was a revelation. Twenty years later she described it in a eulogistic lecture in Dublin in honour of JBY: "In the house of Mr. Yeats I found myself in what seemed to me a wonderful society, a society where ideas were valued above all other possessions ... where first I learned what con-versation meant .... Here I might pour out voice and heart without obstruction, here pride of country, intellectual speculation, creative aspirations were fostered and not frowned on .... In the Irish men and women I met under Mr. Yeats's roof I was having my first contact with a movement that was bringing about a revolution in thinking and feeling in my own country ...."

Given the nationalism aboil in the young poet, who was already scribbling privately, the oil portrait is somewhat formal. JBY had made preliminary sketches (figs. 70, 71) which are anything but formal, more illustrative of the kitten ready to pounce, which was how he observed her character – she was to become the wit and lampoonist of the Irish renaissance. Here he gives her a fragile look, and paints a romantic image, more distant than the three-quarter length of the artist Clare Marsh, who was slightly younger, and which he painted with more daring about the same period. Her head, with starry brown eyes framed in translucent skin, is crowned quietly by red-gold hair drawn back and parted. Her slender neck issues from a frothy lace collar that drapes her shoulders, and trails down the bosom of her dark dress. Light coming from the left plays about her forehead and her cheek, flattering her wide-nostrilled nose and mobile lips, which are slightly parted. The background is ultramarine (to complement her hair) touched with red, and with black to echo her dress. Her head is highlighted with a stroke of white behind, lifting the density of the surrounding colour.

The freedom of the brushwork is typical of JBY's work from now on: criss-cross strokes dancing in the background, while the artist 'stills' the face with short, dexterous touches of the brush. JBY had only recently returned to oil portraits and was to paint Susan's portrait again, once as *Autumn* for a Dublin restaurant.

Susan Mitchell and JBY remained warm friends throughout life. She worked as a journalist, assistant to George Russell on the *Irish Homestead*. Her mystic and satirical verse was collected in *The Living Chalice* and *Odes to the Immortality of Certain Persons in Ireland* (both 1908). When JBY moved to New York, she became one of his principal correspondents, and he made her the heroine of one of his short stories.

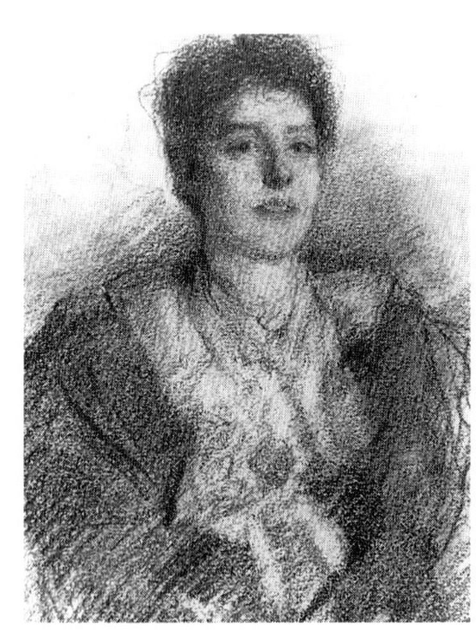

Fig. 70 J.B. Yeats, *Susan Mitchell, ca.* 1899 (Sligo County Museum)

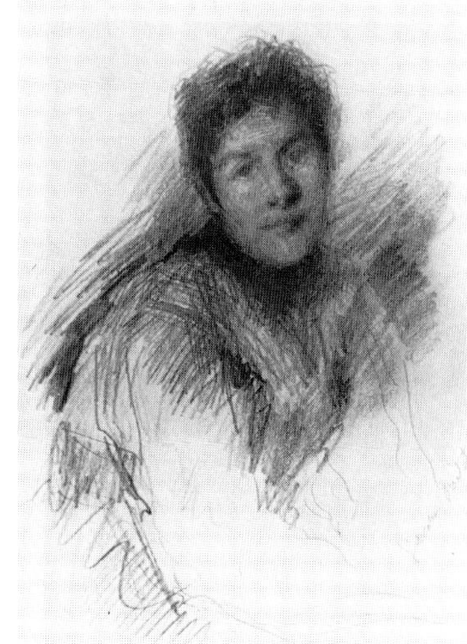

Fig. 71 J.B. Yeats, *Susan Mitchell, ca.* 1899, pencil (Michael Yeats Collection)

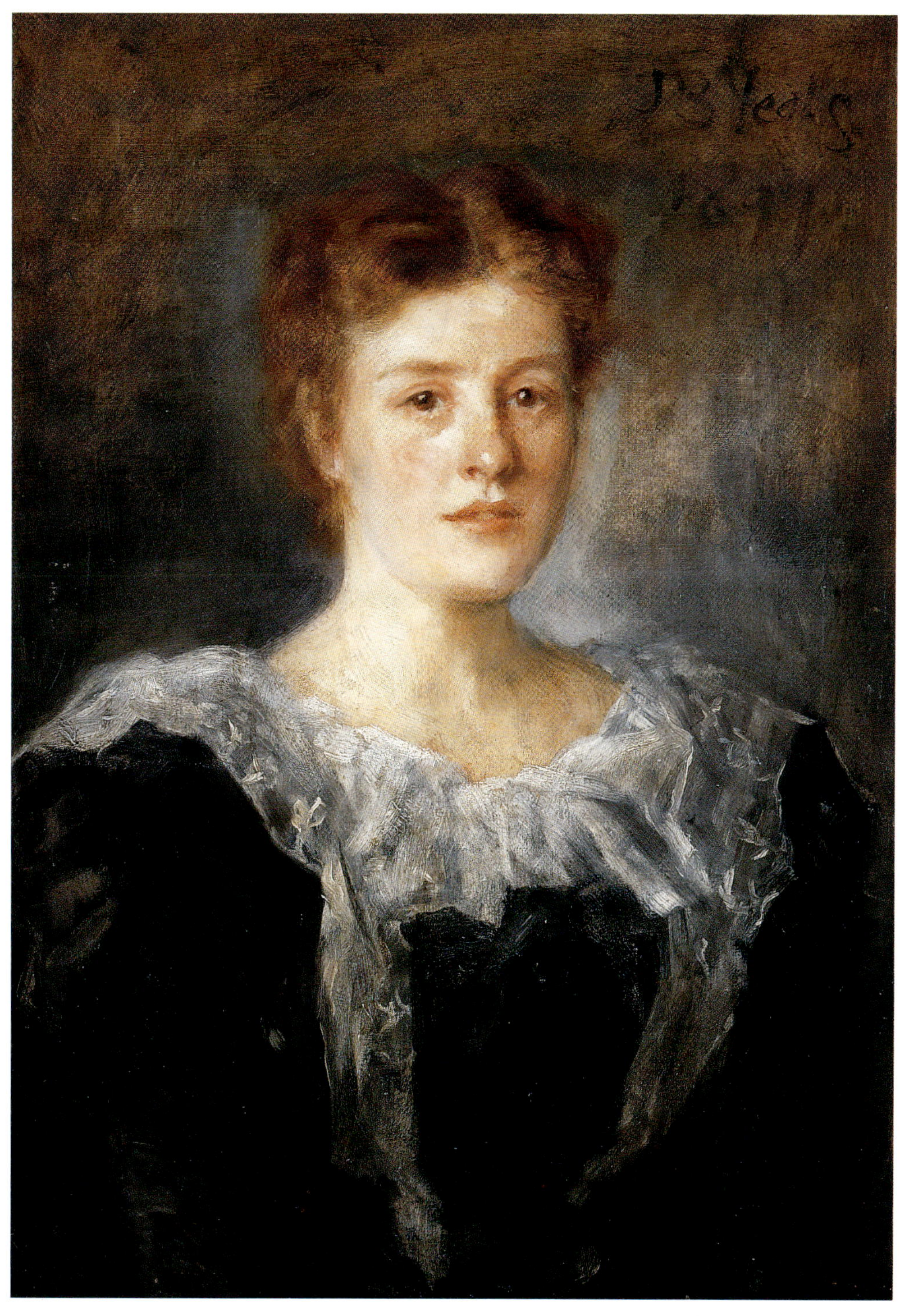

"Iam glad to say," JBY reported to Lady Gregory (2 January 1900), "at last, after only three sittings, I have painted a good portrait of Willie, a head and shoulders. I have painted as if in full tide of talk." The picture makes an interesting comparison with the gouache portrait of 1898 (see p. 88), substituting for its gloomy trance an exciting freshness and energy.

JBY always sought a poetic image in WBY, and here he represents him half-length, at a slight angle against a grey ground where light hovers elusively. A lock of black hair falls over the writer's left brow, the *pince-nez* poised delicately before his bright brown eyes, which gaze dreamily through the glass. His full red lips part, showing his teeth, as if speaking earnestly, elatedly.

The artist has highlighted the intellectual brow, the face narrowing beneath it elfishly, his cheeks appearing almost hollow. The poet wears a black coat, partially buttoned, with his black tie fastened in a lavish bow. He looks entranced, and as if risen up to speak. The gleaming black of his hair and garments make his whole persona arresting, surrounded by the neutral colour of the background which is shot with dark green.

Some years later WBY wrote to John Quinn (7 January 1908), "My father always sees me through a mist of domestic emotion." With all its contrived dynamism – and it is a memorable portrait, in essence true to the sitter though without the depth of some of his other portrayals – it has something of the spirit of simple intensity that may be seen in JBY's portrait of his wife (see p. 54). Perhaps he thought of her as he painted. Of course Susan's portrait shows a subdued personality. Here we have a vital, undaunted spirit: and JBY looks on them both objectively, affectionately.

The year 1900 was to change JBY's life, and give him the fresh start that from time to time he craved. His invalid wife died the day after he had finished the portrait, freeing him from a suffocating responsibility. While his attachment for Susan Pollexfen had been genuine, he had been totally unsuited to the bonds of marriage, and now he was free to travel with an easy conscience. He went to Paris for two weeks, and with Lily stayed near Jack in Devon; and he absorbed himself in painting. "I think I have greatly advanced, as indeed I have given almost the whole of the year to portrait painting," he wrote to O'Leary (29 October 1900). "Hitherto I have done it on occasions when by some luck I had the chance, but this last year I have done nothing else." His portraits begin to show an ease and a confidence as never before.

JBY, writing on 19 November 1901 to John Quinn, who wanted to buy some of his work, mentioned this portrait. "Since it was painted two years ago it has hung in my son's sitting room", and he offered it to Quinn for £20. In 1926, it returned to Ireland and was presented to the National Gallery by Mr C. Sullivan and Mrs Julia Anderson in memory of John Quinn.

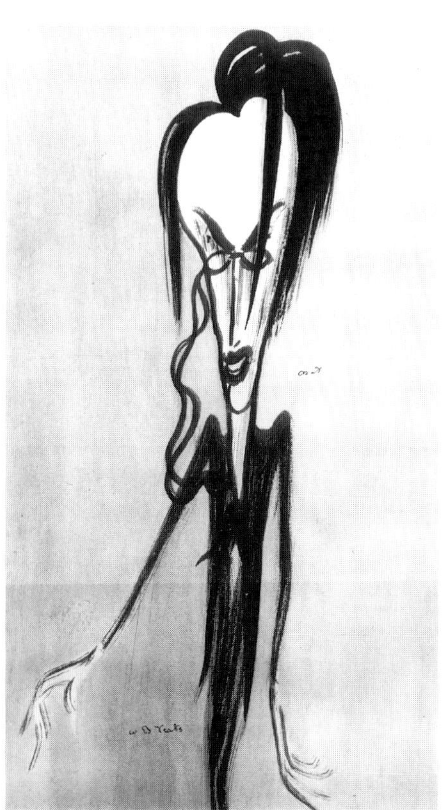

Fig. 72 Max Beerbohm, *William Butler Yeats*, ink and watercolour on paper, 32 × 18.7 cm, NGI 3773

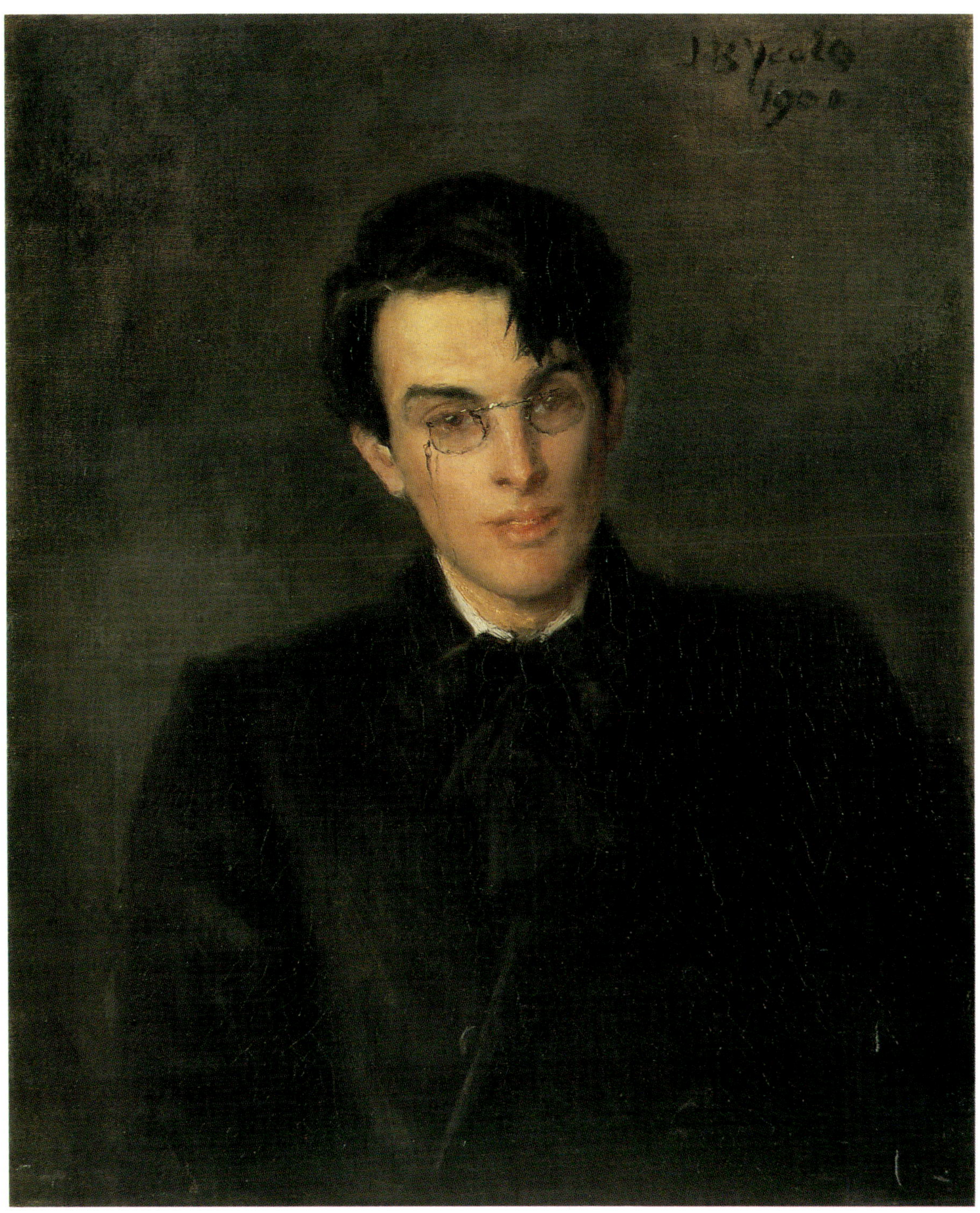

William Butler Yeats

1900, oil on canvas, 77 × 64 cm, NGI 872

JBY drew his daughter Lily (1866–1949) continually. She modelled all but one of the characters – the one being Man Friday – in his illustrations to the sixteen volumes of Defoe commissioned by the publisher Dent in 1894. Besides his childhood portrait of her, he painted her twice in oil, the first version (Michael B. Yeats Collection) being shown in the RHA in 1899. It was the year after she herself had shown a painting of cornflowers, the only occasion on which she exhibited in the Academy. JBY had told Sarah Purser in July 1897 that he had been working for a year and a half on Lily's portrait. Since Lily had spent practically all of 1896 away, he had probably started the portrait before she went and completed it when she returned. In the case of the 1900 portrait, work was initially dedicated and rapid. JBY and Lily stayed for three weeks in Devon near Jack, where, JBY told Clare Marsh (26 July 1900), "I worked all day in Jack's studio, he also being busy there, and Lilly was sitting to me." Nonetheless, he still felt the painting needed finishing touches back in London, early in 1901, when he dated it.

JBY's brush worked fluidly in the inspired manner

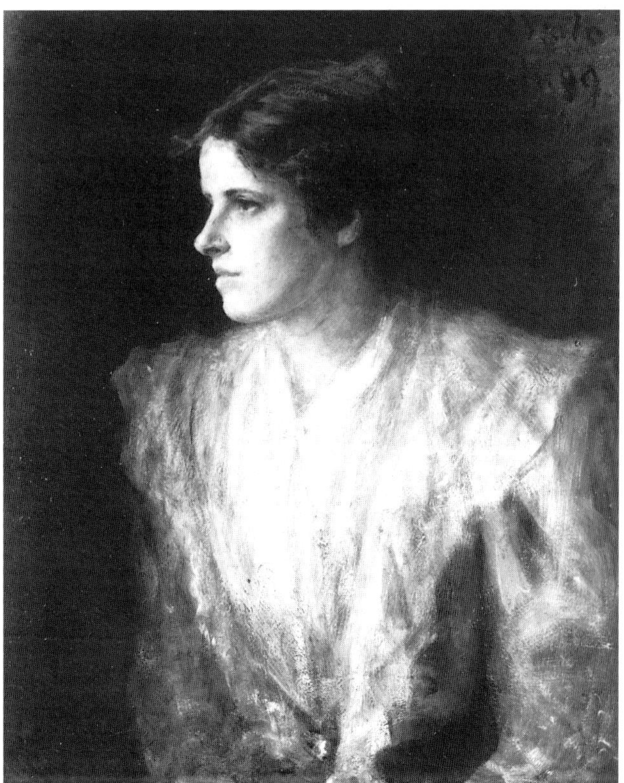

he had now attained. The portrait is engagingly simple. Three-quarter-length, Lily occupies two thirds of the picture, sitting in a chair with polished arm on the right of the painting. She sways slightly as she fixes her bright brown eyes on the viewer with unwavering gaze. She has an immediate presence, meriting the large scale JBY had decided on with a view to sending the portrait to the Royal Academy.

Her dark hair parted in the middle is piled in a bun on top. A square jaw gave her a severe appearance, judging by photographs, but she could look pretty, and facing her father her face softens, the eyes look warm, the full lips, though straight, almost twitch, the firm chin is tenderly described. The back of her head is surrounded with an aura, a practice the painter continued as he painted the personalities of the Irish renaissance. The freshness of her complexion and her gentle expression are complemented by the radiating white of the chiffon blouse she wears, the leg-o'-mutton sleeves embroidered in gold about the cuffs with further embroidery on the shoulders. Her string of coral with its pendant has swung slightly to one side with the twist of her body. JBY has added a touch of coral colour in the buckle of her black belt. Her clasped hands rest in the lap of her beige skirt, an emerald ring on the upper one. This green has been picked up in the formal dark background as a rich sheen, lightened above with amber tones.

It is a formal portrait in which the sitter is charmingly informal. JBY has overpainted the clothing, but the warmth of Lily's personality and her rapport with the artist make it one of JBY's great successes. "I am making a real effort this time for the RA," he wrote to Sarah Purser (14 March 1901), "a portrait of Lilly and another of Lolly." They were both rejected, which led to Sarah Purser's historic exhibition in Dublin that autumn.

Lily, JBY used to say, was the least intellectual of his children. She trained as an embroideress with William Morris's daughter May, and in 1902 joined Evelyn Gleeson at Dun Emer, later setting up the Cuala Industries with her sister Elizabeth Corbet (Lolly) Yeats.

Fig. 73 J.B. Yeats, *Lily Yeats*, 1899, oil on canvas, 76 × 63.5 cm (Michael B. Yeats Collection)

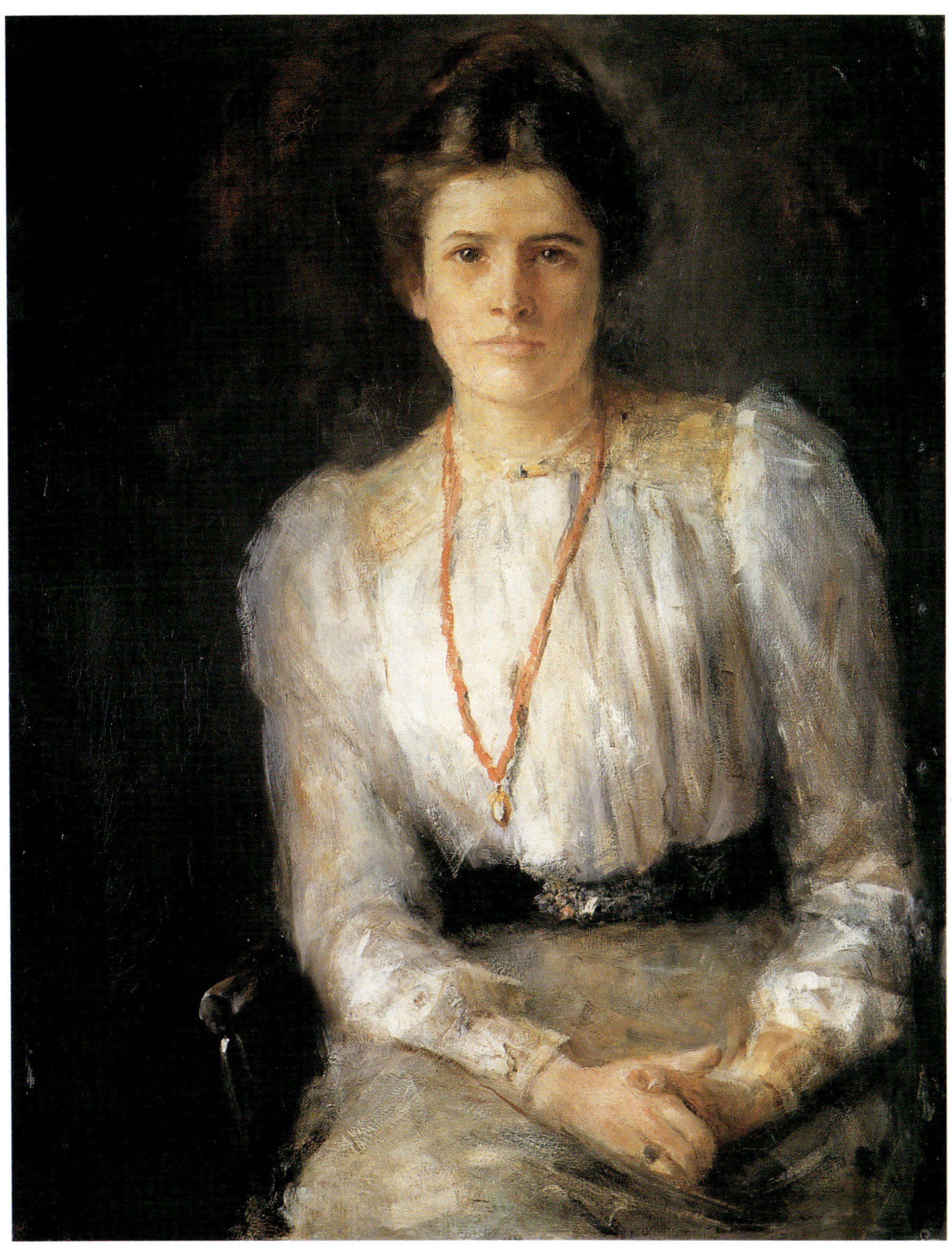

Susan Mary (Lily) Yeats

1900–01, oil on canvas, 91 × 71 cm, NGI 1180

In 1899, JBY told Rosa Butt, daughter of Isaac Butt (see p. 46 and next page), who was then living in Chelsea, that for some time he had had a "much cherished project" – to get sittings from her for a portrait (fig. 74). By the end of October 1900 the portrait was painted, seemingly in a matter of days, which was unusual for JBY. "When painting you I never knew a moment of fatigue mental or physical," he told Rosa; and, "I wish those sittings had lasted one week longer."

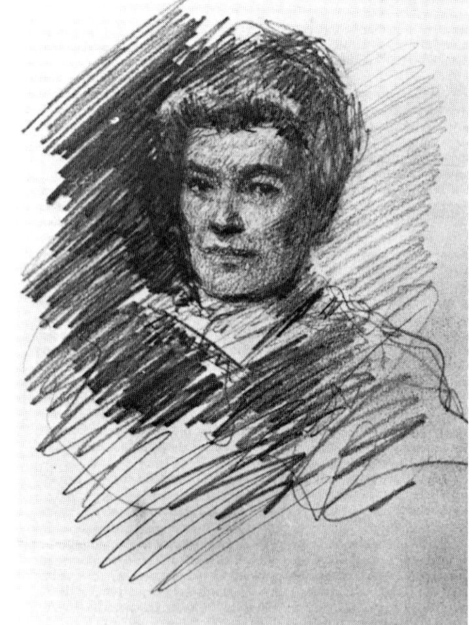

Fig. 74 J.B. Yeats, *Rosa Butt, ca.* 1900, pencil, 34.5 × 24.5 cm (Michael B. Yeats Collection)

JBY, who had recently become a widower, and who so often railed against wives in general, found himself greatly attracted towards this woman in her sixties, a few months older than himself. There has been speculation as to how far the affair progressed, but an examination of the letters he wrote her, now in the Bodleian Library, suggests that, while there was a genuine affection which they kept private for the next twenty years, Rosa Butt refused to consider a permanent bond feasible. JBY's ardour resembled his admiration for other, younger women friends, in that the sentiment, unde-

niably profound, still resided in the mind.

"The whole mischief is this," he wrote to her ([19] December 1900): "when I first saw you you were a woman grown (as well as growing) and I a hobblede-hoy – now a hobbledehoy has terrible passions ... – I thought you the most beautiful woman I ever saw (still think it) – I think it was the peculiar ['perfect' is crossed out] poise of your head & your eyes like those of a wild creature at once pensive & wild – *you are still like this* – here there is not one atom of alteration .... I have been puzzling how to describe the poise of your head. I put in the word perfect because I could not think of any other & 'peculiar' is rather worse – I think *valliant* [*sic*] would have been better. At any rate you look as if you would play dice with fate or father Time & *almost* come off victor."

Such thoughts no doubt passed through JBY's head while he was painting the portrait: he could not dissociate her from her father, Isaac Butt the Irish leader, who had had the same charisma for him. Her letters, he told her, had "the same vital quality – such sentences like a spark struck from an anvil." Her features, for all their feminine grace and charm, betray an uncommon inner strength. Her bright brown eyes, like her father's, under distinctive grey eyebrows, look as if a mischievous twinkle had preceded the pensive mood; the firm characterful lips speak of a strong will patiently controlled.

JBY has represented the monochrome black of her high-collared dress and of the stitched detail of the bolero jacket with skill: but nothing is allowed to detract from the calm head, poised "valliantly", a provocative ribbon crowning the grey hair. The surrounding aura in the mother-of-pearl ground complements the warmth and brilliance of her complexion. In all it is a lively and poetic conception of a thinking woman of distinguished personality.

The artist Mary Swanzy, who negotiated the gift of the portrait to the National Gallery (her father was Rosa Butt's first cousin), told Dr MacGreevy that the portrait had been offered to the Tate Gallery in London, "who sent 'a young lady' to view it and refused the offer".

1900, oil on canvas, 92 × 71 cm, NGI 1724

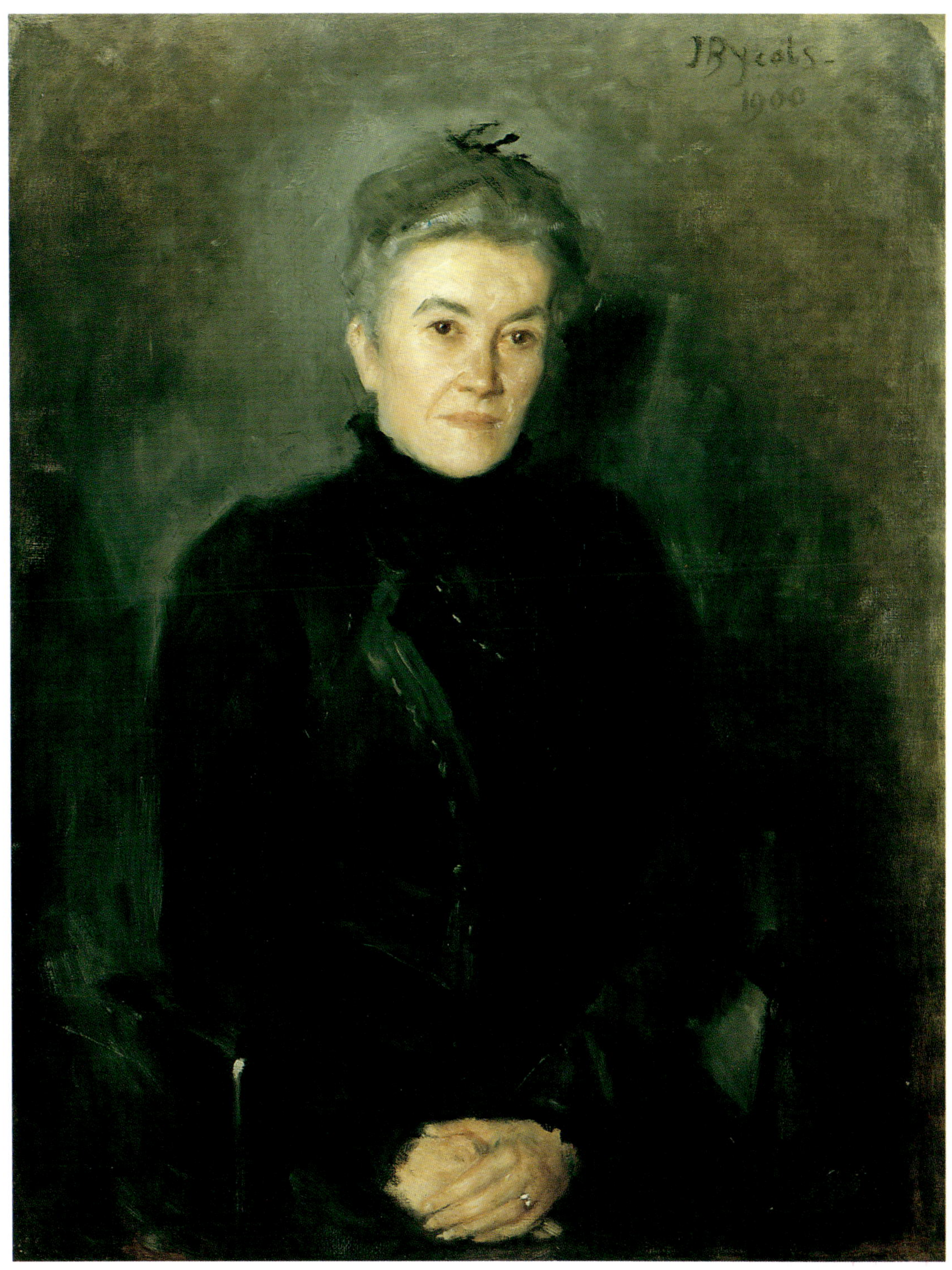

Isaac Butt (1813–1879), from Glenfin in County Donegal, was a friend of JBY's father at Trinity College in the 1830s, and, despite his unquestioning Unionism, he remained a close friend, WBY naming one of his sons after him. He advised JBY when he was at Trinity about taking up the Bar as a profession. It was at this point, during the Fenian trials, that the lawyer abandoned his conservative outlook and began his campaign for Home Rule.

In May 1876, though he was still not confident that he had completed his "apprenticeship" as a portrait painter, JBY felt he must make renewed efforts to gain commissions, and approached Butt, who was now leader of the Irish Party in the House of Commons. The older man responded well, inviting the artist to the House of Commons for dinner, and sitting for him on 25 May at Nettleship's studio, after which there was at least one more sitting. The artist worked in chalk, the medium in which he was most at ease. He had made a pen-and-ink sketch of Butt at the Four Courts ten years before (National Library of Ireland), but now represented him more formally, turned three-quarters to the left, his eyes regarding the spectator.

The original chalk, from which our portrait was copied, is now in the National Portrait Gallery in London, presented by Butt's granddaughter, Lady Ball, in 1952. As in the *Pippa* drawings of the 1870s (see pp. 48 and 50) and other work of the time, the artist's line in it is strong and pictorial. The dense even shading surrounding his head, and the uncompromising focus on detail, emphasize the irregularity of his features and make his hair appear all blown to one side of his head.

The chalk drawing, regarded widely as the finest likeness of Butt, was probably the posthumous portrait of the Irish leader exhibited by Yeats at the Royal Hibernian Academy in 1880, since Yeats is not known to have asked Butt to sit for him again.

Yeats had an undying admiration for Butt, telling his friend Dowden many years later, "Such is the charm of personality that the man who has it is forgiven, though his sins be scarlet – for instance lovable Isaac Butt"; and his affection for the man, and his admiration, are visible in what is an idealized, yet at the same time honest, portrayal. Butt was ousted a year after the portrait was taken by Parnell, himself a charismatic personality – though JBY did not like him – and he died in May 1879.

Rosa Butt, the sitter's daughter, lent the drawing to the *Loan Collection of Pictures* of Hone and Yeats arranged by Sarah Purser in Dublin in 1901. It was then that the National Gallery of Ireland commissioned this copy of it for the Portrait Gallery. Yeats informed John Quinn (19 November 1901) that he had just done a replica of his black chalk portrait of Isaac Butt for the Gallery for £15. The copy, nearly twice the size of the 1870s' drawing, while remarkably faithful to the original, is worked in Yeats's later impressionist manner, with pale soft shading filling the area around the sitter, the more *sfumato* style softening individual features without disturbing their vitality. The artist has exchanged the dramatic realism of the original for a detached, statesmanlike mood, in keeping with the portrait's rôle in the Irish National Collection, without making his likeness any less urgent and convincing.

Isaac Butt

1901 (from an original of 1876), black chalk with white highlights on paper, 69.9 × 56 cm, NGI 2442

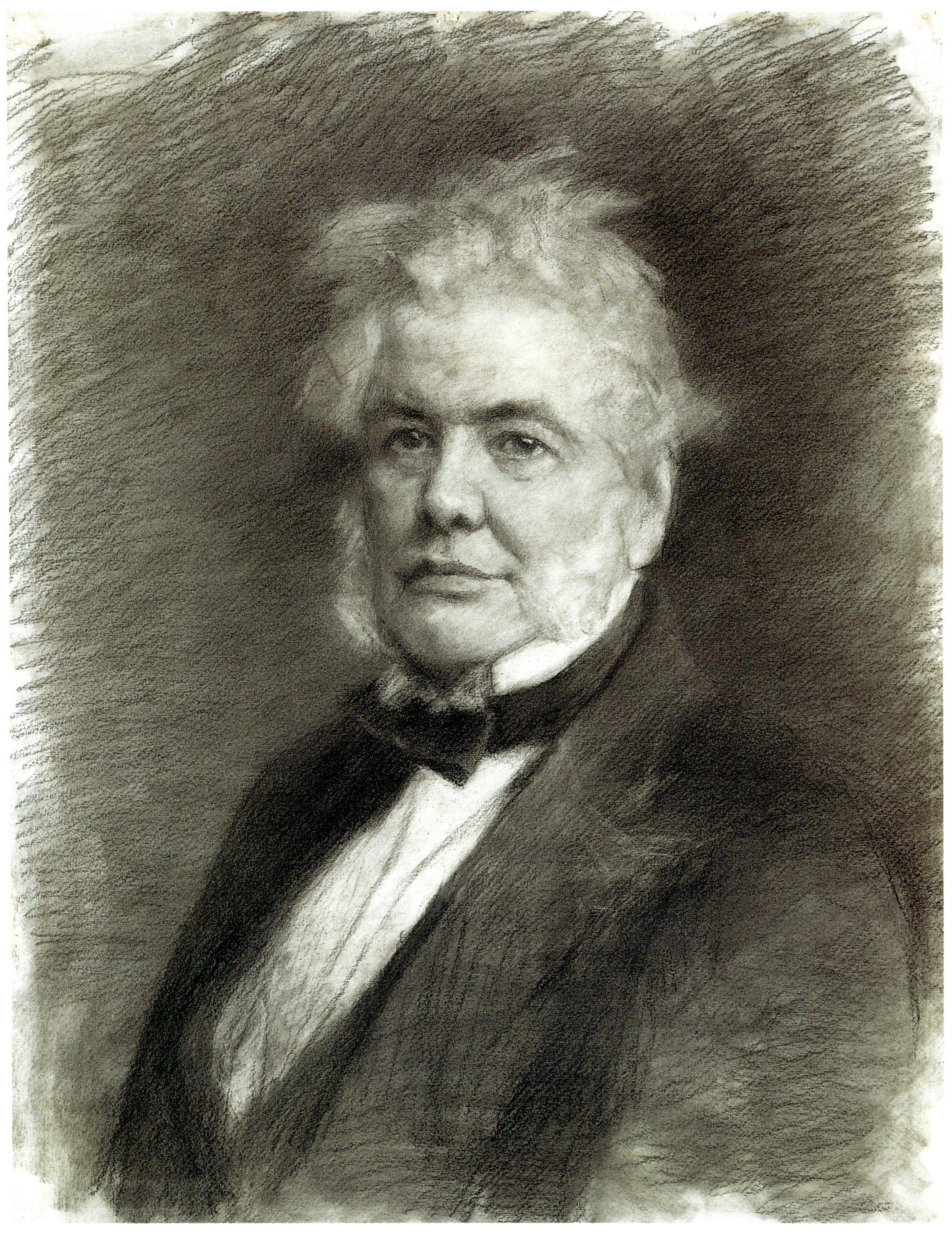

The two portraits of W.K. Magee (1868–1961), like that of Butt (previous page), were among the first commissions resulting from the joint exhibition of Yeats and Hone organized by Sarah Purser in 1901. The exhibition, in the rooms of the Royal Society of Antiquaries, at no. 6, St Stephen's Green – next to JBY's old studio (now occupied by Walter Osborne) – ran for two weeks, from 21 October to 3 November, and was to be the turning point in JBY's career. While financially he was little better off than before, he was now to find himself elected official portraitist of an episode in Irish history which was recognized as historic even as it was unfolding.

Pencil sketches, which he enjoyed, brought him no more than 3 guineas at most. The first likeness of Magee was executed in November 1901, and was commissioned by Lady Gregory to add to the collection of literary portraits she had initiated in 1897. The December sketch belonged to Magee himself.

Both drawings show a man with a neat oval head, a short lock of hair falling on his right temple, the curve of which is echoed in the sickle line of his trim full moustaches – thus interesting shapes are drawn out on an otherwise bland countenance. A bright spot in each eye, indicative of mental alertness, is repeated more dimly on the tip of his nose. Unusually, the artist has spread the light evenly over his face, instead of focussing the attention on a bright forehead. But the triangle of gleaming spots – in counterpoint to the moustache droop, and more muted in the December drawing – immediately creates a centre of visual interest, suggesting a self-contained character, and determined, according to his firm mouth and decisive chin. Collar and tie are precisely in place, the coat (in as much as it is described) is dapper.

JBY sees a silent man. In the first drawing he listens rather distantly, holding himself back, but nevertheless communicating slightly. The following month, in the December drawing, he represented the sitter perhaps as he had requested, in a more formal way, half turned to the right, eyes downcast, looking away reflectively. The mood now is subdued, the shadows lighter, he is carried away in his own thoughts.

William Kirkpatrick Magee was born in Dublin, the son of a Presbyterian minister, and was Assistant Librarian at the time in the National Library of Ireland. One of A.E.'s *protégés*, referred to by WBY as "AE's farmyard", he edited *Dana* in 1904, and wrote occasional, often acid, essays and articles under the pseudonym 'John Eglinton', some of which were published at Dun Emer in 1905. JBY, writing from America, remembered his "logical mind"; he also noted his "trick of criticism" to which he adds "an admiration for the *fait accompli* which makes him turn eyes of admiration so constantly on things English". Magee later retired to Wales and then to England, rather than remain in the newly constituted Free State. He published *A Memoir of AE* after Russell's death. Another half-length sketch of Magee by JBY, dated 1905, is in Colby College, Maine.

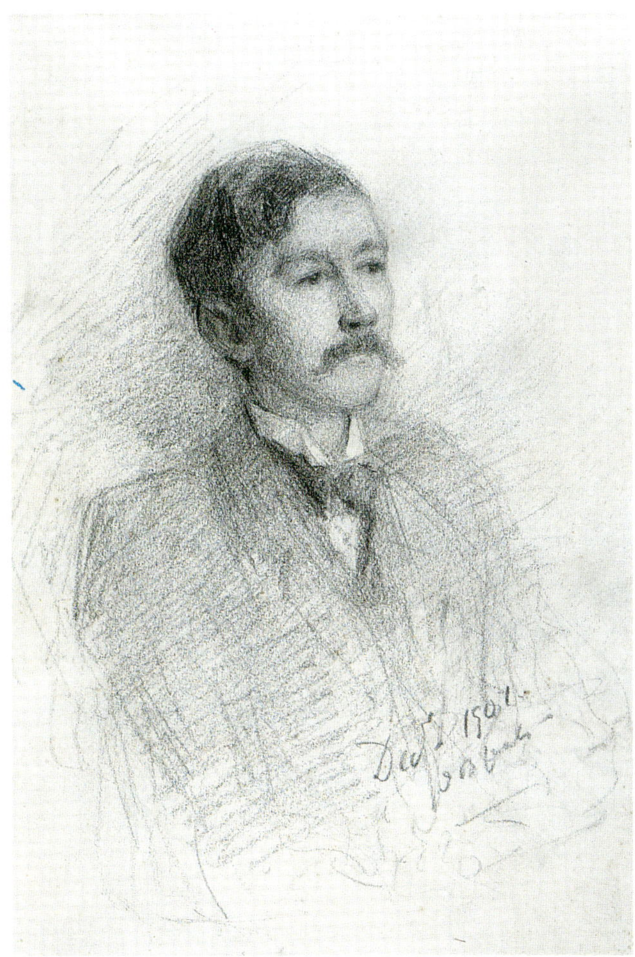

W.K. Magee

December 1901, pencil on unevenly cut buff paper,
38 × 26.8 cm, NGI 2985

W.K. Magee

November 1901, pencil on buff paper, 29.2 × 21.3cm, NGI 2944

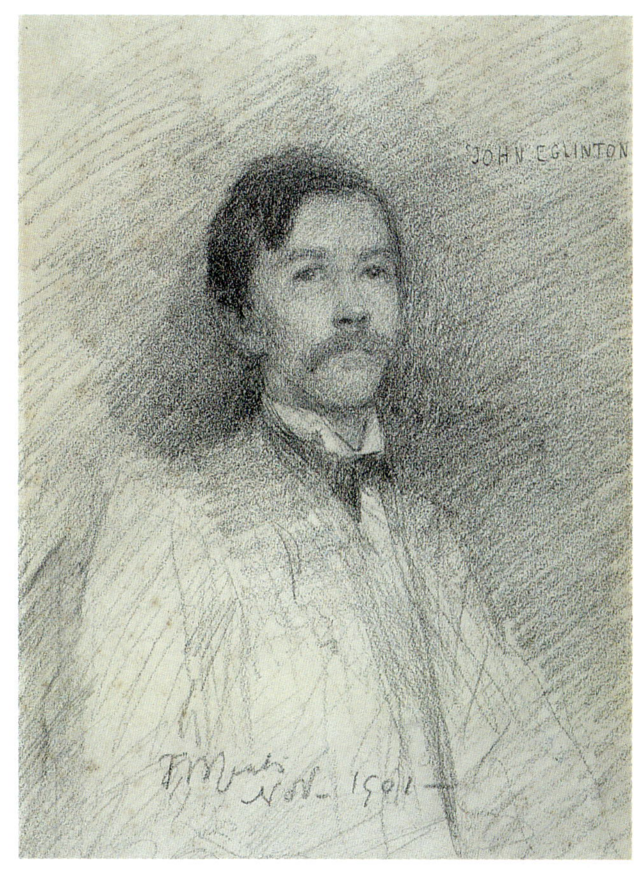

While JBY's exhibition had given him an *entrée* into Dublin society, and his old friends did not stint the hospitality that gave him opportunities to meet potential sitters, he was no more forward in acquiring commissions than he had ever been, and he was still diffident about financial matters. He demanded only £5 for his portrait of Mrs Lenny, whom he had probably met at some dinner party – this was at a time when he should have been in a position to charge ten times that amount.

And his portrait lacks zest. One suspects the artist had little interest in his sitter. Her age was not a problem – he painted, and continued to paint, the patriarchal John O'Leary. But with Mrs Lenny, to start with, conversation was lacking. The old lady, an old-fashioned white cap covering her grey hair, looks patiently, slightly anxiously, at him, her head inclined. She wears a white shawl over her high-collared dress, of which the blackness is relieved by a gold ornament. While the artist has captured her features and personality skilfully, lighting her face and garments gently from the right, the wine-coloured ground does little to flatter the pale face and the dullness of her cap and wrap – this though JBY was accomplished at painting white, and at making it vibrant. This portrait is a fine example of the type of commission he avoided through his reluctance to go out and seek work. Mrs Lenny may have been difficult. The canvas has been extended along the upper edge, throwing the whole image out of proportion, which suggests that – after it was completed – she insisted that it must fit into a particular frame.

His inbuilt self-deprecation made JBY constantly attempt uncalled-for changes in his work in order to attain the perfection he aimed for. Mrs Lenny, according to the artist Mary Swanzy's account, "kept an eye on old John Yeats when he was painting the portrait, since he was inclined to dwell too much on the lights: and when she considered the picture to be finished she took it from him, had it glazed and framed for exhibition in the RHA. At varnishing day John Yeats removed the glass and decided to improve on the lights, adding a blob of impasto on the right side of the cap."

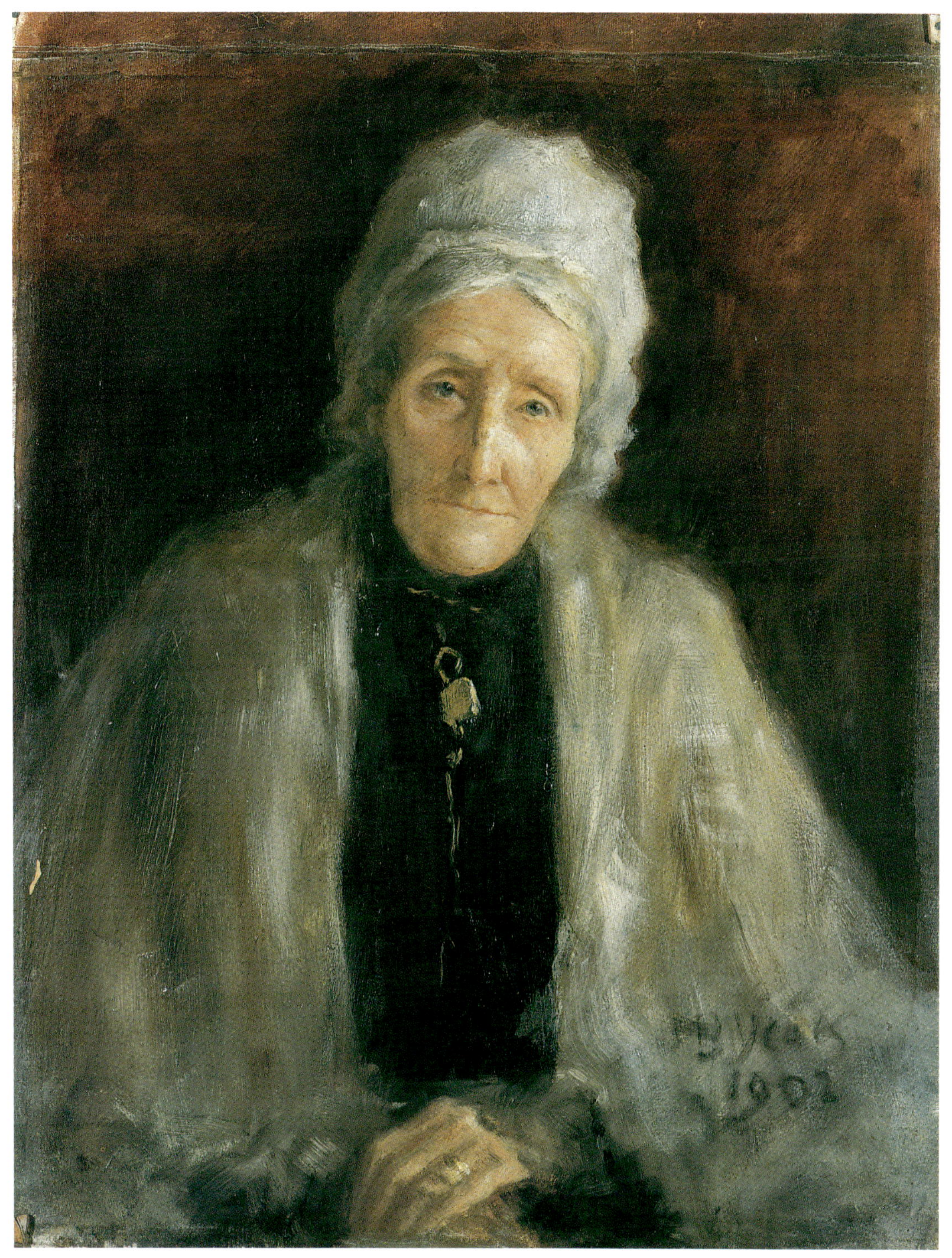

The pencil portrait of Standish James O'Grady (1846–1928) was another commission from Lady Gregory for her gallery of distinguished Irish writers. O'Grady would have been of particular interest to her since they had both re-created the history and legend of Ireland at a time when nationalism bred a craving for the Celtic past and for the recovery of an ancient heritage. O'Grady, the son of a Church of Ireland clergyman in Castletown Berehaven in Cork, had trained as a barrister, but turned from the Bar to journalism, editing *The Daily Express* (Dublin) and later *The Kilkenny Moderator* and founding the short-lived *All-Ireland Review* in 1900. He published his *History of Ireland: Heroic Period* in 1878, and wrote popular historical novels that had a wide-reaching influence. JBY had illustrated O'Grady's *Finn and his Companions*, a story for children published by Fisher Unwin ten years before.

JBY, who had been disappointed about some commissions which had not materialized, confirmed with Lady Gregory in May that she really wanted a likeness of the writer before taking this relaxed portrait, O'Grady leaning back serenely in a chair, looking dreamily into the right distance. The pencilling throughout is dominant, and sometimes dense, leaving no area of paper untouched. The background is diversely scribbled, creating soft directions of movement. The only light is to be found in the sitter's face, which is almost totally without shadow, and the top of the chair against which he rests his head, and to a lesser degree in his hand, which is fully drawn, lying on the chair arm. The other side of his body dissolves into the nebulous gloom of the background.

The drawing has been inscribed, perhaps autographed by O'Grady, across the left-hand corner. JBY sketched him also in 1907, at Sandymount near Dublin (Colby College Collection, Maine). He painted his portrait in oils for Hugh Lane (Hugh Lane Municipal Gallery) and in 1904 did a second oil portrait of O'Grady, this time for John Quinn (see p. 120).

Pencil portrait of Standish James O'Grady

1902, pencil on paper backed by board, 34 × 22.6 cm, NGI 2936

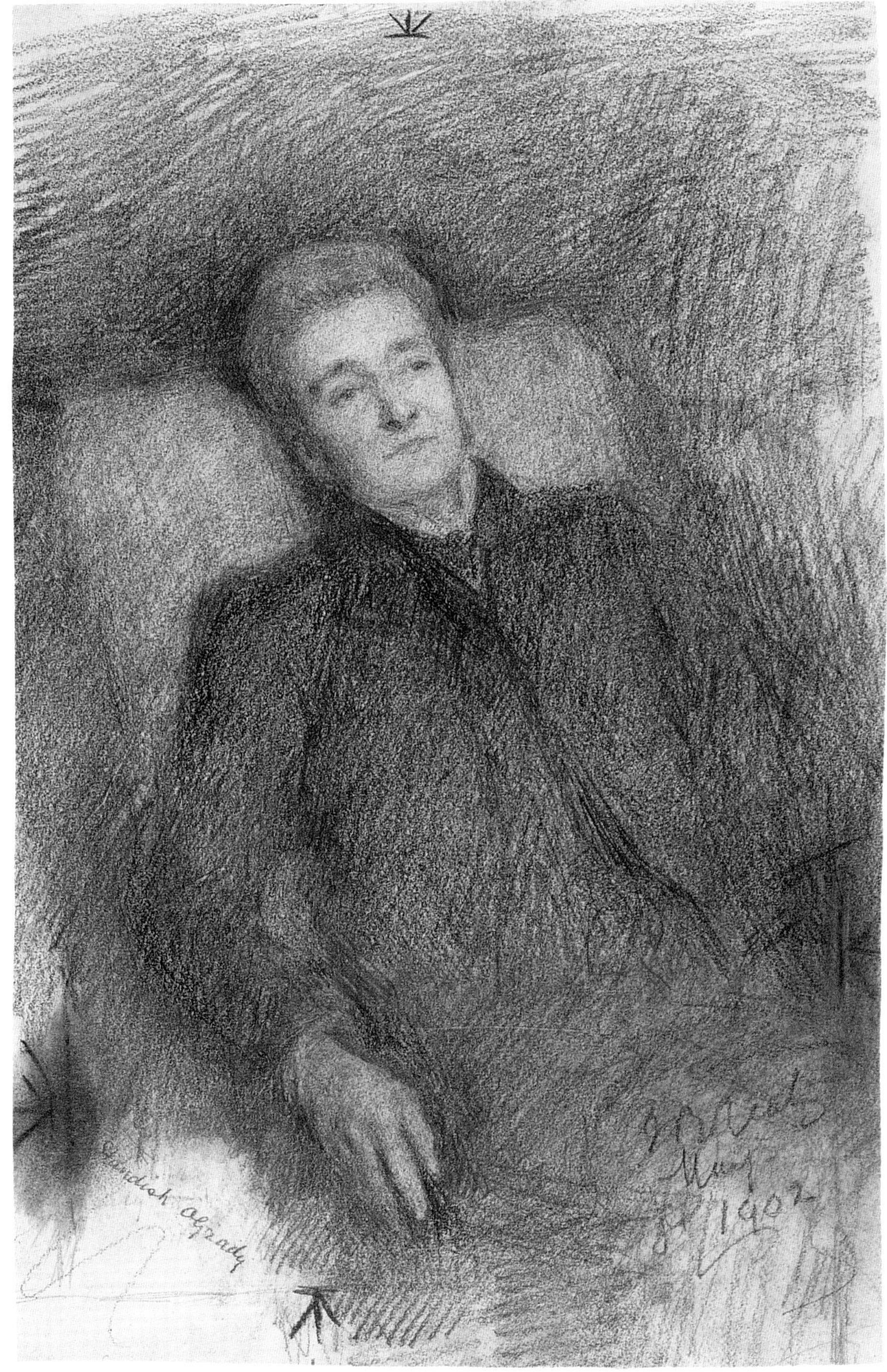

This undated portrait of the German scholar of Celtic languages, Kuno Meyer (1858–1919), taken from a sketchbook, is thought to date from 1903, when JBY was making sketch portraits of other scholars such as Walter Starkie and Father Dineen (sketchbooks, Michael Yeats Collection). Another pencil portrait of Meyer, dating from March 1903, is in Sligo Museum. Here the artist has depicted the head and shoulders turned to the right, the side of the face silhouetted against the buff paper. Dr Meyer's hair has receded, revealing a broad handsome crown above deep-set thoughtful eyes which are gazing into the distance. He has a branching moustache and a thick trim beard, and a slightly obstinate look; though JBY has concentrated on the expression of dedication and self-confidence reflected in eyes that burn with loyalty to *das Vaterland*. JBY has made a powerful portrait head, cross-hatched around the collar, and then finished it off with a looping scribble line which wanders at will, and completes the image intriguingly.

Kuno Meyer, born in Hamburg and educated at Leipzig University, was a lecturer in Teutonic languages at Liverpool University, and later took the chair of Celtic Philology in Berlin. With R.I. Best (who owned the drawing for many years before bequeathing it to the National Gallery of Ireland) and John Strachan, he founded the Dublin School of Irish Learning in 1903.

About the time JBY returned to Ireland they became friendly. Intellectually they must have found each other's company stimulating. In March 1907, JBY dined with Meyer and Oliver Elton; but years later, in New York, he remarked to Elton with distaste how Meyer took colour from his environment like a chameleon. Despite the fact that he had been employed in England for years, Meyer had come to New York shortly after the War started as an agent for the German cause. When the *Lusitania* went down, torpedoed by the Germans, JBY cooled towards him. "The *Lusitania* stands forever between me and Kuno Meyer", he wrote to his brother Isaac.

Kuno Meyer is now remembered for his translations of Old Irish Poetry, including 'The Hermit's Song' and 'The Crucifixion'.

Pencil portrait of Kuno Meyer

ca. 1903, pencil on paper, 19.7 × 11.9 cm, NGI 3311

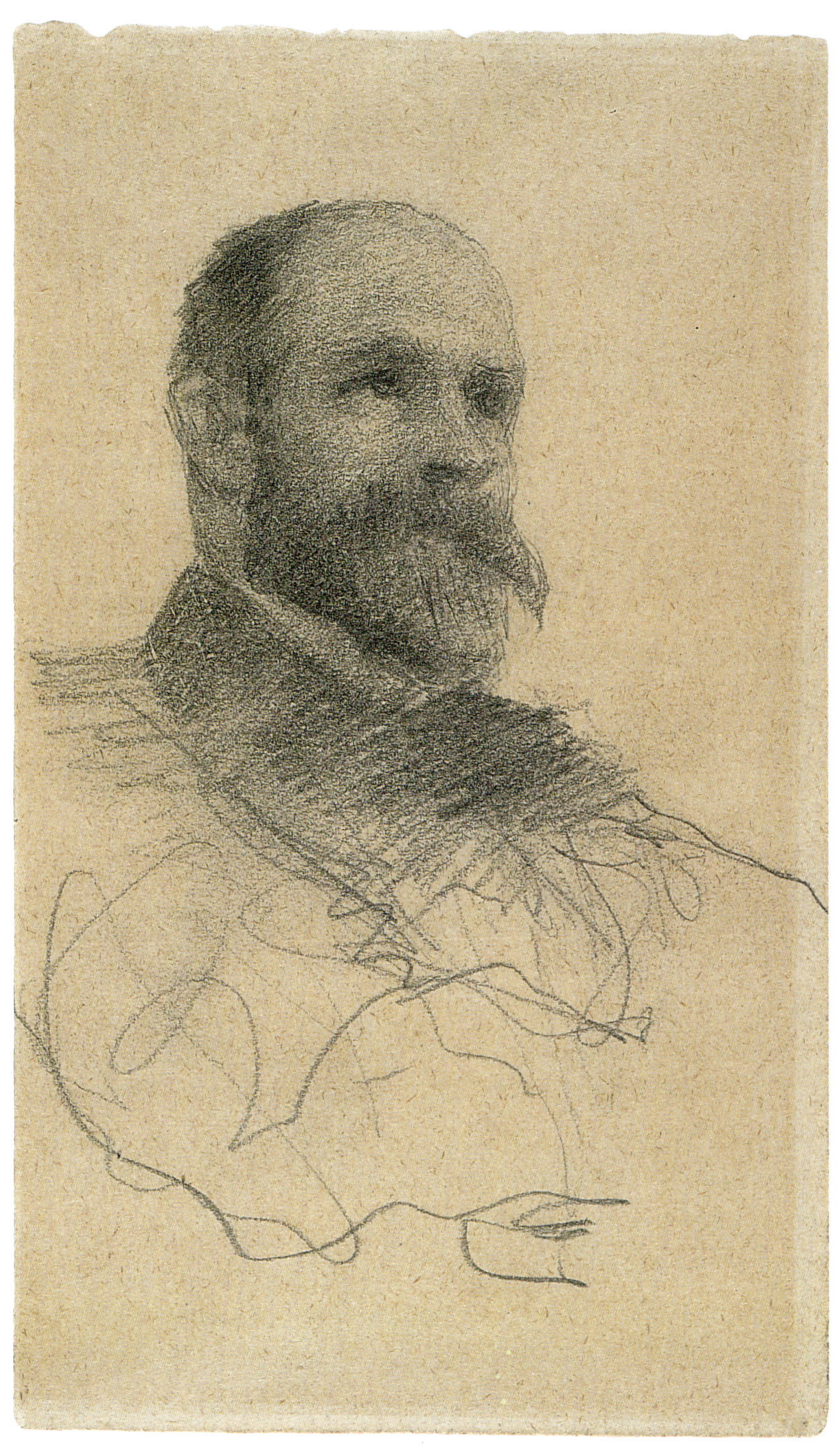

During the spring of 1903, Hugh Lane commissioned from JBY twenty head-and-shoulders portraits of luminaries, Irish or part-Irish, for his modern gallery. He was supportive in helping JBY to retrieve his old studio at no. 7, St Stephen's Green; but JBY found the choice of sitters, many drawn from the Dublin establishment, a burden. Even with sitters more to his liking he worked slowly.

He painted Douglas Hyde (Hugh Lane Municipal Gallery), one of the twenty, at Coole, where they were both guests; and Lady Gregory's sister-in-law, Mrs Algernon Persse, pleased with the portrait, requested JBY to paint her for a fee of £25. He took years off her age, as those who saw her picture exhibited at the RHA in 1904 felt; and Lady Gregory, painted at the same time, looks like a startled schoolgirl. It is a charming portrait, but it completely misses the forceful, incipiently arrogant, nature of the sitter which was caught so convincingly in a bust by Epstein (Hugh Lane Municipal Gallery), also commissioned by Lane, and by Orpen (National Gallery of Ireland). At the same time, those portraits lack the warmth that JBY's painting undoubtedly conveys.

JBY had told Lady Gregory some years before (26 August 1899), "When Jack's wife with wifely glee told how Jack did everything you told him to do, my brother

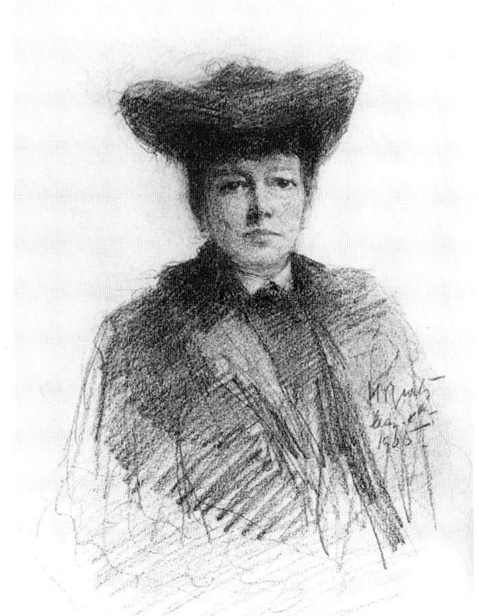

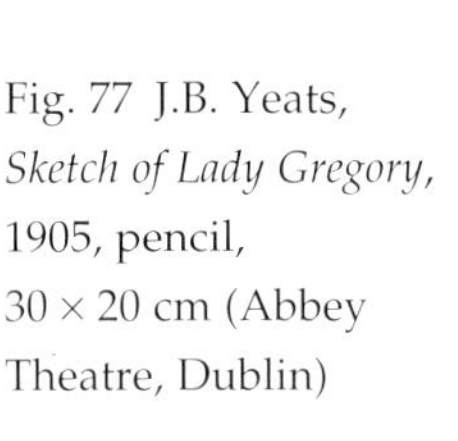
Fig. 77 J.B. Yeats, *Sketch of Lady Gregory*, 1905, pencil, 30 × 20 cm (Abbey Theatre, Dublin)

said, 'there is no resisting those courageous eyes' "; and he seemingly remembered Isaac's comment when painting this portrait, concentrating on the clear hazel eyes gazing steadily out of the picture. Her expressive eyebrows, the long nose and mobile characterful mouth are there, but subordinate to the eyes filled with a heroic light.

The artist has painted her bust length, wearing a dark-blue jacket over a dress with a high collar decorated with lace. Above it, her complexion appears quite red. Her hair is drawn back severely. She has been placed far down in the canvas, which is unusual with JBY, and which contributes to the diminution of her image. Green-gold paint dances in the background. This has been applied sparingly, so that the texture of the canvas is very apparent: and it may be that Lady Gregory removed the picture as soon as she felt it was finished, before he might be tempted to overpaint it.

Isabella Augusta Persse, aunt of Hugh Lane, was one of the younger daughters of Dudley Persse, of Roxborough, County Galway. She married Sir William Gregory, twice her age, in 1880, and went to live at Coole Park. They shared literary interests and a liking for travel. After his death she edited his letters, and collected local folklore, which she translated from Irish and published in popular form. In 1897, she met W.B. Yeats and invited him to Coole. With Edward Martyn, they formed the Irish Literary Theatre, which led to the foundation of the Abbey Theatre in Dublin in 1904, for which they both wrote plays. Her influence on W.B. Yeats was great. "She has been to me mother, friend, sister and brother," WBY wrote. "I cannot realise the world without her – she brought to my wavering thoughts steadfast nobility." JBY and Jack Yeats also shared her hospitality and patronage; and her collection of pencil portraits commissioned from JBY probably inspired Quinn and Lane to commission their series of oil portraits. But JBY reacted against her influence over his son – and this may have been a factor when he came to paint her portrait.

Lady Gregory
1903, oil on canvas, 62 × 52 cm, NGI 1318

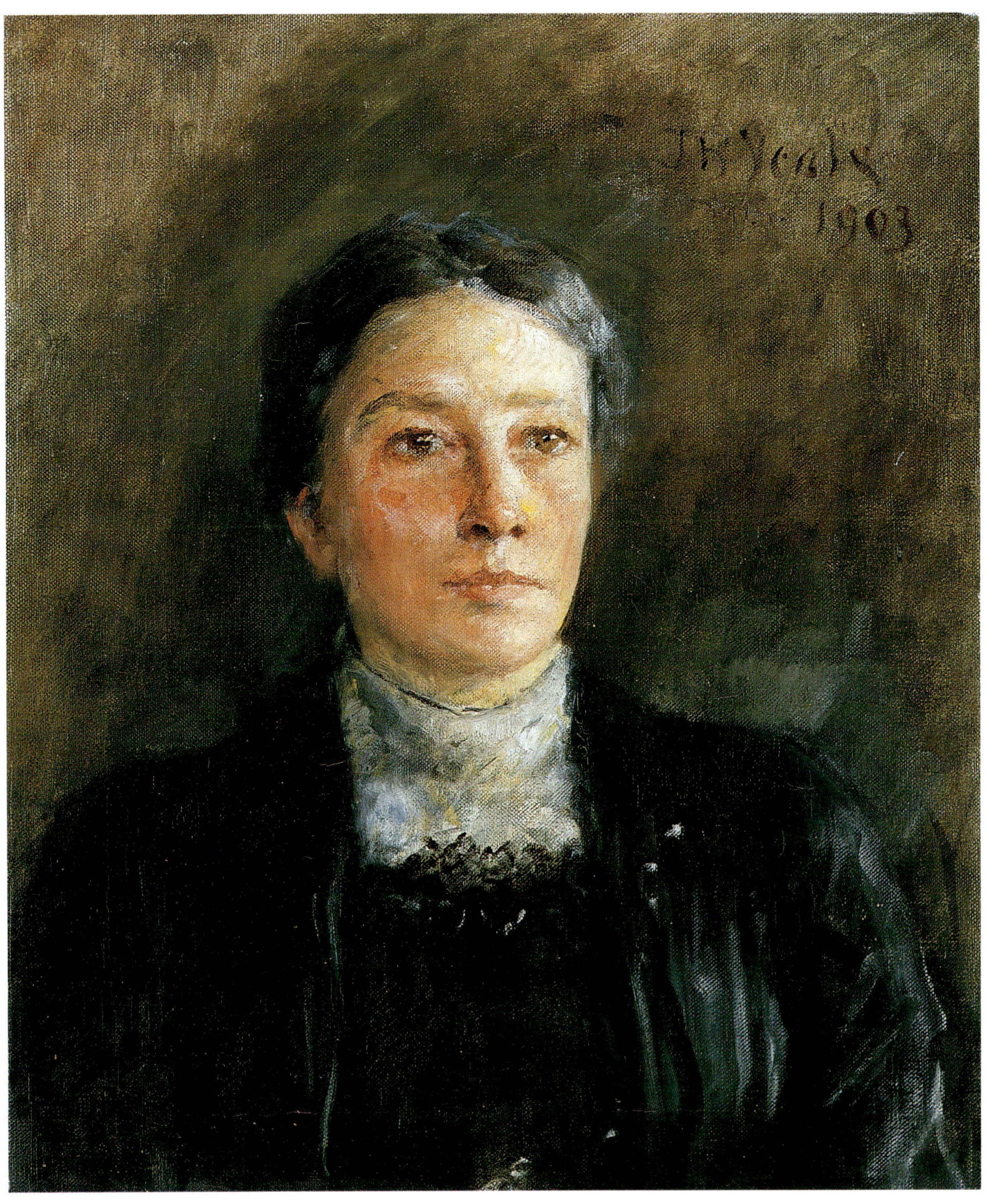

When John Quinn, the American lawyer turned collector, came to Ireland in 1902, he purchased from JBY the portrait of WBY (p. 96) in which he had been interested, and commissioned portraits of O'Leary, Hyde and Russell, for £20 each (see also pp. 82–87). According to Russell (A.E.), JBY had already embarked on his portrait in August. "My Sundays are engaged sitting to your father who is working on a portrait some eccentric American wants painted of me," he told WBY. The portrait was not finished until 1903, when Yeats persuaded Quinn to let him submit it to the RHA for the annual exhibition. JBY was to paint another portrait of A.E., for the foyer of the Abbey Theatre, the following year (fig. 78).

Quinn also commissioned a sketch of A.E. for reproduction in the book of poetry which he was helping the author to publish, and it was ready by May 1903. JBY was dissatisfied with the first version and made a second sketch. "I think it is better myself," Russell informed Quinn. "I am fierce occasionally, but not so fierce as in the first sketch, and am vain enough to wish this more placid likeness which I send would appear instead." This oil portrait, which preceded the sketch, is certainly not placid, but what fierceness it has is probably the result of the artist's endeavour to capture the sitter's visionary eyes, which (ringed by the frame of his monocle) look like those of an eagle or hawk. Though it is not dissimilar from the pencil portrait of 1898 (p. 87) in approach, JBY has captured a greater, perhaps a more mature, intensity in the mystic poet/painter's gaze. A.E. looks directly at the viewer – and beyond. He communicates in his usual warm way, but looks through at the same time to some world on a higher plane that is visible only to himself.

He sits on an upright library chair, with two knob finials on the back and fluting detail down the uprights of the arms, leaning his arms in a relaxed way, his long legs crossed, and the portrait gives a clear impression of his height even though it is only a three-quarter view. His thick brown hair falls casually on his brow; his lips, buried in his thick beard, seem to part. His fair skin is set off by the brightness of his white collar, and by the blue of his suit and his necktie. The painter has paid attention to his "long fingered visionary" hands, which, with the tilt of his arms, seem to counterpoint his head from below. JBY seemed to find shapes and movements to make his portraits visually interesting and alive. Behind, and all around Russell, a reddy gold ground complements the colour of his suit, besides suggesting an aura of harmonious light.

George Russell, the Lurgan-born mystic, friend and colleague of WBY, always published his poetry and signed his paintings with his pseudonym, 'A.E.'. A member of the Dublin branch of the Theosophical Society for ten years, before being employed by the Irish Agricultural Organisation Society as a banks' organizer, he later became a founder member of the Dublin Hermetic Society. He was involved with the Irish National Theatre Society for a time, and became editor of *The Irish Homestead* from 1905, continuing as editor of *The Irish Statesman*, which Sir Horace Plunkett founded in its place. He played a crucial rôle on the Peace Committee formed during the 1913 Strike in Dublin, and also in the Irish Home Rule Convention of 1917. Today he is remembered for his paintings rather than for his poetry, visionary landscapes in an inimitable style, peopled by beings from a divine world.

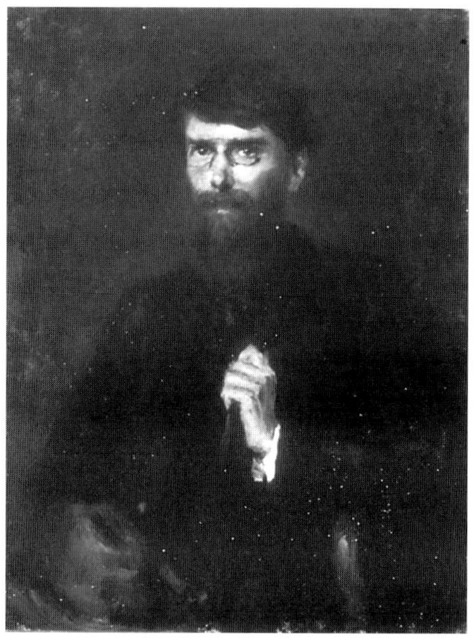

Fig. 78 J.B. Yeats, *George William Russell (A.E.)*, 1904, oil on canvas, 112 × 87 cm (Abbey Theatre, Dublin)

George William Russell (A.E.)

1903, oil on canvas, 112 × 87 cm, NGI 871

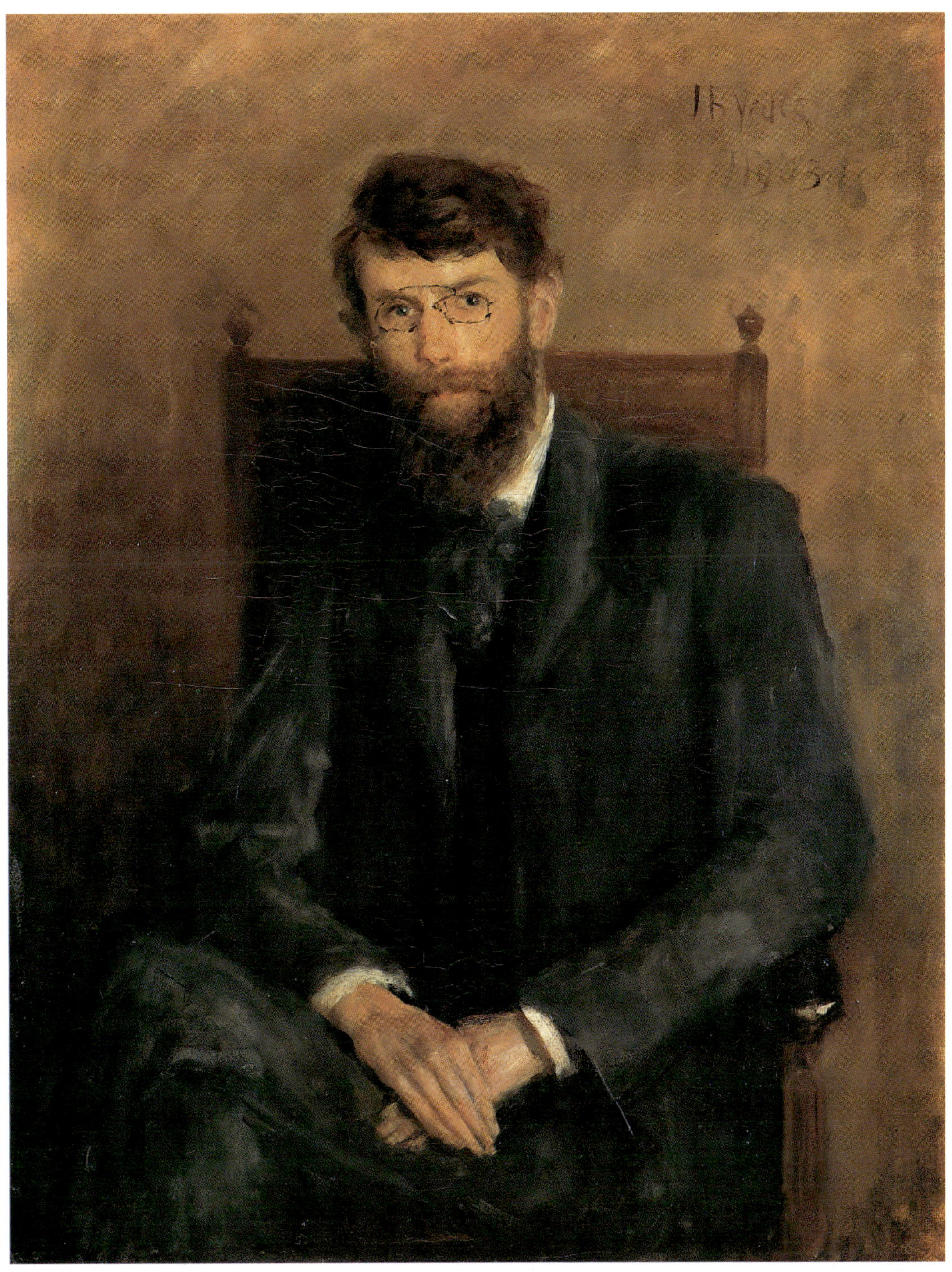

JBY had a great respect for Hugh Lane, but they did not always agree, and Lane's impatience to see his commission (see p. 112) completed made the artist even more uncertain of himself. Lady Gregory remembered that JBY "had not liked being interrupted in the heat of argument by having his clothes brushed from neck to ankle by Hugh". He resented Lane putting roses in the bowls in the studio. While JBY exulted at his success with Sir Antony MacDonell (Hugh Lane Gallery; MacDonell's family thought it made him "look like the devil"), he found three sittings with the Viceroy, Lord Dudley, and with John Redmond, leader of the Irish Party (who refused to come back), not sufficient, and told Lady Gregory, "I cannot work miracles in three sittings." She felt that other portraits commissioned from him – Synge, Plunkett, Edward Dowden and William Fay – were not his best work: "He has the artist's caprice of choosing his own subject, he does not work well in bonds."

Lane decided to resolve the situation in a competition with William Orpen, which JBY approached happily as he divined that Orpen – younger than his sons, but his rival – painted "like an old master", while he himself was "modern and impressionist". They were both to paint Lane's sister Ruth. Lane found Orpen to be the successful contestant, and asked him to complete the commission given to JBY, to do MacDonell again, with Birrell, Mahaffy and Davitt, all now in the Hugh Lane Gallery.

JBY never showed any resentment, and was probably relieved to be free of politicians and diplomats. His portrait of Ruth Lane is a sympathetic one, intimate rather than commanding – Lane, who commissioned her portrait from Mancini a year later, evidently favoured more formal, showy work. The young woman sits at a slant in an upright chair, of which the back is vaguely seen to the left, but looks toward the viewer with big lustrous eyes, very like those of her brother. Her dark hair is piled up in a simple fashion on her head and parted in front, exposing a wide fair forehead – making it almost square, in much the same way as in a photograph of her as a child. She wears no jewellery, only a simple grey dress with a band of red and yellow and a ruched frill about the neckline, finished with a tiny bow. A stole is cast carelessly around her.

Augusta Ruth Lane (1880–1959) was the daughter of Adelaide Persse, Lady Gregory's sister, who had made an unfortunate marriage with the Reverend James William Lane. The only surviving sister among four brothers, she was always close to Hugh, and is said to have played a crucial part in the drawing up of his original will. When her parents separated in 1893, she spent part of the time in Germany with her father and the other part with her mother in Dublin. In 1905, she married James Hickman Shine, a country gentleman of the south of Ireland, who died in 1912. She then joined Hugh at his house in Cheyne Walk, London, and looked after Lady Wolseley's garden at Glynde. According to Lord Wolseley she was the most beautiful girl he had ever seen. Subsequently she married Captain T.C. Heaven, who died less than a year later.

She told Alec Martin, who negotiated the sale for Thomas MacGreevy, who later presented the picture to the National Gallery, "I was 'sitting' for about six weeks, he probably got bored with the sitter, I got rather tired myself!"

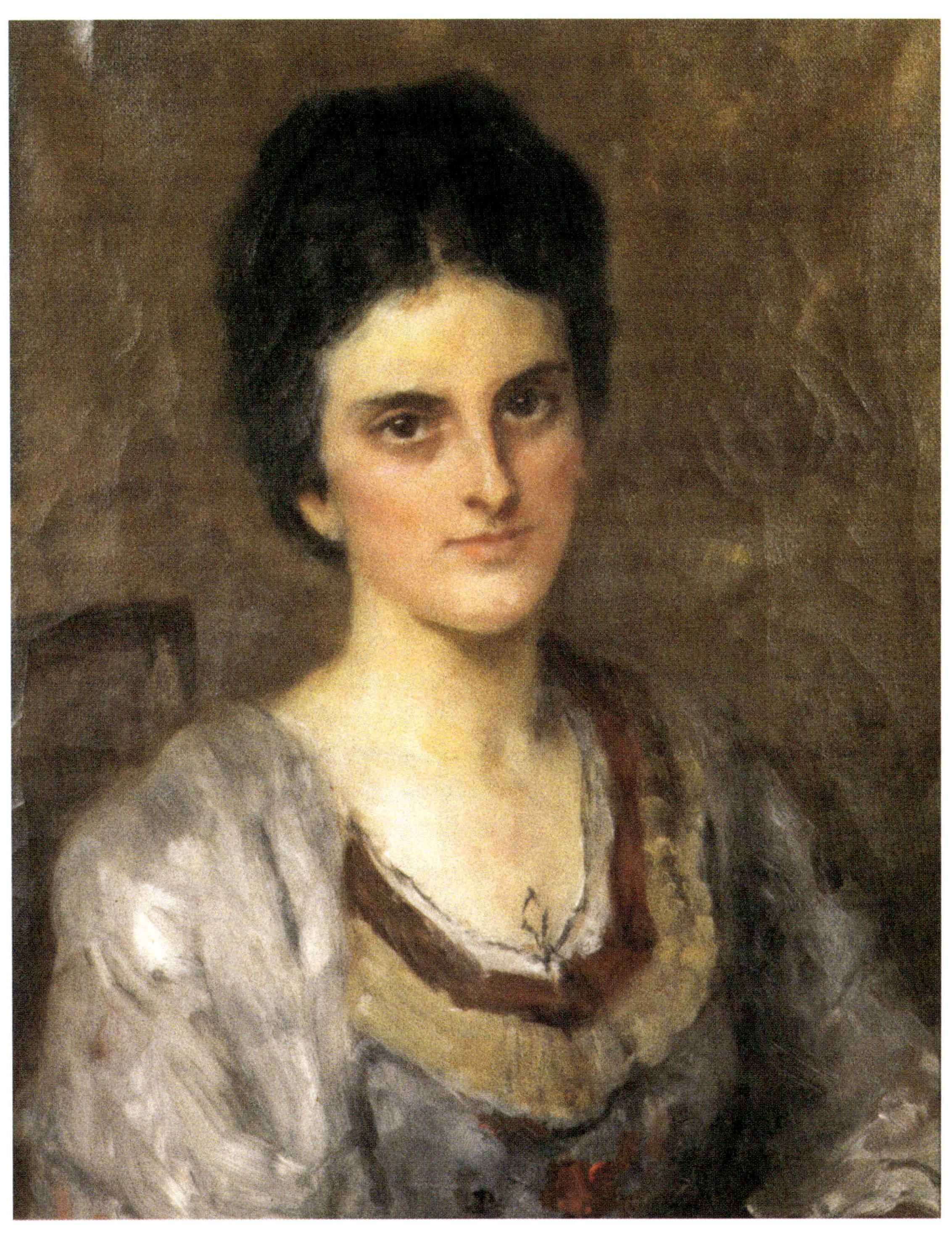

Ruth Lane

1904, oil on canvas, 60 × 51.5 cm, NGI 1800

JBY's portrait of John O'Leary painted for John Quinn is undoubtedly the masterpiece of his career. He had known O'Leary well since his return from exile, both in Dublin and London. He had painted his portrait twice before (pp. 76 and 82). There are numerous sketches indicating that O'Leary was of great interest to him artistically. WBY thought his great head "worthy of a Roman coin". JBY sees him in different guises. O'Leary, after his arrest for high treason during the Fenian campaign in 1865, was sentenced to twenty years' penal servitude, five of which were spent in Mountjoy Jail, and in Pentonville and Portland Prisons in England, and fifteen in exile in France. In NGI 1963 he has the alertness of a man let out from the dark; NGI 595 casts him as a thinker; NGI 869 is like an amalgamation of the two. A photograph of him, taken at prison only hours after receiving his sentence, has the same aspect of thoughtful suffering, the deep furrows under the eyes, as in the 1904 portrait.

JBY conceived the portrait in magnificent Venetian style, with a swathe of curtain behind the patriarchal image, which is life-size, yet towering and portentous, with compelling eyes evocative of ageless wisdom. He is seated quite casually in a library chair with padded arms, on which his elbows rest. One leg is thrown over the other, and he looks straight at the viewer, his slender-fingered hand lying on the broad brim of the voyageur's hat perched on his knee. He wears a dark-grey coat and grey suit, with a glimpse of white shirt at his breast. His golden brown hair, parted always in the same way, is longer now, more wavy, and shot with white. The artist, who made a feature of the square luxuriance of the beard in previous portrayals, now emphasizes its length and whiteness. Despite his increased age, O'Leary's eyes are as bright and blue as ever. He is illuminated with a brilliance from the left, which casts deep shadows about his nose; and the background is golden brown, complementary with the greys of his garments. The portrait is painted in the artist's most flowing 'impressionist' manner, and he is obviously inspired and exhilarated by this further visual encounter with a man for whom he had such admiration.

John O'Leary, after editing *Poems and Ballads of Young Ireland* with WBY, published his *Recollections of Fenians and Fenianism* in 1896 and two years later became President of the 1798 Association – his badge of office is in the National Museum. At the beginning of the Boer War, he made himself unpopular with the authorities as head of the newly formed Transvaal Committee, encouraging support for the Boer cause. Whistler remained a friend from his early Paris days, and visited Dublin especially to see him, and to dine with him at the Shelbourne Hotel on 20 August 1900. O'Leary died in Dublin on 16 March 1907, not long before JBY himself left Ireland. "Romantic Ireland's dead and gone," wrote WBY, "it's with O'Leary in the grave."

The portrait was exhibited almost immediately, at Lane's exhibition of Irish art in the London Guildhall in the spring of 1904. After he moved to New York, JBY exhibited with the Independents (April 1910), borrowing the *John O'Leary* from Quinn; and the portrait was exhibited with the Independents again in November 1910.

John O'Leary

1904, oil on canvas, 112 × 87 cm, NGI 869

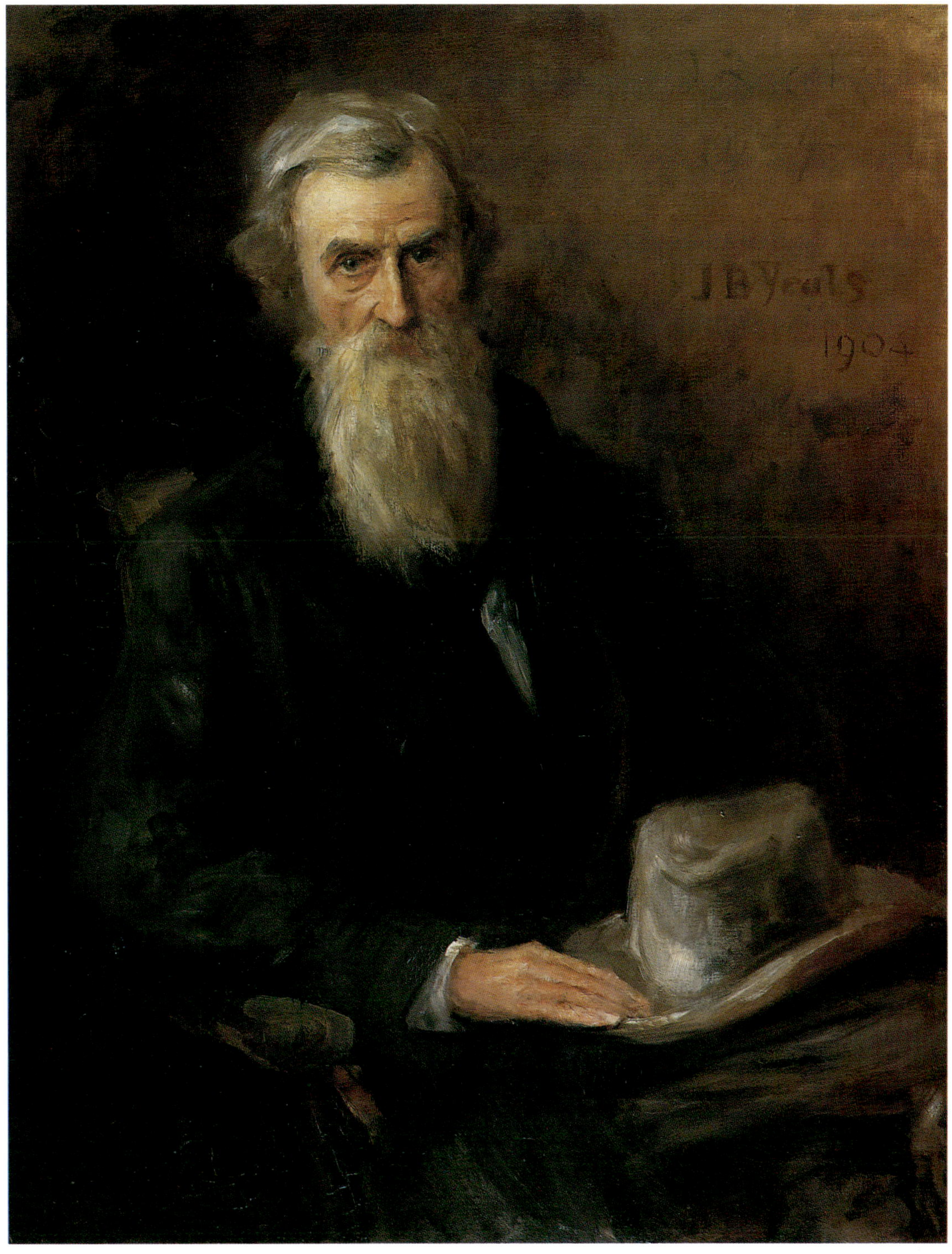

JBY received Quinn's commission to paint Standish James O'Grady (see also p. 108) in 1903, "which, however," he told Rosa Butt, as he was going off to Coole, "is quite hopeless and impossible – tho' he also is shortly to be at Lady Gregory's" (20 August 1903; Bodleian Library). The following year he was still having difficulties getting O'Grady to sit, though the price had been agreed, £20. At the end of October Quinn and the O'Gradys met at the Abbey Theatre, and Quinn enlisted Mrs O'Grady's help: O'Grady was finally persuaded to attend JBY's studio the next morning.

Even then there were difficulties: O'Grady was wearing a blue tie, which JBY metamorphosed into red, but Quinn wanted a white tie, and went out and bought one. "The precious hour and a half that he was there," Quinn told Lily, "was largely taken up by the interruptions of five or six 'irrelevant' persons, who seemed to have plenty of time to loaf and who didn't seem to care whether they wasted each other's time". The following Sunday, Quinn visited JBY, and found him working the hands from an "oversize model". "Quinn suggested that Colum pose, but Colum's hands proved too small, and so Quinn ended up posing himself until two-thirty, when he went off to the Nassau Hotel to dinner with Lady Gregory and W.B. Yeats."

Nevertheless the artist painted a splendid large and authoritative portrait, on a par with the O'Leary canvas (see previous page), though hardly so romantic. JBY had already painted O'Grady for a group of subscribers (fig. 79; the portrait was later acquired by Hugh Lane), which was when he learned how elusive the writer was. Russell told Lady Gregory (for whom O'Grady was "that 'Fenian Unionist' ... who had carried the heroic ideas of the Red Branch into the economic questions of the day") that the likeness was "striking, grim though, like some terrible warrior of ancient days. It should have this legend attached to it, 'O'Grady – his Financial period'; that would explain the grim look. Poor Mr. Yeats painted him under difficulties. He was always starting up to walk about the room. The world could not contain his spirit when the financial question incarnated itself in him. It is a path leading to the stars he sees, not the recovery of paltry pence."

This portrait of 1904, which preserves the same earthy background colouring as the Lane painting, is a much more benign portrayal. O'Grady sits in an upright chair, the polished back introducing a square about his shoulders from which his elbows break out. His hands rest relaxedly on a knee and on a chair arm. He is illuminated lightly from the left. His striking face – another potential square – with thick bushy eyebrows above deep-set, shining blue eyes, is framed by his iron-grey hair, by grey sideburns and by the wings of his white collar. The amber glow of his skin contrasts with the austerity of his priest-like dress.

JBY has captured the appearance of an inspired man who has sat down in genial mood, crossed his legs, and made ready to talk at leisure. Apart from his influential writings about the Irish past, O'Grady had been a classicist, and a distinguished hurler and orator, before he commenced his career as a journalist. He visited JBY in New York ten years later, "for enjoyable talks", as JBY wrote to his daughter Lily.

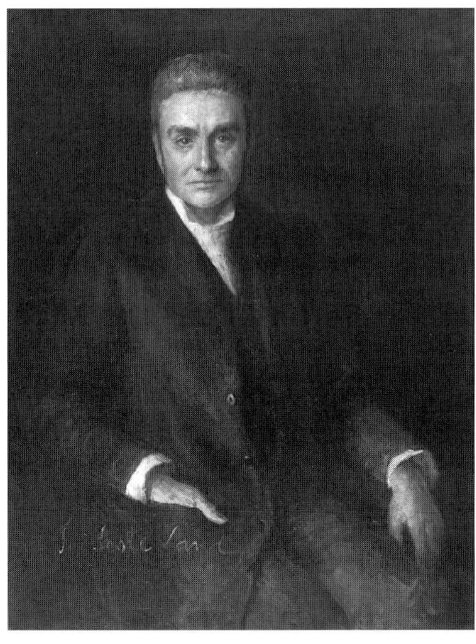

Fig. 79 J.B. Yeats, *Standish James O'Grady*, oil on canvas, 110.5 × 85 cm (Hugh Lane Municipal Gallery, Dublin)

Standish James O'Grady

1904, oil on canvas, 112 × 87 cm, NGI 870

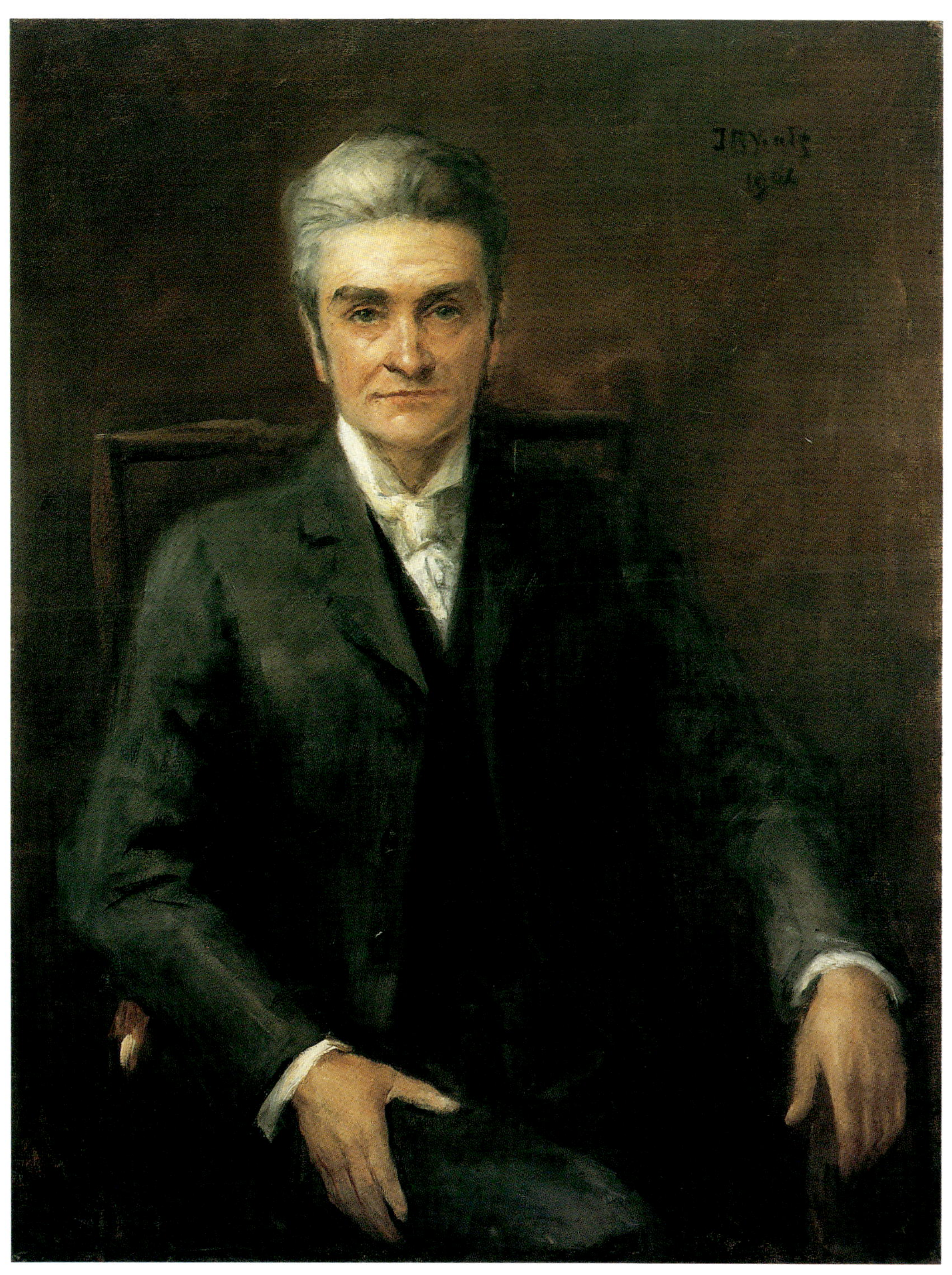

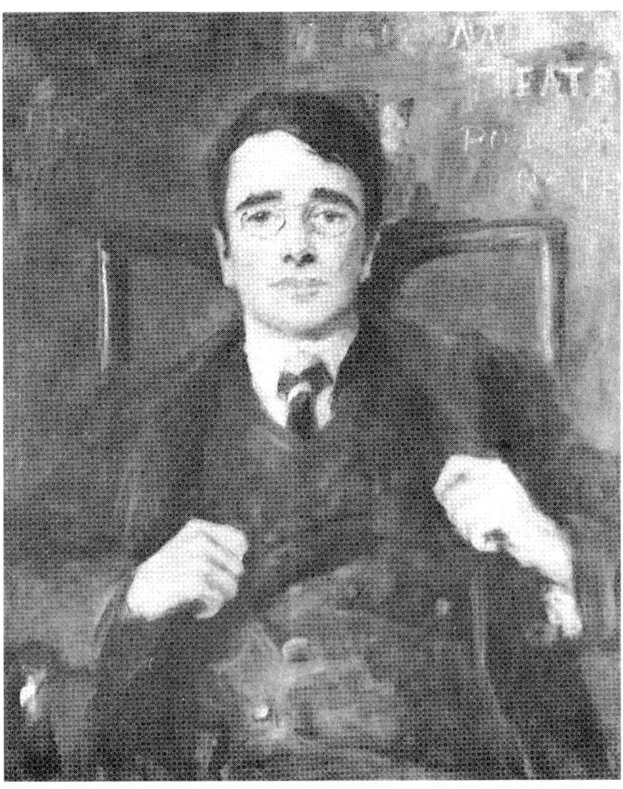

Fig. 80 J.B. Yeats, *W.G. Fay*, 1904, oil on canvas,
111 × 86 cm (Abbey Theatre, Dublin)

JBY made this sketch for Lady Gregory in August 1904, probably independently of the oil he made of the sitter for Hugh Lane and of the Abbey Theatre oil painted earlier in the year (fig. 80), and probably for little or nothing. The likeness might have been taken at rehearsal. Fay is seen in left profile, a long-stemmed pipe in the side of his mouth, looking appraisingly at something, his forehead slightly wrinkled. The head is carefully described with soft shading, the eyes strain through the *pince-nez* balanced on his nose. His body is filled in roughly, one arm propped, on a chair perhaps, the other lying idle along some support in the foreground. Then a fine line has clarified the head and the collar, wandering more coarsely about the rim of his coat.

William George Fay (1872–1947) and his brother Frank, of the Ormonde Dramatic Society and the Inghinidhe na hÉireann theatrical company in Dublin, were natural actors, one a brilliant comedian, the other a beautiful speaker of poetry. They admired WBY's beginnings of a national drama, and joined him and Miss Horniman in creating the Irish National Theatre Society and the Abbey Theatre. A clash of personalities a short time after this portrait was taken resulted in a rift and the foundation by the Fays of the rival dramatic company, the Theatre of Ireland.

JBY and Willie Fay took to each other, the artist finding "the comedian", as he called him, pleasant company, genial and sweet-tempered, either discussing his "engaging" philosophy of life coloured by theosophy, or able to sit in silence without shifting. To Fay, JBY seemed uncontrollably restless while painting his oil portrait. "He walked back and forward all the time, only halting now and again to use a tiny mirror from his pocket to see by reflection how the picture was getting on. Also he talked all the time ... the most entertaining talk ...."

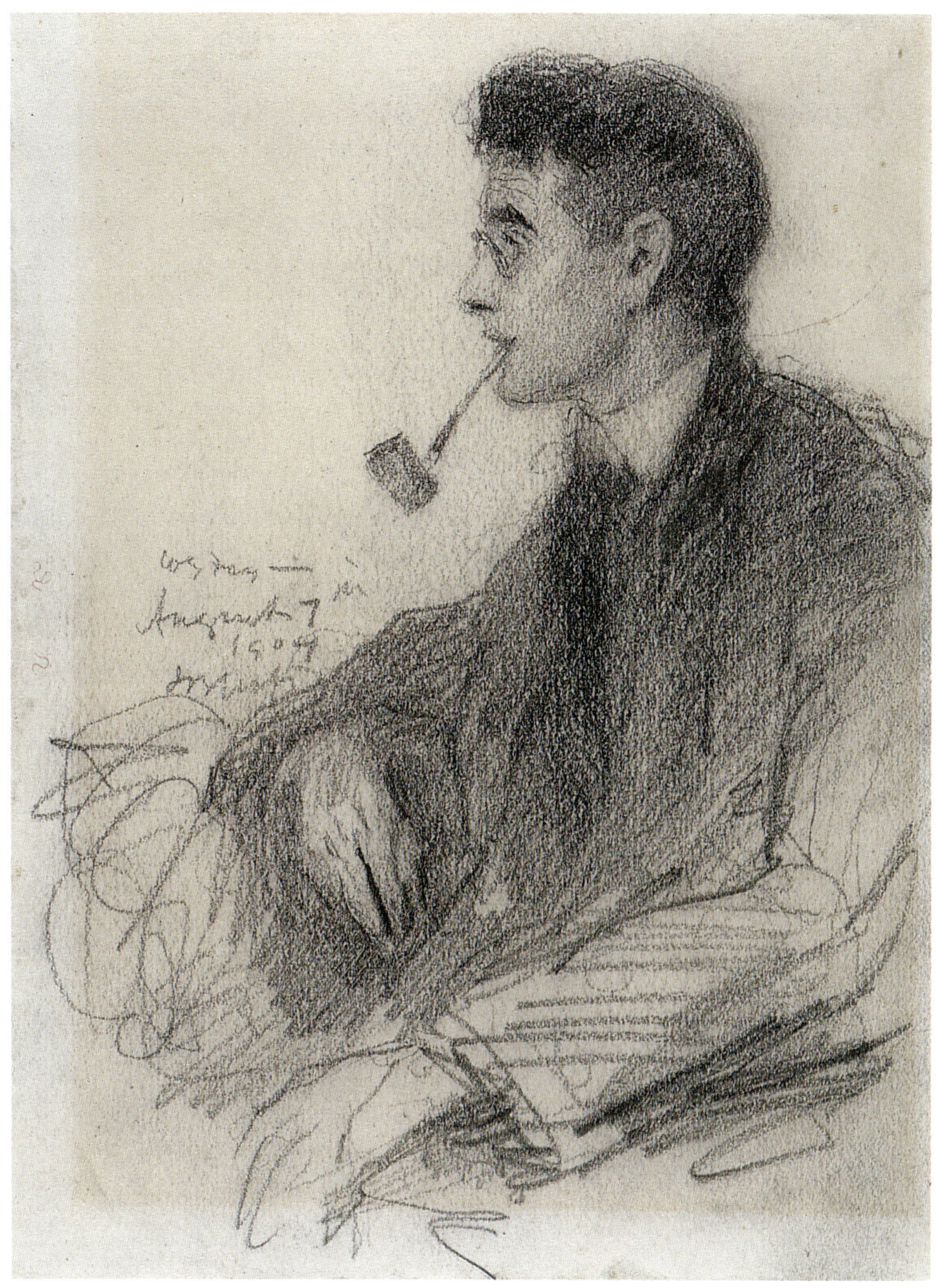

Pencil portrait of William George Fay

1904, pencil on paper, 17.5 × 13.1 cm, NGI 2946

In 1904, JBY painted two portraits of Máire Walker, generally known by her stage name Máire Nic Shiubhlaigh. The portrait which the actress refers to in her book was painted for the Abbey Theatre (fig. 81), and has always hung in the foyers of the old and the new Abbey with the portraits of Lady Gregory, Miss Horniman and the Fay brothers. Lennox Robinson, describing the portraits in the Abbey collection, praised Máire Nic Shiubhlaigh as an actress, adding, "She lacked the power of Sara Allgood and she hadn't the *diablérie* of Sara's sister, Máire O'Neill ... but she had a grace and a charm and a poetic beauty that was all her own."

The smaller portrait, now in the National Gallery, was probably painted first. It was ready to be included in Hugh Lane's ill fated St Louis Exhibition early in 1904, and is less formal than the Abbey picture, where the actress sits in an library chair, against a background of floral paper and wearing a black lace evening dress, her hands folded demurely in her lap. Here she is more relaxed, sitting in a similar high-backed chair, posed likewise at an angle towards the left, but throwing her arms out to rest on the chair arms, and inclining her head back and down towards the viewer, her eyes gazing pensively into the distance.

There is almost a feeling of temperament in the awkward and attractive angle at which she poses, caught so effectively by the artist. She wears a ravishing turquoise dress with a bloused effect, drawn in to a minute waist at odds with her wide shoulders. He has enjoyed finding in her flawless cheeks the pink of the scarf knotted at her throat, just as he has revelled in the floating texture of her gown and the dashes of darker blue there. He relates the colours of her auburn hair and brown eyes, and a warm terracotta tone in her complexion, to the polished wood behind her shoulders; and he has picked these colours up in dancing tones in the deep acquamarine background. It is a painterly, dreamy portrait, and captures all of the "delicacy and charm" remarked on by Lennox Robinson.

Máire Walker was an ardent nationalist, and began her acting career in 1900 in what was one of the smaller nationalist clubs in Dublin, Inginidhe na hÉireann, acting in patriotic *tableaux vivants* at the Antient Concert Rooms in Brunswick Street (now Pearse Street). It was here that she met Willie Fay, and with others they joined WBY in establishing the Irish National Theatre Society, out of which the Abbey Theatre grew. She regarded Frank Fay's insistence on the importance of words and the beauty of the speaking voice as a unique development in theatre, and felt that Yeats's early verse-plays would not have been as effective had it not been for Fay's coaxing forward the peculiar inflections in the Irish voice.

Within a year of the foundation of the Abbey, many of the players, including Nic Shiubhlaigh, withdrew because they felt that the original co-operative policy was not being honoured. As a consequence they set up the Theatre of Ireland, and it was not until November 1910 that Máire Nic Shiubhlaigh was persuaded to act with the Abbey company again.

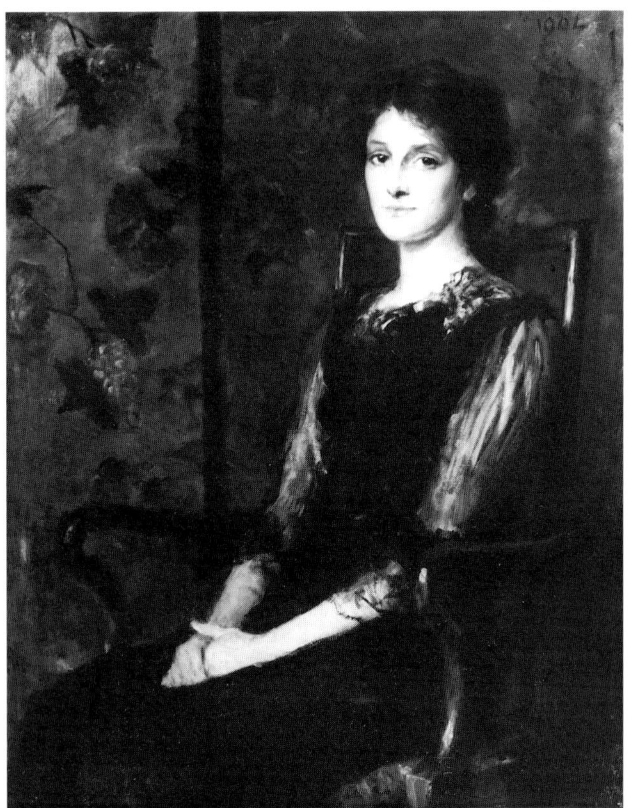

Fig. 81 J.B. Yeats, *Máire Nic Shiubhlaigh*, 1904, oil on canvas, 110 × 85 cm (Abbey Theatre, Dublin)

Máire Nic Shiubhlaigh

1904, oil on canvas, 91 × 71 cm, NGI 4621

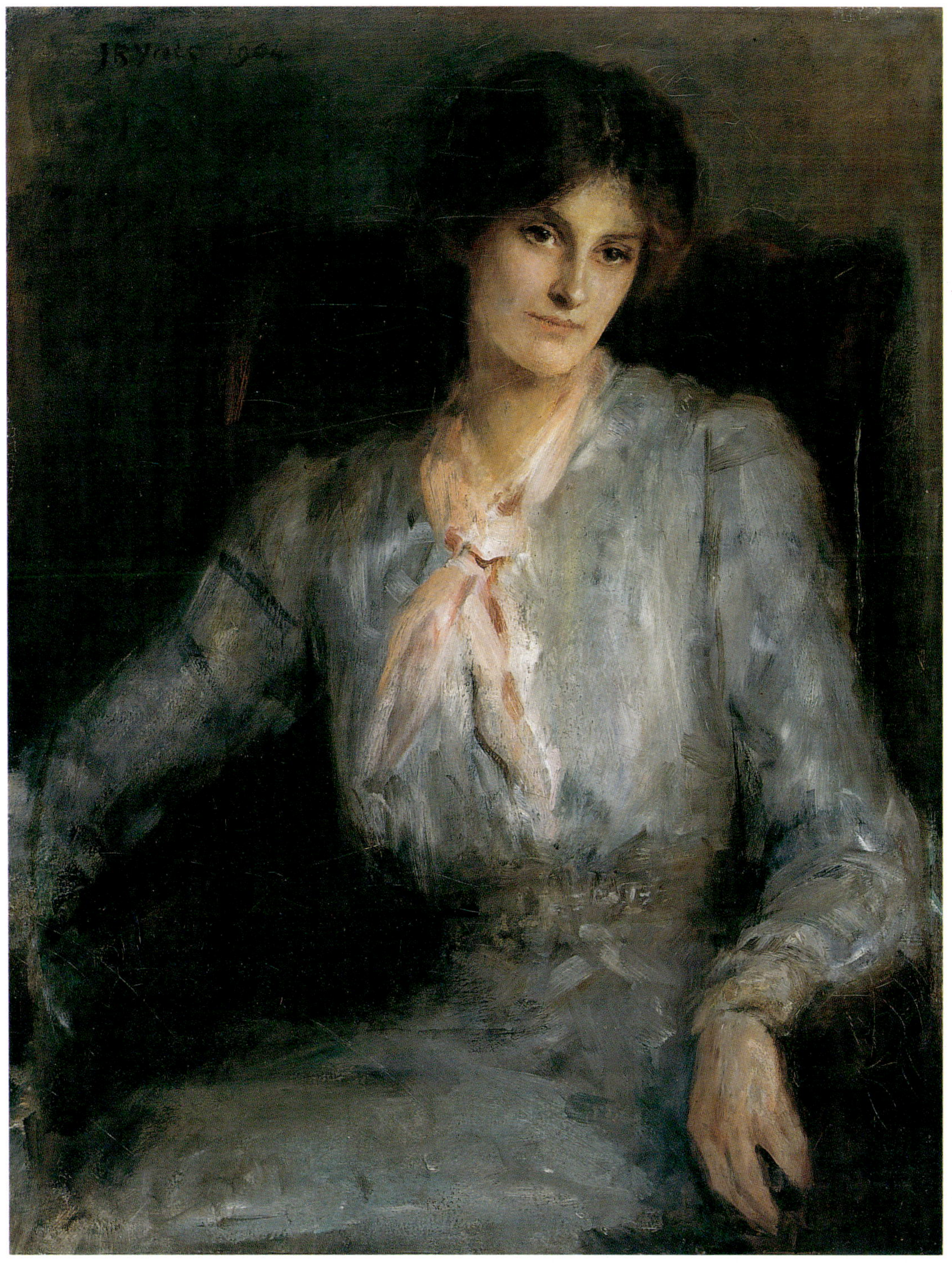

This pencil portrait of J.M. Synge (1871–1909), from Lady Gregory's collection, must be a preliminary study for the oil portrait commissioned by Lane (Hugh Lane Municipal Gallery), on which JBY worked in 1905. William Murphy has pointed out that JBY made two other sketches of Synge the same year, and Ann Saddlemyer notes altogether six drawings by JBY of Synge.

This, the earliest of the group, was taken in January 1905, probably during rehearsals for *In the Shadow of the Glen*, the play which made the diarist Joseph Holloway prophesy that Synge would be the rock on which the Irish National Theatre Society would come to grief.

The writer is seen in a casual pose, as JBY preferred to find his sitters, even in oils. He sits on a stool, perhaps, placed against a wall with his arms crossed. The drawing is similar to the picture of April 1905 in the Abbey Theatre collection (fig. 82), though this is a more powerful study, the writer's head leaning right back, casting a small shadow against the pale surface, while his eyes rove in the distance in dream. The artist draws the attention delicately to his moustache, spreading in a gentle arc above the smigín of beard, and punctuating his face below the spreading eyebrows that shelter the large, wide-set eyes. The beard continues the vertical of the nose and its flared nostrils. JBY also draws out the angles of the heavy-set face attractively, using the neat hair and the high shirt collar, from which Synge's tie has worked free, as frame. The rest of the three-quarter-length figure is sketched loosely, and shaded, finished off with loose cross-hatching.

J. M. Synge lived in Paris after he graduated until his meeting with WBY, who urged him to go to the Aran Islands and to bring to literature a life that had never been expressed. His plays, using local lore for themes, and full of a wild harsh poetry derived from idioms of the Gaelic-speaking inhabitants, disturbed Irish nationalists when they saw them on the Abbey stage, and compared them unfavourably with their romantic notions of an idealized Ireland. Jack Yeats illustrated Synge's books on Aran, Wicklow and Kerry with his line drawings, while WBY placed Synge, one of the literary advisers to the Abbey Theatre, among the greats of the age. He died at a tragically early age, in 1909, after a long fight with persistent illness.

Synge and JBY enjoyed their sessions together in his studio as the oil portrait was painted, and conversation flowed. One of JBY's finest hours, commemorated by his son in his poem 'Beautiful, Lofty Things', was when he defended the dramatist against the hostility of the audience, standing on the Abbey stage during the riots occasioned by *The Playboy of the Western World*, 'his beautiful mischievous head thrown back'. Synge's peasant, JBY declaimed, 'was a real, vigorous, vital man, though a sinner'. He was working on Synge's portrait in oils at the time, which he kept altering and never finished; and the end result, for all its conversational mood and evident likeness, lacks the light touch of his pencil sketches of the playwright.

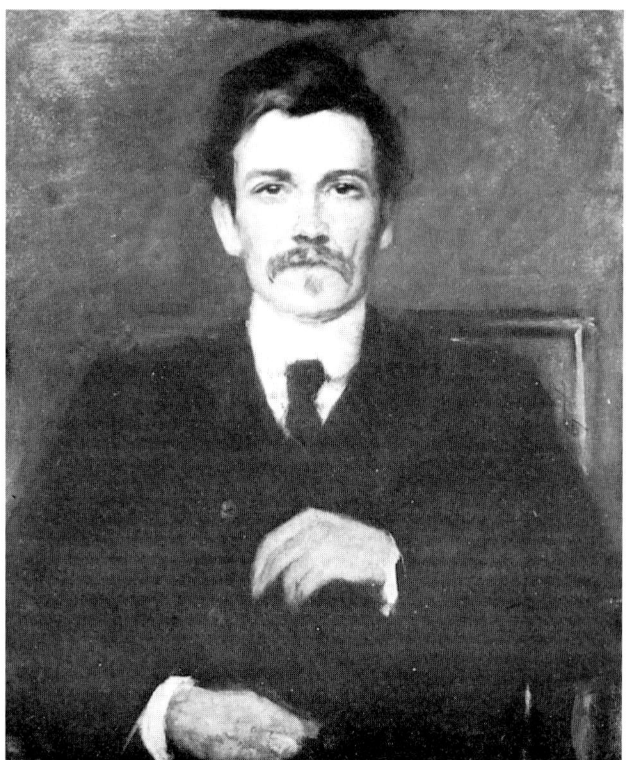

Fig. 82 J.B Yeats, *J.M. Synge,* 1905, oil on canvas, 76 × 62 cm (Abbey Theatre, Dublin)

Pencil portrait of John Millington Synge

1905, pencil on paper, 31.6 × 25 cm, NGI 2937

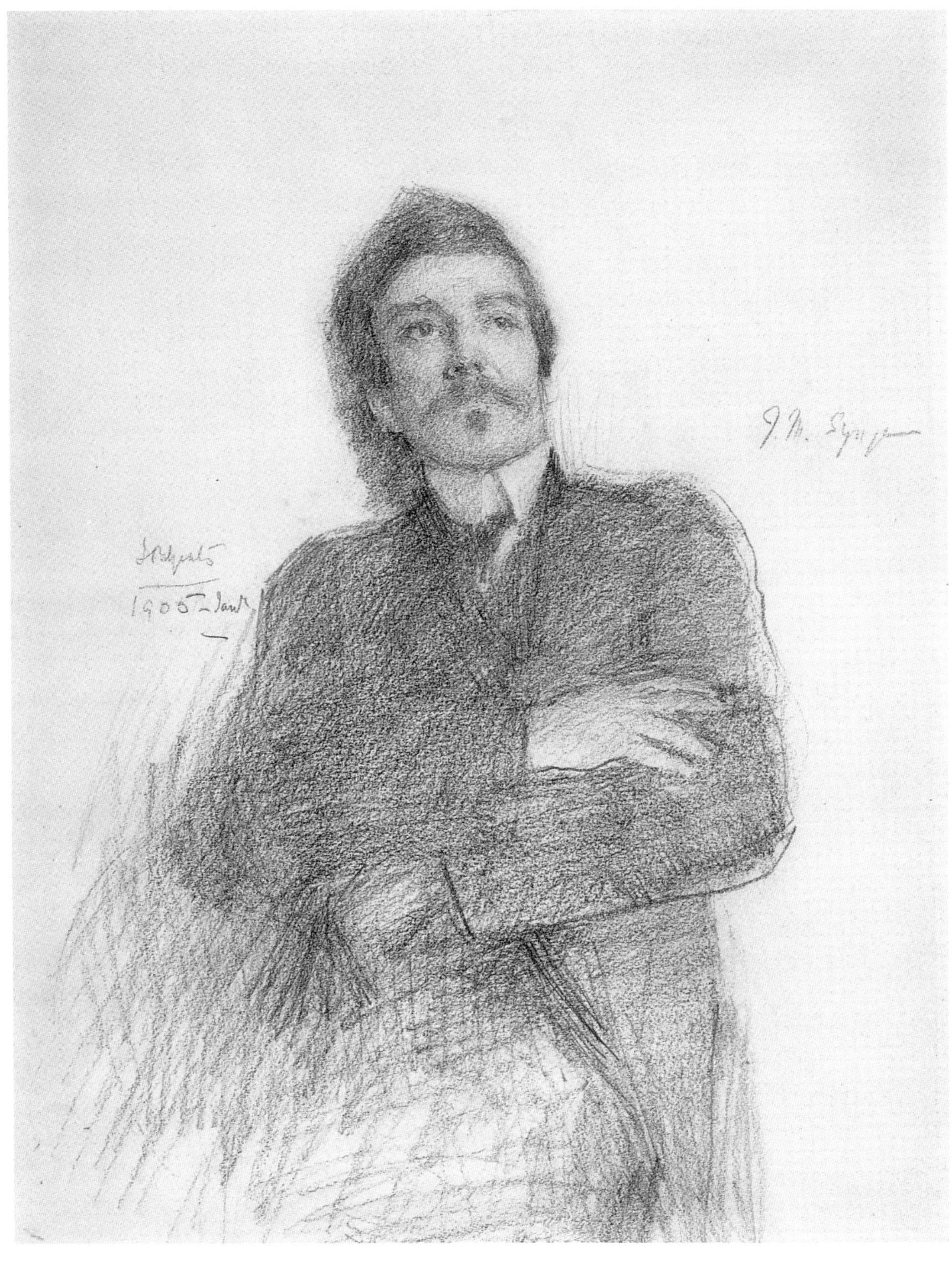

JBY met the Irish lexicographer Father Patrick S. Dineen (1860–1934) when Lily and her assistants at the Dun Emer workshop were working on the sodality banners for the new cathedral at Loughrea. Father Dineen advised on the saints' names which were embroidered in Irish on the banners. Writing from Gurteen Dhas, his home with his daughters in Church-town, County Dublin, the artist told Rosa Butt in August 1903 that he had been arguing with Father Dineen about the tyranny of the Roman Catholic Church. He told John Quinn, "It is not every day that a Protestant has a chance of buttonholing a priest, and I seized my chance to say what I am always wanting to say to Catholics". Two years later he was still at it, talking over religious questions with Father Dineen, and the "queer things" the future might hold (20 May 1905; Bodleian Library).

Father Dineen seems to listen to the artist's out-pouring talk with grave amusement. He crosses his arms, exposing a band of white cuff, which, amid the blackness of his clerical coat (in this work JBY has fin-ished off the body as well as the head), offers a rhyth-mical counterpoint to the slight curve of his starched clerical collar. His face seems curiously young under his thinning hair. He was forty-five when the portrait was finished – it may have been embarked on two years before. He has a broad wrinkled forehead on which the lights dwell, as also on the tip of his well shaped nose. His deep blue eyes gaze intently at the artist, eyebrows tilted in a slightly anxious pose, though his generous mouth is calm and humorous. His complexion is fresh.

The background dances with blue and caramel and darker tones, the colours reflecting the colour of his skin and eyes. It is a picture of a contented scholarly man, who can be friendly, and controlledly emotional. Pádhraig Ua Duinnín gave his years of scholarship to the Irish Texts Society, of which Douglas Hyde was president, bringing out eight important volumes between 1900 and 1927. His first work was an edition of O'Rahilly, and he had published the first edition of *Foclóir Gaedhilge agus Béarla* (his famous Irish dictionary) the year before the portrait was painted. In 1908 he edited Keating's *History of Ireland.* The stereotypes of his dictionary being destroyed by fire during the 1916 Rising, he set out to compile a new edition, more than twice the size of the first, in which, he commented, the effort was made "to net the chief living elements of the language while there was still time". A native-speaker of the Connacht dialect, he had based his first dictio-nary to a large extent on recollections of idioms from childhood, as well as on more recent observations and his wide reading of old and modern Irish literature; but in the second edition he relied on speakers and schol-ars of dialects from all over Ireland, and the new volume, published also by the Irish Texts Society, became a standard work of reference, still used today. His portrait remained in the Yeats family until it was presented to the National Gallery of Ireland by WBY in 1928.

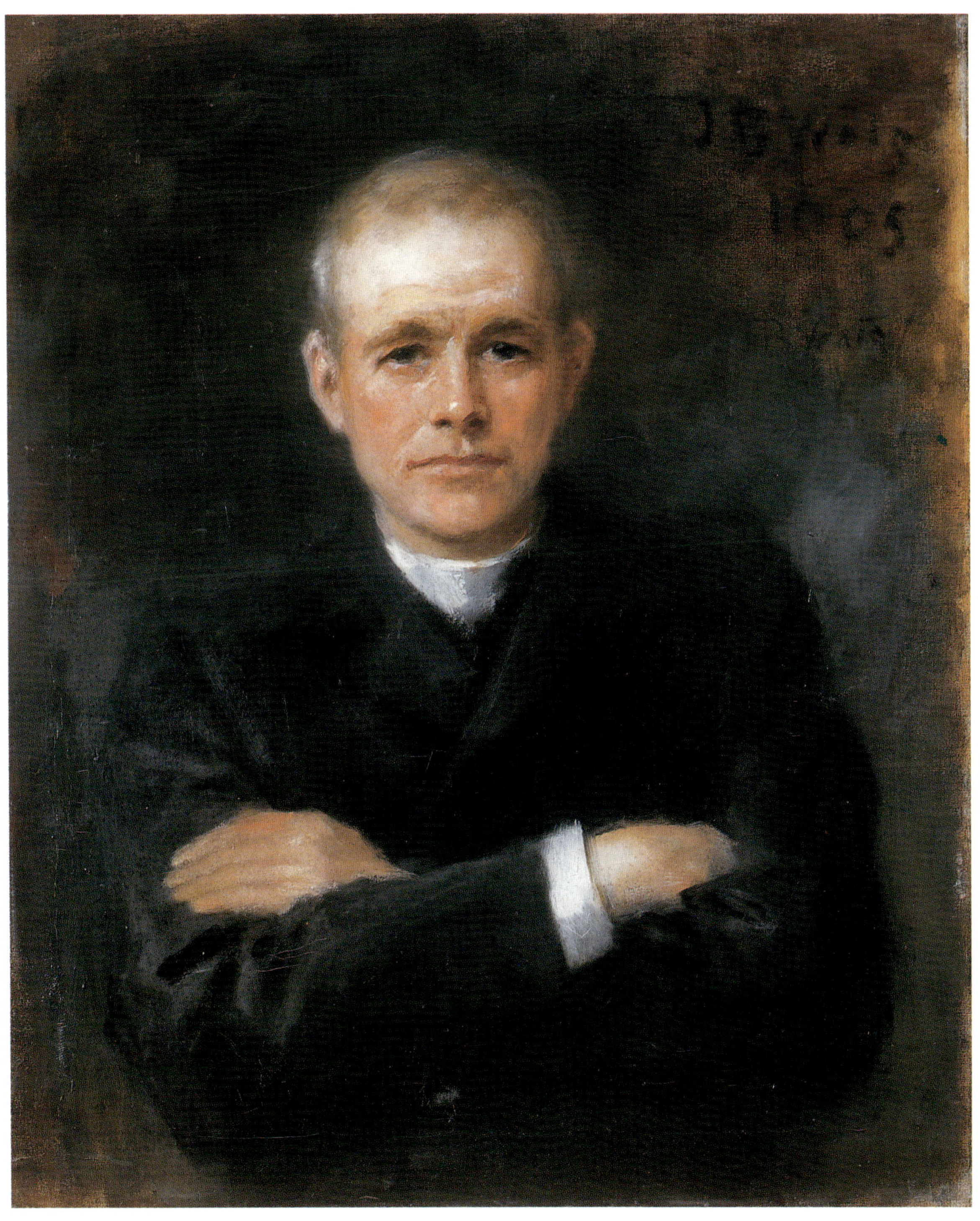

Reverend Patrick S. Dineen

1905, oil on canvas, 77 × 64 cm, NGI 910

J BY's sketch of Hugh Lane looks like an impromptu drawing made while Lane was visiting his studio, talking of his plans for a gallery of modern art in Dublin, or seeing how the remaining portraits he had commissioned were progressing. The artist no doubt seized a piece of white card while Lane looked around, and began to draw the connoisseur's face, making a cobweb of lines out of which the alert dominant eyes, the aristocratic nose and the firm mouth surmounted by a small flourishing moustache emerge. JBY's way of shaping his subject from within an invisible abstract frame is evident here, where spidery lines project beyond the neat outline. The artist has used an unusually hard pencil for this date. Lane's body has been pencilled in roughly, one arm propped up, the other holding a drawing perhaps, the tie and lapels not yet completed.

With all its brevity, the artist has conveyed instantly the symbol of authority that Lane was to him, his head held high like a commander-general overlooking his forces, his distinctive heavy-lidded eyes looking confidently before him. He is a man of action, a moving force, a man who gets things done. JBY kept the drawing, and it was presented to the National Gallery by his daughters many years later.

Hugh Lane (1875–1915) was one of the leading international art experts of his generation. After training at Colnaghi's, and spending a short period at the Marlborough Gallery, he opened his own gallery in London in Pall Mall Place, where he made a fortune through his expertise as a dealer. A visit to his aunt Lady Augusta Gregory, at Coole in 1900, and subsequently to Dublin, brought him into contact with the leading writers and artists of the Irish renaissance. In 1903, he commissioned a series of portraits of distinguished Irish people from JBY, later asking William Orpen to complete the series (see pp. 112, 116).

He founded the Gallery of Modern Art in Harcourt Street, Dublin, in 1908. Here his modern portraits were

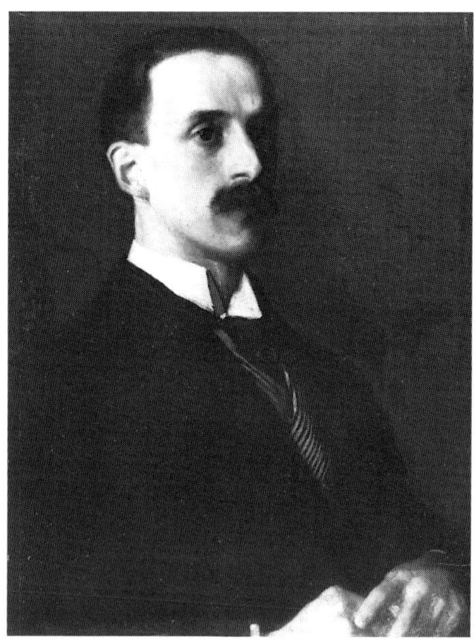

Fig. 83 Sarah Cecilia Harrison, *Sir Hugh Lane*, oil on panel, 41 × 31 cm (NGI 1280)

exhibited, with 154 works of art which he had collected; and he received a knighthood for his services to art. Some years later, when the Corporation failed to build a permanent gallery to house the pictures, he made a will bequeathing thirty-nine of his modern Continental paintings, including Manet and Renoir, to the National Gallery in London.

Not long after this he was appointed Director of the National Gallery of Ireland, in succession to Walter Armstrong. During his all too brief directorship, he presented masterpieces by El Greco and Veronese to the Gallery, later bequeathing to it magnificent works by Titian, Goya, Poussin and others. Before sailing to New York in 1915, he revoked his will in favour of the Dublin Municipal Gallery, but the codicil was unwitnessed. When he went down with the *Lusitania*, the original bequest was upheld, and his aunt Lady Gregory spent the remainder of her days appealing the decision.

Pencil portrait of Hugh Lane

1905, pencil on white card, 17.5 × 12.7 cm, NGI 2866

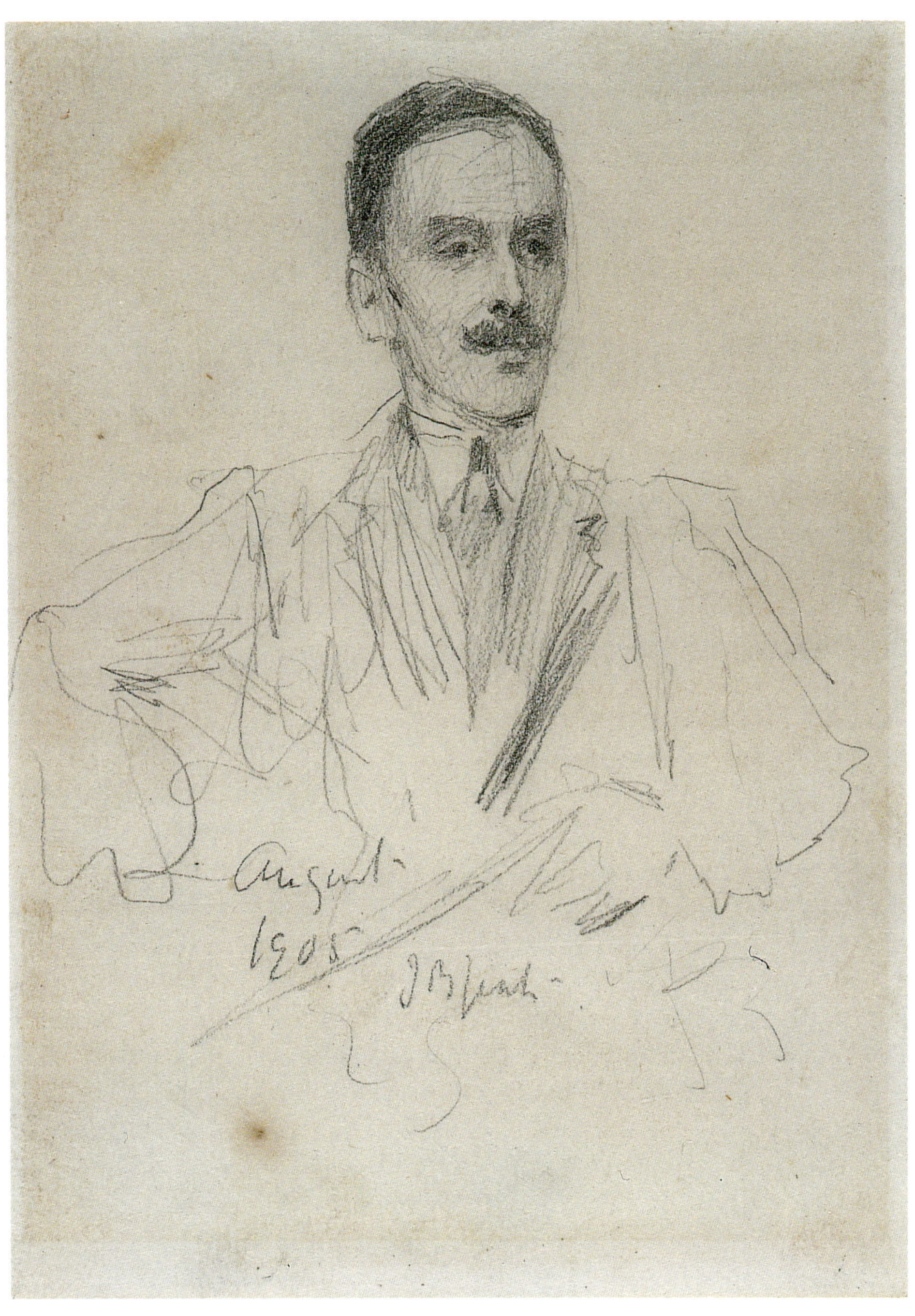

JBY, reporting on his portrait of the novelist George Moore (1852–1933), in an undated letter to Rosa Butt (Bodleian Library), told her that Moore had had one sitting "and went away I think favourably impressed by his portrait so far as it is painted". This portrait of a man who had been painted by Manet and Degas, and who had himself desired to be a painter, was commissioned by Quinn in August 1905. JBY was given a second – it turned out to be the final – sitting by early September. Two months later Lily was able to tell Quinn, "The George Moore is very good and does not make people laugh. All other portraits of him do." But the portrait dragged on. Moore was planning to leave Ireland, and Quinn grew nervous. He wrote to Lily on 23 January 1906, "Isn't there some way by which you can induce Moore to come to the studio and have the portrait finished? Above all, if you manage to get Moore there, can't you so manœuvre things that 'irrelevant' and 'immaterial' persons [who diverted the artist with their conversation] can be excluded?"

The picture is firmly signed and dated *1905*, and evidently JBY did not lift a brush to it in 1906. Lily and George Russell were of the opinion that the portrait was "remarkably good, and could not be more like", though the artist did not agree. However, she told Quinn (6 May 1906), "Another sitting with George Moore in a truculent mood would most likely spoil the portrait." And the picture is all the better for having been left alone. The paint is used sparingly, the brush has been directed sensitively to the face, merging the highlights skilfully with the skin pigments. The lightly painted background, in a smoky blue, revealing the canvas at the edges, complements the fresh, live image, and one feels that the artist has at last achieved the truly impressionistic touch with which he identified himself.

In essence, of course he has not identified with Impressionism, which he comprehended only by instinct. Moore is dressed in dark coat, waistcoat and black tie. The colours are conservative, though all are treated broadly giving the quality of a sketch – exactly as the artist wished. His main interest, as always, is the sitter's face, and his ovoid head and thin grey hair,

which is parted, allowing a lock to fall over his brow. The writer is inclined slightly to the right, eyes lowered in reflective thought. His walrus moustache reaches to each side of his face with a flourish, his lip projecting below it. His luminous complexion and the blueness of his eyes are compelling.

Moore, who was born on his father's estate, Moore

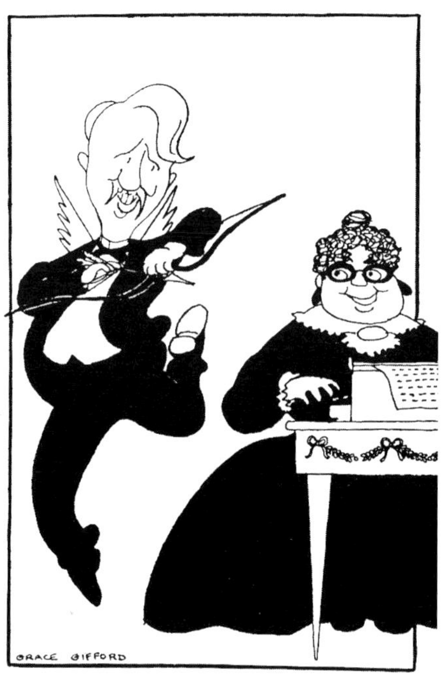

Fig. 84 G. Gifford, *Cupid and Psyche* [satirical portraits of George Moore and Susan Mitchell], in *The Irish Review*, September/November 1914

Park, in County Mayo, trained briefly for the priesthood, but decided to study painting in Paris, where he knew Manet, Degas, Picasso and other artists, and became an art critic. He next turned to writing novels, achieving great success with *Esther Waters*, *The Lake* and other books. His collaboration as a dramatist with his cousin Edward Martyn and WBY brought him to Dublin for ten years, where he abandoned Roman Catholicism for the Church of Ireland. Susan Mitchell and others ridiculed him for his self-importance, and she lampooned him vigorously. Moore's autobiographical trilogy, *Hail and Farewell*, the first volume of which was published shortly after he left Ireland for good in 1911, treated everyone maliciously except George Russell; Susan Mitchell retaliated in an elegant prose satire (1916), which greatly injured his vanity.

George Moore

1905, oil on canvas, 77 × 64 cm, NGI 873

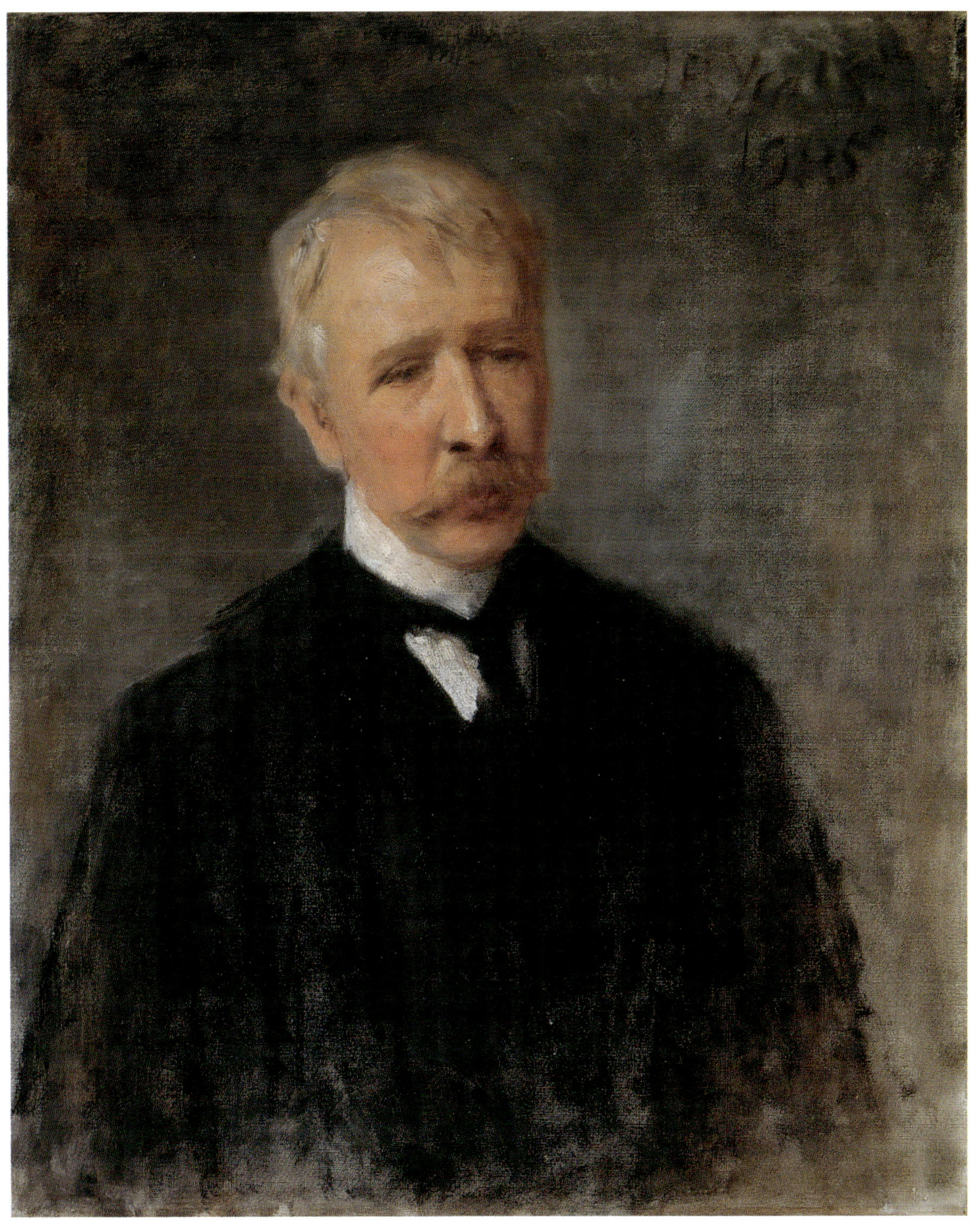

When Hugh Lane commissioned a portrait of Douglas Hyde from JBY, his aunt Lady Gregory was sceptical, considering what had happened when her sketch portrait of An Craoibhín Aoibhinn (see p. 84) was in the making – "It will be difficult to get Dr. Hyde to sit again," she wrote to Hugh. "He caught cold and got a little cross at the last sitting". The portrait for Lane was painted, after many sittings, at Coole in the summer of 1903, JBY working against a deadline for which he was late. Lady Gregory found him "the most trying visitor possible in a house", as she told Quinn years later. He dropped socks anywhere, and cared only for his brushes, his palette and his paints. "Space and time mean nothing to him," she said, "he goes his own way, spoiling portraits as hopefully as he begins them, and always on the verge of a great future!"

The 1903 portrait in the Hugh Lane Municipal Gallery (fig. 85), nevertheless, has everything of serenity, and gives no hint of the tensions in its vicinity. Hyde's eyes shine out of his heart-shaped face above his profuse moustache with equanimity. In contrast, this oil of 1906, commissioned by Quinn, has everything of strain, even suggesting a coolness on the part of Hyde, who clasps his hands tightly and stares out of the canvas with an intent expression, his eyes gleaming, his mouth set, in so far as it can be seen through the hirsute growth depending from his upper lip. The portrait was commissioned before the George Moore (see previous page), and by late April 1905 was nearly ready, according to Lily, but she advised Quinn to be firm about a deadline. JBY seems to have returned to it for nearly a year before he was satisfied, and overpainted the image, perhaps thus contributing to the stiffness.

Hyde is seated in the high-backed mahogany chair that features in other portraits, the gleam of polished wood helping to define the spatial dimensions of the central image. His neatly brushed short hair frames the round pate on which the light dwells, thus underlining for the viewer that this is a man of intellect. His dark eyes gaze out steadily and compellingly. He wears a black suit and a red tie, the colour of which is echoed in the vibrant red brown that surrounds the sitter, and settles in a pool about the back of his head.

Douglas Hyde (1860–1949), son of a Roscommon rector, had collected and published the traditional love songs and religious songs of his native county, and scored a success with his play *Casadh an tSugáin* when it was performed in a double bill with *Diarmuid and Grania* by WBY and Moore in 1902. The Gaelic League which he had founded, and which celebrated its centenary in 1993, had by now five hundred and fifty branches around Ireland, where the Irish language and Irish culture were pursued peaceably. President since its foundation, he toured America lecturing and seeking funds; but the political element in a body which he had conceived as non-political and non-sectarian proved too strong for him, and in 1915 he was forced to resign. He was Professor of Modern Irish in University College, Dublin, from 1908 to 1932, a Senator of the Free State, and in 1937 was elected the first official President of Ireland.

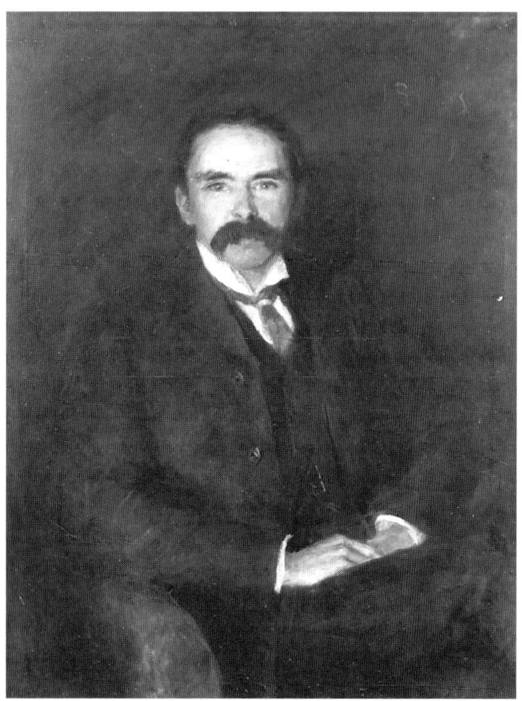

Fig. 85 J.B. Yeats, *Douglas Hyde*, 1903, oil on canvas, 110 × 85 cm (Hugh Lane Municipal Gallery, Dublin)

Douglas Hyde

1906, oil on canvas, 107 × 86 cm, NGI 874

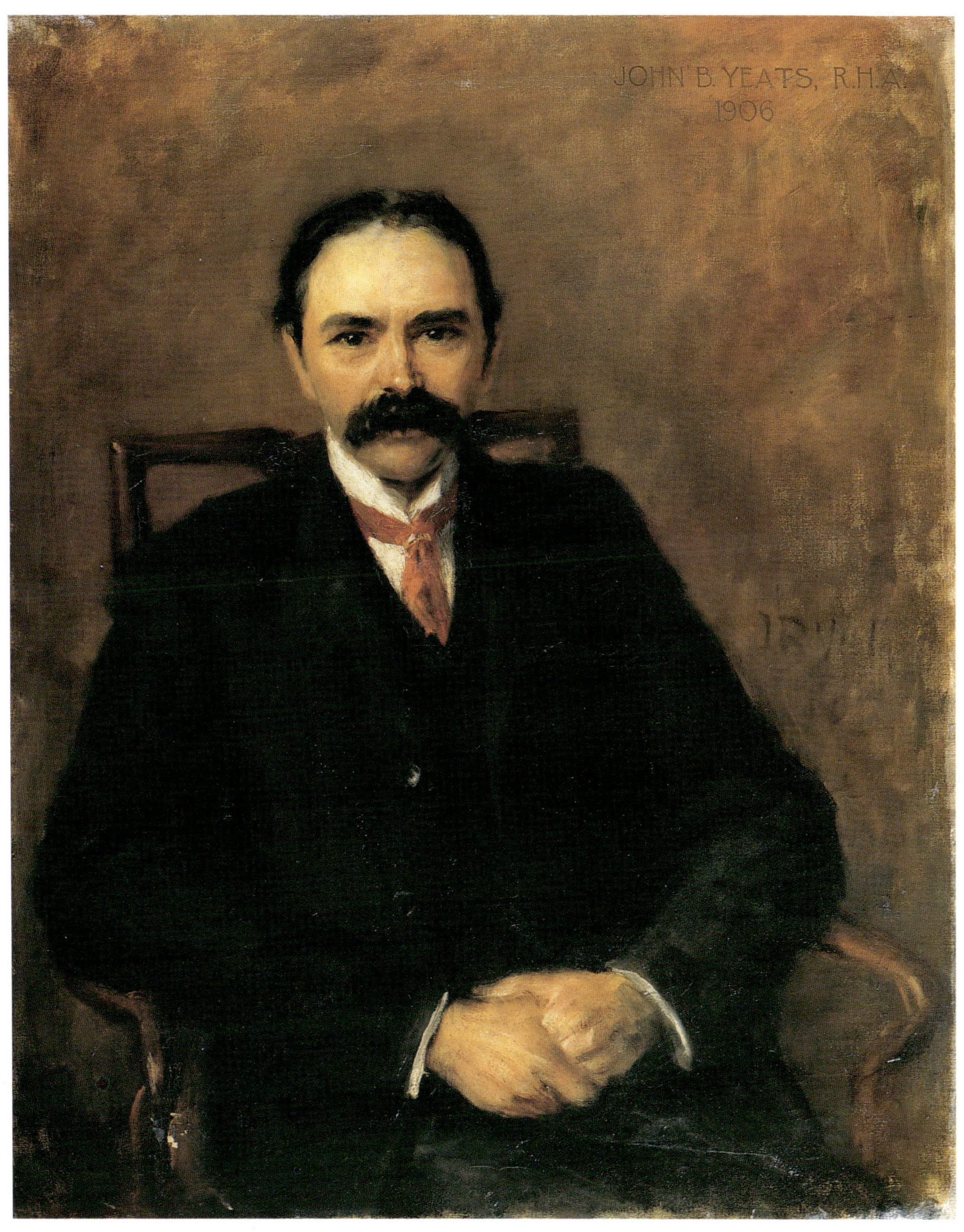

Richard Irvine Best (1872–1959) was Assistant Director of the National Library of Ireland when he commissioned this pencil portrait from JBY. It is a sympathetic sketch, in a frontal half-length pose, the body slanting slightly to the right with the customary quiet counterpoint.

The sitter's heavy-lidded eyes are lowered as in thought. His face is calm and reflective. He wears a moustache and short hair as was fashionable at the time. JBY has shaded rapidly behind his head, clearly outlined with a delicate pointing of angles, and he has darkened the right side of his head to increase the mood of reserve. Otherwise light plays evenly over the lightly modelled head. The shoulders and arms of the sitter are sketched in more vaguely, his right hand in embryo outline grasping what looks like the top of a stick.

Born in Derry in 1872, R.I. Best became a distinguished scholar in the field of Celtic studies. His career started in 1901, when George Russell persuaded Arthur Griffith to publish his translation of M.H. d'Arbois de Jubainville's book on the *Irish Mythological Cycle* in the *United Irishman*; and he later published conclusive evidence that the script of *Lebor na Huidre* was by more than one scribe, as well as editing *The Book of Leinster* and the *Annals of Innisfallen*. With Kuno Meyer (p. 110) and John Strachan he founded the School of Irish Learning in Dublin in 1903, and he remained secretary of it for the twenty years of its existence. From 1924 he was Director of the National Library of Ireland. He was appointed Senior Professor in the Dublin Institute of Advanced Studies in 1940, and in 1948 became chairman of the Irish Manuscripts

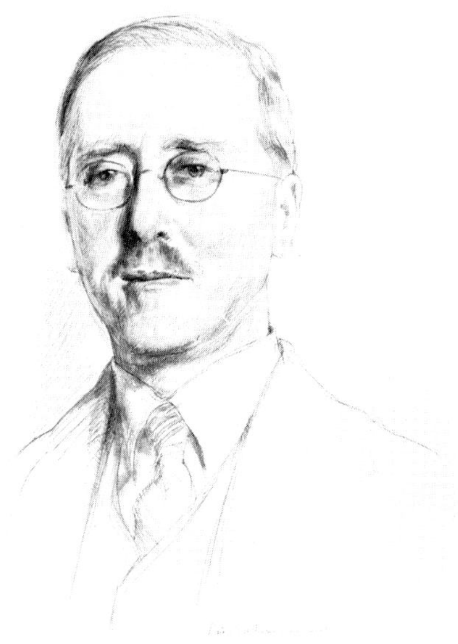

Fig. 86 Seán O'Sullivan, *Richard Irvine Best*, pencil on paper, 51.8 × 42.9 cm (NGI 3559)

Commission until he retired in 1956.

Richard Best was a connoisseur and collector of paintings, often small in scale, and bequeathed not only this drawing to the National Gallery of Ireland but also four pictures by Jack B. Yeats, including *Islandbridge Regatta*. Other paintings from his collection may be found in galleries around Ireland. He was portrayed again in pencil by Seán O'Sullivan in July 1938 (fig. 86). There are two oil portraits of R.I. Best, one by Sarah Cecilia Harrison painted in 1928 (National Gallery of Ireland), and a later likeness by James Sleator (Royal Irish Academy).

Pencil portrait of Richard Irvine Best

1906, pencil on unevenly cut paper, 34.5 × 25 cm, NGI 3307

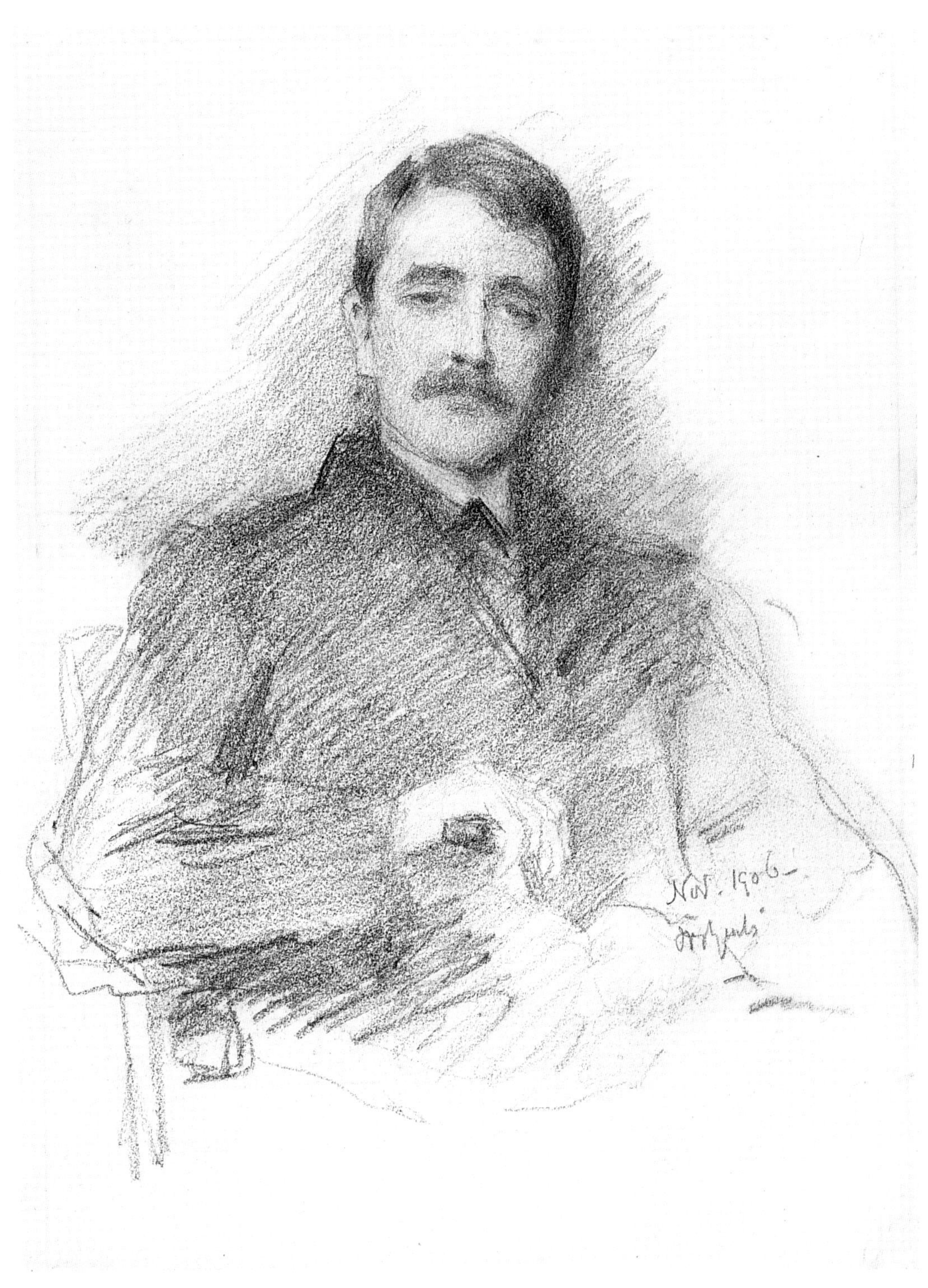

Edith Oldham (1868–1950) was a gifted pianist. In 1906 she married Dr Richard Best (see previous page), the Celtic scholar, then Assistant Director of the National Library of Ireland. JBY knew her brother Charles Hubert Oldham, founder of the Contemporary Club, to which he had belonged in the 1880s, and where he met all the leading intellectuals and liberal thinkers of the day, witnessing the burgeoning of Protestant nationalism in its many aspects (see pp. 64–70).

Drawing Edith Best in January 1907, he did not represent her in conversation, but sketched her in the drawing room of her house – perhaps when on a social visit there – as she played the piano. The sketch is an informal one. Best may have thought a head and shoulders would have been too austere. JBY has captured the atmosphere of subdued light at evening, and, judging by the brief way in which the piano and the chair are sketched, did not have a great deal of time. Edith Best is seen in right profile, full length, the artist appreciative of the trim elegance of her full sleeves, the shoulder ruffle of her blouse and the swirl of her spreading skirt. She is engrossed in her playing. JBY has outlined her features delicately and sensitively; but at the same time he suggests the movement of one who has only just sat down to play. Any sentimentality attached to such a scene has been obviated by the vigorous, almost defiant, strong lines with which he has finalized the outline. The legs of the piano and the lines of the music rest might almost echo the vibrations of some dramatic chords.

With her husband, Edith Best helped to organize the Dublin Féis Ceoil, an annual musical competition that continues to this day. Nearly twenty years later, in 1924, Sarah Cecilia Harrison made a portrait of Edith Best in wash and pencil, now in the collection of the National Gallery of Ireland (fig. 87).

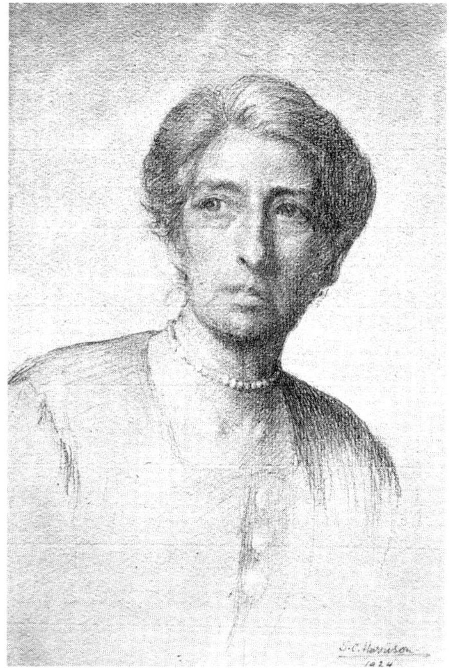

Fig. 87 Sarah Cecilia Harrison, *Mrs Edith Best*, 1924, pencil and wash on paper, 30 × 20.6 cm (NGI 3042)

Mrs Best at the piano

1907, pencil on paper, 22.7 × 14 cm, NGI 3310

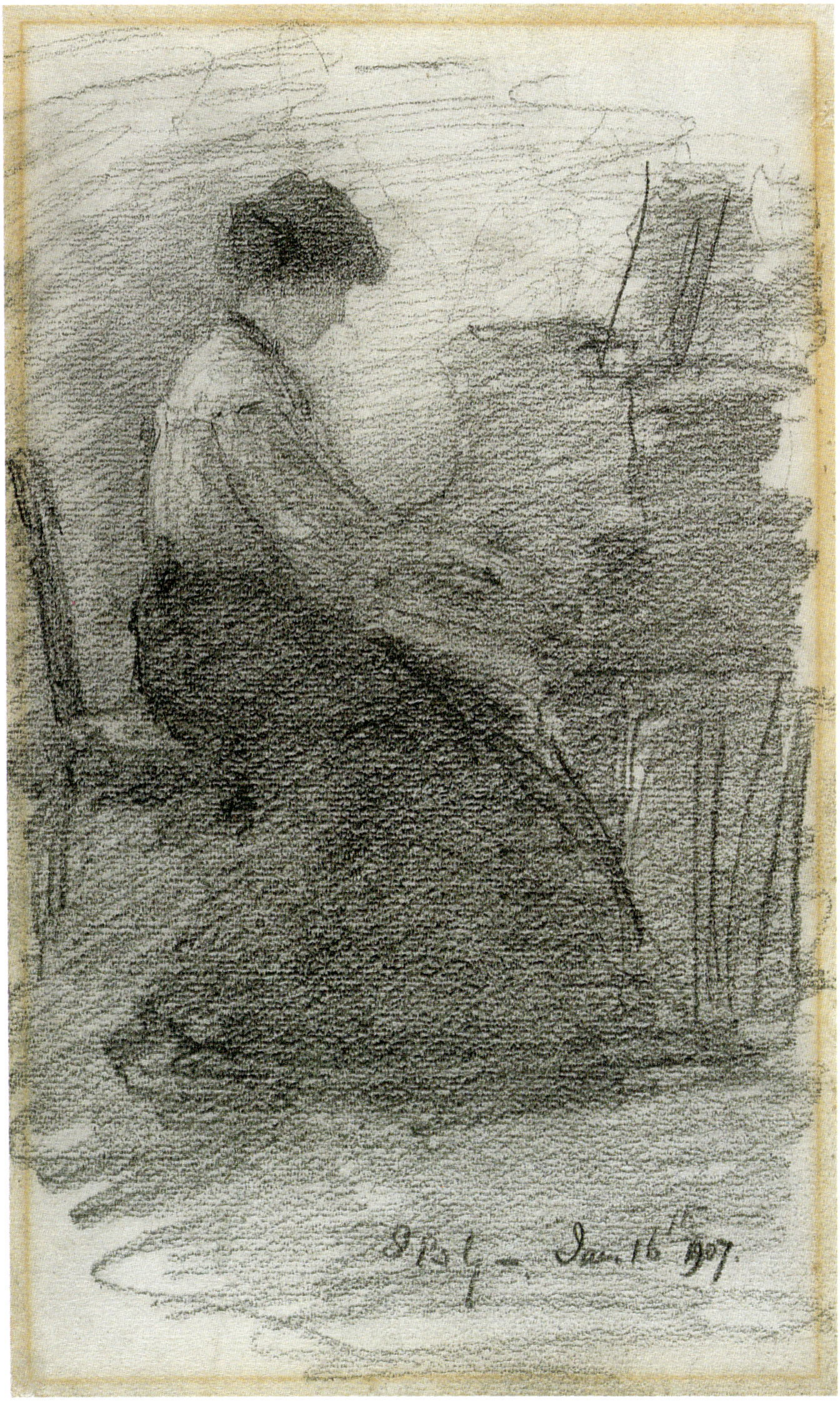

The identification of the subject of this drawing has been disputed by William Murphy, although, since it comes from the Kerrigan collection (see next page) and the figure has a marked resemblance to Maud Gonne MacBride, there seems little reason to object. JBY may have made the watercolour from memory, recalling Maud Gonne in the title rôle of *Cathleen Ni Houlihan* by WBY in the Irish National Theatre Society production in early April 1902, which was received with acclaim. (Critics, though, were

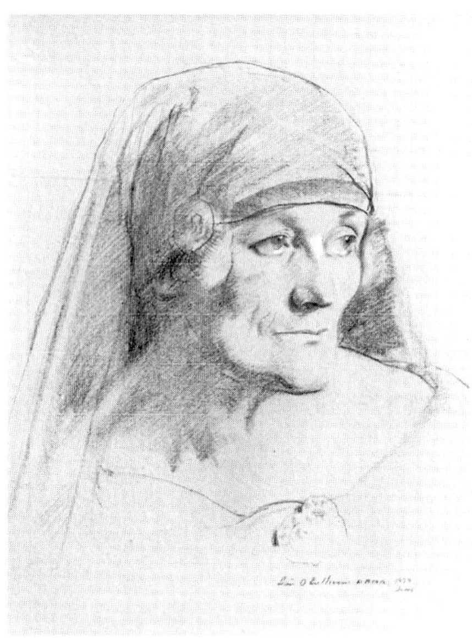

Fig. 88 Seán O'Sullivan, *Maud Gonne*, 1929, red chalk and charcoal with white highlights on brown card, 36.6 × 29.8 cm (NGI 3538)

inclined to attribute her success to her ability as a nationalist agitator rather than as an actress!) Or it may have been done on the occasion of one of Maud Gonne's fleeting visits to Dublin, surreptitiously after her separation from Major MacBride, and specifically to discuss the monthly publication *Bean na hÉireann* which she and Helena Molony proposed setting up in 1907. JBY at the time was working on an oil-painting, *Erin*, which he finished in August. "Erin wont behave as I want her to," he had written to Rosa Butt in July. "She would look like a young lady ... now I have short-

ened her nose and she does not look so beastly lady-like, the hussy –." Perhaps his watercolour of Maud Gonne put the idea of *Erin* in his mind.

Whatever the origins of the watercolour, it is unique in JBY's œuvre, a drawing perhaps intended for illustration, but in colour wash rather than monochrome. The young woman wears a long, loose plum-coloured dress and brown cloak, the hood framing her face. She raises both arms in supplication, gazing upward with an exalted expression, her lips parted. The static figure is silhouetted against the white paper on which it has been worked in scarlet lake and vandyke brown, the image contained within a loose painterly outline, reinforced here and there with crayon.

Maud Gonne (1866–1953) became known to the Yeats family in January 1889, when she called on JBY at Blenheim Road in London, with an introduction from John O'Leary. The family were aware that her chief interest was in WBY, who was instantly infatuated, and whose verse she was to inspire for over twenty years. The daughter of an Irish colonel, she had been brought up in France, and returned to Dublin about 1882, "marching on to glory over the hearts of the Dublin youths", as Elizabeth Yeats put it. Her beauty was arresting. She was tall, with a Junoesque figure, and she quickly made an impact in an Ireland on the verge of change as she adopted causes, speaking on behalf of the Land League at meetings in Dublin, and soon becoming an ardent nationalist. In Paris she lived for some years with Lucien Millevoye, a journalist and politician many years older than herself, by whom she had two children. With WBY she established a branch of the Irish League in Paris. She shared his interest in Celtic mysticism; and she was one of the vice-presidents of the Irish National Theatre Society, founded in 1902. In 1903 she married Major John MacBride (later executed for his part in the 1916 insurrection). She parted from him after two years.

Her autobiography, *A Servant of the Queen*, was published in 1938. A late bust portrait of her, by Laurence Campbell, is in the Hugh Lane Municipal Gallery of Modern Art; and a late pencil portrait by Seán O'Sullivan is in the National Gallery of Ireland (fig. 88).

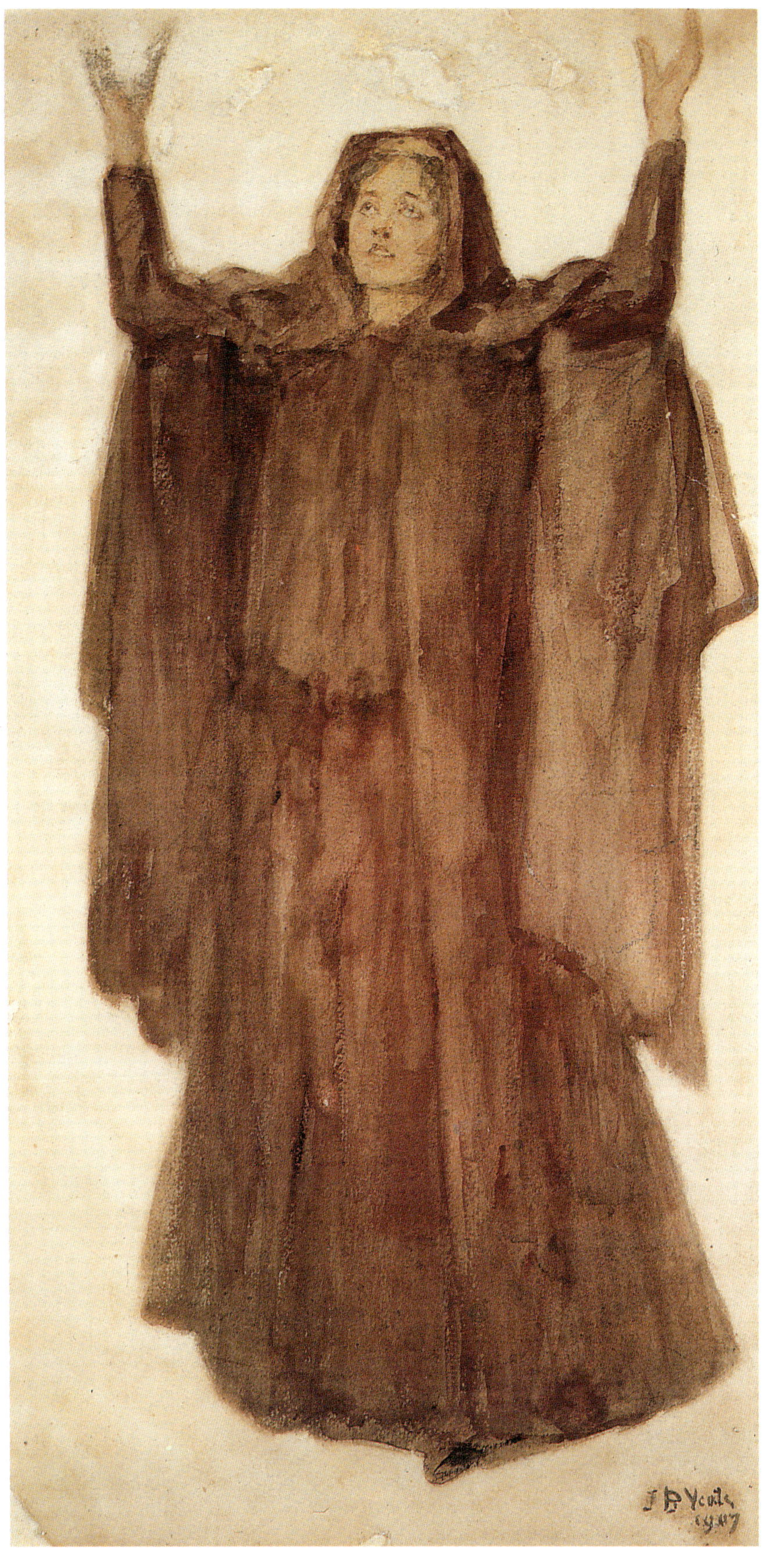

Maud Gonne MacBride

1907, pencil, watercolour and crayon on
paper, 46 × 24 cm, NGI 7712

y 1911, JBY, who had left Dublin supposedly on a short trip in late December 1907, was well settled in New York. He had one direct contact with Dublin in November, when his pupil, the artist Clare Marsh, came to stay at White Plains with some cousins; and another when the Abbey Players visited New York in the autumn/winter of 1911 on tour. Quinn commissioned JBY to do drawings of eight of the players – J.M. Kerrigan, Sydney J. Morgan, Arthur Sinclair, Fred O'Donovan, J.A. O'Rourke, Udolphus Wright, Sara Allgood and Eithne Magee – which he intended to present to the Abbey Theatre.

By Christmas Eve, JBY had finished only two of the sketches. It was difficult to get the actors to sit, and Kerrigan failed to keep his first appointment. Nevertheless JBY finished the sketches before the end of the month. He thought the Kerrigan was good. But Quinn was critical, and told him to get O'Donovan and Kerrigan to sit a second time. "If these two are done over, and Kerrigan, now looking like an old woman, is turned into a young man, I want to have them all reproduced," he wrote (16 February 1912). In the end JBY had to sketch on the *Campania* the night they sailed, when the company was "merry", he told Clare Marsh. The sketch of Kerrigan is dated *1911*, so he may have spent the evening reworking the original drawings rather than making a new set.

The technique here differs from that of his Dublin sketches in that he uses a harder pencil, and creates his lights by exposing small areas of virgin card. The sketch of J.M. Kerrigan, too, aims at a rapid realism rather than musing in poetic vein on the personality before him, as he had been wont to do in his Dublin studio. J.M. Kerrigan (1885–1964), a Dubliner, who had played a variety of rôles in his career with the Abbey Theatre, would have interested him. But here he rests mute, looking rather weary, perhaps dazed after finding his way to JBY's studio, or having been taken away from the farewell party for a short spell. JBY has worked around his clean-shaven face, moulding it with a light cobweb of shading, and he has stressed the thick mop of short hair that tucks down at each side in front of the big ears, and the fine eyes, gazing earnestly. The rest is rendered briefly, the broad shirt collar and tie, the buttoned waistcoat, the upper coat.

The following year, Lady Gregory mounted an appeal in the United States to raise money to build a gallery of modern art in Dublin, to house her nephew Hugh Lane's collection. One fund-raising device was a square of Irish linen, unhemmed, measuring 48 × 46 cm, sold by the Abbey Players for $1.00 (fig. 89). It was stamped with reproductions of the eight sketches of the Abbey players done for Quinn, some of them autographed. A quotation from one of Lady Gregory's plays accompanies the sketches, with beneath it the final lines of WBY's poem 'To a Wealthy Man who Promised a Second Subscription to the Dublin Municipal Gallery if it were Proved the People Wanted Pictures'.

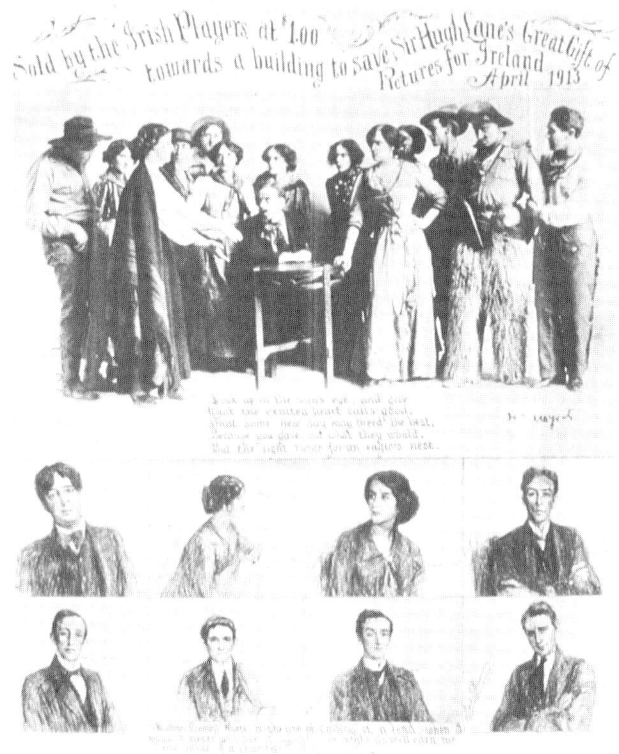

Fig. 89 Abbey Handkerchief, 1912 (private collection)

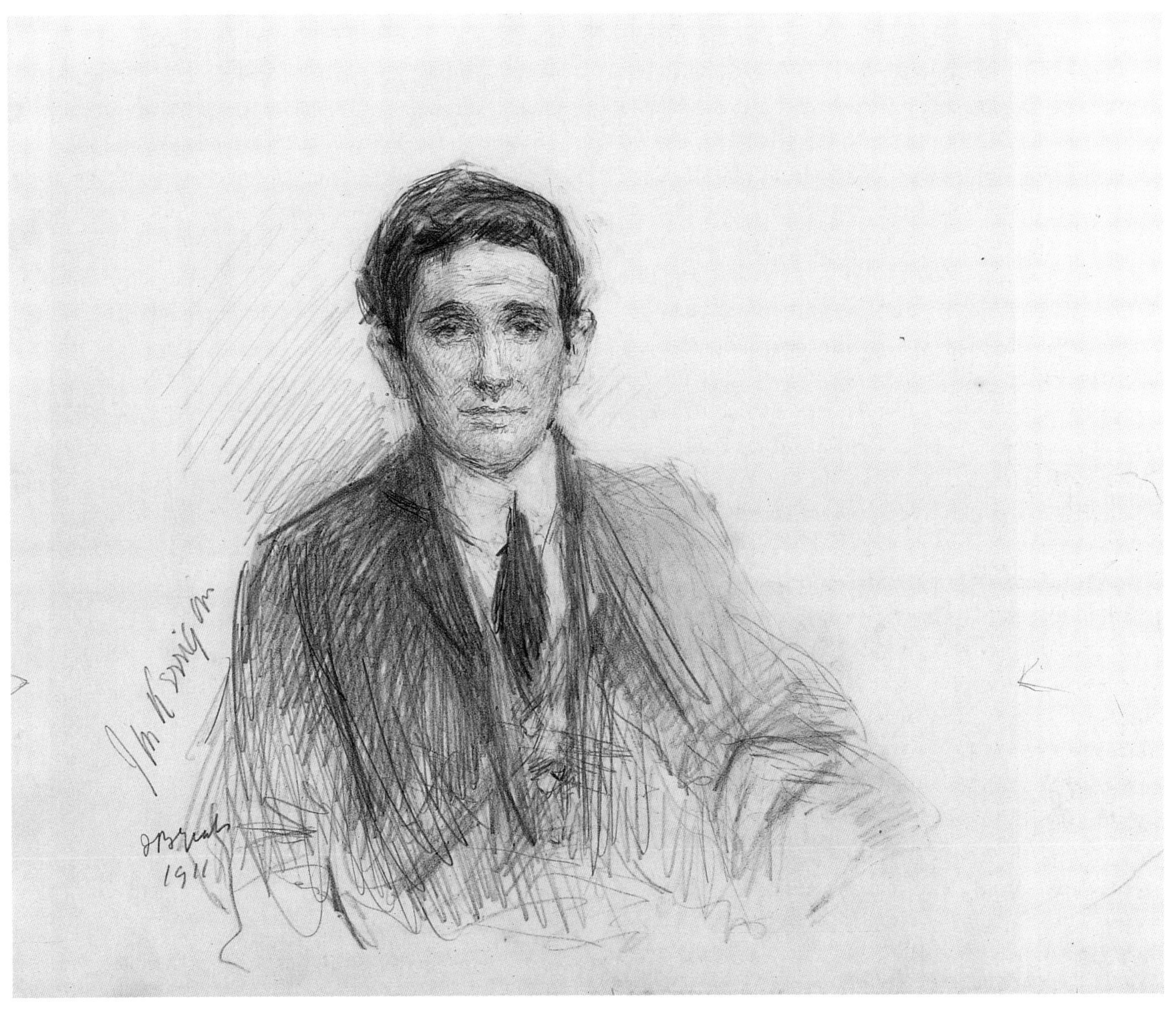

JBY's first contact with Mrs Mary Tower Lapsley Caughey was in August 1915. Her husband, a Pennsylvanian engineer, was absent from home all week, and Mrs Caughey arranged cultural events, inviting JBY to lecture in December. In July 1916 he stayed again at her house twelve miles from Pittsburgh, this time to paint her portrait. Of Ulster Presbyterian extraction but emancipated (criticized by the locals for her refusal to go to prayer meetings), she was found by JBY clever and attractive. She talked to him of WBY, knew every line of his son's poetry and could discuss Browning. She herself wrote poetry. "What I have seen I can praise in a qualified way," he wrote to Rosa Butt (1 July 1916). To add to the pleasure of his visit, the house was on the edge of a moor surrounded by bushes full of exotic birds. JBY described himself as being "in a saturnalia of vanity and emotion" – "in England I would be nobody, here I am *some*body". He was fêted at lunch parties by women who aspired to being intellectual, "the only men present being butlers or postmen".

By mid-August he had painted four portraits, three of them full length, "and as regards these three *the heads of two of them done in one sitting*. I seemed to the people a maker of myracles". These two portraits, which he told Rosa Butt (1 July 1916) were "effective sketches", must be the portrait of Mrs Caughey's daughter (see next page) and NGI 1727, where Mrs Caughey stands with one hand on her hip, the other on the back of a chair, gazing at the artist with a coquettish expression on her face. Her brown hair is piled on her head in a top knot. An open door gives a brief glimpse of another part of the house.

"Then I started another for which Mrs. Caughey got a special dress – an evening dress, black and made of some fluffy material with bare arms, bare bosom etc. and this I worked on, stipulating that it would not be considered finished till I *myself was satisfied*. – how we fought over it! again and again I was told that it had been perfect and that I in my obstinacy would go on and had spoiled it and that she was no longer interested etc. – there were tears in her eyes, she sat and would not speak and I only laughed and kept on. It came to the last morning and she declared herself at last to be appeased and satisfied, and as it was the last morning I agreed – but the husband ... arrived, and he said it is wonderful, everything is perfect and beautiful *except the face*. Then Mrs. Caughey was indignant with him and said she did not care about his opinion and that the picture was for herself and to please herself – I know perfectly well why she liked the portrait and he did not – she looked 25 whereas in reality she is 40 – so backed up by the husband's opinion I set to work and had my own way and made her look 40. It was only a matter of ten minutes work. And Mrs. Caughey was as angry as ever, but the husband came in and was delighted, and everyone says it is the best of all."

Mrs Caughey sits on a high-backed Jacobean-style chair, leaning slightly to one side. Her pert face looks mildly impatient, her eyebrows raised, the large hazel eyes defiant. The whole dark image looks arresting, and formidably modern, against the greeny pink background. JBY handles the brush more tightly than in his Dublin period, uses the paint more assertively. It is a challenging rather than a dreamy image or an encounter with a thinker. The picture is of a practical woman, totally in command of the age and ethos that have come her way.

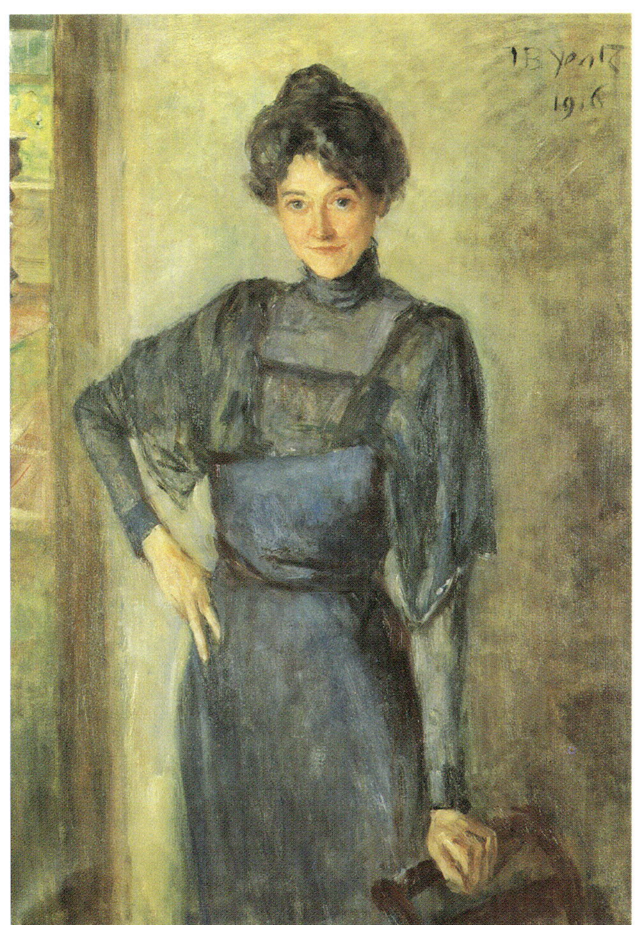

Mrs Mary Tower Lapsley Caughey standing

Oil on canvas, 102 × 71 cm, NGI 1727

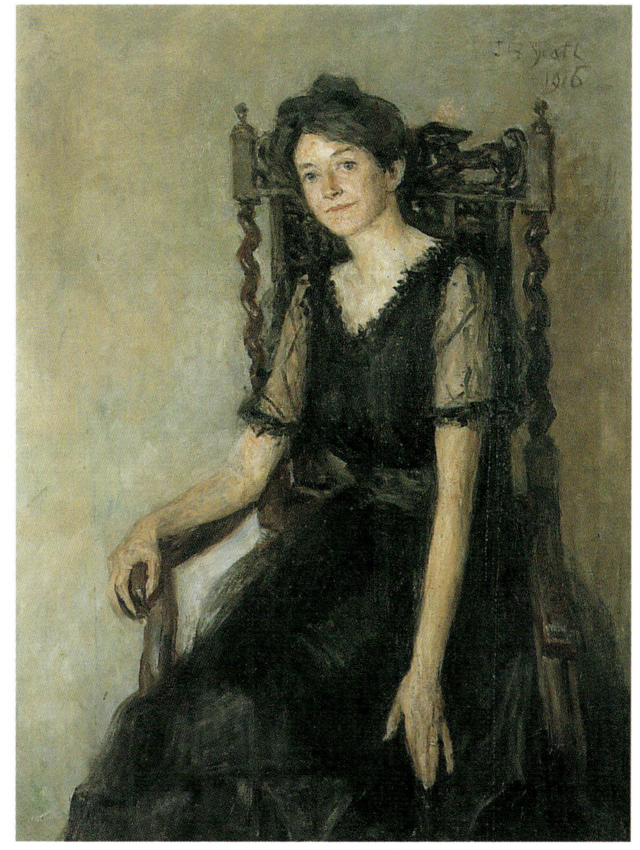

Mrs Mary Tower Lapsley Caughey seated

Oil on canvas, 102 × 76 cm, NGI 1726

It was through Mrs Caughey Guest (1901–1964) of Cincinnati, Ohio, that the three Caughey portraits by JBY (see previous page) came into the National Gallery. Presenting the portraits of her mother in October 1963, she wrote to Dr MacGreevy, then direc-tor of the Gallery, "I wish you could see another por-trait, which he made of me: it also has the same lovely brilliant colors .…" JBY's work was not currently in vogue in the States. "Particularly I am annoyed by people who complain that his colors are too somber. It is for this reason that I am glad for your museum to have these two portraits." Subsequently Mrs Guest bequeathed her own portrait to be presented to the National Gallery on the death of her husband, George Martin Guest.

Mary Lapsley Caughey (later Mrs Guest) was fifteen when this portrait was painted at her mother's house in Ohio Road, Sewickley, in Pennsylvania. According to JBY the portrait was done in one sitting (to Rosa Butt, 11 August 1916; Bodleian Library), though it is in no way unfinished: he must have worked quickly. She sits in the same chair with the elaborately carved back as her mother in NGI 1726. This time the chair is turned to the right and, in a favourite pose of the artist's, the sitter turns her head to look straight at the spectator. She is tall, her adolescent figure made more graceful by the full white dress, divided by broad black bands at the waist and in the skirt, and edged with black ribbon at the wrists and the neckline. Her thick brown hair, parted and gathered into two loose plaits framing her neck at either side, falls down into her lap, where she holds a magazine. There is a ring on the little finger of her right hand.

While JBY's style had changed somewhat since his move to New York, as a result of his association with the Ashcan School and the more avantgarde painters, his views on the essential art of portraiture had not altered; and he gives the shy, serious young sitter all

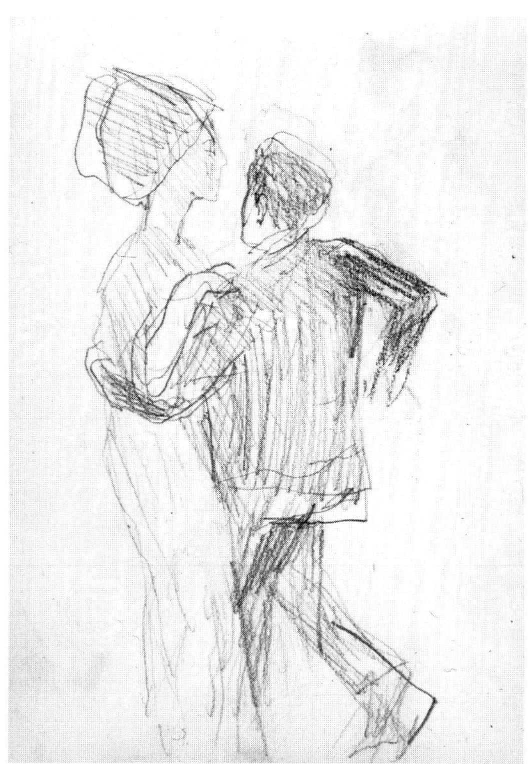

Fig. 90 J.B. Yeats, *Couple dancing*,
from an American sketchbook, *ca.* 1916
(Anne Yeats Collection)

of his attention, silhouetting her within the contained shape of the wooden chair against a background alive with dancing pigment. At the same time, there is an ele-ment of narrative in these American portraits. Part of a door is described to the right, a brown and red cush-ion sticks out from behind the girlish figure, and her fingers play with the book she holds in her lap, as she keeps her eye fixed dutifully on the artist.

Writing to Rosa Butt from New York in August 1916 about his experiences as he painted the Caughey por-traits, JBY added, "Happy as I was at Sewickley I was glad to get back."

1916, oil on canvas, 105 × 84 cm, NGI 1821

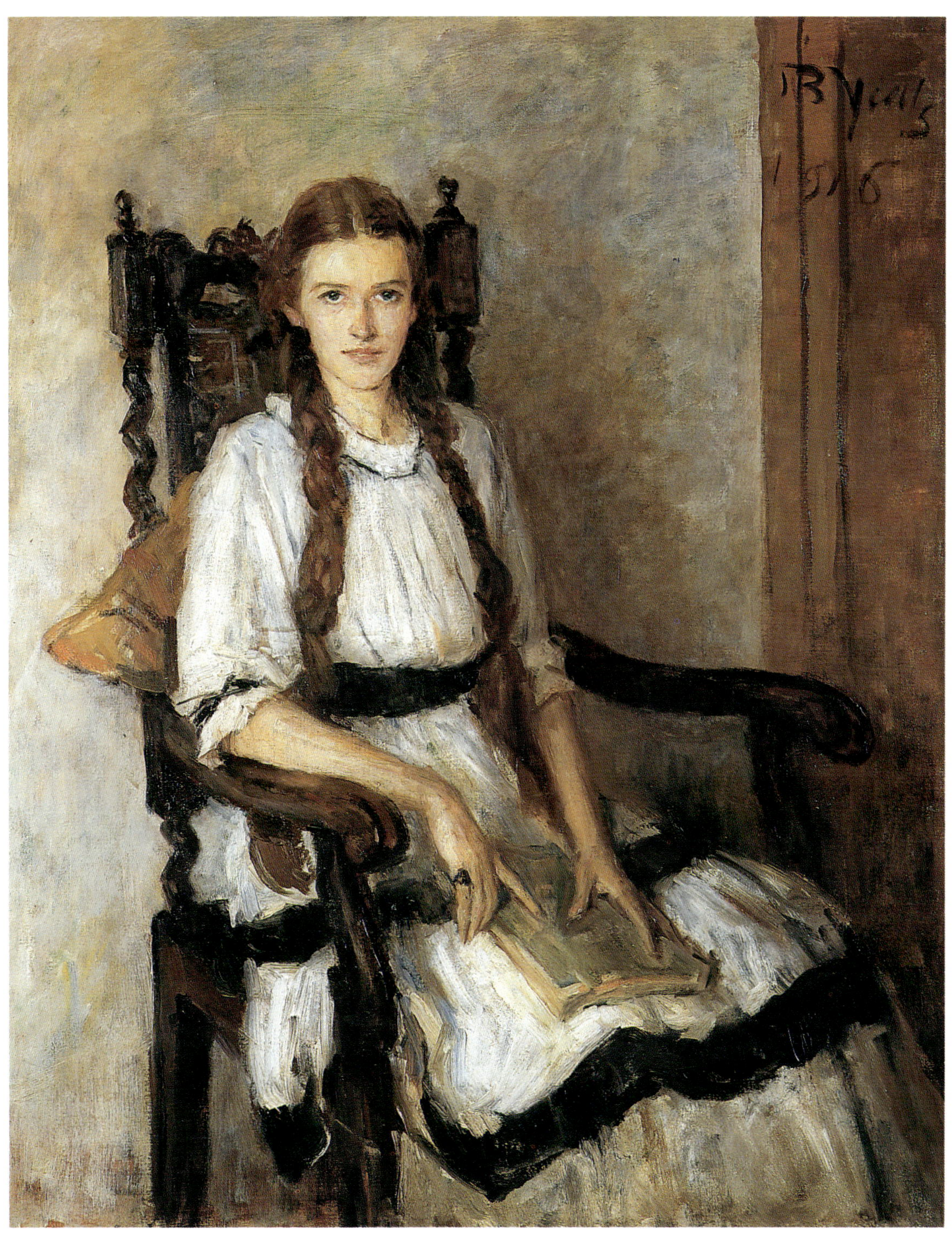

JBY's pencil portrait of Ernest Boyd (1887–1946), journalist and literary historian, made less than eighteen months before his death, is as lively as any of his sketch portraits. Like all his American work, though, it is much more realist in approach than his Dublin 'impressionist' likenesses, and his technique is more robust, more 'post-impressionist' (though of course he never associated this term with his own work). Instead of the fine soft shading, gone over time and again to darken it gradually, he contrasts the white of the card with dabs of shading and broad cross-hatching, which darken, or build up, form. This explicit manner tends to create an alert rather than a dreamy figure. However, the exigencies of the final outline (the line itself a pleasure in the delicacy of its movement), together with his sympathy for the sitter, make this a sensitive, if somewhat formal, portrait.

The viewer is directed straight to the sitter's intelligent face, as might be expected, but the body is well described, seated at the slight angle JBY preferred, with head turned to look straight at the viewer (see fig. 91). Boyd has a well groomed beard, short hair and regular features; and he wears a bow tie about his wing collar. While the upper background is clear of shading, around the base of the drawing the artist has scribbled with charcoal, thus anchoring the bust image firmly within the spatial frame.

Ernest A. Boyd is best remembered for his pioneer history of the modern Anglo-Irish literary movement. A Dubliner, he worked in the British Consular Service from 1913 to 1920, acting also as literary adviser to the Talbot Press. When the Talbot Press published JBY's *Essays*, he looked for first refusal on his autobiography. In 1920 he moved to New York, to devote himself to writing, and he also edited the works of Guy de Maupassant. From 1932 he edited *The American Spectator*.

JBY spent his last Christmas with the Boyd family; and Boyd was among those who met for dinner in the spring of 1922 to honour JBY's memory two months after his death, at the Petitpas boarding house in which he had lived for the final twelve years of his life. Pádraic Colum was there, as were the painters Robert Henri and John Sloan of the Ashcan School with whom JBY associated, and JBY's patron of long standing, John Quinn. In his tribute in the *Literary Review* (11 February 1922), Ernest Boyd had called JBY "the youngest of old men".

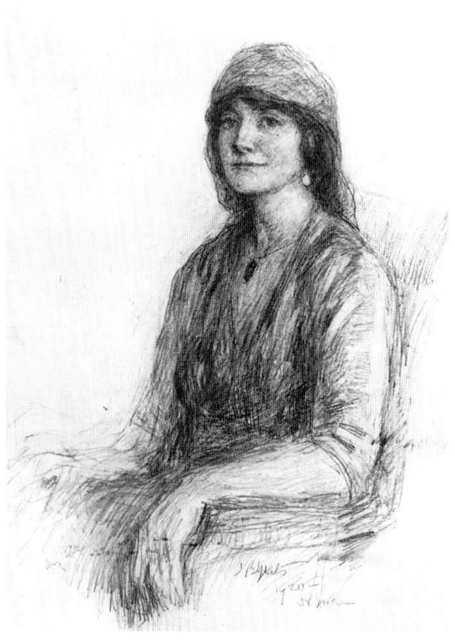

Fig. 91 J.B. Yeats, *George (Mrs W.B.) Yeats*, 1920, pencil, 49.5 × 36 cm
(Michael B. Yeats Collection)

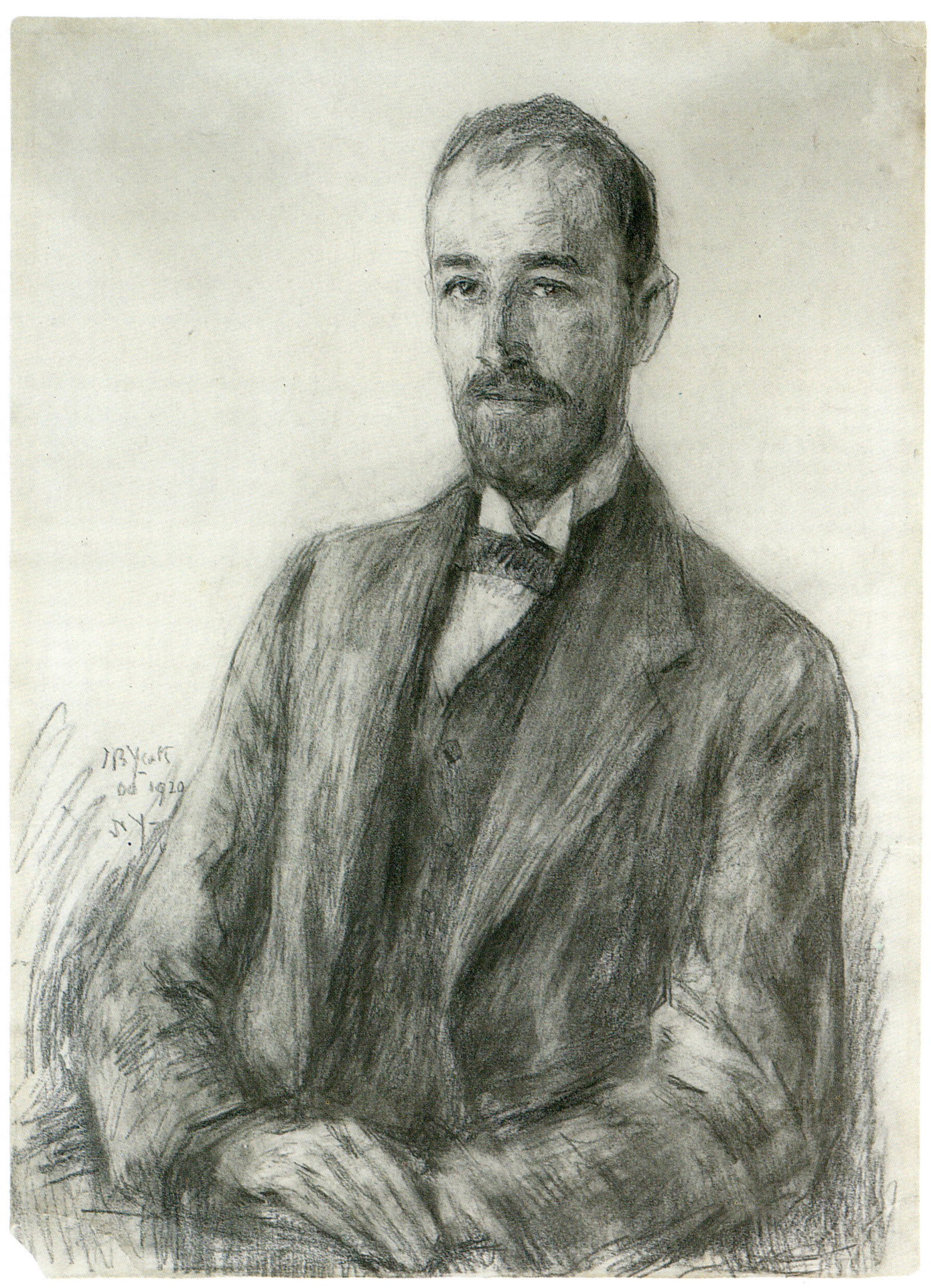

While John Quinn's commission for the famous oil self-portrait (fig. 92) dates from February 1911, and the artist tackled the subject with enthusiasm almost straightaway, there is no evidence that the canvas was started at that time. The self-portrait had to go through a series of manifestations before JBY clarified the final image. In *Life and the Dream*, Mary Colum described the artist's dingy room in the Petitpas boarding house where he lodged, with an iron bed, a cheap worn rug and "an easel on which was always erected a portrait at which he tinkered day after day".

However, the sketch had always been the ultimate for JBY in portraiture, and he may have embarked on the self-sketches as a result of having had to use a chalk self-portrait of 1902 (where the optical effect of the mirror image plays its part) to illustrate his *Essays Irish and American*, published in June 1918. He had frequently included sketches of himself in letters to correspondents back in Ireland, but during 1919 he began to compose more formal self-sketches. Quinn commissioned two, promising to pay $25 each on delivery – with the self-portrait in oil – and by October JBY had completed the near full-length pencil work which he inscribed, "Myself seen through a glass darkly" (Foster-Murphy Collection). NGI 19,341, inscribed *To John Quinn from JBYeats 1920*, is probably the second sketch made for this commission. Like the sketch of January 1920 in the National Portrait Gallery, London (which is similar though it includes a raised hand with pencil), this is a simple bust portrait, a rather pensive portrayal. The eyes fix themselves on those of the viewer with an intense sadness. The head with its wispy hair, huge ears and neatly shaped beard has a faint shadow behind it.

In August 1920 JBY told his daughter Elizabeth that he was making black-and-white studies for the oil, and reassured Quinn, "I think that now I see my way, and not till now." The second self-portrait sketch in the collection (NGI 6313) relates directly to the final oil, and may be counted as a direct study. In this half length the head is still dreamy in comparison with the buoyancy of the painting, and preoccupied in mood, with a slightly anxious expression, but the glass-fronted bureau, piled with untidy books, which is developed more fully in the oil, appears behind him. The right hand, holding what might be a stick of charcoal, is raised as if the artist has been arrested momentarily at the moment of creation. The shadow behind his head is now a veritable aura, as in his most inspired portraits.

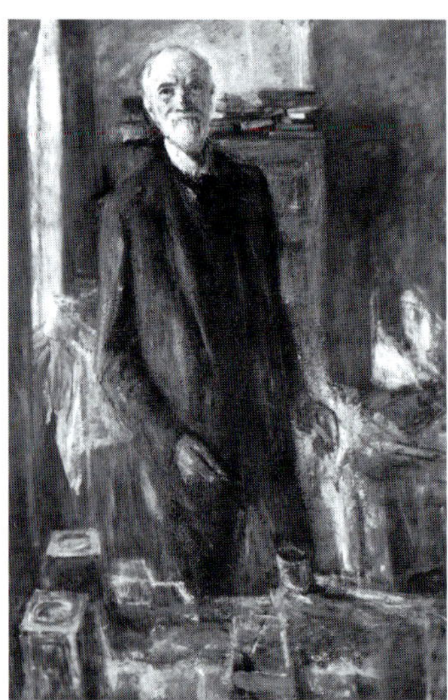

Fig. 92 J.B. Yeats, *Self-portrait*, 1920–22, pencil, 54 × 41.5 cm (Michael Yeats Collection)

Sketch self-portrait

Pencil with some crayon on buff paper, 48.4 × 37.8 cm, NGI 6313

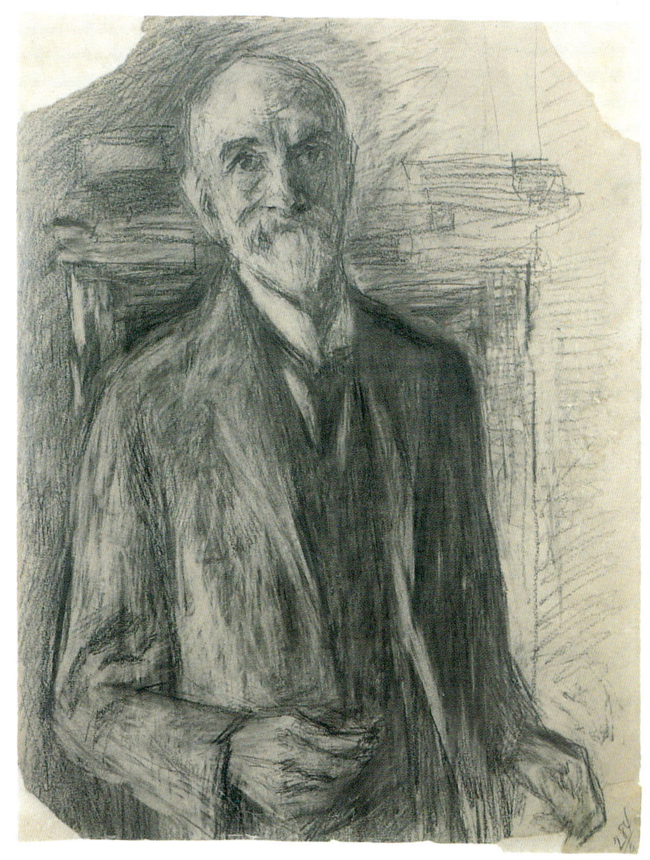

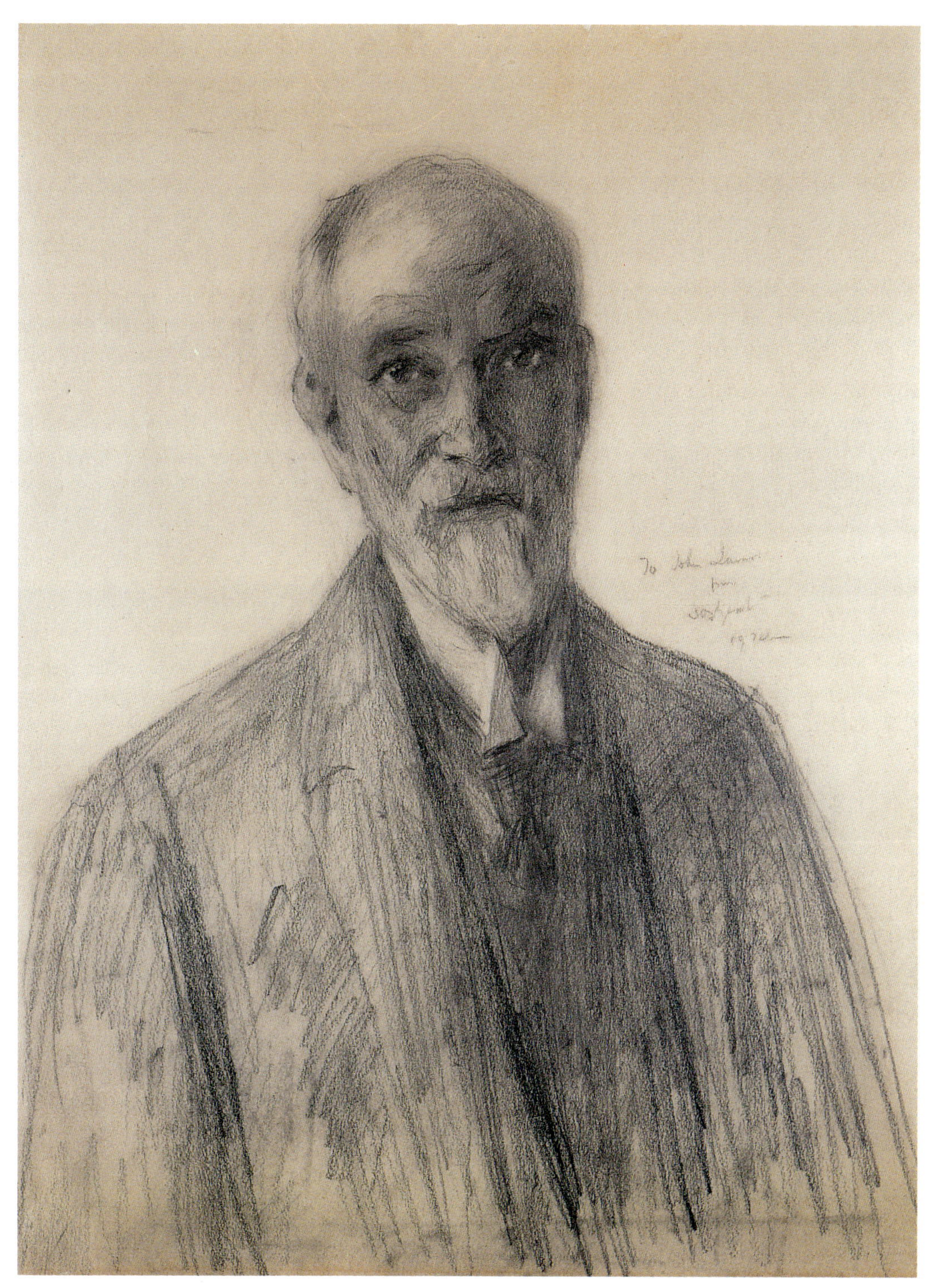

William Butler Yeats 1865–1939

William Butler Yeats, the eldest child of John Butler Yeats and his wife, Susan Pollexfen, was born in Sandymount, Dublin, on 13 June 1865, while his father was a law student at the King's Inns. Not long afterwards JBY moved to London to train at Heatherley's Art School, so that WBY's infancy and youth were spent with a father who was still a student, and who expounded his ideas and discoveries incessantly to his eldest son, whom he seems to have regarded as his special responsibility. It was WBY who was regularly privy to his father's celebrated conversations with those who frequented JBY's studio when it was in York Street and later in no. 7, St Stephen's Green.

WBY refused to go to Trinity, where his father had been. However, JBY always insisted that as a part of education every one should have an experience of art school. His daughters were at the Metropolitan School of Art, in Kildare Street, in 1883; and WBY attended the School from May 1884 until April 1886 (apart from some classes at the RHA Schools), where, he tells in *Reveries*, he was taught by his father. Fellow students were John Hughes and Oliver Sheppard, later prominent sculptors, and George Russell (A.E.), the poet and painter, with whom he was associated in the theatre and other cultural projects throughout his life. They were influenced by French art through magazines.

WBY "longed for Pre-Raphaelitism" in place of life drawing, but, he wrote, came out unable to compose anything but a portrait. *Head of a boy*, which is unsigned, belonged to his friend the poet Katharine Tynan, who referred to it in *The Years of the Shadow* (p. 241) as "a boy's head in chalk by W.B. Yeats, a relic of his art student days". WBY had had several poems published in the *Dublin University Review* by Charles Oldham, of the Contemporary Club, when Oldham brought him to see Katharine Tynan, already an established poet. She saw him as a tall lanky youth, "a gentle dreamer". Their friendship blossomed as he abandoned the palette to concentrate on his poetry.

Head of a boy is a romantic colourful image of a boy viewed in left profile, head bowed on his breast – perhaps resting his arms on a table. Only his bust is shown, his shoulder and upper arm forming a single ochre mass. His face, with a long-lashed dark eye and red lips, his black shining hair and his red cap, becomes the focus of the painting.

The student work is perhaps based on fifteenth-century prototypes, but with a nineteenth-century pleasure in colour. The transparent paint has been rubbed in some places to give the effect of light on the ochre garment, and in shady areas has been applied in an opaque wash. Light hatching in fine pen has been added to sharpen up areas around the eye, the nose and the side face. The whole concept is sensitively treated, with a breadth of image, the paint being applied very smoothly.

When he became interested in psychical research and mystical philosophy, which the rational-minded artist could not tolerate, WBY broke away from his father's influence. However, his late poetry is full of artistic allusions, influenced by his predilection for the Pre-Raphaelites and the Symbolists, as well as for certain contemporary painters, and he welcomed his father's portraits as illustrations to his own publications. His own pastels and watercolours are rare (fig. 94).

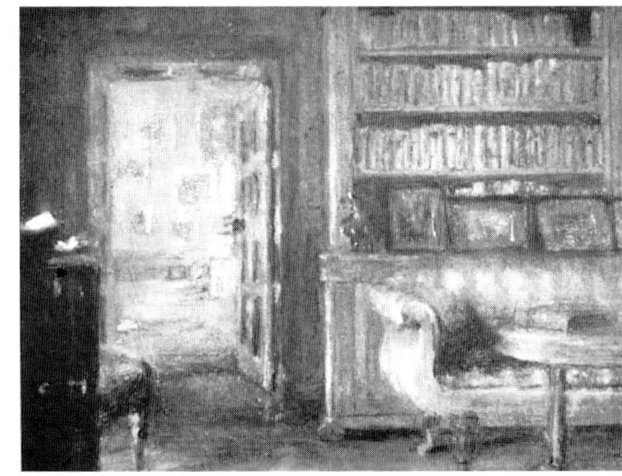

Fig. 94
W.B. Yeats,
*The Library,
Coole House*
(Michael Yeats
Collection)

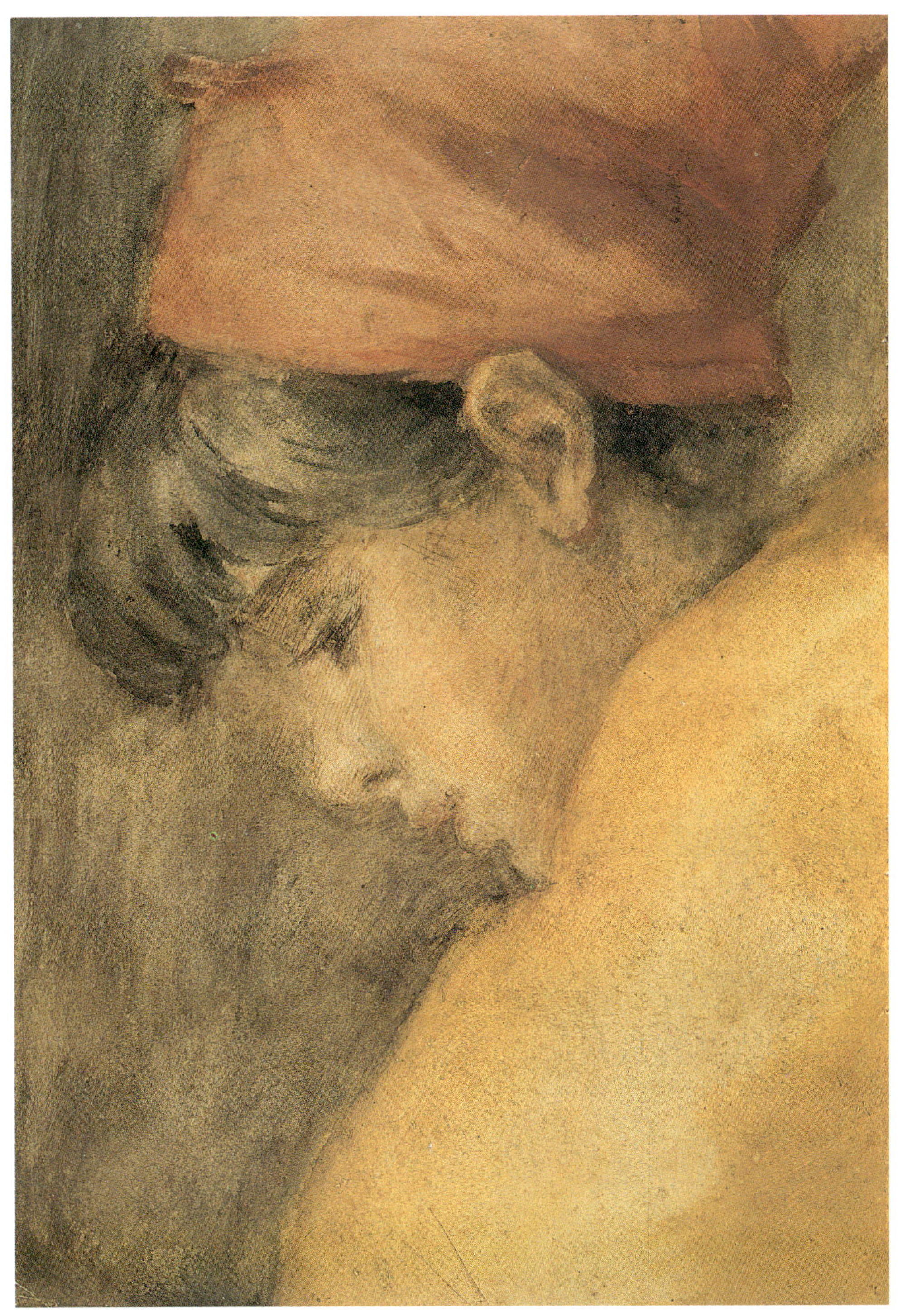

Susan Mary (Lily) Yeats 1866–1948

Susan Mary Yeats was the only one of JBY's children born in Sligo, and she felt a close identity with the place. Though named after her mother, she was always known by her family name 'Lily', and she signed her work 'Lily Yeats'. Her psychic tendency was inherited from the Pollexfen family as was her interest in genealogy, and she became the family chronicler, identifying for posterity the sitters and possible dates of many of JBY's sketches.

When the family settled in Bedford Park, London in 1887, Lily was apprenticed to William Morris's daughter, May, who ran an embroidery workshop at Kelmscott House in Oxfordshire. She spent nearly six years there, staying with the workshop when it moved to Hammersmith. She showed a flower painting at the Royal Hibernian Academy in 1898, but returned to embroidery, exhibiting with the newly established Arts and Crafts Society of Ireland from 1899.

When, in 1902, Evelyn Gleeson founded an arts and crafts co-operative for women at Dundrum in Dublin modelled on the Kelmscott workshops, she invited the Yeats sisters to join her, Lily to supervise embroidery, and Lolly to establish a printing press. The name Dun Emer (Emer's fort) was chosen for the venture – Emer the wife of the ancient Irish hero Cuchulain was renowned for her beauty, wit and needlework – and those involved in the Celtic revival wanted to mirror those legendary times in modern artistry, using only Irish materials. Classes in painting and the Irish language were organized for the working girls employed: and one of the first commissions was the embroidering of a set of sodality banners for the new cathedral in Loughrea, County Galway (see pp. 166–169).

Lily Yeats exhibited at the New York Irish Exhibition in January 1908, returning to negotiate a separation from Evelyn Gleeson and Dun Emer. Evelyn Gleeson continued to weave carpets and tapestries. The Yeats sisters set up their own embroidery and printing workshops at Churchtown, south of Dublin, in a cottage set in fields with "a wide view of the Dublin mountains" and adopting Cuala, the Old Irish name of the local barony, for their business.

Lily's designs tended to be influenced by her brother Jack's *Broadside* manner in their bold outline but they had a pictorial bent of their own. She often made several versions of subjects that were designed by her sister or herself.

She worked *Cornfield with poppies* in 1941 for her distant cousin David Meredith, then aged sixteen. A simple country scene, akin to her series of *Meadows*, it is dominated by the purple hill in the background, which is framed by tall foxgloves and stylized meadowsweet. In the foreground a stile leads to a ripe field of corn. The daisies and poppies crowding the verge push at the wooden fence (compare fig. 95). It all looks three-dimensional by dint of the different stitches used, especially the chain stitch and French knot, and through the subtlety of the colour tones. The deep blue of the fabric sky (where birds are flying) reaches down the sides of the picture. The shading is distinctive, the space between stitches altering to create the mistiness of distance.

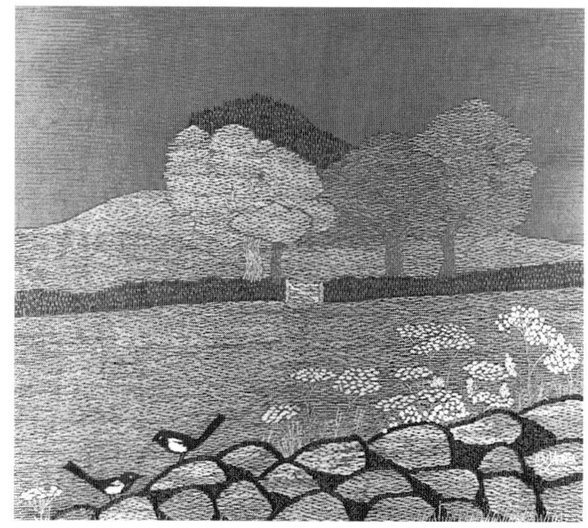

Fig. 95 Lily Yeats, *The stone wall* (NGI Yeats Archive)

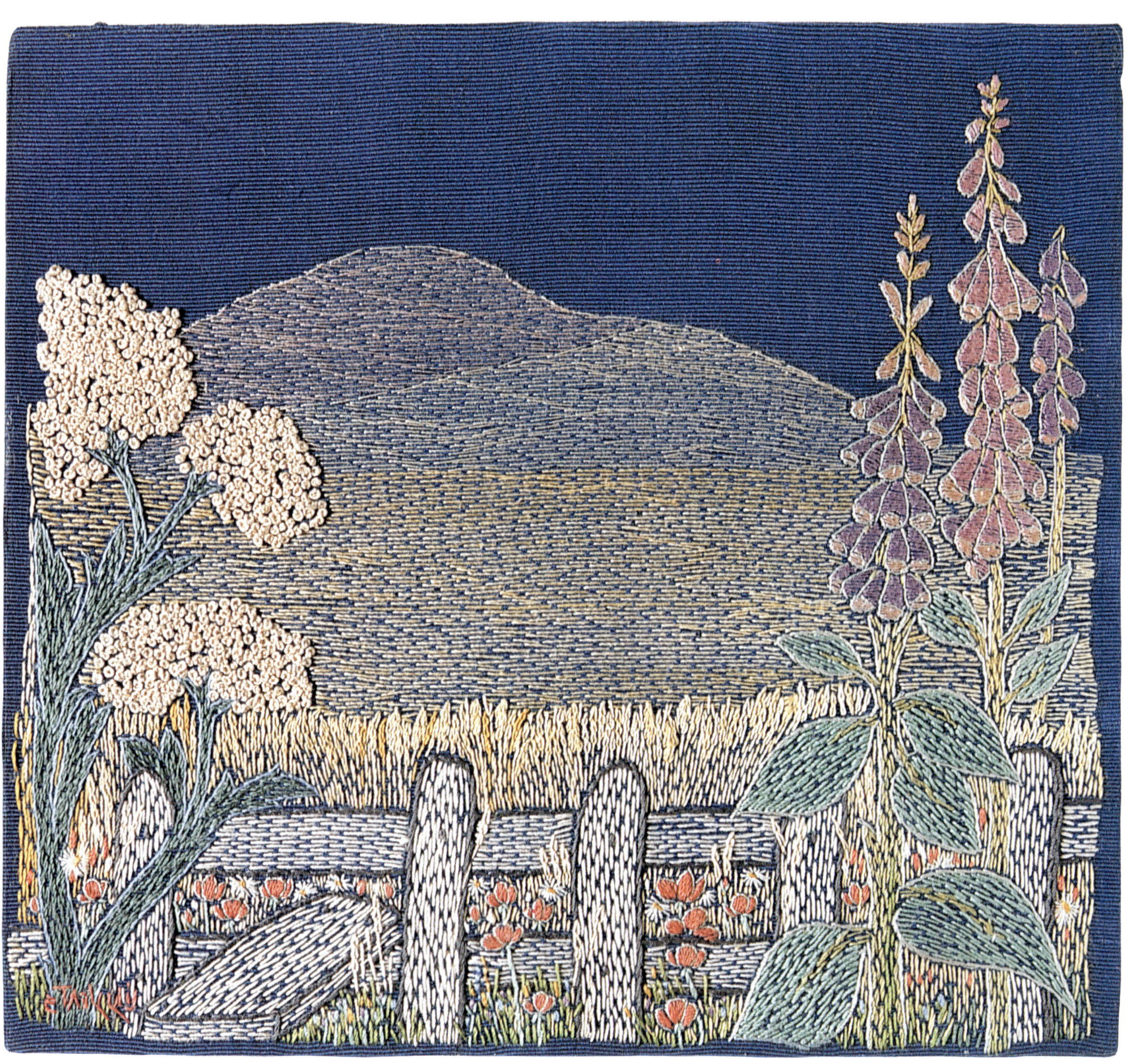

Elizabeth Corbet (Lolly) Yeats 1868–1940

Elizabeth (or Lolly) Yeats was the founder of the Dun Emer and Cuala Presses, celebrated for their essential contribution to the Irish literary renaissance. Her brother, WBY, editor and director, published his first editions under the Cuala imprint. The poet John Masefield told Lily Yeats, "Your sister did very much to make your Brother what he was, and to keep the Irish movement linked with the progress of the arts rather than with violent political upheaval."

Originally Elizabeth Yeats trained as a Froebel teacher; but she had seen private printing at first hand at Kelmscott House, where Lily worked with May Morris. Through the Morris family, the Yeats family had their first taste of the Arts and Crafts movement, and Lily and Lolly took readily to Evelyn Gleeson's proposal in 1902 that they should introduce art workshops to Dublin. Within a matter of weeks, Elizabeth had trained as a printer manager and the Dun Emer Press was launched in the spring of 1903 with *In the Seven Woods* by WBY. Each page of her books was characterized by its classic plainness. She soon started publishing hand-coloured prints and Christmas cards, designed by her brother Jack and herself and others,

and training assistants to finish them by hand in watercolour.

The first issue of *A Broadside* was printed at Dun Emer in June 1908, after which this series of ballads and modern poems illustrated by Jack B. Yeats continued to be published monthly from the Cuala Press until 1915 (there are three original drawings for *A Broadside* in the National Gallery collection), with further editions in 1935 and 1937. During thirty years of printing, Elizabeth Yeats produced sixty books, by A.E., Lady Gregory, Synge, Hyde, Gogarty, Tynan and others. During the early years, her own prints for Dun Emer and Cuala (fig. 96) are signed *E.C.Y.*

Elizabeth Yeats was also a watercolourist, and taught in London for ten years, continuing to teach painting when she returned to Ireland. She published four brushwork manuals: *Brushwork* (1895), *Brushwork Studies of Flowers, Fruits and Animals* (1898), *Brushwork Copy Book* (1899) and *Elementary Brushwork Studies* (1900), in which she first showed latent skills as a book designer.

Cashlauna Seilmide: the studio shows the exterior of Jack B. Yeats's studio in Devon, a building of wood and brick with a high pitched roof and a front veranda supported by pillars, set on a hillside surmounted by a small wood of trees coming into leaf. There are saplings at either side of the path that winds down the hill from it, and a bank of over-large primroses in the right foreground.

Elizabeth Yeats, who painted the watercolour when she visited her brother in Devon at Cashlauna Seilmide ('Snail's Castle') in April 1900, follows her principle of drawing with the brush particularly when depicting the angular lines of the young trees. Her palette is similar to that of Jack Yeats at that period, with purply shadows and a veridian green, but her matching of tones is less assured. She captures admirably the freshness of the April day and the spring sunlight on the gable end of the building.

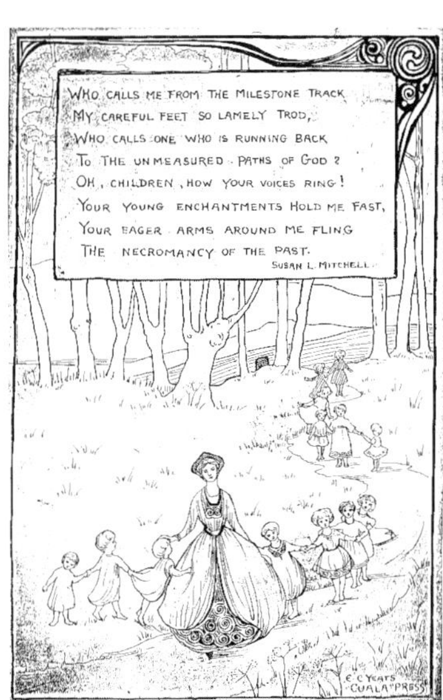

Fig. 96 Elizabeth Yeats, *Who calls me from the milestone track*, Cuala Card (Anne Yeats Collection)

Cashlauna Seilmide: the studio

1900, watercolour on artists' board, 54.5 × 36.5 cm, YArcECY1

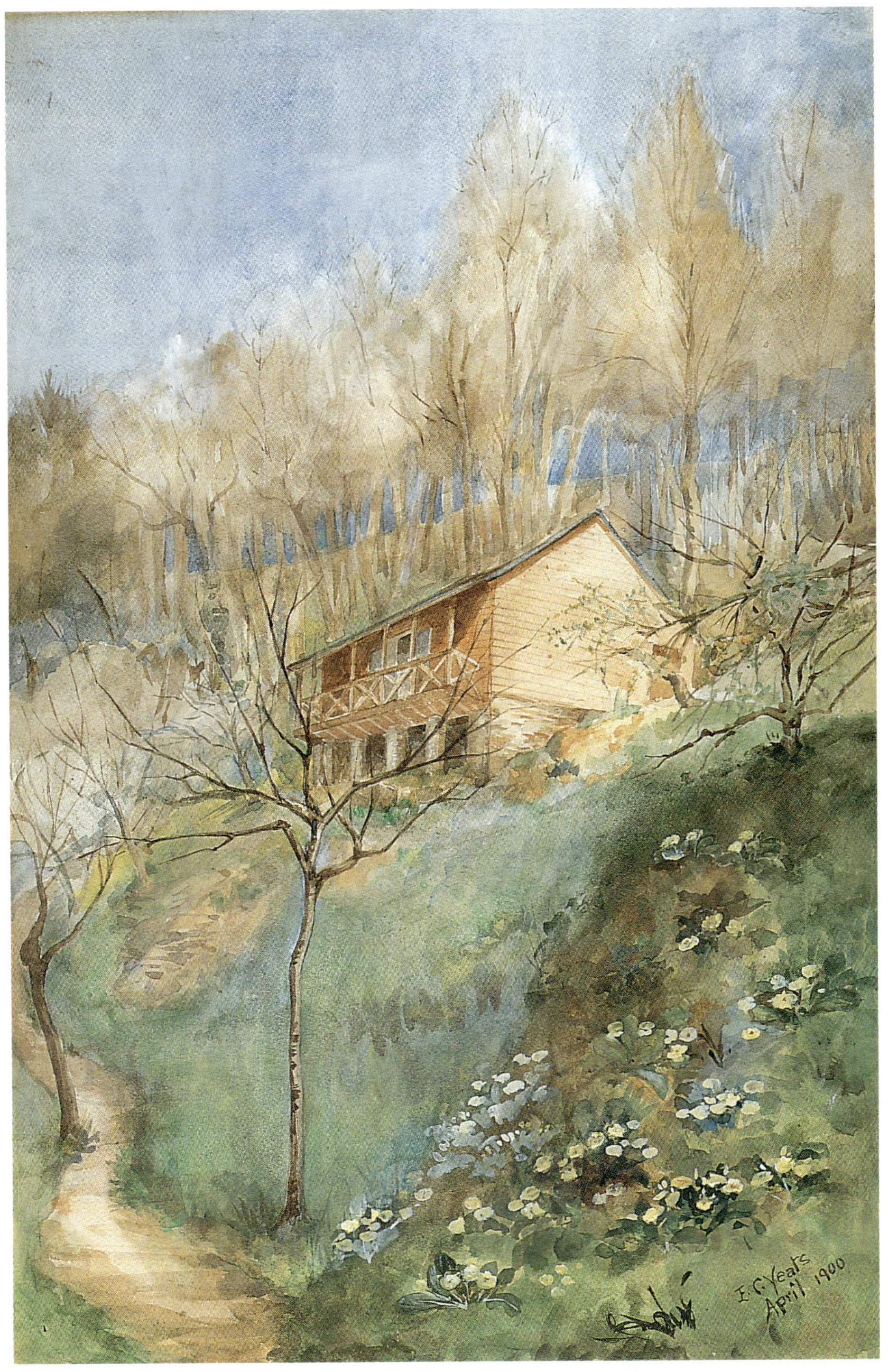

Jack B. Yeats 1871–1957

In 1899, Jack B. Yeats and his wife spent a holiday with J.C. Miles on the Norfolk Broads near Yarmouth, Jack sketching a great deal on Hickling Broad (fig. 97). This was probably in the early part of July, not long after they had returned from Paris (see Chronology). For Yeats, the water of sea and river had an enduring fascination; and his knowledge of these waters led people to believe that he had been a sailor during his youth, he was so well acquainted with nautical lore. Much of this lore he had picked up on his grandfather's trading vessels, which plied between Sligo and Liverpool, and in which he and his brother WBY travelled to England. The route around the north coast of Ireland is described vividly by WBY in the first chapter of *John Sherman and Dhoya*.

Elsewhere, Jack Yeats cultivated his interest in boats on the quays of Sligo and Galway where he sketched; in Dublin's dockland; and, more pleasurably, at Coole, where he joined in boat races on the lake with Robert Gregory, WBY and their young contemporaries; or about the coast of Donegal where he rowed with his wife. In Devon he lived for years beside the sea. The Norfolk Broads were a new and welcome experience for him.

The three companion watercolours in this collection (pp. 158–163) may have been executed *in situ*, as they were worked on a drawing block. Yeats seems to have been chiefly preoccupied with the boat itself. In the first, the yacht heels over in a fresh wind, the peak of the sail thrusting in a diagonal direction upward into the top left-hand corner of the painting, in a tension of movement away from the mast. The mast makes a less challenging thrust across the central space. In counterpoint, the water churning in the wake of the boat leads the eye into the picture from the lower left-hand corner; opening up the interesting shapes created on each side of the vessel, in the sky and in the sea.

Ignoring these skilful and unobtrusive elements of construction, one can see that the subject is invested with lyricism, and treated with a freshness that is typical of Yeats's watercolours between 1897 and 1899. A blue verging on purple is dominant, applied with a broad flexible stroke and with an experienced eye to the effect of natural light and space. A visit to Venice the year before must have affected the artist's colouring, making it warm and emotional. The boat is described with a masterly, yet sensitive, line and the rest of the details are sketched in briefly in the first of a trio of studies of the yacht which show Yeats the watercolourist at his most sophisticated.

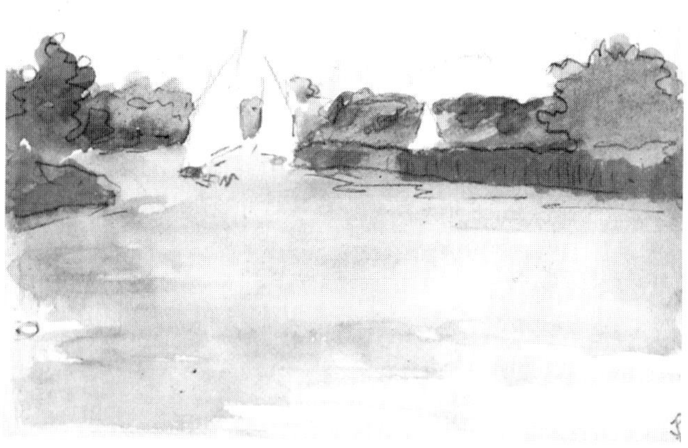

Fig. 97 Jack B. Yeats, *On Hickling Broad*, from a sketchbook (Theo Waddington Archive)

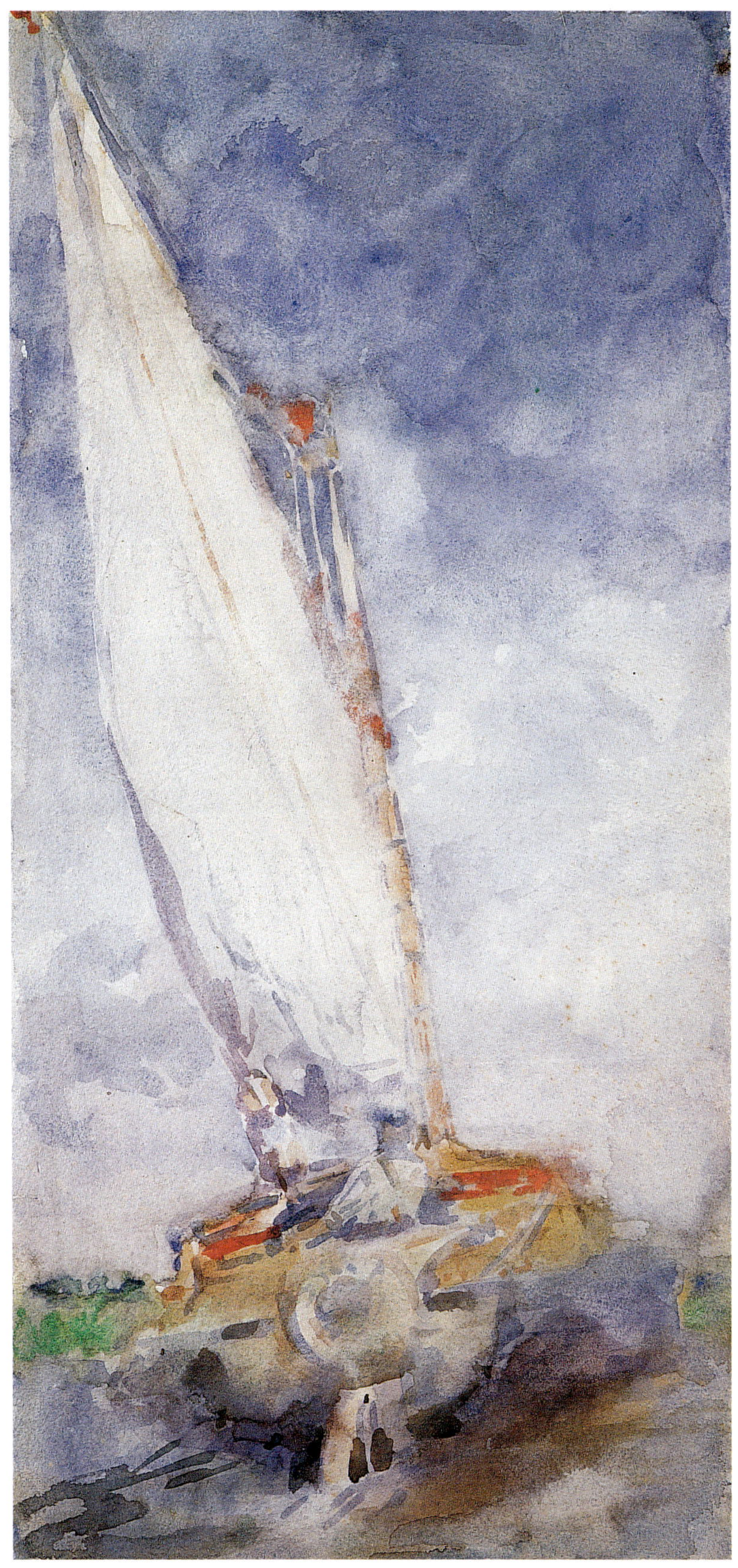

On the Broads

1899, watercolour on paper, 35.5 × 17 cm,
NGI 6318

O*n Deck*, the second of the Norfolk water-colours, through a wide expanse of barely tinted paper conjures up the sensation of the nearness of the yacht's prow when the eye has dropped from the coastline and the surrounding water to become totally involved in the floating vessel. The sail, represented as a wavy rectangle through which the distant coastline (painted first) may be seen, seems to dominate the painting with its moody colour. The trees and water appear ghostly in comparison with the solidity of the yacht's deck, which forges forward, bearing the unseen sailors along purposefully in the wind.

Yeats places the mast's base in the upper centre of the composition, a pivot on to which the upright pole, the straining lines of the sail, the pale shadow of the flat skyline hinterland and the curves of the deck converge. The picture, in this way, is divided into three provocative shapes. Of these, the near empty arc of the deck in the foreground is the most prominent, suggesting most of the movement and excitement of the picture through its aggressive thrust and the intimation of human presence.

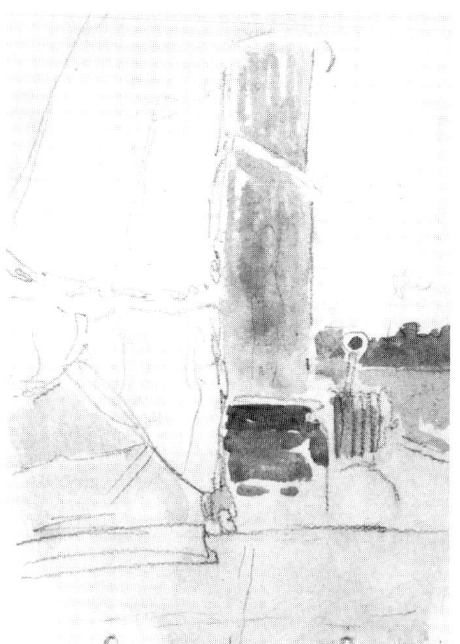

Fig. 98 Jack B. Yeats, *On the Broads,* from a sketchbook (Theo Waddington Archive)

On deck, on the Broads

1899, watercolour on paper, 17 × 35.5 cm, NGI 6319

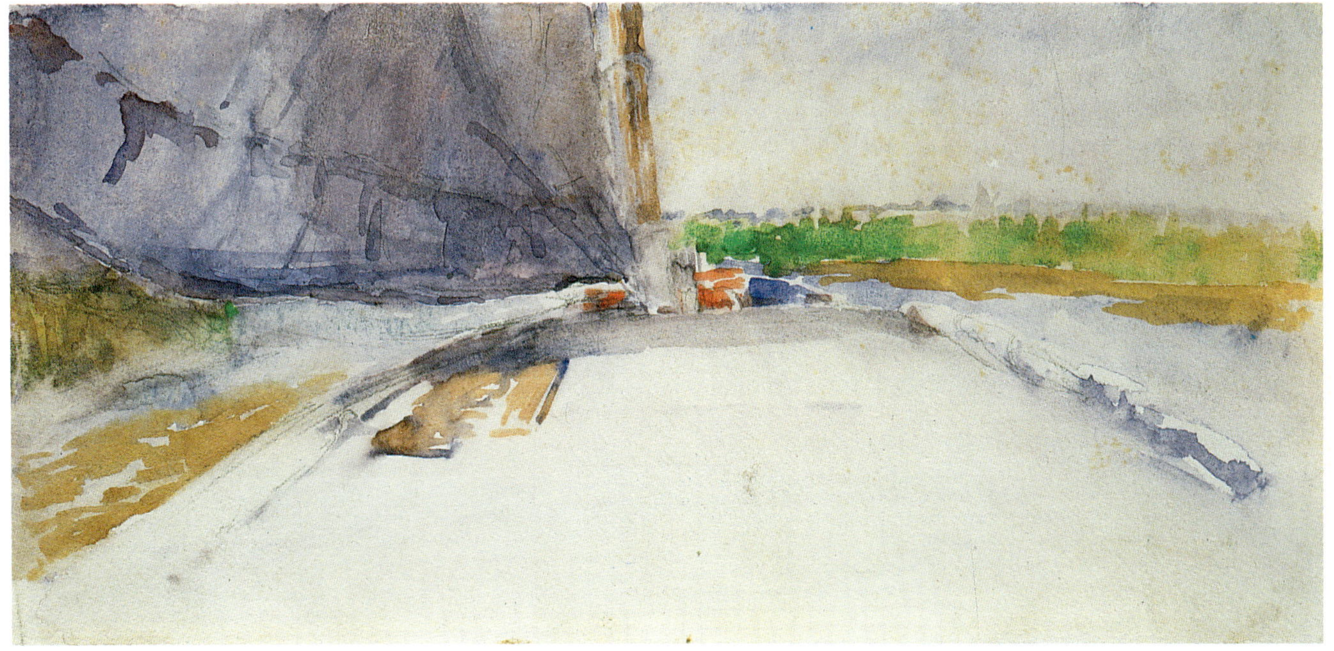

The third of Yeats's studies painted on the Norfolk Broads (see previous pages), *Below deck* is a view of the inside of the cabin of J.C. Miles's yacht. It is painted a warm brown, varied with the play of green that reflects into the cabin from the grassy coastline. Through the row of horizontal windows, a yacht in full sail may be seen.

The cabin itself is rendered as an interior space without detail except for the globular lamp that hangs to the upper right of the centre, and which reproduces the suggestive reflections from elsewhere in the cabin on a more intimate scale. The lamp also is the agent whereby the lines of the low windows are carried upward and joined in a single line to the rim of the ceiling, above the barely indicated door. This creates a linear movement in what might be a still picture, were it not for the rocking light expressed so vividly in the paint. The touch of red on the window adds a further lively element.

The constriction of the cabin is emphasized by the pools of shadow here and there, and by its dimness in contrast with the loosely sketched vignettes of landscape glistening beyond the windows.

Jack Yeats painted a fourth watercolour in this series, which shows his friend J.C. Miles looking into the cabin of a wherry. This he presented to Miles's great-granddaughter as a christening present from "her great grand Godfather" in December 1942. The watercolour is still in the possession of the family.

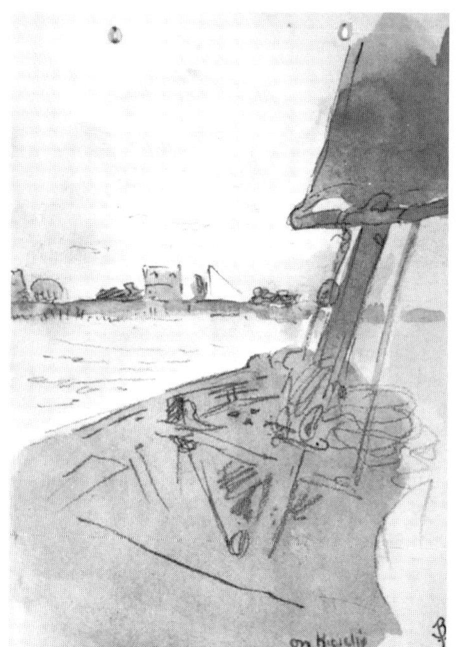

Fig. 99 Jack B. Yeats, *On the Broads*, from a sketchbook
(Theo Waddington Archive)

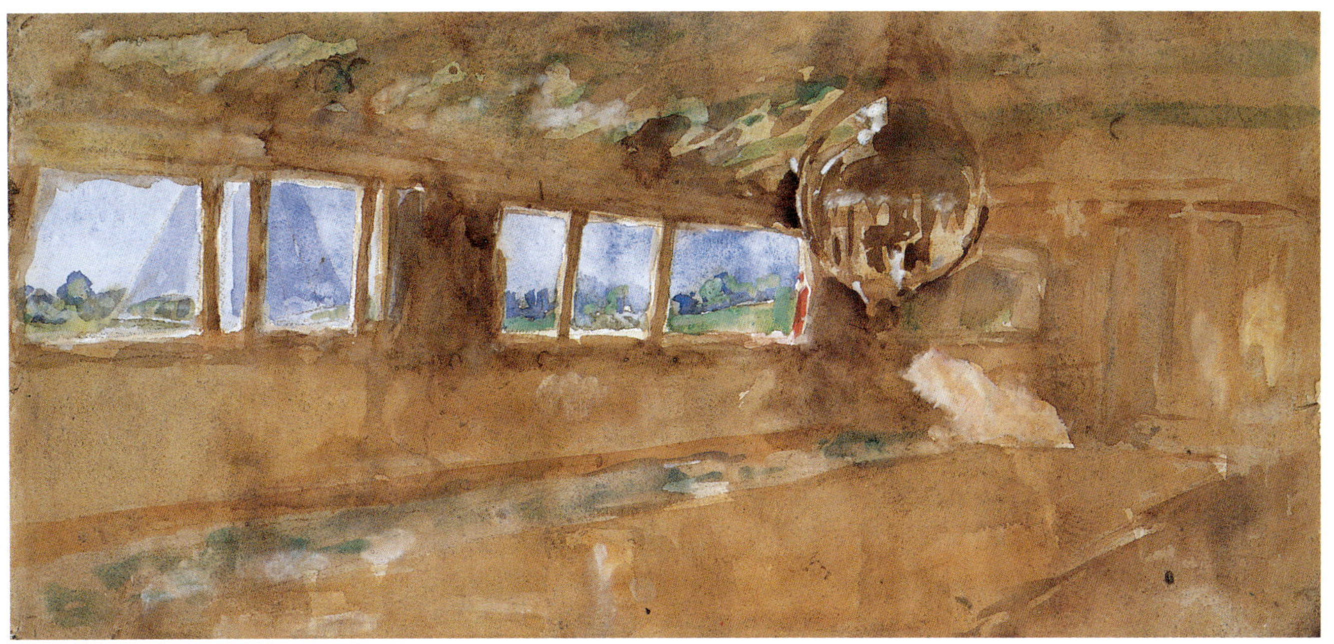

Below deck, on the Broads

1899, watercolour on paper, 17 × 35.5 cm, NGI 6320

Since his youth, Jack B. Yeats had been captivated by the ballad singers of Sligo, who carried bundles of crudely printed broadsides for sale and demonstrated the quality of their ware by performance. He began to collect broadsides of the eighteenth and nineteenth centuries as a young man. He made many watercolours and oil paintings of ballad singers; and later in life used the wandering singer in paintings such as *Eileen Aroon* (the title is the refrain of an Irish love song) as a symbol for inspiration (see further p. 184 and fig. 109).

In 1900, he came in contact with a young American artist, Pamela Colman Smith, who shared his enthusiasm for folk culture. She had published Jamaican folktales for children, which she illustrated in a decorative style akin to Walter Crane. After leaving Jamaica, she visited the Yeats family in Bedford Park, London, in 1899; and subsequently she stayed with Jack and his wife at their house, Cashlauna Seilmide, in Devon. She and Jack evolved *A Broad Sheet*, which they persuaded Elkin Mathews, London, to publish, and which came out monthly from January 1902 until the end of 1903. Two or three poems or ballads with hand-coloured illustrations were printed on one side of a sheet of paper in amplified artistic imitation of the traditional balladsheet. The illustrations by Jack Yeats and Pamela Colman Smith are in strong linear styles, both derived from the traditional woodcut, yet easily distinguished from one another for their individuality.

Several poets contributed to *A Broad Sheet*, WBY, John Masefield and A.E. (George Russell) among them; and there were traditional ballads, translated from Irish, Danish and French.

Pamela Colman Smith had many enthusiasms, and, after the first year of *A Broad Sheet*, she lost interest. In January 1903 she retired; Jack Yeats continued to produce the publication on his own, continuing to hand-colour every number of each issue until the end of 1903, when he brought it to a close.

The County of Mayo is Yeats's illustration to a well known Irish ballad, translated by George Fox and printed in *A Broad Sheet* in July 1903. With nostalgia, the verses recall the gaiety and prosperity in Mayo before the writer was forced to emigrate. It is one of many poems of the transition period that lament the passing of the Gaelic dominion and the changes that came about under a foreign ruler. The poet, in fact, devotes most of the poem to the pernicious state of affairs in his native county under the usurper: but Yeats chooses to see the speaker beginning his exile on board ship, illustrating the couplet which is inscribed on the back of the drawing:

'Tis a bitter change from those gay days
 that now I'm forced to go,
And must leave my bones in Santa Cruz
 far from my own Mayo.

The emigrant is seen, half length, with a background of a seventeenth-century galleon, looking moodily into space, his face cupped between his hands, his elbows resting on his knees. A wide-brimmed black hat frames his bearded, tragic face. The sleeves of his coat are slashed elegantly and fastened with buttons. The opening of his shirt is laced. Behind him is the ship's sail. A figure climbs the rigging and the sea may be glimpsed beyond that again. To the bottom right, in the corner of the detailed drawing, appears the face of the ship's captain, impassive and fatalistic, in charge of the ship that hurries the emigrant away from his beloved County of Mayo.

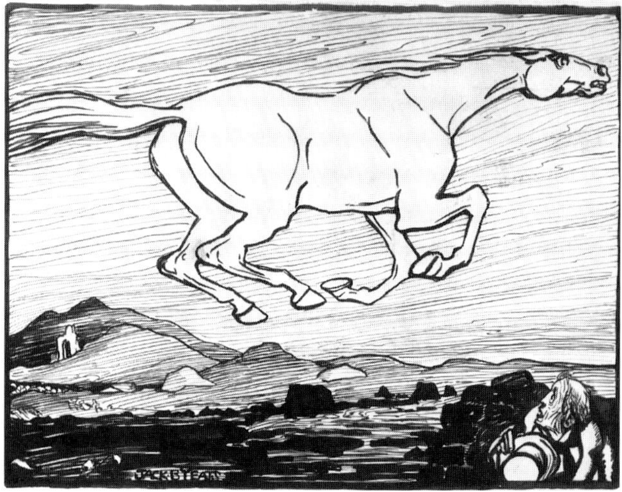

Fig. 100 Jack B. Yeats, *The Pooka*, in *A Broad Sheet*, January 1902 (private collection)

The County of Mayo

1903, pen and ink, and watercolour, on card, 15.6 × 20.2 cm, NGI 3830

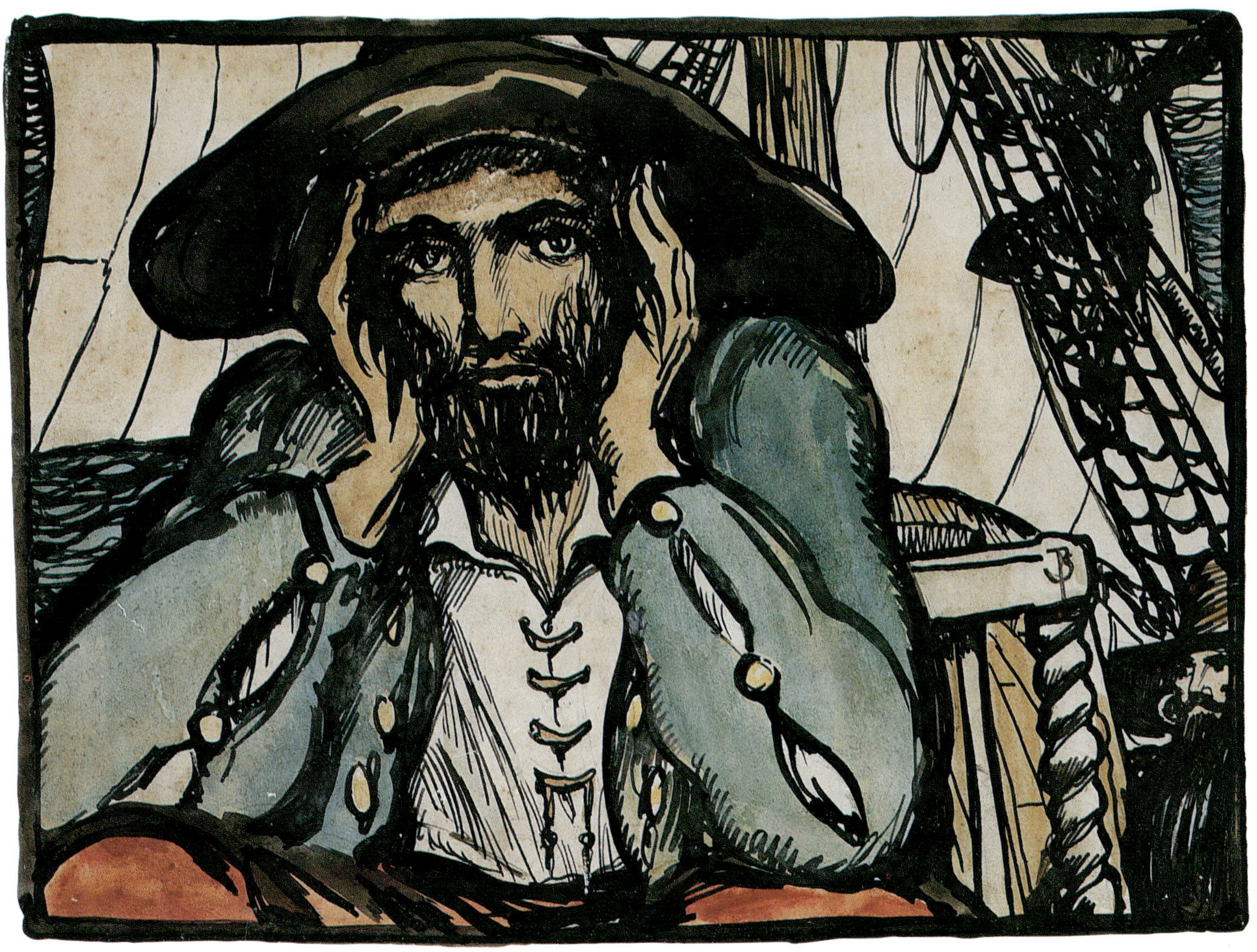

I n 1903, Jack B. Yeats and his wife Mary Cottenham Yeats were invited to design sodality banners for the new cathedral at Loughrea, in County Galway. These sodalities were in honour of the Sacred Heart, and met once a month in the cathedral for Mass, the men one Sunday, the women the following Sunday. The sodalities were divided into groups, and banners, each depicting a saint, were put up among the pews to denote where each group should sit.

Jack Yeats designed the Sacred Heart banner, and all of the men saints', except for St Patrick's and St Laurence O'Toole's, which were designed by A.E. (George Russell); Cottie Yeats designed all the women saints', except St Bridget's, which Pamela Colman Smith designed, and St Agnes's, designed by Jack Yeats. Yeats made further cartoons for Sts Aloysius, Alphonsus and Diochu, which were not used. The banners were embroidered at the Dun Emer workshop by Lily Yeats and her assistants, using wool and silk thread on linen; and the twelve banners were exhibited at Dun Emer, Dundrum, County Dublin on 4 and 11 February 1904, before going to Loughrea.

About 1930, Mrs Oliver St John Gogarty commissioned a series of four banners from Jack and Lily Yeats,

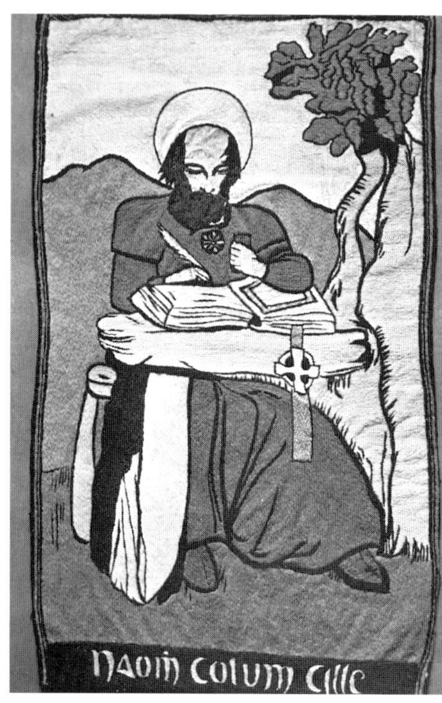

Fig. 101 Lily Yeats, *Naomh Colum Cille (St Columba)*, banner, wool and silk embroidery on linen, 78 × 49 cm (Loughrea Cathedral)

one of which was a St Colmcille identical with the Loughrea Colmcille (fig. 101). This is signed with a B monogram in the finished embroidery, which was done on silk poplin, and is now in the National Museum of Ireland.

St Colmcille or Columba, one of the most striking personalities of the early Celtic Church, was born at Gartan in Donegal in 521, a member of the royal Uí Néill family. His father was the great-grandson of Níall of the Nine Hostages. Colmcille studied with St Finian of Moville and St Finian of Clonard; and also with St Mobhi, at Glasnevin in Dublin, after which he returned to the north of Ireland. He was given an oak wood as the site for his church Doire Choluim Cille, now better known as the City of Derry.

While at the monastery of St Finian of Moville, Colmcille, who was a noted scholar, asked permission to make a copy of Finian's Psalter; but he was refused. Colmcille secretly made his own copy. This led later to a major battle, at the foot of Ben Bulben in County Sligo, and Colmcille's eventual self-imposed exile from Ireland to Iona where he founded his famous monastery. The transfer design shows him engaged at work copying, his quill pen in one hand, his ink pot in the other. Yeats's humour contrives a convenient table for him in the open in the shape of a dolmen-like slab perched upon the lower branch of a stunted oak.

The *Cathach*, a Psalter in the collection of the Royal Irish Academy in Dublin, is believed to be Colmcille's controversial copy of St Finian's Psalter. St Colmcille died in AD 597.

The prickmarks made in the linen on which this design is drawn, and the absence of facial detail, indicate that this was one of the transfers made at Dun Emer to enable the embroideress to translate the cartoon image accurately on to her material, prior to working the banner with the threads. The original St Colmcille cartoon by Jack B. Yeats, from which the transfer was taken, is in Áras an Uachtaráin, the residence of the President of Ireland.

Transfer design for *St Colmcille banner*

1903, ink on linen, 94.1 × 54.9 cm, NGI 7946

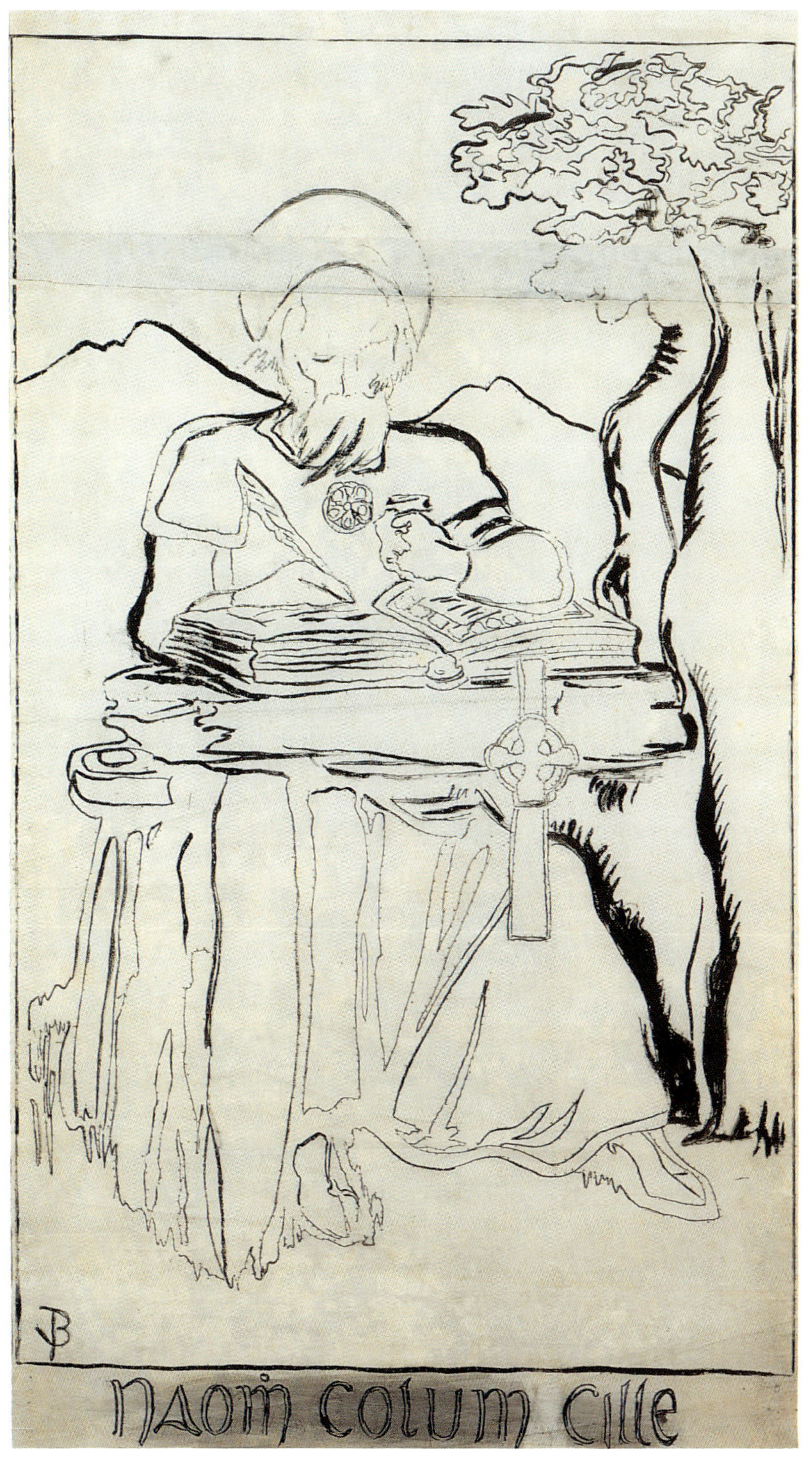

This is one of the transfer designs used in the working of the Loughrea banners during 1903–04 (see previous page). Jack B. Yeats's original cartoon for St Asicus is in Sligo County Library and Museum. Asicus (Irish: Assith), patron saint of the Diocese of Elphin of which Sligo is a part, is said to have been one of St Patrick's priest-craftsmen, and a skilled metalworker.

According to legend, St Asicus either told a lie quite innocently, or else had a lie told about him; and as a penance he retreated, quite unnecessarily, to Slieve League where he built himself a hermitage. After that, he moved to an island off the west coast of Ireland. He remained in isolation for seven years, after which he was persuaded to return to Elphin; but he died before he reached Elphin, at Rathcooney, Ballintra.

In the Loughrea banner, he wears a red habit. He holds a book, to show his clerical status, and lays his hand on the top of a bell, which he himself may have cast and which bears images of a round tower and a rabbit on it, both symbolizing the victory of chastity. All the Loughrea banners are embroidered in strong rich colours, with the figures silhouetted against backgrounds of gold.

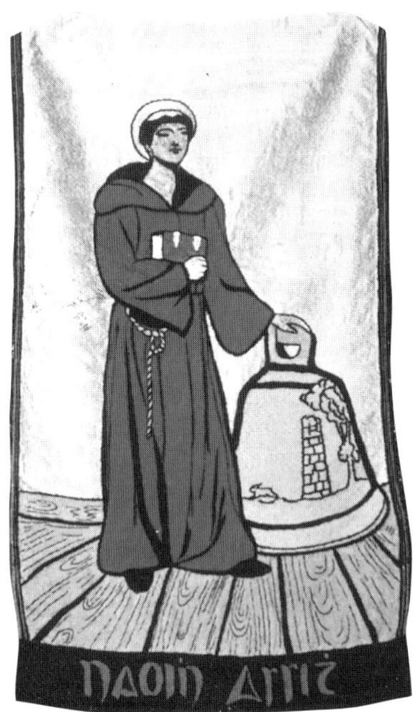

Fig. 102 *Naomh Assith (St Asicus)*, banner, wool and silk embroidery on linen, 83 × 49.5 cm (Loughrea Cathedral)

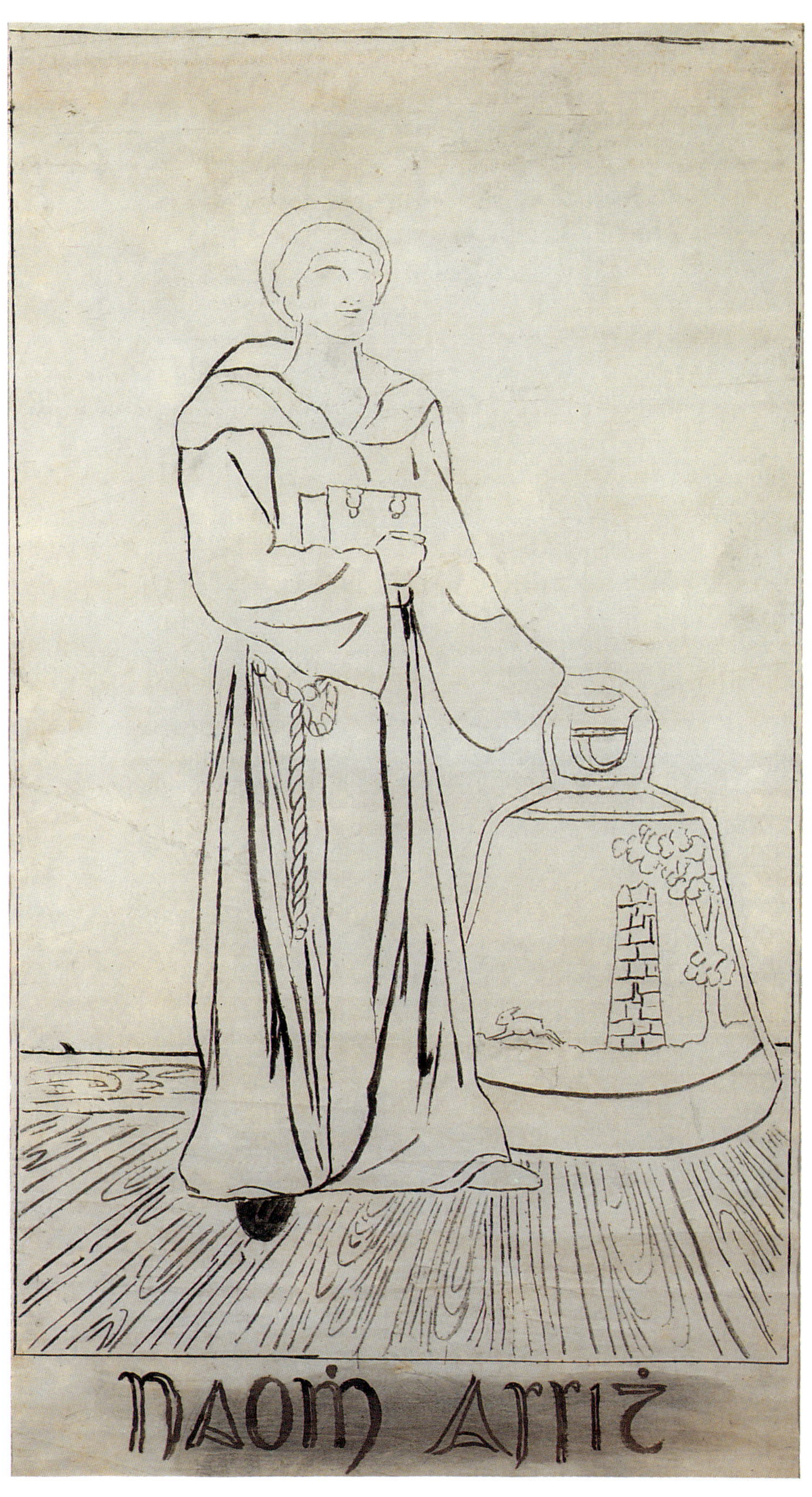

*Transfer design for
St Asicus banner*

1903, ink on linen, 95.2 × 55.4 cm,
NGI 7947

In June 1905, J.M. Synge and Jack B. Yeats visited West Galway and Mayo to investigate the impoverished areas of Ireland (in the care of the Congested Districts Board) on behalf of *The Manchester Guardian*. Synge wrote twelve articles for the paper, and Yeats provided fifteen illustrations for the articles. The editor was impressed with the collaboration and invited Synge to do a further series on 'Irish types', which Yeats might have illustrated, but the articles were never written.

When the opportunity came to publish Synge's œuvre posthumously, W.B. Yeats felt that the *Guardian* articles were of inferior quality, and that they should not be included in the *Collected Works*. They were not reprinted until the second edition of Synge's prose was edited by Alan Price in 1966, the volume including Yeats's accompanying illustrations. Jack Yeats, however, coloured and exhibited some of his original drawings in the 1920s, and developed images from them in his oils, regarding his association with Synge as one of the inspirational experiences of his life. *Many ferries* (p. 256), for example, is based on one of the *Manchester Guardian* drawings, *The Dinish ferryman*.

The ink drawing *The causeway of Lettermore*, published in Synge's article 'Among the Relief Works', inspired *The causeway bridge*, a watercolour which the artist exhibited in Dublin the following year and in London in 1908 (New York Public Library, Berg Collection). Like the drawing, the watercolour shows Synge, Yeats and a jarvey travelling across the causeway bridge that links Lettermore in South Connemara with the island of Gorumna. Synge is depicted looking down nervously at the water. The ink drawing lacks the warm blues and browns of the watercolour, but it is a lively scene with an element of humour in the silhouette. The jarvey's scarf flies behind him in the wind. The pony, which is making good speed, tosses its head as it canters. Yeats with his broad-brimmed hat seems to smile at Synge, seated firmly on the jolting side-car as they roll along only feet above the strong currents swirling around the foot of the bridge. Small as the drawing is, Yeats has captured the atmosphere of the locality splendidly, the breadth of the landscape and the sense of limitless sky.

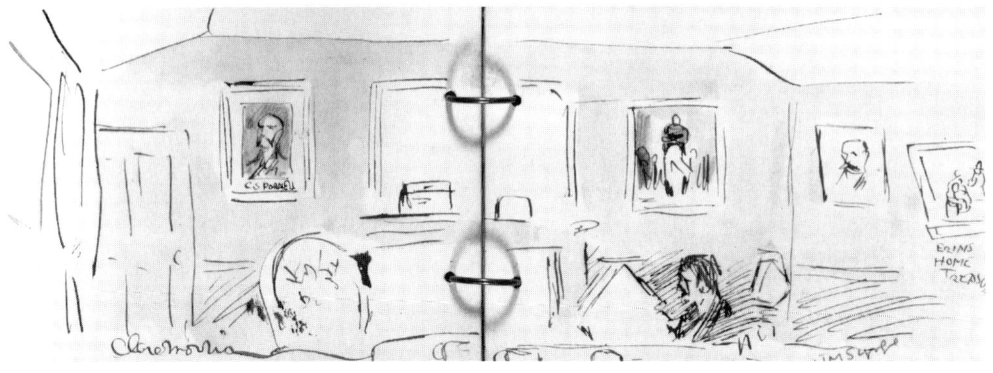

Fig. 103 Jack B. Yeats, *J.M. Synge at Claremorris*, from a sketchbook (NGI Yeats Archive)

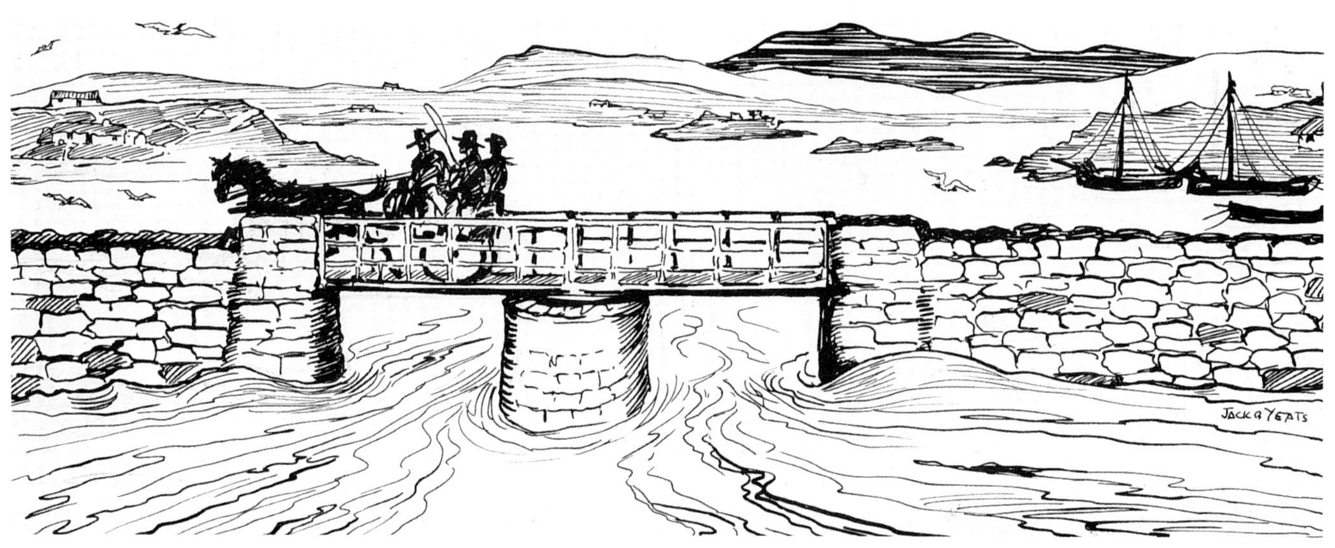

The causeway of Lettermore

1905, pen and ink on card, 9.5 × 24 cm, NGI 19,395

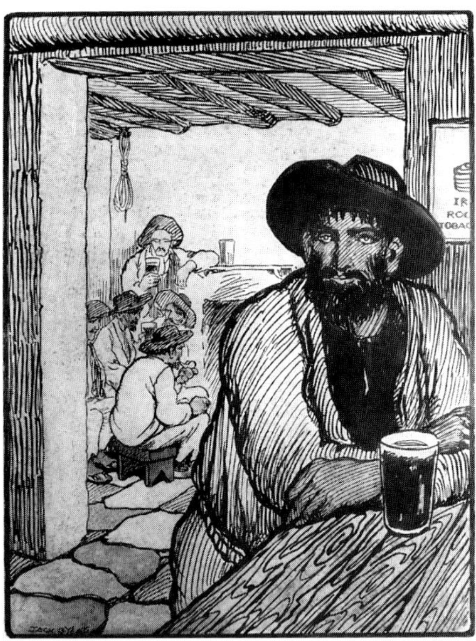

Fig. 104 Jack B. Yeats, *Porter*, from *The Aran Islands* by J.M. Synge, pen and ink and watercolour, 29 × 23 cm (private collection)

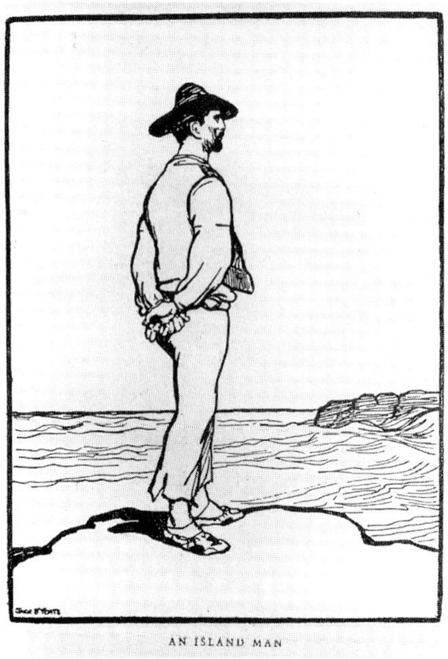

Fig. 105 Jack B. Yeats, *An Island man*, from *The Aran Islands* by J.M. Synge, pen, ink and watercolour, 30.5 × 23 cm (Sligo County Library and Museum)

'Aranmore', the name Yeats uses here for the largest of the three Aran Islands off the coast of Galway, is more generally known as 'Inishmore', which means 'big island'. J.M. Synge uses the term 'Aran Mór' in his book *The Aran Islands*; and the islanders themselves refer to the big island as 'Árann'. Jack Yeats painted this watercolour after he had visited the Irish-speaking districts of South Galway with Synge in the summer of 1905.

An islandman stands on the quay of some local harbour in South Galway, the mast of his hooker rising from the water below him. The background to his striking figure may be the artist's memory of Aranmore, and the hill beside Kilronan, the main town on the island; though if the man has sailed in at Carna or Ros Muc it may well be the cone of Cashel Hill that is seen on the edge of the inlet. He has evidently come on business of some kind in his hooker. There has always been constant traffic between the island and the mainland.

The combination of warm mauves and gold that characterizes this watercolour was used elsewhere by Yeats at this period. The water is a golden colour beyond the rocks, reflecting the light yellow of the smooth pale sky. The hill, mauve with heather and gold with gorse, repeats the conical shape of the man's wide-brimmed hat, of the kind worn in Galway at this date, and seems to guard him from the ravages of the Atlantic Ocean on the barren west coast. He stretches his legs on the jetty, confident and self-contained.

The islander wears a coat over his fisherman's jersey, a pair of tweed or flannel trousers and shoes rather than the pampooties described by Synge, and with which Yeats provides the Aran islanders (fig. 105) in his illustrations to Synge's book *The Aran Islands*, published in 1907 (see *A four-oared curagh*, p. 176). The lighting is typical of the soft, spray-filled atmosphere of the Connemara seaboard.

The man from Aranmore

1905, chalk and watercolour on Whatman board, 38 × 27.3 cm, NGI 6317

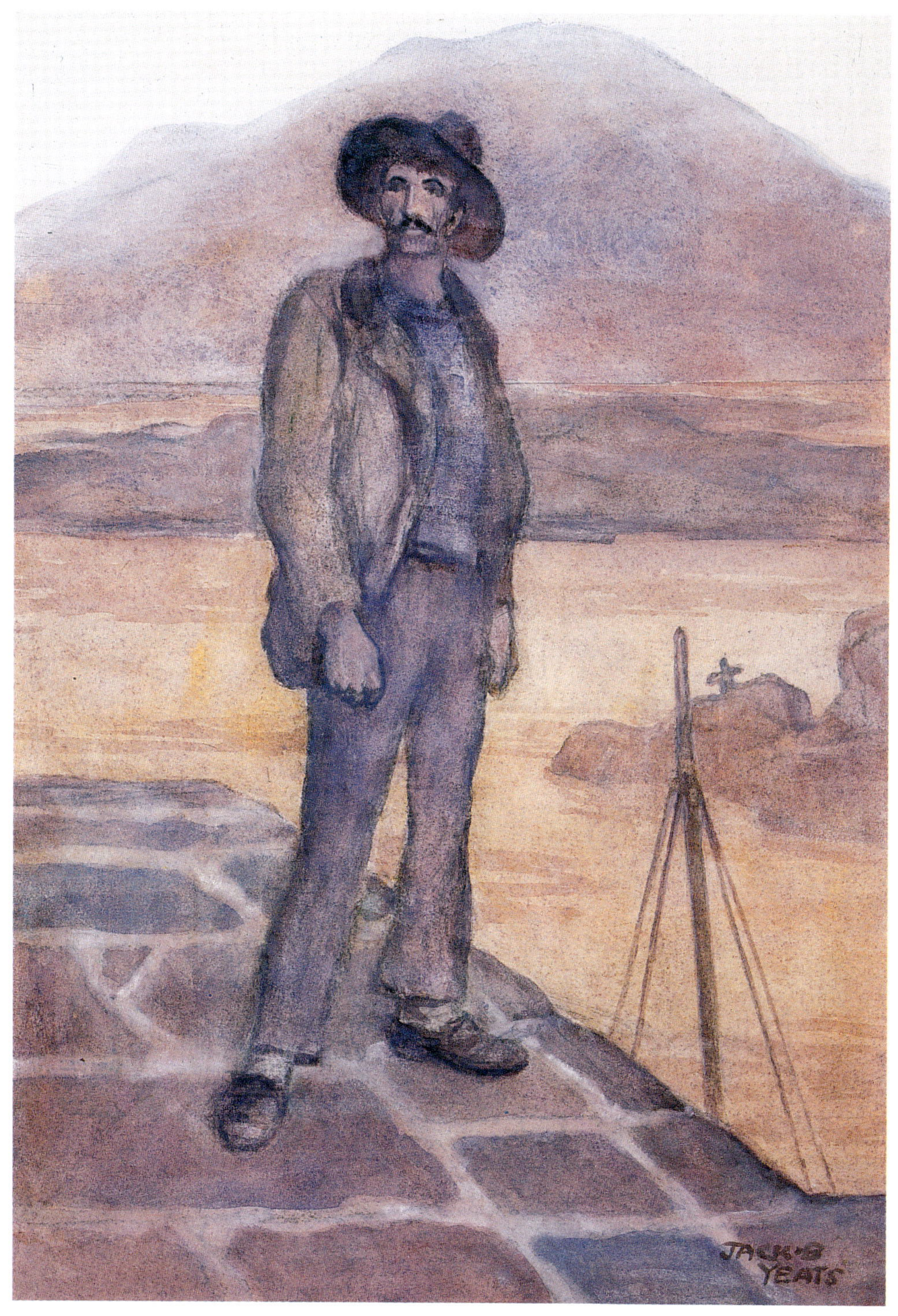

Visiting Baillie's Gallery in London in February 1905 to see the exhibition Jack Yeats shared with three other artists, the critic Arthur Symons wrote, "To go into the room where these forty sketches in watercolour hang in happy confusion is to go into a child's paradise. There is next to no drawing, and the colour, though it has often a queer kind of emotion, is often mere fun. But what vitality, what expressiveness, what a sense of the drunk and disorderly side of existence, of 'rum and barnacles', of pirates and beggars and blind pipers and shows and races! ... In his way he is as much a visionary as his brother …."

Other critics rather extravagantly saw in the modest-sized watercolours a glimpse of the dark side of Manet, though the Dublin *Freeman* felt the pictures were generally "gloomy" and vague, leaving everything to the imagination of the spectators. *Rum and barnacles* was shown again in October of the same year in the Leinster Hall, which was "draped in an inoffensive and deprecating shade of green" for the occasion. The Dublin critics took Yeats's work extremely seriously since he was already regarded as the artist who fitted best within the context of the Gaelic revival, and every one in society and of literary or artistic standing visited the show. "Mr. Yeats's exhibition this year shows a great advance on any of his preceding ones and marks him out as a really capable exponent of that evasive Irish spirit which never appears in the 'French' work of his friend, weird Mr. George Russell," commented the *Irish Society and Society Review*, whose critic welcomed the toning down of colour in compositions that were essentially "virile".

'Virile' is probably a good description for *Rum and barnacles* with its energetic narrative. Partly because of the provocative title and certainly because of the lively way the scene is presented, the watercolour attracted a great deal of attention, and considerably more than *The man from Aranmore* (see previous page), also shown at the Dublin venue. The story has been associated in various forms with seafishing villages all over the world. A cask of rum encrusted with barnacles has been thrown up by the sea, and the task of the villagers is to retrieve the precious liquor before the authorities hear of its existence. Here, in the Sligo village of Rosses Point, which was a continual inspiration for Yeats (more recently a new wide road has obliterated the original coastline), everyone is enlisted in the hurry, the local youths getting great entertainment out of the event. Yeats explained to viewers that while they were carrying the rum away in their pails the coastguards arrived. However, since the cask was not yet empty, the people poured buckets of seawater into it and so spoiled the rum for them.

It is a vivid evening scene, the dimming light playing a part, as does the interpretation of individual character. Yeats would continue to paint scenes from the Irish life he wanted to record even as he moved to oil some years later: and this robust pleasure in the bizarre events of reality forms the backbone of the subject-matter of his maturity.

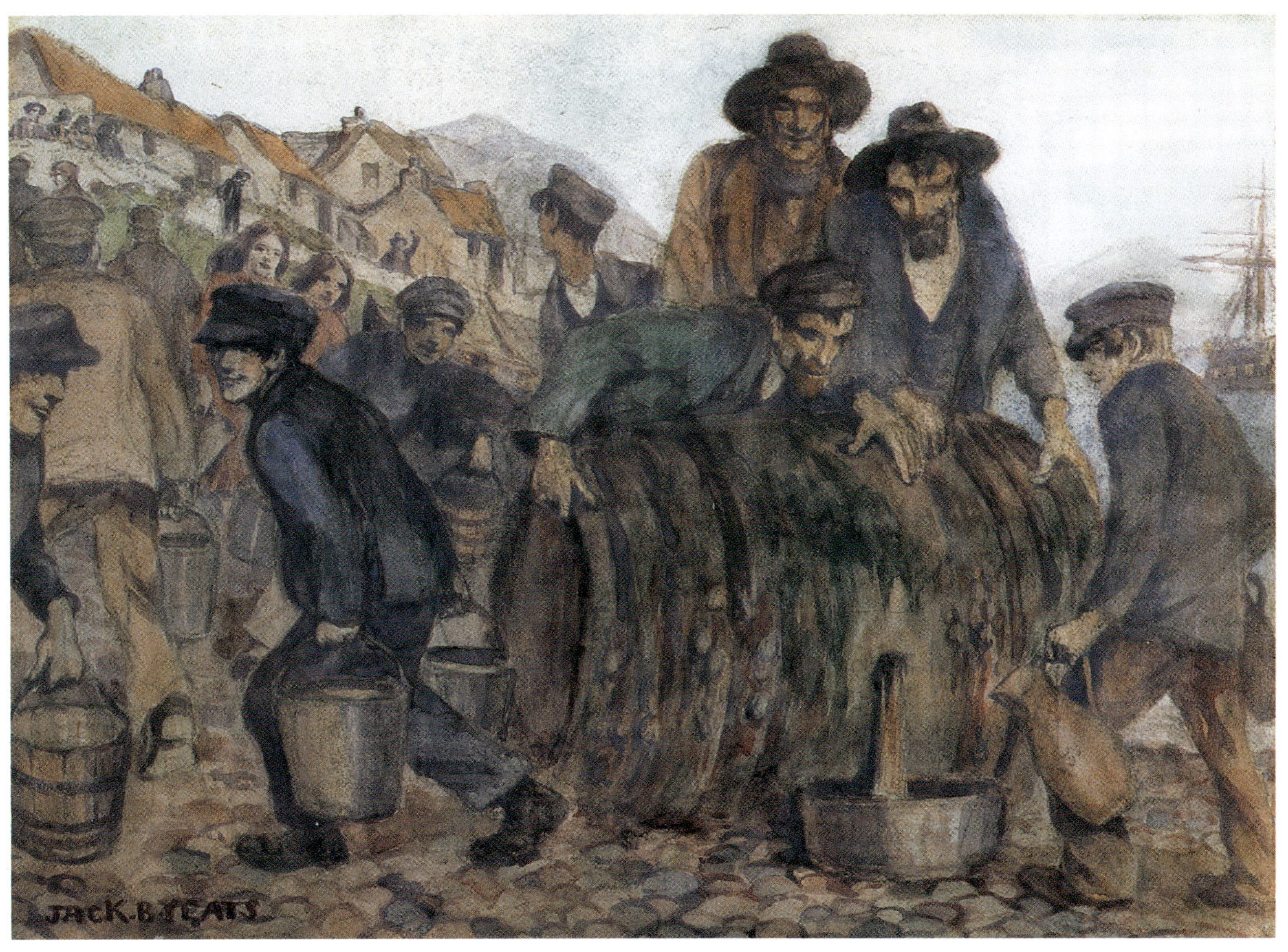
JACK·B·YEATS

J.M. Synge spent a few weeks on the Aran Islands every year between 1898 and 1902, and in 1907 published his book *The Aran Islands* for which Yeats provided twelve illustrations, including *A four-oared curagh.* ('Curagh' is Synge's adaptation of the Irish word usually rendered 'curragh' in English.) Each of these pen-and-ink drawings describes the islanders' activities, on sea, in the public house, gathering kelp, thatching; one only refers to Synge himself. The drunken man who carried the playwright's bag from Galway Quay to the station on one of his return journeys from Aran, and thought the baggage was heavy with gold when it was really books, caught Yeats's imagination. These Aran drawings are similar in style to the illustrations (see p. 170) for Synge's articles in *The Manchester Guardian* and not as mannered as in *A Broad Sheet* of a few years previously (see p. 164). The water-colour wash was added at a later date.

Curraghs were used by the Aran islanders, and by people of the Galway mainland, as a fleet and convenient form of transport about the coast, hookers being employed for heavy freight and fishing in deeper water: and they are still used today (though not in such numbers), often with an outboard motor. Synge mentions four-oared curraghs and three-oared curraghs in his book:

"Early this morning the man of the house came over for me with a four-oared curagh – that is, a curagh with four rowers and four oars on either side, as each man uses two – and we set off a little before noon.

"It gave me a moment of exquisite satisfaction to find myself moving away from civilisation in this rude canvas canoe of a model that has served primitive races since man first went on the sea.

"We had to stop for a moment at a hulk that is anchored in the bay, to make some arrangements for the fish-curing of the middle island, and my crew called out as soon as we were within earshot that they had a man with them who had been in France a month from this day.

"When we started again, a small sail was run up in the bow, and we set off across the sound with a leaping oscillation that had no resemblance to the heavy movement of a boat.

"The sail is only used as an aid, so the men continued to row after it had gone up, and as they occupied the four cross seats I lay on the canvas at the stern and the frame of slender laths, which bent and quivered as the waves passed under them."

Synge set out from Inishmore on a brilliant April morning, but, before they reached Inishmaan, the middle island, a thunderstorm broke out. Yeats, in this study of *A four-oared curagh*, gives a vivid impression of the fickleness of the swelling wave, not only through the crest that tosses away from the boat, but is nearly as high as its prow, but in the tense, melancholy expressions of the three islanders whose faces are visible. The fourth turns to look at the corner of the island to be seen beyond the huge wave.

There is nothing else but the blank sky and the rising water. Three of the islanders wear the wide-brimmed Spanish-style hat, and they all wear the typical collarless shirt, pampooties (cowskin sandals), a tweed waistcoat or a báinín coat, and trousers of grey flannel.

The diagonal line of the vessel across the picture is repeated by Yeats in an oil painting some fifteen years later. In *Off the Donegal Coast* (Crawford Municipal Art Gallery, Cork) a curragh is in genuine difficulty, caught on a similar wave swell, which rises ominously above the strip of land visible in the distance.

Yeats wrote to John Quinn on 28 July 1906 that the illustrations to Synge's book had been completed for some time. There are copies of *The Aran Islands* dated 1906; but publication was delayed, and it was not released until April 1907.

A four-oared curagh

1906, pen and ink and watercolour on card, 29.9 × 23.8 cm, NGI 3825

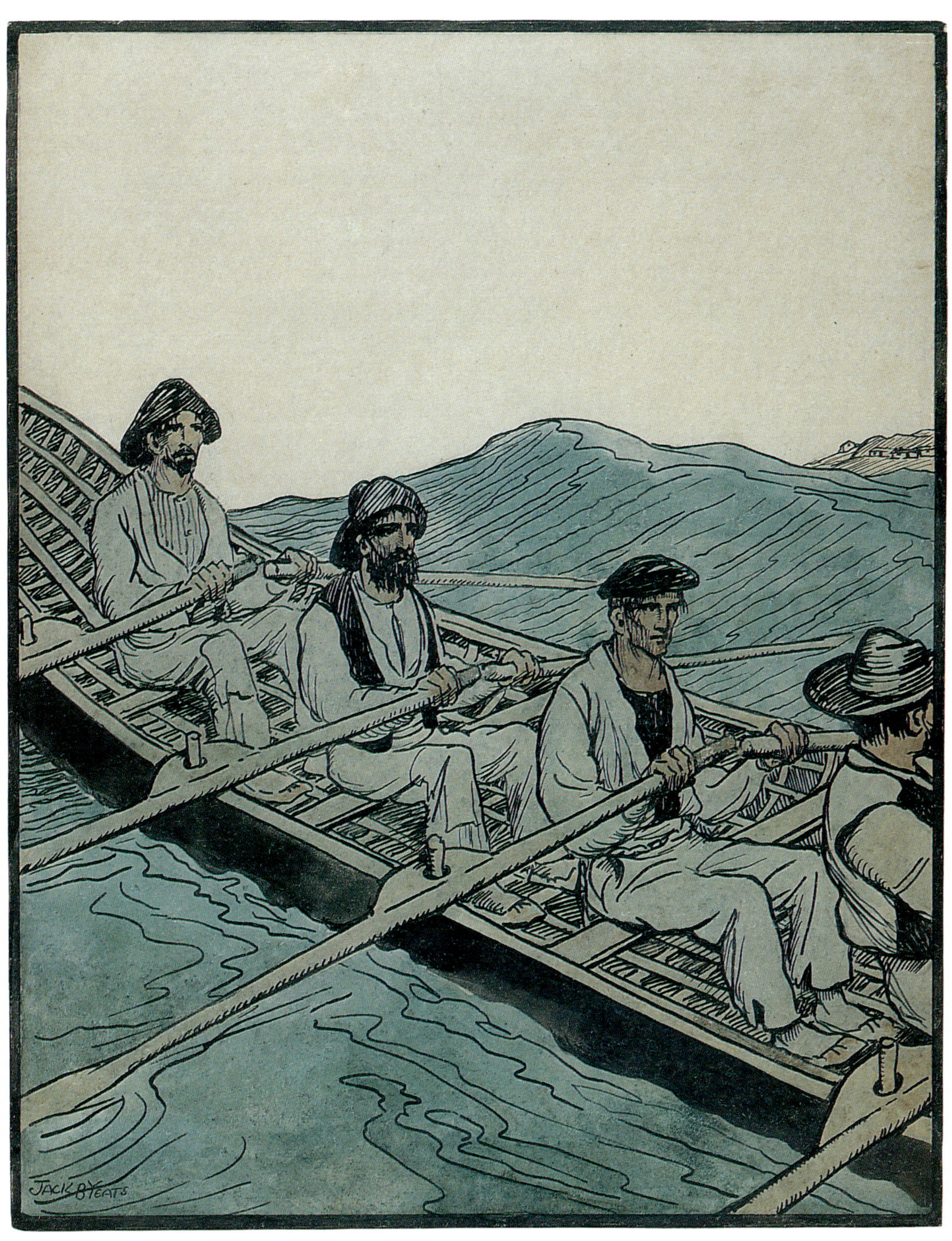

Lough Gill, a very beautiful lake, lies to the south-east of Sligo town. It is set among woods and covered with islands, among them Innisfree, an overgrown rock which inspired WBY to write his famous poem. Jack Yeats paid his annual visit to Ireland in the summer and early autumn of 1906, but sketched little when he was in Sligo. He probably did this watercolour on the spot, working on a drawing block. With two studies similar in approach, depicting the Gara stream behind his house in Devon, it is one of his few straight watercolour landscapes of this year, though he did many subject drawings and watercolours, and he made small sketches in Connemara.

He was beginning to take landscape seriously and for the next few years would take his oil paints with him as he travelled about the west. "It is no pleasure," he wrote to his friend, the American collector John Quinn, "to sit on a desolate coast, perched on a damp rock, with the cold showers sweeping over you and your paint and a drop on the end of your nose."

While there is no reason to believe that these conditions prevailed while he was painting Lough Gill, this picture was certainly not painted on a pet day. The blue-grey of the sky and the darker water convey little of the romance associated with Lough Gill. It relates rather to the series of grey landscapes of the Irish coast which he embarked upon from 1910 onwards for a decade. These were on exactly the same scale as this watercolour, but painted in oil. Yeats, at this period, seems to have been deliberately rejecting the moderns, though he had visited Paris and had seen contemporary exhibitions while in London. Like Walter Sickert, the British Impressionist who maintained a low-toned palette and concentrated on a harsh reality, Jack Yeats, in his early landscapes, kept a neutral harmonious tone and a generalized broad effect to seek what was most important to him, a reality that was unspectacular. In his studies of Irish scenery, which are portraits of a coastline in calm, rather than in storm, he captured the grey misty atmosphere admirably.

Lough Gill is a realistic representation of the lake on a typical Irish day. The water registers the passing breezes in its dark ruffles. The foliage of the islands is broadly sketched with thick wet paint, while the near rocks are worked firmly. The rest of the picture, water and sky, floats, and in some places melts, with shadow shapes drawn in with the brush after the initial washes were dry. A few touches of more vivid colouring foretell the artist's palette of future years.

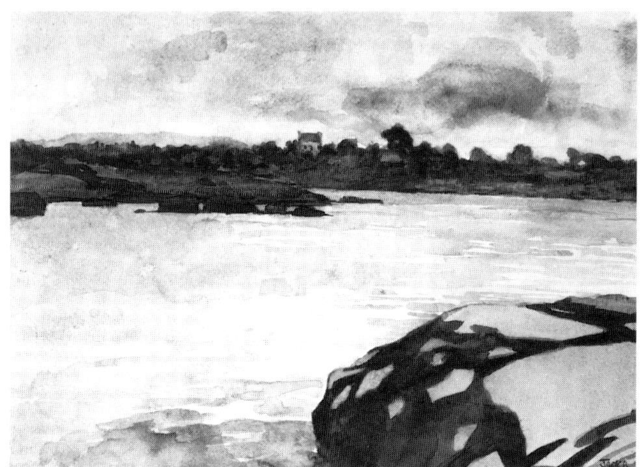

Fig. 106 Jack B. Yeats, *The Lake at Coole*, 1908, watercolour, 24.5 × 35 cm (private collection)

Lough Gill, County Sligo

1906, watercolour on paper, 25.6 × 36.8 cm, NGI 6321

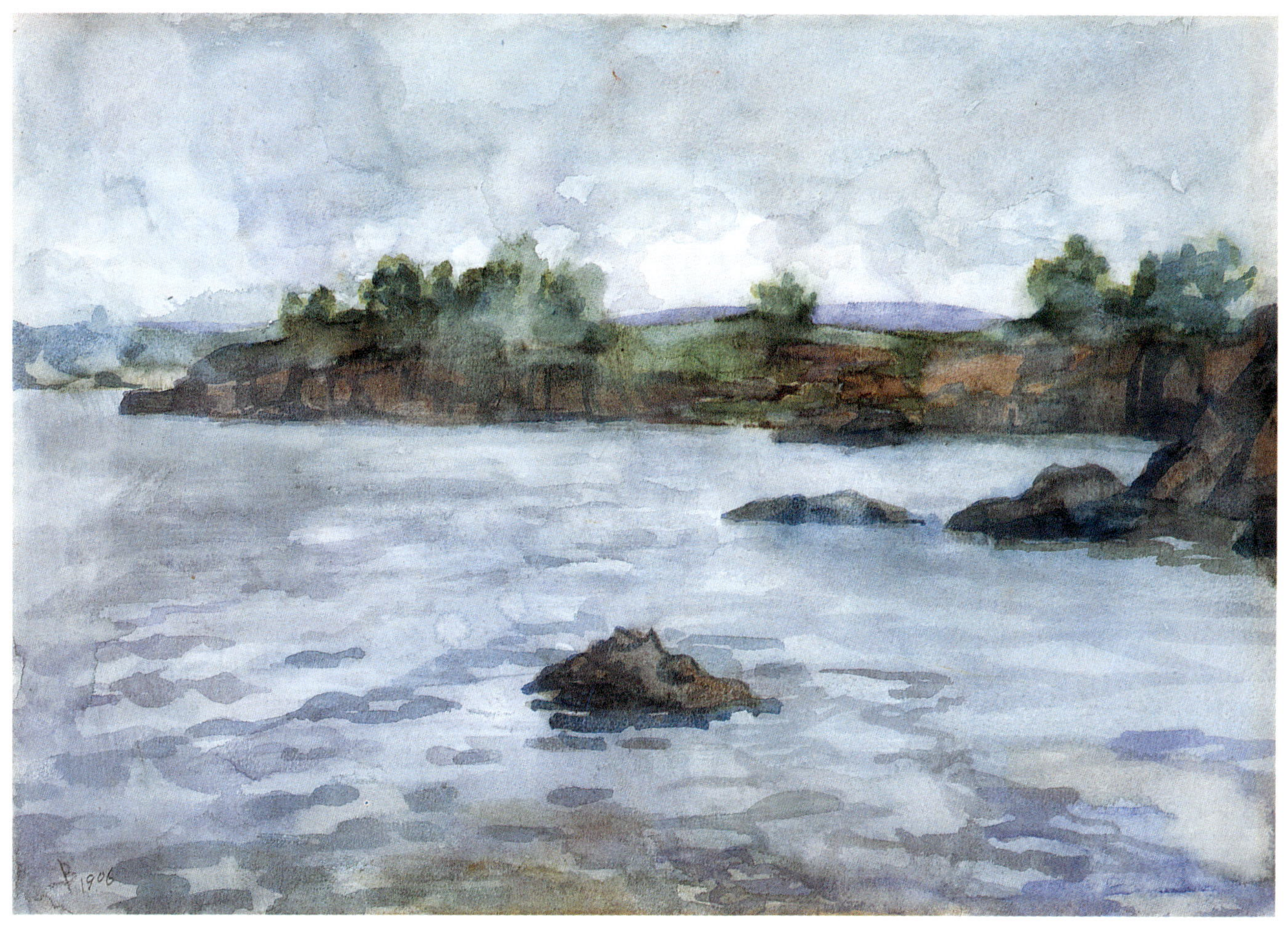

In 1908 Jack B. Yeats revived *A Broad Sheet* (see p. 164), taking *A Broadside* as title for the new publication. The format of *A Broadside* differs from that of *A Broad Sheet*. There are four quarto-size pages, formed from one sheet folded over, with the final page left blank. Yeats's practice was to put one or two ballads or poems with two small line-block illustrations by himself in the first two pages, and to fill the third page with a single uncoloured drawing, often one he had made some years before. *The wake house* may be such a drawing, or it may have been made especially for the new publication. It is reproduced on the third and last page of the October issue of *A Broadside*, 1908.

The wake was not a subject from Jack Yeats's normal Sligo experience. With his Protestant background, he is unlikely to have attended a wake in Sligo. He may have been to one in Galway, or heard descriptions from Lady Gregory at Coole; or his friendship with Synge may have been the source of this drawing. Two of Synge's plays, *Riders to the Sea* and *The Shadow of the Glen* – both of which appeared in print the year the two men set off for the west together – revolve around the wake, a traditional Irish death ritual; and in *The Aran Islands*, Synge describes what he saw of an old woman's wake, and the keening by the graveside, on Inishmaan. "The grief of the keen is no personal complaint for the death of one woman over eighty years, but seems to contain the whole passionate rage that lurks somewhere in every native of the island."

The Irish wake, an ancient custom which has largely died out now, was a vigil that took place in country parts, spanning the period from the time of death to the funeral. Relations and neighbours came to pay their respect to the corpse, laid out in a place of honour in the main room of the house, with candles head and foot. The company were regaled with pipes and tobacco, and poitín or porter, while those present reminisced; and the keening was usually carried out by a group of professional mourners, joined by whoever was moved to emotional expression.

Yeats's drawing shows none of the religious or convivial practices, but describes one of the social aspects of the wake house. A storyteller, perhaps the local shanachie, is holding his audience spellbound in front of the turf fire, before which a dog is slumbering. The small cottage 'room' (off the kitchen, where, presumably, the coffin lies), with its heavy wooden beams, is undecorated apart from the holy picture above the mantleshelf. The woman of the house stands in the doorway. At the window, a face gazes in at the crowded scene. The sense of excitement Yeats instils in the urgent expression of the speaker, and in the various characterful people gathered around him – young and old, locals and returned Americans – suggests that the storyteller's tale has to do with more than eulogy of the departed neighbour. It recalls the resurgence of Irish nationalism during the early years of the century, which is the theme of other drawings and paintings by the artist about this time.

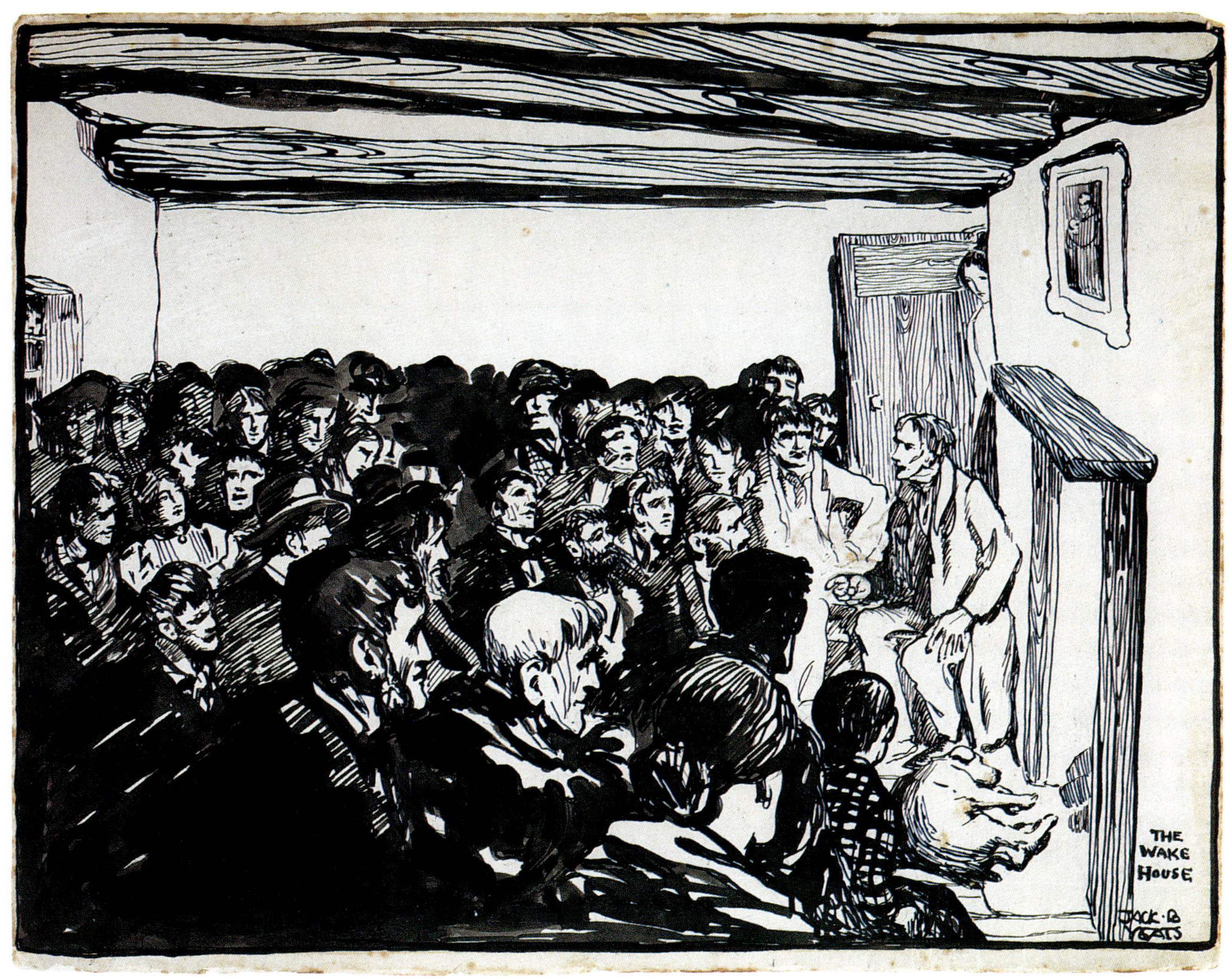
THE
WAKE
HOUSE
JACK·B
YEATS

During his youth Yeats had watched the pilots negotiating the Garavogue, or walking in the vicinity of the look-out shelter at Rosses Point (this is how he depicts the pilot in *Life in the west of Ireland*, fig. 107). Later, the pilot became a metaphysical image for him, on a par – in his view of Sligo as epitomizing life in general – with the lighthouse and the Metal Man (p. 194), which protect Sligo seamen in their separate ways. The pilot in Yeats's imagery is as important as the sea captain, and shares the side-car with the captain and the jarvey as he returns to his home in Sligo from the anchored ship at Rosses Point in at least two of his paintings.

This drawing of the pilot going out to the ship is of an anecdotal nature, and echoes the comedy of his early black-and-white journalism in the 1890s. Arriving at the side of the steamship in a splash of waves, the pilot's craft is made fast with a rope cast by a seasoned sailor, who looks down from the deck with guarded hostility. A young waiter on the cabin deck pauses with a tray in his hand to look down, swaying perilously towards the flimsy railing, his coat caught by the wind. Two small boys enjoying the excursion in the pilot's boat are securing one oar amidst laughter, while a sailor on the other side of the small boat puts up the other.

The drawing is alive with linear movement. The flexible pen-and-ink style is ideal for Yeats's reading of human character. It is a taut composition. The placing of the central figures, whose covert glances indicate a clash of personalities, is reinforced by the strong diagonals of the ropes. Above the moody old tar, the juxtaposition of the radiating rigging and details of the vessel structure creates a visual impression of ceaseless activity that is increased by the energy with which the

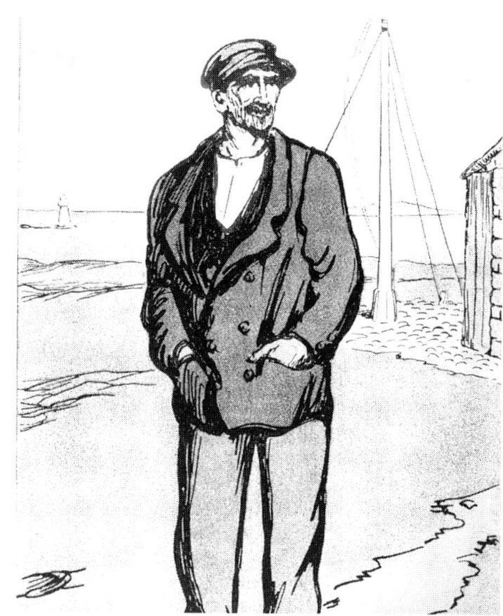

Fig. 107 Jack B. Yeats,
The pilot in *Life in the West of Ireland*, 1912,
pen, ink and watercolour, 20.5 × 13.5 cm
(private collection)

banner of steam furls across the top of the picture and by the vigour of the waves that churn and jolt at the ship's base.

Like *The wake house* (see previous page) and the *Illustration to 'The Felons of our Land'* (see next), *The pilot* was used in *A Broadside*. While he probably illustrated the ballad about the time it was printed, the other two drawings were very likely made at an earlier date and included by Yeats when the situation demanded it. They share a style which he had perfected for his interpretation of western Irish life, an original style of his own continued in the *Life in the West of Ireland* drawings (see further p. 188), which likewise defy an exact dating.

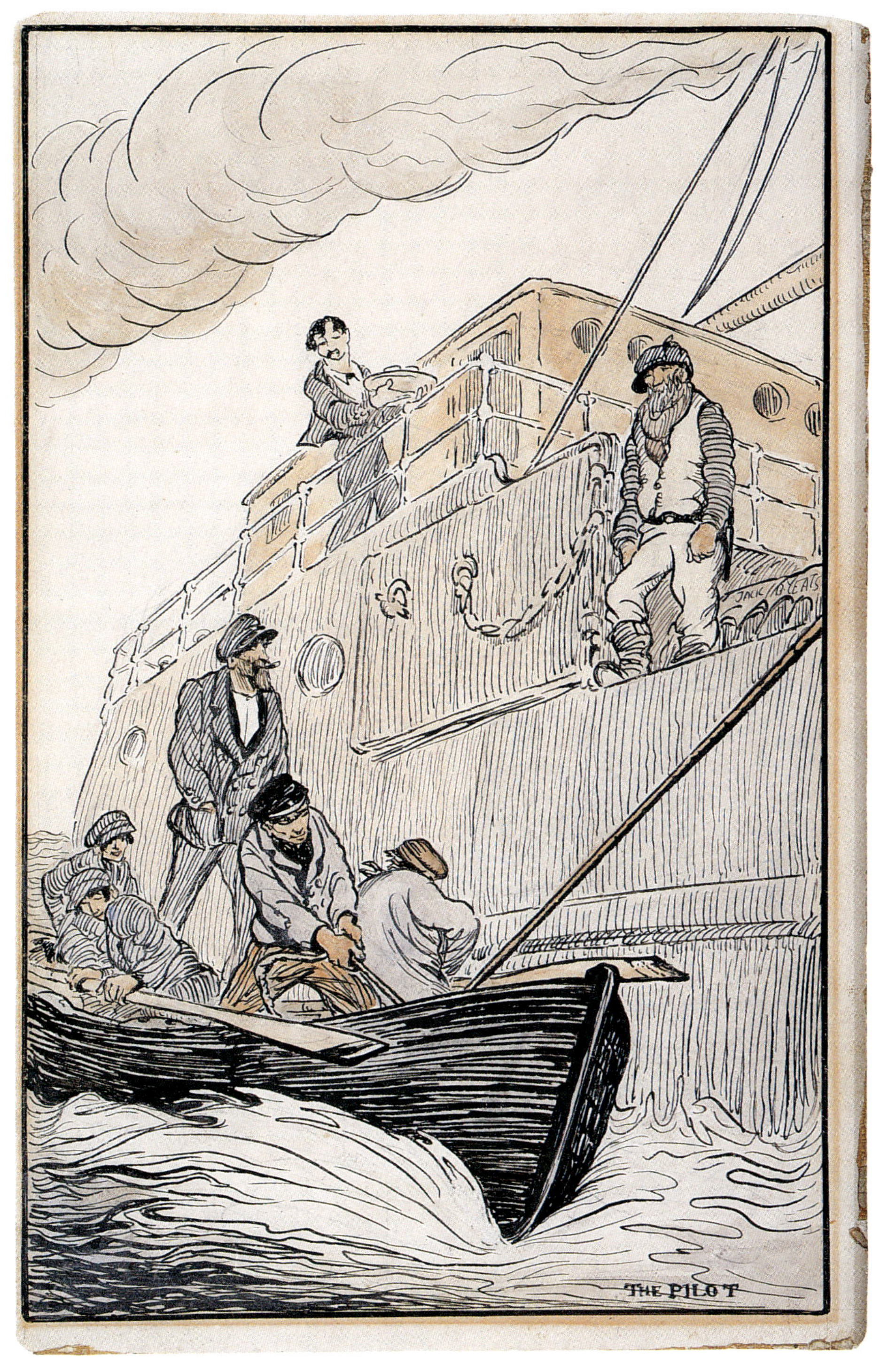

The pilot

ca. 1910, pen and ink and watercolour on card,
27.2 × 18 cm, NGI 3826

The ballad 'The Felons of our Land', published by Yeats in 1910, was found in a popular Glasgow publication, *The Home Rule Song Book*, which he kept in his library. In the book he marked the first verse of the second part of the ballad for use in *A Broadside*:

> And though they sleep in dungeons deep,
> Or flee, outlawed and banned,
> We love them yet, we can't forget
> The felons of our land.

Yeats does not illustrate the contents of the ballad. At all periods his tendency was to show the ballad singer and the audience, and to add the ballad itself in the form of a title for his drawing or painting. In later life he would develop the innuendos derived from a ballad's theme in some kind of wide-reaching metaphor. Even at this early stage, however, the image is more than an illustration of an entertainment at a race meeting. The men who gather round the ballad singer react in various ways, their characters cleverly drawn

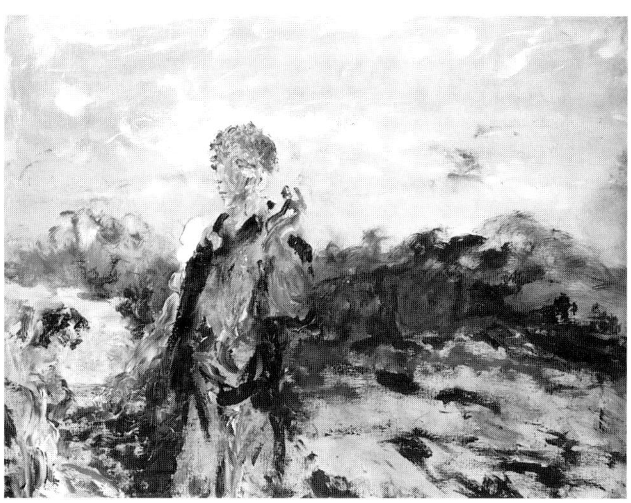

Fig. 109 Jack B. Yeats, *Eileen Aroon*, 1953, oil on canvas, 91.5 × 122 cm (private collection)

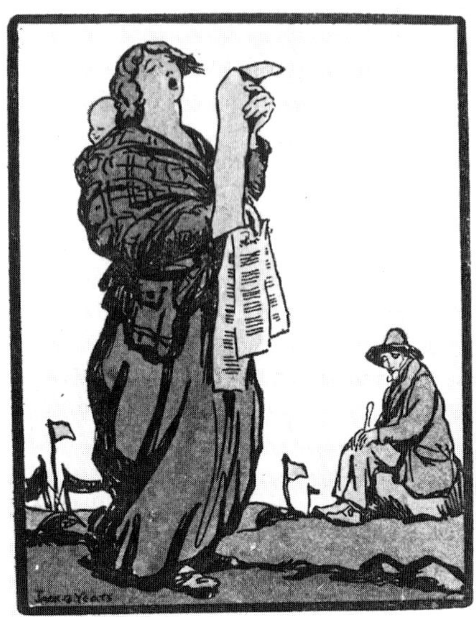

Fig. 108 Jack B. Yeats, *Illustration to 'Lament for the death of Eoghan Ruadh O'Neill, commonly called Owen Roe O'Neill'* from *A Broadside*, February 1910, pen and ink and watercolour, 14.5 × 11.5 cm (private collection)

by the artist, very likely based on people he had observed in Sligo (this ballad singer appears elsewhere in his œuvre). One man seems aggressive, another inspired, others are affected by the melody; while an old man on his stick to the right looks as if he could tell a few stories about these same 'felons' – the patriots whose sacrifice for their country had ended in disaster.

Behind the group, beyond the stone fence on which a woman (who might be Cathleen Ni Houlihan, or Mother Ireland) is seated, and beyond the ploughed field behind her, a race meeting is in full progress, and we can see among the flags and tents a winning jockey surrounded by bystanders.

Some pencil sketches on the reverse side of the card, romantic studies of young women, have been scribbled out by whoever made them. They are quite unlike Yeats's manner and may be doodles by his wife Cottie (Mary Cottenham Yeats), herself an artist, who illustrated some of the Cuala cards.

In May 1915, *A Broadside* came to a close at the end of its seventh year. Yeats continued to hand-colour reprints from it for the Cuala Industries in the form of calendars or greeting cards until early in 1926 when he told his sister Elizabeth that he would do it no longer. He intended to devote himself to his painting.

Illustration to 'The Felons of our Land'

1910, ink and watercolour on card, 30.5 × 19.5 cm, NGI 19,412

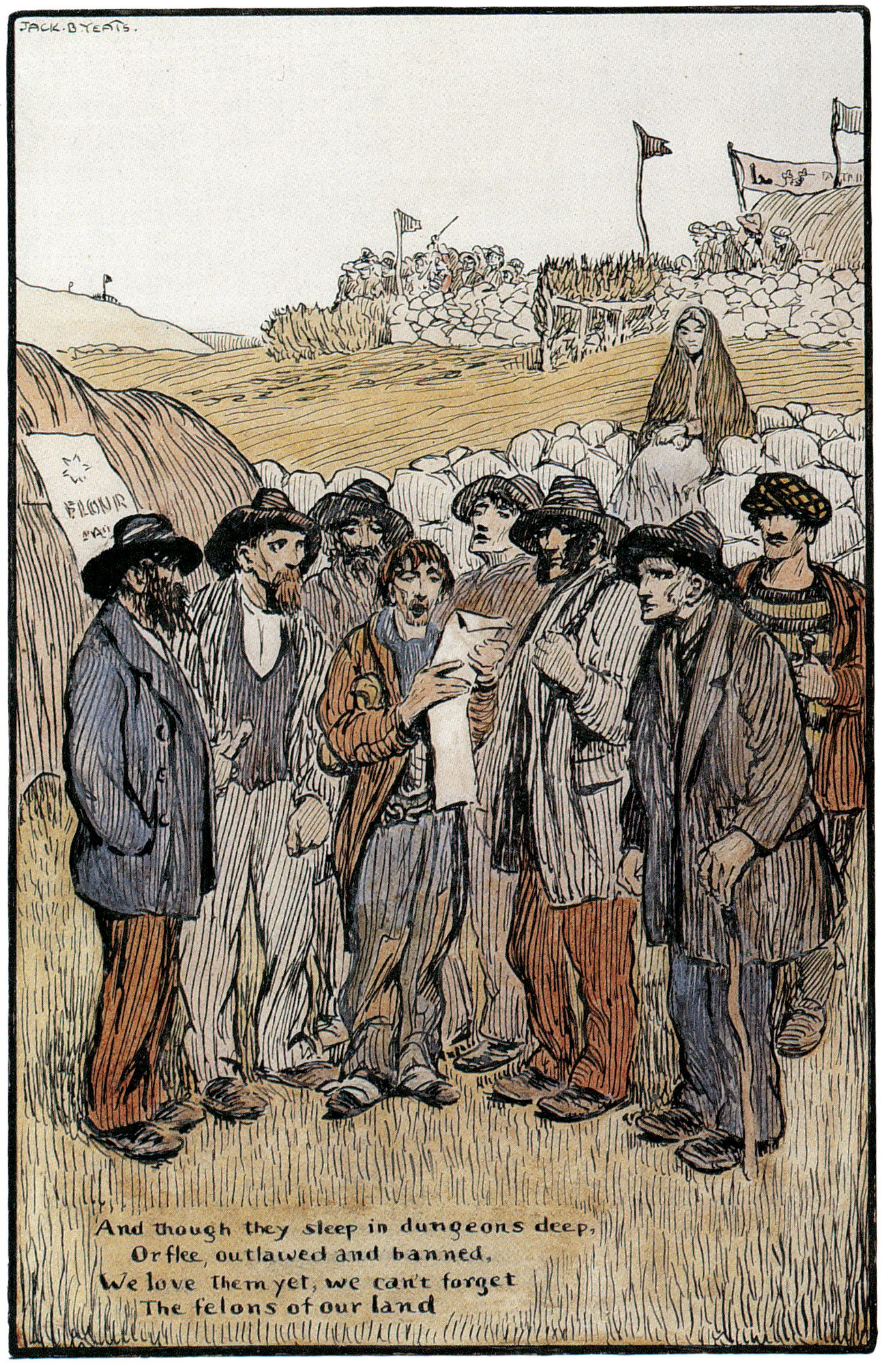

Some of Yeats's earliest drawings were of the circus, one of the high points of the Sligo of his youth. In watercolour, and then in oil, he recalled special aspects: the circus poster, advent of fantasy and athletic marvel; the procession, with the magnificent wagon holding high the superfolk and oddities; the clown, a lasting symbol for Jack Yeats, as for other artists and poets; the acrobats and their beautiful horses; even the company drudge. It was the human element of the travelling show that affected him most deeply.

The circus chariot is one of his more unusual circus themes, though he did a black-and-white drawing of the same subject in *A Broadside* in September 1908 (fig. 110) depicting the charioteer parading as part of the circus procession through a country town. In *Ah Well* he remembers a similar form of entertainment in London or Liverpool, "... chariot races in a circus tent under a long glass roof, and the way the outer wheels used to spray up the sand and dust when the driver spun his team at the turn". In this watercolour, the charioteer exercises his horses in an Irish landscape. He leans backwards dangerously, in his low-slung vehicle, leaving the circus tent behind him on the low horizon as his piebald horses gallop through driving rain.

The low horizon is common in Yeats's work of this period, partly deriving from his experience of western Irish landscape, but used deliberately as a compositional device to accentuate character, in this case a grim and determined man. Whether considered in terms of fantasy, or of real life, this man is obsessed with what he is doing. Like him, the horses are rendered as separate personalities, and their being silhouetted against the rain cloud assists this exercise.

The watercolour is painted in the thick solid manner of his later watercolours. The grey colouring is relieved by the glowing carmine of the horses' harness and the ruby of the man's cloak, while touches of green crayon create muted highlights.

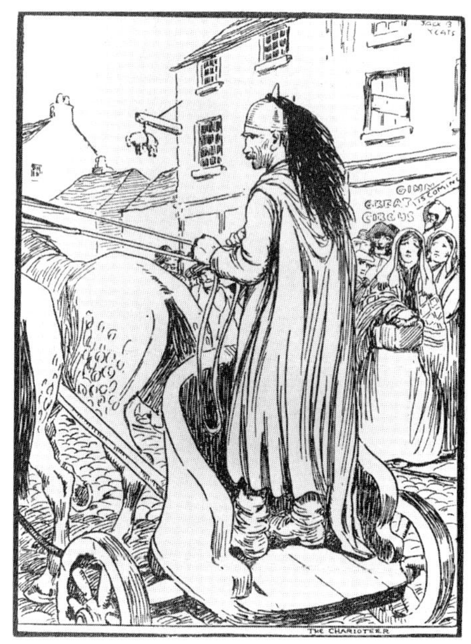

Fig. 110 Jack B. Yeats, *The charioteer* in *A Broadside*, September 1908, Indian ink and watercolour, 25.5 × 19 cm (private collection)

The circus chariot

1910, watercolour and crayon on paper, 25.4 × 35.5 cm, NGI 6316

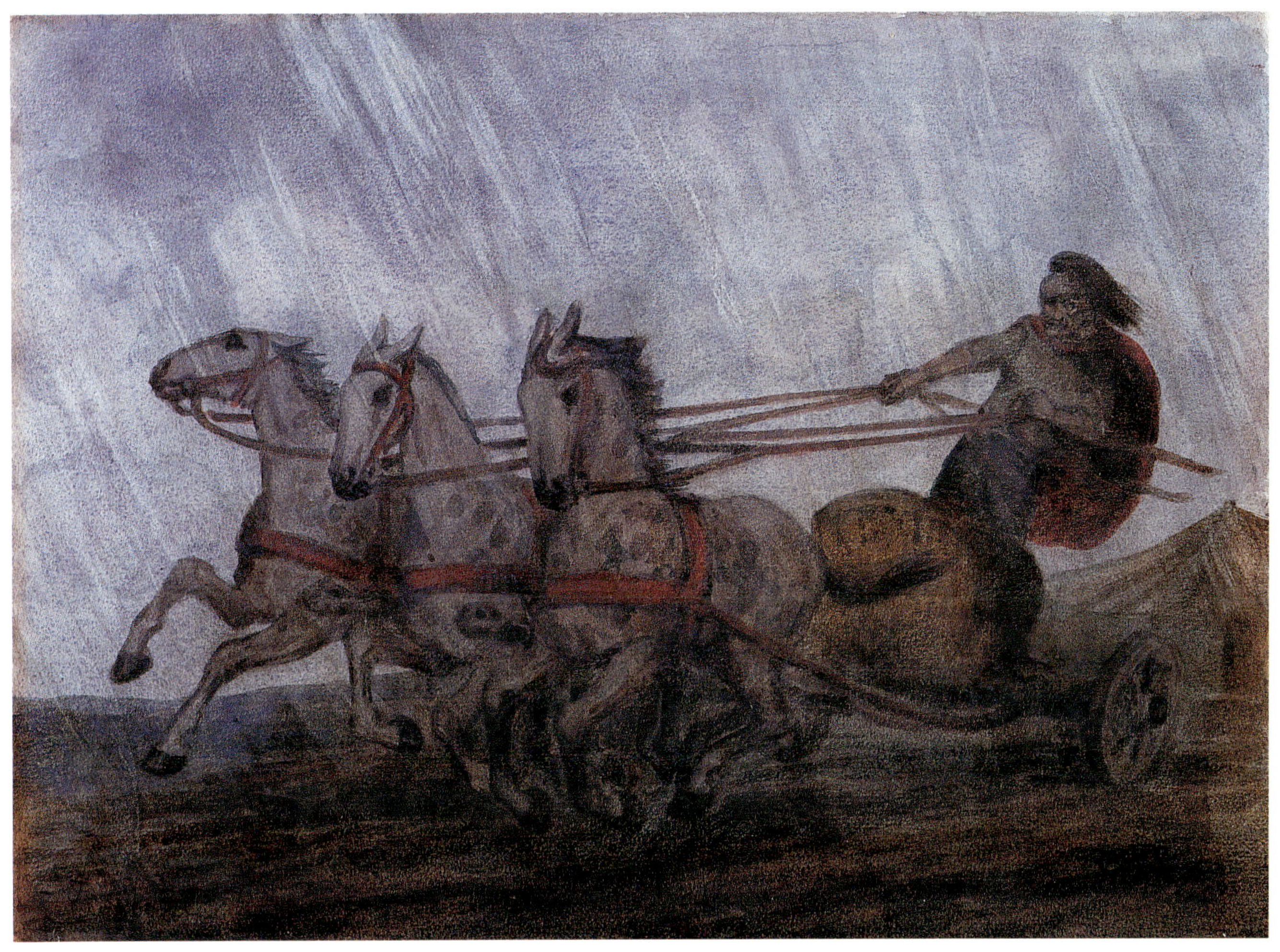

The is one of the drawings for *Life in the West of Ireland*, published in 1912. In 1898, on his annual visit to Ireland, Jack Yeats, who had been drawing and painting every kind of subject that he encountered around the district where he lived in Devon, found himself deeply moved by the centenary celebrations of the 1798 rising. Witnessing the nationalist fervour, perhaps becoming aware for the first time of the movement that was afoot, was a keystone in his development. He seems to have made up his mind from that moment to make the Irish way of life his theme.

His exhibition in London, in February 1899, was entitled *Sketches of Life in the West of Ireland*; and he continued to use the same title for exhibitions for many years. Out of the numerous watercolour and pen-and-ink scenes and character studies grew the book of original pen drawings and reproductions of paintings, *Life in the West of Ireland*. It was a summing up of his objective, satirical and affectionate record of contemporary rural life.

Yeats had also come to a point in his career when he realised that he must break away from the image he had earned as an anecdotal illustrator, if he was to develop his skill as a serious oil-painter. When asked to illustrate *Irishmen All* the following year, therefore, he worked on a larger scale, in oil, and he exhibited the pictures afterwards as individual paintings. Two years later, in 1915, he did his last black-and-white drawings for *A Broadside*, which the Cuala Press had published monthly for seven years, and his illustrating from then on was sporadic.

So the book *Life in the West of Ireland* represents a signing off from years of artistic journalism, the artist's final statement as an objective commentator. He had started life as an artist reporter, covering boxing matches and race meetings for *Paddock Life* and other papers in his black-and-white sketches and cartoons. After ten years working for many illustrated papers, earning a living with his pen, he had turned to watercolour, to give a full visual commentary on the west of Ireland, as he knew it, a counterblast to the stage Irishman image of nineteenth-century British art. His observations have their own humour, as this drawing

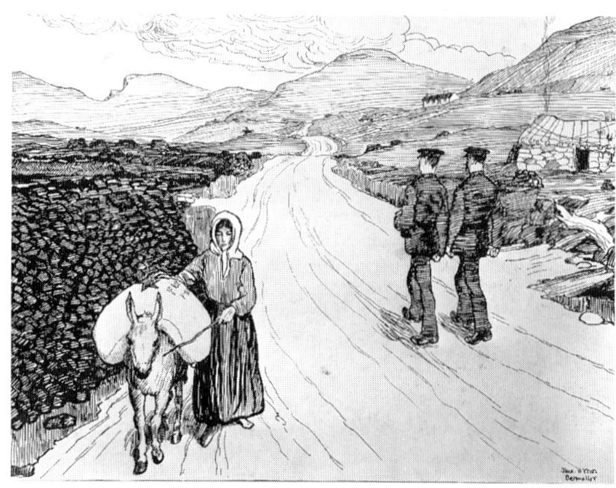

Fig. 111
Jack B. Yeats,
Belmullet, in
*The Manchester
Guardian*,
8 July 1905

of a poteen distillers' trial demonstrates. Yeats had been present at such a court case in the summer of 1909. Poteen, as the caption in the book explains, is illicit whisky, made generally around the coasts of Ireland.

An old man in Carraroe had told Synge and Yeats, when they were travelling there, that the making of poteen had been a great trade in the past. "You'd see the police down on their knees blowing the fire with their own breath to make a drink for themselves and then going off with the butt of an old barrel, and that was one seizure, and an old bag with a handful of malt, and that was another seizure, and would satisfy the law; but now they must have the worm and the still and a prisoner, and there is little of it made in the country".

Yeats's poteen makers, seen from behind in the bottom centre of the drawing, look newly brushed for the unsavoury occasion, and awkwardly uncomprehending as the clerk offers one of them a bible on which to make his oath. There are expressions of malicious glee or concern among the crowd around them in the courtroom, but generally the mood is one of sympathy, and of apprehension about the allegation. Above the huge official desk rise the impassive faces of the magistrates, each admirably characterized, the confident rectitude of the law underlined by their elevation against the uncluttered wall which is decorated with a few official posters. Yeats's gift at creating in a few lines such a human situation is at its height in this drawing.

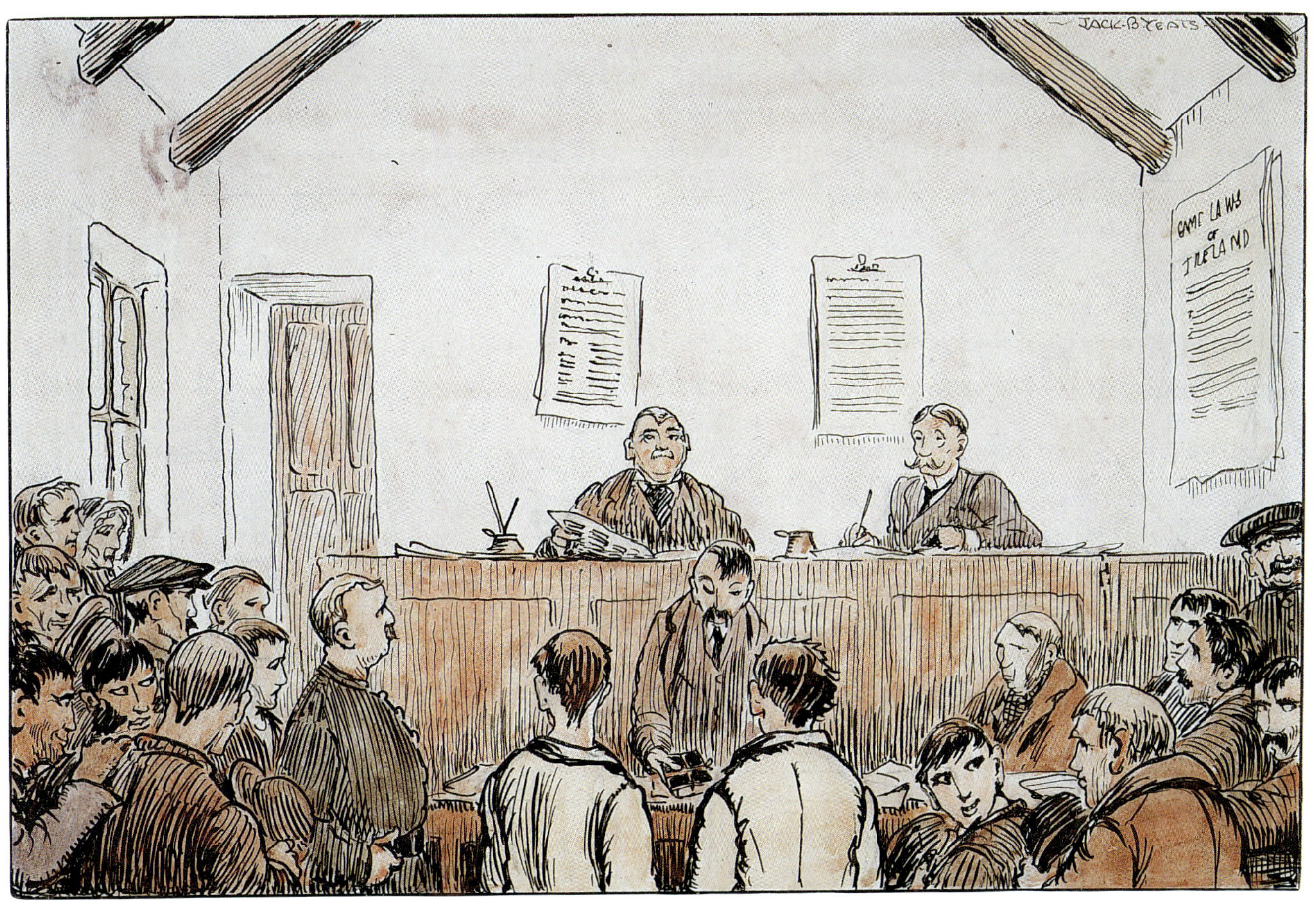

The poteen makers

ca. 1912, pen and ink and watercolour on card, 13 × 20.5 cm, NGI 7882

D uring the earlier part of his career, Yeats depicted many shops, seeing them as the social and economic centres of small town life in the west. He obviously found enjoyment in drawing this country shop, which is the first of the illustrations to *Life in the West of Ireland*.

Everything is stocked here, from hair oil, nutmeg, wallpaper and fabric to hob-nailed boots, rope and lanterns. The proprietress dominates the left centre of the picture, in her neat, buttoned blouse, trimmed at the throat with a brooch. She sits on a tall-backed stool, behind the counter, holding an account book with firm, wrinkled fingers, and running her small, hard, spectacled eyes down a row of names and figures. Her tight mouth, encased in flabby jowls, is devoid of expression. Yeats took her likeness from a sketch he made, when travelling in North Mayo with Synge in 1905, of a Mrs Jordan, leaning on the counter of her shop in Belmullet (figs. 112, 113). The other characters, and the detail of the store, he added later when he drew this picture.

The country woman leaning over the counter, clutching a thin purse, looks earnestly into the business woman's face, in the manner of the time. She is probably illiterate, and can read the face more easily than the book.

Yeats's instinctive sense of compositional balance places a harp in exact counterpoint to the proprietress's head, right of the centre, thus, appositely, satirizing one current form of Irish nationalism. Enthusiastic about a liberated Ireland, this merchant is incapable of mercy to a fellow Irishwoman. James Stephens was making similar observations in his writing on nationalism about this time.

To drive home this point about the twisted nature of human affairs, Yeats places the proud figure of a western man in the right foreground, perhaps gently satirizing him. He turns his back, in typical fashion, on the women's private affairs, closing his eyes, no doubt dreaming of the world beyond the shop walls. This world is shown by the artist – as a roof top and a glimpse of the sky – reflected in the small mirror hanging from the middle rafter. The man wears a collarless coat and a gansey, and fastens his flannel trousers with a knotted rope. The wide hat, for Yeats, suggested vision and romance.

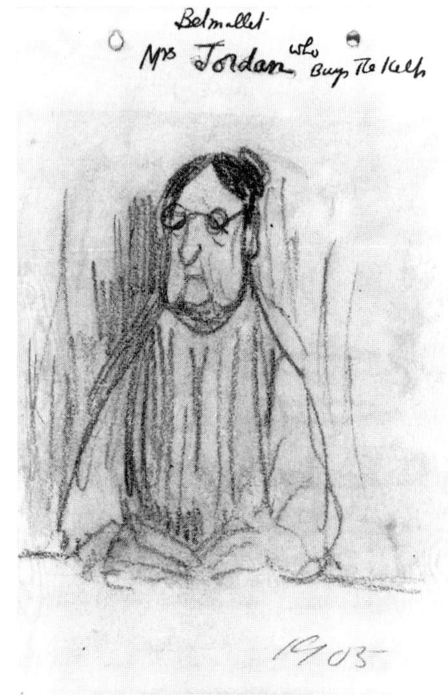

Fig. 112 Jack B. Yeats, *Belmullet: Mrs Jordan who buys the kelp*, from a sketchbook, 1905 (NGI Yeats Archive)

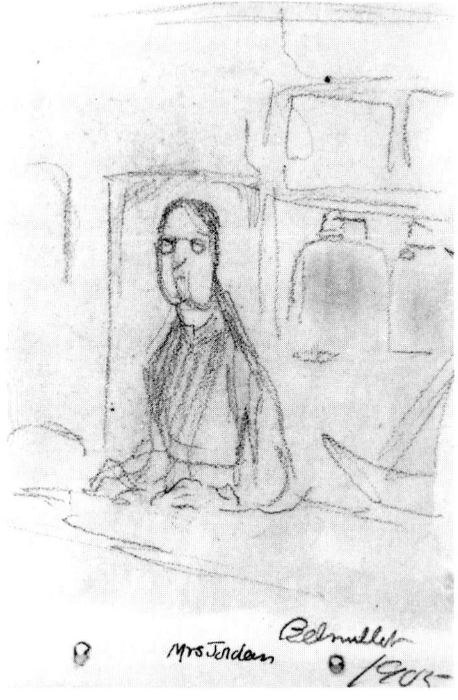

Fig. 113 Jack B. Yeats, *Mrs Jordan, Belmullet*, from a sketchbook, 1905 (NGI Yeats Archive)

The country shop

ca. 1912, pen and ink and watercolour on card, 26.6 × 19.5 cm, NGI 3829

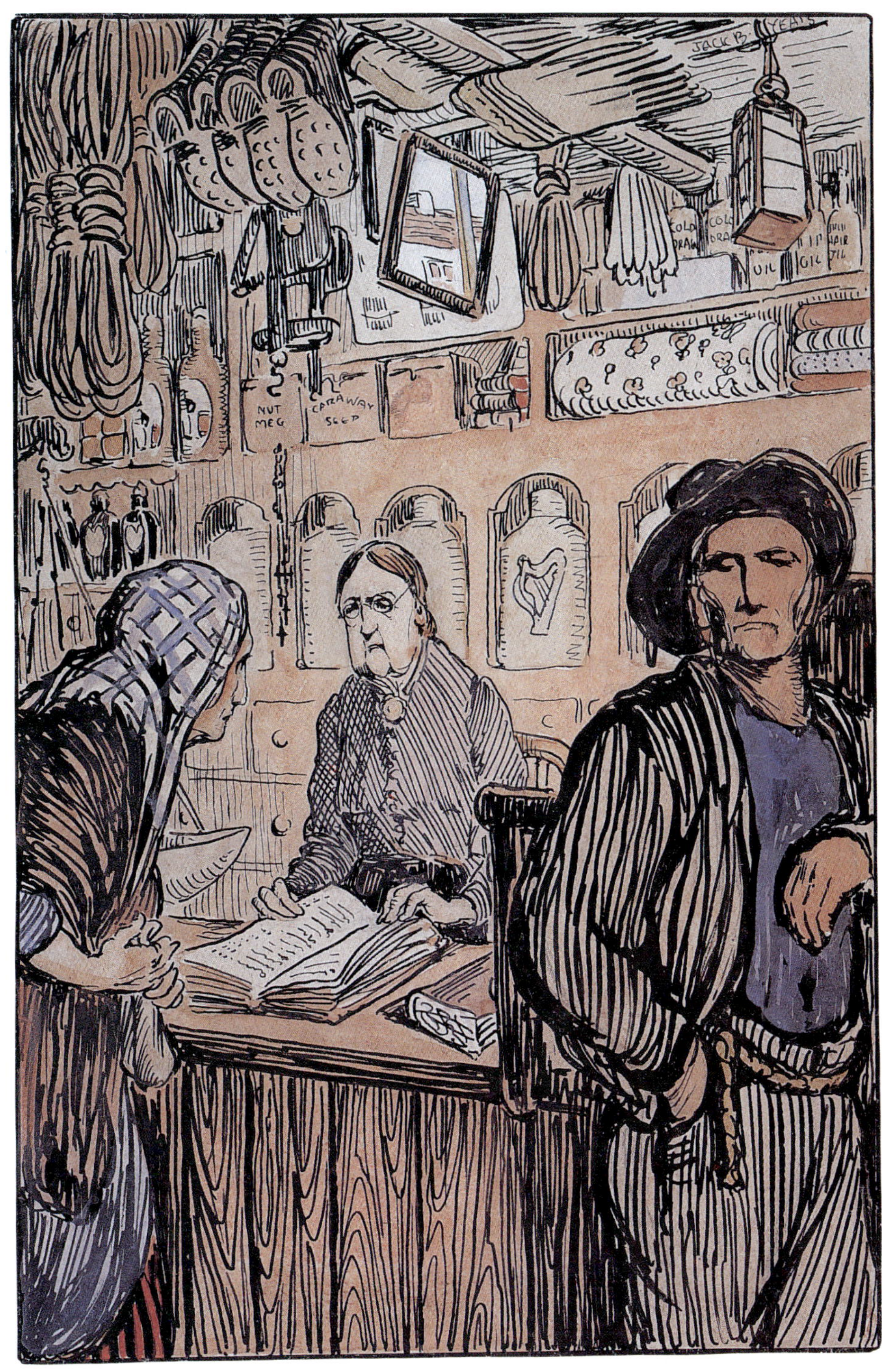

"After a gale the seaweed which is piled on the coast by the waves is gathered for manure" is Yeats's note to this drawing in *Life in the West of Ireland.* He made several drawings of kelp gatherers for J.M. Synge. Synge dedicated a whole article of his series on Connemara life for *The Manchester Guardian* in 1905 to the kelp-making industry. In his view it was a worthwhile, long-standing occupation, entailing much hard work, but often subject to the duplicity of middlemen. It had not received support from the Congested Districts Board, or from the Department of Agriculture and Technical Instruction for Ireland.

Yeats's drawing shows Connemara men gathering seaweed, not for sale, but probably for their own use, to manure the rocky thin-soiled patches of field in the west. The atmosphere of the stormy day, lowering over the misty hills, and the curved strand is pictured vividly. Gusts of wind drive the laden carts up the beach from the shallow water, where the men have been spearing the floating seaweed with poles or pitchforks. A boy, to the right, leads a donkey with dripping creels; but most of the work is done with horses and carts. Several are returning to the strand, empty.

Yeats places one of his typical westerners, with wide-brimmed hat, in the left foreground, surveying the busy scene from the floor of his cart, his horse rearing up as it reaches the end of the stony boreen that leads on to the strand. A gleam of light breaks unevenly over this onlooker, and over the near part of the strand, as so often happens in cloudy weather in the west. Artistically, it creates a sense of larger space and distances the background; and it provides a moment of immediacy.

There are forty line-drawings in *Life in the West of Ireland*, referring to places or incidents Yeats sketched between 1900 and 1912. All are worked in the consistent, stylized manner he adopted for pen-and-ink illustration after completing *A Broad Sheet*. However, the fact that the drawings are more or less uniform in size and manner of presentation suggests that they were executed as a set, over a not too prolonged period, and probably close to the date of publication.

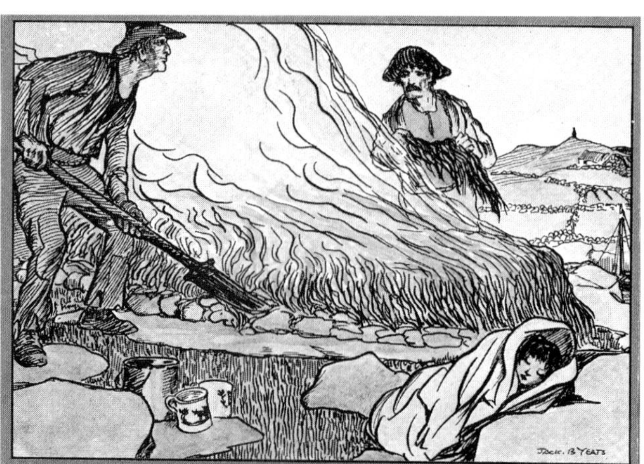

Fig. 114 Jack B. Yeats, *Kelp burning*, from *The Manchester Guardian*, 24 June 1905

Gathering seaweed

ca. 1912, pen and ink and watercolour on card, 17.7 × 25.3 cm, NGI 3828

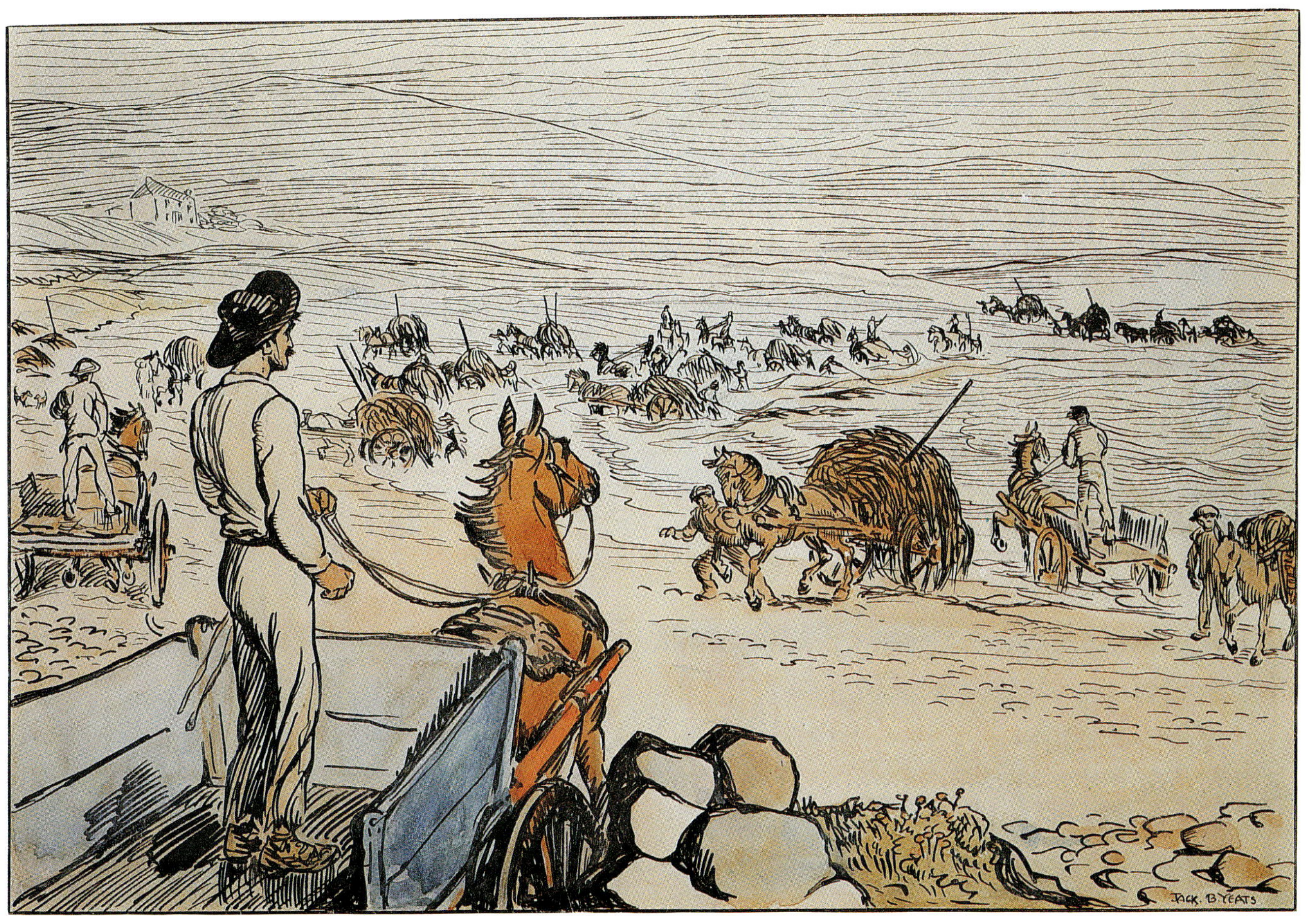

Rosses Point lies five miles to the north-west of Sligo town, where Jack Yeats spent his boyhood. He commemorated those days in his watercolour of 1900, *Memory harbour* (fig. 115), which contains many images he was to develop in later works. It was the peninsula of Rosses Point he depicted as his harbour of memories, with the smoke of the summer house of his cousins the Middletons rising from behind a hillock. The Metal Man, with boys boating near it, occupies a prominent position.

In this drawing for *Life in the West of Ireland*, the Metal Man is viewed from a southward position. A relic of the Napoleonic era, this twelve-foot high figure, in royal blue sailor's jacket, white trousers and black tie, points down from his stone pedestal to where ships may find a safe channel beside a coastline prone to silting. The day is calm. The water is gently purled with waves. Two small boys weigh their oars for an instant to wave up to the marine effigy, whose characterful presence added to the young Yeats's visits to Rosses Point. Cottages on the mainland are seen on the low skyline.

Yeats centres the drawing at a point between the horizon line and the rim of the stone pedestal, so that the height of the silhouetted Metal Man may be appreciated as much by the spectator as by the boys. Their boat floats diagonally in the lower part of the drawing. Their arms, stretched in a counter-diagonal upwards, create a jerk of movement in contrast with the vertical and horizontal stability of the rigid Man. Like the other *Life in the West of Ireland* drawings, *The Metal Man* has been finished with a wash of blue and brown watercolour, the blue being dominant in this instance.

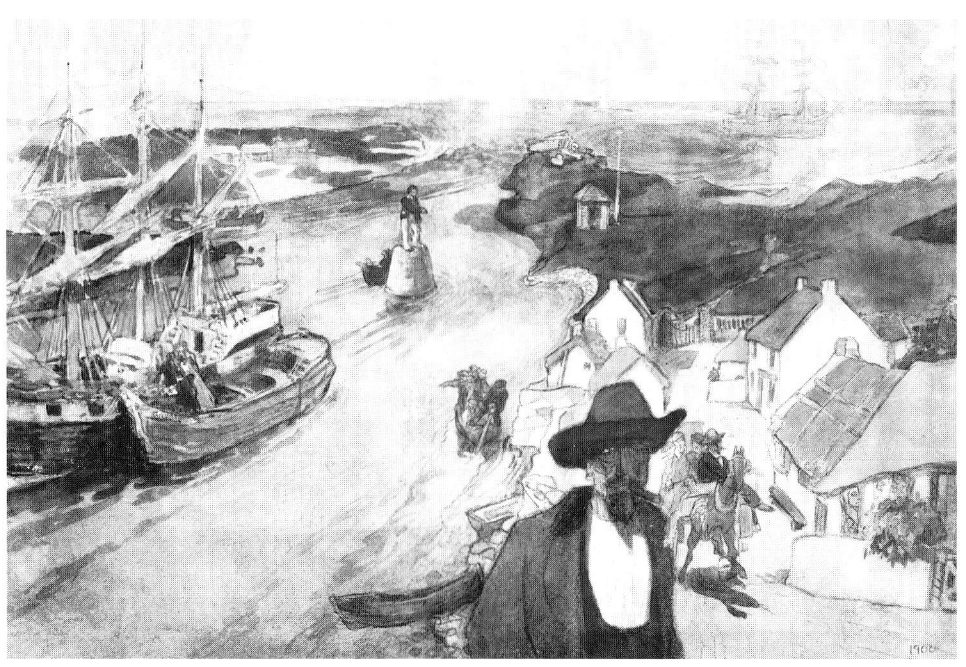

Fig. 115 Jack B. Yeats, *Memory harbour*, 1900, watercolour and crayon on card,
31 × 47 cm (Michael B. Yeats Collection)

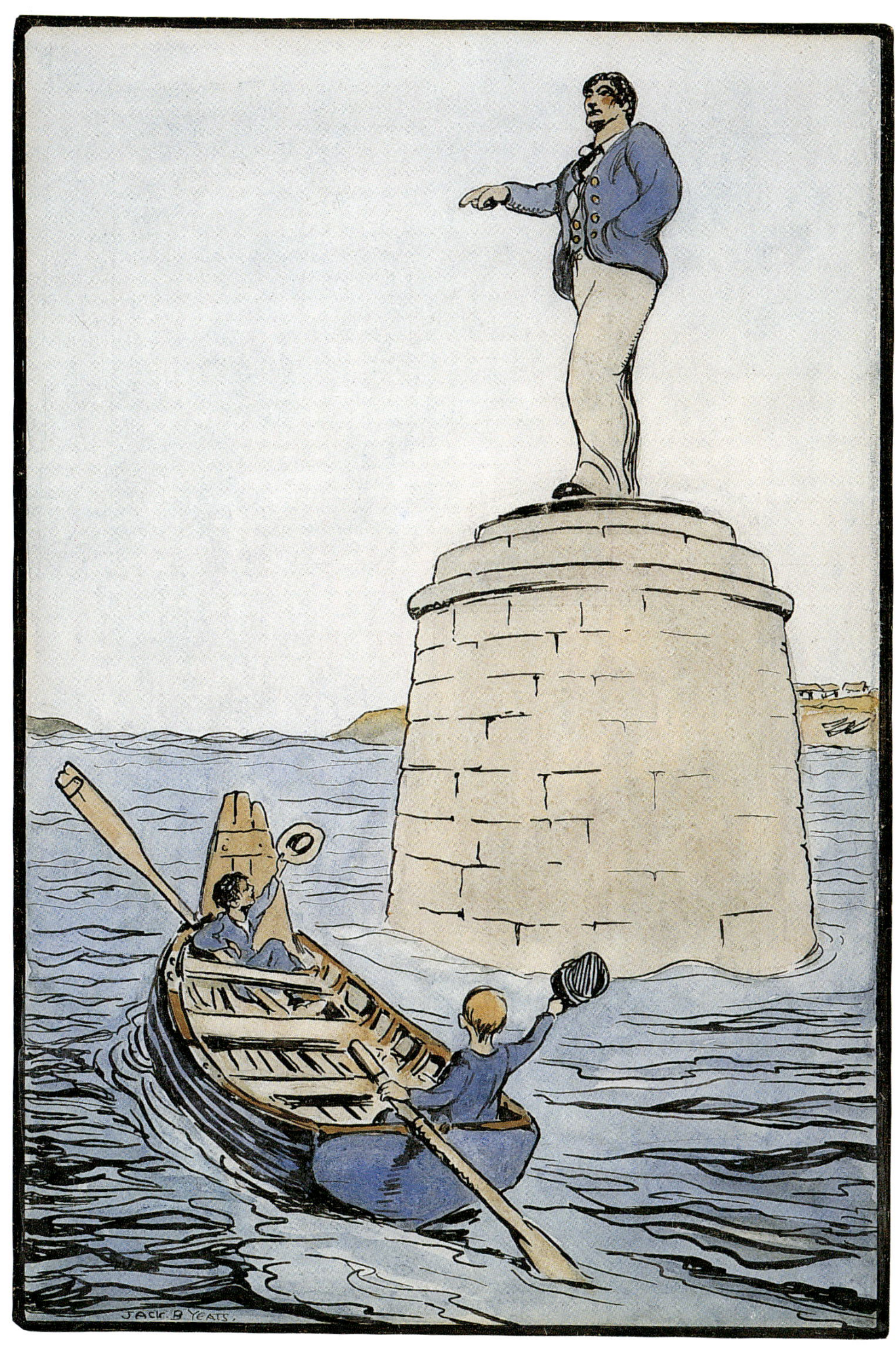

Jack Yeats's interest in miniature drama derived from a fascination with nineteenth-century prints. From an early period, he collected the melodrama designs of Redington and Pollock, and under their influence devised his own miniature stage, for which he wrote and designed children's plays, beginning with *James Flaunty: or the Terror of the Western Seas*, published by Elkin Mathews in 1901 (fig. 116). Edward Gordon Craig became interested in the artist's activities, and later, when creating settings for WBY's drama, used cut-out figures made by Jack Yeats and his wife Cottie in a model theatre, moving a lighted candle about the scenery to judge the effects that shadow and absence of detail might make on a stage. WBY wanted "'impressions' of the world his characters lived in, rather than "exact pictures of any moment in a play".

Jack Yeats, in turn, was influenced by Craig's experiments, so that when he designed a backcloth for his brother's play *The King's Threshold* in 1913, while maintaining his personal style (somewhat developed since his miniature drama days), he reached a level of abstraction that is uncharacteristic, but, interestingly, closest to his illustration to WBY's poem 'Cathleen the Daughter of Houlihan', which he included in *A Broad Sheet* (April 1903).

The simple outline of a range of hills, filled in with black ink, and the smooth green foreground, broken by a pattern of intertwined lines to the left, refer directly to the text of *The King's Threshold*, which was originally performed by the Abbey Theatre in 1903, with Celtic-style designs by Miss Horniman. In the play, the poet Seanchan goes on hunger strike in pursuit of the poets' right to maintain their traditional rôles as members of the king's council. Fasting on the steps of the king's palace, he grows progressively weaker and more delirious. He insists that not only have the poets been denied the king's court, but that creative inspiration has been banished as well.

> You have driven away
> The images of them that weave a dance
> By the four rivers in the mountain garden.

Later, he embroiders the image of the visionary garden, making it equivalent with paradise:

> The four rivers that run there,
> Through well-mown level ground,
> Have come out of a blessed well
> That is all bound and wound
> By the great roots of an apple tree.

Jack Yeats's simple mountainscape comes straight out of his west of Ireland experience, being the back of the King's Mountain in the Ben Bulben range, viewed from near Ballintrillick in County Sligo. He refers to Seanchan's delirious words, and depicts the "well-mown level ground" with the four rivers and their tributaries, which represent the mountain garden of the poet's imagination in the play. In this way the poetic plane, in the generalized impression his brother demanded, is achieved while, true to his own way, he maintains the silhouette of the definite locality to which the legend relates.

The play was performed at the Abbey Theatre in 1913 and was received with acclaim. "With the help of Mr. Gordon Craig's design and Mr. Jack B. Yeats's backcloth, a very beautiful scene was arranged," wrote a reviewer. "It was quite simple in construction, showing merely two sets of steps opposite each other, and a background of mountain and sky. The lighting, which was admirably contrived, was of a soft and subdued nature, and anything of a glaring effect was strictly avoided .... Such work as this ... shows us the Abbey Theatre at its very best."

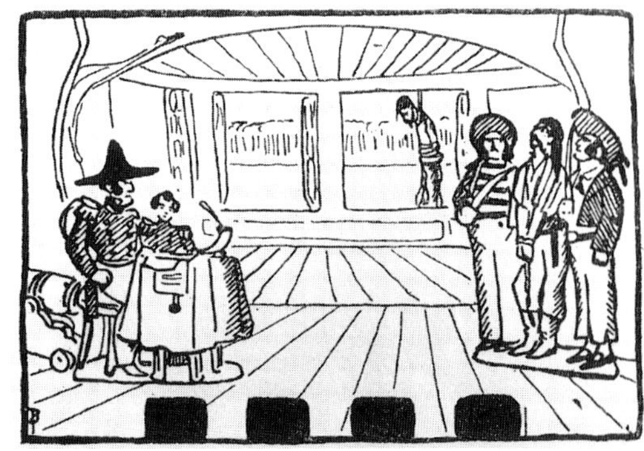

Fig. 116
Jack B. Yeats,
James Flaunty,
Scene IV, 1901
(NGI Yeats
Archive)

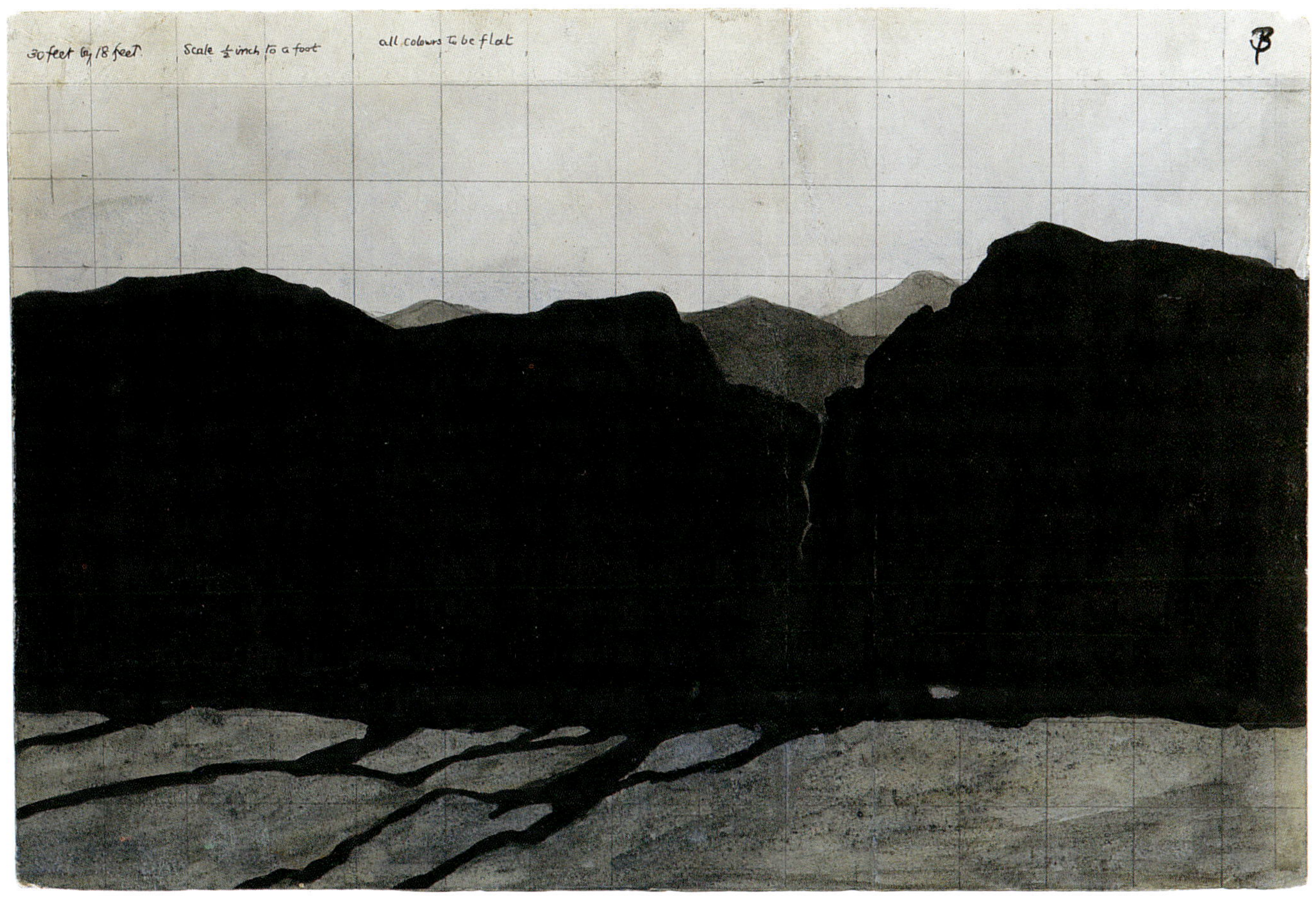

Design for a mountain backcloth for
The King's Threshold

1913, ink, pencil and watercolour on card, squared for transfer, 24.8 × 37.5 cm, NGI 6322

The priest is one of twelve oils painted by Yeats as illustrations to *Irishmen All* by George A. Birmingham, published in London in October 1913. There are twelve chapters, each describing an Irish type – policeman, squire, politician, country gentleman, shop assistant and so on – and Yeats provided a portrait for each chapter. Many of the author's professional types have been given a fictional name, the personality undoubtedly being inspired by some person or people he had known; but, when addressing himself to the parish priest, Birmingham had no particular cleric in mind, and he talked about the profession in a general way. "How are we to estimate … the character of Irish priests?" he wrote. "Can we estimate it at all? I confess that I shrink from making the attempt. But of this I feel sure, that the stability and strength of the Roman Catholic Church in Ireland depend upon her having among her priests a large number of men of the Spirit".

George A. Birmingham was the pseudonym of Canon James Owen Hannay (1865–1950), himself a priest of the Church of Ireland and Rector of Westport, County Mayo, for a time. His humorous, often caustic, novels about Irish life were not always well received: and, disillusioned with the state of affairs in his country, he emigrated to England. His book *The Lighter Side of Irish Life* (1911) was illustrated with watercolours by the Scottish artist Henry W. Kerr. *Irishmen All* was more serious, assessing officialdom and the major and minor professions in a satirical but not unkind way.

He found a sympathetic illustrator in Jack Yeats, who had been painting Irish characters, with similar satire, for a decade, and who had already provided black-and-white drawings for several of George Birmingham's stories in *A Celtic Christmas* over the years. Yeats seems to have received a list of chapter headings, with perhaps a summary of the author's intentions, and that was all. Neither saw the other's work beforehand. Yet the novelist wrote to him delighted at how well illustrations and text complemented each other.

Yeats's early oils, like his watercolours, were often of an illustrative character, so it is not surprising that he chose to do these illustrations in oil. He had abandoned watercolour at this date and was to exhibit these works as independent paintings. The subject-matter fitted perfectly with the theme he had been pursuing over the past fifteen years as *Life in the West of Ireland*. Birmingham's Irishmen were drawn from all over the country, whereas Yeats's illustrations were rooted in the west he knew, *The politician* having the recognizable shape of Ben Bulben in the background.

As was characteristic with his watercolours, he silhouetted most of the characters against a backdrop of their locality, particularly effective in the case of *The priest*, suggesting his emblematic dominance in rural life. Yeats's priest is obviously a particular personality, surprisingly close in appearance to his friend the Reverend T.A. Harvey, who was to become Church of Ireland Bishop of Cashel, and whom, interestingly, he did not use as model for his illustration of *The minister*. *The minister* is seen by George Birmingham as unambitious and forgotten, in his "utterly remote little rectory". This priest is a vibrant and uncompromising leader, walking the roads of his parish, and no doubt instrumental in the erection of the building at which men are working in the background of the picture. He is at the same time, with his ascetic appearance, one of the "large number of men of the Spirit" whom George Birmingham describes.

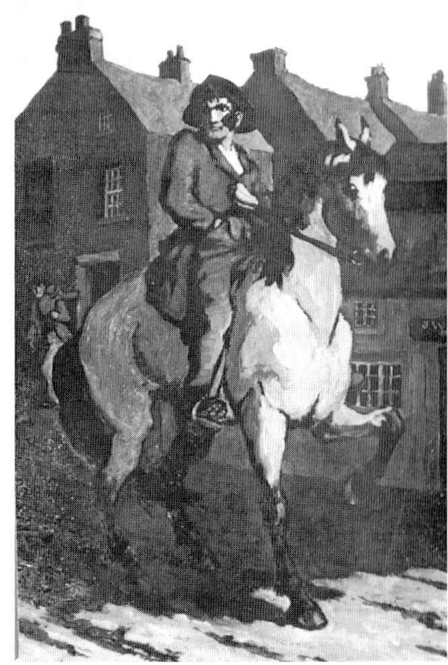

Fig. 117 Jack B. Yeats, *The farmer*, oil on panel, 36 × 23 cm, 1913 (private collection)

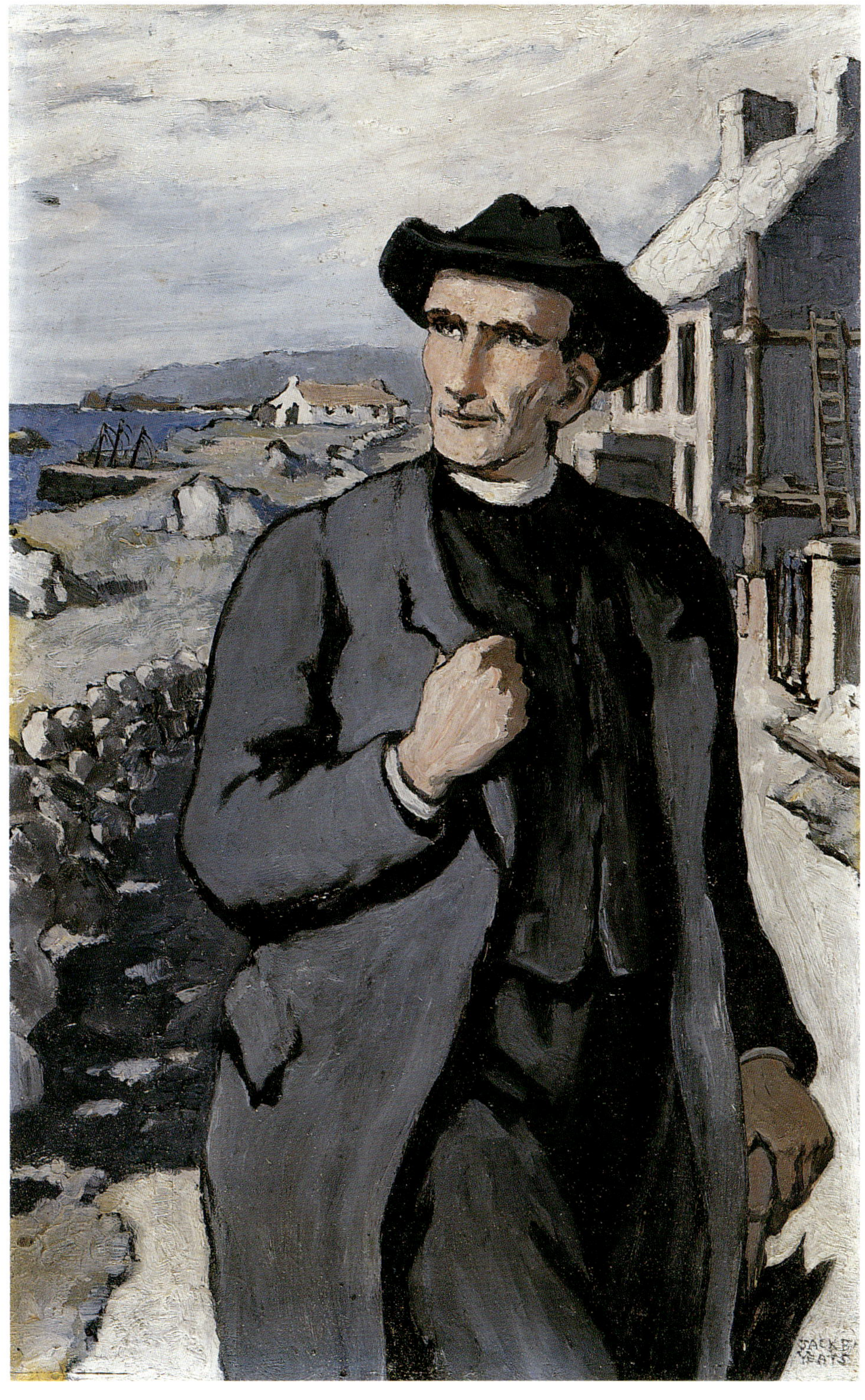

Jeremiah O'Donovan Rossa, born in Roscarbery, County Cork, in 1831, was tried for complicity in the Fenian Conspiracy in 1859. After his release, he became business manager of *The Irish People*, but he was rearrested in 1865 and sentenced to penal servitude for life. At a later date he was exiled, under amnesty, to America, where he edited *The United Irishman*. After his death in 1915 he was brought home to Dublin where he lay in state in the City Hall.

Jack Yeats attended the City Hall and made full notes afterwards of what he had seen. A photograph of the lying-in-state, taken from *The Daily Sketch*, 30 July 1915, and preserved among the artist's personal papers, may have prompted him to make this drawing and may also have suggested the structure of the composition. The drawing was never worked up into a painting. It is in BB pencil, with a little cross-hatching mainly rubbed with a finger.

Though sketching roughly, the artist has conveyed the solemnity of the occasion. Three statues grace the left background of the rotunda of the City Hall, between lightly indicated columns. Each wears a black drape. The open coffin, swathed in a tricolour, is raised up on a black platform and flanked by a crucifix and four tall candles. A soldier to the right (lightly described), his hands resting on his rifle, watches the procession of men, heads bared, winding about the bier and then moving out through the door in the right background. The ghostlike forms, so individual and expressive, are forerunners of Yeats's expressionist human outlines in oil paintings from the late 1920s onwards.

The top of the candle on the left is in the exact centre of the drawing, with a gap opened in the procession, to the right of it, whereby the coffin may be properly seen. The expressions of the men in the right foreground are compact and immediate; the row of the back of heads in the left foreground – those who have moved on – suggests the blankness and anonymity of public grief; while the varied movements and expressions of those disappearing in the middle distance add a further dimension to this occasion of national mourning.

The fact that he notes twice in the inscription that the drawing is done from memory is a strong indicator of the increasing importance Yeats would attach to memory from this period – though factual memory for him would not be long in becoming artistic memory, with a licence to arrange a composition to convey more than a photographic record is capable of doing. In this pencil drawing, Yeats has amalgamated fragments culled from observation and from memory into one single pictorial sketch. His later reliance on memory as the inspirational source for his paintings was to allow manifold incursions of the imagination to transform his work.

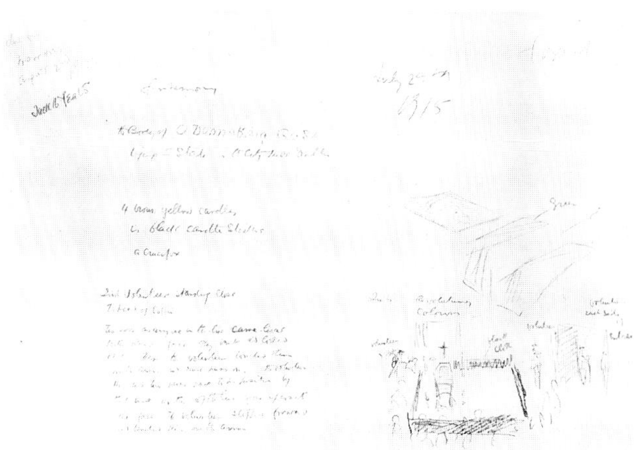

Fig. 118 *The lying-in-state of O'Donovan Rossa*, 1915 (verso)

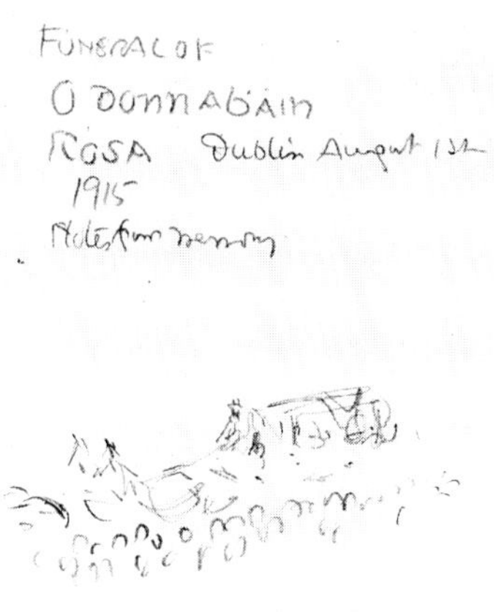

Fig. 119 Jack B. Yeats, *Funeral of O Donnabáin Rosa, Dublin, August 1st 1915. Notes from memory* (NGI Yeats Archive)

The lying-in-state of O'Donovan Rossa

1915, pencil on paper, 25.5 × 36 cm, NGI 3780

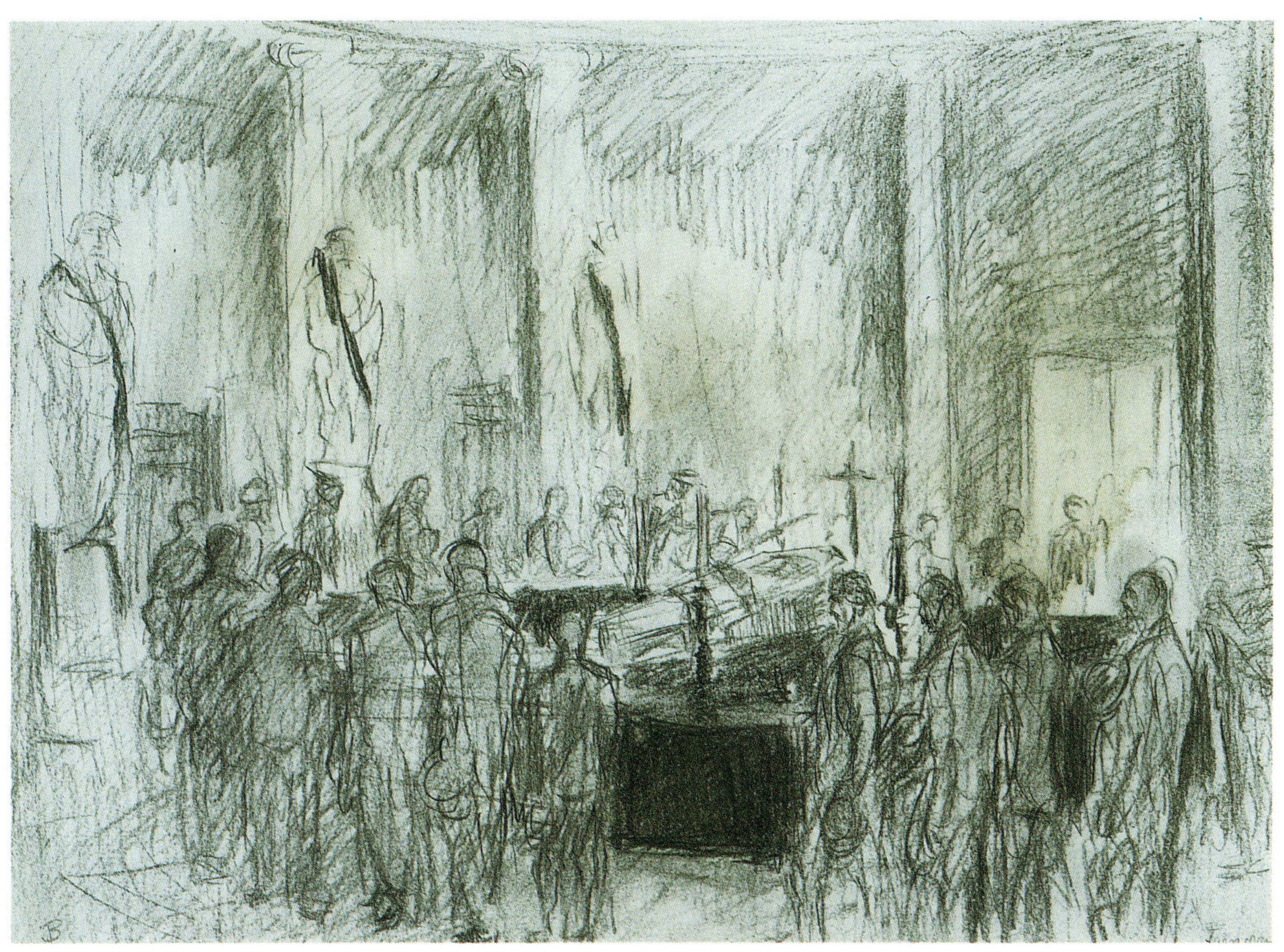

The gathering of the jockeys on their mounts before the race began was a subject that fascinated Degas (see fig. 20); but, while there are certain similarities between the artists at an earlier phase of Yeats's career, in *Before the start* Yeats concentrates on contrasts of character as well as on purely spatial revelations. His three jockeys, silhouetted against a pale sky, exude determination, nervousness and aggression; their horses, in their turn, reflect these different moods in their expressive heads and ears. Three local heroes, they tower above the tight-packed heads of their expectant neighbours, who are dressed in their best and eagerly await the start of the race.

Yeats inserts a suspicious face, peeping out from the centre of the crowd, as a humorous comparison with the serious countenances of the competitors, and to inject a warmer element into the otherwise anonymous crowd, who present their backs to the spectator. The variety of hats in the foreground as such is interesting. The flat-crowned wide-brimmed hat in the centre was worn in Galway at the turn of the century, and the hat with the higher crown to its left may be seen on *The man from Aranmore* (p. 172).

Yeats silhouetted his figures like this against seemingly empty space in many of his early paintings. The motif of the silhouetted jockeys, strengthened by the outline of the starting post with streaming flag (dividing the picture into a horizontal rectangle and a smaller vertical space), seems to have struck him first when he was in Kerry in 1913, and he made various sketches of this kind to use in future compositions. In a different way, the erect flag in *A lake regatta* (p. 216) draws the indeterminate space surrounding it towards a focal point.

Yeats had been painting race-meeting subjects for many years, and continued to do so in a more fanciful way throughout his life (see fig. 120). Colours, as is typical of this early period, are firm and evocative, and the format is still conservative. One of the pleasures of the painting is in the decisive brushwork. The paint is applied expressively, with the thick impasto contained within strong outlines. *Before the start* dates from 1915, and was highly commended at the Aonach Exhibition at the Royal Dublin Society Horse Show in 1922.

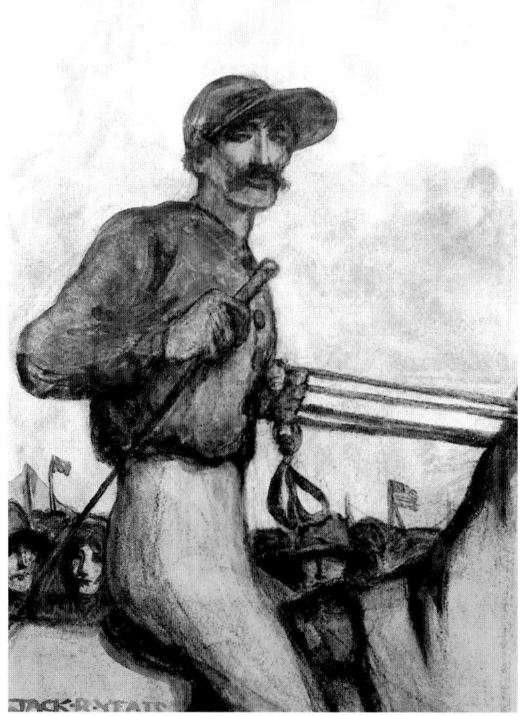

Fig. 120 Jack B. Yeats, *The country jockey*, watercolour, *ca.* 1902, crayon and watercolour, 35.5 × 25.5 cm (private collection)

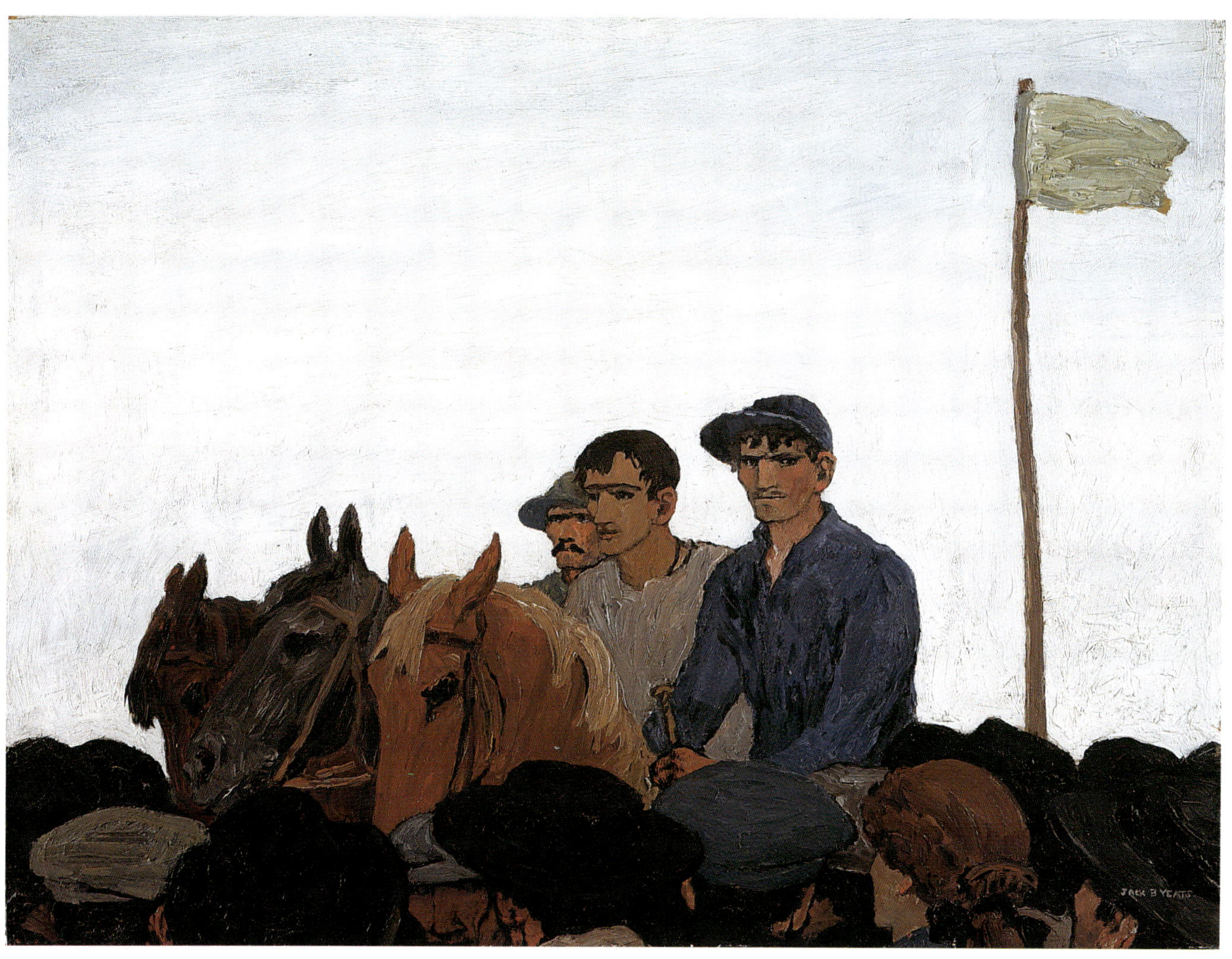

The circus and circus life were among Yeats's richest sources of subject-matter (see p. 186). In this picture of 1916, he paints two bare back-riders, balancing themselves on the rump of a piebald horse, spreading out their arms as it canters round the ring of a travelling circus in Sligo. One acrobat wears a red jacket with blue sleeves, the other blue with red sleeves, and they stand out against the blackness of the tent canvas in their night act, lit only by the flare on the central post.

Alongside the horse a clown gallops outrageously, imitating man and beast at one and the same time, waving his hat in defiance of his ridiculous performance. To Yeats, as to other artists such as Rouault, and writers like his brother WBY, the clown was a ready image of man's tragic situation, comical, pathetic, courageous and ready to try anything; expressive of man's various attributes, whether despicable or admirable. In his last paintings, the clown is sublimated, but here Yeats maintains the simple narrative manner of his first-period oils. At the same time, he makes full play of the opposing diagonals of the moving horse and the energetic figures, and of the verticals and horizontals of the tent posts and the striped canvas, of the uncertain glimmer of light resting on the essential details, and of the brooding figure of the countryman, sitting at the edge of the ring, watching with intense concentration.

Yeats's use of oil was at its heaviest at this stage, with broad criss-crossed strokes and very obvious brushwork creating the compacted shapes and interesting shadows. The impasto is applied in a dancing pointillist manner in the lower part of the picture. As his manner grew more fluid, he was to abandon the vertical compositions of his early years altogether, and to paint henceforward horizontal pictures, his scale increasing in the more important paintings as the years progressed.

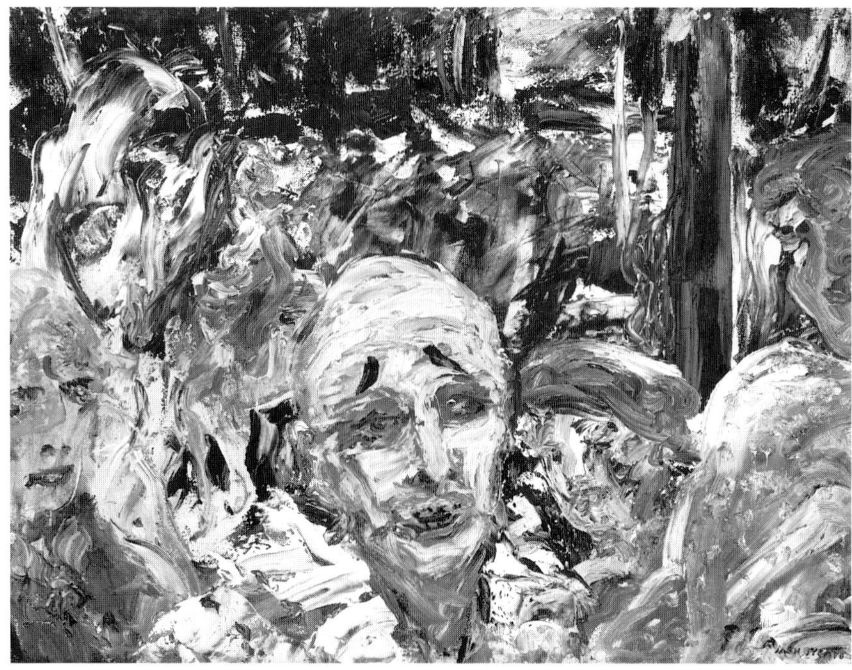

Fig. 121 Jack B. Yeats, *The clown among the people*, 1932,
oil on canvas, 46 × 61 cm (private collection)

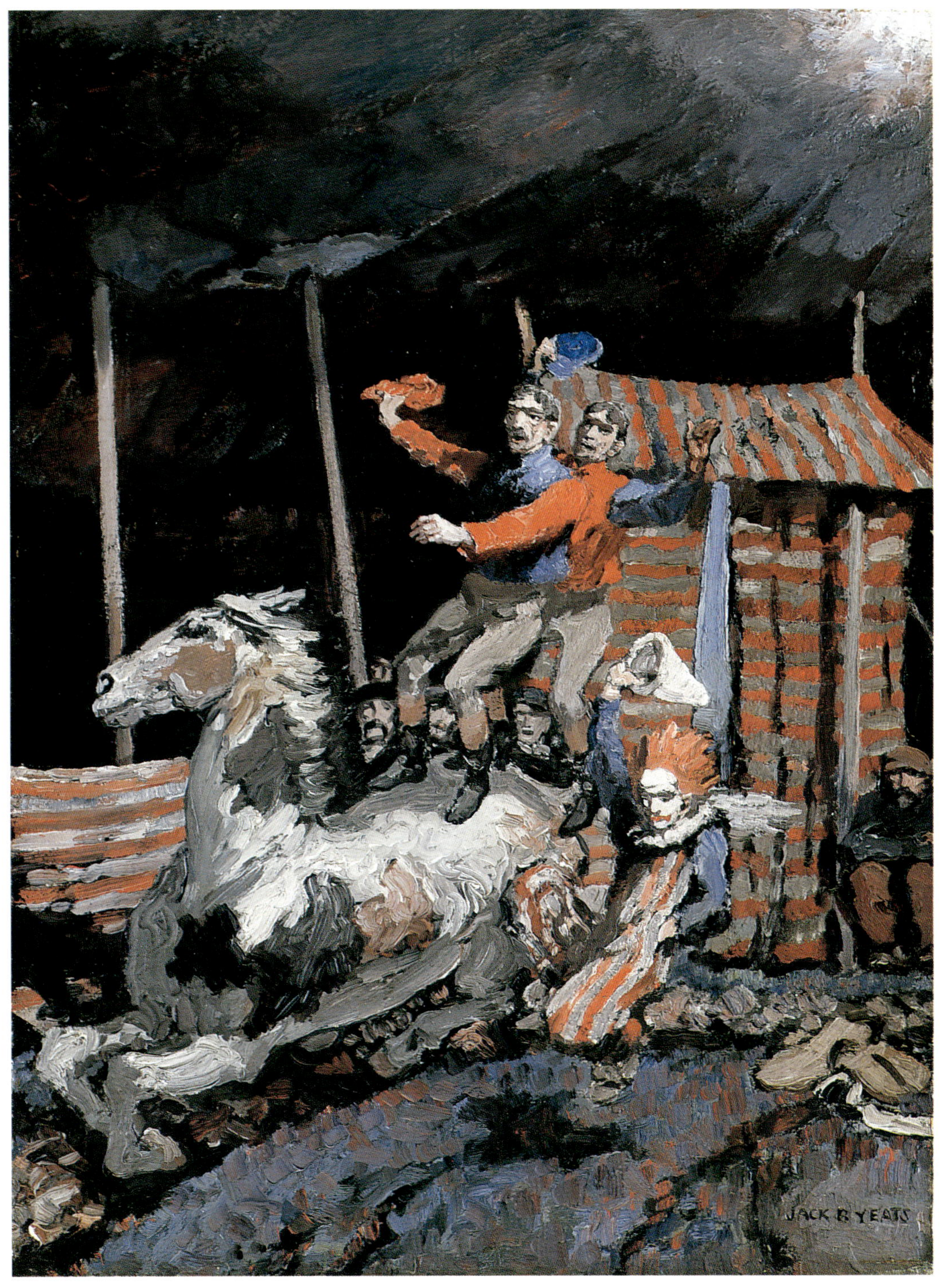

Jack Yeats was not a portrait painter. He painted his wife in *Portrait of a lady*, in 1926; did an admirable likeness of Masefield in watercolour; and made stencil images of Synge and his father. Otherwise, his portraits are chance sketches in his notebooks, with the exception of the series of self-portraits he made in the 1920s, beginning with this pencil study and a pen-and-ink head of 1914–20. It may have been his father's profession as a portrait painter that inhibited him, despite the fact that he himself was capable of a very good likeness. Equally, he may have found the formality of portrait painting confining. It is interesting, however, that he drew this sketch about the time that his father was completing his major self-portrait that he had worked on for years in New York.

Jack Yeats, who had sat to his father as a boy and as a young man, shows himself at fifty, standing at his easel in a corner of his own studio. His hand holding the pencil is indicated hazily, hovering at the edge of the paper. His face appears as an intense mask, in a good if rigid likeness, as he studies his reflection minutely. The rest of the image is freely worked, with Yeats's relaxed mastery of line rendering the confident stance, his unemployed hand in his pocket, the legs firmly apart.

Deep, mobile shadows create pleasing variations of outline and texture in the plain, baggy, waistcoated suit – nothing outrageous, by way of artistic showmanship, but the plain garb of an ordinary man of the day. There is no attempt to decorate, or artificially arrange, the interior. It is simply the corner of a bare room, which the artist lifts from its emptiness with cross-hatching, scribbling and black shading, relieved by light coming from an unseen window to the left.

That Yeats regarded this as a study in light and shade is evident from the addition of some light-green

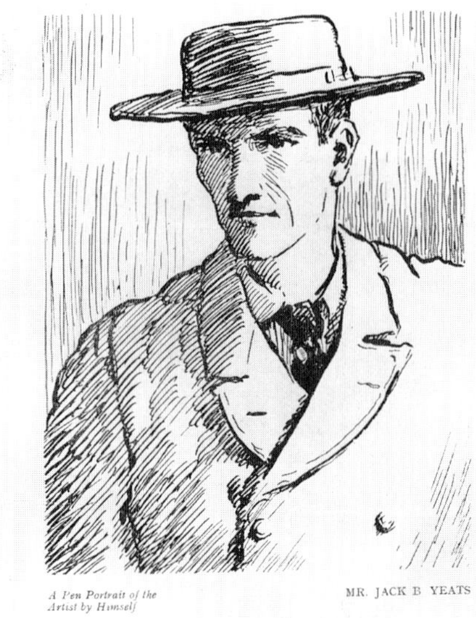

Fig. 122 Jack B. Yeats, *A Pen Portrait of the Artist by Himself*, from *T.P.'s Weekly*, 18 July 1914

chalk down the centre of the drawing, highlighting that portion of the sketch. The soft blunt pencil sometimes scrapes the surface, and this contributes to the mobile effect of light. Other self-portraits of the 1920s are in pen and ink, showing the artist's head and shoulders, and they are pensive in mood (fig. 122). They present an image of isolation, of a certain melancholy. Out of this initial period of introspection emerged the major works of reminiscence, where the artist is represented as a ghost image, wandering among boxing rings, or the circus and theatre of his youth, linking the emotion of particular past experiences to the well furnished vision of old age.

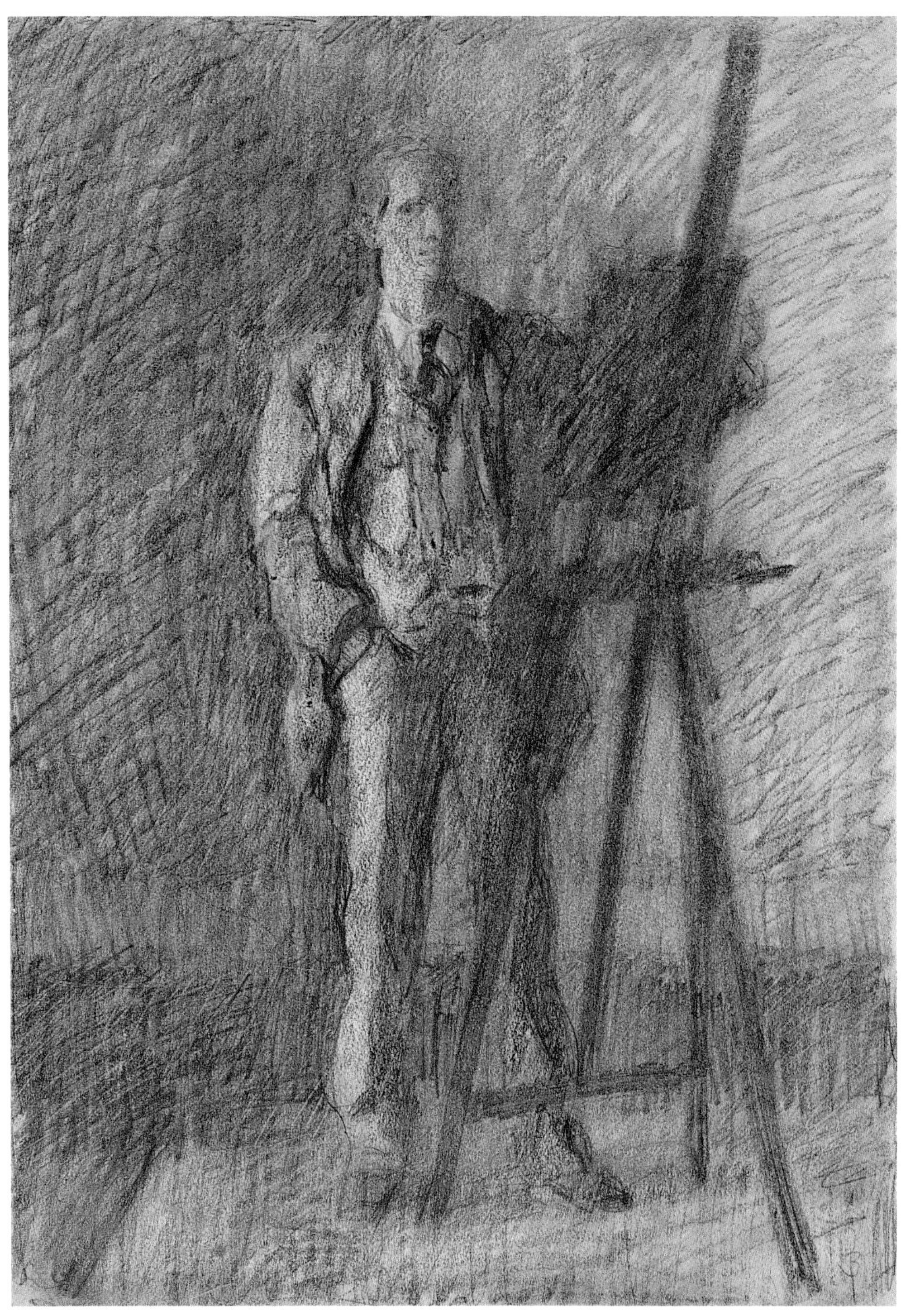

Yeats was ill in 1916, and deeply affected by the seeming failure of the Easter Rising. As a result his approach to his painting changed. He lost interest in the dramatic and heroic propensities of his Sligo and western subjects, and, instead, travelled about the south, painting and widening his knowledge of the Irish coast. He moved to the city and sketched a good deal in Dublin, particularly on the quays and at the Grand Canal Docks in Ringsend.

Alongside this intensified study of land and dockscape, he was developing his awareness of the importance of memory, which carried with it the notion of 'half-memory' and its effect on the artist's consciousness, out of which his mature fantastical style was to evolve.

Draughts, painted in 1922, is an excellent example of one of his direct studies of cityscape of this period. However, the two seamen engrossed in their game in the foreground were probably painted from memory. Their faces and their poses are as characterful as any of the Sligo sailors he painted. Yeats was always fascinated by games and the various forms of entertainment of ordinary people, and had sketched children playing pitch and toss at the Grand Canal Docks. The view, with the lock gate to the right, and the dock wall to the left, with one of the masted boats that were frequently seen at the time beyond, forms a framework for their game of chance and skill. Yeats always painted a masted boat when he had the opportunity.

But this picture has a contemplative quality and a new element of affection for his subject, which was a feature of Yeats's rather sober-coloured scenes of this date. The mood contrasts with the pure reportage of his early style and preludes the elated emotion of his later work. The loose paintwork in the surrounding view, described with a relaxed broad brush and little exact definition, is characteristic of the early phase of his middle period. Relieving the sombre greys that clothe the rows of buildings above the dock basin are the rust of the scarf worn by the moustached man in the foreground and the pink pieces of the draught set. The only other colour is the green of the weeds on the pier, the same green tinging the masted boat and lighting the surface of the canal basin water.

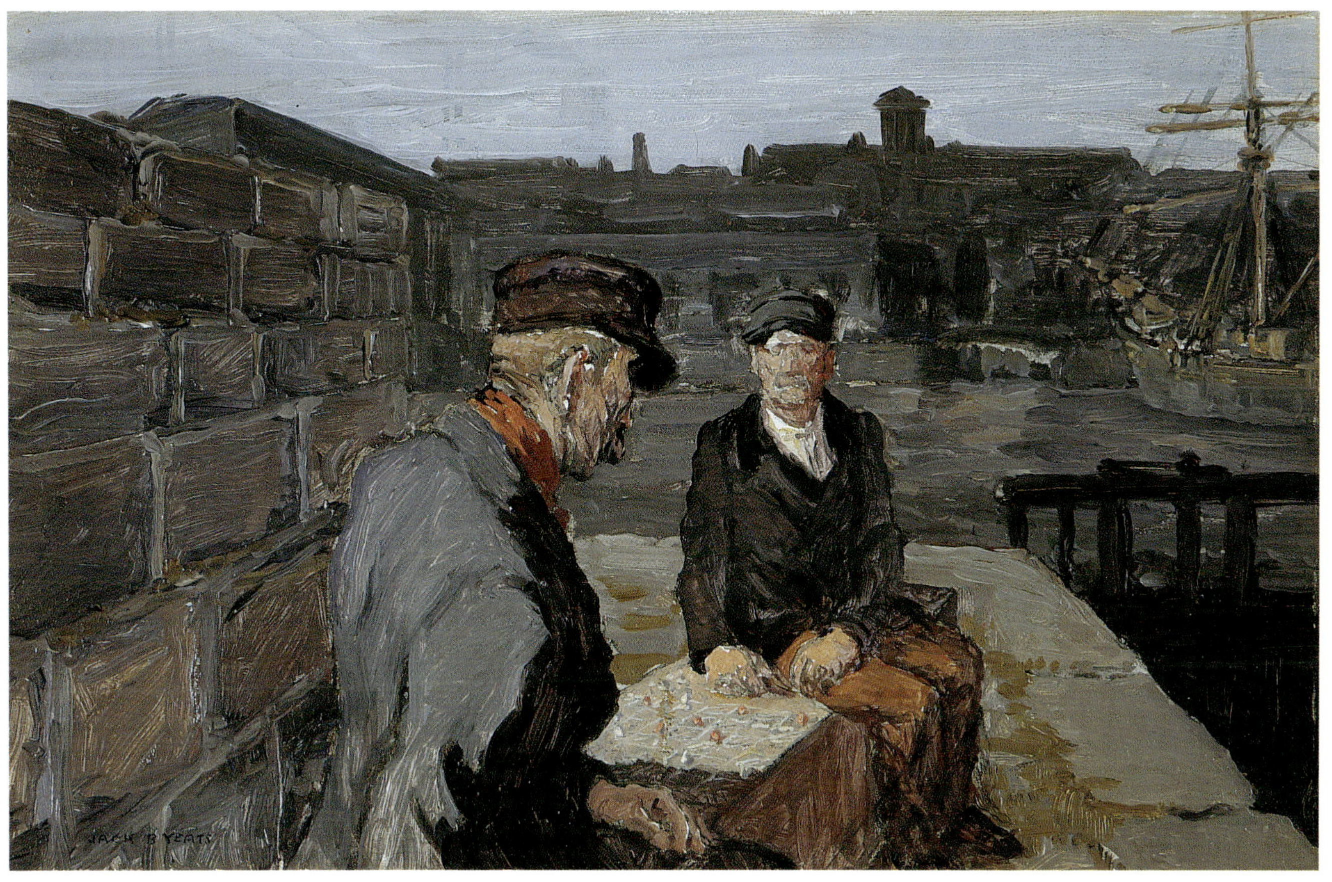

During the early 1920s, Yeats painted several tram subjects, in what can be seen as a coming to terms with modern urban life. He had lived in Greystones, beside the sea, when he first returned to Ireland from Devon, but in 1917 moved into Dublin to live in Marlborough Road, in Donnybrook, not far from the centre of the city. During the next few years, he deliberately turned from the images of adventure and nostalgia that had preoccupied him since his youth, and addressed himself to images of a New Ireland, which became a hope after the Sinn Fein Convention in 1918 and found an unillustrious truncated reality in 1921. Yeats was apolitical by nature, but in his sympathies supported the Republicans. Nevertheless, despite his inner anguish at the defeat of the Easter Rising and the unsatisfactory compromise that emerged, his art gathered strength, and he has left some of the most vivid descriptions of the life of the ordinary Dubliner in the early days of the Free State, as well as a few important visual records of contemporary political happenings.

In the tram of 1923 shows two young Dublin women gathered into a gossiping group with an older woman in a corner of the Lucan train, while a man in hat and coat sits hunched up on his own at the far end of the seat. They are passing the walls of the Phoenix Park, which act as a backcloth beyond the tram window. Yeats exhibited the painting as *In the tram*, but described it as 'In the Lucan Tram', or 'The Merry Wives of Lucan'. The faces and figures of the women carry all the subtleties of expression that Yeats had developed during his study of human character over the years; but such a close confrontation with feminine subjects was a new departure for Yeats, and the elegant movement of the woman who holds the centre of the picture, and the swanlike stoop of her companion on the very right, anticipate his romantic women to come.

His style at this date had become so confident and free that he had abandoned the firm outline he had used formerly, and rendered the representational images – Manet-like – with a new technical freedom and lightness of paint. The colours are still fairly sombre, relieved by the warm hues of the geometric shapes of tinted glass in the tram ventilators, which make a harmonious pattern against the wall beyond the windows.

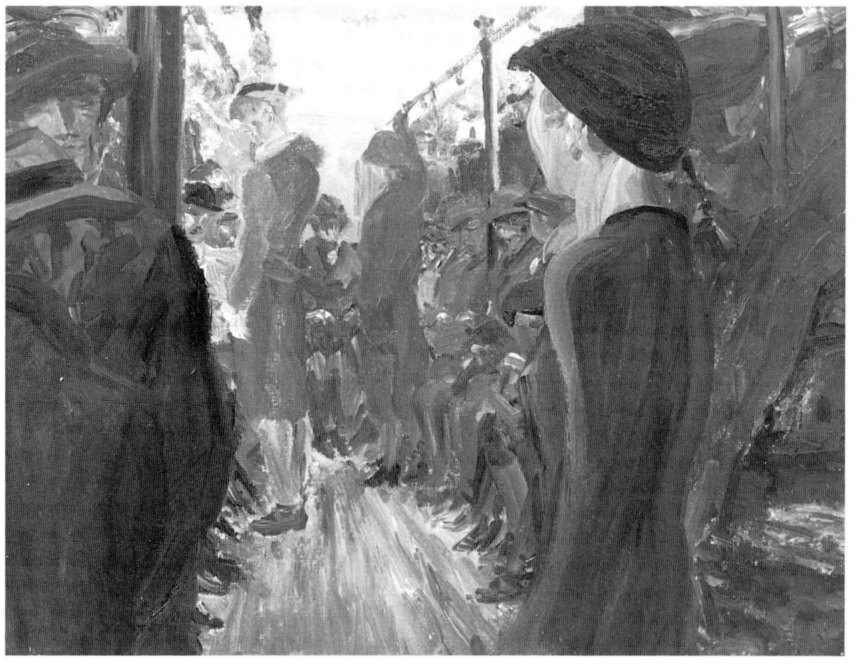

Fig. 123 Jack B. Yeats, *A full tram*, 1923, oil on canvas, 46 × 61 cm (private collection)

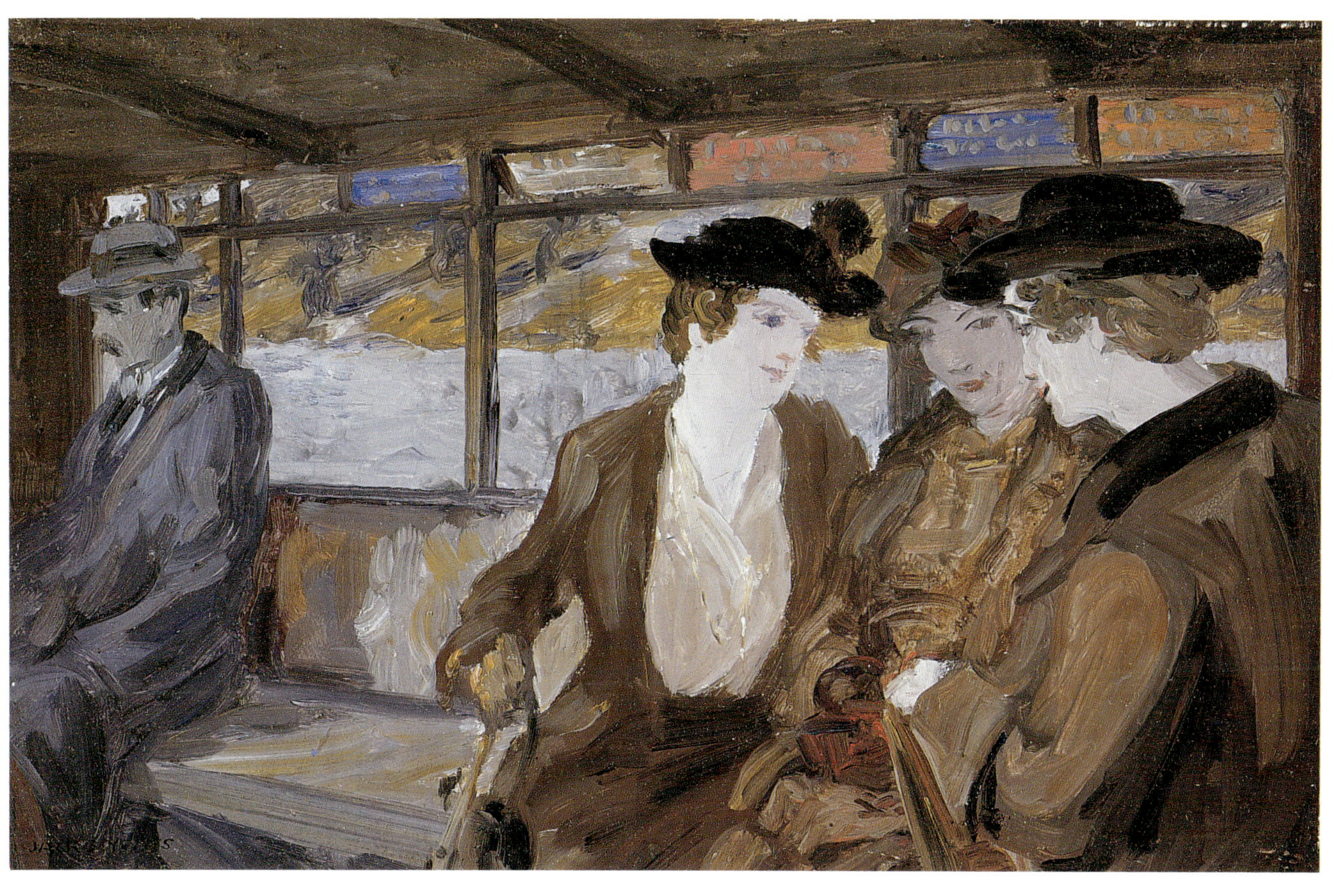

his picture of 1923 in Yeats's transitional style, recording the annual Swim down the River Liffey through Dublin city, shows a return to capturing the thrill of sporting events, abandoned for a time while the artist concentrated on quieter, less arresting subjects during the early 1920s. The Liffey Swim had been instituted as a city event in 1920, and recently celebrated its seventy-fifth anniversary. By contrast to the relaxed reaction to the event in the 1990s, the occasion seems to have been of much greater importance in its early years, though it is noticeable that Yeats has exerted his artistic license in the matter of perspective in order to include every element of excitement that he can. He brings in not only the spectators in the foreground crowding the riverside on Bachelor's Walk, and those with a grandstand view on the trams passing behind them, but also the people thronging O'Connell Bridge in the middle distance and on the quay opposite.

A wide range of types of every age and standing in society is depicted skilfully from behind. Their graduated posture, as they lean forward to watch the swimmers progressing down the river, produces an illusion of movement in the classical manner.

The man in the brown hat, picked out to the left of centre (near a woman in a yellow hat), may well be the artist himself taking notes. Certainly the man appears as a detached observer, similar to the artist sketching in the foreground whom Yeats would have seen in Irish eighteenth-century topographical landscapes. It suggests also the active association of the painter with what he paints, which was to become so important to Yeats in his later subjective work.

Despite his use of traditional tools, though, the style is modern and confident, the artist having abandoned the characteristic strong outline of his early figurative oils. Brushstrokes are broad and free. Colours are rich, with highlights applied directly from the paint tube: and the whole gives the impression of having been painted with great rapidity. Emotion is now implemental in the composition, expressed in the actual application of paint, and in colour that is deliberately intrusive. Thus red – positive and aggressive – tints the water around the desperate striving of the near figure. The spectators are painted in passive greens and blues, and pink in the clouds reflects the general mood of optimism.

Yeats was conscious that this was one of his major works and, in the Royal Hibernian Academy Annual Exhibition of 1925, priced it highly for him, at £300. It was awarded a silver medal at the Paris Olympic in 1924. *The Liffey Swim* was the first Jack B. Yeats painting acquired by the National Gallery of Ireland, a donation from the Haverty Bequest.

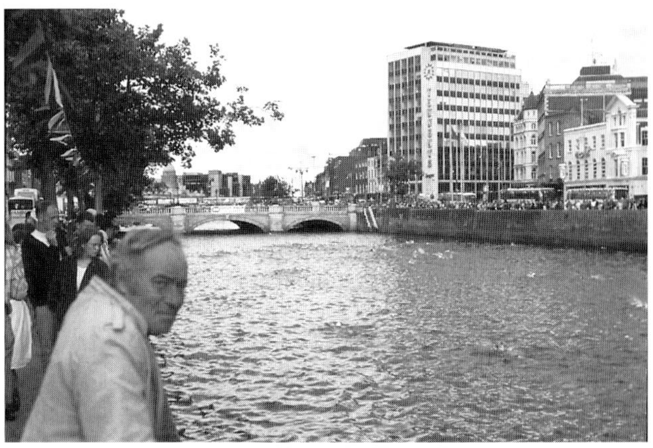

Fig. 124 The seventy-fifth anniversary of the Liffey Swim, Dublin, September 1995

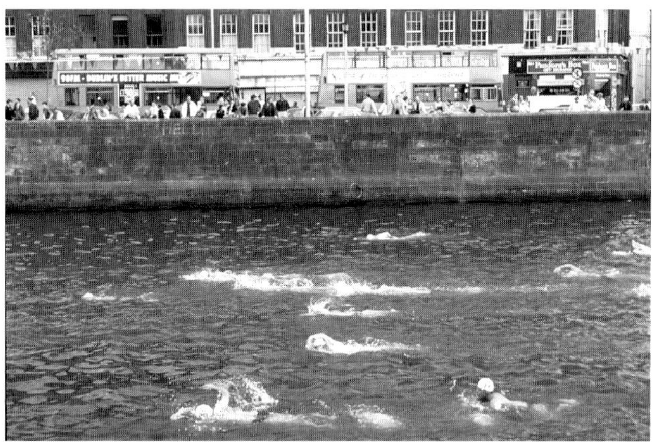

Fig. 125 The seventy-fifth anniversary of the Liffey Swim, Dublin, September 1995

The Liffey Swim

1923, oil on canvas, 61 × 91 cm, NGI 941

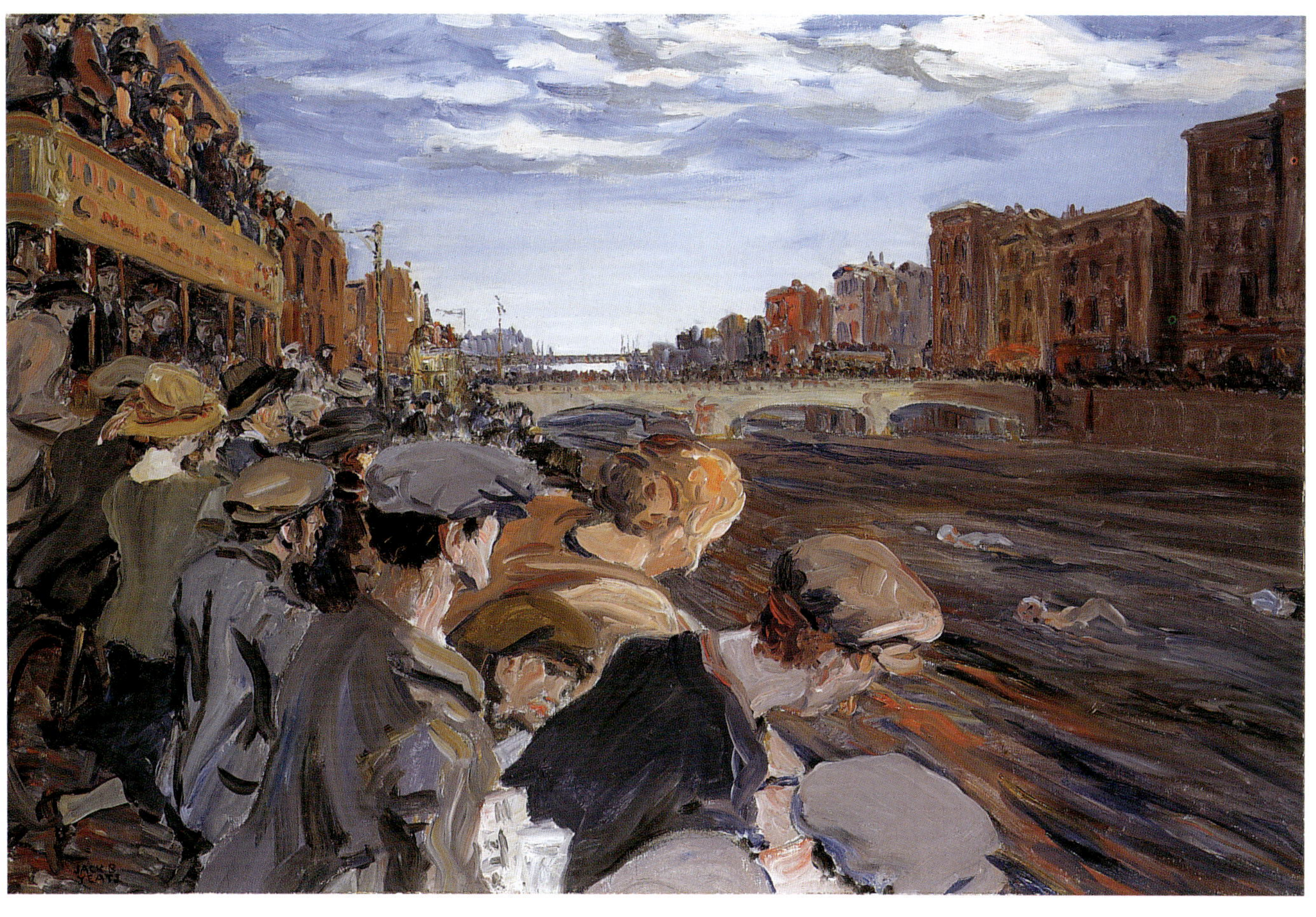

OVERLEAF
Detail of *The Liffey Swim*

213

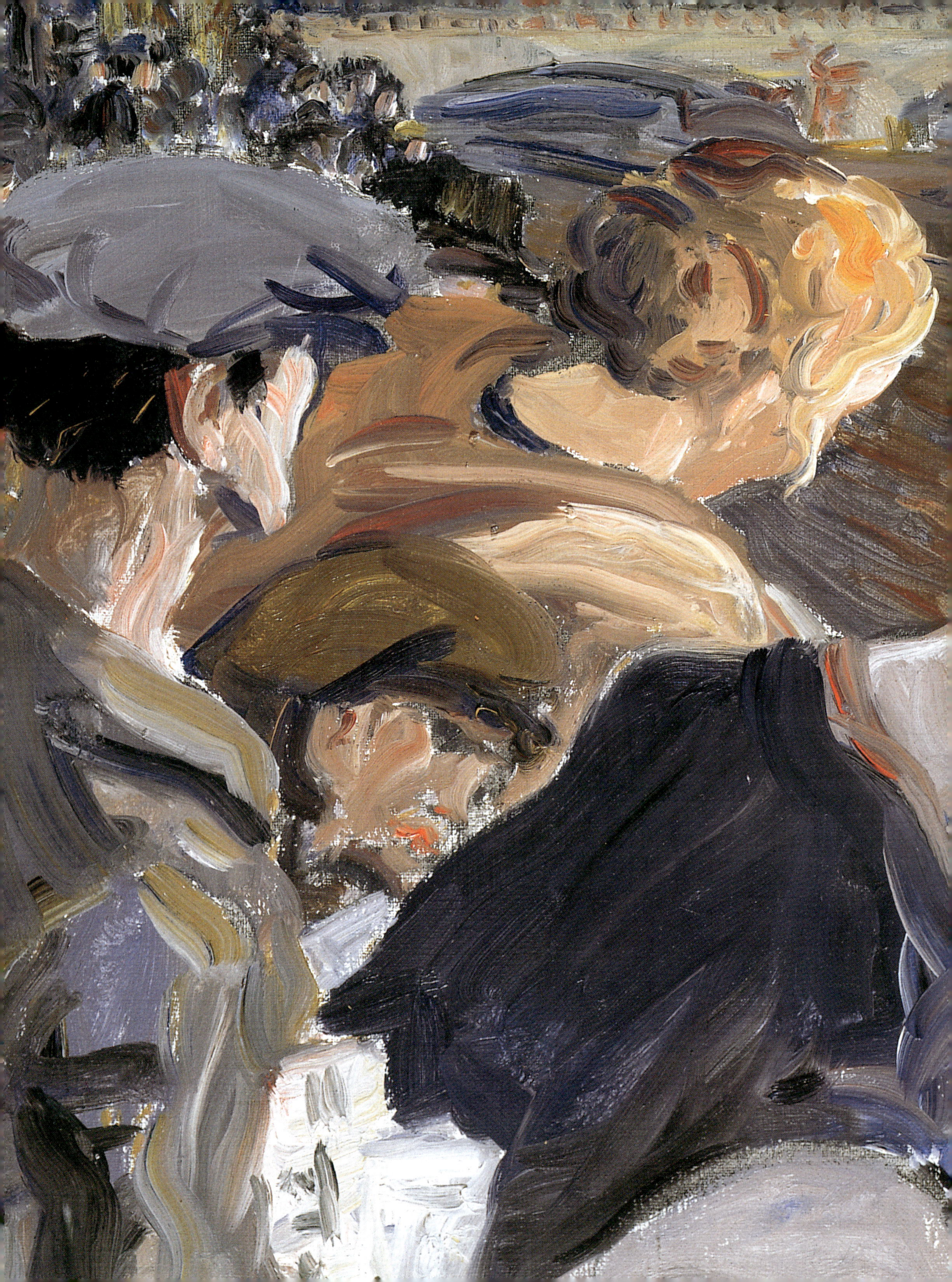

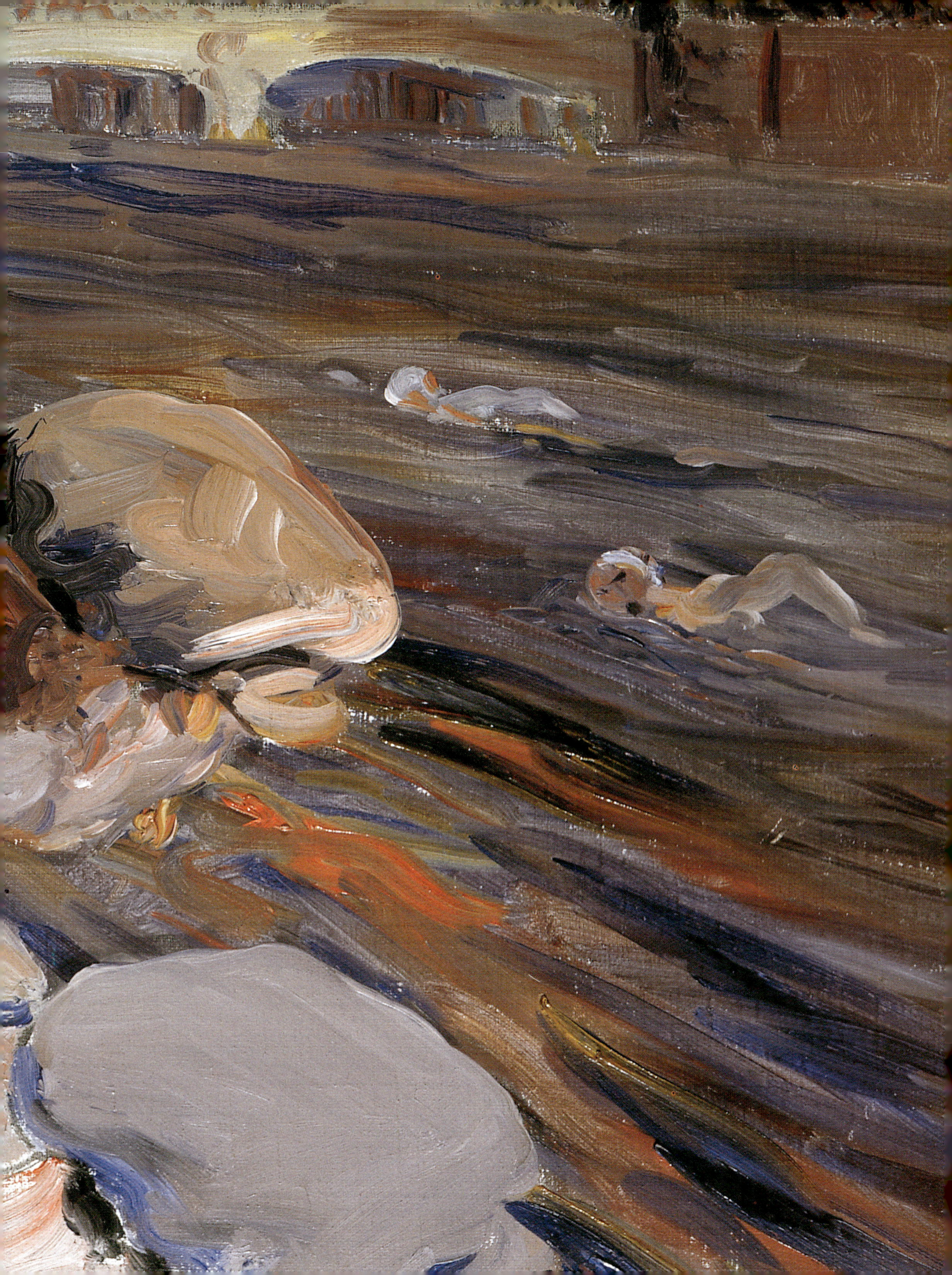

In 1923, Yeats paid a visit to Lady Gregory at Coole Park in County Galway and found material for several small paintings, including *A lake regatta*. It is very different from the black-and-white drawing *Regatta* (fig. 126) in his book of 1912, *Life in the West of Ireland*. There the competing boats are caught in a squall of rain and the artist dwells on the panic of the young rowers, finding an element of comedy in the not too stormy conditions. This oil view, on the other hand, depicts a fair windy day, presumably on Lough Cutra near Gort, with puff-ball clouds riding in the sky, which are reflected in the deep blue and green ruffle of the lake. Three boats, one a curragh, steady themselves in the water, meeting together so that the rowers can confer before the race starts. Another boat, outlined on the water to the right, is approaching to join the conference. A man in the bow of the boat to the left wears the wide-brimmed low-crowned hat typical of Galway at the time.

Yeats's skills in composition are quietly manifest at this period. At the centre of the picture, the man with the white boater and the flag provide a counterpoint to the two men in waistcoats and shirt sleeves seated in the red boat on the left. Another figure standing in the centre of the right-hand boat acts as a similar asymmetrical foil to the end of the oar on the left, belying the apparently accidental arrangement of the figures: and these verticals act as essential pivots in an otherwise predominantly horizontal composition.

All the same, the group of men and their boats are not the main interest, as they would have been in the early Yeats. The sense of a larger world about them – of which they are a minute portion – is the magnet for the viewer: the unmeasured depth of the water on which they float, the remoteness of the green bank and the smooth-faced mountain, and the infinite space of the sky.

The picture is painted with long curving strokes of rich colour lying one beside the other, bringing up the foreground of the picture with broad touches of thick impasto. It has a fine spatial perspective; and the natural atmosphere of a typical summer day in Ireland is splendidly conveyed.

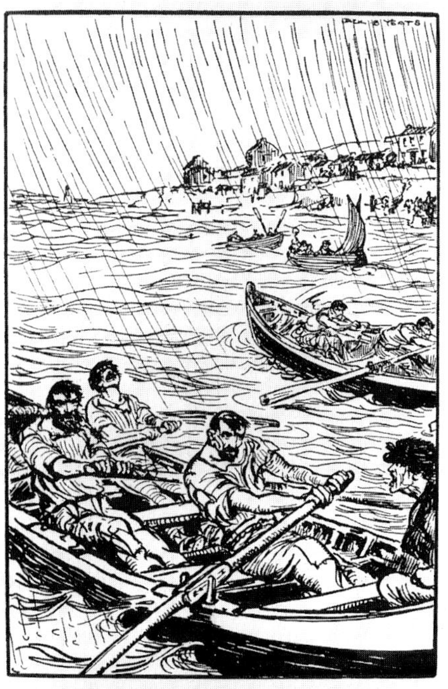

Fig. 126 Jack B. Yeats, *Regatta*, from *Life in the West of Ireland*, 1912 (Yeats Archive)

A lake regatta

1923, oil on panel, 23 × 36 cm, NGI 1406

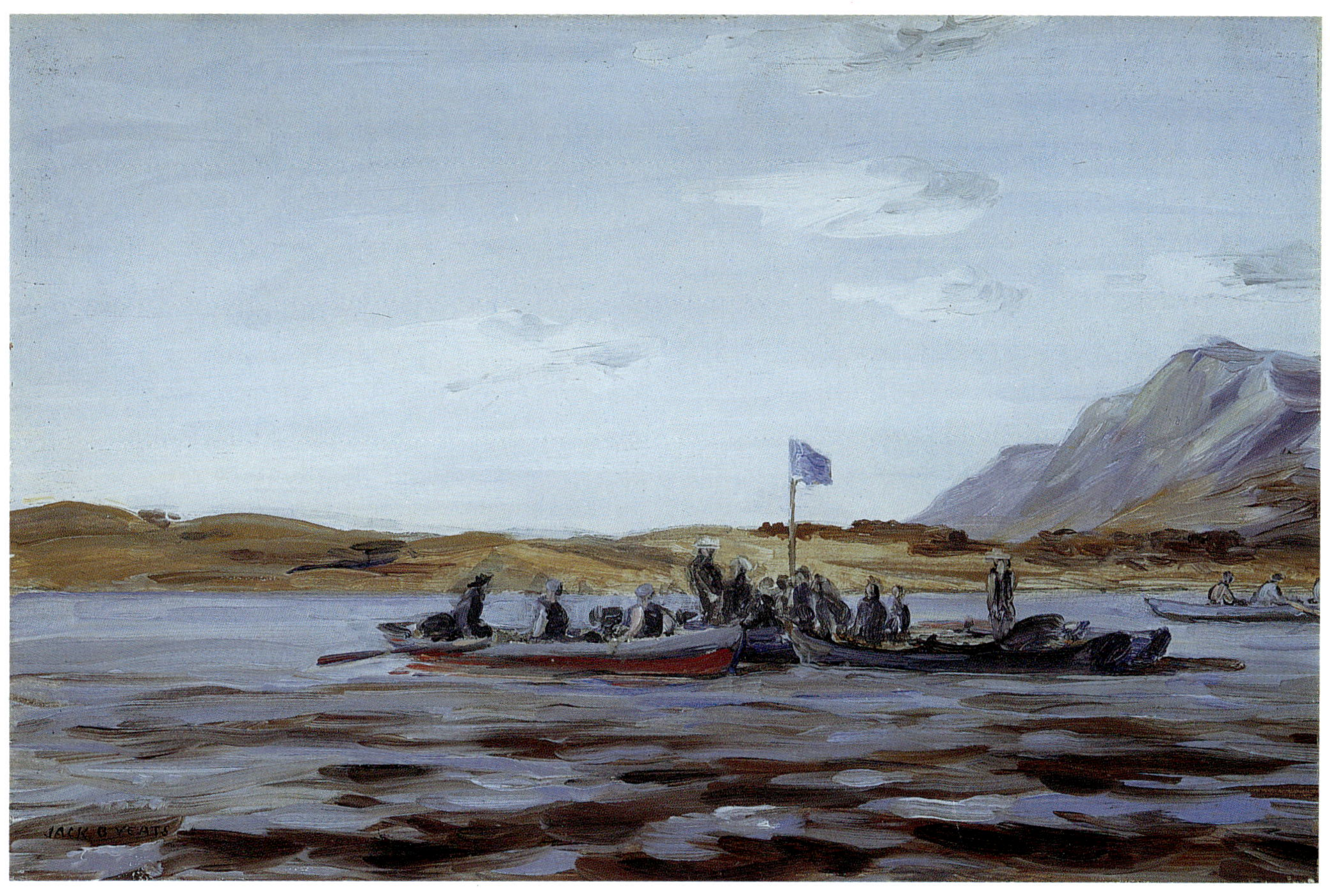

The small weir is unusual among Yeats's land-scapes of this period in that it has the appearance of being a sketch done *in situ*. The two cows on the far bank of the stream – unique in his work: a donkey was a far more likely subject for him – are caught grazing among great boulders in a lush patch, and depicted with rapid thick strokes of a brush that is extraordinarily expressive. The river water is a rich blue, with touches of brown and green, and pink wild flowers on the near bank (perhaps valerian) stand up against the light-green churning of the weir. The blue sky, with fluffy white clouds, conveys the breezy summer weather immediately.

Yeats had painted his first oil landscapes from about 1906 in the open air, and told the American collector John Quinn how he and his wife would hire a boat when they were in the west, and row out to some island, where he would paint. This unpeopled view certainly has a fresh, unplanned look, as if it were brushed on impulse during one of his rambles about Coole Park. It is even suggestive of the artist's desire to school himself to draw directly on to canvas, without preliminary formalities, a technique which was to be the essence of his late style.

Jack B. Yeats was a less frequent visitor to Coole than his brother WBY; though he owed much to Lady Gregory's energetic support when he mounted his first exhibitions in Dublin, and he paid periodic visits to her in her Galway home. It is not without significance that this vivid little sketch was in the collection of the artist Evie Hone, who also painted landscape, and who adopted a similarly free and rich-coloured manner in the painting of her stained-glass windows.

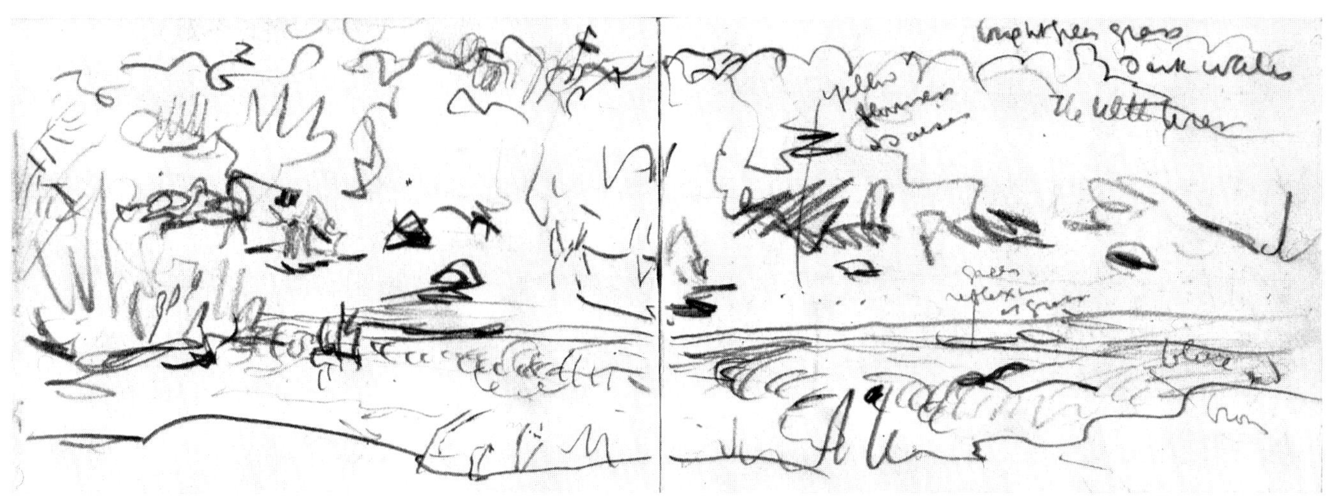

Fig. 127 Jack B. Yeats, *The little weir*, from a Coole sketchbook, 1923 (NGI Yeats Archive)

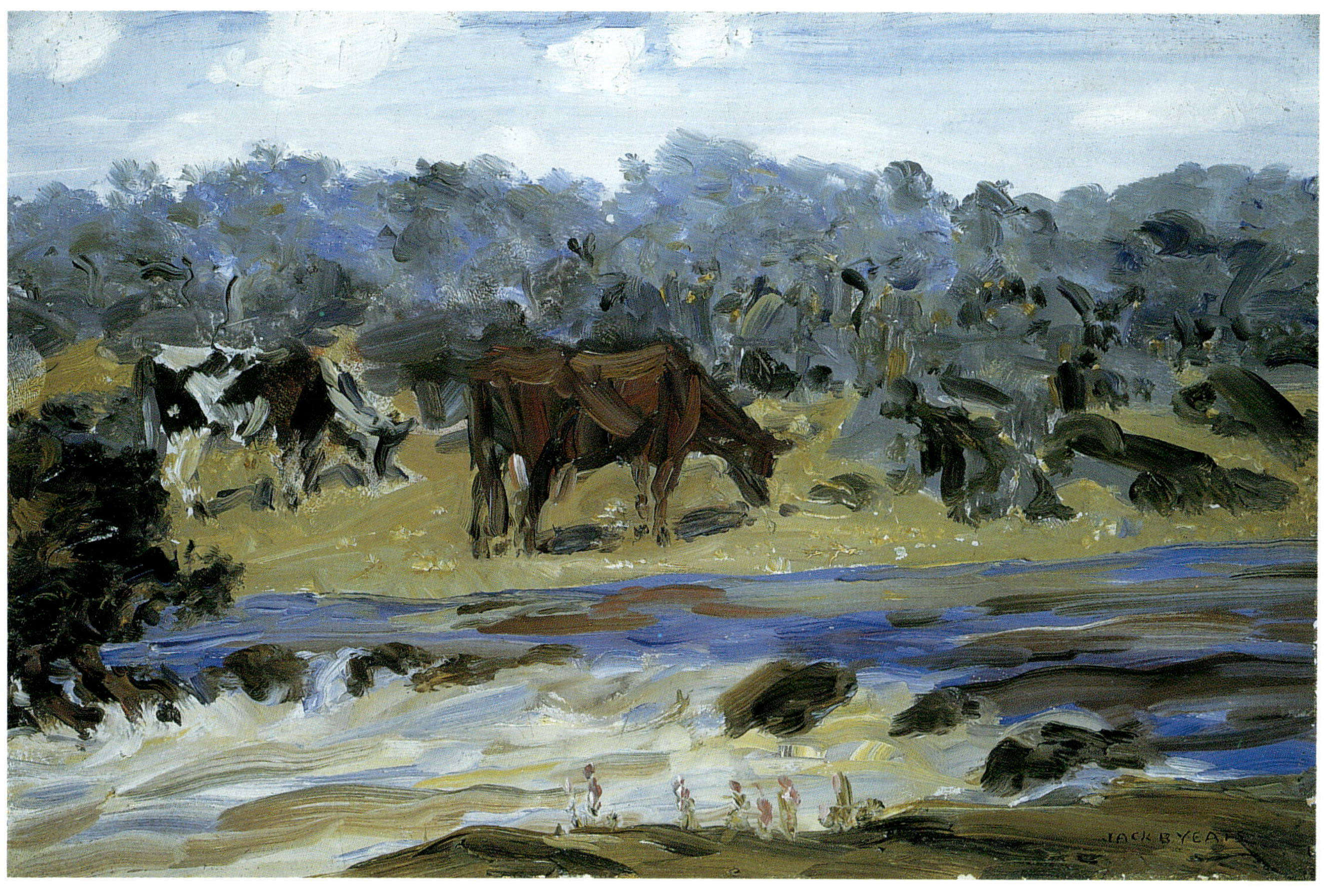

The annual regatta of Dublin University Boat Club is held on the River Liffey at Islandbridge, just beyond Kilmainham. Yeats in this painting constructs his composition in much the same way as in *The Liffey Swim* (see p. 212). It is based on a diagonal, with the heads and backs of spectators occupying the triangle created on the left, while more people watch from the far bank. There is far less definition of detail in the Islandbridge painting, however, and the excitement of the event is largely intimated through the potent colour. The expanse of water in front of the boats, too, intensifies the feeling of urgency, its emptiness demanding the straining athletes to hurry forward and fill it up.

The river is framed by rich-green banks, by darker green trees and by the multi-coloured group in the left foreground. Painted in a vivid indigo, with streaks of lighter blue and black, it shows the artist moving towards an even freer style. So does the partially described boy with yellow hair in the foreground. He draws the eye into the picture, giving the impression of being half-in, half-out, so as to persuade viewers that they too can step in and become an intimate part of the event. This anonymous image of youth was acquiring increasing importance for Yeats during the 1920s and was to appear regularly in his late work as a symbol for optimism.

Slightly smaller than *The Liffey Swim*, this painting of 1925 demonstrates the breadth of the artist's development over a matter of two years to something beyond inspired reportage, and involving a deliberately subjective viewpoint. The theme is still impersonal, being the record of a public sporting event; but the inner sensuality of landscape is now savoured by the artist, who imbues it with his own feelings of tension and excitement. The cloudy atmosphere, the lush grass, the cool liquidity of the water, are sensed rather than described, the personality of artist and viewer dominating the external image. It is a kind of Expressionism, but still deliberately rooted in recognizable experience, and distinguishable from the poetic metaphor that Yeats developed during the 1930s. The rich and confident use of paint is typical of the artist's mature middle period style, and the painting is an excellent example of his work.

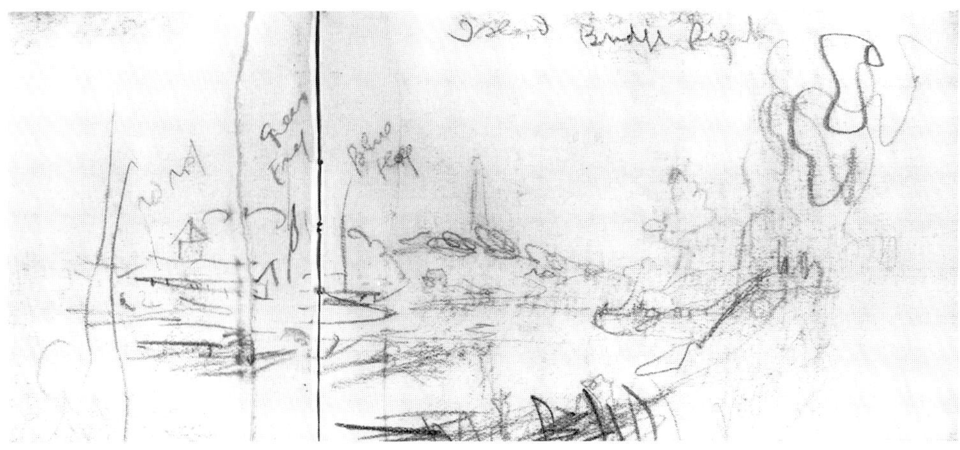

Fig. 128 Jack B. Yeats, *Islandbridge Regatta*, from a Coole sketchbook, 1925 (NGI Yeats Archive)

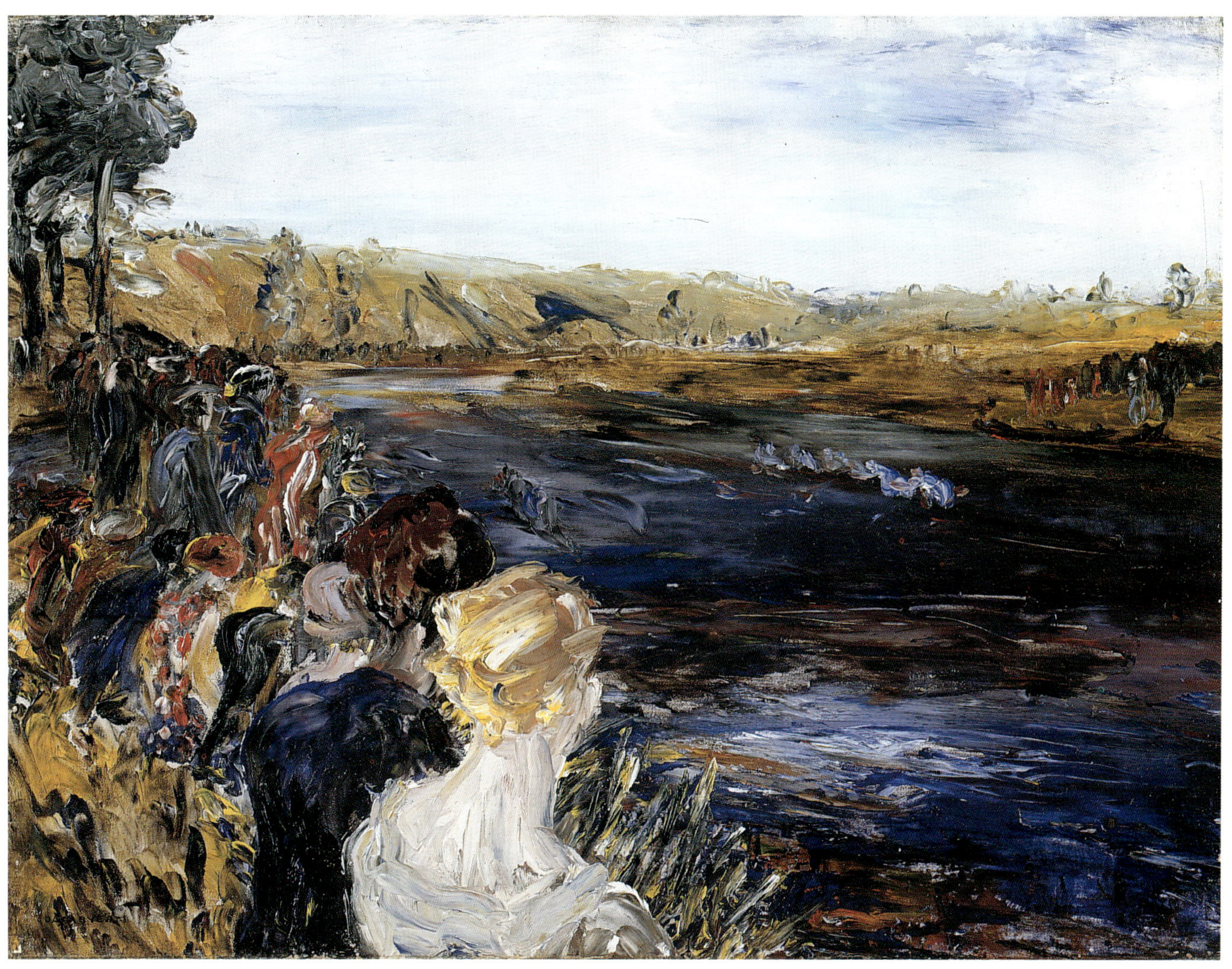

There are several paintings of flower girls by Jack B. Yeats. The most famous is *Bachelor's Walk, in memory* (fig. 129), where he commemorates a political incident in the gesture of a flower girl. She strews flowers where innocent bystanders have been shot down by the army in 1914 during disturbances at a peaceful demonstration by the Irish Volunteers. Somewhat later, *In Capel Street* (Crawford Municipal Gallery, Cork) is a simple study of a forlorn girl sitting with her baby on a doorstep. The strange juxtaposition of beautiful plants beside their squalid vendors, in the run-down Dublin of the 1920s, seems to have haunted Yeats. By contrast, *Flower girl, Dublin*, is optimistic in tone.

We see the outside of a shop in the centre of the city. The lighted interior is represented vaguely in pale green and yellow. The exterior paintwork is a deep blue; and these colours are carried on to the pavement by the figure of the man with a hat, hands in pockets, who is coming out of the shop door. A flower girl offers a tray of violets to the lady in the centre of the picture. The latter's red cloche hat and scarf pick up the colour of a red rose lying on the girl's arm. Her brief shawl, her apron and short dress, and her sickly face and bare head are compared with the elegant brown coat of the lady, whose pink complexion is well made up.

To the right are the shadowy shapes of two men, one leaning against a lamp post. These derelicts, and the flower girl, are in the dimmer half of the painting, while the red-hatted lady and the man are surrounded with colour and light. The brushwork is untidy. Paint is applied in vertical, horizontal or scribbled strokes; all adding up to a confusion and emotion about the subject. The figures though have been sketched with authority, the impasto gleaming sensually. The verticals of shop and lamp post form comprehensible intervals, which hold the characters together and create a firm structure.

Already the figures of the women have acquired a romantic quality, partly to do with their womanhood, partly to do with the flower girl's lovely, ephemeral ware. Yeats, about this time, adopted the rose as a personal symbol, fastening one to his easel while he worked.

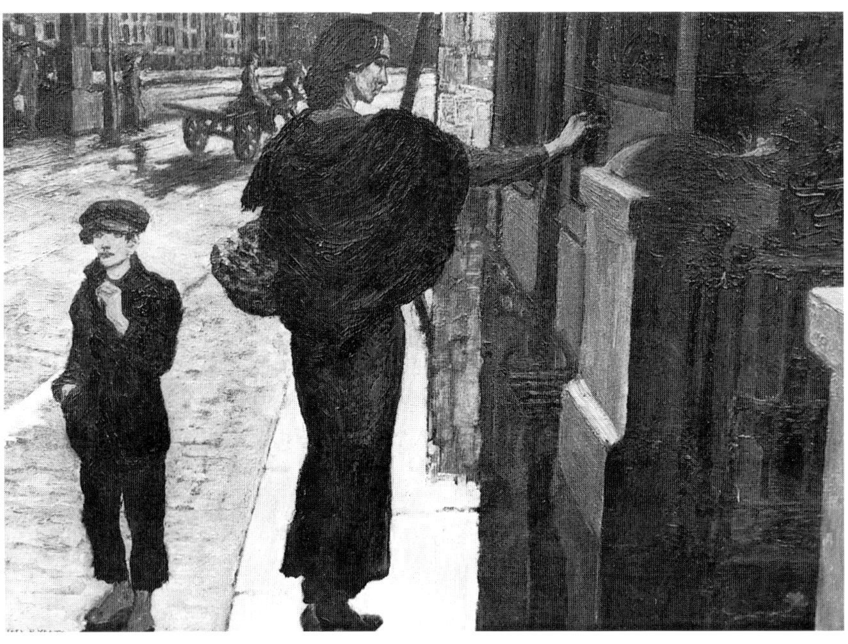

Fig. 129 Jack B. Yeats, *Bachelor's Walk, in memory*, 1915,
oil on canvas, 46 × 61 cm (Lady Dunsany Collection)

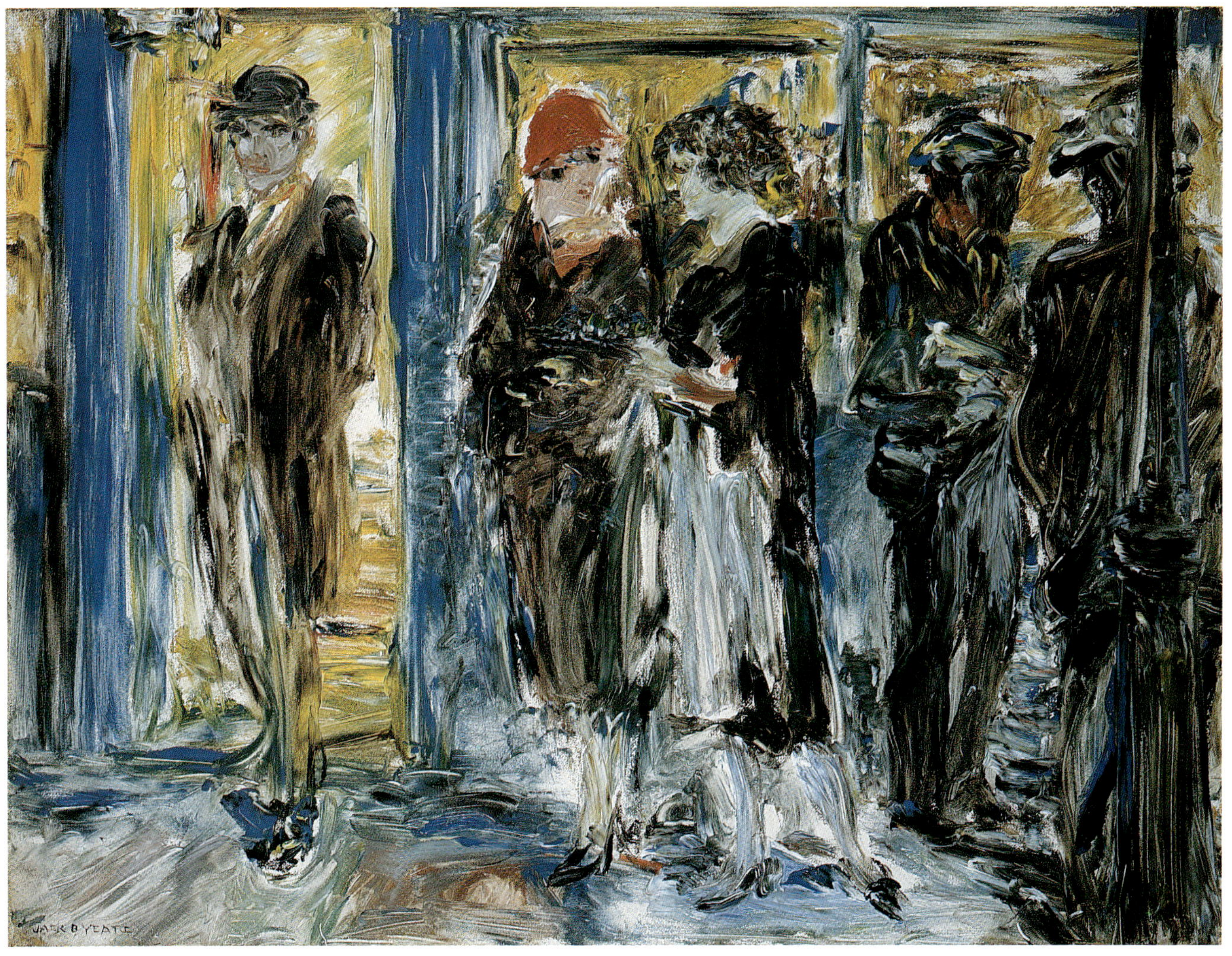

Yeats painted three pictures of Dublin workmen in 1928 – *Quaysiders*, *The readers* (showing a jarvey leaning over the shoulder of a flower girl who is reading a book) and *Dinner hour at the docks*, all simple studies of the non-events that are the nub of everyday living. In each, the compassion of the artist for ordinary people is evident, expressing itself in the simply sketched freedom of the paint, which flows as freely as the emotion he feels towards his subject. "The Beautiful is the Affection that one person or thing feels for another person or thing, either in life, or in the expression of the arts," he told Thomas MacGreevy, a former Director of the National Gallery of Ireland; and, in a speech to the Irish Race Congress in Paris in 1922, he said, "The roots of True Art are in the affections, no true artist stands aloof".

During the 1920s Yeats had been finding himself drawn more and more into his subjects, so that, even though this portrayal of a man taking his sandwiches in a shelter during a break of work is simply descriptive, the presence of the artist can be sensed. The man is undersized, not attractive despite his ample moustache. He seems pinched into his occupation, sitting beneath an oversized hat, and he eats in silence, in unappealing surroundings.

The swanlike curve of his wife, turning towards him, creates a gesture of release and beauty in the centre of the painting, her tall supple form, backed by the strong vertical of the shelter's opening, suggesting a movement of protection and love towards this shrimp of society, cramped by what it has denied him. The complementary green behind his figure adds a tenderness to the scene.

Through a door to the left is a glimpse of one of the trucks stationed beside the docked ship, whose loading and unloading provides the man's unremarkable and exigent pattern of life. The colours echo the sombre theme.

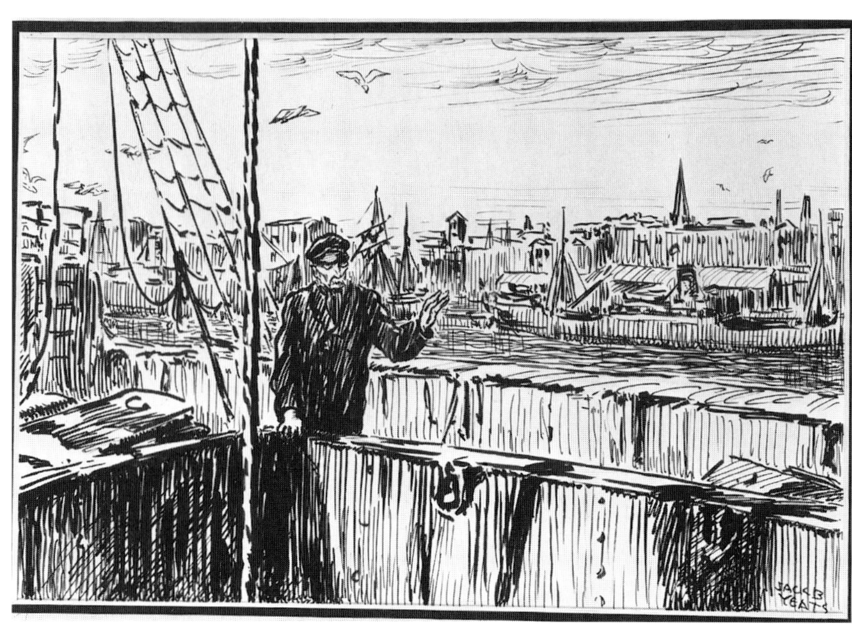

Fig. 130 Jack B. Yeats, *Liffeyside, ca.* 1920, ink, 20 × 30 cm (private collection)

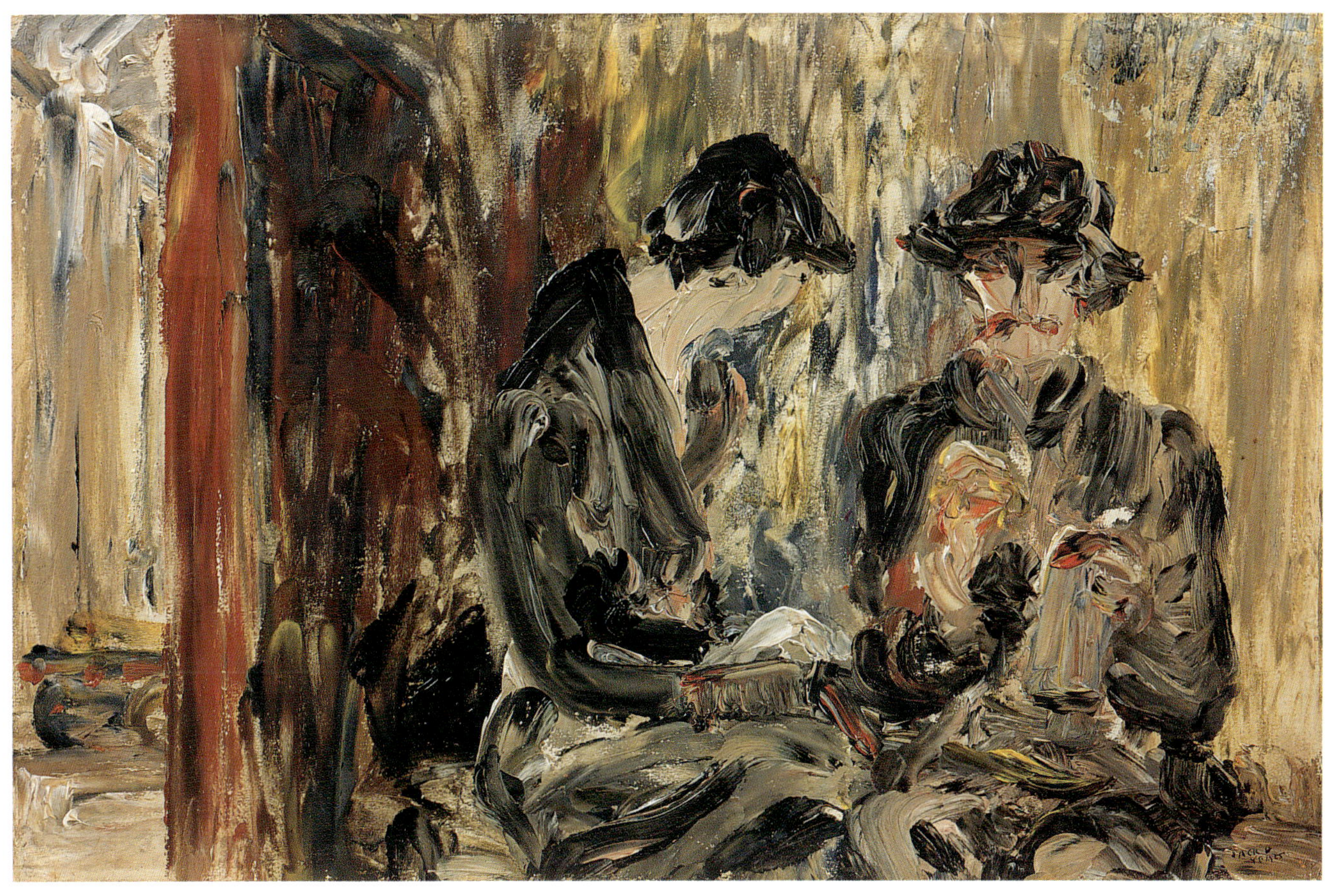

J ack Yeats painted many dark pictures in 1929, the year he moved to live in Fitzwilliam Square in the centre of Dublin. It was a time when he was trying his hand at writing again, but in a more serious and reflective way. James Joyce, who bought two of his Liffey paintings that year, said that he and Yeats had "the same method". The artist's first full-length book, *Sligo*, loaded with reminiscence which is released in an enigmatic verbal stream, was published in 1930.

Yeats was now attaching more significance to time and its passing, in the form of farewells or nostalgic looks at a past which, whether experienced or not, forms part of the consciousness of everyone. *June night*, however, is astonishingly free from any sort of sentiment. It is a straight study of a night in June, viewed through a paned window which frames the sky. The casing is rimmed with the glow of the setting sun. The sky is calm and pale, with tops of green trees visible below the window.

Inside the room, the shapes of furniture have been reduced to dark abstractions as the eye of the painter is concentrated on the dying light outside. Only a mirror to the right captures a faint reflection of the blue sky and the fading yellow gleams. There are touches of colour through the predominantly brown tones which liven the gloom. There is a sense of a presence in the room, even of movement, but no one is definitely described.

During the 1930s, Yeats painted various interiors (see fig. 131), modern and historical, usually with some human life. This small painting is a study in light at a particular time of day, in a particular place, and so it captures its unique moment. Nature and man are here set side by side in the complete vision of things.

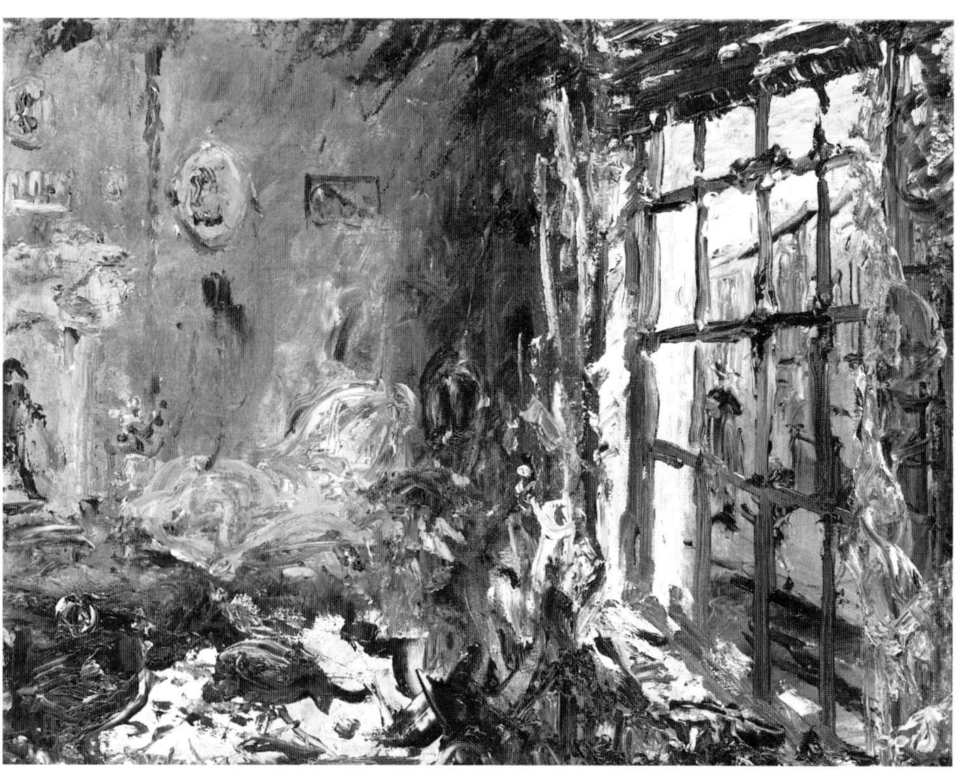

Fig. 131 Jack B. Yeats, *A room in Sligo*, 1935,
oil on canvas, 46 × 61 cm (Theo Waddington, London)

1929, oil on panel, 23 × 35 cm, NGI 4595

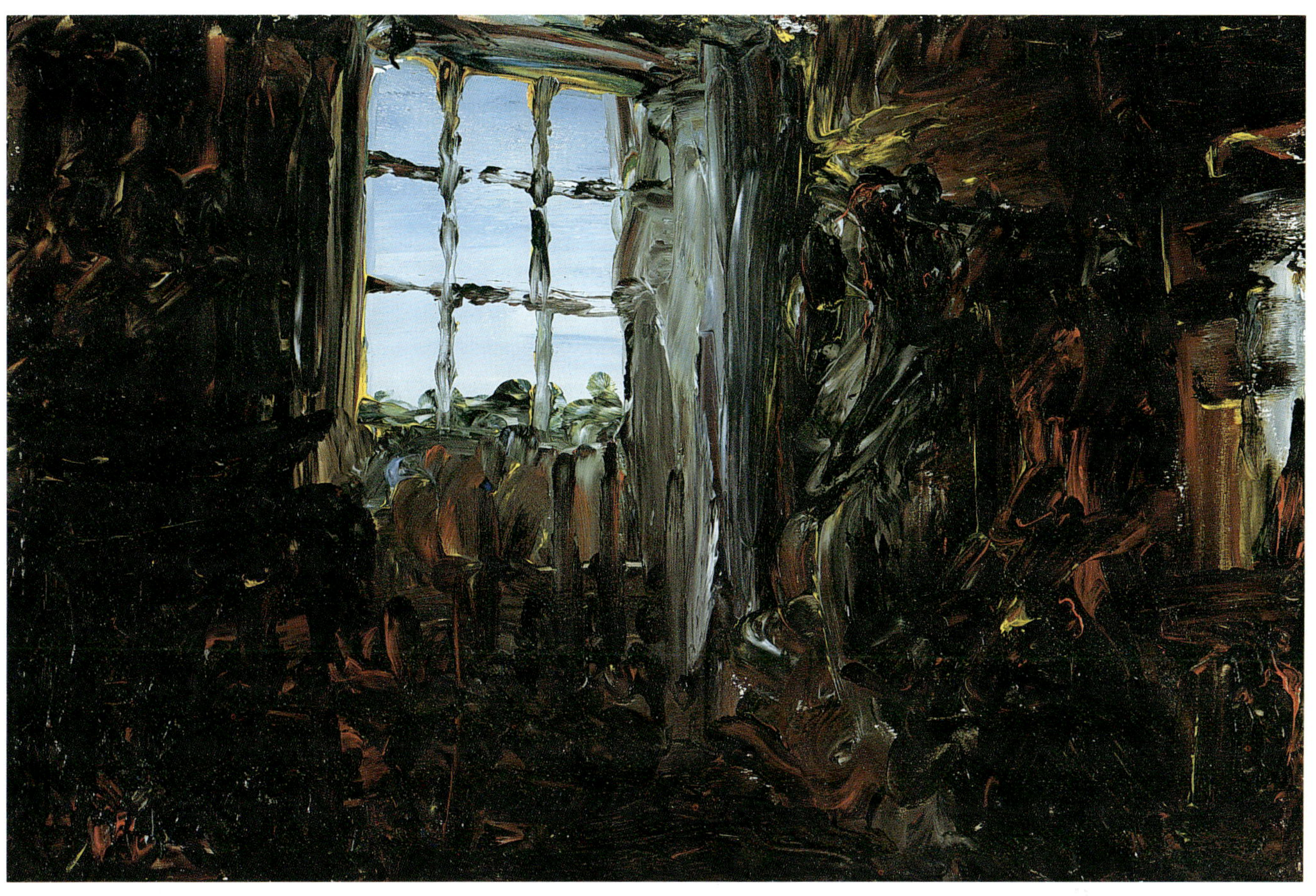

This is a view of the Pigeon House Power Station from the North Bull Island in Dublin Bay. While Paul Henry was encouraging painters to study the mysterious beauties of the west, Yeats was not the only Irish artist of his time to attempt less picturesque aspects of his country's landscape. Estella Solomons painted the power station (fig. 132) with similar Impressionism, looking in a more south-westerly direction; and George Atkinson did a series of etchings of the hydro-electric construction on the River Shannon (fig. 133) as it was being built between 1925 and 1929.

The Electricity Supply Board's power station occupied the Pigeon House Fort on the eighteenth-century South Wall of the port of Dublin for many years, until it was replaced by the present construction with its two spectacular chimneys. The Pigeon House Fort – so called after an innkeeper named Pigeon who provided accommodation and refreshment for packet-boat passengers – was built on the site of the inn in 1748 and altered at various times. Its distinctive outline was a feature of Dublin Bay. The Poolbeg lighthouse at the other end of the wall provided the only variation in an otherwise flat maritime view. The lighthouse in Sligo Bay was drawn and painted many times by Yeats, but here he concentrates on the murky shape of the Pigeon House Power Station in an industrialized seascape, with the contrast of the distant hills beyond. The carmine chimney, with its banner of indigo smoke, stands out, stark and raw, against the tossed blue and white sky. To the left is the soft undulation of the Sugar Loaf Mountain. In the foreground lies the flat grass and sand of the Bull Wall Island, built up by the tides over the years, and now a bird sanctuary; and beyond it the strip of sea bounding the South Wall.

Yeats's style of 1930 is thoroughly painterly. The dry pigment is tossed lightly on to a barely treated board. Thick impasto, swept across this initial ground with a palette knife, creates a third dimension through the sheer vivacity of the paint. Textural detail, to supply natural movement in a figureless landscape and a feeling of the air, has been rendered by scoring the paint with the point of the brush handle or the knife in places. It is a loose, vibrant style, which became typical of the artist's small non-metaphorical landscapes over the decade that followed.

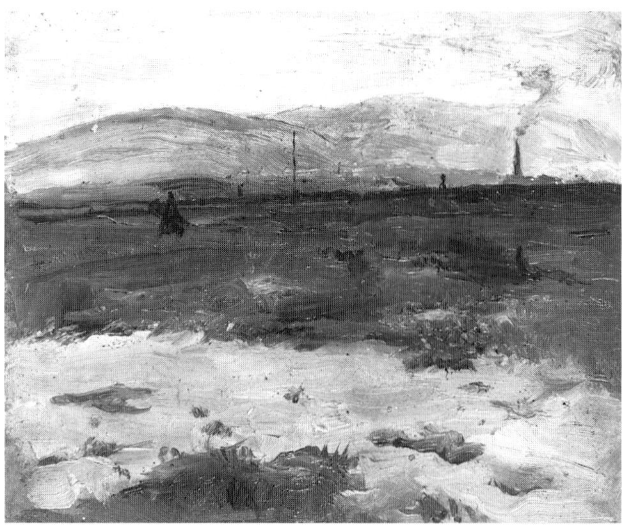

Fig. 132 Estella Solomons, *View from the Bull*, 1920–25, oil on board, 14 × 18 cm (private collection)

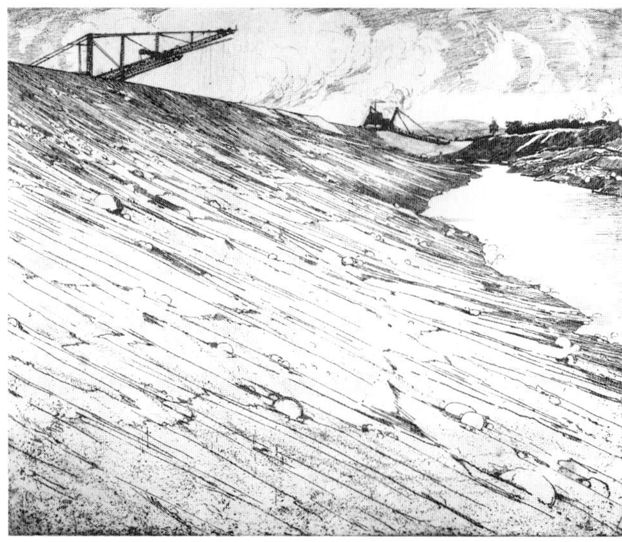

Fig. 133 George Atkinson, *Shannon, Scheme no. 1. Keeper Mountain* (Crawford Art Gallery, Cork)

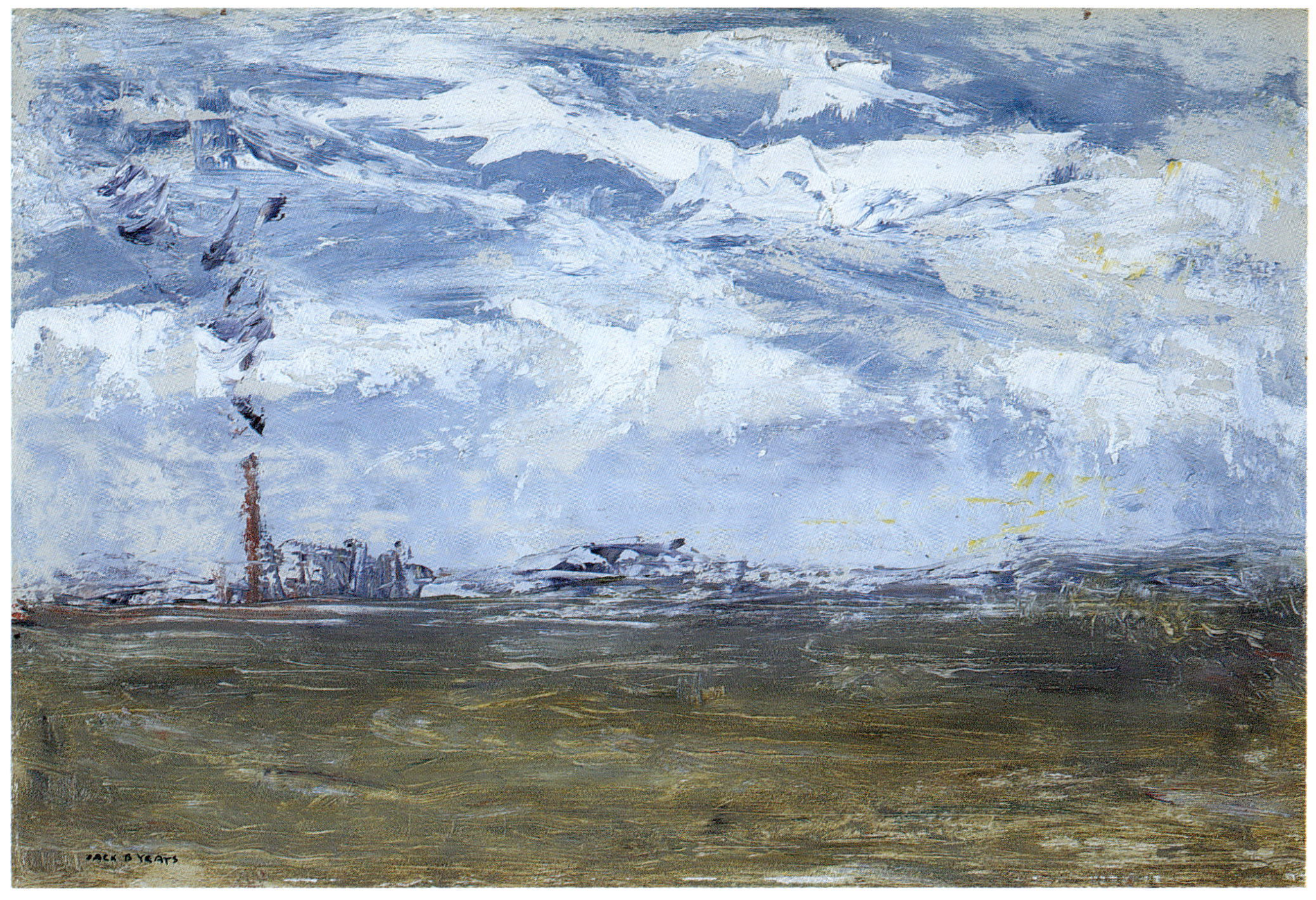

Jack B. Yeats painted comparatively little during
the 1930s, as compared with the 1940s, his most
productive phase, because he was then writing seriously. He published *Sligo* in 1930 and *Sailing, Sailing
Swiftly* in 1933, besides other works which have led to
his being evaluated on a level with Samuel Beckett,
with whom he had contact about this time.

His literary mood turned his mind to literary interests of the past. The subject of *About to write a letter*
(1935) has been drawn from *The Fancy*, a small book
which John Masefield and Yeats edited and illustrated
together in 1906. A collection of poems originally published in 1820 under the pseudonym Peter Corcoran,
The Fancy may have appealed to Yeats because Corcoran's parents were alleged to have been Irish, from Carlow. The poet Corcoran was training to be a lawyer, but
had been drawn to the cult of 'The Fancy', fraternizing
with dissolute young men whose lives centred around
pugilism and companion cruel sports. Corcoran was
genuinely interested in boxing as a skill, but he tried
to extricate himself from his foolish addiction when he
met the sister of a friend and fell in love. Instead of
sport, she now become the subject of his poetry.

She was away on a visit when he found himself again
attracted to sparring and the attendant indulgences of
drink and betting. During an exchange of letters, it

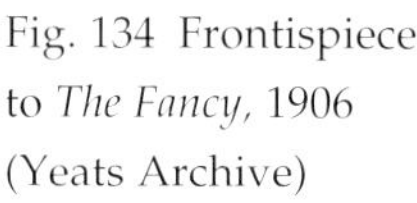
Fig. 134 Frontispiece
to *The Fancy*, 1906
(Yeats Archive)

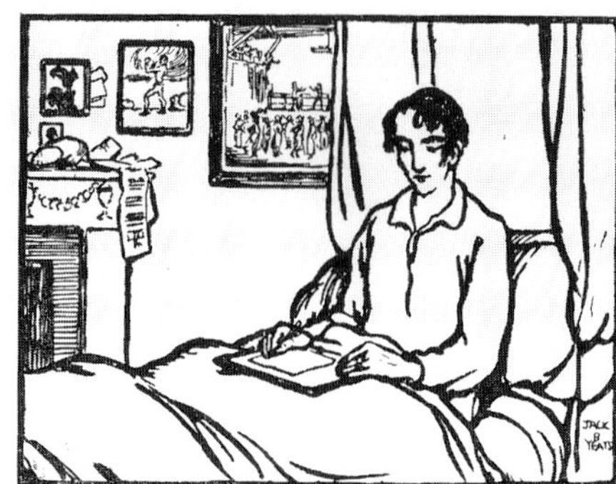

became clear that his fiancée had no sympathy for him,
despite his declared love for her. A coolness arose.
When Corcoran went into a decline, she refused to be
present at his bedside, and he died.

Yeats managed to identify the real author of *The
Fancy* as John Hamilton Reynolds, a close friend of

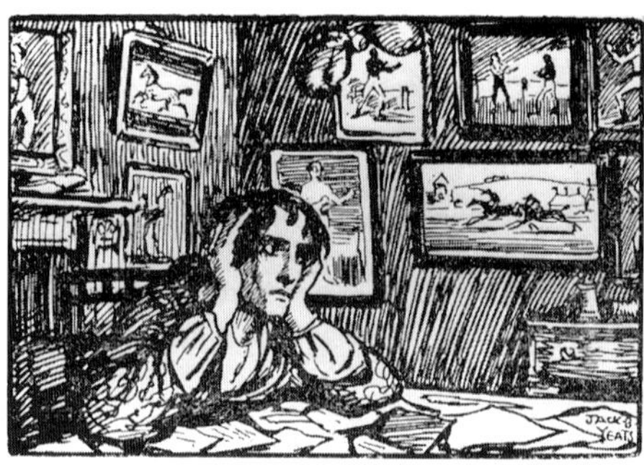
Fig. 135 Illustration to *Stanzas* in *The Fancy*,
1906 (Yeats Archive)

Keats. The poems were Reynolds's farewell to the wild
days of his own youth. Keats was in Rome, fatally ill.
Their circle was breaking up. He himself had started
work in a lawyer's office and would soon marry.

Yeats, in this painting, thirty years after he and Masefield had republished Reynolds's book, shows a young
man looking exceedingly pallid, hovering in front of a
table on which writing materials are placed. His
appearance is similar to that of the dying poet, drawn
by Yeats in his illustrations for the frontispiece (fig. 134)
and for *Stanzas* (fig. 135) in *The Fancy*. What is most
remarkable about the picture is the richness of the
colour: the scarlet of the table cover, flecked with shadows from the flickering lamp; the deadly white of the
man's face, the dense black of his coat and the ruby rust
of his hair; the wall behind, shaded with the green of
memory, and melancholy blue, highlighted with
moments of yellow.

The only immediately recognizable images in the
picture frames are the large silhouette of a lady, which
seems to bend towards him; and some dim outlines of
horses at rest, or racing. The picture centres on the inviting table with waiting pen and paper, on the man
imprisoned in his tragic thoughts, and the romantic
womanly image isolated in her frame, linking them
together in an inverted triangle in the middle of the
painting.

The Vermeer-like theme arouses questions, partially
posed in the title, which viewers must answer in their
own way.

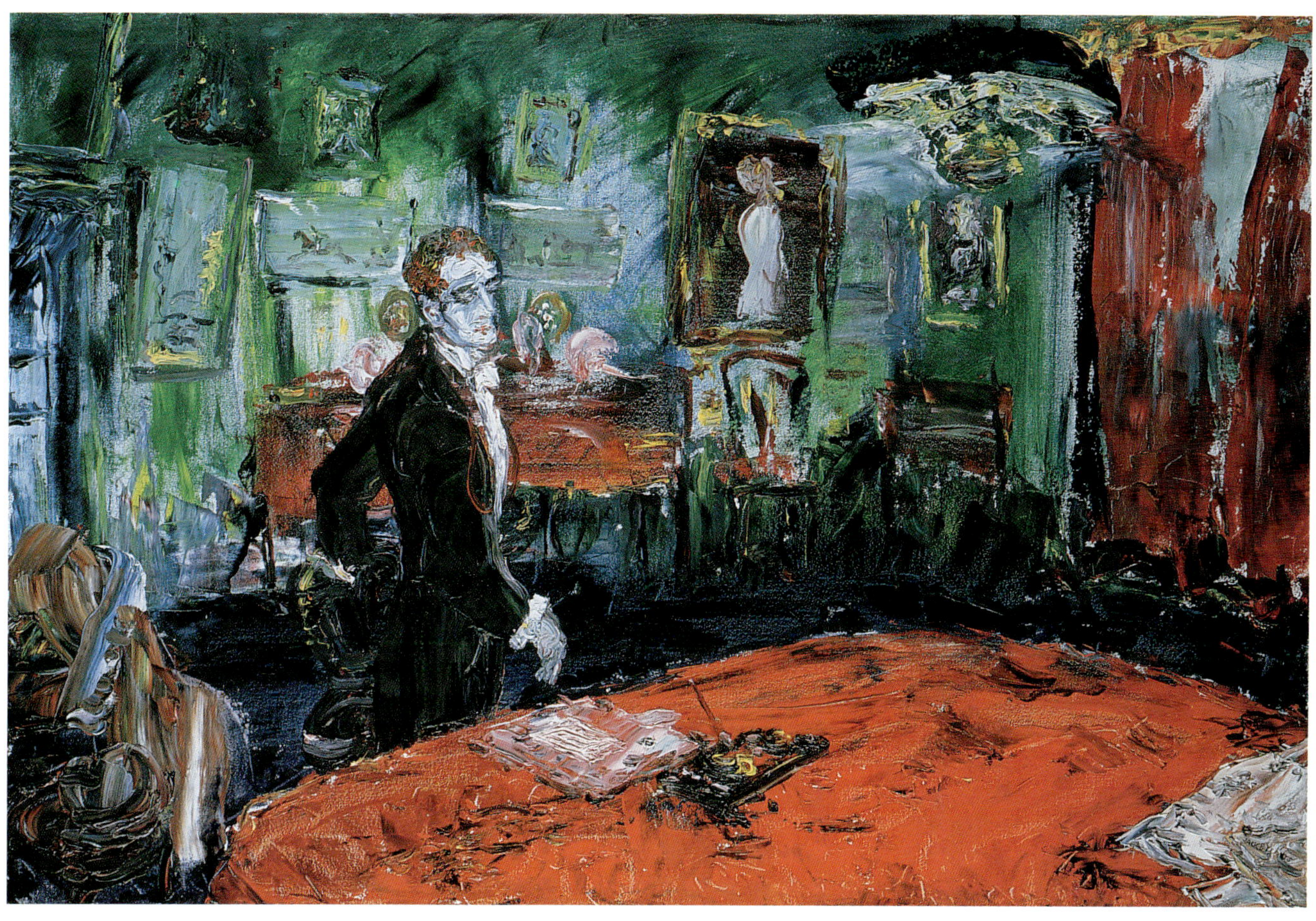

About to write a letter

1935, oil on canvas, 91 × 61 cm, NGI 1766

Jack B. Yeats and Samuel Beckett first met early in 1931, when, with an introduction from Tom Mac-Greevy, Beckett visited the artist in his studio. The young writer was immediately impressed, as much by Yeats's self-reliance in his work and his determination to remain independent, as by the individual canvases which became a constant visual stimulus to him. He later compared Yeats's work with that of T.S. Eliot when identifying 'the new' in the contemporary arts as a breakdown or lack of interaction between subject and object. "The artist who is aware of this may state the space that intervenes between him and the world of objects; he may state it as no-man's land, Hellespont or vacuum, according as he happens to be feeling resentful, nostalgic or merely depressed. A picture by Mr. Jack Yeats, Mr. Eliot's 'Waste Land', are notable statements of this kind."

When Beckett was in Dublin, the two men walked occasionally together around Yeats's usual haunts, or drove out to Lucan to walk, often wordless in each other's company. At Yeats's 'At Homes' and at his exhibitions Beckett had the opportunity of seeing the artist's latest work and he made notes on it.

In 1936 he wrote ecstatically to MacGreevy, "The new stuff, some of it, is superb. One small picture especially, *Morning*, almost a skyscape, wide street leading into Sligo looking west as usual, with boy on a horse, 30 pounds. If I had ten I would beard him with an easy payments proposition. But I have not …. Do you think he would be amenable to instalments [?] It's a long time since I saw a picture I wanted so much" (29 January 1936; TCD MS 10402).

The painting was shown in London in the spring of 1936, after which Beckett arranged to buy it directly from the artist in his studio, borrowing £10 to pay the first instalment, and paying off the rest gradually, each payment being recorded meticulously by the artist in his book.

Compared with other more fanciful pictures of the 1930s, *A morning* is a simple scene. A youth with a pack on his back, and mounted on a chestnut horse, pauses in a wide market street lined with cottages to look westward in farewell to where he has come from. He is one of Yeats's travellers, who turn up in every guise in his paintings and prose, here on an untold mission on a day of strong wind, though the gleam of light in the pale sky and the lifting clouds suggest that the omens are good.

Within the unity of the scene, a fragile moment on a peripheral corner of the spinning earth, the freshness of air, the light and dark of the shadows and the solidity of horse and rider are very real. Yeats has room for a humorous note, horse and cat communicating tentatively while the man is carried away in private thoughts. The economy of the image, worked from the thinnest of brushwork to a lush, rapidly applied impasto – all in pearly tones that are shot with vibrant colour – appealed to Beckett who had said to Yeats the year before, "This inhuman landscape evokes – provokes – the inhuman in oneself". He described it to MacGreevy as "always morning, and a setting out without the coming home". Beckett's cousin Morris Sinclair felt that the painting represented "the going forth … a reserve of strength" (Lois Overbeck, Martha Fehsenfeld to the author, 1 December 1991).

A morning

1935–36, oil on panel, 23 × 36 cm, NGI 4628

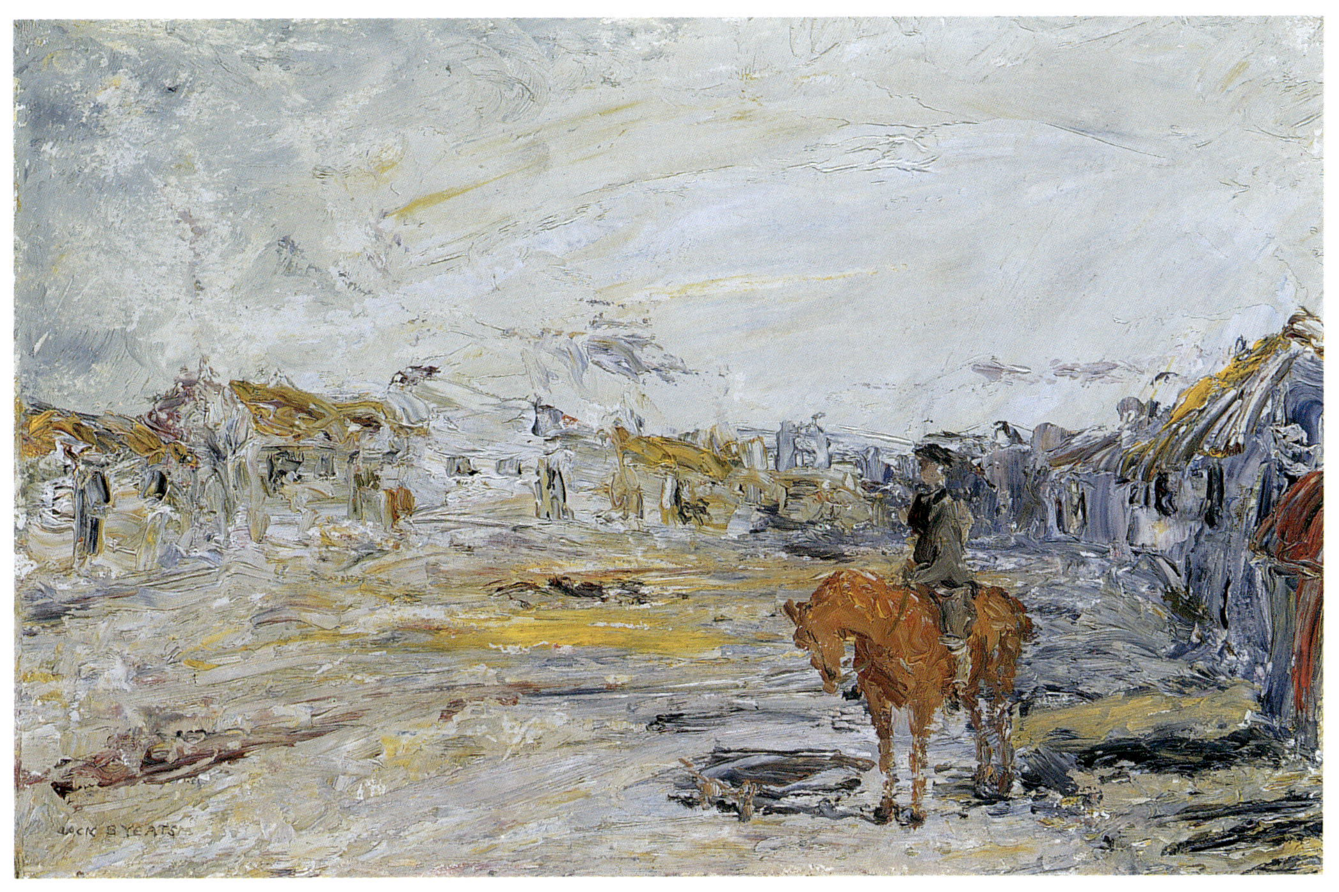

After spending his first Dublin years in Donnybrook, Yeats moved to Fitzwilliam Square in the centre of Georgian Dublin, on the edge of Fitzwilliam Place, a wide handsome street with a direct view of the Dublin mountains. His city subjects now assumed a romantic mood, especially in the last years of the 1930s, and reminiscence became an important element of his compositions. In 1936, he painted *Donnelly's Hollow* (fig. 136), a landscape of the curragh with its monument to the celebrated boxer, Dan Donnelly, showing himself in wide-brimmed hat and coat, an isolated figure in the centre of the picture going with others to view the site of the famous encounter between the Irish pugilist and the English champion Cooper.

Likewise, *A morning in a city* of the following year shows him strolling in a place of past and present memories. The two rows of Georgian houses, which line the street in which he walks, glow a dull red in the early morning light, and the warm colour of the brickwork stains the light and mood of the city – a phenomenon that has largely become a forgotten beauty since the extensive demolition of such terraces in more recent years.

Dim figures hurry or walk collectedly through the streets: an efficient girl going towards the office, a man bent over his barrow, the postman with his sack, a business man rather leisured; and, beyond him, a newspaper boy, who was a favourite subject with Yeats – a twentieth-century Hermes. A figure emerges from a lighted doorway in the house to the left. All are ghosts, along with the barely indicated dog; all are part of the continual fluctuation of life under the yellow and white pale sky, which is infinitely distant, but visible above the roofs, with pink fingers of light breaking through to the blue of daytime.

The artist is part of this busy procession of the various professions, some lowly and others more fortunate; but he is separate also. He contemplates the dim mass all around him, and soaks in the scene from a cocoon of loneliness, wandering in isolation against the indigo shadow of the old houses beyond and the green of the trees in the square. In some paintings, his mode of reminiscence was more personal, and idiosyncratic in its references, but here his mood is Wordsworthian, quickened to the spirit of the city itself and of the people who inhabit it. He is endorsing his identification with city life and, at the same time, making his artistic detachment plain.

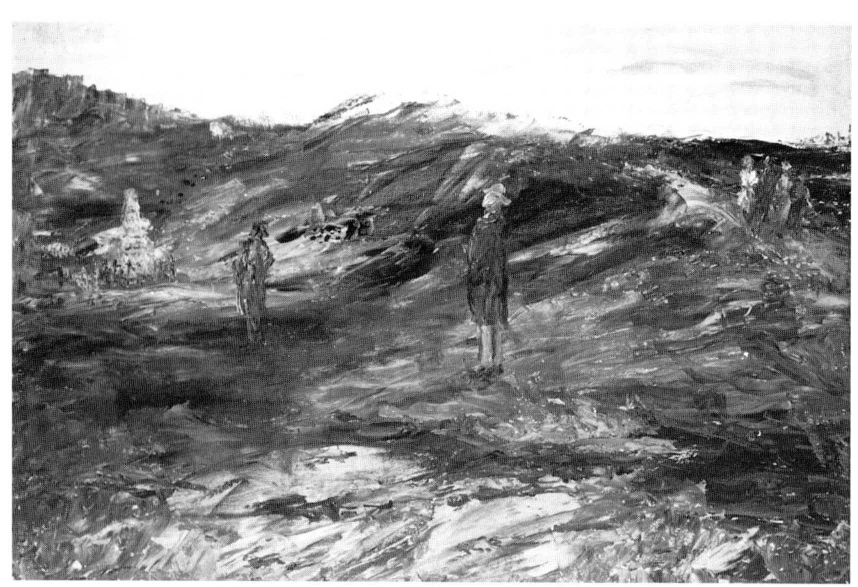

Fig. 136 Jack B. Yeats, *Donnelly's Hollow*, 1936,
oil on canvas, 61 × 91.5 cm (private collection)

A morning in a city

1937, oil on canvas, 61 × 91 cm, NGI 1050

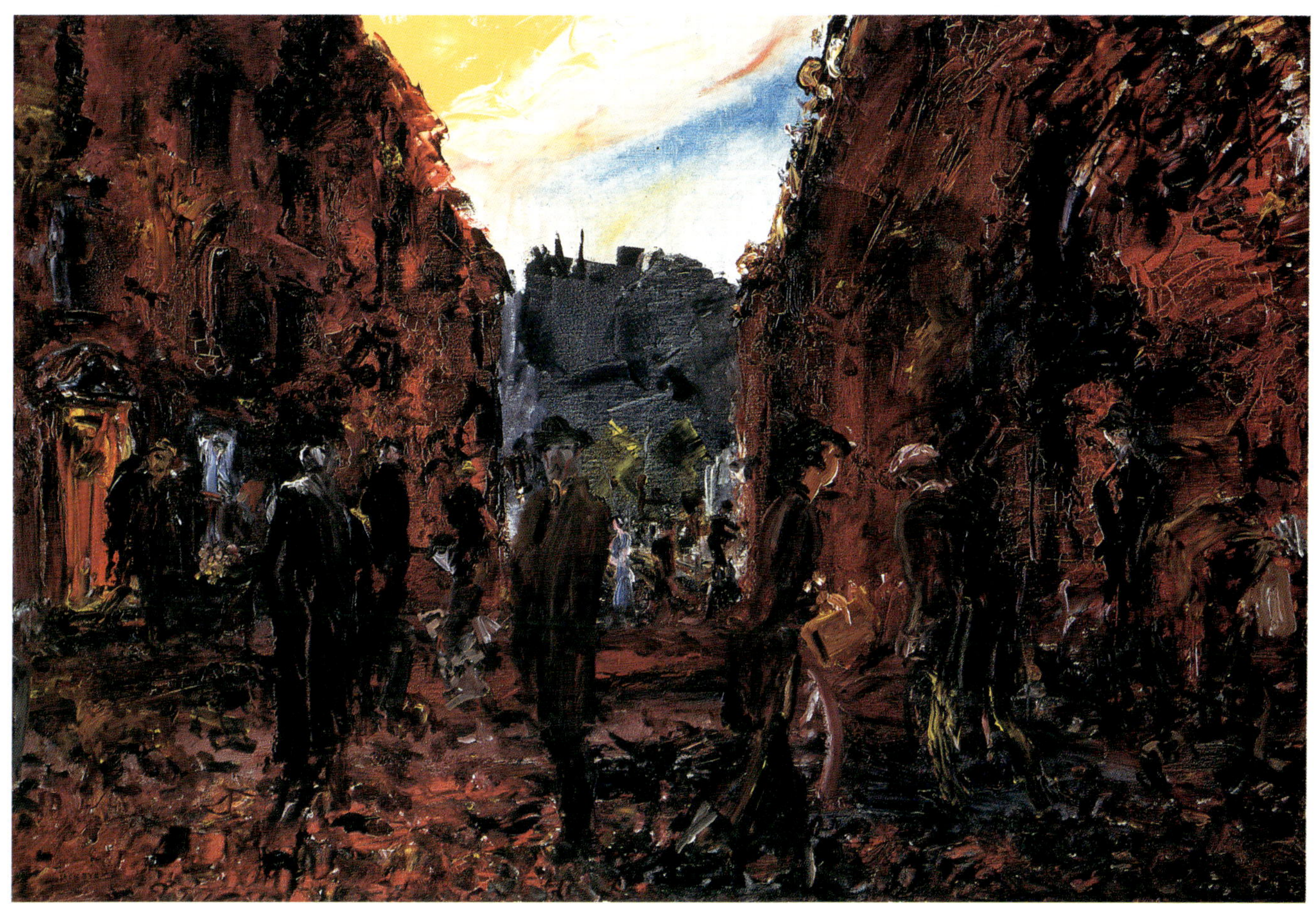

Yeats "grows Watteauer and Watteauer", Samuel Beckett observed to Thomas MacGreevy in 1938. Something of Watteau's seemingly inconsequential fantasies in the realms of Cythera, which Yeats echoed in *A race in Hy Brazil* (fig. 137), may be seen in this picture. A group of actors in full theatrical costume alight from the long car in which they are travelling and play out their rôles in the shallow waters below Glencar Waterfall, in County Sligo. Yet, for Yeats as for Watteau, the mythical event was far from inconsequential. He was summing up his debt to two nineteenth-century entrepreneurs who had been the source of imaginative delight for him during his youth and early manhood, and whose memory he would carry with him through life.

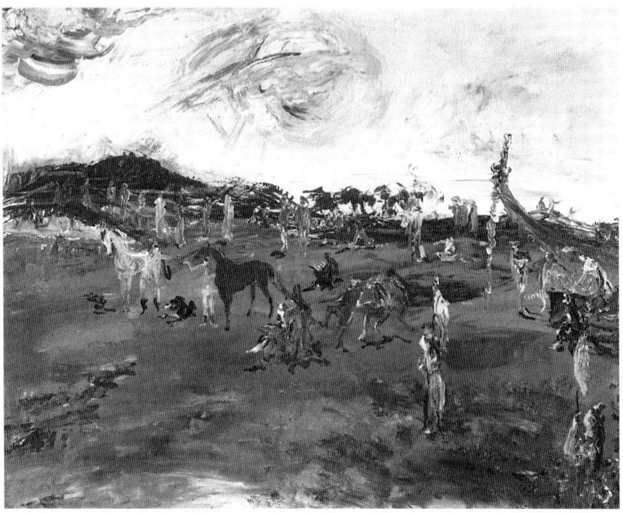

Fig. 137 Jack B. Yeats, *A race in Hy Brazil*, 1937, oil on canvas, 71 × 91.5 cm (Allied Irish Banks Collection)

The long car, or Bianconi car as it was often called, was a large version of the Irish side-car and, during the nineteenth century, a common and dependable form of travel in the western midlands. It could hold twenty passengers and was drawn by four, or sometimes three, horses. The latter 'triangle' of horses was known as 'the unicorn', and is depicted here by Yeats in front of the Bianconi car which is seen in part.

Charles Bianconi was a native of Tregolo near Milan, who came to Ireland in 1802 to travel with another Italian selling prints and statuettes. When he set up business on his own, he realised the need for some form of public transport apart from the mail coach and, in 1815, started a one-horse stage car, travelling between Clonmel and Cahir. His business spread all over the south and west of Ireland, and into part of the north; after the establishment of the railway he ran cars to the railway termini.

Dion Boucicault, who changed his name from the Dublin Huguenot form of Boursiquot, went to London to act when he was seventeen, and quickly made his name as a virtuoso. He soon founded his own company, which produced his numerous melodramas. His three Irish plays are still popular today: *The Colleen Bawn* (1860), *Arrah na Pogue* (1864) and *The Shaughraun* (1874), which is set during the Fenian rising of 1866. Boucicault's melodramas would have been the first plays Yeats saw, performed by travelling actors, who no doubt arrived in Sligo on a Bianconi car.

At least two of the characters in the painting are identifiable: Clare Ffolliott, in a dark-green riding dress, holding a black Spanish hat, with feathers and a gold loop, standing beside the 'unicorn' of horses; and Conn the Shaughraun in hunting coat and a shabby black velvet hunting cap. Other recognizable characters from *The Shaughraun* are Captain Molineaux, Robert Ffolliott (the hero declaiming), and the priest Father Dolan. The young man in green, with exquisitely drawn buckle shoes, is Myles-na-Coppaleen; and the hunchback halfway up the waterfall is Danny Mann – both of them from *The Colleen Bawn*. The warm, sometimes subterfuge, colours and the active brushwork suggest the sharpness and confusion of memory, memory that has been embellished. The figures sparkle with the light of Glencar Falls, so that the actors' action – in their enthusiasm almost bathing themselves in the stream – accords with metaphysical ideas about the sanctity of water in Yeats's late books. The hillside itself admits unexpected light through a gap, at the top of the picture. Plants, roughly indicated, bend towards the fall, which glows with pink – the warmth of memory – as it flows down to the shallow stream below.

In memory of Boucicault and Bianconi

1937, oil on canvas, 61 × 92 cm, NGI 4206

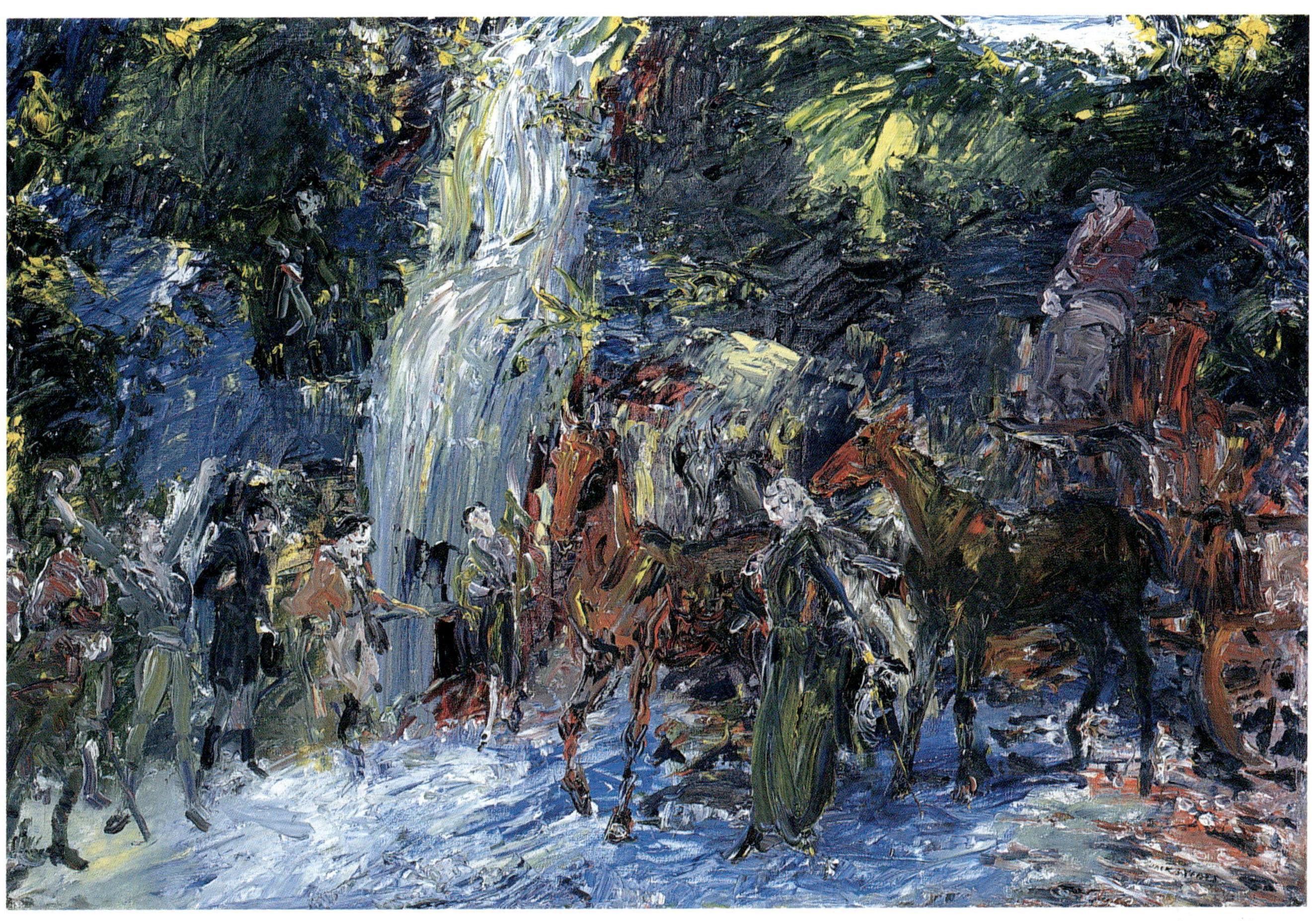

*F*our scenes in search of characters are four stage sets without figures, painted by Yeats in 1942 and first exhibited at the theatrical exhibition in the Contemporary Picture Galleries in Dublin in November of that year. They may have been painted especially for the exhibition. Originally framed separately (as they are now), they were framed together by Yeats for a time to prevent them being separated. The echo in the title of Pirandello's *Sei personaggi in cerca d'autore* (*Six characters in search of an author*), 1921, not only indicates Yeats's fascination for modern drama, but is a reminder of his personal association with the Theatre of the Absurd.

Yeats had always enjoyed theatre, and particularly the melodrama of the early years of this century, which he imitated in his plays for miniature stage such as *James Flaunty, or the Terror of the Western Seas* (1901) (fig. 116, p. 196) and *The Treasure of the Garden* (1902) (fig. 138). During the 1930s he returned to playwriting. *Harlequin's Positions* was produced at the Abbey Theatre in 1939, *La La Noo* in 1942 and *In Sand* in 1949. In them he knit his enjoyment of popular drama with a deeper, more contemporary approach, influenced by cinema, which also had its effect on his paintings of this period.

This set of pictures *cum* stage sets was made at the time when he was endeavouring to interest producers in his dramatic work. In all his plays he provided detailed descriptions of the sets and precise instructions for the positioning of the characters. The action seemed to unfold visually in his mind as quickly as the dialogue poured out; but the visual element of the drama was very often complicated when it came to stage production. He admitted to Ria Mooney in 1949 when offer-

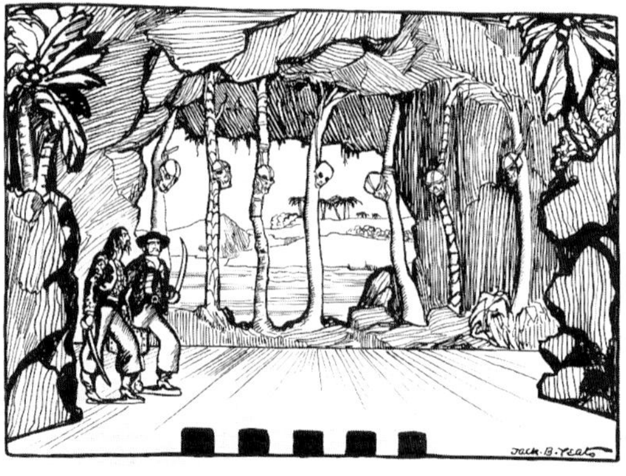

Fig. 139 Jack B. Yeats, *The Scourge of the Gulph*, Scene III (NGI Yeats Archive)

ing her plays, "All have elaborate scenery and mechanical devices, which would be expensive, and which, when I wrote these plays, I thought important. Now I know, with the fine players and producers available, they are mostly fussy and of no importance."

In their simplicity, *Four scenes in search of characters* look back to his first – juvenile – dramas, composed for the village children at Strete while he lived in Devon, and afterwards published by Elkin Mathews, London. These small plays had sets 'in search of characters', who would be created in his own and the childrens' imaginations. Following the tradition of Victorian pioneers of miniature theatre, he drew backcloth scenes against which his cut-out figures gesticulated in frozen attitudes, while he recited and roared, and added excitement with smoke and bells and startling illumination.

Scene I of the *Four scenes in search of characters*, set in Naples, recalls the adventures in foreign parts of his early heroes, though none of his miniature dramas was set in Italy. Vesuvius in the background is pouring flames straight up into the dark-blue sky. In the foreground is a terrace looking on to the sea. The buildings to each side have coloured awnings and inviting entrances, and the scattered chairs, the grotto-like arch and the opening in the balustrade where there must be a path up from the sea are ready for action. The choppy sea and the volcanic mountain are the only signs of life so far. "Now Character," Yeats is saying, "make your entrance."

Fig. 138
Jack B. Yeats,
*The Treasure of the
Garden,* Scene II (NGI
Yeats Archive)

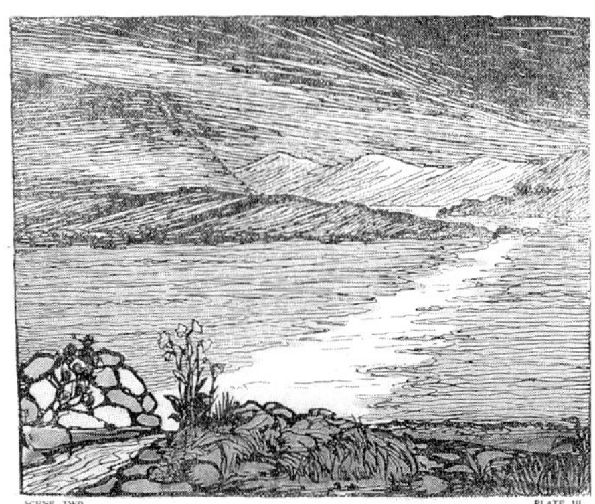

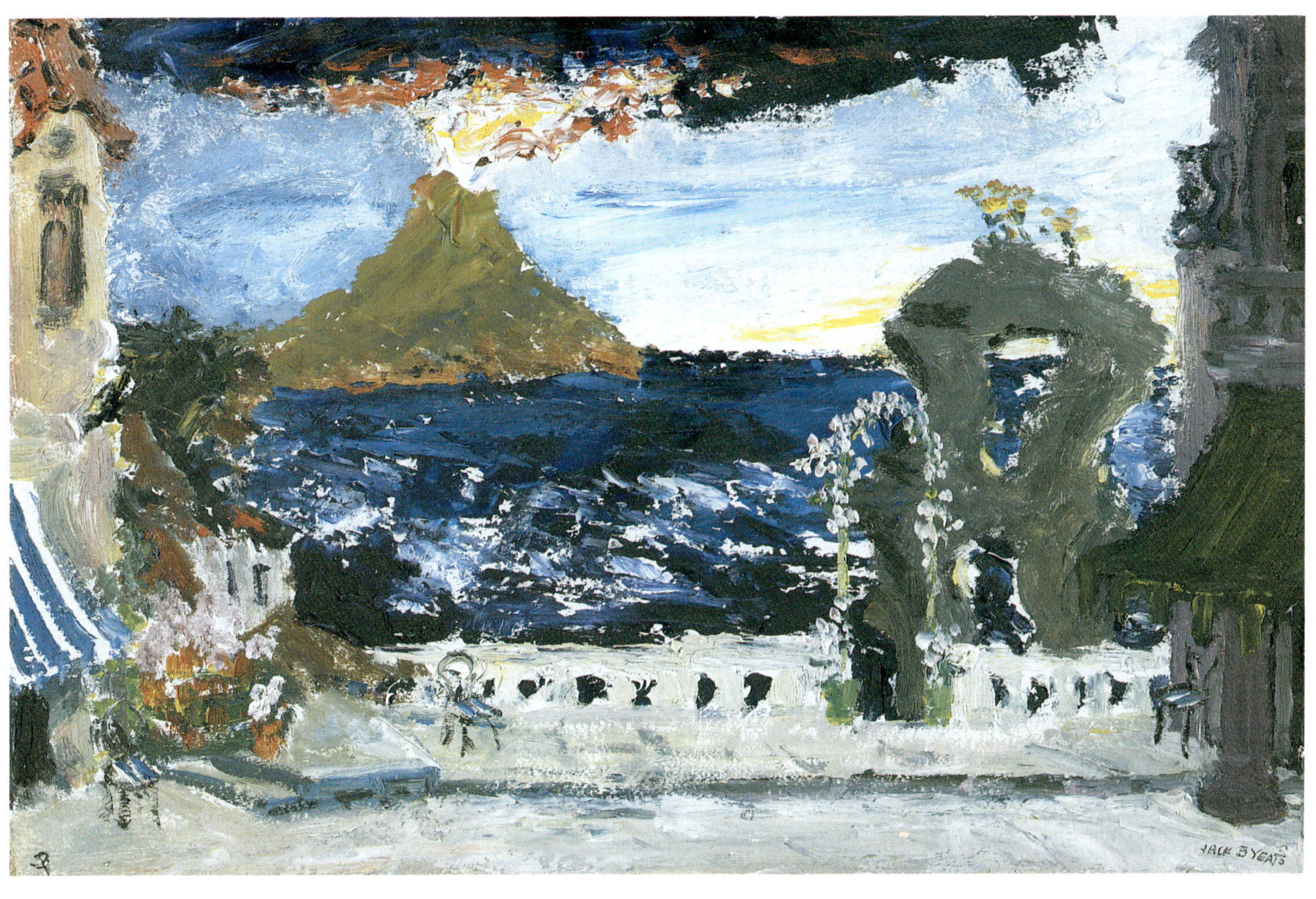

OVERLEAF

Detail of *Beginning with Naples*, Scene I

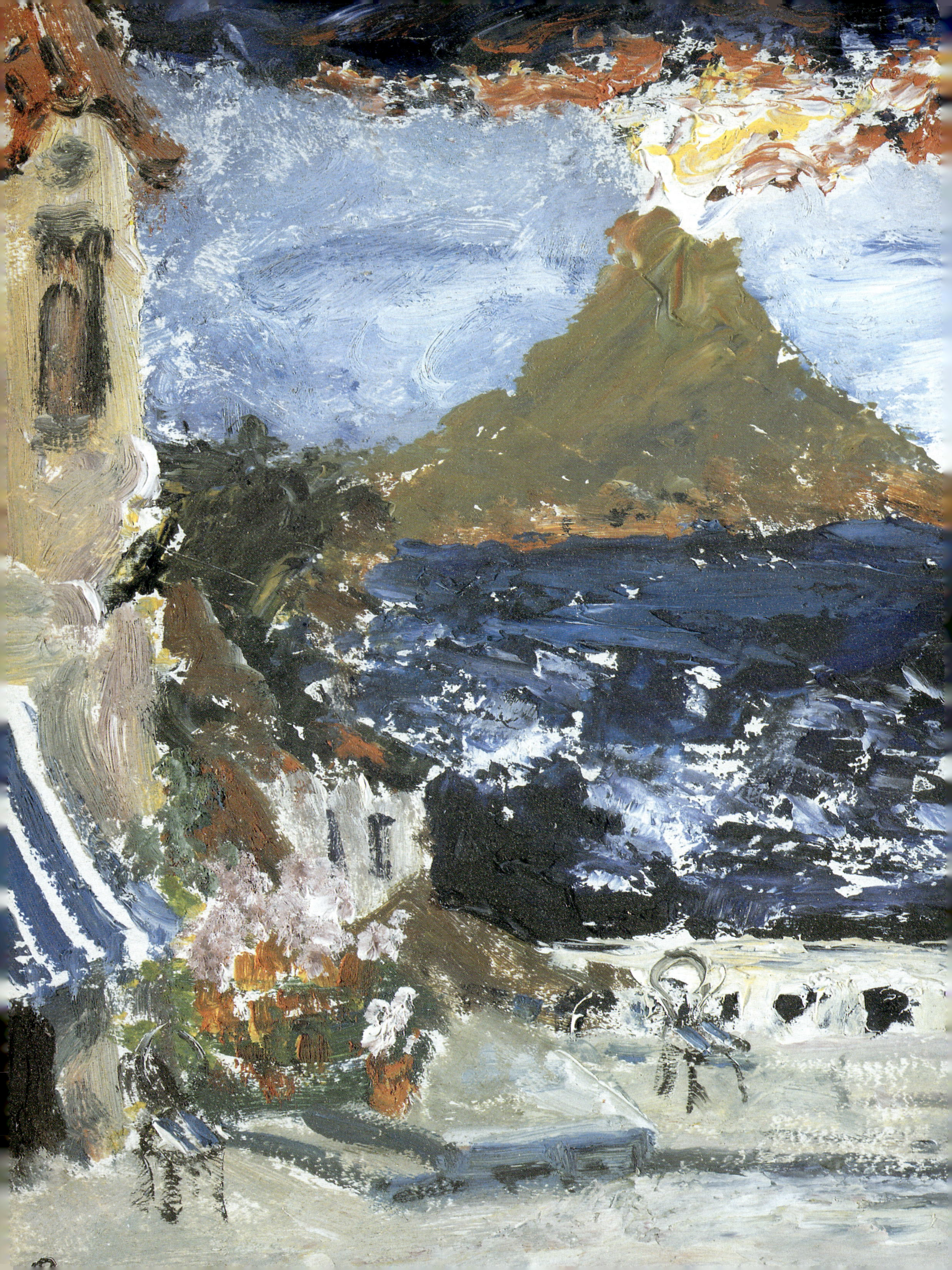

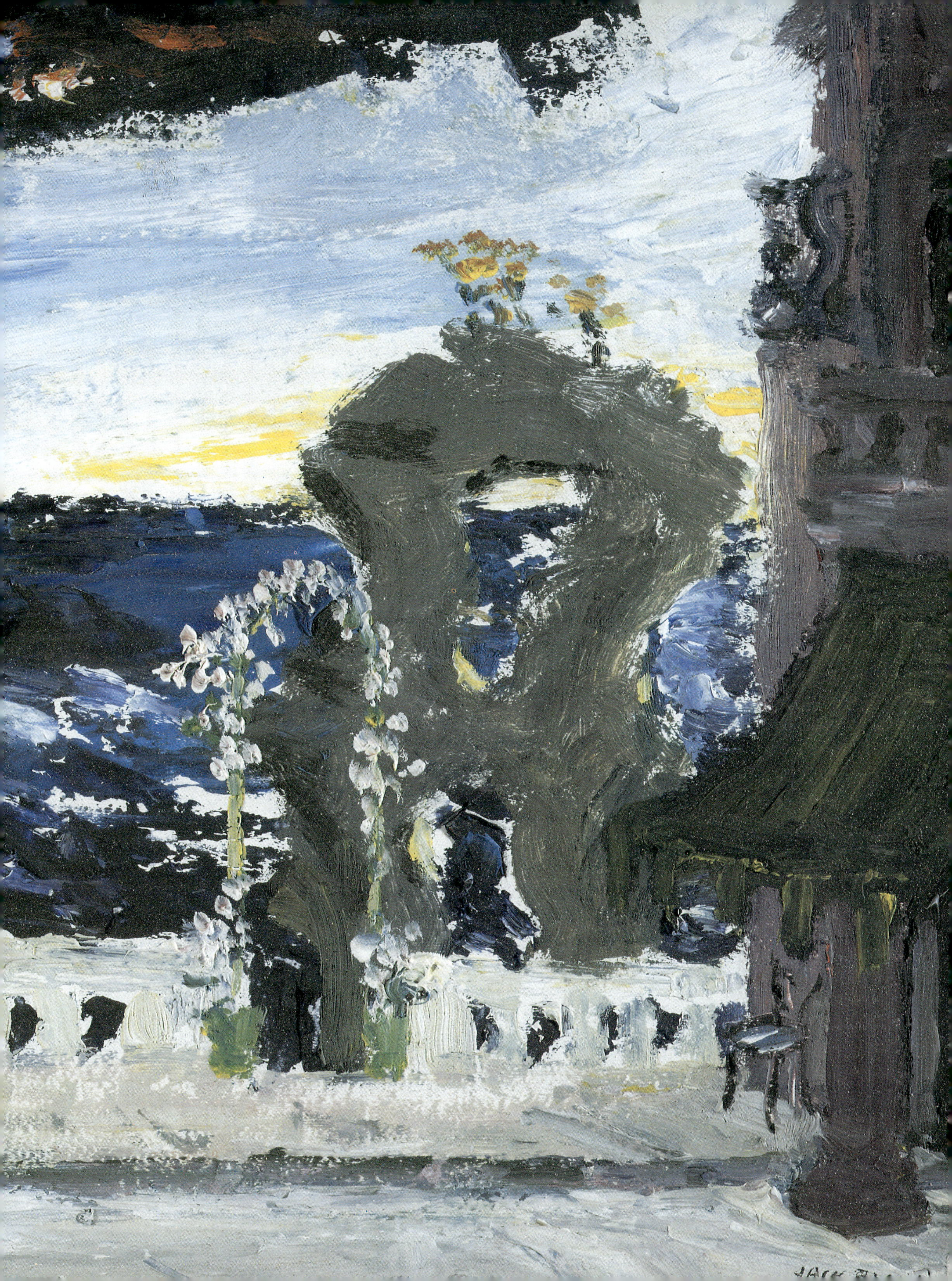

Three of the four stage scenes (see previous and following pages) relate to Yeats's paintings of the 1930s,
when he was interested in interiors, and particularly in
the gracious interiors of the eighteenth and early nineteenth centuries (he himself lived in Fitzwilliam
Square, in Dublin, where some of the choicest houses
of that period are to be found). This second scene is
such an interior. We look at the wall of a drawing room,
with wide sash windows through which low fields and
a blowy pale sky may be seen. The room is carpeted in
green, with blue walls and some ancestral portraits on
the walls. Chairs are placed in anticipation as in Scene I,
and to the right is an open door, with a white mat in
front of it.

An air of morning freshness permeates the room.
One is aware now that these scenes are as much about
time as about event. The cold Naples terrace (Scene I)
was lit with a streak of dawn yellow in the sky, and here
the day has moved on some hours. Between them, the
four scenes describe a sequence of the day's progression.

All four scenes are painted with a light sketchy
touch, so that the walls are made to appear obviously
artificial, as on a stage, the cardboard structure mask-
ing the real world outside.

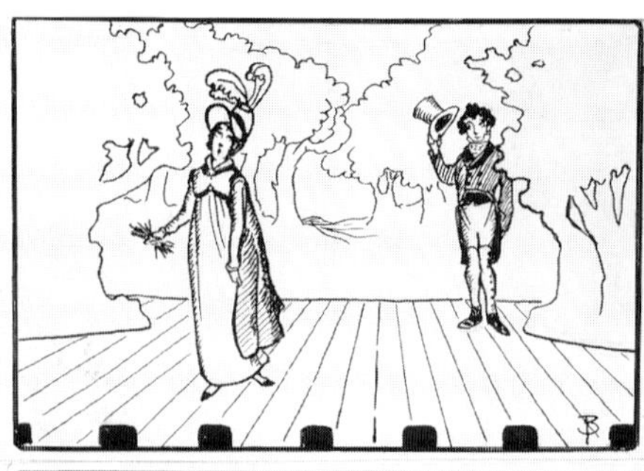

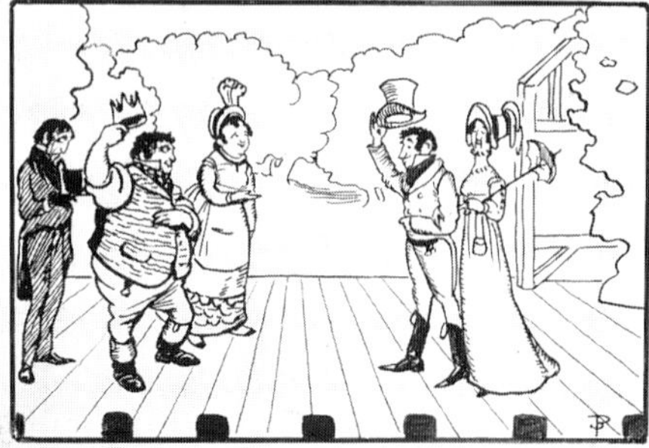

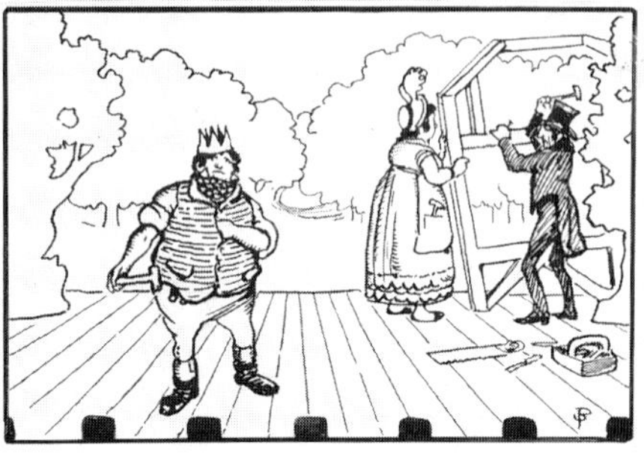

Fig. 140 Jack B. Yeats, Illustrations to *King
Tims the First*, Scenes I and II, in *The Fancy*,
1906 (NGI Yeats Archive)

1942, oil on panel, 23 × 35.5 cm, NGI 4582

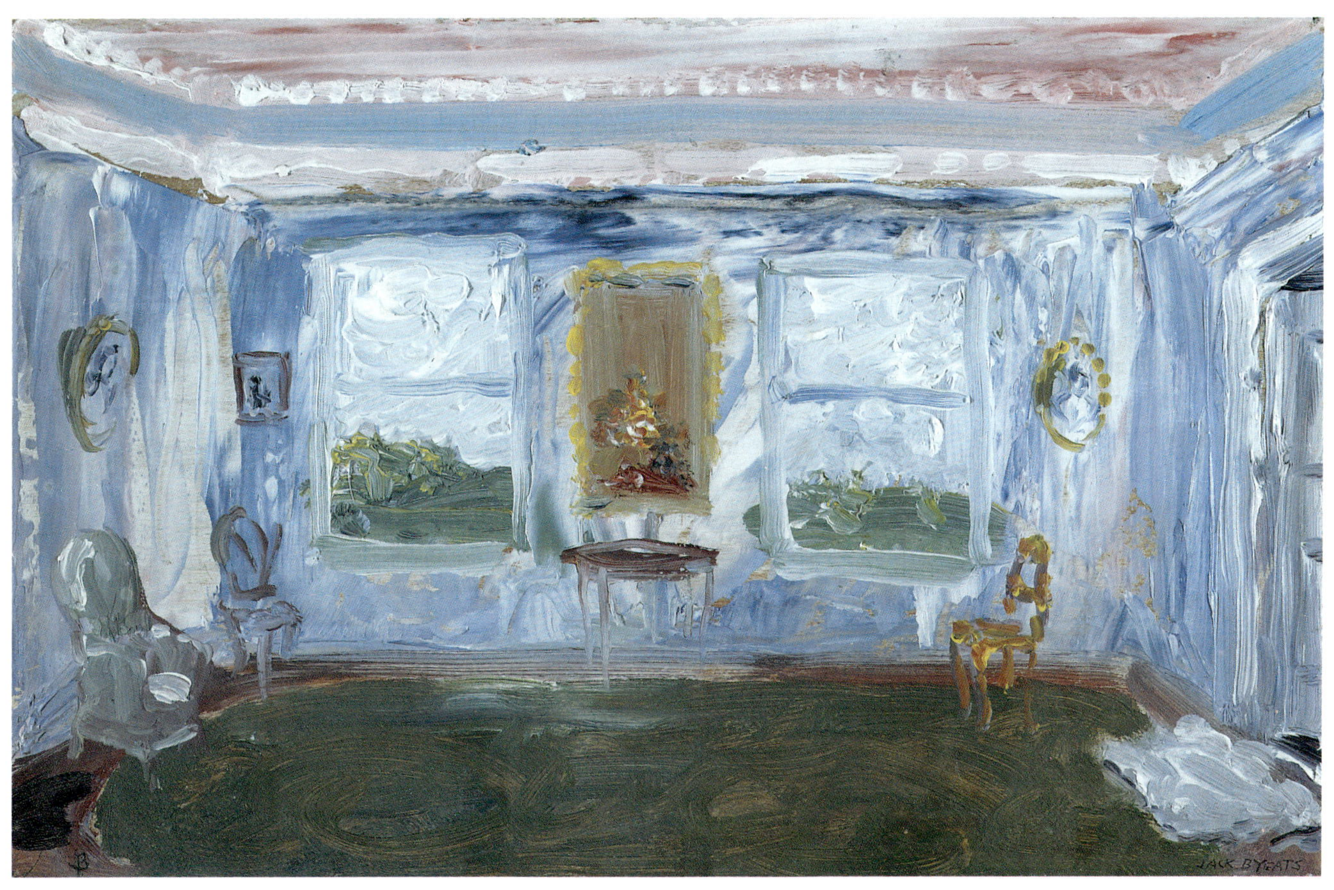

Scene III of the *Four scenes in search of characters* is the most complex of the group. Yeats, who has written a short detailed description in pencil and ink on the back of each of the panels, notes on this that it is a "street of houses a side window right", adding that there are three doors with busts over each, and strips of drugget over the carpet from the doors.

The resulting scene is an interior like a dining room rather than a street, with the pedimented doors Yeats mentions (a bust framed within each pediment) and panelling covering the lower walls. The side window frames a vase of flowers. A wide paned window on the left affords a distant view, a cityscape. A highly polished dining table occupies the centre stage. This time only one chair is provided for the characters whom the scenes may find.

Yeats is suggesting a dual rôle for his scene. As a room it is adaptable at the drop of a hat for a different function or action. The drugget strips lead to the doors like paths, so that it can be used as a street simply by withdrawing the furniture. At the same time he is being deliberately enigmatic. His purpose seems to be to create the notion of a street within a room, placing the outside beside what is within. If we take the backdrop to be the façade of a house, where can the doors lead, when the windows already indicate that there is landscape beyond? The house façade is an empty shell. The illusion of drama, the duality of the real and the absurd, and the readiness of the audience to accept all this, is evidently pursued here by the artist, who, in verso inscriptions on all the small panels, persists with the overall title, *Beginning with Naples*.

Colouristically, this painting is predominantly a subdued plum-toned pink, painted very lightly. The only brightness is in the windows, a pale-blue light that is picked up in the deeper blue of the chair seat and elsewhere. This is the afternoon of a moody Continental day.

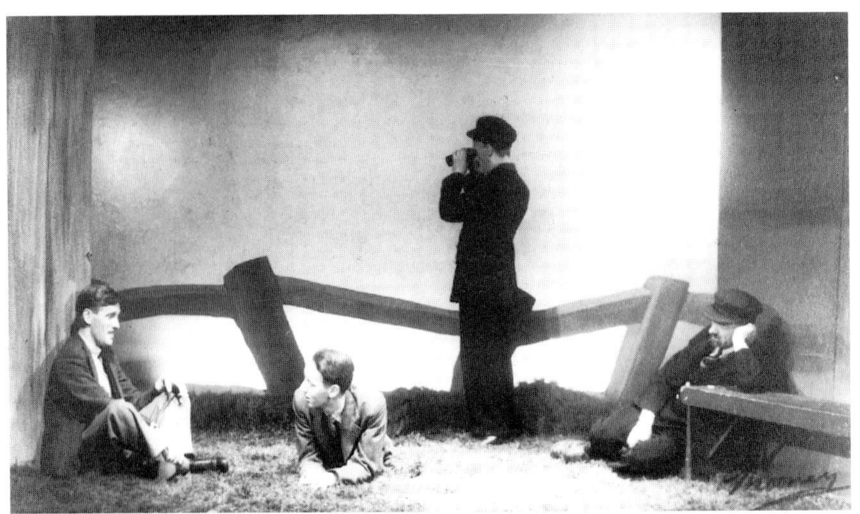

Fig. 141 Jack B. Yeats, Set design for *Harlequin's Positions*, Act III, performed by the Abbey Experimental Theatre, 5 June 1939

Four scenes in search of characters:
Beginning with Naples, Scene III

1942, oil on panel, 23 × 35.5 cm, NGI 4583

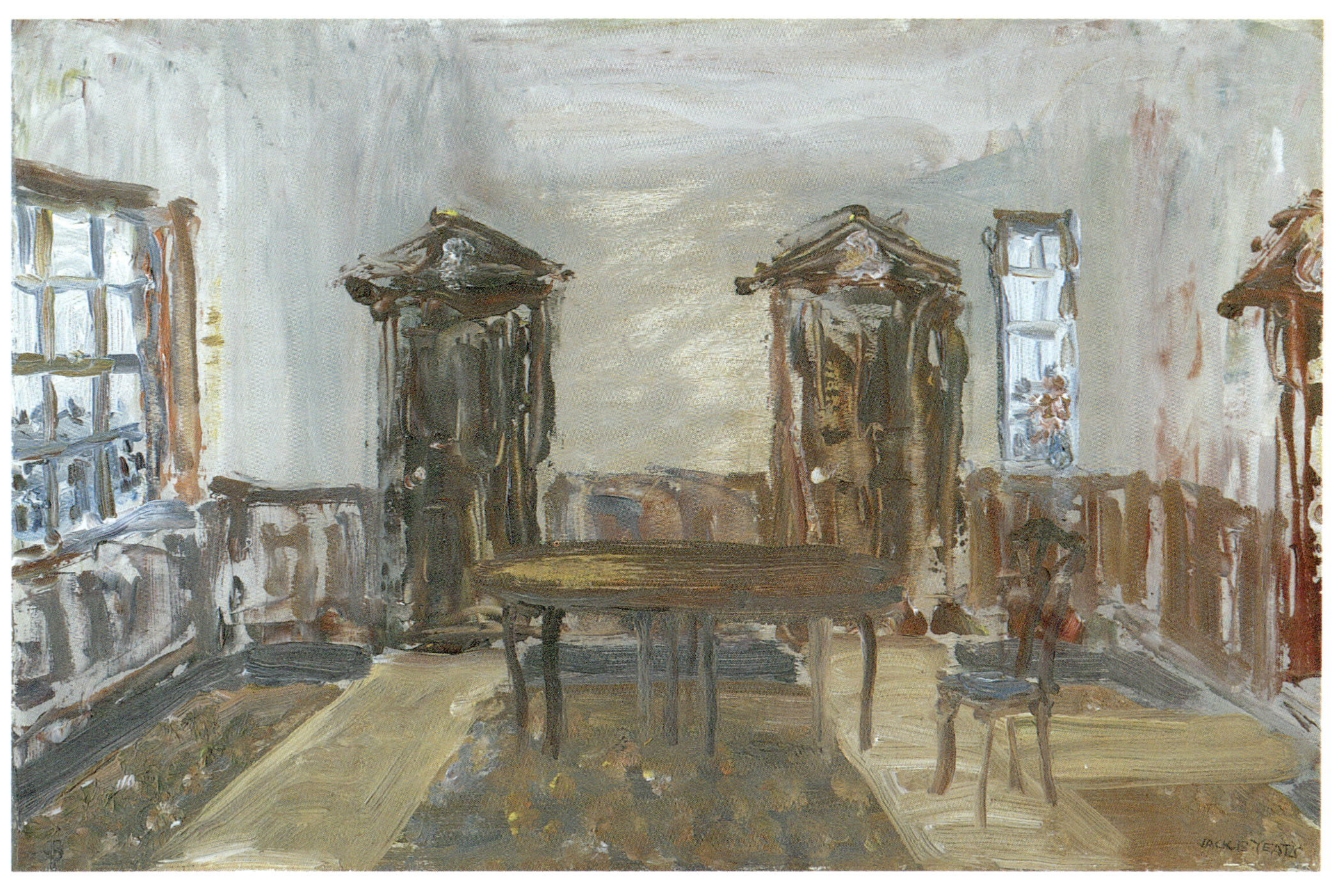

Scene IV of *Beginning with Naples* has returned to the Ireland Yeats painted during his late life, often with metaphorical figures in some kind of visionary ritual. On the reverse of the panel he has noted "bog and mountain top back cloth", with an "uncarpeted yellow floor", and a "curtain over door left". In his picture there is a large paned window reaching to the floor at the back of the stage, opening in French doors on the right, giving access straight on to the bog and mountain top.

Following the time sequence of the other three scenes in search of characters, this scene is coloured with the yellow and mauves of evening. Like other paintings of the period, which deal with death and farewell, there is a bed, or rather a flat gilded couch, which imparts an air of finality to this act of the drama – should it unfold.

The colour of the gold sky is repeated in the floor of the interior, which reflects the shape of the windows dully on the polished boards, capturing also a hint of the red of the heather bogland and the dying sun.

The four scenes are reminiscent of the sequence of rose paintings which Yeats completed half a dozen years before (see fig. 142), showing a rose plucked and fresh, then fading in "the ante room of the Rose's Shadow Land", after which he painted it "departing", as he told Thomas Bodkin. These were occasions when his imagination would not be satisfied with a single image.

The elegance of the stage sets suggest the past; but they have been constructed, or painted, in the present; and the small scenes are alive with anticipation of a future when characters from past and present will invade the sets – themselves presences, as Yeats has painted them – to take up dramatic positions. Yeats's quixotic humour is at work here, picking up the paradox implied in the notion of *Six Characters in Search of an Author*. Nevertheless, with all his instructions and visual planning, Yeats in these paintings, like Pirandello in his play, knows that he must enlist the assistance of the spectator in creating the characters for whom the scenes search.

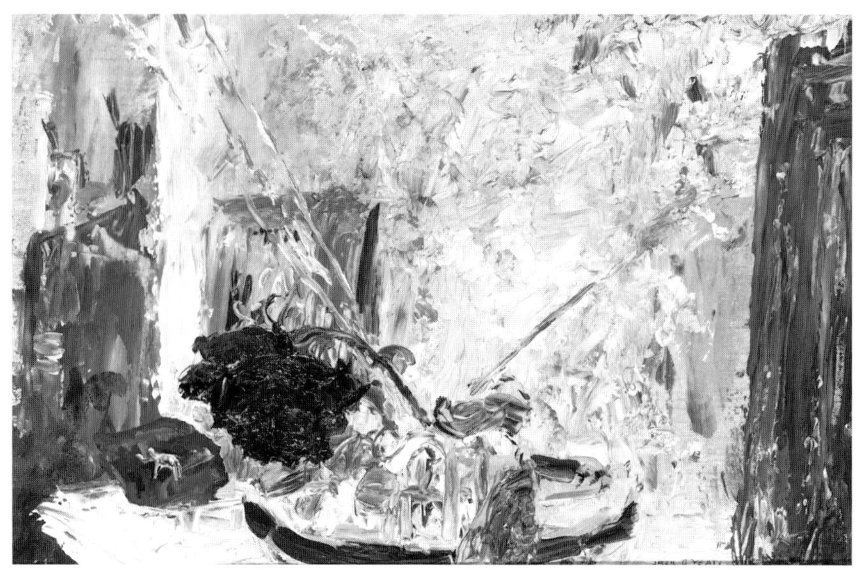

Fig. 142 Jack B. Yeats, *A rose dying*, 1936,
oil on panel, 23 × 35.5 cm (private collection)

1942, Oil on panel, 23 × 35.5 cm, NGI 4584

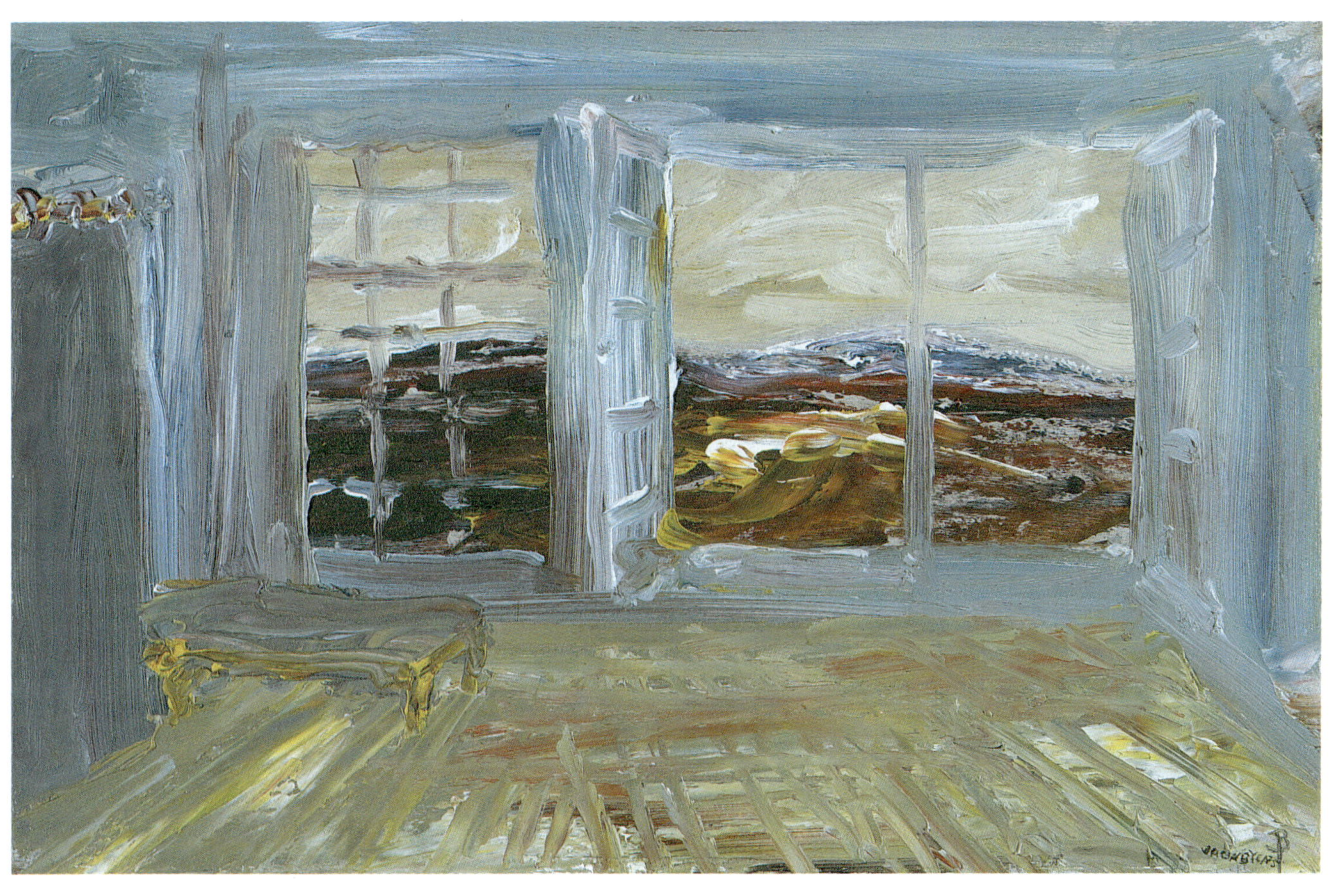

The rose was an important symbol for Jack B. Yeats, as it was for his brother WBY, whose book *The Secret Rose* was the apogee of his early writing. But while for WBY the associations with mysticism and alchemy were compelling, for Jack Yeats the rose imaged for him the love of his country – one of the traditional names for Ireland is 'Róisín Dubh' ('The little black rose' or 'My dark Rosaleen'). He used the rose in various forms in his œuvre, and from an early point in his career regarded the rose as his personal inspiration, painting with one pinned to his easel, as he recorded in his middle-period picture *The scene painter's rose*.

James White has described how, when his work was treated insensitively at a dinner held in his honour at the Dublin Arts Club, Yeats was appalled. "It had seemed to me that our greatest artist had been damned with faint praise by a number of condescending speakers. Later that night when he arrived home his wife gave him a pink paper rose with which someone had presented her at the dinner. He went into his studio and thereupon tied the rose to an easel. 'I made a vow then,' he told me, 'that from thence forward all my work would be *sub rosa*; I would never again discuss the meaning of my pictures. For too long I had endeavoured to think of communicating. Not any more.'"

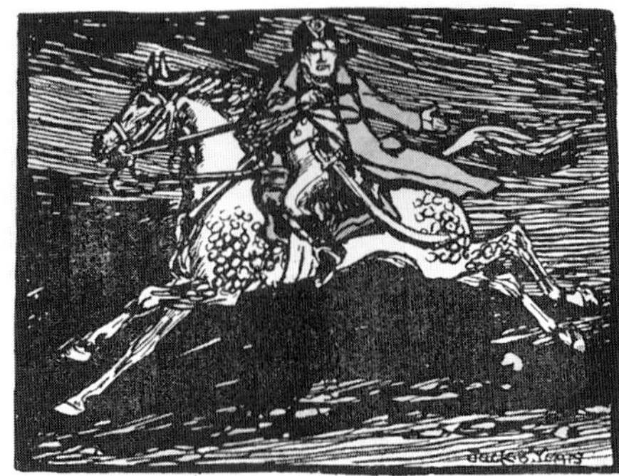

As a result he painted *This grand conversation was under the rose*, taking the title from an Irish political ballad of the Napoleonic period, *The Grand Conversation under the Rose*, which he had illustrated in *A Broad Sheet* in August 1903. On the reverse of the canvas he has inscribed *That Grand Conversation was under the Rose*;

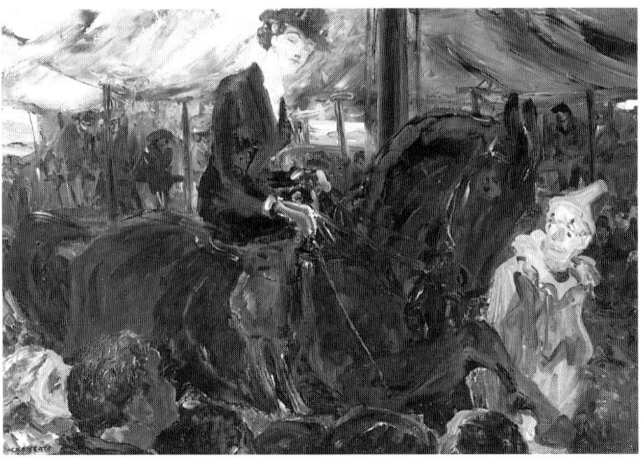

Fig. 144 Jack B. Yeats, *The Haute École act*, 1925, oil on canvas, 61 × 91.5 cm (private collection)

but he always referred to the picture as *This grand conversation*, and exhibited it under this title. The painting ignores the content of the ballad, and turns to the circus, which was dear to the artist's heart – a metaphor encapsulating for him the whole of life, with its high points, its risks, its impermanence. However, he takes the circus performers out of their usual context, the ring, and shows them in the wings of a circus tent, as they rest between acts. The *Haute École* rider, still beautiful and remote, leans against her horse, gazing proudly into the distance. But the clown, the buffoon and misfit who simulates undying, unrequited love for her in the ring, reveals himself now as a fellow performer. He relaxes and drinks his cup of tea quietly as he sits on an orange box. They communicate silently as members of the same circus troupe, meeting as they do in their private capacity as actors 'under the rose' (*sub rosa*) which she has elevated on her riding whip.

Yeats's metaphor, with a certain whimsy at this level, penetrates deeply into the private life of the artist, and may be regarded as a personal statement on his part. The elegant *Haute École* rider is the artist's inspiration. The clown (another common symbol in his work) is the artist, and the grand conversation is their meeting together creatively – *sub rosa*, secretly, 'under the rose'.

1943, oil on canvas, 35.5 × 53 cm, NGI 4576

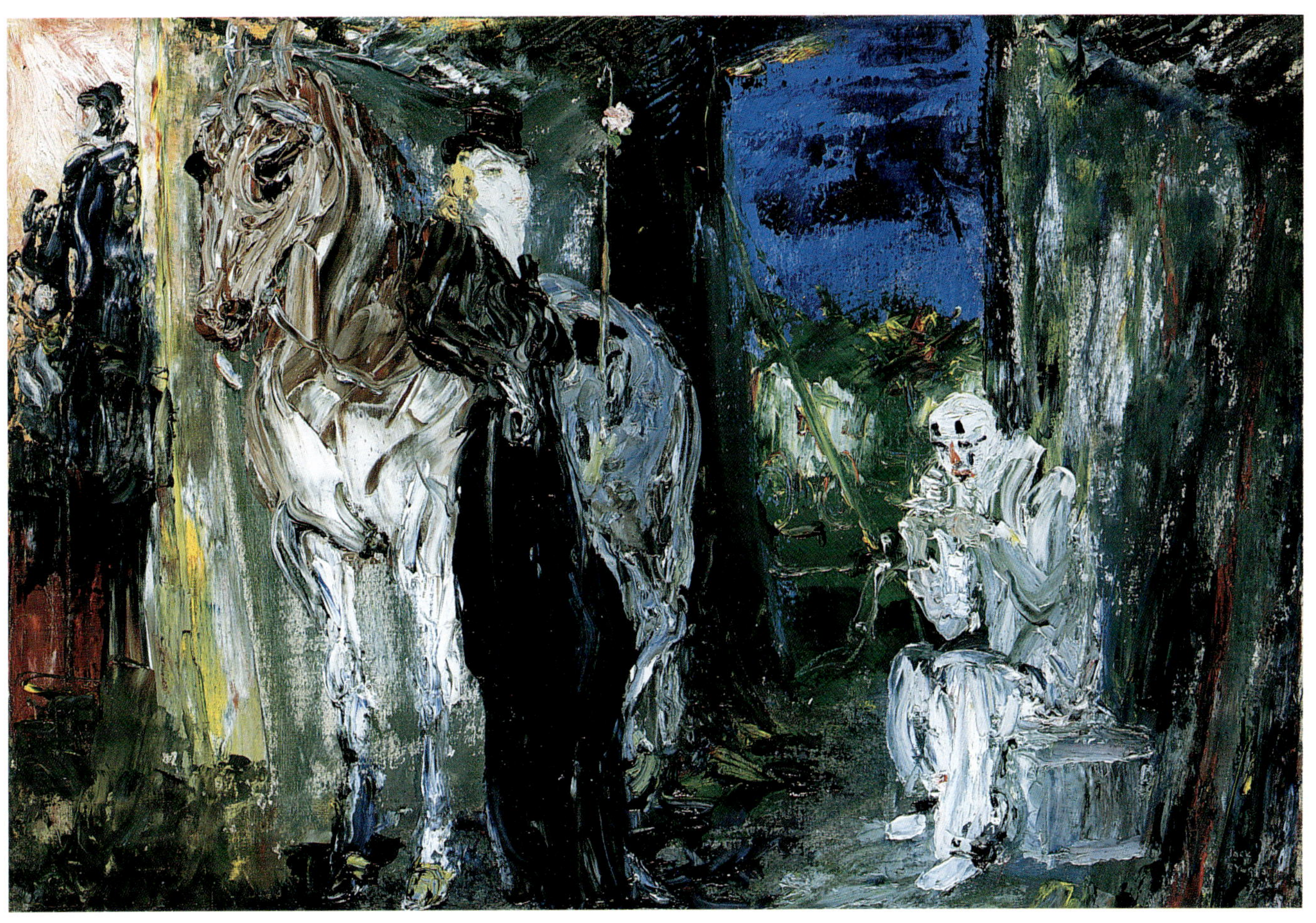

eats used the form of remembrance generally associated with tombs – 'In memory of' – in the titles of several of his paintings as a form of tribute to those who have enhanced the quality of life. But he wanted to take the notion of memory right out of the graveyard, away from the "tons of sculptural marble" he refers to in his play *In Sand* (first performed in 1949). *In Sand*, indeed, makes this idea its theme.

No flowers, of 1945, while set in a graveyard, draws the mind away from the funereal marble to the loving action of the living which can link them with the dead. An old man – presumably someone Yeats happened to see – has no flowers; so he offers leaves instead as tokens of remembrance.

He is in a large cemetery, though in a sparsely filled area. He bends his knee between two newly dug mounds in the left foreground. He wears a black hat and coat, his rust-coloured trousers picking up the colour of the earth around him, and in his left hand he clutches some greenery which he is strewing on to one of the graves. Behind him some tombstones are briefly indicated, and beyond and to the right of the path dividing the graveyard are buildings and deciduous trees, whose light blue and green contrast with the dull conifers to the left of the path.

The conifers create darkness in the left half of the picture, symbolic of the man's grief and confusion. The triangle of sky is tossed with blue and white, in thick impasto. The foreground is painted thinly and ruminatively, as compared with the sparkle of the brighter portion of the picture, yet these soft pinks and green have a quiet emotional energy, so that, despite the pathos of the old man's memorial gesture, he seems surrounded with a glowing and pleasantly coloured buoyancy, which surely must engage him once he has passed through the immediate cloud.

The 1940s were a period of gradual separation for Jack Yeats, when, one by one, the members of his family were passing away. Yet, despite his genuine sorrow, he continued to paint pictures of extraordinary elation and poetic symbolism.

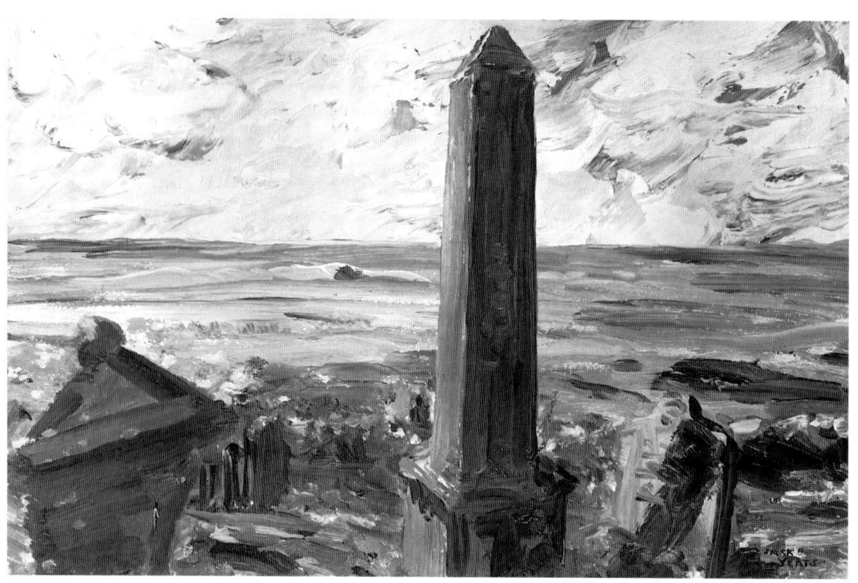

Fig. 145 Jack B. Yeats, *In memory of the crew of the Port Yarrock of Glasgow*, 1925, oil on canvas, 23 × 35.5 cm (private collection)

No flowers

1945, oil on canvas, 61 × 92 cm, NGI 4031

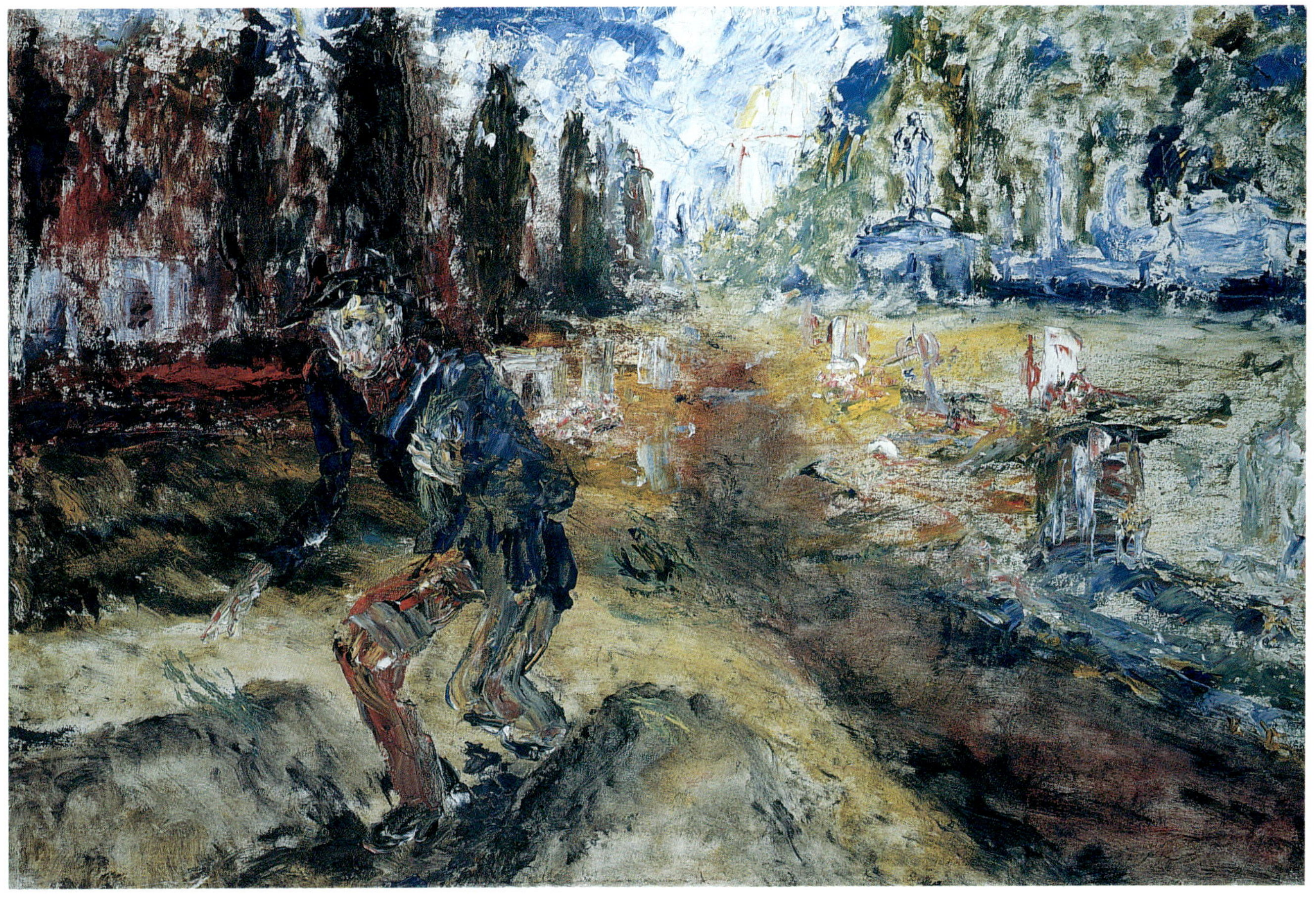

M*en of destiny* was painted in 1946, thirty years after the Insurrection led by Pádraic Pearse in Dublin. Yeats cannot have been unaffected by the fact that the Second World War had recently ended, or that De Valera's hopes of finally establishing a republic would soon be realised.

He used a similar form of composition, with figures silhouetted as they walk on a promontory, in *Two travellers* (fig. 146). Two tramps meet on a peninsula, with sea surrounding them, and a mountain in the distance. They are on the move, but it is also clear that they are travellers through life as well as landscape.

Men of destiny is more idealistic in its conception. Through a richly coloured image of the Sligo fishermen he had watched in his youth – fastening their masted boats when they disembark at Rosses Point – the artist remembers similar men who had left their daily employment at various times to fight for freedom. The name of the painting recalls Ireland (known as 'Inis Fáil' or 'Land of Destiny'), as well as De Valera's republican party ('Fianna Fáil' – 'Warriors of Destiny'), who had fought for absolute independence. Yeats, at this stage of his career, regarded his subjects in a wide context, and no doubt saw not only the future of Ireland but the future of Europe depending on ordinary men such as these. All men of vision, the painting suggests, are 'men of destiny'.

The two dominant characters, approaching in the foreground, walk in a relaxed but confident way, the foremost figure, on the left, throwing back some remark to his companion. They are presented as anonymous figures, at the same time as heroes, the one vermilion and gold, the other gold and royal blue, sublimated by the rays of the setting sun. Their boat, moored at the end of the point, is sketched clearly in yellow and pink, in the artist's unmistakeable manner. Another fisherman, mainly yellow in outline, who has just stepped

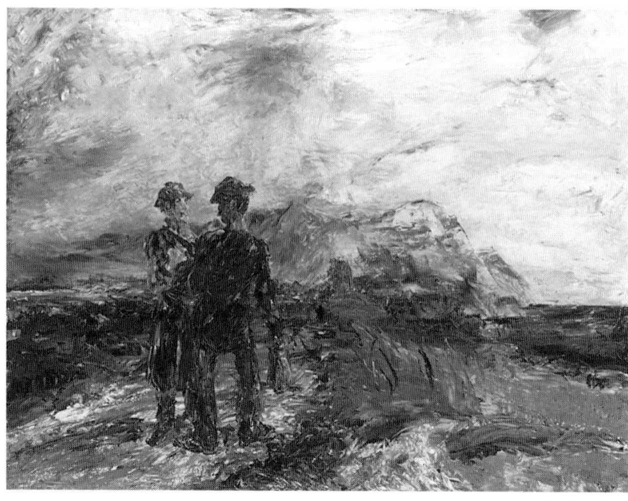

Fig. 146 Jack B. Yeats, *Two travellers,* 1942, oil on canvas, 91.5 × 122 cm (Tate Gallery, London)

ashore, turns to follow them.

The whole painting is alive with exuberant colour, mostly royal blue, indigo and greens, heightened with vermilion and lemon yellow and white. The sky, flaming with energy, is reflected in the foam of the dark tossing sea, and in the rich colours of the headland, which seems a mass of gorse yellow and other vibrant tones – vermilion, pink, sage and turquoise. Yeats controls his emotional use of colour so as to create a crescendo of idealized vision.

The picture was bought by the Committee who organized the Jack B. Yeats National Loan Exhibition in the National College of Art with money remaining from the exhibition. Yeats himself encouraged them to buy *Dublin: Number One ferry, dinner hour*, a painting of 1927; but *Men of destiny* was chosen by the Committee and presented to the National Gallery of Ireland.

Men of destiny

1946, oil on canvas, 51 × 69 cm, NGI 1134

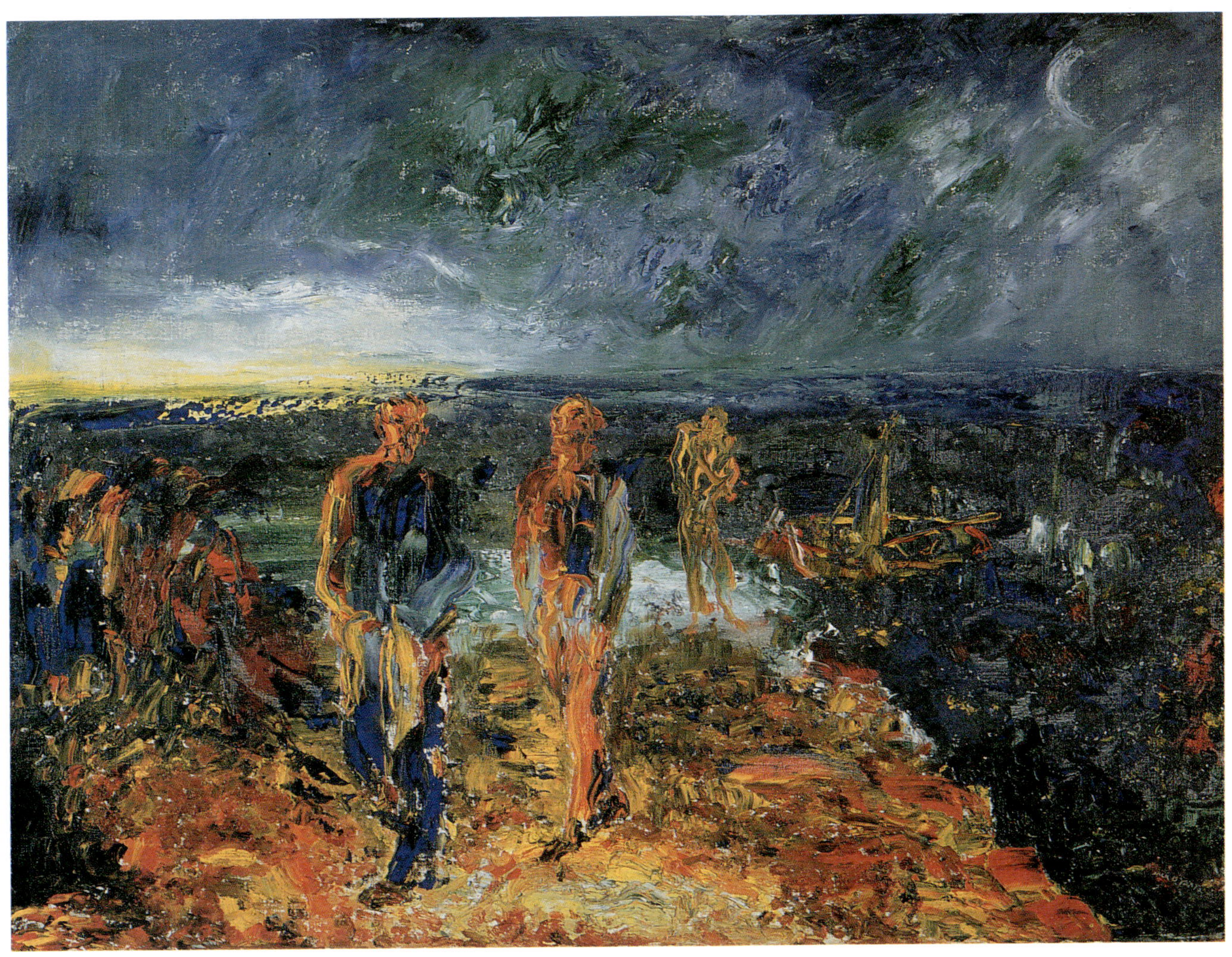

Among the paintings of intense emotion or eso-
teric imagery in Yeats's late career, *Above the
fair* comes as a refreshing throwback to the
manner and themes of his earliest work. The colours –
and every colour is employed – are not so demanding
as in *Men of destiny* (previous page). The style is visibly
graphic, with little vignettes stolen from former watercolours and early oils. Here Yeats puts together a grand
panorama of the fair characters he has known.

The farmer, seen in miniature in the distance, trots
on his chestnut mare, near a horse and cart which dis-
appears down the road into the far landscape, spread
between Ben Bulben and Knocknarea. In the nearer
foreground, tinkers like those he was painting around
1905 emerge, with their dark ominous faces. The upper
part of a girl wearing a tragic mask of the 1920s is
squeezed in between them. To the right, burly farmers,
of his *Life in the West of Ireland* days, bargain below the
beautifully drawn head of a red and gold horse, rearing upwards.

A strong and vivid pattern of fair day in a town in
the west materializes, despite the generally bare effect
of the lightly primed canvas and the lack of dominant
areas of paint. Yellow, red, blue, green, gold, black,
grey, white, all touch the canvas at various points, and
make a mosaic of life and the sensual ferment of human
experience.

Above the fair (which, like the circus, in Yeats's late
schemata becomes a metaphor for human life) rises a
tiny, yellow-haired boy, straddled on an enormous
grey. His expression is solemn, as he raises his small
arm in a gesture of prayerful vision to the pale tinted
sky. The blaze of yellow, near his mount's head, seems
to enlarge his sober ecstasy. Yeats, as he grew older,
was seeing the hope of the future in youth.

One of the pleasures of this large canvas lies in the
variety of human characters, sometimes very nasty,
jostling in the foreground, and their contrast with the
sublimated child lifted above them, whom they largely
ignore.

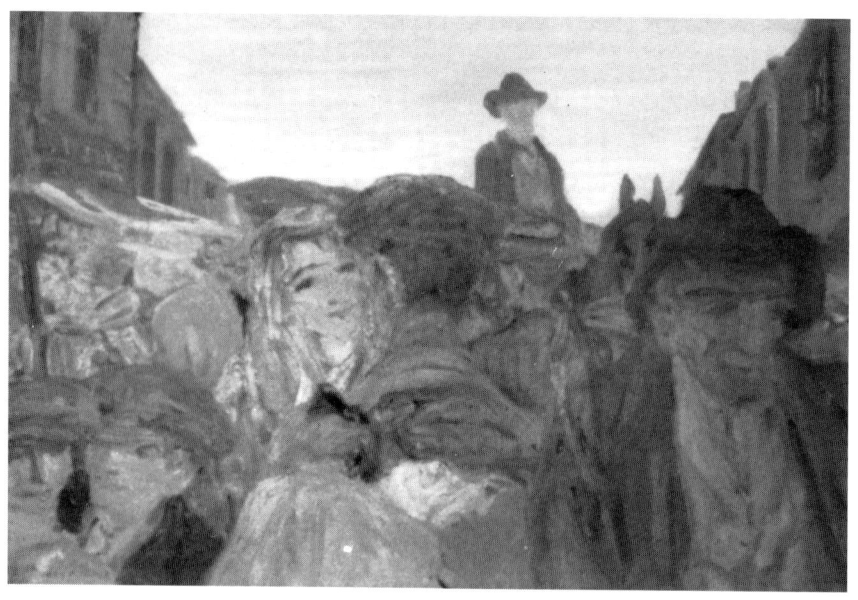

Fig. 147 Jack B. Yeats, *Fair Day, County Mayo*, 1925,
oil on canvas, 61 × 91.5 cm (private collection)

Above the fair

1946, oil on canvas, 91 × 122 cm, NGI 1147

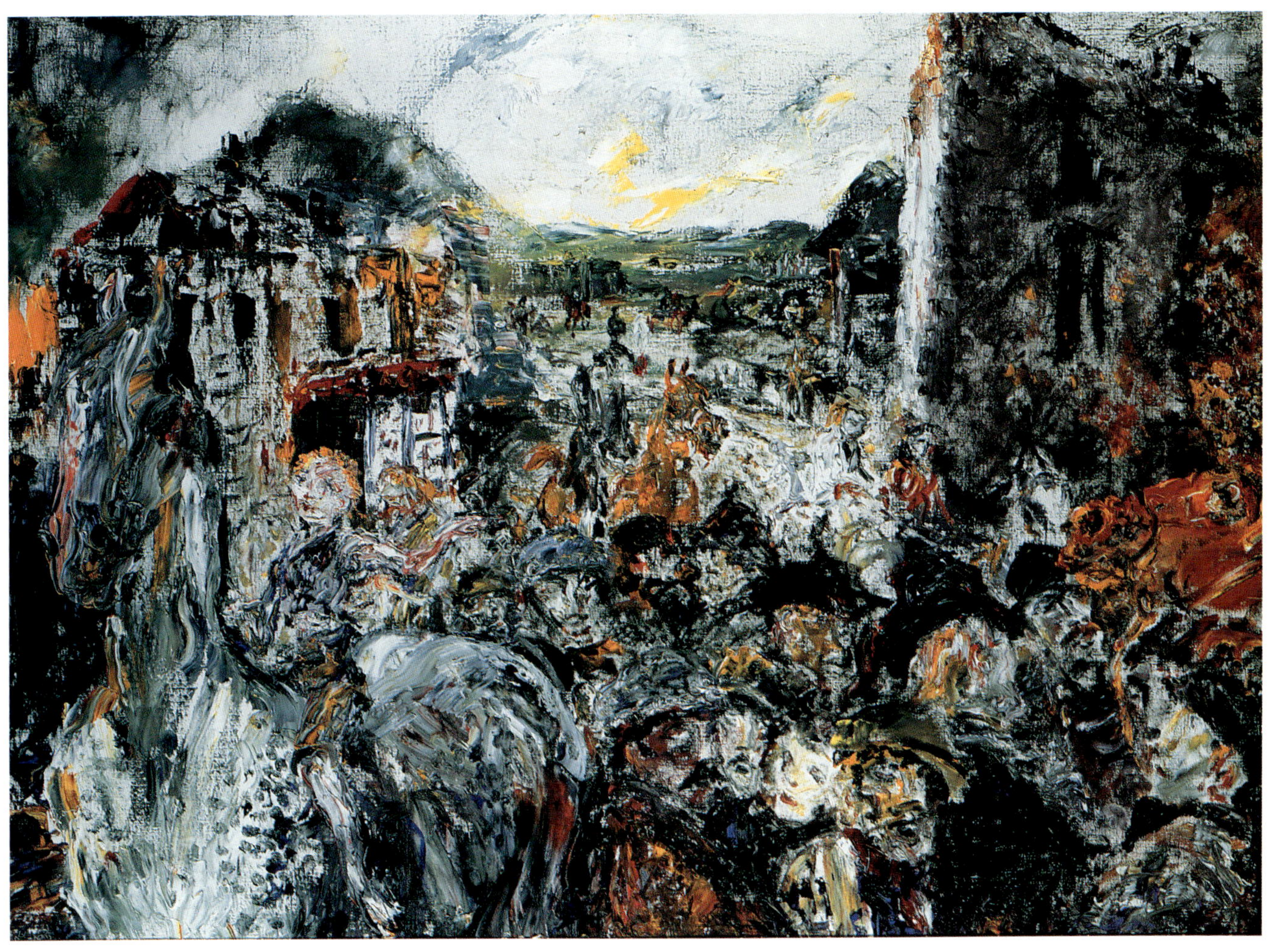

Many ferries is essentially a narrative painting, relating to a memory of 1905. The half-length man with the hat, in the foreground, refers directly to some illustrations Yeats made for J.M. Synge in *The Manchester Guardian* that year (see p. 170). In the month of June, they made a tour together through the poverty-stricken areas of Connaught, then called the 'congested districts'. Synge reported what they had seen, and described the conditions of life there in a series of articles, each of which Yeats illustrated with one or two drawings. The view he recalls in *Many ferries*, of 1948, was to be seen from the top of Dinish Island, at the end of a string of islands in the Gorumna group, off the south coast of Connemara. The larger islands had been joined to the mainland by a series of causeways, but Dinish was still reached by ferry from Furnace.

In one of his articles, Synge describes how, as they looked towards Dinish from Furnace, they saw a man on the far bank gesturing wildly, and shouting at them continually as he rowed his boat over to them. He showed them how they could climb into the boat from a rocky ledge, and, in great excitement at seeing two strangers, he told them the story of his life, about his time in America acting as interpreter for the emigrants and about his misfortunes since he had returned.

Yeats did two pen-and-ink portraits of the ferryman (figs. 148, 149), one poling his boat with an oar near some rocks, the other sitting inside his boat, pulling on both oars as he approaches the island. In both, he wears the broad-brimmed caubeen of the oil painting in which Yeats reconstructs the view of the islands Synge described in his *Manchester Guardian* article. "Afterwards he took us up to the highest point of the island, and showed us a fine view of the whole group and of the Atlantic beyond them, with a few fishing-boats in the distance, and many large boats nearer the rocks rowing heavily with loads of weed."

In Yeats's painting, the ferryman stands on a hillock, looking down at the string of islands, painted richly in green and yellow, between which fishermen in curraghs are rowing. The tiny islands stretch out in a deep-blue sea that grows mauve in the distance and seems to find its horizon in the gleam of yellow in the roughly brushed sky. Yeats obviously re-creates the view with the glory of memory, but, as elsewhere, the episodic nature of life seems to fascinate him. With the help of reminiscence, he imagines the experience of the ferryman, gazing down at the view he has introduced to the two strangers.

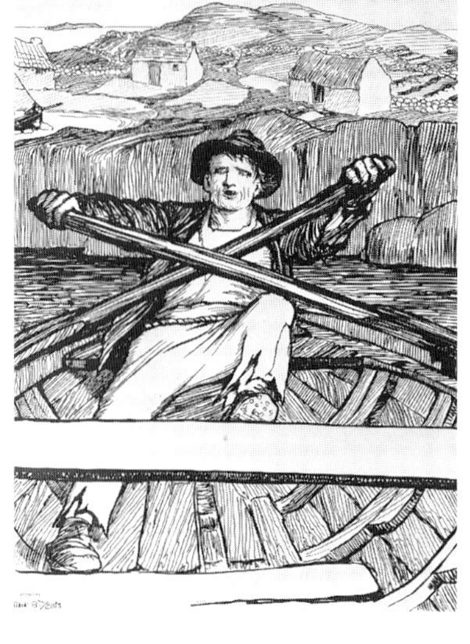

Fig. 148 Jack B. Yeats, *The Dinish ferryman*, from *The Manchester Guardian*, 21 June 1905 (Yeats Archive)

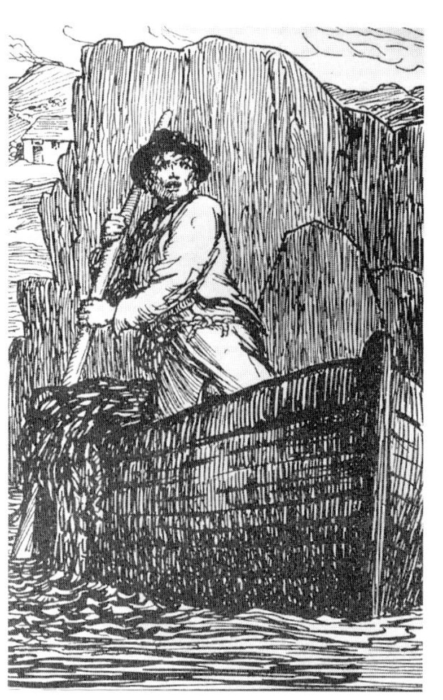

Fig. 149 Jack B. Yeats, *The ferryman of Dinish Island*, from *In Wicklow, West Kerry and Connemara* by J.M. Synge, 1911 (Yeats Archive)

Many ferries
1948, oil on canvas, 51 × 69 cm, NGI 1550

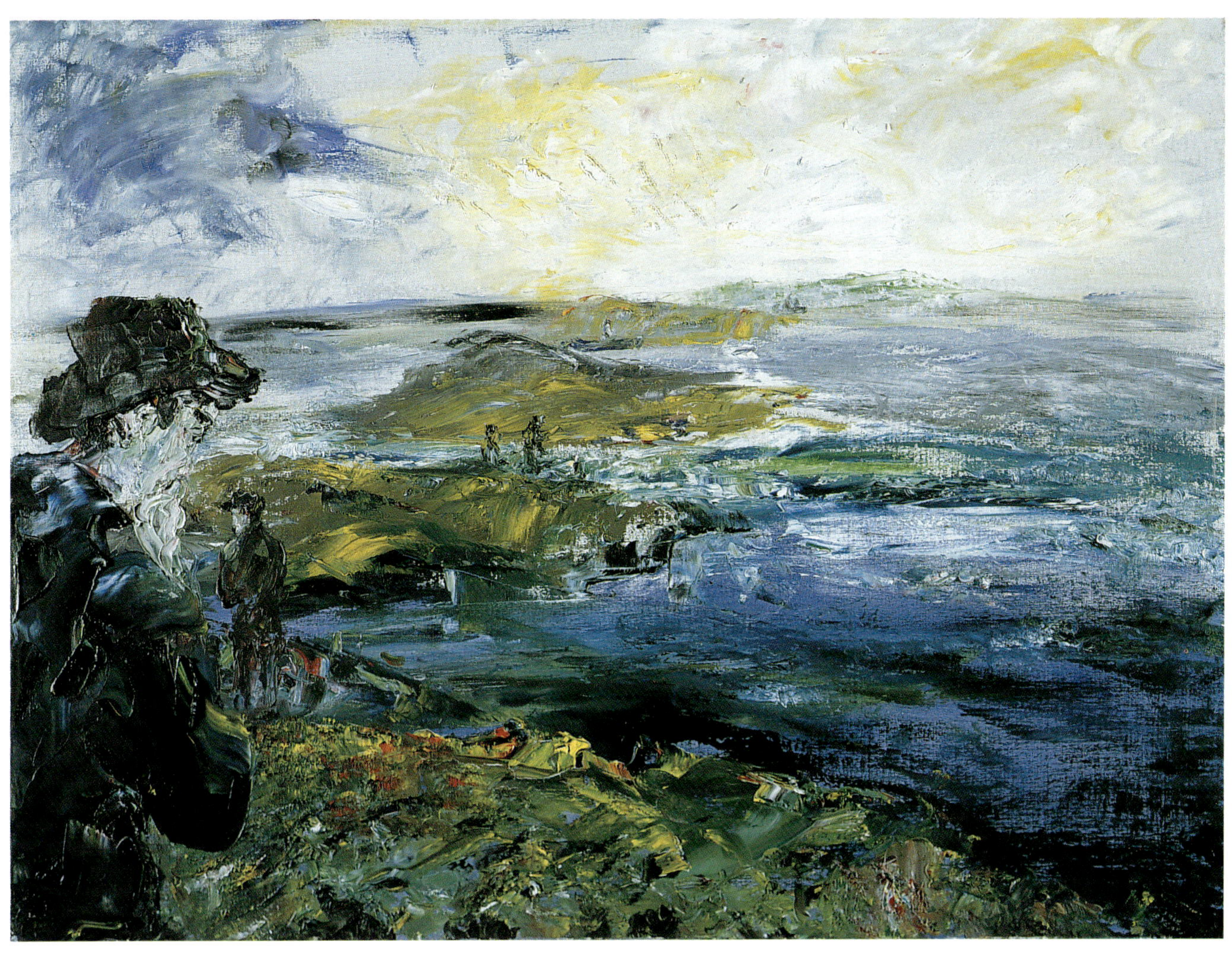

Since the early 1930s, Yeats had been giving serious thought to the transience of life. In his play *The Deathly Terrace*, he may sound frivolous when talking about 'leg pulling': yet the humour conceals a deep questioning. "There is always coming nearer the day," says the tramp, Nardock, "when the last pullable leg will be pulled. A poet has shown us the sadness of the last man, the hangman with no one in the world left to pull his legs. But I see another picture of the last man looking with desolate eyes searching for the last leg but two, just to pull it, and his mind will be brimming with splendid schemes for leg pulling – too late, and he could not stoop to pull his own leg".

In *The last dawn but one*, through the image of the circus striking camp (because it is believed to be unlucky to stay on in the same place), Yeats considers the day of 'the last pullable leg'. The landscape is overcast by the ominous deep blue and red in the sky, which tinges the figures packing huge trunks, taking down tents, assembling their gear. A man on horseback supervises the proceedings. He is ready to go, turning his back on the pending storm that broods above, and heading towards the lighter, yet equally cloudy part of the sky.

The figures are tense, and like shadows. They can see ahead only as far as the dawn of the following day, so uncertain is their way of life.

Yet there are good auguries. Two figures in the foreground are radiant with a golden yellow. On a half of the dismantled Big Wheel, a child stands up, regardless of the urgent activity of the anonymous performers round about; and, in the left foreground, there is a pool of water – water now had religious connotations for Yeats – with yellow flowers flourishing on the banks.

The style is typical of the late 1940s, the paint being used to stain the canvas in an economical fashion. Imagery is supplied with rich blobs and squeezes of pigment, the artist often drawing with the tube of paint, and modifying the result by scoring away with his knife or with the handle of his paintbrush.

Meeting the dawn (fig. 150), also painted in 1948, and picking up at a different point the core theme of the circus's departure, is more optimistic in mood. Similar figures form a procession. Led by the cloaked rider on his horse, and a man with a banner, and a donkey, they move together towards a lighted sky.

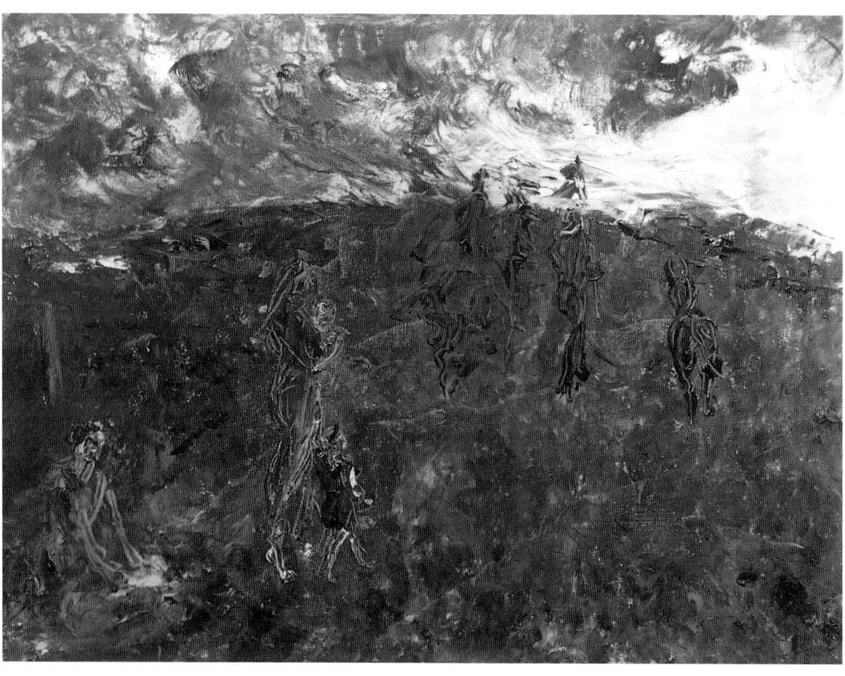

Fig. 150 Jack B. Yeats, *Meeting the dawn*, 1948, oil on canvas, 51 × 68.5 cm (private collection)

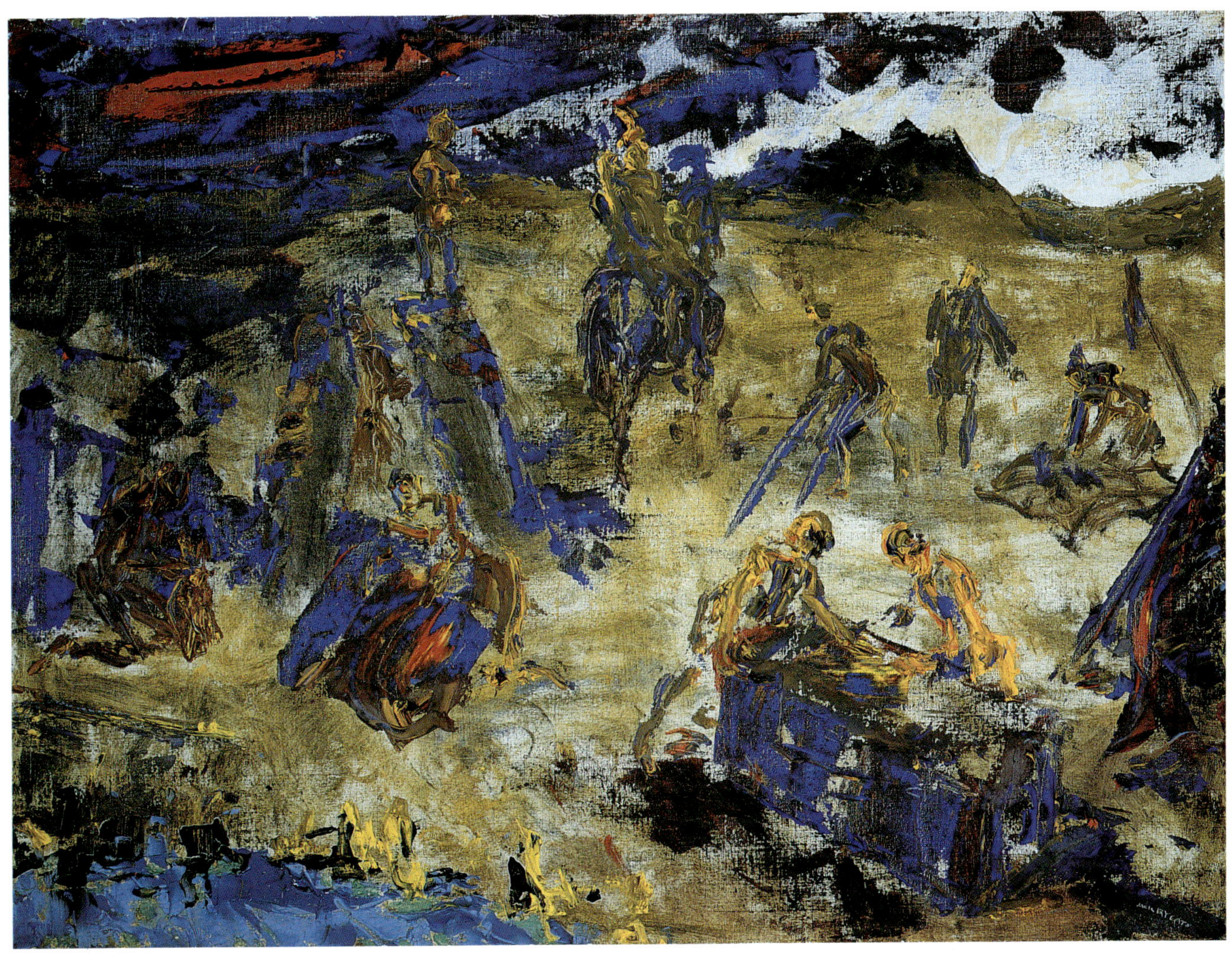

The last dawn but one

1948, oil on canvas, 51 × 69 cm, NGI 1906

As he grew older, Yeats's landscapes became progressively more visionary, so that earth, water, air and light seemed all to reach some metaphysical plane where the physical world is allied with the heavenly. The landscapes are still recognizably Irish in their colouring, and in their changeable weather, their wealth of little lakes and streams, and their mountainous hills. But emotionally Yeats seemed to gather up the countryside which he had studied in detail as a young man, and transform through a personal ecstasy this land he loved so deeply.

The men and women in these late paintings – the tramps and tinkers and ballad singers and sailors which we are familiar with in earlier works – are transformed too, and caught up in the ecstasy of the artist, so that they become one with the landscape. This is a landscape which is capable of any emotion, because all emotion is part of living; and Life is what his painting continues to be about, though now it is a vision of Life which can express the unseen as well as the seen. Yeats remained concerned about the suffering, bereavement and loneliness of this life (as in *Grief*, p. 264), but put it into a perspective measured by a simple belief in an ultimate joy which can be reached through vision. His peripatetic characters in *Shouting* (fig. 151) release themselves into the visionary state through the physical act of making sound in landscape. In *Glory* (1952), a little child hoisted on the shoulders of two old men carols aloft, in his noisiness rejoicing in the mere fact of existence. "I call out 'Glory'," Yeats wrote in his book *Ah Well*; "and every one of you gets a lift in the upper garret of his stomach, isn't that so?"

The singing horseman, a medium-sized painting, is one of his most joyous images, a simple rendering of a bareheaded youth mounted on a yellow horse, clasping his hands together and singing his heart out to the heavens. His face and hands are fringed with gold, carrying him far above the immediate sphere, to beyond the tossed blue sky. His horse is transformed too, blended lyrically into his mood of ecstasy, turning into gold in a landscape which itself loses its look of solidity. The young man is a traveller through life, like so many of Yeats's characters, who settle nowhere, but take life as it comes, reaching moments of insight like this into a life that is indescribable. His horse, an opaque transparency, seeming greater than its master though wed to him in a relationship of love and understanding, has a wide penetrating eye that looks inward and can confidently see all.

Anna Russell told Jack Yeats that *The singing horseman* was her sister's favourite painting, and he responded, "I got a thrill out of man and horse when I painted them" (16 July 1952; National Gallery of Ireland Archive).

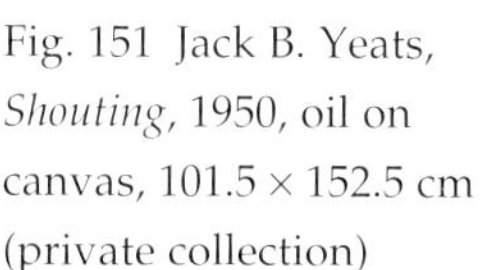

Fig. 151 Jack B. Yeats, *Shouting*, 1950, oil on canvas, 101.5 × 152.5 cm (private collection)

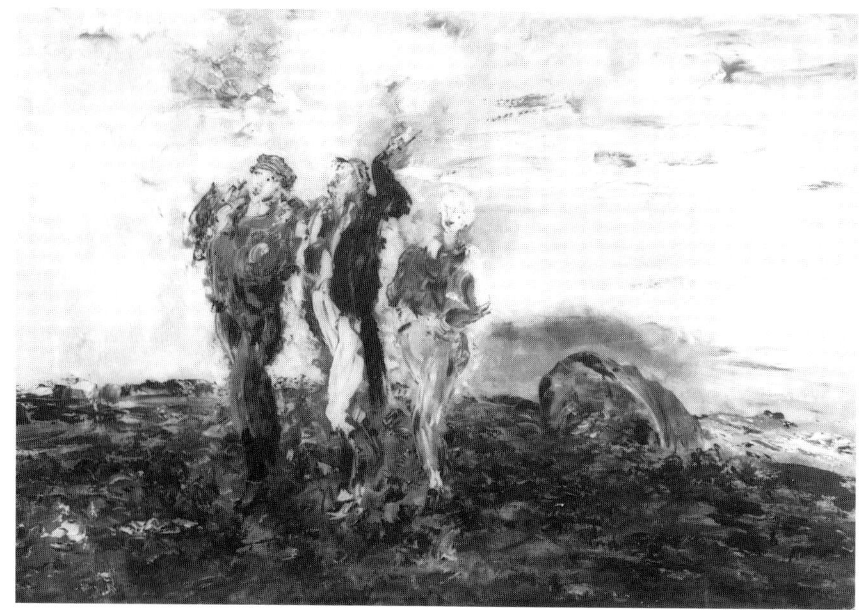

1949, oil on canvas, 61 × 91.5 cm, NGI 4524

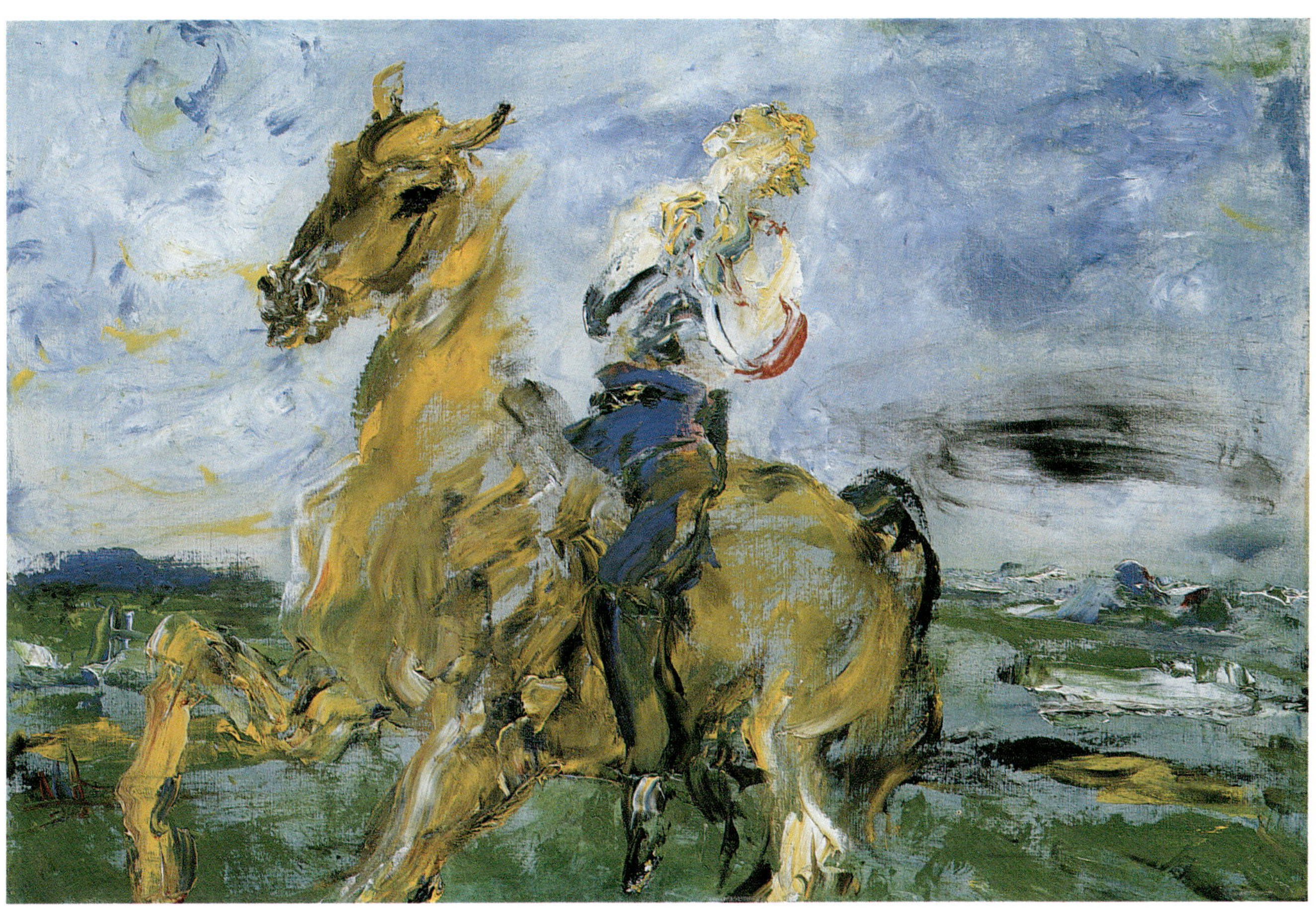

This small painting of 1949 has two clear images in it: a spotted horse to the left, gleaming with white and with the red and gold of its saddle and harness; and the figure of a cowboy to the right, doffing his hat to the horse – which seems to turn its head towards him – as he prepares to stride forth into the yellow of sunlight. Yeats shows us a child in a fairtent, who is so caught up in his imagination that, when he dismounts from the merry-go-round, he is still the skilled horseman he imagined himself to be, and still

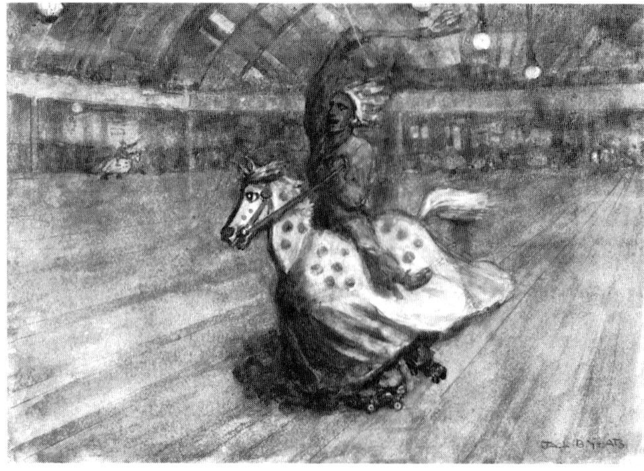

Fig. 152 Jack B. Yeats, *Crystal Palace, ca.* 1903, watercolour, 18 × 26.5 cm (private collection)

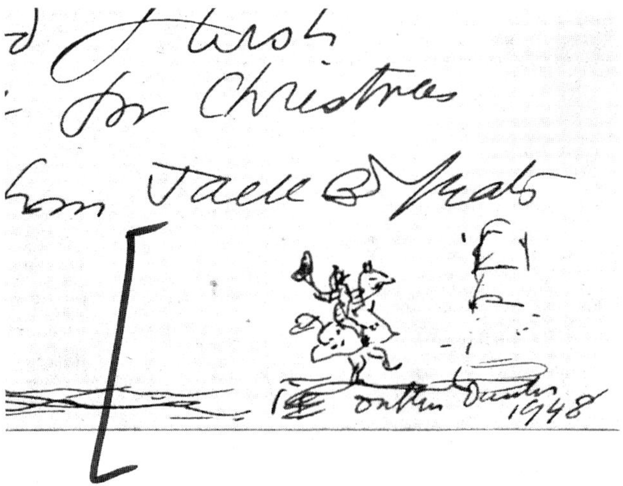

Fig. 153 Jack B. Yeats, *Sketch of a hobby horse,* from a letter to Anna Russell, 1948 (NGI Archive)

tied emotionally to the toy that accompanied him into his dream. The heroic figure, represented as a dramatic outline rather than as a body with volume, appears in other theatrical paintings by Yeats.

The title refers to the romantic poem 'The Arab's Farewell to his Steed' by Caroline Norton, granddaughter of Richard Brinsley Sheridan. Yeats illustrated the first verse of her poem directly in a later painting, *My beautiful, my beautiful!* (fig. 156, p. 268).

> My beautiful, my beautiful that standest meekly by,
> With thy proudly-arched and glossy neck, and dark
>   and fiery eye!
> Fret not to roam the desert now with all thy winged
>   speed;
> I may not mount on thee again! – thou'rt sold, my
>   Arab steed!

The poem describes the Arab owner's emotion as he struggles to persuade himself to sell his horse, and Yeats captures the bond of man and beast superbly in his large painting.

Here, however, the mood is light and humorous, a moment of theatre. Yeats was recalling, in drawings of the same period, the skaters he had witnessed at the Crystal Palace in London. These were dressed as Red Indians, riding on other performers who were disguised as hobby horses with skirts hiding their feet (fig. 152). He drew them from memory (fig. 153), jovially converted; and painted them in another guise in *The attack on the Deadwood coach* (1943), an oil with drollery similar to this painting.

He expects us to be taken in, at first glance, by the lifelike head and torso of the horse in *The cavalier's farewell*. Gradually it dawns on us that it has no legs, and is only part of the fair. The youthful 'cavalier', also, may be expected to make a very different farewell from the lament of the Arab in the poem. Quite apart from the two striking images, the strong bright colours surrounding them lend ornament to the witty fantasy.

The cavalier's farewell to his steed

1949, oil on board, 36 × 46 cm, NGI 1374

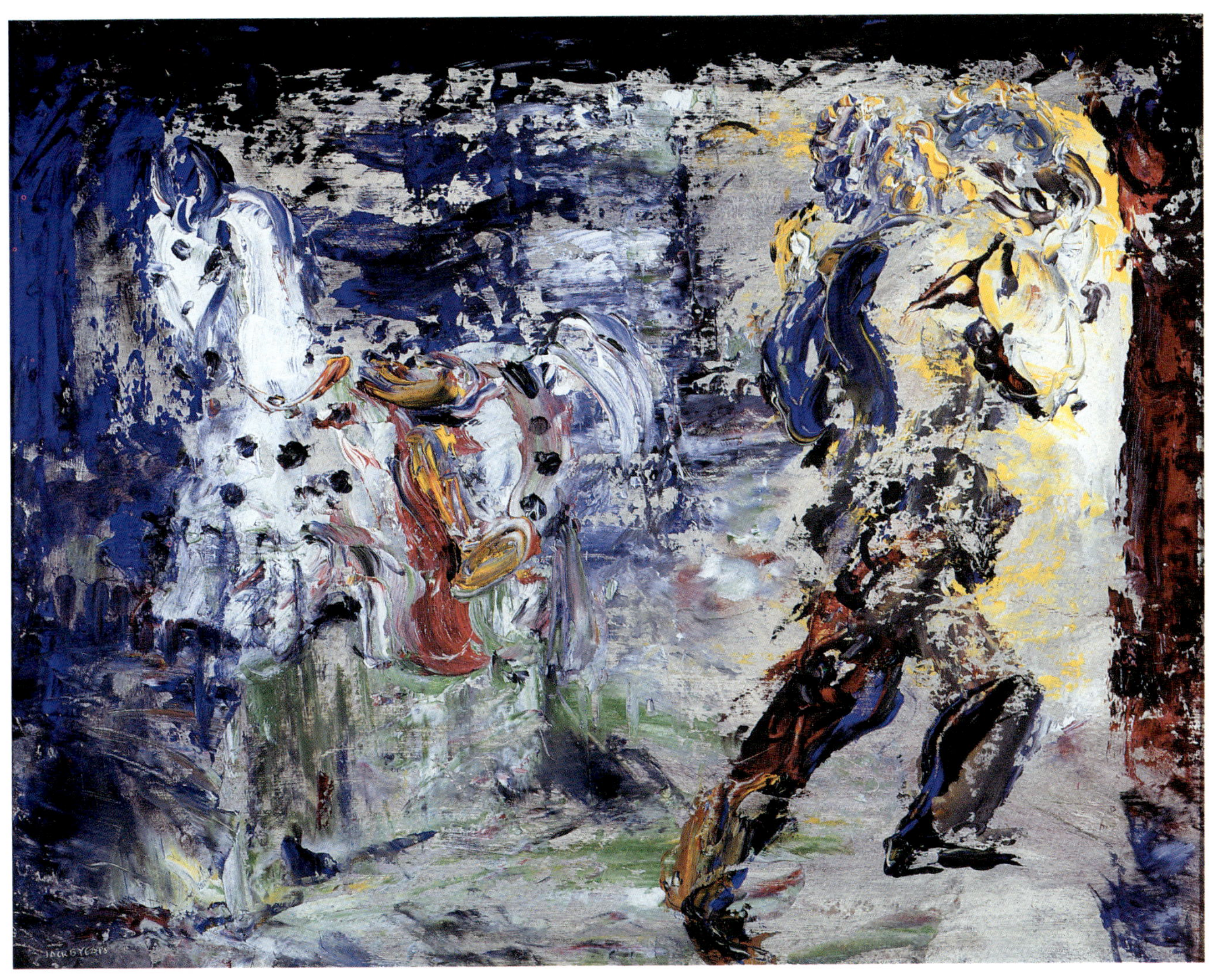

*G*rief is one of Yeats's more outspoken paintings. He had treated the subject of war and its effects some years before in *Tinkers' encampment; the blood of Abel* (1940) where murder has been committed at night in a tinker's camp. The huge implications of the spilling of blood – in a society where we are all related – grows to even vaster proportions as we see the distance the tinkers have come, crossing mountain and river to reach the camp, drawn magnetically

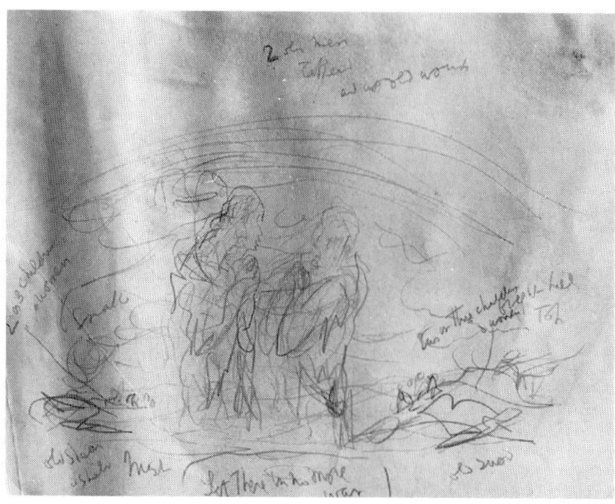

Fig. 154 Jack B. Yeats, *Let there be no more war*, from Yeats's final workbook, *ca.* 1950 (Yeats Archive)

to review, and to try to understand, the event.

However, around 1951, when this picture was painted, Yeats was exploring particular human emotions in his pictures. *Grief* seems to originate from a sketch he made in his last workbook, which he entitled *Let there be no more war* (fig. 154). Two figures are indicated in the centre of the drawing, as "2 old men tattered with old wounds"; and women and children lie, among weapons, near them. There is a snake, and further armour, and mist. The sketch was simply an initial thought and has little to do with the final picture, but, like other scribblings in the same book, it seems to have been an essential means of holding on to the germ of an idea until there was time to paint it. Yeats's mind, especially during the last years, was ceaselessly inventive.

The theme is projected powerfully in the oil painting. Through the simplest images, Yeats conveys his utter abhorrence of war. For such a large painting, the detail is comparatively brief. Two rows of houses, one facing the other – as in *Above the fair*, indicating a typical Irish country town – are laconically described; and between them pours a crowd of angry fighting men, painted in a tossing indigo which is broken only by the green of a figure in the left foreground, who may be fleeing from the soldiers. Their leader, an apocalyptic phantom on a white horse, framed between the houses, gestures aggressively. He and the head of his horse occupy a position just above the exact centre of the painting, the horse's head and the man's head being equidistant from the left and right edges of the painting.

It is possible that Yeats may have seen a reproduction of *Guernica*, and that this prompted him to an Irish interpretation of the same theme. Unusual in his work, the face of his destroyer bears a resemblance, in its distortion, to some of Picasso's heads deriving from African carvings. Yet the subject is represented otherwise in his own original manner. The destroyer is surrounded with brilliant red, giving the effect of flames.

In the foreground, an old man with white hair and face crouches, dazed, looking at the blood dropping into his hands. A mother, in a typical Yeatsian pose of feminine protectiveness, puts her arm around a small child and inclines her head towards him. He has yellow hair, and in some ways is the dominant image in the painting, the prototype of the joyful, entranced boy in *Above the fair* (p. 254), isolated to the right of the picture's centre in a cocoon of bare canvas, which iterates the transparency of his innocence. His hands and the lower part of his body are red with blood.

To the right of the mother and child, the courtyard of the old house is bare and empty, merely stained with a melancholy blue and touches of green and yellow. Their world seems devastated. The wounded man, though, is still linked with the world of action, where the landscape confronting the agile soldiers and their silhouetted guns throbs with colour, and the rich cobalt of the house wall that frames the left side of the picture adds a further vitality to the violent area of the painting.

Grief

1951, oil on canvas, 102 × 153 cm, NGI 1769

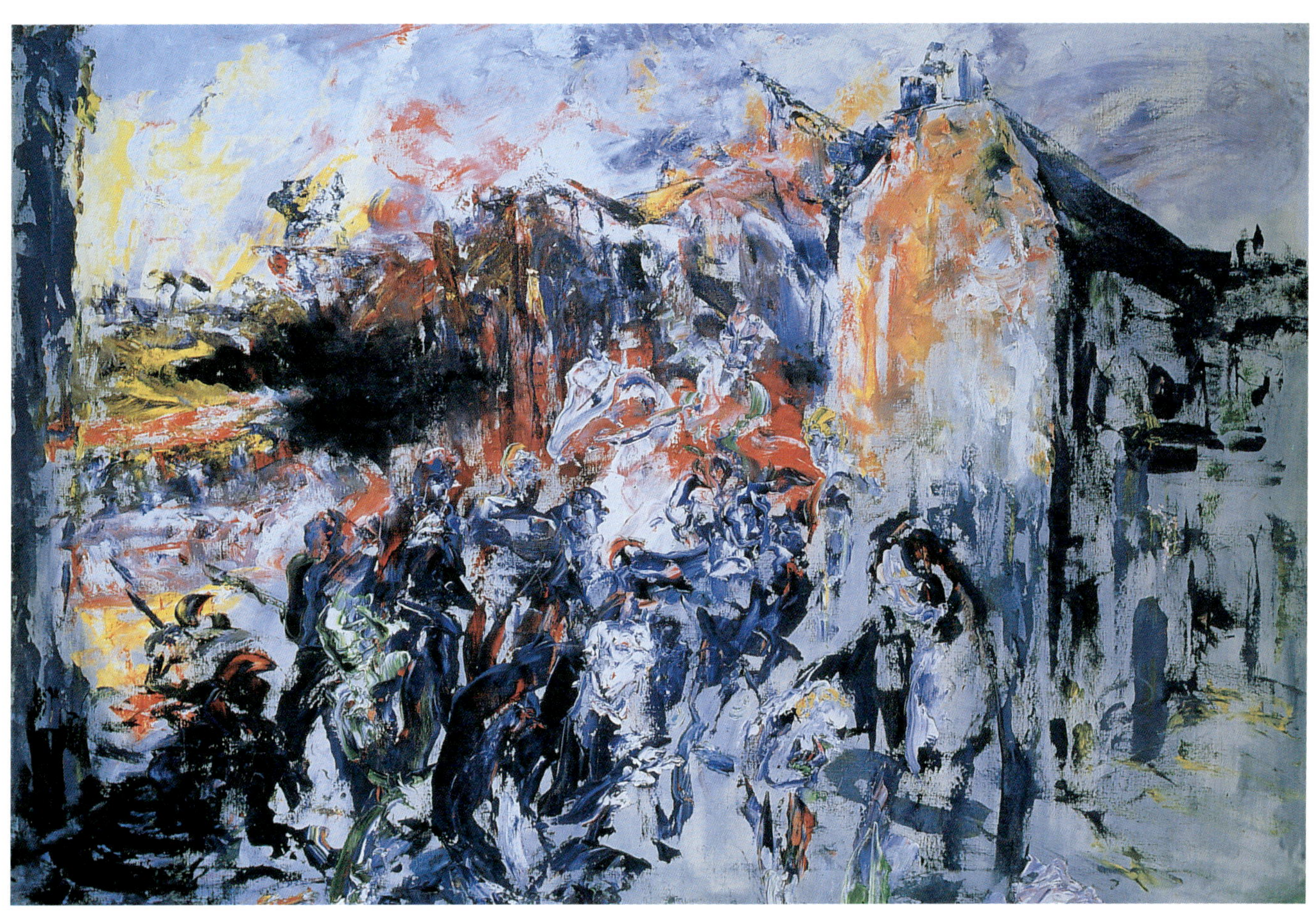

OVERLEAF
Detail of *Grief*

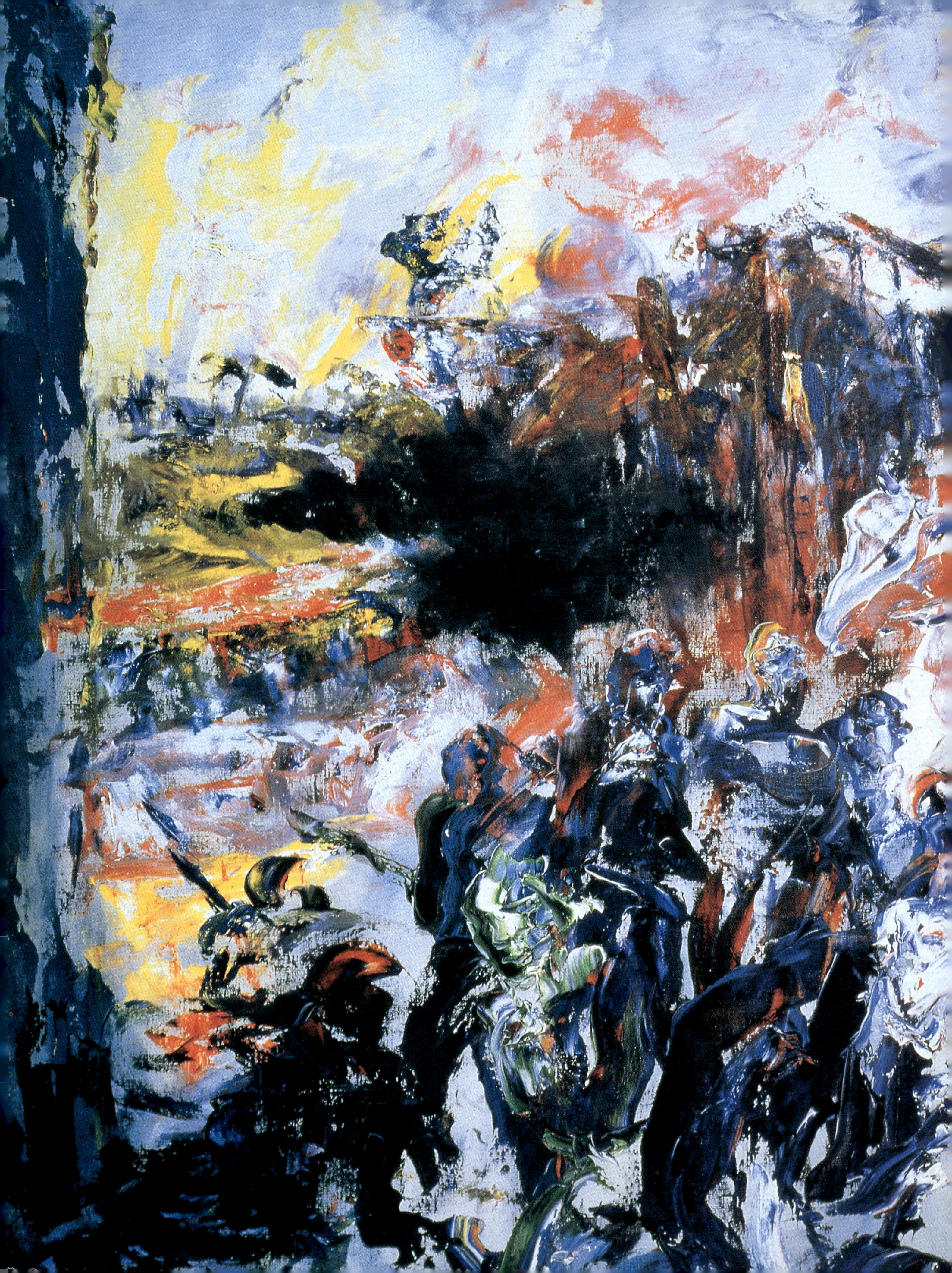

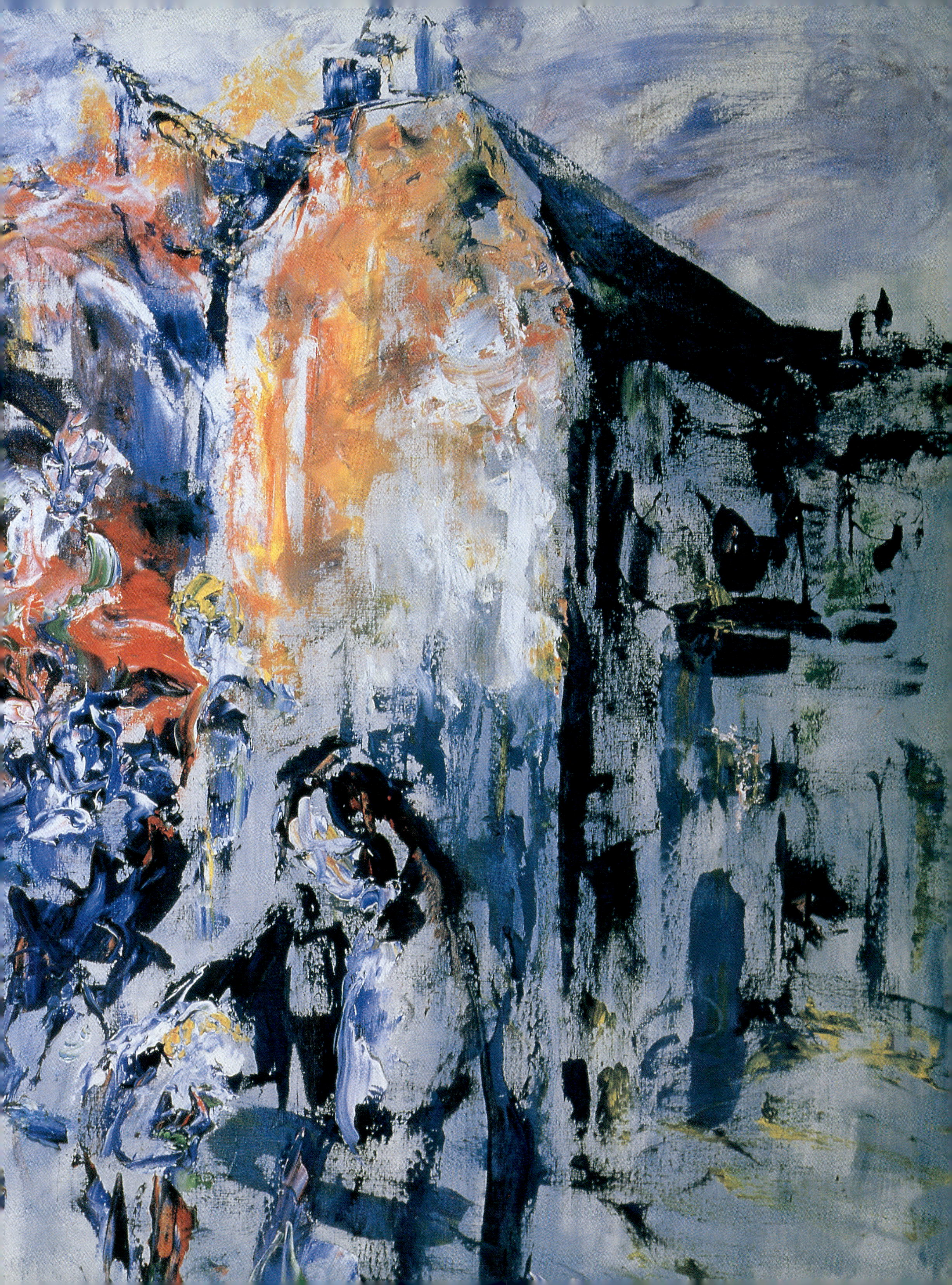

Yeats painted many horse paintings during his career. Though he never claimed to have been a horseman himself, he showed a great affection for horses from his earliest days, when he drew *Rumbo the circus horse* (fig. 155) for the illustrated magazine *Judy*, and included horses in watercolour subjects, depicting life as lived in the west of Ireland in the first years of this century. One of his most charming late paintings is of a herd of ponies galloping around a seated figure, in a meadow below Ben Bulben.

This three-quarter-length horse, in a clearing in a wood, hears the call of its master and responds instantly, galloping from the shadow of the trees towards a light leafy tunnel, at the end of which the man's figure may be seen silhouetted against the daylight. The drawing of the horse, with a tossing brush which highlights the horse's face and the ridge of his back with touches of yellow, is confident. It is one of

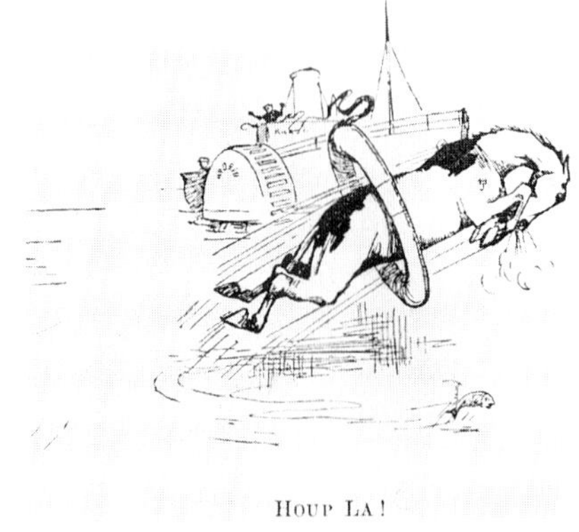

Fig. 155 Jack B. Yeats, *Rumbo the circus horse,* from *Judy,* 28 June 1893

Yeats's most energetic horse images. It breathes vitality and intelligence.

The contrast of shade and light, clearly marked in a diagonal line falling across the right of the picture, is beautifully managed. Touches of red, in vertical lines to right and left of the painting and at the entrance to

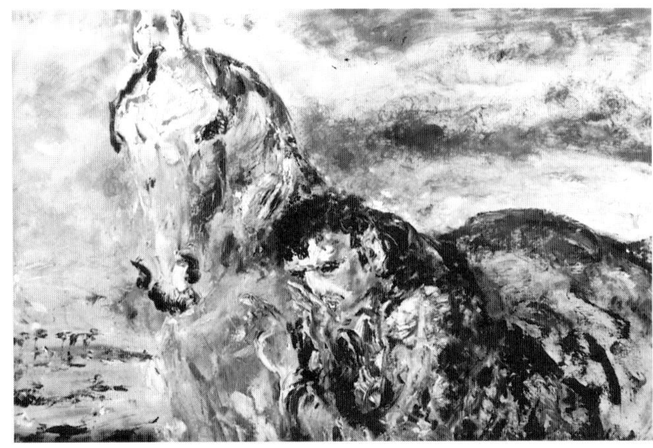

Fig. 156 Jack B. Yeats, *My beautiful, my beautiful!*, 1953, oil on canvas, 101.5 × 152.5 cm (private collection)

the tunnel, inject a forceful element into a picture that is predominantly blue, green, yellow and white. The mood is happy.

The horse's excitement at the proposed expedition with its master is a metaphor for Yeats's own positive attitude to life. He saw it as a progression towards a goal, if possible with a sympathetic companion. Thus the artist sets out on the picaresque journey of his book *The Charmed Life* (1938) as Mr No Matter travelling with Bowsie. That the goal is unstated, and may in fact never be reached, seems irrelevant. It is the road that is of interest to Yeats.

For the road is a painting of affection, expressing the silent understanding that can exist between two living creatures, and which he expressed in a more emotional way in *My beautiful, my beautiful!*, his great horse painting of 1953 (fig. 156). In a wider way, *For the road* implies the peace that is to be found beyond any kind of understanding, after the term in the thicket, and after the journey through the tunnel have been effected. It was painted in 1951.

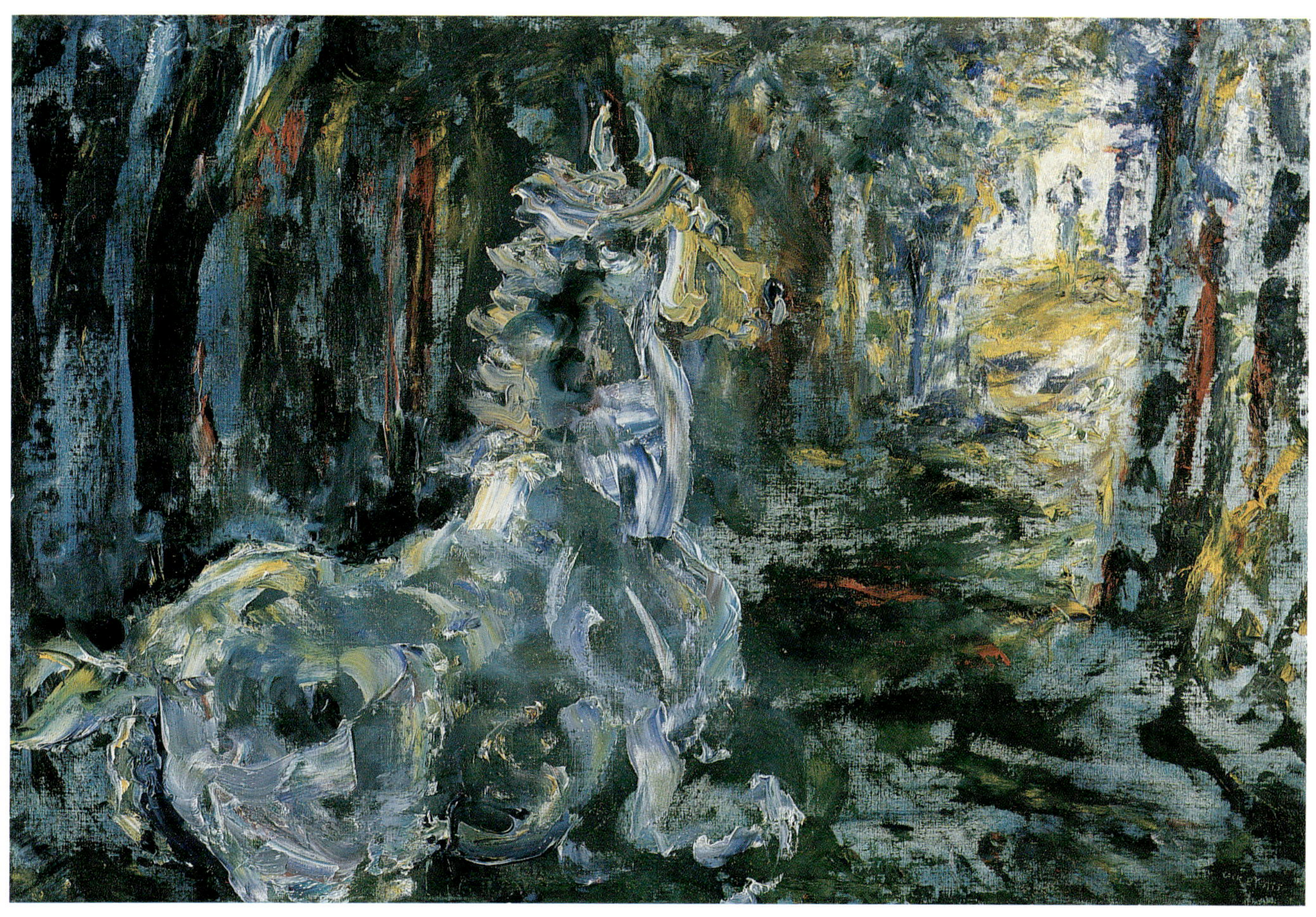

Anne Yeats born 1919

reativity in the Yeats family did not end with the spectacular achievement of the two generations whose genius spanned art and literature in Ireland for nearly a century. Currently, among the younger generation, there is a turn towards music and performance; but Anne Yeats, born in 1919, daughter of WBY, has preserved the succession of painters. From an early age she pursued an artistic career.

Her first work, after training at the Royal Hibernian Academy Schools under Maurice MacGonigal and Henry Tisdall, was as a stage designer, assistant to Tanya Moseiwitch in the Abbey Theatre. After a time at the Paul Collin School of Theatre Design in Paris, she returned to the Abbey as chief designer, making costumes and sets for some of her father's plays, as well as for others by Shaw, Lady Gregory and Austin Clarke, and the first production of her uncle's play *Harlequin's Positions*.

During the 1940s she decided to become a painter, though continuing as a freelance designer for a time. She participated in the first Irish Exhibition of Living Art in 1943, becoming closely associated with it, and so involved with the growing avantgarde of the day. She drew much in her early days from an identification with Parisian painters like Picasso, Matisse and Braque, whom she experienced initially in reproduction, and studied further during a second visit to Paris.

Her interest in the marginalized individuals of the Dublin streets led her to an exploration of loneliness, often with its comic side – visual wit has always been an important facet of her style. From her earliest period she painted the solitary people whom she observed about the Dublin streets and parks near her studio in Mount Street. These are objective studies in which the mannered style plays as important a part as her interest in individual character. Women in particular are a preoccupation, from the street walker to a young girl reading a letter or a woman watching the world through her window. Solitary women, she has said, are "probably me". Even in groups she draws attention to the gulf between people. In this painting of washerwomen resting during their work she represents them as separated by space and by their individual thoughts.

Women and washing was painted after a visit to Sicily in 1965. The artist spent six weeks touring there, as well as exploring the inland region. Her other paintings of Sicily are brightly coloured, but the sombre tones in this picture were dictated by the dark dress of the women and by the contrast of bright sunlight with the shadow. The absence of colour led her to round and simplify her images, and was eminently suitable for subject-matter of this kind, treated by the artist at a time when women's issues were beginning to be taken seriously. The picture was painted between June 1965 and July 1966, and exhibited for the first time in September 1966. When she lent it to the Jack B. Yeats Centenary Exhibition in Sligo Museum in 1971 she altered the title to *Women and washing, Sicily*.

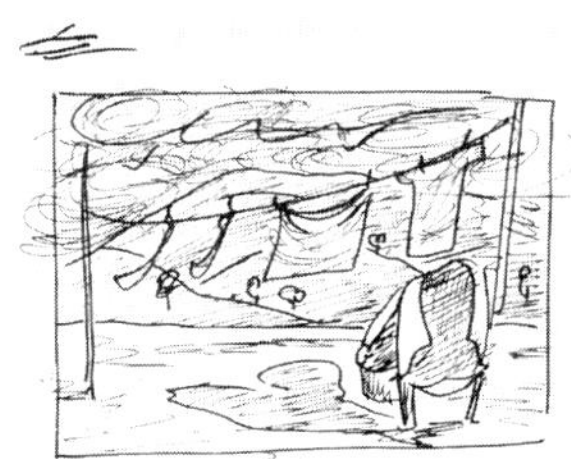
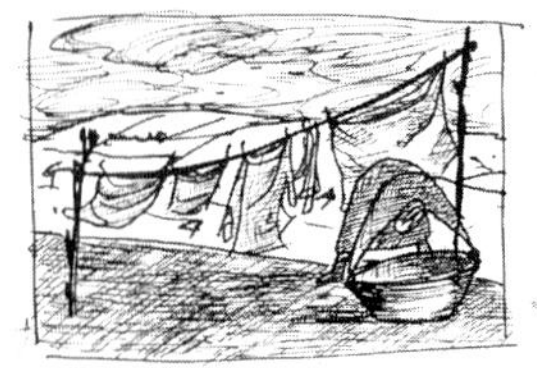
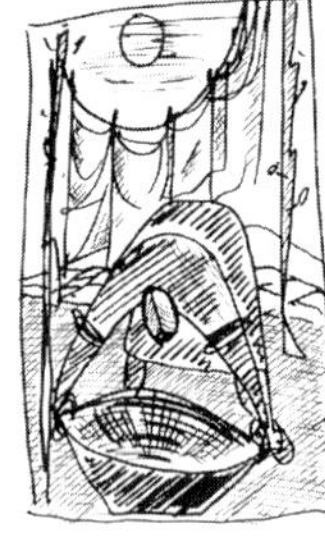

Fig. 157 Anne Yeats, *Woman and washing*, from a sketchbook (Anne Yeats Collection)

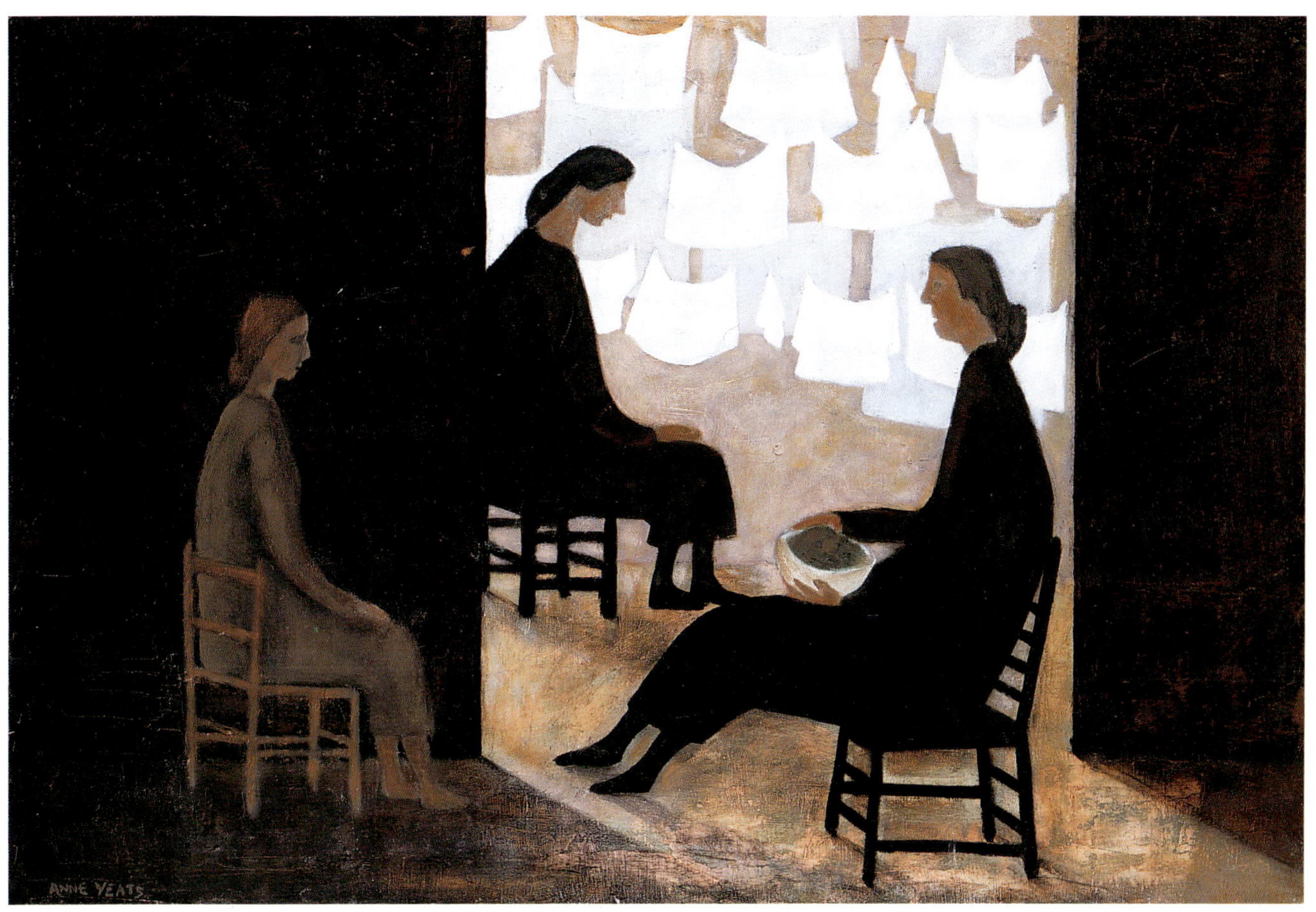

Technique has always been a major preoccupation with Anne Yeats. At an early stage she devised her own ink-and-wax manner, letting colour run into the hollows of coarse watercolour paper to create visual ambiguities in landscapes and figure scenes. This technique was soon developed in watercolour and wax, in which she worked larger portraits and character studies.

Still lifes of a later period were an occasion for further experimentation. She took butter muslin, soaked it in diluted oil pigment and pressed it to the canvas. When the fabric was removed, it left an imprint full of ambiguities, on which she superimposed apples or oranges or lemons. Her cloth technique has expanded over twenty years, in various manifestations, more recently in compositions with cat or bird, where the ambiguity between the artificial and what is observed initiates an underlying tension. For *Call down the hawk* (Samuel Beckett Theatre, Trinity College, Dublin), rags rather than muslin were used to spread the deep-blue pigment about the canvas, so creating a background of unceasing movement on to which she glazed the hawk image.

In *Green cloth floating* and companion water paintings of 1993 the muslin cloth print, combining with the overall colour, takes on an illusion of liquidity. It floats in a fusion of blue and green movement, created by sweeping strokes of the brush, which carries notions of abundant subliminal life. In this background, the cloth can appear almost as a human incursion, bending this way and that, but preserving a curious mythology of its own.

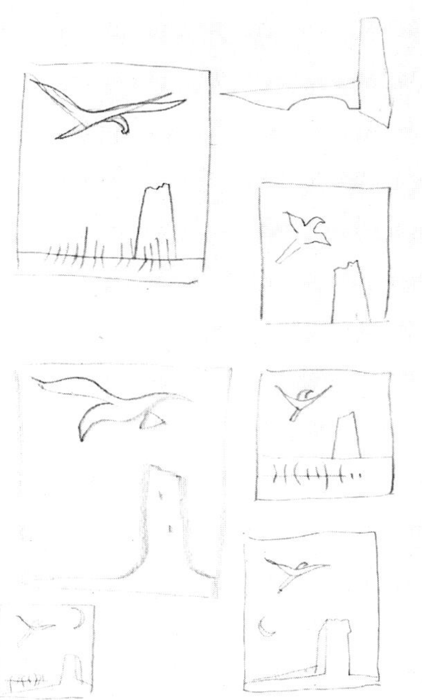

Fig. 158 Anne Yeats, *Hawk studies*, from a sketchbook (Anne Yeats Collection)

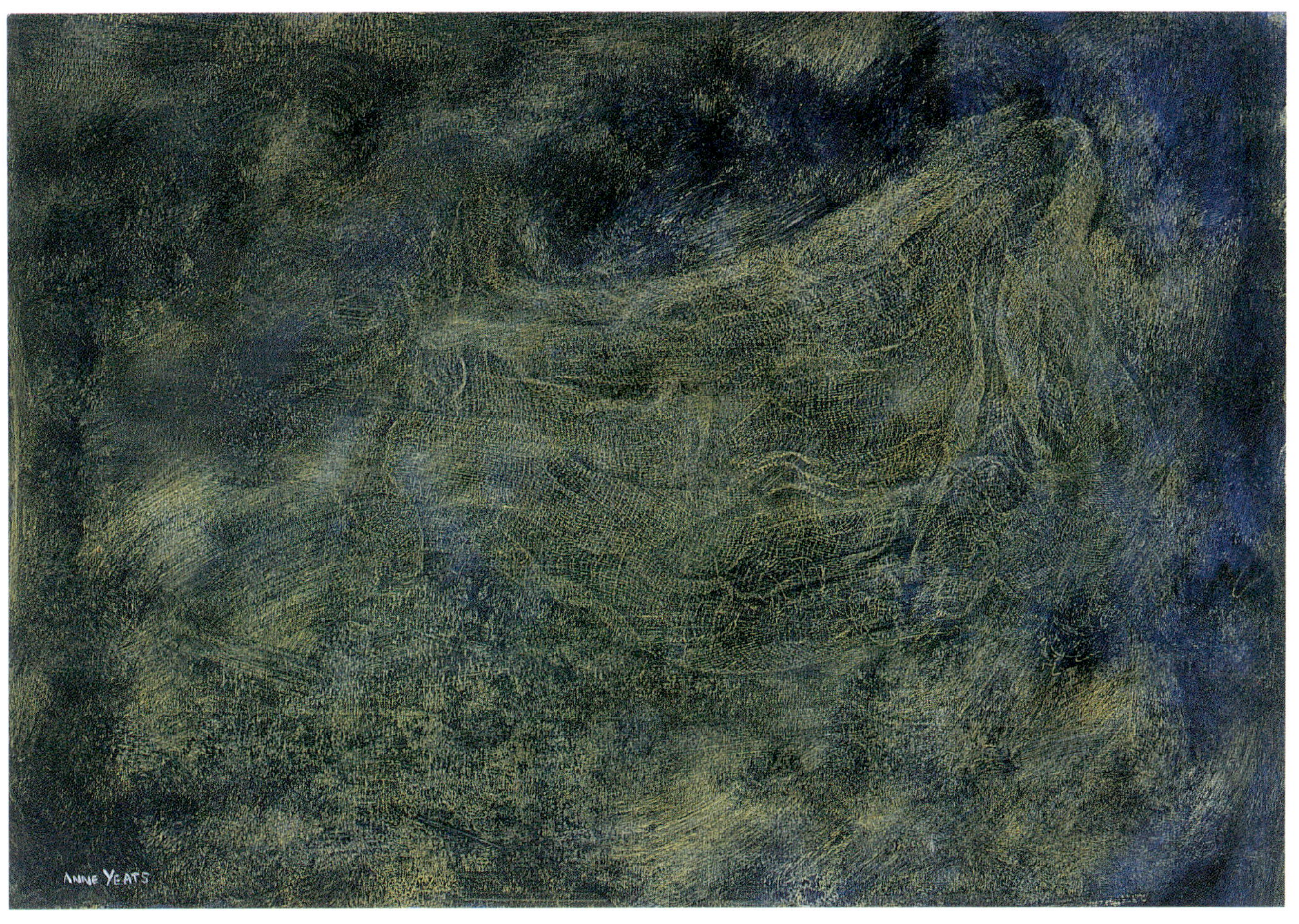
ANNE YEATS

Apparatus Criticus

John Butler Yeats
1830–1922

Sketch of James Whiteside,
QC, in court, 1866

NGI 2575, p. 46
Pencil, pen and sepia on paper
20.2 × 20.5 cm
Inscribed *Right Honble James Whiteside*
February – 1866 speaking in the
Fitzgerald will case
EXHIBITION
1972, Dublin, National Gallery of
Ireland, *Paintings and Drawings by*
John Butler Yeats from the Collection of
Senator Michael B. Yeats and the
National Gallery of Ireland, no. 7
PROVENANCE
Bought from the artist in 1904 for the
National Gallery of Ireland
Historical and Portrait Gallery

Pippa Passes, 1870–72

NGI 3531, p. 48
Gouache on paper, originally laid
down on wooden panel from which it
was removed in 1972
48 × 34 cm
EXHIBITIONS
1871, London, Dudley Gallery, *Group*
Exhibition
1873, Dublin, Industrial Exhibition
Palace, *Loan Museum of Art*, no. 620
1901, Dublin, no. 6, St Stephen's
Green, *Loan Collection of Pictures by*
Nathaniel Hone, R.H.A. and John
Butler Yeats, R.H.A., no. 71
1961, Manchester and Dublin, *W.B.*
Yeats: Images of a Poet, no. 197
1965, Dublin, National Gallery of
Ireland, *W.B. Yeats: A Centenary*
Exhibition, no. 92

1971, Cork, Crawford Municipal
Gallery, *Rosc Chorcaí: Irish Art in the*
19th century, no. 135
1972, Dublin, National Gallery of
Ireland, *Paintings and Drawings by*
John Butler Yeats from the Collection of
Senator Michael B. Yeats and the
National Gallery of Ireland, no. 2
1991, Dublin, National Gallery of
Ireland, *Irish Watercolours and*
Drawings, no. 75
LITERATURE
Murphy 1978, pp. 68–69, 74
M. Bourke, *Sacred Heart Messenger*,
September 1984, 'Pippa Passes'
pp. 47–49 (ill.)
National Gallery of Ireland: *Fifty Irish*
Drawings and Watercolours, 1986,
p. 36 (ill.)
Cullen 1987, pp. 21–22 (fig. 3)
P. Butler, *Three Hundred Years of Irish*
Watercolours and Drawings, 1990,
p. 164 (fig. 184)
PROVENANCE
Presented, Mr A.C. Hunt, 1962

Pippa, 1870

NGI 3253, p. 50
Black chalk on cream paper, originally
mounted on board
35 × 38 cm
Signed *JBY 1871*
EXHIBITIONS
1965, Dublin, National Gallery of
Ireland, *W.B. Yeats: A Centenary*
Exhibition, no. 93
1971, Cork, Crawford Art Gallery,
Rosc Chorcaí: Irish Art in the 19th
Century, no. 135
1972, Dublin, National Gallery of
Ireland, *Paintings and Drawings by*
John Butler Yeats from the Collection of
Senator Michael B. Yeats and the
National Gallery of Ireland, no. 3
LITERATURE
Murphy 1978, pp. 68–69, 74

M. Bourke, *Sacred Heart Messenger*,
September 1984, 'Pippa Passes',
pp. 47–49
Cullen 1987, pp. 40–41
Pyle 1989, pp. 10–11
PROVENANCE
Purchased from the Westminster Bank
Ltd in 1952

Landscape, 1871

NGI 3254, p. 52
Gouache on paper, originally lined
and attached to a stretcher backed by
canvas
25.2 × 35.1 cm
Signed: *JBY 1871*
EXHIBITION
1972, Dublin, National Gallery of
Ireland, *Paintings and Drawings by*
John Butler Yeats from the Collection of
Senator Michael B. Yeats and the
National Gallery of Ireland, no. 4
PROVENANCE
Purchased from the Westminster Bank
Ltd in 1952

The artist's wife, ca. 1875

NGI 1179, p. 54
Oil on canvas
61 × 71 cm
EXHIBITIONS
1965, Dublin, National Gallery of
Ireland, *W.B. Yeats: A Centenary*
Exhibition, no. 77
1971, Sligo and Dublin, *Jack B. Yeats*
and his Family, no. 56
1972, Dublin, National Gallery of
Ireland, *John Butler Yeats and the*
Irish Renaissance, no. 95 (plate 2)
PROVENANCE
Miss Lily Yeats; bequeathed to the
Friends of the National Collections
of Ireland, who presented it to the
National Gallery of Ireland in 1949

Hester Dowden as a child, 1879

NGI 1395, p. 56
Oil on canvas
76 × 63 cm
EXHIBITIONS
1881, Dublin, Royal Hibernian
    Academy, no. 112
1901, Dublin, no. 6, St Stephen's
    Green, *Loan Collection of Pictures by
    Nathaniel Hone, R.H.A. and John
    Butler Yeats*, R.H.A., no. 7
1907, Dublin, *International Exhibition*,
    no. 167
1965, Dublin, National Gallery of
    Ireland, *W.B. Yeats: A Centenary
    Exhibition*, no. 59
1972, Dublin, National Gallery of
    Ireland, *John Butler Yeats and the
    Irish Renaissance*, no. 91
PROVENANCE
Mrs Edward Dowden; Dr Travers
    Smith, from whom it passed to Mrs
    Lennox Robinson; purchased from
    Mrs L. Robinson in 1959

Frances Elizabeth Geoghegan as a child, ca. 1882

NGI 1343, p. 58
Oil on canvas
46 × 36 cm
EXHIBITION
1972, Dublin, National Gallery of
    Ireland, *John Butler Yeats and the
    Irish Renaissance*, no. 107
PROVENANCE
Bequeathed by Mrs Geoghegan in
    1956

Jack B. Yeats as a boy, ca. 1883–84

NGI 1142, p. 60
Oil on canvas
61 × 51 cm
EXHIBITIONS
1883, Dublin, Royal Hibernian
    Academy, no. 366
1951, Amsterdam, State Museum, *Irish
    Exhibition*, no. 57
1965, Dublin, National Gallery of
    Ireland, *W.B. Yeats: A Centenary
    Exhibition*, no. 80
1971, Sligo and Dublin, *Jack B. Yeats
    and his Family*, no. 55
1972, Dublin, National Gallery of
    Ireland, *John Butler Yeats and the
    Irish Renaissance*, no. 94
LITERATURE
Murphy 1978, p. 120
Ronald Anderson, *Irish Arts Review*, III,
    no. 3, autumn 1986, 'Whistler in
    Dublin 1884', pp. 45–51
PROVENANCE
Presented by Mr Jack B. Yeats, in
    accordance with the wishes of his
    deceased wife, in 1947

A young man of his country's service, 1885

NGI 19,238, p. 62
Black chalk, pencil and monochrome
wash on watercolour paper
35.7 × 25.6 cm
Stamped on verso DUBLIN SKETCHING
CLUB
Signed *JBYeats Decr. 3d 1885*
EXHIBITION
1986, Dublin, National Gallery of
    Ireland, *Acquisitions 1984–86*, no. 72
LITERATURE
Burlington Magazine, CXXVII, November
    1985, pp. 838–39, no. 4 (fig. 4)
PROVENANCE
Presented by Mr Peter B. and Mrs
    Susanne S. Franz, Michigan, in
    memory of his grandmother, Sarah
    L'Estrange Mahon (1827–1924), June
    1985

Sketches made at the Contemporary Club, 1886

(Six sketches mounted together, NGI 6078–83)

EXHIBITIONS
1901, Dublin, no. 6, St Stephen's
    Green, *Loan Collection of Pictures by
    Nathaniel Hone, R.H.A. and John
    Butler Yeats, R.H.A.*, no. 14
1972, Dublin, National Gallery of
    Ireland, *Paintings and Drawings by
    John Butler Yeats from the Collection of
    Senator Michael B. Yeats and the
    National Gallery of Ireland*, no. 21
LITERATURE
D. Daly, *The Young Douglas Hyde*,
    1974, pp. 75–77
M. Macken, *Studies*, March 1939,
    'Yeats, O'Leary and the
    Contemporary Club', pp. 136–42
H. Nicholls, *Irish Times*, 20–21
    December 1965, 'Memories of the
    Contemporary Club'
Cullen 1987, p. 54
PROVENANCE
Donated or sold by the artist to the
    Contemporary Club in 1886;
    presented by the then secretary of
    the Club, Mr Nicholl, to the
    National Museum in 1945;
    transferred from the Museum to the
    National Gallery of Ireland in 1966

William Morris at the Contemporary Club, April 1886

NGI 6078, p. 64
Pencil on buff paper
16.8 × 19 cm
Inscribed: *Author of "Earthly Paradise"*
W. Morris
LITERATURE
Murphy 1978, pp. 147 (ill.), 149,
    156–57
Cullen 1987, pp. 54–55

Professor Sullivan, President of University College, Cork, and William Morris

NGI 6079, p. 64
Pencil on paper
16.9 × 11.5 cm
Inscribed [beside head] *Professor Sullivan President of Cork College*

Arnold White and Mohini Chatterji, April 1886

NGI 6080, p 64
Pencil on paper
16.9 × 14.6 cm
Inscribed [under White] *Arnold White English Radical* [under Chatterji] *Mohini* [bottom edge] *April 17 1886*

John O'Leary

NGI 6081, p. 66
Pencil on unevenly cut paper
16.8 × 22 cm
Inscribed *"God in Heaven Id sooner march on Kerry – " John. O. Leary*
LITERATURE
Murphy 1978, p. 141 (ill.)

Dr MacDonnell reasoning with Mr Russell

NGI 6082, p. 66
Pencil on paper
16.8 × 11 cm
Inscribed *Dr Macdonnell reasoning* [inserted over 'arguing'] *with Mr Russell*
LITERATURE
E. O'Brien and A.O. Crookshank with Sir G. Wolstenholme, *A Portrait of Irish Medicine. An Illustrated History of Medicine in Ireland*, 1984, p. 46

Mr Taylor

NGI 6083, p. 66
Pencil on paper
16.8 × 20.3 cm
Inscribed *Mr. Taylor* [in top left corner] *26th*
LITERATURE
Murphy 1978, p. 143 (ill.)

(Nine sketches mounted together, NGI 7357–65)

Inscribed and signed on original mount: *Contemporary Club 1886 J B Yeats*
EXHIBITIONS
1901, Dublin, no. 6, St Stephen's Green, *Loan Collection of Pictures by Nathaniel Hone, R.H.A and John Butler Yeats, R.H.A.*, no. 15
1972, Dublin, National Gallery of Ireland, *Paintings and Drawings by John Butler Yeats from the Collection of Senator Michael B. Yeats and the National Gallery of Ireland*, no. 16
LITERATURE
M. Macken, *Studies*, March 1939, 'Yeats, O'Leary and the Contemporary Club', pp. 136–42
H. Nicholls, *Irish Times*, 20–21 December 1965, 'Memories of the Contemporary Club'
D. Daly, *The Young Douglas Hyde*, 1974, pp. 75–77
PROVENANCE
Donated or sold by the artist to the Contemporary Club in 1886; presented by the then secretary of the Club, Mr Nicholl, to the National Museum in 1945; transferred from the Museum to the National Gallery of Ireland in 1966

Arthur Patton, Mr Taylor (?) and T.W. Russell MP

NGI 7357, p. 68
Pencil on paper
16.7 × 21.7 cm
Inscribed [top right] */86* [part of word] [under left hand figure] *Arthur Patton* [under figure on extreme right] *T.W. Russell M.P.*

William Thomas Stead, of the Pall Mall Club, London

NGI. 7358, p. 68
Pencil on unevenly cut buff paper
7.8 × 7.8 cm
Inscribed *Mr Stead. of the Pall Mall*

Mr Oldham

NGI 7359, p. 68
Pencil on buff paper
16.6 × 13 cm
Inscribed *Mr Oldham*
LITERATURE
Murphy 1978, p. 140

Mr Bailey

NGI 7360, p. 68
Pencil on buff paper, unevenly cut
16.5 × 7.9 cm
Inscribed *Mr. Bailey*

Alfred Percival Graves

NGI 7361, p. 70
Pencil on paper
7.8 × 7.2 cm
Inscribed *A. Graves – poet*

Mr Crooks and Mr Doherty

NGI 7362, p. 70
Pencil on paper
16.7 × 18 cm
Inscribed: [under the left figure] *Mr. Crooks* [under right hand figure] *Mr. Doherty who built O'Connell Bridge*

Mr Bailey, Mr Walker and Mr J. Hogg

NGI 7363, p. 70
Pencil on buff paper
16.7 × 23 cm
Inscribed [under figure on left] *Mr. Bailey* [under central figure] *Mr. Walker* [under figure on right] *Mr. I. Hogg*

George Coffey and Mr McNiffe

NGI 7364, p. 70
Pencil on buff paper, unevenly cut
7.9 × 10.3 cm
Inscribed [over the left figure] *G. Coffey* [over the right hand figure] *Mr. McNiffe*

Mohini Chatterji

NGI. 7365, p. 70
Pencil on paper, unevenly cut
16.7 × 13.4 cm
Inscribed *Mohini*

Pencil portrait of William Butler Yeats, 1886

NGI 3256, p. 72
Pencil on paper
15 × 23.5 cm
Signed *JBYeats*
LITERATURE
Murphy 1978, p. 137
Cullen 1987, pp. 58–59
PROVENANCE
Presented by Miss Alice Digby, with four other drawings, in 1944

A group of four portrait sketches, 1886–87?

LITERATURE
Murphy 1978, p. 163, 165, 169
PROVENANCE
Presented by Miss Alice Digby in 1944

Seated lady

NGI 2727, p. 74
Pencil on paper
23.5 × 15 cm
Signed *JBYeats*

Gentleman smoking a cheroot

NGI 2986, p. 74
Pencil on paper
19.3 × 11.7 cm
Drawing on verso of a man wearing a tam-o'-shanter

Lady and gentleman in conversation

NGI. 3257, p. 74
Pencil on paper
23.5 × 15 cm
Signed *JBYeats*

Standing lady

NGI 7683, p. 74
Pencil on paper
23.5 × 15 cm
Signed *JBYeats*

John O'Leary, 1887

NGI 1963, p. 76
Oil on canvas
92 × 71 cm
Signed *JBYeats 1887*
EXHIBITION
1887, Dublin, Royal Hibernian Academy, no. 132
PROVENANCE
Transferred from the National Museum in 1969

Jack B. Yeats, 1890

NGI 4040, p. 78
Oil on canvas
61 × 51cm
Signed *JBY '90* [indistinctly]
EXHIBITIONS
1967, London, St Michael's Vicarage, Bedford Park, *Artists and Architecture of Bedford Park 1875–1900*, no. 10e (ill.)
1972, Dublin, National Gallery of Ireland, *John Butler Yeats and the Irish Renaissance*, no. 113 (plate 7)
PROVENANCE
Presented by Mr V. Waddington, 1972

Violet Osborne, 1891

NGI 4032, p. 80
Oil on canvas
61 × 51 cm
Signed *JB Yeats 1891*
EXHIBITION
1972, Dublin, National Gallery of
Ireland, *John Butler Yeats and the
Irish Renaissance*, no. 111
LITERATURE
J. Sheehy, *Walter Osborne*, Cork
(Gifford & Craven) 1979, no. 90
PROVENANCE
Miss V. Stockley Bequest, 1971

John O'Leary, 1891

NGI 595, p. 82
Oil on canvas
91 × 71 cm
EXHIBITIONS
1891, Dublin, Royal Hibernian
Academy, no. 203
1901, Dublin, no. 6, St Stephen's
Green, *Loan Collection of Pictures by
Nathaniel Hone, R.H.A. and John
Butler Yeats, R.H.A.*, no. 53
LITERATURE
Murphy 1978, p. 235
R. Anderson, *Apollo*, 1986, 'Whistler:
an Irish rebel and Ireland', pp.
254–58
J.B. Yeats, 1972, p. 4
PROVENANCE
John O'Leary; bequeathed to the
National Literary Society, who
presented it to the National Gallery
in 1908

Pencil portrait of Douglas Hyde, 1898

NGI 2947, p. 84
Pencil on paper
32 × 25.2 cm
Signed *JBY*[eats] *1898* [twice]
EXHIBITIONS
1901, Dublin, no. 6, St Stephen's
Green, *Loan Collection of Pictures by
Nathaniel Hone, R.H.A. and John
Butler Yeats, R.H.A.*, no. 32
1965, Dublin, National Gallery of
Ireland, *W.B. Yeats: A Centenary
Exhibition*, no. 40
1972, Dublin, National Gallery of
Ireland, *Paintings and Drawings by
John Butler Yeats from the Collection of
Senator Michael B. Yeats and the
National Gallery of Ireland*, no. 35
LITERATURE
G. O'Malley and D.T. Torchiana, *Irish
Renaissance: A Gathering*, p. 57: edd.
R. Skelton and D.R. Clark, 'John
Butler Yeats to Lady Gregory: new
letters'
PROVENANCE
Purchased, Coole Park, Lady Gregory
Sale, 1932

Pencil portrait of George William Russell (A.E.), 1898

NGI 2943, p. 86
Pencil on paper with a faint
watermark
31.8 × 25.2 cm
Signed *JBYeats 1898 Jany*
EXHIBITED
1901, Dublin, no. 6, St Stephen's
Green, *Loan Collection of Pictures by
Nathaniel Hone, R.H.A. and John
Butler Yeats, R.H.A.*, no. 38
PROVENANCE
Purchased, Coole Park, Lady Gregory
Sale, 1932

Wash study portrait of William Butler Yeats, 1898

NGI 2942, p. 88
Monochrome watercolour with
gouache, mounted on board
35.6 × 25.3 cm
Signed *JBYeats 1898*
EXHIBITIONS
1961, Manchester and Dublin,
W.B. Yeats: Images of a Poet, no. 12
1965, Dublin, National Gallery of
Ireland, *W.B. Yeats: A Centenary
Exhibition*, no. 3
1972, Dublin, National Gallery of
Ireland, *Paintings and Drawings by
John Butler Yeats from the Collection of
Senator Michael B. Yeats and the
National Gallery of Ireland*, no. 36
1976, Dublin, National Gallery of
Ireland, and Dallas, Museum of Fine
Arts, *Irish Watercolours 1675–1925*,
no. 53
1991, Dublin, National Gallery of
Ireland, *Irish Watercolours and
Drawings*, no. 74
LITERATURE
Murphy 1978, p. 203
Cullen 1981, p. 64
PROVENANCE
Purchased, Coole Park, Lady Gregory
Sale, 1932

Pencil portrait of Jack B. Yeats, 1899

NGI 2945, p. 90
Pencil on paper
29 × 22.8cm
Signed *JBYeats May* [indistinctly] –
1899 –
Inscribed on reverse *Post to Lady Gregory, Coole Park, Gort, Galway, Ireland*
EXHIBITION
1972, Dublin, National Gallery of Ireland, *Paintings and Drawings by John Butler Yeats from the Collection of Senator Michael B. Yeats and the National Gallery of Ireland*, no. 45
PROVENANCE
Purchased, Coole Park, Lady Gregory Sale, 1932

Pencil portrait of Edward Martyn, 1899

NGI 2941, p. 92
Pencil on Whatman paper
28.3 × 22.8 cm
Signed *JBYeats 1899*
Inscribed *Edward Martyn* [in another hand]
EXHIBITIONS
1901, Dublin, no. 6, St Stephen's Green, *Loan Collection of Pictures by Nathaniel Hone, R.H.A. and John Butler Yeats, R.H.A.,* no. 33
1972, Dublin, National Gallery of Ireland, *Paintings and Drawings by John Butler Yeats from the Collection of Senator Michael B. Yeats and the National Gallery of Ireland*, no. 47 (plate 15)
LITERATURE
Murphy 1978, p. 238
PROVENANCE
Purchased, Coole Park, Lady Gregory Sale, 1932

Susan L. Mitchell, 1899

NGI 1298, p. 94
Oil on canvas
79 × 56 cm
Signed *JB Yeats 1899*
EXHIBITION
1972, Dublin, National Gallery of Ireland, *John Butler Yeats and the Irish Renaissance*, no. 112 (plate 24)
LITERATURE
Irish Arts Review, 1988, p. 90
H. Pyle, *Irish Arts Review Yearbook 1991–92*, 'External things and images', pp. 165–70 (ill.)
PROVENANCE
Purchased from the poet's niece, Miss K. Brabazon, in 1954

William Butler Yeats, 1900

NGI 872, p. 96
Oil on canvas
77 × 64 cm
Signed *JB Yeats 1900*
EXHIBITIONS
1946, Edinburgh, Society of Scottish Artists
1961, Manchester and Dublin, *W.B. Yeats: Images of a Poet*, no. 14
1965, Dublin, National Gallery of Ireland, *W.B. Yeats: A Centenary Exhibition*, no. 2
1966, Dublin, National Gallery of Ireland, *Cuimhneachán 1916*, no. 140
1971, Sligo and Dublin, *Jack B. Yeats and his Family*, no. 64
1972, Dublin, National Gallery of Ireland, *John Butler Yeats and the Irish Renaissance*, no. 115 (plate 3)
1974, Columbus, Toledo and St. Louis, *Aspects of Irish Art*, no. 76
LITERATURE
'The heroic energy of Cuchulain', *Apollo*, October 1966, p. 257 (ill.)
M. Wynne, *National Gallery of Ireland: Fifty Irish Painters*, 1983, p. 42 (ill.)
PROVENANCE
Purchased from the artist by John Quinn; Quinn Sale, 1926, purchased by Mr C. Sullivan and presented to the National Gallery in memory of Mr J. Quinn

Susan Mary (Lily) Yeats, 1900–01

NGI 1180, p. 98
Oil on canvas
91 × 71 cm
Signed *JB Yeats 1901*
EXHIBITIONS
1904, London, Guildhall, *Loan Collection of Irish Pictures*
1965, Dublin, National Gallery of Ireland, *W.B. Yeats: A Centenary Exhibition*, no. 76
1972, Dublin, National Gallery of Ireland, *John Butler Yeats and the Irish Renaissance*, no. 117 (plate 5)
LITERATURE
Cullen 1987 (fig. 1)
PROVENANCE
Presented to the Gallery by the Friends of the National Collections of Ireland in 1949

Rosa Butt, 1900

NGI 1724, p. 100
Oil on canvas
92 × 71 cm
Signed *JB Yeats 1900*
EXHIBITIONS
1901, Dublin, Royal Hibernian Academy, no. 186
1965, Dublin, National Gallery of Ireland, *W.B. Yeats: A Centenary Exhibition*, no. 48
1966, Nenagh, St Joseph's Hall, *1916 Jubilee Exhibition*
1972, Dublin, National Gallery of Ireland, *John Butler Yeats and the Irish Renaissance,* no. 116
PROVENANCE
Presented by Sir William Ball (whose wife was a niece of Rosa Butt), 1960

Isaac Butt, 1901 (from an original 1876)

NGI 2442, p. 102
Black chalk with white highlights on paper
69.9 × 56 cm
EXHIBITIONS
1902, Cork, Fitzgerald's Park, *International Exhibition*, no. 491
1965, Dublin, National Gallery of Ireland, *W.B. Yeats: A Centenary Exhibition*, no. 28
1970, Dublin, National Gallery of Ireland, *Art and Oratory*, no. 60
1972, Dublin, National Gallery of Ireland, *Paintings and Drawings by John Butler Yeats from the Collection of Senator Michael B. Yeats and the National Gallery of Ireland*, no. 15
LITERATURE
T. de V. White, *The Road of Excess*, 1946, p. 198
Irish Review, III, no. 35, January 1914, frontispiece, facing p. 553
PROVENANCE
Commissioned from the artist in 1901 for the National Gallery of Ireland Historical and Portrait Gallery

Two pencil portraits of W.K. Magee (John Eglinton)

W.K. Magee, November 1901

NGI 2944, p. 104
Pencil on buff paper
29.2 × 21.3cm
Signed *JBYeats Nov–1901–*
Inscribed JOHN EGLINTON [by another hand]
EXHIBITIONS
1965, Dublin, National Gallery of Ireland, *W.B.Yeats: A Centenary Exhibition*, no. 69
1972, Dublin, National Gallery of Ireland, *Paintings and Drawings by John Butler Yeats from the Collection of Senator Michael B. Yeats and the National Gallery of Ireland*, no. 53
LITERATURE
Cullen 1987, p. 87
PROVENANCE
Purchased, Coole Park, Lady Gregory Sale, 1932

W.K. Magee, December 1901

NGI 2985, p. 104
Pencil on unevenly cut buff paper
38 × 26.8 cm
Signed *Decr 1901. JBYeats –*
EXHIBITIONS
1965, Dublin, National Gallery of Ireland, *W.B. Yeats: A Centenary Exhibition*, no. 39
1972, Dublin, National Gallery of Ireland, *Paintings and Drawings by John Butler Yeats from the Collection of Senator Michael B. Yeats and the National Gallery of Ireland*, no. 52 (plate 23)
LITERATURE
Cullen 1987, p. 87
PROVENANCE
Presented to the Gallery, through his brother J.H. Magee, by W.K. Magee, 1943

Mrs Lenny, 1902

NGI 1004, p. 106
Oil on canvas
66 × 51 cm
Signed *JB Yeats 1902*
EXHIBITION
1902, Dublin, Royal Hibernian Academy, no. 60
PROVENANCE
Miss K. Lenny Bequest, 1938

Pencil portrait of Standish James O'Grady, 1902

NGI 2936, p. 108
Pencil on paper backed by board
34 × 22.6 cm
Signed *JBYeats May 3rd 1902*
Inscribed *Standish O'Grady* [in another hand]
EXHIBITIONS
1965, Dublin, National Gallery of Ireland, *W.B. Yeats: A Centenary Exhibition*, no. 38
1972, Dublin, National Gallery of Ireland, *Paintings and Drawings by John Butler Yeats from the Collection of Senator Michael B. Yeats and the National Gallery of Ireland*, no. 55
1980, Chicago, *Ireland's Literary Renaissance: 20th century portraits*
LITERATURE
Murphy 1978, p. 275
PROVENANCE
Purchased, Coole Park, Lady Gregory Sale, 1932

Pencil portrait of Kuno Meyer, ca. 1903

NGI 331, p. 110
Pencil on paper
19.7 × 11.9 cm
On reverse *Kuno Meyer, drawing by J.B. Yeats RHA about 1900*
EXHIBITION
1972, Dublin, National Gallery of Ireland, *Paintings and Drawings by John Butler Yeats from the Collection of Senator Michael B. Yeats and the*

National Gallery of Ireland, no. 49
(plate 25)
LITERATURE
Murphy 1978, pp. 249, 321 *etc*
PROVENANCE
Bequeathed by Dr R.I. Best in 1959

Lady Gregory, 1903

NGI 1318, p. 112
Oil on canvas
62 × 52 cm
Signed *JB Yeats 1903*
EXHIBITIONS
1965, Dublin, National Gallery of
   Ireland, *W.B. Yeats: A Centenary
   Exhibition*, no. 68
1966, Nenagh, St Joseph's Hall, *1916
   Jubilee Exhibition*
1972, Dublin National Gallery of
   Ireland, *John Butler Yeats and the
   Irish Renaissance*, no. 119 (plate 13)
1987–88, London, Barbican Art
   Gallery, *The Edwardian Era*
PROVENANCE
Presented to the Gallery by the
   Friends of the National Collections
   of Ireland, 1956

George William Russell (A.E.), 1903

NGI 871, p. 114
Oil on canvas
112 × 87 cm
Signed *JB Yeats 1903*
EXHIBITIONS
1903, Dublin, Royal Hibernian
   Academy, no. 84
1965, Dublin, National Gallery of
   Ireland, *W.B. Yeats: A Centenary
   Exhibition*, no. 55
1967, Dublin, National Gallery of
   Ireland, *George Russell (AE):
   Centenary Exhibition*
1972, Dublin, National Gallery of
   Ireland, *John Butler Yeats and the
   Irish Renaissance*, no. 120 (plate 19)
1979–80, Dublin, National Gallery of
   Ireland, and London, Fine Art
   Society, *The Abbey Theatre
   1904–1979*, no. 12

LITERATURE
Letters from A.E., ed. A. Denson, 1961,
   pp. 43, 49
PROVENANCE
Commissioned from the artist by John
   Quinn; Quinn Sale, 1926, purchased
   by Mr C. Sullivan and presented to
   the National Gallery in memory of
   Mr J. Quinn

Ruth Lane, 1904

NGI 1800, p. 116
Oil on canvas
60 × 51.5 cm
EXHIBITION
1972, Dublin, National Gallery of
   Ireland, *John Butler Yeats and the
   Irish Renaissance*, no. 105
LITERATURE
A. Gregory, *Hugh Lane's Life and
   Achievement*, 1921, pp. 34–40, 160–61
Murphy 1978, p. 272
B. Dawson, *Images and Insights*, 1993,
   p. 15
PROVENANCE
Purchased from Mrs Heaven
   through Sir Alec Martin by Dr T.
   MacGreevy, who presented it to the
   National Gallery in 1966

John O'Leary, 1904

NGI 869, p. 118
Oil on canvas
112 × 87 cm
Signed *JB Yeats 1904*, and inscribed
with the same
EXHIBITIONS
1904, London, Guildhall, *Loan
   Collection of Irish Pictures*
1910, New York, Independent Artists,
   Spring & Autumn Exhibitions
1951, Amsterdam, State Museum, *Irish
   Exhibition*, no. 48
1961, Manchester and Dublin,
   W.B. Yeats: Images of a Poet, no. 93
1964, Dublin, National Gallery of
   Ireland, *National Gallery of Ireland
   1864–1964: Centenary Exhibition*, no.
   174

1965, Dublin, National Gallery of
   Ireland, *W.B. Yeats: A Centenary
   Exhibition*, no. 61
1966, Dublin, National Gallery of
   Ireland, *Cuimhneachán 1916*, no. 24
1971, Sligo and Dublin, *Jack B. Yeats
   and his Family*, no. 72
1972, Dublin, National Gallery of
   Ireland, *John Butler Yeats and the
   Irish Renaissance*, no. 123 (plate 9)
1980, Chicago, *Ireland's Literary
   Renaissance: 20th Century Portraits*,
   no. 3
LITERATURE
Cullen 1987, fig. 2
J.B. Yeats 1923, p. 42
PROVENANCE
Commissioned from the artist by John
   Quinn; Quinn Sale, 1926, purchased
   by Mr C. Sullivan and presented to
   the National Gallery in memory of
   Mr J. Quinn

Standish James O'Grady, 1904

NGI. 870, p. 120
Oil on canvas
112 × 87 cm
Signed *JB Yeats 1904*
EXHIBITIONS
1906, Dublin, Royal Hibernian
   Academy, no. 76
1970, Dublin, *Art and Oratory:
   Bicentenary of the College Historical
   Society*, no. 82
1972, Dublin, National Gallery of
   Ireland, *John Butler Yeats and the
   Irish Renaissance*, no. 125 (plate 10)
LITERATURE
A. Gregory, *Hugh Lane's Life and
   Achievement*, 1921, p. 35
Reid 1968, p. 29
Murphy 1978, pp. 277, 430
PROVENANCE
Commissioned by John Quinn in 1904;
   Quinn Sale, 1926, purchased by Mr
   C. Sullivan and presented to the
   National Gallery in memory of Mr J.
   Quinn

Pencil portrait of William George Fay, 1904

NGI 2946, p. 122
Pencil on paper
17.5 × 13.1 cm
Signed *WGFay – August 7th 1904 JBYeats*
EXHIBITION
1965, Dublin, National Gallery of Ireland, *W.B.Yeats: A Centenary Exhibition*, no. 126
1972, Dublin, National Gallery of Ireland, *Paintings and Drawings by John Butler Yeats from the Collection of Senator Michael B. Yeats and the National Gallery of Ireland*, no. 77
LITERATURE
M. Nic Shiubhlaigh and E. Kenny, *The Splendid Years*, 1955, pp. 5–8, 57–58 *etc*
Murphy 1978, pp. 249, 276
M. O hAodha, *Pictures at the Abbey*, 1983, pp. 11–12, 24
PROVENANCE
Purchased, Coole Park, Lady Gregory Sale, 1932

Máire Nic Shiubhlaigh, 1904

NGI 4621, p. 124
Oil on canvas
91 × 71 cm
Signed *JBYeats 1904* [twice]
LITERATURE
M. Nic Shiubhlaigh and E. Kenny, *The Splendid Years*, 1955
M. O hAodha, *Pictures at the Abbey*, 1983, pp. 36–38
PROVENANCE
J.E. Taylor, Chapellier Gallery, New York, from whom purchased by Mrs J. Murray Mitchell, Lismore, Fort William, in August 1966; presented to the National Gallery of Ireland by Nicholas Burke, in memory of his mother Mrs J. Murray Mitchell, in 1996

Pencil portrait of John Millington Synge, 1905

NGI 2937, p. 126
Pencil on paper
31.6 × 25 cm
Signed *JBYeats 1905 – Jany J.M. Synge*
EXHIBITIONS
1965, National Gallery of Ireland, Dublin, *W.B. Yeats: A Centenary Exhibition*, no. 110
1967, London and New York, *Drawings from the National Gallery of Ireland*, no. 92
1972, Dublin, National Gallery of Ireland, *Paintings and Drawings by John Butler Yeats from the Collection of Senator Michael B. Yeats and the National Gallery of Ireland*, no. 72
1979–80, Dublin, National Gallery of Ireland, and London, Fine Art Society, *The Abbey Theatre 1904–1979*, no. 7
LITERATURE
Murphy 1978, p. 285
Ed. A. Saddlemyer, J.M. Synge, *Letters to Molly*, 1971, p. 148
PROVENANCE
Purchased, Coole Park, Lady Gregory Sale, 1932

Reverend Patrick S. Dineen, 1905

NGI 910, p. 128
Oil on canvas
77 × 64 cm
Signed *JB Yeats, 1905* [with a second, fainter signature]
EXHIBITION
1972, Dublin, National Gallery of Ireland, *John Butler Yeats and the Irish Renaissance*, no. 127
LITERATURE
P. O Conluain and D. O Céileachair, *An Duinníneach*, 1958, ill. p. 64
Murphy 1978, p. 249
PROVENANCE
Presented by Mr W.B. Yeats in 1928

Pencil portrait of Hugh Lane, 1905

NGI 2866, p. 130
Pencil on white card
17.5 × 12.7 cm
Signed *August 1905 JBYeats*
EXHIBITIONS
1965, Dublin, National Gallery of Ireland, *W.B. Yeats: A Centenary Exhibition*, no. 60
1967, London and New York, *Drawings from the National Gallery of Ireland*, no. 93
1972, Dublin, National Gallery of Ireland, *Paintings and Drawings by John Butler Yeats from the Collection of Senator Michael B. Yeats and the National Gallery of Ireland*, no. 73 (plate 14)
LITERATURE
C.J. White, *Master Drawings*, 1967, pp. 411–12, 'The Dublin drawings in London'
T. Crombie, *Apollo*, LXXXV, June 1967, p. 460, 'Drawings from Dublin'
PROVENANCE
Presented by Miss Lily and Miss Elizabeth Corbet Yeats in 1919

George Moore, 1905

NGI 873, p. 132
Oil on canvas
77 × 64 cm
Signed *JB Yeats 1905*
EXHIBITIONS
1951, Amsterdam, State Museum, *Irish Exhibition*, no. 45
1965, Dublin, National Gallery of Ireland, *W.B. Yeats: A Centenary Exhibition*, no. 113
1972, Dublin, National Gallery of Ireland, *John Butler Yeats and the Irish Renaissance*, no. 126 (plate 17)
1974, Columbus, Toledo and St. Louis, *Aspects of Irish Art*, no. 74
1979–80, Dublin, National Gallery of Ireland and London, Fine Art Society, *The Abbey Theatre 1904–1979*, no. 14
1980, Chicago, *Ireland's Literary*

Renaissance: 20th Century Portraits,
no. 18
LITERATURE
A. Stewart, *National Gallery of Ireland:
Fifty Irish Portraits*, 1984, p. 43 (ill.)
PROVENANCE
Commissioned from the artist by John
Quinn in 1905; Quinn Sale, 1926,
purchased by Mr C. Sullivan and
presented to the National Gallery in
memory of Mr J. Quinn

Douglas Hyde, 1906

NGI 874, p. 134
Oil on canvas
107 × 86 cm
Signed *JBYeats 1906* [faintly]
Inscribed *John B. Yeats, RHA 1906*
EXHIBITIONS
1972, Dublin, National Gallery of
Ireland, *John Butler Yeats and the
Irish Renaissance*, no. 128 (plate 18)
1979–80, Dublin, National Gallery of
Ireland and London, Fine Art
Society, *The Abbey Theatre 1904–
1979*, no. 17
LITERATURE
A. Gregory, *Hugh Lane's Life and
Achievement*, 1921, p. 36
Murphy 1978, p. 286
PROVENANCE
Commissioned from the artist by John
Quinn; Quinn Sale, 1926, purchased
by Mr C. Sullivan and presented to
the National Gallery in memory of
Mr J. Quinn

Pencil portrait of Richard Irvine Best, 1906

NGI 3307, p. 136
Pencil on unevenly cut paper
34.5 × 25 cm
Signed *Nov. 1906 – JBYeats*
EXHIBITION
1972, Dublin, National Gallery of
Ireland, *Paintings and Drawings by
John Butler Yeats from the Collection of
Senator Michael B. Yeats and the
National Gallery of Ireland*, no. 74
PROVENANCE
Bequeathed by the sitter in 1959

Mrs Best at the piano, 1907

NGI 3310, p. 138
Pencil on paper
22.7 × 14 cm
Signed *JBY – Jan 16th 1907*
Inscribed [on reverse in pencil]
Best Esq.
EXHIBITION
1972, Dublin, National Gallery of
Ireland, *Paintings and Drawings by
John Butler Yeats from the Collection of
Senator Michael B. Yeats and the
National Gallery of Ireland*, no. 76
PROVENANCE
Bequeathed by Dr R.I. Best in 1959

Maud Gonne MacBride, 1907

NGI 7712, p. 140
Pencil, watercolour and crayon on
paper
46 × 24 cm
Signed *JBYeats 1907*
LITERATURE
Murphy 1978, p. 584, n. 44
PROVENANCE
Purchased from Mrs Kerrigan, Cork,
1974

Pencil portrait of J.M. Kerrigan, 1911

NGI 3290, p. 142
Pencil on heavyweight card
27.3 × 33 cm
Signed *JBYeats 1911*, and autographed
by J.M. Kerrigan
EXHIBITIONS
1965, Dublin, National Gallery of
Ireland, *W.B. Yeats: A Centenary
Exhibition*, no. 136
1972, Dublin, National Gallery of
Ireland, *Paintings and Drawings by
John Butler Yeats from the Collection of
Senator Michael B. Yeats and the
National Gallery of Ireland*, no. 83
(plate 31)
1979–80, Dublin, National Gallery of
Ireland and London, Fine Art

Society, *The Abbey Theatre 1904–
1979*, no. 26
1980, Chicago, *Ireland's Literary
Renaissance: 20th Century Portraits*,
no. 32
LITERATURE
Murphy 1978, pp. 390–91, 405
M. O hAodha, *Pictures at the Abbey*,
1983, pp. 8, 18
Cullen 1987, pp. 102–05
PROVENANCE
Presented by the Friends of the
National Collections of Ireland in
1956

Two portraits of Mrs Mary Tower Lapsley Caughey, 1916

EXHIBITION
1972, Dublin, National Gallery of
Ireland, *John Butler Yeats and the
Irish Renaissance*
LITERATURE
Murphy 1978, p. 435
PROVENANCE
Presented by Mrs M. Lapsley
Caughey-Guest in 1961

Mrs Mary Tower Lapsley Caughey standing

NGI 1727, p. 144
Oil on canvas
102 × 71 cm
Signed *JB Yeats 1916*

Mrs Mary Tower Lapsley Caughey seated

NGI 1726, p. 144
Oil on canvas
102 × 76 cm
Signed *JB Yeats 1916*

Mary Lapsley Caughey, 1916

NGI 1821, p. 146
Oil on canvas
105 × 84 cm
Signed *JB Yeats 1916*
EXHIBITION
1972, Dublin, National Gallery of
Ireland, *John Butler Yeats and the
Irish Renaissance*, no. 130
PROVENANCE
Mrs M. Lapsley Caughey-Guest,
Bequest, 1967

Pencil portrait of Ernest Boyd, 1920

NGI 3288, p. 148
Charcoal and pencil on card
50.7 × 38 cm
Signed *JBYeats Oct 1920 NY–*
EXHIBITION
1972, Dublin, National Gallery of
Ireland, *Paintings and Drawings by John
Butler Yeats from the Collection of
Senator Michael B. Yeats and the
National Gallery of Ireland*, no. 85
(plate 26)
PROVENANCE
Presented by Mrs McKinley Hayes in
1955

Two sketch self-portraits, 1920

Sketch self-portrait

NGI 6313, p. 150
Pencil with some crayon on buff
paper
48.4 × 37.8 cm
Signed *To John Quinn from JBYeats
1920 –*
EXHIBITION
1988, Dublin, National Gallery of
Ireland, *Acquisitions 1986–8*, no. 31
PROVENANCE
Purchased from the Dawson Gallery,
Dublin, 3 October 1951 by Mr John
L. Sweeney, USA; Máire MacNeill,
Bequest in memory of her husband,
John L. Sweeney, 1987

Sketch self-portrait

NGI 19,341, p. 150
Charcoal on buff paper
49.5 × 39.4 cm
Inscribed with numbers in lower
corners
EXHIBITIONS
1971, Sligo, *Jack B. Yeats and his Family*,
no. 78
1976, Dallas, *Exhibition of Irish Art*
1980, Chicago, *Ireland's Literary
Renaissance: 20th century portraits*,
no. 8

LITERATURE
Murphy 1978, pp. 384–86, 398,
498–501
Cullen 1987, pp. 108–11
PROVENANCE
Given by the artist to Mrs Ernest Boyd
in New York, from whom it passed
to Helen H. Peck; presented to the
National Gallery by Evelyn Murray,
Washington, in 1966

William Butler Yeats 1865–1939

Head of a boy, 1887

NGI 3018, p. 152
Pencil, ink and watercolour on paper
35.5 × 26.5 cm
EXHIBITIONS
1961, Manchester and Dublin, *Images
of a Poet*, no. 196a
1965, Dublin, National Gallery of
Ireland, *W.B. Yeats: A Centenary
Exhibition*, no. 96
1988, Dublin, Hugh Lane Municipal
Gallery, *Yeats at the Hugh Lane
Municipal Gallery of Modern Art,
Dublin*, no. 46
LITERATURE
Foster 1997, pp. 36, 254
PROVENANCE
Purchased from Miss P. Hinkson, 1948

Susan Mary (Lily) Yeats 1866–1948

Cornfield with poppies, 1941

YMUS LY1, p. 154
Silk thread embroidered on blue
poplin
25.5 × 28 cm
Signed *Lily Yeats*
LITERATURE
Lewis 1994
Irish Arts Review Yearbook, XIV, 1997,
  G. Lewis, 'Three rediscovered
  embroideries by Lily Yeats'
PROVENANCE
David Meredith, Achill and United
  States; presented to the Yeats
  Museum in his memory by his
  brother John Meredith in 1996

Elizabeth Corbet (Lolly) Yeats 1868–1940

Cashlauna Seilmide: the studio, 1900

YARCECY1, p. 156
Watercolour on artists' board
54.5 × 36.5 cm
Signed *E.C.Yeats April 1900*
LITERATURE
Lewis 1994
W.M. Murphy, *Family Secrets: William
  Butler Yeats and His Relatives*, 1995,
  pp. 86–264
Hardwick 1996
PROVENANCE
Donated to the National Gallery of
  Ireland by Anne Yeats, as part of
  the Jack B. Yeats Archive, in 1995

Jack B. Yeats 1871–1957

On the Broads, 1899

NGI 6318, p. 158
Watercolour on paper
35.5 × 17 cm
Inscribed [verso] *On the Broads*
EXHIBITIONS
1961, London, Waddington Galleries,
  Jack B. Yeats: Early Watercolours,
  no. 57
1967, London, Victor Waddington,
  *Jack B. Yeats: Early Drawings and
  Watercolours*, no. 55
1971–72, Dublin and New York, *Jack
  B. Yeats 1871–1957: A Centenary
  Exhibition*, no. 13
1986, Dublin, National Gallery of
  Ireland, *Jack B. Yeats in the National
  Gallery of Ireland*, no. 1
PROVENANCE
Purchased from Victor Waddington,
  London, in 1967

On deck, on the Broads, 1899

NGI 6319, p. 160
Watercolour on paper
17 × 35.5 cm
EXHIBITIONS
1961, London, Waddington Galleries,
  Jack B. Yeats: Early Watercolours,
  no. 55
1967, London, Victor Waddington,
  *Jack B. Yeats: Early Drawings and
  Watercolours*, no. 56
1971–72, Dublin and New York, *Jack
  B. Yeats 1871–1957: A Centenary
  Exhibition*, no. 14
1986, Dublin, National Gallery of
  Ireland, *Jack B. Yeats in the National
  Gallery of Ireland*, no. 2
PROVENANCE
Purchased from Victor Waddington,
  London, in 1967

Below deck, on the Broads, 1899

NGI 6320, p. 162
Watercolour on paper
17 × 35.5 cm
EXHIBITIONS
1961, London, Waddington Galleries,
    Jack B. Yeats: Early Watercolours,
    no. 56
1967, London, Victor Waddington,
    *Jack B. Yeats: Early Drawings and
    Watercolours,* no. 57
1971–72, Dublin and New York, *Jack
    B. Yeats 1871–1957: A Centenary
    Exhibition,* no. 15
1986, Dublin, National Gallery of
    Ireland, *Jack B. Yeats in the National
    Gallery of Ireland,* no. 3
PROVENANCE
Purchased from Victor Waddington,
    London, in 1967

The County of Mayo, 1903

NGI 3830, p. 164
Pen and ink and watercolour on card
15.6 × 20.2 cm
Signed with monogram
Inscribed [verso] *The County of Mayo
"'Tis a bitter change from those gay days
that now I'm forced to go, And must leave
my bones in Santa Cruz far from my own
Mayo." 17th Century Ballad*
EXHIBITIONS
1920, Dublin, Mills Hall, *Jack B. Yeats:
    Drawings and Pictures of Life in the
    West of Ireland,* no. 38
1972, Lund, Konsthall, *From Yeats to
    Ballagh,* no. 41
1986, Dublin, National Gallery of
    Ireland, *Jack B. Yeats in the National
    Gallery of Ireland,* no. 4
1990, Monaco, Centre de Congrès, and
    Dublin, National Gallery of Ireland,
    Images in Yeats, no. 4
LITERATURE
Jack B. Yeats, ed., *A Broad Sheet,* no.
    19, July 1903 (ill.)
Queen's University College, Belfast,
    Fête Supplement, May 1907, p. 33
    (ill.)

PROVENANCE
Purchased by Mrs Alice Stopford
    Green in 1920; William A. Cadbury,
    whose executors presented it to the
    National Gallery in 1966

Transfer design for St Colmcille banner, 1903

NGI 7946, p. 166
Ink on linen
94.1 × 54.9 cm
Inscribed [bottom left] with
monogram, [lower edge] *Naom Colum
Cille* [in Irish script]
EXHIBITIONS
The banner embroidered from this
    design was exhibited:
    1971–72, Sligo and Dublin *Jack
    B. Yeats and his Family,* no. 85
This design was exhibited:
    1986, Dublin, National Gallery of
    Ireland, *Jack B. Yeats in the National
    Gallery of Ireland,* no. 5
LITERATURE
Irish Homestead, 13 February 1904,
    'Irish saints at Dun Emer', p. 134
D.D.C. Mould, *The Irish Saints,* 1964,
    pp. 93–105
P. Larmour, *Irish Arts Review,* I, no. 4,
    Winter 1984, 'The Dun Emer Guild',
    pp. 24–28, ill.
PROVENANCE
Dun Emer Guild; Miss Lily Yeats of
    Cuala Industries gave it and other
    designs for the Loughrea banners to
    her assistant, Miss Hyland, *ca.* 1940;
    Thomas MacGreevy purchased the
    designs *ca.* 1958, and presented this
    design and NGI 7947 to the National
    Gallery of Ireland

Transfer design for St Asicus banner, 1903

NGI 7947, p. 168
Ink on linen
95.2 × 55.4 cm
Inscribed [lower edge] *Naom Assit* [in
Irish script]
EXHIBITIONS
The original cartoon for the banner
    and the banner itself were exhibited:
    1971–72, Sligo and Dublin, *Jack B.
    Yeats and his Family,* nos. 12 and 88
This design was exhibited:
    1986, Dublin, National Gallery of
    Ireland, *Jack B. Yeats in the National
    Gallery of Ireland,* no. 6
LITERATURE
Irish Homestead, op. cit. above
D.D.C. Mould, *op. cit.* above
P. Larmour, *op. cit.* above
PROVENANCE
Dun Emer Guild; Miss Lily Yeats of
    Cuala Industries gave it and other
    designs for the Loughrea banners to
    her assistant, Miss Hyland, *ca.* 1940;
    Thomas MacGreevy purchased the
    designs *ca.* 1958, and presented this
    and NGI 7946 to the National Gallery
    of Ireland

The causeway of Lettermore, 1905

NGI 19,395, p. 170
Pen and ink on card
9.5 × 24 cm
Signed *Jack B. Yeats*
EXHIBITIONS
1962, Dublin, Dawson Gallery, *Jack B.
    Yeats: Watercolour and Pen and Ink
    Drawings,* no. 67
1964, Derry and Belfast, Arts Council
    of Northern Ireland, *North West Arts
    Festival,* no. 51
1971–72, Dublin and New York, *Jack
    B. Yeats 1857–1957: A Centenary
    Exhibition,* no. 5, ill.
LITERATURE
The Manchester Guardian, 17 June 1905,
    p. 7 (ill.)

J.M. Synge, *Collected Works*, vol. II,
    1966, p. 300, ill.
Pyle 1989, pp. 87–89
PROVENANCE
Dawson Gallery, Dublin; sold in 1962
    to Miss Elizabeth Coyne, Dublin,
    who bequeathed it to the National
    Gallery of Ireland in 1992

The man from Aranmore, 1905

NGI 6317, p. 172
Chalk and watercolour on Whatman
board
38 × 27.3 cm
Signed *Jack B. Yeats.*
Inscribed [verso] *Man from Aranmore*
EXHIBITIONS
1905, Dublin, Leinster Hall, *Jack B.
    Yeats: Pictures of Life in the West of
    Ireland*, no. 23
1908, London, Walker Art Gallery, *Jack
    B. Yeats: Pictures of Life in the West of
    Ireland*, no. 28
1961, London, Waddington Galleries,
    Jack B. Yeats: Early Watercolours,
    no. 11
1964, Derry and Belfast, Arts Council
    of Northern Ireland, *North West Arts
    Festival*, no. 10
1967, London, Victor Waddington,
    *Jack B. Yeats: Early Drawings and
    Watercolours*, no. 17
1971–72, Dublin and New York *Jack
    B. Yeats 1857–1957: A Centenary
    Exhibition*, no. 12
1986, Dublin, National Gallery of
    Ireland, *Jack B. Yeats in the Nationbal
    Gallery of Ireland*, no. 7
1990, Monaco, Centre de Congrès, and
    Dublin, National Gallery of Ireland,
    Images in Yeats, no. 6
LITERATURE
Pyle 1989, pp. 44 and 87–90 (ill.)
PROVENANCE
Mrs Nancy Pulvertaft; purchased from
    Victor Waddington, London, in 1967

Rum and barnacles, 1905

NGI 19,443, p. 174
Watercolour on paper
28 × 36 cm
Signed *Jack B. Yeats*
EXHIBITIONS
1905, London, Baillie's Gallery,
    *Painting, Drawings and Sketches by
    J.H. Donaldson, Jack B. Yeats, Elinor
    Monsell and Mrs Norman*, no. 8
1905, Dublin, Leinster Hall, *Jack B.
    Yeats: Pictures of Life in the West of
    Ireland*, no. 15
LITERATURE
A. Symons, *Outlook*, 18 February 1905,
    p. 225, 'Watercolours and toys'
PROVENANCE
Sold by the artist to W. Marmion,
    1945; private collection, Dublin;
    purchased in Clifden, County
    Galway, in 1972 by Mrs Hortense
    Feldblum, New York, who
    presented it to the National Gallery
    of Ireland in 1997

A four-oared curagh, 1906

NGI 3825, p. 176
Pen and ink, and watercolour on card
29.9 × 23.8 cm
Signed *Jack B. Yeats*
EXHIBITIONS
1917, Birmingham, *Theatre Exhibition*
1972, Lund, Konsthall, *From Yeats to
    Ballagh*, no. 43
1986, Dublin, National Gallery of
    Ireland, *Jack B. Yeats in the National
    Gallery of Ireland*, no. 8
LITERATURE
J.M. Synge, *The Aran Islands*, 1907 (ill.)
J.M. Synge, *Collected Works*, vol. II, ed.
    A. Price, 1966, 'The Aran Islands',
    pp. 47–184 (ill.)
PROVENANCE
Purchased in Birmingham by William
    A. Cadbury, whose executors
    presented it to the National Gallery
    in 1966

Lough Gill, County Sligo, 1906

NGI 6321, p. 178
Watercolour on paper
25.6 × 36.8 cm
Signed with monogram *1906*
EXHIBITIONS
1961, London, Waddington Galleries,
    Jack B. Yeats: Early Watercolours,
    no. 58
1964, Derry and Belfast, Arts Council
    of Northern Ireland, *North West Arts
    Festival*, no. 41
1986, Dublin, National Gallery of
    Ireland, *Jack B. Yeats in the National
    Gallery of Ireland*, no. 9
PROVENANCE
Purchased from Victor Waddington,
    London, in 1967

The wake house, ca. 1908

NGI 3827, p. 180
Pen and ink on paper
22.5 × 29.4 cm
Signed *Jack B. Yeats*
Inscribed *THE WAKE HOUSE*
EXHIBITIONS
1913, Dublin, Black & White Artists'
    Society of Ireland
1986, Dublin, National Gallery of
    Ireland, *Jack B. Yeats in the National
    Gallery of Ireland*, no. 10
LITERATURE
Jack B. Yeats, *A Broadside*, no. 5,
    October 1908 (ill.)
E. Marriott, *Manchester Quarterly*, CXIX,
    July 1911, 'Jack B. Yeats: Pictorial
    and Dramatic Artist' (ill.)
PROVENANCE
Presented by the executors of William
    A. Cadbury in 1966

The pilot, ca. 1910

NGI 3826, p. 182
Pen and ink, and watercolour on card
27.2 × 18 cm
Signed *Jack B. Yeats*
Inscribed *THE PILOT*
EXHIBITIONS
1918, Dublin, Mills Hall, *Jack B. Yeats: Drawings and Pictures of Life in the West of Ireland*, no. 34
1986, Dublin, *Jack B. Yeats in the National Gallery of Ireland*, no. 12
LITERATURE
Jack B. Yeats, *A Broadside*, no. 11, second year, April 1910 (ill.)
PROVENANCE
Purchased by William A. Cadbury in 1918, whose executors presented it to the National Gallery in 1966

Illustration to 'The Felons of our Land', 1910

NGI 19,412, p. 184
Ink and watercolour on card
30.5 × 19.5 cm
Signed *Jack B. Yeats*
Inscribed *And though they sleep in dungeons deep, Or flee, outlawed and banned, We love them yet, we can't forget The felons of our land.* [verso; in blue crayon] *Reduce to 5 inches* [in pencil] *please mount in stone grey the same as I used at my exhibition grey mount* [over rough drawing of mount]
EXHIBITIONS
1922, Dublin, no. 7, St Stephen's Green, *Jack B. Yeats: Drawings and Pictures of Life in the West of Ireland*, no. 27
LITERATURE
A Broadside, no. 1, third year, June 1910 (ill.)
R. Lynd, *Rambles in Ireland*, 1912, ill. in col. as 'The Treason Song'
Pyle 1989, pp. 94–96
PROVENANCE
Sold to Hugh Martin in 1922; placed on permanent loan in the National Gallery of Ireland by Mrs Iona and Caitríona McLeod, 1994, in memory of their stepfather, Patrick J. Little, TD

The circus chariot, 1910

NGI 6316, p. 186
Watercolour with crayon on paper
25.4 × 35.5 cm
Signed *Jack B. Yeats* [also] *J* in pencil and monogram
Inscribed [verso] *a circus chairiot* [sic]
EXHIBITIONS
1910, Dublin, Leinster Hall, *Jack B. Yeats: Pictures of Life in The West of Ireland*, no. 5
1967, London, Victor Waddington, *Jack B. Yeats: Early Drawings and Watercolours*, no. 1
1967, London, St. Michaell's Vicarage, Bedford Park, *Artists and Architecture of Bedford Park 1875–1900*, no. 11a
1971–72, Dublin and New York *Jack B. Yeats 1971–1957: A Centenary Exhibition*, no. 24
1986, Dublin, National Gallery of Ireland, *Jack B. Yeats in the National Gallery of Ireland*, no. 11
LITERATURE
Jack. B. Yeats 1942; repr. 1974
PROVENANCE
Mrs Nancy Pulvertaft; purchased from Victor Waddington, London, 1967

The poteen makers, ca. 1912

NGI 7882, p. 188
Pen and ink, and watercolour on card
13 × 20.5 cm
Signed *Jack B. Yeats*
EXHIBITIONS
1923, Dublin, no. 7 St Stephen's Green, *Jack B. Yeats: Drawings and Pictures of Life in the West of Ireland*, no. 36
1962, Dublin, Dawson Gallery, *Jack B. Yeats: Watercolours and Pen and Ink Drawings*, no. 54
1986, Dublin, National Gallery of Ireland, *Jack B. Yeats in the National Gallery of Ireland*, no. 13
LITERATURE
Jack B. Yeats 1912, ill. p. 23

PROVENANCE
Purchased from the Dawson Gallery in August 1966 by Mrs Beryl S. Austrian, New York; Seamus Kelly, by whom bequeathed to the Gallery, through Mrs Austrian, in 1979

The country shop, ca. 1912

NGI 3829, p. 190
Pen and ink, and watercolour on card
26.6 × 19.5 cm
Signed *Jack B. Yeats*
EXHIBITIONS
1914, Dublin, Black & White Artists' Society of Ireland
1970, Dublin, *Watercolour Society of Ireland Centenary Exhibition*, no. 107
1986, Dublin, National Gallery of Ireland, *Jack B. Yeats in the National Gallery of Ireland*, no. 14
LITERATURE
Jack B. Yeats 1912, ill. p. 1
PROVENANCE
William A. Cadbury, whose executors presented it to the National Gallery in 1966

Gathering seaweed, ca. 1912

NGI 3828, p. 192
Pen and ink, and watercolour on card
17.7 × 25.3 cm
Signed *Jack B. Yeats*
Inscribed [verso] *Gathering Seaweed*
EXHIBITIONS
1917, Birmingham, *Theatre Exhibition*
1970, Dublin, *Watercolour Society of Ireland Centenary Exhibition*, no. 111
1972, Lund, Konsthall, *From Yeats to Ballagh*, no. 45
1986, Dublin, National Gallery of Ireland, *Jack B. Yeats in the National Gallery of Ireland*, no. 15
LITERATURE
Jack B. Yeats 1912, ill. p. 35
J.M. Synge, *Collected Works*, vol. II, ed. A. Price, 1966, 'The Kelp Makers', pp. 307–09

PROVENANCE
Purchased by William A. Cadbury, whose executors presented it to the National Gallery in 1966

The Metal Man, ca. 1912

NGI 3831, p. 194
Pen and ink, and watercolour on card
30.4 × 34.5 cm
Signed *Jack B. Yeats*
EXHIBITIONS
1917, Birmingham, *Theatre Exhibition*
1986, Dublin, National Gallery of Ireland, *Jack B. Yeats in the National Gallery of Ireland*, no. 16
LITERATURE
Jack B. Yeats 1912, ill. p. 31
PROVENANCE
Purchased in 1917 by William A. Cadbury, whose executors presented it to the National Gallery in 1966

Design for a mountain backcloth for The King's Threshold, 1913

NGI 6322, p. 196
Ink, pencil and watercolour on card, squared for transfer
24.8 × 37.5 cm
Signed with monogram
Inscribed *30 feet by 18 feet Scale ½ inch to a foot all colours to be flat.* [verso]
Mountain Back cloth for Kings Threshold. October 1913. For the Abbey Theatre.
EXHIBITION
1986, Dublin, National Gallery of Ireland, *Jack B. Yeats in the National Gallery of Ireland*, no. 17
LITERATURE
W.B. Yeats, *Plays for an Irish Theatre: with Designs by Gordon Craig*, 1911
H. Pyle, *Studies*, Summer/Autumn 1977, '"Men of Destiny" – Jack B. Yeats and W.B. Yeats: The Background and the Symbols', pp. 188–213, ill. plate 5

PROVENANCE
The artist's estate; Victor Waddington, by whom presented to the National Gallery in 1968

The priest, 1913

NGI 1804, p. 198
Oil on panel
36.3 × 23.3 cm
Signed *Jack B. Yeats*
EXHIBITIONS
1917, Birmingham, *Theatre Exhibition*
1986, Dublin, National Gallery of Ireland, *Jack B. Yeats in the National Gallery of Ireland*, no. 18
1990, Monaco, Centre de Congrès and Dublin, National Gallery of Ireland, *Images in Yeats*, no. 7
LITERATURE
G. Birmingham, *Irishman All*, 1913, p. 184 (ill.)
Pyle 1989, pp. 114–15, ill. plate 5
PROVENANCE
Purchased at the Birmingham exhibition by W.A. Cadbury, whose executors presented it to the National Gallery in 1966

The lying-in-state of O'Donovan Rossa, 1915

NGI 3780, p. 200
Pencil on paper
25.5 × 36 cm
Signed with monogram
Inscribed [verso] *done from memory August 2nd 1915 – Jack B Yeats – from memory – the Body of O Donnabáin Rosa lying in State in the City Hall Dublin – 4 brown yellow candles in black candle sticks – a crucifix – Irish Volunteer standing close to head of coffin – As soon as anyone in the line came level with Rossa face they bent and looked at it Then the Volunteer touched them on the arm and said pass on. The Volunteer then took two paces back to his position by that time another of the line was opposite the face the Volunteer stepped forward and touched them on the arm – July 29th 1915*

EXHIBITIONS
1966, Dublin, National Gallery of Ireland, *Cuimhneacháin 1916*, no. 32;
1971–72, Dublin and New York, *Jack B. Yeats 1871–1957: A Centenary Exhibition*, no. 6
1986, Dublin, National Gallery of Ireland, *Jack B. Yeats in the National Gallery of Ireland*, no. 19
PROVENANCE
The artist's estate; purchased from the Dawson Gallery, Dublin, in 1965

Before the start, 1915

NGI 1549, p. 202
Oil on canvas
46 × 61 cm
Signed *Jack B. Yeats*
EXHIBITIONS
1915, Dublin, Royal Hibernian Academy, no. 149
1915, Dundalk, *Oireachtas*
1916, London, Grafton Galleries, *Allied Artists Association 8th Salon*
1918, Dublin, Mills Hall, *Jack B. Yeats: Drawings and Pictures of Life in the West of Ireland*, no. 12
1919, London, Little Art Rooms, *Jack B. Yeats: Drawings and Pictures of Life in the West of Ireland*, no. 14
1921, Edinburgh, Royal Scottish Academy
1922, Dublin, *Aonach*
1924, Paris, *Olympic Exhibition*
1927, Liverpool, Walker Art Gallery, *Autumn Exhibition*, no. 890
1933, Chicago World Fair
1964, Dublin, Municipal Gallery of Art, and Belfast, Ulster Museum, *Friends of the National Collections of Ireland*, no. 131
1971–72, Dublin and New York, *Jack B. Yeats 1871–1957: A Centenary Exhibition*, no. 30
1986, Dublin, National Gallery of Ireland, *Jack B. Yeats in the National Gallery of Ireland*, no. 20

PROVENANCE
Purchased in 1949 from the
Waddington Galleries, Dublin, by
Mrs Julia Egan, by whom it was
bequeathed to the National Gallery,
through the Friends of the National
Collections of Ireland, in 1960

The double jockey act, 1916

NGI 1737, p. 204
Oil on canvas
61 × 46 cm
Signed *Jack B. Yeats*
EXHIBITIONS
1917, Dublin, Royal Hibernian
Academy, no. 48
1917, London, Grafton Galleries, *Allied
Artists Association 9th Salon*
1936, London, Leger Galleries, *The
Circus*, no. 76
1945, Dublin, National College of Art,
*Jack B. Yeats: National Loan
Exhibition*, no. 14
1986, Dublin, National Gallery of
Ireland, *Jack B. Yeats in the National
Gallery of Ireland*, no. 21
PROVENANCE
Purchased by Dr P. MacCarvill in
1945, from whom it passed to Dr
Eileen MacCarvill; purchased Shaw
Fund, 1963

Self-portrait, ca. 1920

NGI 3319, p. 206
Pencil on paper
35.5 × 25.3 cm
Inscribed [verso] *Myself, about 1920*
EXHIBITIONS
1961, Dublin, Dawson Gallery, *Jack B.
Yeats: Watercolours and Pen and Ink
Drawings*, no. 39
1964, Derry and Belfast, *Arts Council of
Northern Ireland, North West Arts
Festival and May Festival*, no. 54
1965, Dublin, National Gallery of
Ireland, *Jack B. Yeats: A Centenary
Exhibition*, no. 73

1967, London and New York,
Wildenstein, *Drawings from the
National Gallery of Ireland*, no. 101
(ill.)
1971–72, Dublin and New York, *Jack B.
Yeats 1871–1957: A Centenary
Exhibition*, no. 8
1986, Dublin, National Gallery of
Ireland, *Jack B. Yeats in the National
Gallery of Ireland*, no. 22
PROVENANCE
Presented to the National Gallery by
Victor Waddington in 1961

Draughts, 1922

NGI 31407, p. 208
Oil on panel
23 × 36 cm
Signed *Jack B. Yeats*
EXHIBITIONS
1922, Dublin, Stephen's Green Gallery,
*Jack B. Yeats: Drawings and Pictures of
Life in the West of Ireland*, no. 4
1945, Dublin, National College of Art,
*Jack B. Yeats: National Loan
Exhibition*, no. 33
1986, Dublin, National Gallery of
Ireland, *Jack B. Yeats in the National
Gallery of Ireland*, no. 23
1988, Dublin, Hugh Lane Municipal
Gallery of Modern Art, *Yeats at the
Hugh Lane Municipal Gallery of
Modern Art, Dublin*, no. 51
PROVENANCE
Purchased in 1922 by Richard Irvine
Best, who bequeathed it to the
National Gallery in 1959

In the tram, 1923

NGI 31408, p. 210
Oil on panel
23 × 36 cm
Signed *Jack B. Yeats*
EXHIBITIONS
1923, Dublin, Stephen's Green Gallery,
*Jack B. Yeats: Drawings and Pictures of
Life in the West of Ireland*, no. 17
1924, London, Gieves Art Gallery,
Paintings of Irish Life, no. 5
1980, Dun Laoghaire, Town Hall, *A
Borough Portrait*, no. 50
1986, Dublin, National Gallery of
Ireland, *Jack B. Yeats in the National
Gallery of Ireland*, no. 24
1988, Dublin, Hugh Lane Municipal
Gallery of Modern Art, *Yeats at the
Hugh Lane Municipal Gallery of
Modern Art, Dublin*, no. 54
1990, Monaco, Centre de Congrès and
Dublin, National Gallery of Ireland,
Images in Yeats, no. 12
PROVENANCE
Purchased from the Waddington
Galleries, Dublin, in 1942, by
Richard Irvine Best, who
bequeathed it to the National
Gallery in 1959

The Liffey Swim, 1923

NGI 3941, p. 212
Oil on canvas
61 × 91 cm
Signed *Jack B. Yeats*
EXHIBITIONS
1924, Paris, *Olympic Exhibition*
1925, Dublin, Royal Hibernian
Academy, no. 64
1926, London, Arthur Tooth, *Jack B.
Yeats: Paintings of Irish Life*, no. 28
1926, Liverpool, Walker Art Gallery,
Autumn Exhibition, no. 74a
1939, San Francisco, World Fair
International Business Machine
Corporation, *Contemporary Art of 79
Countries*
1945, Dublin, National College of Art,
*Jack B. Yeats: National Loan
Exhibition*, no. 35

1965, Waterford, Municipal Gallery, *Jack B. Yeats: Loan Exhibition*, no. 18

1971–72, Dublin and New York, *Jack B. Yeats 1871–1957: A Centenary Exhibition*, no. 46

1986, Dublin, National Gallery of Ireland, *Jack B. Yeats in the National Gallery of Ireland*, no. 25

1988, Dublin, Hugh Lane Municipal Gallery of Modern Art, *Yeats at the Hugh Lane Municipal Gallery of Modern Art, Dublin*, no. 52

1990, Monaco, Centre de Congrès and Dublin, National Gallery of Ireland, *Images in Yeats*, no. 11

LITERATURE

M. Wynne, *National Gallery of Ireland: Fifty Irish Painters*, 1983, p. 50 (ill.)

PROVENANCE

Purchased from the artist by the Trustees of the Haverty Bequest in December 1930 and presented to the National Gallery in 1931

A lake regatta, 1923

NGI 1406, p. 216

Oil on panel

23 × 36 cm

Signed *Jack B. Yeats*

EXHIBITIONS

1923, Dublin, Stephen's Green Gallery, *Jack B. Yeats: Drawings and Pictures of Life in the West of Ireland*, no. 13

1986, Dublin, National Gallery of Ireland, *Jack B. Yeats in the National Gallery of Ireland*, no. 26

PROVENANCE

Purchased at the exhibition by Richard Irvine Best, who bequeathed it to the National Gallery in 1959

The small weir, Coole, 1923

NGI 1309, p. 218

Oil on panel

25 × 37 cm

Signed *Jack B. Yeats*

EXHIBITIONS

1924, London, Gieves Art Gallery, *Jack B. Yeats: Paintings of Irish Life*, no. 6

1924, Dublin, Engineers' Hall, *Jack B. Yeats: Pictures of Life in the West of Ireland*, no. 23

1945, Dublin, National College of Art, *Jack B. Yeats: National Loan Exhibition*, no. 41

1986, Dublin, National Gallery of Ireland, *Jack B. Yeats in the National Gallery of Ireland*, no. 27

PROVENANCE

Purchased from the artist by Father Dempsey, Clontarf, in 1933; Mrs Josephine MacNeill lent it to the National Loan Exhibition; it was purchased from the Dawson Gallery, Dublin, by Evie Hone, who bequeathed it to the National Gallery in 1955

Islandbridge Regatta, 1925

NGI 1409, p. 220

Oil on canvas

46 × 61 cm

Signed *Jack B. Yeats*

EXHIBITIONS

1927, Birmingham, Ruskin Galleries, *Jack B. Yeats: Paintings of Ireland*, no. 29

1931, Dublin, Engineers' Hall, *Jack B. Yeats: Paintings*, no. 10

1932, London, Leger Galleries, *Jack B. Yeats: Ireland and Irish Life*, no. 13

1945, Dublin, National College of Art, *Jack B. Yeats: National Loan Exhibition*, no. 46

1986, Dublin, National Gallery of Ireland, *Jack B. Yeats in the National Gallery of Ireland*, no. 28

1988, Dublin, Hugh Lane Municipal Gallery of Modern Art, *Yeats at the Hugh Lane Municipal Gallery of Modern Art, Dublin*, no. 56

1990, Monaco, Centre de Congrès and Dublin, National Gallery of Ireland, *Images in Yeats*, no. 16

PROVENANCE

Purchased from the artist in 1942 by Richard Irvine Best, who bequeathed it to the National Gallery in 1959

Flower girl, Dublin, 1926

NGI 1905, p. 222

Oil on canvas

46 × 61 cm

Signed *Jack B. Yeats*

EXHIBITIONS

1926, New York, *Society of Independent Artists*

1928, London, Arthur Tooth, *Jack B. Yeats: Paintings*, no. 26

1929, Dublin, Engineers' Hall, *Jack B. Yeats*, no. 26

1939, San Francisco, World Fair International Business Machines Corporation, *Contemporary Art of 79 Countries*, no. 12

1986, Dublin, National Gallery of Ireland, *Jack B. Yeats in the National Gallery of Ireland*, no. 29

1988, Dublin, Hugh Lane Municipal Gallery of Modern Art, *Yeats at the Hugh Lane Municipal Gallery of Modern Art, Dublin*, no. 57

LITERATURE

Pyle 1992, no. 97

PROVENANCE

Purchased from the artist in 1939 by International Business Machines Ltd, New York, who presented it to the National Gallery in 1969

Dinner hour at the docks, 1928

NGI 1791, p. 224
Oil on panel
23.5 × 36.5 cm
Signed *Jack B. Yeats*

EXHIBITIONS
1929, London, Alpine Club Gallery, *Jack B. Yeats: Paintings*, no. 6
1938, Dublin, Royal Hibernian Academy, no. 188
1939, Dublin, 5 South Leinster Street, *Jack B. Yeats: Exhibition of 11 Paintings*, no. 1
1939, Dublin, 5 South Leinster Street, *Loan and Cross-Section Exhibition of Contemporary Paintings*, no. 15
1945, Dublin, National College of Art, *Jack B. Yeats: National Loan Exhibition*, no. 67
1986, Dublin, National Gallery of Ireland, *Jack B. Yeats in the National Gallery of Ireland*, no. 30

PROVENANCE
Given by the artist to the F.R. Higgins Memorial Fund in April 1941; presented to the National Gallery by Mrs R.M. Smyllie, in memory of R.M. Smyllie, in 1966

June night, 1929

NGI 4595, p. 226
Oil on panel
23 × 35 cm
Signed *Jack B. Yeats*
Inscribed on reverse *A June Night*

EXHIBITIONS
1929, Dublin, Engineer's Hall, *Jack B. Yeats: Paintings*, no. 30
1945, Dublin, National College of Art, *Jack B. Yeats: National Loan Exhibition*, no. 72

PROVENANCE
Placed in the National Gallery of Ireland on permanent loan by Mrs Iona and Caitríona McLeod, 1994, in memory of their stepfather, Patrick J. Little, TD

Power station, 1930

NGI 1370, p. 228
Oil on panel
24 × 36 cm
Signed *Jack B. Yeats*

EXHIBITIONS
1930, London, Alpine Club Gallery, *Jack B. Yeats: Paintings*, no. 18
1931, Dublin, Engineers' Hall, *Jack B. Yeats: Paintings*, no. 19
1986, Dublin, National Gallery of Ireland, *Jack B. Yeats in the National Gallery of Ireland*, no. 31
1988, Dublin, Hugh Lane Municipal Gallery of Modern Art, *Yeats at the Hugh Lane Municipal Gallery of Modern Art, Dublin*, no. 61

PROVENANCE
Purchased at the 1931 exhibition by Mrs Augustine Henry; acquired by Mr and Mrs Raymond French, who presented it to the National Gallery in 1957

About to write a letter, 1935

NGI 1766, p. 230
Oil on canvas
91 × 61 cm
Signed *Jack B. Yeats*

EXHIBITIONS
1935, Dublin, Royal Hibernian Academy, no. 83
1936, London, Dunthorne Gallery, *Jack B. Yeats: Recent Paintings*, no. 13
1936, Pittsburgh, Carnegie Institute, *International Exhibition of Paintings*, no. 107
1945, Dublin, National College of Art, *Jack B. Yeats: National Loan Exhibition*, no. 86
1951–52, Boston/Washington/San Francisco/Colorado Springs/Toronto/Detroit/New York, *Jack B. Yeats: A First Retrospective American Exhibition*, no. 15
1969–71, Helsinki/Göteborg/Norrköping/Stockholm/Copenhagen/Bielefeld/Bonn/Saarbrücken/London/Leeds/Glasgow/Dublin, *Modern Irish Painting (Comhairle Ealaíon)*, no. 50
1971–72, Dublin/New York, *Jack B. Yeats 1871–1957: A Centenary Exhibition*, no. 60
1986, Dublin, National Gallery of Ireland, *Jack B. Yeats in the National Gallery of Ireland*, no. 32

LITERATURE
H. Pyle, *Irish Arts Review*, II, no. 1, Spring 1985, '"About to Write a Letter": Jack B. Yeats in Search of Fantasy in the Company of John Masefield", pp. 43–47
Brian P. Kennedy, *Irish Arts Review Yearbook*, IX, 1993, 'The Oil Painting Technique of Jack B. Yeats', pp. 115–23 (col. repro.)

PROVENANCE
Purchased in 1944 from the artist by Richard McGonigal, SC, from whose estate it was purchased in 1964

A morning, 1935–36

NGI 4628, p. 232
Oil on panel
23 × 36 cm
Signed *Jack B. Yeats*
Inscribed on verso in ink (in another hand) *Aut 1935, April 1936*

EXHIBITION
1936, London, Dunthorne Gallery, *Jack B. Yeats: Recent Paintings*, no. 27

LITERATURE
E. O'Brien, *The Beckett Country: Samuel Beckett's Country,* 1986, p. 155
Knowlson, J., *Damned to Fame: The Life of Samuel Beckett*, 1996, pp. 224, 747
A. Cronin, *Samuel Beckett: The Last Modernist*, 1996, p. 227

PROVENANCE
Sold in 1936 to Samuel Beckett, Dublin and Paris, who later presented it to Jack MacGowran, Dublin; private collection, London, 1972; bought by the National Gallery with the help of the Bryan Guinness Charitable Trust, in 1996

A morning in a city, 1937

NGI 1050, p. 234
Oil on canvas
61 × 91 cm
Signed *Jack B. Yeats*
EXHIBITIONS
1937, Dublin, Royal Hibernian
Academy, no. 121
1939, San Francisco, World Fair
International Business Machines
corporation, *Contemporary Art of 79
Countries*
1945, Dublin, National College of Arts,
*Jack B. Yeats: National Loan
Exhibition*, no. 89
1951–53, Boston/Washington/San
Francisco/Colorado Springs/
Toronto/Detroit/New York, *Jack
B. Yeats: A First Retrospective
American Exhibition*, no. 7
1953, Dublin, Municipal Gallery of
Modern Art, *An Tóstal: Irish Painting
1903–1953*, no. 44
1965, Waterford, Municipal Gallery,
Jack B. Yeats: Loan Exhibition, no. 20
1986, Dublin, National Gallery of
Ireland, *Jack B. Yeats in the National
Gallery of Ireland*, no. 33
LITERATURE
Brian P. Kennedy, *Irish Arts Review
Yearbook*, IX, 1993, 'The Oil Painting
Technique of Jack B. Yeats',
pp. 115–23 (col. repro.)
PROVENANCE
Purchased from the artist by the
Trustees of the Haverty Bequest in
February 1938 and presented to the
National Gallery in 1941

In memory of Boucicault and Bianconi, 1937

NGI 4206, p. 236
Oil on canvas
61 × 92 cm
Signed *Jack B. Yeats*
EXHIBITIONS
1939, Dublin, Royal Hibernian
Academy, no. 29
1939, Dublin, 5 South Leinster Street,
*Jack B. Yeats: Exhibition of 11
Paintings*, no. 6

1940, Dublin, Contemporary Pucture
Galleries, *Jack B. Yeats: Paintings*,
no. 9
1942, Dublin, Contemporary Picture
Galleries, *In Theatre Street*, no. 1
1945, Dublin, National College of Art,
*Jack B. Yeats: National Loan
Exhibition*, no. 100
1946, Edinburgh, *Society of Scottish
Artists*, no. 157
1951–52, Boston/Washington/San
Francisco/Colorado Springs/
Toronto/Detroit/New York, *Jack
B. Yeats: A First Retrospective
American Exhibition*, no. 20
1961, Sligo, Town Hall, presented by
Sligo Art Society, *Jack B. Yeats: Loan
Collection*, no. 1
1963, London, Waddington Galleries,
Jack B. Yeats: Paintings, no. 14
1971–72, Dublin/New York, *Jack
B. Yeats 1871–1957: A Centenary
Exhibition*, no. 79
1980, Dun Laoghaire, *A Borough
Portrait*, no. 51
1986, Dublin, National Gallery of
Ireland, *Jack B. Yeats in the National
Gallery of Ireland*, no. 34
LITERATURE
MacGreevy 1945, pp. 28 and 30 (ill.)
Pyle 1989, pp. 129–31
H. Pyle, *Eire–Ireland*, Summer 1983,
'Many Ferries: Jack B. Yeats and J.
M. Synge', pp. 24–25
PROVENANCE
Purchased from the Contemporary
Picture Galleries by Harold Jacob in
1940; Mr and Mrs F.L. Vickerman;
John Huston, who presented it to
the National Gallery in 1977

Four scenes in search of characters: Beginning with Naples – Scene I, 1942

NGI 4581, p. 238
Oil on panel
23 × 35.5 cm
Signed with monogram and *Jack B.
Yeats*
Inscribed on reverse *Title* [also]
SCENE ONE: NAPLES [written in ink]
*Left and right as seen by Audience Two
steps up on left stand with several tiers of
flowers in pots, one step down practical
steps down under arch on right back
pieced tall rock right back wing on right
painted dark colour*
EXHIBITIONS
1942, Dublin, Contemporary Picture
Galleries, *In Theatre Street*, no. 4
1948, London, Tate Gallery, *Jack B.
Yeats; Loan Exhibition* (not in
catalogue)
LITERATURE
R. Skelton, *The Collected Plays of Jack B.
Yeats* (1971)
Pyle 1989, pp. 138, 145, 154–55
Purser 1991, *passim*
PROVENANCE
Purchased at the exhibition in 1942 by
Leo Smith and sold to Sir John
Rothenstein in 1945; the Lady
Walston; purchased at Sotheby's,
London, for the National Gallery of
Ireland, in 1992

Four scenes in search of characters: Beginning with Naples – Scene II, 1942

NGI 4582, p. 242
Oil on panel
23 × 35.5 cm
Signed with monogram and *Jack B. Yeats*
Inscribed *Title* [also] BEGINNING WITH NAPLES SCENE TWO [written in ink] *Windows without curtains. back cloth green fields trees* [written in pencil] *white mat on right*
EXHIBITIONS
1942, Dublin, Contemporary Picture Galleries, *In Theatre Street*, no. 4
1948, London, Tate Gallery, *Jack B. Yeats; Loan Exhibition* (not in catalogue)
PROVENANCE
Purchased at the exhibition in 1942 by Leo Smith and sold to Sir John Rothenstein in 1945; the Lady Walston; purchased at Sotheby's, London, for the National Gallery of Ireland in 1992

Four scenes in search of characters: Beginning with Naples – Scene III, 1942

NGI 4583, p. 244
Oil on panel
23 × 35.5 cm
Signed with monogram and *Jack B. Yeats*
Inscribed *Title* [also] *Beginning with Naples: SCENE THREE* [written in pencil] *street of houses a side window right three doors busts over each strips of drugget over carpet from doors*
EXHIBITIONS
1942, Dublin, Contemporary Picture Galleries, *In Theatre Street*, no. 4;
1948, London, Tate Gallery, *Jack B. Yeats; Loan Exhibition* (not in catalogue)
PROVENANCE
Purchased at the exhibition in 1942 by Leo Smith and sold to Sir John Rothenstein in 1945; the Lady Walston; purchased at Sotheby's, London, for the National Gallery of Ireland in 1992

Four scenes in search of characters: Beginning with Naples – Scene IV, 1942

NGI 4584, p. 246
Oil on panel
23 × 35.5 cm
Signed with monogram and *Jack B. Yeats*
Inscribed *Title* [also] BEGINNING WITH NAPLES: SCENE FOUR [written in pencil] *Bog and mountain top back cloth uncarpeted yellow floor curtain over door left*
EXHIBITIONS
1942, Dublin, Contemporary Picture Galleries, *In Theatre Street*, no. 4
1948, London, Tate Gallery, *Jack B. Yeats; Loan Exhibition* (not in catalogue)
LITERATURE
Pyle 1992, pp. 438–42
PROVENANCE
Purchased at the exhibition in 1942 by Leo Smith and sold to Sir John Rothenstein in 1945; the Lady Walston; purchased at Sotheby's, London, for the National Gallery of Ireland in 1992

This grand conversation was under the rose, 1943

NGI 4576, p. 248
Oil on canvas
35.5 × 53 cm
Signed *Jack B. Yeats*
Inscribed on verso *That Grand Conversation Was Under the Rose*
EXHIBITIONS
1943, Dublin, Victor Waddington Galleries, *Jack B. Yeats: Later Paintings*, no. 17
1945, Dublin, National College of Art, *Jack B. Yeats: National Loan Exhibition*, no. 123
1961, Sligo, Town Hall, presented by Sligo Art Society, *Jack B. Yeats: Loan Collection*, no. 29
1971–72, Dublin/New York, *Jack B. Yeats 1871–1957: A Centenary Exhibition*, no. 83 (repro.)
LITERATURE
A Broad Sheet, no. 20 (August 1903)
P.W. Joyce, ed., *Old Irish Folk Music and Songs* (1909), pp. 176–77
J. White, *Theatre and the Visual Arts*, 1972, 'Memory Harbour: Jack B. Yeats's painting process', pp. 9–17
H. Pyle, *Studies*, Summer/Autumn 1977, "Men of Destiny" – Jack B. Yeats and W.B. Yeats: the background and the symbols', pp. 204–06 (ill.)
Pyle 1989, pp. 68, 132 (plate 20)
PROVENANCE
Sold at the exhibition in 1943 to one of the patients of Dr Bethel Solomons, who presented it to Dr Solomons; Dr Michael Solomons, from whom it was purchased for the National Gallery of Ireland in 1992

No flowers, 1945

NGI 4031, p. 250
Oil on canvas
61 × 92 cm
Signed *Jack B. Yeats*
EXHIBITIONS
1945, Dublin, Royal Hibernian Academy, no. 28
1948, Leeds, Temple Newsam Gallery, *Jack B. Yeats: Loan Exhibition*
1948, London, Tate Gallery, *Jack B. Yeats: Loan Exhibition*, no. 50
1960, York, City Art Gallery, *Jack B. Yeats: Paintings*, no. 27
1962, New York, Willard Gallery, *Jack B. Yeats: Oil Paintings*, no. 6
1963, London, Waddington Galleries, *Jack B. Yeats: Paintings*, no. 17
1964, Derry and Belfast, Arts Council of Northern Ireland, *North West Arts Festival and May Festival*, no. 57
1967, London, Victor Waddington, *Jack B. Yeats: Oil Paintings*, no. 13
1971–72, Dublin/New York, *Jack B. Yeats 1871–1957: A Centenary Exhibition*, no. 92

1986 Dublin, National Gallery of
Ireland, *Jack B. Yeats in the National
Gallery of Ireland*, no. 35
PROVENANCE
Purchased from the artist in 1947 by
Mrs M. Spiro, later Mrs
Waddington, who presented it to
the National Gallery in 1971

Men of destiny, 1946

NGI 1134, p. 252
Oil on canvas
51 × 69 cm
Signed *Jack B. Yeats*
EXHIBITIONS
1946 Dublin, National College of Art,
*Thomas Davis and the Young Ireland
Movement Centenary Exhibition*, no. 4
1946 Edinburgh, Society of Scottish
Artists, no. 151
1946 Dublin, Royal Hibernian
Academy, no. 57
1948 Leeds, Temple Newsam Gallery,
Jack B. Yeats: Loan Exhibition, no. 66
1951–52 Boston/Washington/San
Francisco/Colorado Springs/
Toronto/Detroit/New York, *Jack
B. Yeats: A First Retrospective
American Exhibition*, no. 6
1953 Dublin, Municipal Gallery of
Modern Art, *An Tóstal: Irish Painting
1903–1953*, no. 42
1956 Belfast, Museum and Art Gallery,
Jack B. Yeats: Paintings, no. 4
1962 Venice, *XXXI Esposizione Biennale
Internazionale d'Arte: Irlanda*, no. 10
1966 Dublin, National Gallery of
Ireland, *Cuimhneacháin 1916*, no. 154
1971–72 Dublin/New York, *Jack B.
Yeats 1871–1957: A Centenary
Exhibition*, no. 94
1986 Dublin, National Gallery of
Ireland, *Jack B. Yeats in the National
Gallery of Ireland*, no. 36
LITERATURE
H. Pyle, *Studies*, Summer/Autumn
1977, '"Men of Destiny" – Jack B.
and W.B. Yeats: The Background
and the Symbols', pp. 188–213 (ill.)

PROVENANCE
Purchased from the artist by the
Committee of the Jack B. Yeats Loan
Exhibition, with the money
remaining from the exhibition, and
presented to the National Gallery of
Ireland in 1946

Above the fair, 1946

NGI 1147, p. 254
Oil on canvas
91 × 122 cm
Signed *Jack B. Yeats*
EXHIBITIONS
1947 Dublin, Victor Waddington
Galleries, *Jack B. Yeats; Paintings*,
no. 18
1948 Leeds, Temple Newsam Gallery,
Jack B. Yeats: Loan Exhibition
1948 London, Tate Gallery, *Jack B.
Yeats: Loan Exhibition*, no. 66
1951–52 Boston/Washington/San
Francisco/Colorado Springs/
Toronto/Detroit/New York, *Jack
B. Yeats: A First Retrospective
American Exhibition*, no. 5
1953 Dublin, Municipal Gallery of
Modern Art, *An Tóstal: Irish Painting
1903–1953*, no. 43
1954 Paris, Galerie Beaux-Arts, *Jack B.
Yeats: Peintures*, no. 13
1956 Belfast, Belfast Museum and Art
Gallery, *Jack B. Yeats: Paintings*, no. 3
1962 *Venice, XXXI Esposizione Biennale
Internazionale d'Arte: Irlanda*, no. 7
1971–72 Dublin/New York, *Jack B.
Yeats 1871–1957: A Centenary
Exhibition*, no. 93
1980 Cork, Crawford Municipal
Gallery, and Belfast, Ulster
Museum, *Rosc Chorcaí 80: Irish Art,
1943–1973*, no. 118
1986 Dublin, National Gallery of
Ireland, *Jack B. Yeats in the National
Gallery of Ireland*, no. 37
PROVENANCE
Purchased from the Victor
Waddington Galleries in 1947, and
presented to the National Gallery by
the Revd Father Senan, OFM, Cap.,
on behalf of a group of private
citizens

Many ferries, 1948

NGI 1550, p. 256
Oil on canvas
51 × 69 cm
EXHIBITIONS
1951 Edinburgh, *United Nations
International Art Exhibition*, no. 71
1964 Dublin, Municipal Gallery of
Modern Art, and Belfast, Ulster
Museum, *Friends of the National
Collections of Ireland Exhibition*, no.
132
1969–71, Helsinki/Göteborg/
Norrköpping/Stockholm/
Copenhagen/Bielefeld/Bonn/
Saarbrücken/London/Leeds/
Glasgow/Dublin, *Modern Irish
Painting (An Chomhairle Ealaíon)*,
no. 56
1971–72 Dublin/New York, *Jack B.
Yeats 1871–1957: A Centenary
Exhibition*, no. 102
1986 Dublin, National Gallery of
Ireland, *Jack B. Yeats in the National
Gallery of Ireland*, no. 38
LITERATURE
J. M. Synge, *Collected Works*, vol. II,
1966, p. 306
H. Pyle, *Eire–Ireland*, Summer 1983,
'"Many Ferries": Jack B. Yeats and
J.M. Synge', pp. 17–35
PROVENANCE
Purchased in 1951 by Mrs Julia Egan,
who bequeathed it to the National
Gallery through the Friends of the
National Collections in Ireland in
1960

The last dawn but one, 1948

NGI 1906, p. 258
Oil on canvas
51 × 69 cm
Signed *Jack B. Yeats*
EXHIBITIONS
1949, Dublin, Victor Waddington
Galleries, *Jack B. Yeats: Oil Paintings*,
no. 7
1951–52, Boston/Washington/San
Francisco/Colorado Springs/
Toronto/Detroit/New York, *Jack B.
Yeats: A First Retrospective
AmericanExhibition*, no. 33;
1953, London, Wildenstein, *Jack B.
Yeats: Recent Paintings*, no. 13
1954, Paris, Galerie Beaux-Arts, *Jack B.
Yeats: Peintures*, no. 39
1956, Belfast, Museum and Art Gallery,
Jack B. Yeats: Paintings, no. 36
1957, Edinburgh, Society of Scottish
Artists, no. 214
1962, Venice, *XXXI Esposizione
Biennale Internazionale d'Arte: Irlanda*,
no. 14
1971–72, Dublin/New York, *Jack B.
Yeats 1871–1957: A Centenary
Exhibition*, no. 100
1986, Dublin, National Gallery of
Ireland, *Jack B. Yeats in the National
Gallery of Ireland*, no. 39
PROVENANCE
Thomas MacGreevy; purchased by the
National Gallery from Messrs.
Whitney, Moore and Keller, Dublin,
in 1969

The singing horseman, 1949

NGI 4524, p. 260
Oil on canvas
61 × 91.5 cm
Signed *Jack B. Yeats*
EXHIBITIONS
1950, Dublin, Royal Hibernian
Academy, no. 38
1951–52, Boston/Washington/San
Francisco/Colorado Springs/
Toronto/Detroit/New York, *Jack B.

*Yeats: A First Retrospective American
Exhibition*
1965, Massachussetts, Hayden Gallery,
*Institute of Technology Loan
Exhibition*, no. 28
1971–72, Dublin/New York, *Jack B.
Yeats 1871–1957: A Centenary
Exhibition*, no. 115 (repro.)
LITERATURE
J.J. Sweeney, *Art News*, April 1951,
'The Yeats who paints', p. 36 (ill.)
*National Gallery of Ireland, Acquisitions
1986–1988*, pp. 72–73 (ill.)
PROVENANCE
Sold by the artist to J.L. Sweeney,
USA, August 1950; presented by
Máire MacNeill Sweeney in his
memory to the National Gallery of
Ireland in 1987

The cavalier's farewell to his steed, 1949

NGI 1374, p. 262
Oil on board
36 × 46 cm
Signed *Jack B. Yeats*
EXHIBITIONS
1965, Waterford, Municipal Gallery,
Jack B. Yeats Loan Exhibition, no. 21
1986, Dublin, National Gallery of
Ireland, *Jack B. Yeats in the National
Gallery of Ireland*, no. 40
PROVENANCE
Purchased in March 1950 by Mrs
Dorothea Case, who bequeathed it
to the National Gallery through the
Friends of the National Collections
of Ireland in 1958

Grief, 1951

NGI 1769, p. 264
Oil on canvas
102 × 153 cm
Signed *Jack B. Yeats*
EXHIBITIONS
1951, Dublin, Victor Waddington
Galleries, *Jack B. Yeats: Paintings*,
no. 21
1955, Dublin, *Irish Exhibition of Living
Art*, no. 28

1957, Edinburgh, Society of Scottish
Artists, no. 211
1962, Los Angeles, Felix Landau
Gallery, *Jack B. Yeats: Paintings*,
no. 11
1971–72, Dublin/New York, *Jack B.
Yeats 1871–1957 A Centenary
Exhibition*, no. 121
1980, Cork/Belfast, Crawford
Municipal Gallery/Ulster Museum,
Rosc Chorcaí '80: Irish Art, 1943–1973,
exhib. cat.
1986, Dublin, National Gallery of
Ireland, *Jack B. Yeats in the National
Gallery of Ireland*, no. 41
LITERATURE
T.G. Rosenthal, *Yeats*, 1966 (The
Masters – 40) p. 8, plate XV
Pyle 1989, pp. 170–71 (ill.)
PROVENANCE
The artist's executors, after which it
was in private ownership;
purchased from the Waddington
Galleries, London, in 1965

For the road, 1951

NGI 4309, p. 268
Oil on canvas
61 × 92 cm
Signed *Jack B. Yeats*
EXHIBITIONS
1953, Dublin, Municipal Gallery, *An
Tóstal: Irish Painting 1903–1953*,
no. 45
1957, Edinburgh, Society of Scottish
Artists, no. 202
1961, Sligo, Town Hall, presented by
Sligo Art Society, *Jack B. Yeats: Loan
Collection*, no. 30
1962, Venice, *XXXI Exposizione Biennale
Internazionale d'Arte: Irlanda*, no. 17
1971–72, Dublin/New York, *Jack B.
Yeats 1871–1957: A Centenary
Exhibition*, no. 126
1986, Dublin, National Gallery of
Ireland, *Jack B. Yeats in the National
Gallery of Ireland*, no. 42
PROVENANCE
Purchased through Victor
Waddington in 1952 by Mr and Mrs
F.L. Vickerman, who presented it to
the Gallery in 1978

Anne Yeats (b. 1919)

Women and washing, Sicily, 1965–66

NGI 4613, p. 270
Oil on canvas
61 × 91.5 cm
Signed *Anne Yeats* [also on verso]
Inscribed [verso] *1965–1966 24″ x 36″
Women and Washing C28 Anne Yeats*
EXHIBITIONS
1966, Dublin, Dawson Gallery, *Anne
    Yeats: Paintings*, no. 18
1971–72, Sligo, County Museum and
    Dublin, Municipal Gallery, *Jack B.
    Yeats and his Family*, no. 104
1995, Dublin, Gorry Gallery, *An
    Exhibition of 18th, 19th and 20th
    century Irish Paintings*, no. 60
LITERATURE
H. Pyle, *Irish Arts Review*, 1994,
    pp. 117–20
PROVENANCE
Mrs George Yeats; bequeathed to
    Anne Yeats; private collection,
    London; Jim O'Connor; Gorry
    Gallery, Dublin

Green cloth floating, 1993

NGI 4602, p. 272
Oil on paper
39.5 × 57 cm
Signed *Anne Yeats*
EXHIBITIONS
1994, Dublin, Taylor Galleries, *Anne
    Yeats*, no. 12
1995, Dublin, Royal Hibernian
    Academy, *Anne Yeats: A
    Retrospective Exhibition*, no. 61
LITERATURE
H. Pyle, *Irish Arts Review*, 1994,
    pp. 117–20
PROVENANCE
Purchased in 1994 by the Friends of
    the National Collections of Ireland
    and presented to the National
    Gallery of Ireland

The lying-in-state of O'Donovan Rossa,
  NGI 3780, p. 200
The man from Aranmore, NGI 6317,
  p. 172
Many ferries, NGI 1550, p. 256
Men of destiny, NGI 1134, p. 252
The Metal Man, NGI 3831, p. 194
A morning, NGI 4628, p. 232
A morning in a city, NGI 1050, p. 234
No flowers, NGI 4031, p. 250
On deck, on the Broads, NGI 6319, p. 160
On the Broads, NGI 6318, p. 158
The pilot, NGI 3826, p. 182
The poteen makers, NGI 7882, p. 188
Power station, NGI 1370, p. 228
The priest, NGI 1804, p. 198
Rum and barnacles, NGI 19,443, p. 174
Self-portrait, NGI 3319, p. 206
The singing horseman, NGI 4524, p. 260
The small weir, Coole, NGI 1309, p. 218
*This grand conversation was under the
  rose*, NGI 4576, p. 248
Transfer design for Saint Asicus banner,
  NGI 7947, p. 168
*Transfer design for Saint Colmcille
  banner*, NGI 7946, p. 166
The wake house, NGI 3827, p. 180

Anne Yeats
Green cloth floating, NGI 4602, p. 272
Women and washing, Sicily, NGI 4613,
  p. 270

Suggestions for Further Reading

Books by John Butler Yeats

Passages from the Letters of J.B. Yeats,
  selected by E. Pound, Dublin (Cuala
  Press) 1917
Essays Irish and American,
  Dublin/London (Talbot
  Press/Fisher Unwin) 1918
Further Letters of John Butler Yeats, ed.
  L. Robinson, Dublin (Cuala Press)
  1920
*Early Memories: Some Chapters of
  Autobiography*, Dublin (Cuala Press)
  1923
*Letters from Bedford Park: A Selection
  from the Correspondence (1890–1922)
  of John Butler Yeats*, ed. W. Murphy,
  Dublin (Cuala Press) 1972

Books by Jack B. Yeats

Life in the West of Ireland, Dublin
  (Maunsel) 1912
Sligo, London (Wishart) 1930
Sailing, Sailing Swiftly, London
  (Putnam) 1933
The Amaranthers, London
  (Heinemann) 1936
The Charmed Life, London (Routledge)
  1938
Ah Well, London (Routledge) 1942;
  repr. 1974
And to You Also, London (Routledge)
  1944; repr. 1974
The Careless Flower, London (Pilot
  Press) 1947
The Collected Plays, ed. R. Skelton,
  London (Secker & Warburg) 1971

Books by Elizabeth C. Yeats

Brushwork, London (G. Philip) 1895
*Brushwork, Studies of Flowers, Fruits and
  Animals for Teachers and Advanced
  Students*, London (G. Philip) 1898
Brushwork Copy Book, London
  (G. Philip) 1899
Elementary Brushwork Studies, London
  (G. Philip) 1900

Biography, Criticism, Letters

D.N. Archibald, *John Butler Yeats* (Irish
  Writers Series), Lewisberg (Bucknell
  UP) 1974
F. Cullen, *The Drawings of John Butler
  Yeats (1839–1922)*, New York
  (Albany Institute of History & Art)
  1987
R.F. Foster, *W.B. Yeats: A Life*, I: *The
  Apprentice Mage, 1865–1914*, Oxford
  (OUP) 1997

J. Hardwick, *The Yeats Sisters: A Biography of Susan and Elizabeth Yeats*, London (Pandora) 1996

Ed. J. Hone, *J.B. Yeats: Letters to his Son W.B. Yeats and Others, 1869–1922*, New York (Dutton) 1946

B.P. Kennedy, *Jack B. Yeats*, Dublin (National Gallery of Ireland) 1991

Ed. F. Kermode and others, *W.B. Yeats: Images of a Poet*, Manchester (University of Manchester) 1961

G. Lewis, *The Yeats Sisters and the Cuala*, Dublin (Irish Academic Press) 1994

T. MacGreevy, *Jack B. Yeats: An Appreciation and an Interpretation*, Dublin (Victor Waddington) 1945

Ed. R. McHugh, *Jack B. Yeats: A Centenary Gathering* (Tower Series of Anglo-Irish Studies III), Dublin (Dolmen Press) 1971

W. Murphy, *The Yeats Family and the Pollexfens of Sligo*, Dublin (Dolmen Press) 1971

W. Murphy, *Prodigal Father: The Life of John Butler Yeats (1839–1922)*, Ithaca and London (Cornell UP) 1978

J.W. Purser, *The Literary Works of Jack B. Yeats*, London (Colin Smythe) 1991

H. Pyle, *Jack B. Yeats: A Biography*, new edn., London (André Deutsch) 1989

H. Pyle, *Jack B. Yeats: A Catalogue Raisonné of the Oil Paintings*, London (André Deutsch) 1992

H. Pyle, *Jack B. Yeats: His Watercolours, Drawings and Pastels*, Dublin (Irish Academic Press) 1993

H. Pyle, *The Different Worlds of Jack B. Yeats*, Dublin (Irish Academic Press) 1994

H. Pyle, 'Call down the Hawk: The Paintings of Anne Yeats', *Irish Arts Review*, x, 1994, pp. 117–20

J. White, *John Butler Yeats and the Irish Renaissance*, Dublin (National Gallery of Ireland) 1972

Edd. H. Pyle and N. Niland, *Jack B. Yeats and his Family*, Sligo (County Library and Museum) 1971

J. White and H. Pyle, *Jack B. Yeats 1871–1957: A Centenary Exhibition*, Dublin (National Gallery of Ireland) 1971

Background

V.W. Brooks, *John Sloan, A Painter's Life*, New York (Dutton) 1955

A. Crookshank and the Knight of Glin, *The Painters of Ireland c. 1660–1920*, London (Barrie & Jenkins) 1978

A. Crookshank and the Knight of Glin, *The Watercolours of Ireland*, London (Barrie & Jenkins) 1994

R. Gordon, *John Butler Yeats and John Sloan: The Records of a Friendship*, Dublin (Dolmen Press) 1978

Ed. N. Gordon Bowe, *Art and the National Dream*, Dublin (Irish Academic Press) 1993

Ed. H. Pyle, *Irish Art, 1900–1950*, Cork (Crawford Municipal Gallery) 1975

Ed. C. Barrett, *Irish Art, 1943–1973*, Cork (Crawford Municipal Gallery) 1980

P. Larmour, *The Arts and Crafts Movement in Ireland*, Belfast (Friar's Bush Press) 1992

L. Miller, *The Dun Emer Press, later the Cuala Press* (New Yeats Papers series), Dublin (Dolmen Press) 1973

B.L. Reid, *The Man from New York: John Quinn and his Friends*, New York (OUP) 1968

Edd. R. Skelton and A. Saddlemyer, *The World of W.B. Yeats*, Dublin/Seattle (Dolmen Press/Washington UP) 1965

J. Thorpe, *English Illustration: The Nineties*, London (Hacker Art Books) 1975

W.B. Yeats, *Autobiographies*, London (Macmillan) 1966

W.B. Yeats, *Collected Letters*, I: *1865–1895*; III: *1901–1904*, ed. J. Kelly, Oxford (Clarendon Press) 1986, 1994

Index

A Yeats Family Tree

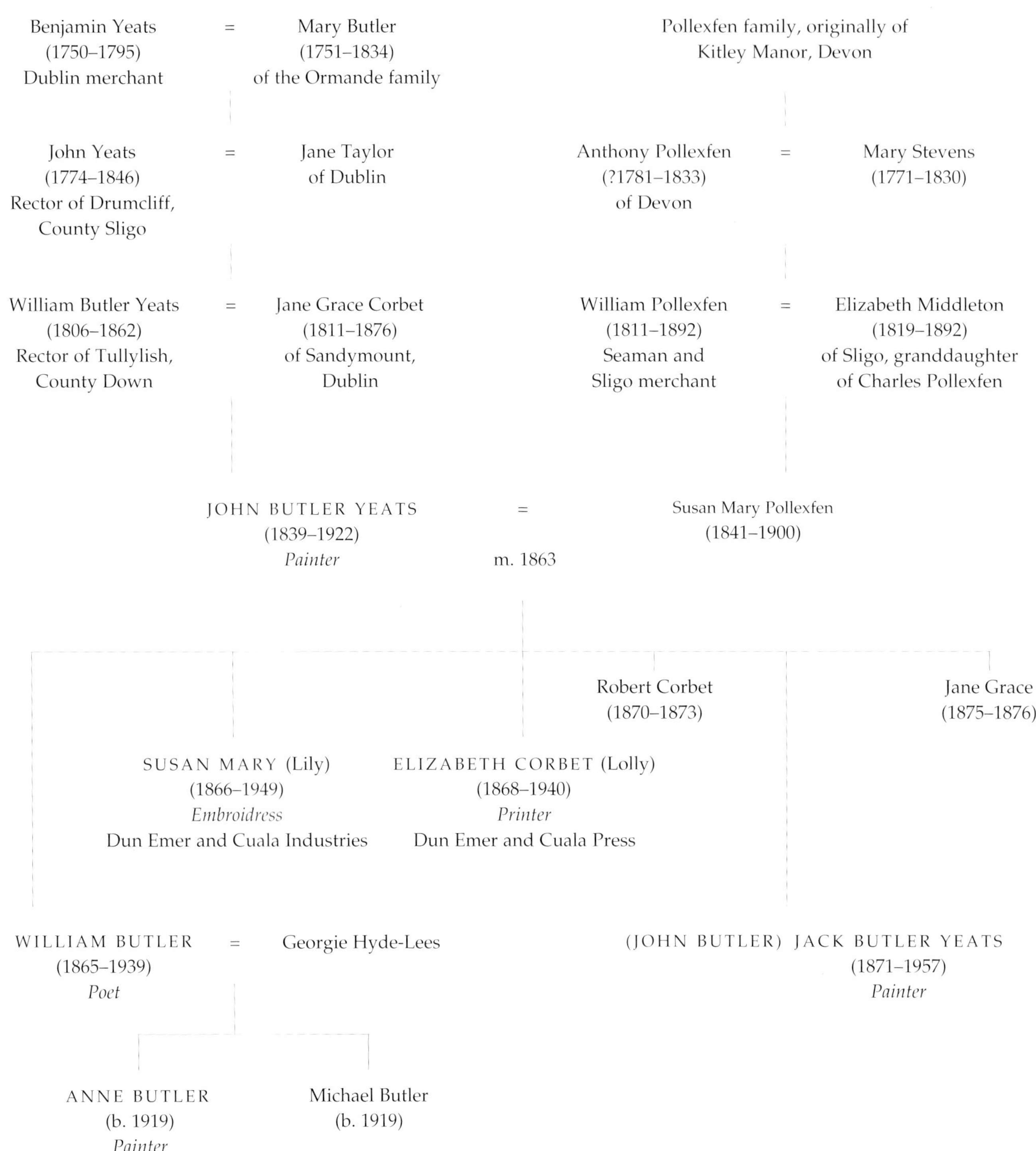